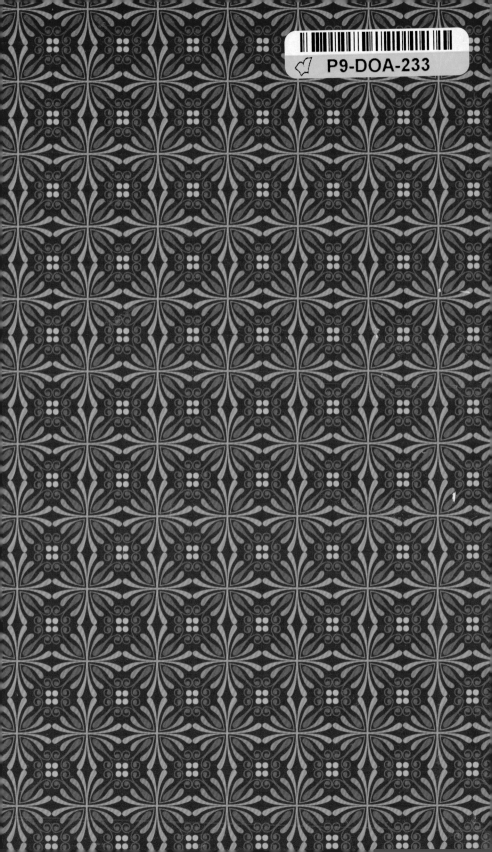

The Book of

Who Said That?

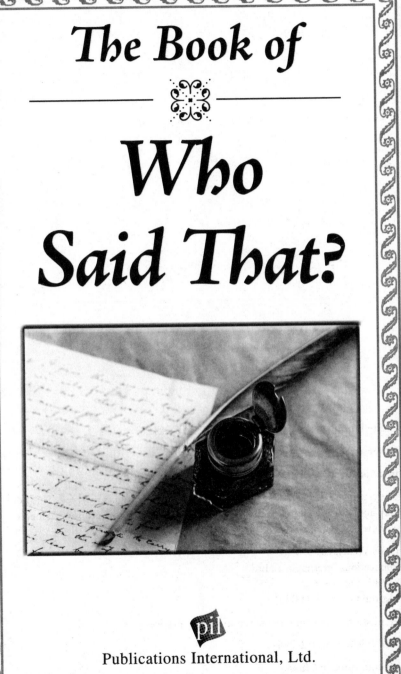

Publications International, Ltd.

Contributing writers: Jim Daley and Marty Strasen

Cover art: Shutterstock.com

Interior illustrations and photography: Shutterstock.com

ISBN: 978-1-68022-754-3

Manufactured in China.

8 7 6 5 4 3 2 1

Contents

✳ ✳ ✳ ✳

Quotations so old they're new again, from luminaries of the ancient world, including Aesop, Aristotle, Bion, Cicero, Confucius, Demosthenes, Diogenes, Epicurus, Herodotus, Julius Caesar, Lao Tzu, Ovid, Pindar, Sophocles, Terence, and more. Find out the origins of these quotations and many more:

"Familiarity breeds contempt."

"Though boys throw stones at frogs in sport, the frogs do not die in sport, but in earnest."

"What is a friend? A single soul dwelling in two bodies."

"Let the punishment match the offense."

"The three hundred poems are summed up in the one line, Think no evil."

Some of the residents of the White House have been witty, some wise, others...quotable for other reasons. Discover the answers to these questions and more:

Which vice president (and later president) called the vice presidency "the most insignificant office that ever the invention of man contrived or his imagination conceived"?

What have the First Ladies thought of life in the White House?

What were the circumstances around the Gettysburg Address?

Which president coined the term "military-industrial complex"?

The quotations in this chapter give an array of viewpoints on war, from generals to foot soldiers to observers, on the topics of glory and suffering. Find out the origins of these quotations and many more:

"Don't fire until you see the whites of their eyes."

"I have not yet begun to fight!"

"It is well that war is so terrible—we should grow too fond of it."

"Theirs not to reason why, Theirs but to do and die."

What poet was called mad, bad, and dangerous to know?

What novelist wrote, "I beheld the wretch—the miserable monster whom I had created"?

Which songwriter declared there was "No business like show business"?

Did Sherlock Holmes really say the words, "Elementary, my dear Watson"?

Chapter 7 ✳ Places   387

For a quick look around the world, read these quotations on travel, countries, and cities. Find out the stories behind these and other quotes:

"For my part, I travel not to go anywhere, but to go. I travel for travel's sake. The great affair is to move."

"Sell a country! Why not sell the air, the clouds and the great sea, as well as the earth? Did not the Great Spirit make them all for the use of his children?"

"Go West, young man."

Chapter 8 ✳ The Human Condition   409

These articles explore the stories behind quotations from philosophers, poets, and others about life, God, truth, duty, freedom, history, and the best way to make one's way in the world. Find out the stories behind these quotations and many more:

"Sometimes a scream is better than a thesis."

"The life of man, solitary, poor, nasty, brutish, and short."

"It is one thing to show a man that he is in error, and another to put him in possession of the truth."

"This world is a comedy to those that think, a tragedy to those that feel."

"If you enquire what the people are like here, I must answer, 'The same as everywhere!'"

"There are only two or three human stories, and they go on repeating themselves as fiercely as if they had never happened before."

"What experience and history teach is this—that people and governments never have learned anything from history, or acted on principles deduced from it."

"I find the great thing in this world is not so much where we stand, as in what direction we are moving: To reach the port of heaven, we must sail sometimes with the wind and sometimes against it—but we must sail, and not drift, nor lie at anchor."

What have people had to say about love, passion, motherhood, marriage, and family? Find out in this chapter.

What popular wedding reading originates with a woman addressing her mother-in-law?

What poet wrote, "How do I love thee? Let me count the ways."

Who really discovered the 'Way to a Man's Heart'?

What novelist had a character suggest, "it's as easy to marry a rich woman as a poor woman"?

Who first suggested that the hand that rocks the cradle rules the world?

Chapter 10 ❄ **Popular Sayings**   **546**

The sayings in this chapter permeate our daily lives...but where did they come from? Find out in this chapter, which answers these questions and many more.

What company first used "always a bridesmaid, never a bride" in their ads?

Did P.T. Barnum really say, "There's a sucker born every minute"?

What incident led a broadcaster to say, "Oh, the humanity!"

John Adams wasn't the first person to say, "Facts are stubborn things." Who was?

Who was the first politician to promise "a chicken in every pot"?

Who wrote, "Those who cannot remember the past are condemned to repeat it"?

Chapter 11 ❄ **The Quotables**   **617**

The orators and writers spotlighted in this chapter didn't limit themselves to one topic. They've left behind hundreds of familiar quotes. From Shakespeare to Twain, Wollstonecroft to Wilde, Johnson to the writers of the Algonquin Round Table, you'll find wit, satire, sharp observations, and more than a few dollops of humor.

Was it Wilde or Twain who said, "I haven't a particle of confidence in a man who has no redeeming petty vices whatsoever"?

Was it Pascal or Montaigne who wrote, "The heart has its reasons, which Reason does not know?

Who wrote more than 500 maxims, including, "Nothing is given so profusely as advice"?

Quotable Quotes

✳   ✳   ✳   ✳

HAVE YOU EVER wondered who first coined the term "cool as a cucumber"? Have you ever heard a quote and figured it was *probably* Mark Twain who said it, but you weren't sure? If so, we've got the book for you. *The Book of Who Said That* provides hundreds of articles that cover the origins of countless quotations and popular sayings. Along with the quotations, you'll find out more about the lives and times of the people who said them. In some cases they were famous and prolific; in other cases they left behind one perfectly-phrased quotation before fading back into obscurity.

With 11 chapters divided into different themes, you'll find quotes for all occasions. Some quotations date back centuries; others were introduced much more recently but have already become part of our shared vernacular.

Read about:

✳ The ancient Greek poet who wrote, "Whom the gods love die young" a few millenia before Billy Joel wrote the song, "Only the Good Die Young."

✳ The sources that influenced Franklin Delano Roosevelt when he said, "The only thing to fear is fear itself."

✳ The naval hero who first coined the term, "Our country, right or wrong."

✳ Whether Hippocrates really said, "First, do no harm."

✳ The woman who wrote the words at the base of the Statue of Liberty.

The Book of Who Said That will inform you about the stories behind quotations you've always known—and introduce you to even more words of wit and wisdom!

Wit and Wisdom from the Ancient World

A Man of Fables

An ancient Greek storyteller who lived between 620–546 BCE, Aesop created more than a hundred fables that have been passed down to this day, and teach simple parables about ethics and morality. The earliest biography of Aesop, The Aesop Romance, *is itself widely recognized to be a work of fiction. As his fables were passed down through the centuries, they were continually translated and revised, and have been adapted to the stage and television. These are a few of his best.*

✳   ✳   ✳   ✳

The Ant and the Grasshopper

IN THIS FABLE, a grasshopper has spent the summer singing, while an ant has worked all summer storing up food for the long winter ahead. When winter does come, the grasshopper begins to starve, and begs the ant for food. The ant admonishes the grasshopper for its idleness and suggests that having sung through the summer, that it tries dancing through the winter. The moral of the fable is to emphasize the importance of hard work and planning against lean times in the future, although counter-fables arose as early as ancient times that stressed the values of compassion and charity.

The Goose That Laid the Golden Eggs

A farmer and his wife find that one of their geese has begun to lay a golden egg every day. They reasoned that this must mean that the goose has a huge lump of gold inside her, and in order to get it right away, they kill the goose and cut her open. But to their surprise, the goose is the same as any other one, and there is no gold. Having hoped to become rich all at once, the pair has lost any chance of the possibility of patiently growing rich instead. "Killing the Golden Goose" has since become a common idiom.

The Lion and the Mouse

A sleeping lion is awakened by a noisy mouse, and the lion becomes enraged. But the mouse begs the lion to forgive it, saying that the mouse is unworthy prey and killing it wouldn't bring any honor to the lion. The lion agrees, and lets the mouse go. Later, the lion is caught in a hunter's net. When the mouse hears the lion roaring for help, it comes to help, gnawing through the ropes to free the lion. The moral of the fable is that mercy will bring its own reward, and that no one is so small that they cannot help someone greater.

The Boy Who Cried Wolf

A shepherd boy, bored, cries out for help from nearby villagers, shouting that a wolf is attacking the flock of sheep. When the villagers come running to help him, the boy laughs at them and admits that there was no wolf. Although the villagers scold and beat the boy, the next day he does it again. After a few days of fooling the villagers like this, the boy is tending his flock when a wolf attacks. The boy cries out for help, but no one will come help him. The English idiom "To cry wolf" for giving a false alarm is derived from this fable.

The Farmer and His Sons

Nearing death, a farmer calls his sons to him in secret, and tells them not to give away the family farm, because there is a great treasure hidden somewhere on the land. After he dies, the sons dig everywhere on the farm, searching for the treasure, but find nothing. But because they have carefully turned over the soil on the farm, the next year the farm's crops flourish as never before, and they realize the hidden meaning in their father's advice: that work is its own reward.

More Wisdom

Here are just a few of the quips that we still use today, courtesy of Aesop.

"Appearances often are deceiving."

"Do not count your chickens before they are hatched."

"No act of kindness, however small, is wasted."

"Familiarity breeds contempt."

"A crust eaten in peace is better than a banquet partaken in anxiety."

"People often grudge others what they cannot enjoy themselves."

"It is thrifty to prepare today for the wants of tomorrow."

"Any excuse will serve a tyrant."

"Beware lest your lose the substance by grasping at the shadow."

"The gods help those that help themselves."

"We would often be sorry if our wishes were gratified."

"Union gives strength."

An Early Wit

His father was a fishmonger and a smuggler, and his mother was a prostitute. The slave of a Greek rhetorician, Bion burned his master's library and gave away his inheritance after his death and fled to Athens, where he became one of the greatest Cynics of the ancient world.

✳ ✳ ✳ ✳

B ION WAS BORN around 325 BCE on the coast of the Black Sea to free parents, but because his father was charged with a number of crimes, his family were sold into slavery when he was still a young man. After making his way to Athens, Bion studied at Plato's Academy, traveled extensively throughout Greece and Macedonia, and eventually became a teacher at the Academy in Rhodes.

Unlike other scholars of his day, Bion was not associated with Platonism, instead joining the Cynics of Diogenes and Antisthenes. Cynics believed that the meaning of life was found by living virtuously and in harmony with nature. They lived simply, eschewing worldly goods and attacking social traditions.

Bion was known for his withering attacks on his opponents, who included the gods, musicians, astrologers, the wealthy, and the devout. His most well-known work, *Diatribes*, ruthlessly satirized people's general foolishness and poked fun at the human condition. He advocated using common sense when dealing with life's problems, no matter how big or small – from the fear of death to poverty to exile and slavery. His writings were widely cited by historians, including Plutarch and Cicero.

Bion died sometime around 250 BCE in Chaclis in Euboea.

The Words of Bion

Here are just some of the many things that Bion is quoted as saying.

"Though boys throw stones at frogs in sport, the frogs do not die in sport, but in earnest."

"How stupid it was for the king to tear out his hair in grief, as if baldness were a cure for sorrow."

"Old age is the harbor of all ills."

"Love of money is the mother-city of all evils."

"The road to Hades is easy to travel; at any rate men pass away with their eyes shut."

"He has not acquired a fortune; the fortune has acquired him."

"Self-conceit is the enemy of progress."

Which Philosopher?

Each quote below is attributed to Socrates, Plato, or Aristotle. Do you know who said what?

✳ ✳ ✳ ✳

1. Liars when they speak the truth are not believed.

a) Socrates

b) Plato

c) Aristotle

2. I am not an Athenian or a Greek, but a citizen of the world.

a) Socrates

b) Plato

c) Aristotle

3. There is only one good, knowledge, and one evil, ignorance.

a) Socrates

b) Plato

c) Aristotle

4. The life which is unexamined is not worth living.

a) Socrates

b) Plato

c) Aristotle

5. No evil can happen to a good man, either in life or after death.

a) Socrates

b) Plato

c) Aristotle

6. What is a friend? A single soul dwelling in two bodies.

a) Socrates

b) Plato

c) Aristotle

7. The basis of a democratic state is liberty.

a) Socrates

b) Plato

c) Aristotle

8. False words are not only evil in themselves, but they infect the soul with evil.

a) Socrates

b) Plato

c) Aristotle

9. Having the fewest wants, I am nearest to the gods.

a) Socrates

b) Plato

c) Aristotle

Answers: 1. c; 2. a; 3. a; 4. b; 5. b; 6. c; 7. c; 8. b; 9; a.

Socrates

Socrates was born in Athens circa 470 BCE. We know about him largely through the writings of his students, including Plato and Xenophon. His method of testing philosophical ideas—the Socratic Method—laid the foundation for Western philosophy and logic.

✳ ✳ ✳ ✳

SOCRATES WAS BORN in Athens circa 470 BCE. It's thought that he worked as a mason before devoting himself to philosophy, and he also briefly served in the Athenian army. He had three sons with his wife Xanthippe, but was not much of a family man, preferring to devote himself to educating Athens' youth.

Socrates taught that philosophy should advance the greater wellbeing of society. He was perhaps the first philosopher to propose a system of ethics based on human reason instead of theological dogma. Because human choices are motivated by the desire to be happy, and because wisdom is couched in knowing oneself, he argued, the more a person knows the better they will be able to reason and make choices that bring true happiness. Socrates thought that this logically meant government worked best when it was ruled by knowledgeable, virtuous, and completely self-aware individuals, or what he called philosopher kings.

Socrates strolled the streets of Athens, asking questions of nobles and commoners alike in an effort to find truths, rather than lecture about what he did know. The Socratic Method of questioning fellow Athenians was designed to force them to think through a problem and realize the conclusion themselves.

Trial and Execution

Athens was undergoing a period of political turmoil during his life, and Socrates publicly attacked what he considered the backwards thinking. As a result, he was arrested, tried for heresy and "corrupting the minds" of Athenian youth. Found guilty, he was sentenced to death by drinking a mixture containing poison hemlock in 399 BCE.

The Father of Philosophy?

Plato was one of the most influential of the ancient Greek philosophers. He founded the famous Academy in Athens, which would devote itself to philosophical and scientific research and education. Plato's extensive works on philosophy, politics and mathematics influenced many of the thinkers of his day and for centuries to come.

✳ ✳ ✳ ✳

PLATO'S INFLUENCE ON his contemporaries is demonstrated by the fact that he is one of the few ancient philosophers whose works were preserved practically in their entirety. Little is known about his early life, but it's believed he was born in Athens or Aegina around 428 BCE. Plato died in 348 or 347 BCE.

Plato wrote extensively, but was modest about recording his own life. He may have traveled in the ancient world before returning to Athens at the age of 40, when he founded the Academy. The Academy endured for nearly three centuries until it was destroyed by the Roman general Sulla in 84 BCE.

Plato developed his philosophical ideas and scientific theories at the Academy. He tackled metaphysics in his argument that universal properties exist independently of any mind or description. This idea, called Platonic Realism, started a centuries-long debate about realism that persists in ontological studies today.

Plato's Theory of Forms, famously explained in his allegory of the cave, argues that the world as it appears is not real, but merely a "copy" of the real world. And his epistemology (or theory of knowledge) holds that knowledge is intrinsic, and learning is actually recalling innate truths.

In *The Republic* Plato laid out his political theory. In brief, he divided society into three classes: producers/workers, warriors/guardians, and rulers or philosopher kings. Written in Socratic dialogue, it remains his most famous work.

Bringing Science Down to Earth

Aristotle's impact on Western knowledge was incredibly profound. He is widely regarded as creating the earliest known comprehensive system of Western philosophy, with contributions to physics, biology, logic, ethics, government, and the arts. His shift from Platonism, which argued for the coexistence of a 'perceptible' reality and an 'imperceptible' one, to Empiricism, which holds that human knowledge is rooted in that which can be observed, was nothing short of revolutionary in its influence.

✳ ✳ ✳ ✳

Born in Greece in 384 BCE, Aristotle joined Plato's Academy in Athens when he was a teenager, and studied there for the next twenty years of his life. While there, he immersed himself in Platonic thought and scientific study.

Following the death of Plato in 347 BCE, Aristotle left Athens to become the head of the Royal Academy of Macedon. He was the royal tutor to Alexander the Great and other future Macedonian kings. His position as Alexander's tutor allowed him to influence world politics at the time: he personally encouraged Alexander to invade Persia and pursue his conquest of Asia Minor. His position also gave him the resources necessary to establish his own school, the Lyceum, where he completed many of his most influential writings.

Some of his most influential works include *Physics*, *On the Soul*, *Metaphysics*, and *Poetics*. Aristotle's wide-ranging studies are generally considered to be not only an index of Greek knowledge at the time, but also constitute the foundation of Western thought for the next two millennia.

After Alexander died in 323, growing anti-Macedonian sentiment in Athens forced Aristotle to flee. Upon leaving, he declared "I will not allow the Athenians to sin twice against Philosophy," referring to the execution of Socrates in Athens in 399 BCE. Aristotle died later that year.

Cicero

A revered orator, philosopher, and statesman, Marcus Tullius Cicero had an enormous influence on the Latin language, Roman ideas about politics and philosophy, and the development of European literature and thought. The European Renaissance was largely inspired by the rediscovery of his writings during the 14th century.

※ ※ ※ ※

CICERO WAS BORN on January 3, 106 BCE, to a wealthy landowner. Early on, he immersed himself in his father's library, and when his father saw this, he took Cicero to Rome to be educated. There he learned Greek philosophy, poetry and rhetoric. He would translate many of the Greek philosophers' works into Latin, making them accessible to a wider audience.

Around 81 BCE, Cicero began his career as a lawyer, and he gained notoriety for his defense of Sextus Roscius against a charge of patricide. His defense courageously challenged the authority of Sulla, who was then dictator, and he won the case. It would not be the last time Cicero challenged those in power.

In 79 BCE, perhaps to escape Sulla's wrath, Cicero travelled to Rhodes to study history and oratory; he would eventually be the greatest classical orator since Demosthenes. (See page 23.) In 75 BCE, he began his political career as a public servant, and later became a praetor (judge) before being elected consul in 63 BCE. In the Senate, Cicero criticized Caesar, refused an offer to join him in a power-sharing Triumvirate, and was exiled from Rome until 57 BCE. He avoided politics for the next few years, concentrating instead on his writing.

Following the assassination of Caesar, Cicero publically feuded with Mark Antony, prompting Antony to declare him an enemy of the state. He fled, but was captured and killed on December 7, 43 BCE.

Cicero's Sayings

Some of Cicero's most famous quotes are as follows:

"There is said to be hope for a sick man, as long as there is life."

"Almost no one dances sober, unless he is insane."

"Cui bono?" ("Who benefits?" or "To whose advantage?")

"Laws are silent in time of war."

"Old age: the crown of life, our play's last act."

"Old men are garrulous by nature."

"A friend is, at it were, a second self."

"That which stands first, and is most to be desired by all happy, honest and healthy-minded men, is dignified leisure."

"Everything has a small beginning."

"If you have a garden and a library, you have everything you need."

"Let the welfare of the people be the ultimate law."

"Let the punishment match the offense."

"Few are those who wish to be endowed with virtue rather than to seem so."

"There is nothing so ridiculous but some philosopher has said it."

Confucius

Born Kong Qui in the Lu state of China during the Spring and Autumn Period of Chinese history, Confucius developed a system of teachings around ethics, family, and education that would become the official imperial philosophy of China for centuries. His work was particularly influential during the Han, Tang, and Song dynasties.

✳   ✳   ✳   ✳

CONFUCIUS WAS BORN circa 551 BCE in the present-day Shandong Province in China. Very little is known of his early life, and accounts vary so widely that some claim he was born into poverty while others assert he was raised as part of a royal family of the Chou Dynasty.

During his life, several rival Chinese states were competing with the Chou Dynasty, which at the time had ruled for more than five centuries. The resulting turmoil undermined traditional Chinese principles and led to a period of moral decline. Confucius seized upon this opportunity to begin spreading teachings that were focused on restoring traditional values based around compassion. His philosophy was couched in the simple idea called *ren*. The idea includes the dual tenets of loving others and practicing self-discipline in what was perhaps the earliest recorded instance of the Golden Rule.

With regard to family, he advocated for family loyalty, ancestor veneration, and respect of elders by children and wives by husbands.

The concept of self-discipline also infused Confucius' political philosophy. He taught that leaders had to exercise self-discipline so that they could lead by a positive example, treating their followers with respect and compassion while remaining humble in their position of power. Confucius taught that leaders could inspire their subjects to respect the rule of law by teaching them to be virtuous and unite using ritual decorum and good manners.

Confucius promoted a philosophy of education based on the Six Arts of archery, calligraphy, chariot-driving, computation, music, and ritual. He believed that the main purpose of education was to teach the people to lead lives of integrity and honor. He attempted to restore the traditional values of generosity, respectability and ritual in Chinese society through his educational philosophy.

Major Writings

Many of the most influential works of classical Chinese writing including all of the *Five Classics* were written or edited by Confucius. Among others, he revised the *Book of Odes* and the *Book of Documents*, a classic historical work on ancient China. He also wrote a history of the nobles of Lu, a vassal state during the Zhou dynasty, called *The Spring and Autumn Annals*.

Confucius' political and philosophical beliefs are collected in the *Lunyu*, which may have been composed by his disciples. It is one of the Four Books that were published by Zhu Xi in 1190 CE, and that make up the core of Confucianism. *Lunyu* was translated into English as *The Analects of Confucius*.

Confucius died in Qufu in 479, a year after his son Tzu-lu was killed in battle. At the time of his death, he believed his teachings had had no real impact on Chinese culture or society, but by the fourth century BCE, he had become widely regarded as a brilliant philosopher and sage who had not received the proper recognition during his life.

During the Han Dynasty in the second century BCE, Confucius' philosophy had become the foundation of the official state ideology, and he remains one of the most influential thinkers in Chinese history.

The Sayings of Confucius

Here is a selection of some of Confucius' beliefs:

"Smooth words and fawning looks are seldom found with love."

"The young should be dutiful at home, modest abroad, careful and true, overflowing in kindness for all, but in brotherhood with love. And if they have strength to spare they should spend it on the arts."

"He that rules by mind is like the north star, steady in his seat, whilst the stars all bend to him."

"The three hundred poems are summed up in the one line, Think no evil."

"Learning without thought is naught; thought without learning is dangerous."

"Lift up the straight, put away the crooked; and the people will be won. Lift up the crooked, put away the straight; and the people will not be won."

"A man without love, what is courtesy to him? A man without love, what is music to him?"

"Loveless men cannot bear need long, they cannot bear fortune long. Loving men find peace in love, the wise find profit in it."

"Whilst thy father and mother are living, do not wander afar. If thou must travel, hold a set course."

"We shall seldom get lost if we hold to main lines."

"A great soul is never friendless: he has always neighbours."

"Love is to conquer self and turn to courtesy. If we could conquer self and turn to courtesy for one day, all below heaven would turn to love. Does love flow from within, or does it flow from others?"

"Rank thy work above success, will not the mind be raised? Fight the bad in thee, not the bad in other men, will not evil be mended?"

"If good men were to govern a land for an hundred years, cruelty would be conquered and putting to death done away with."

"What is governing to a man that can rule himself? If he cannot rule himself, how shall he rule others?"

The Second Sage

"Never has a man who has bent himself been able to make others straight."

✳ ✳ ✳ ✳

BORN NEARLY A century after Confucius, Mencius (or Mengzi, "Master Meng") would eventually become known as "The Second Sage" for his contributions to Confucianism. He collated and interpreted Confucius' teachings, and helped form them into a comprehensive philosophy to which he added his own ideas and teachings.

Like Confucius, little is known about Mencius' life, although the biographer Sima Qian, who also wrote about Confucius, said he was born in Lu in northeast China during the Warring States Period following the collapse of the Zhou Dynasty.

Mencius is best known for is his belief that human nature is inherently good, a concept he called *xing shan*. He taught that a characteristic of a person can be part of the person's nature even if it is not expressed. For example, bearing fruit is a characteristic of orange trees. Even if most orange seeds do not develop into trees that bear fruit, Mencius said, they retain the characteristic as part of their nature. Like an orange seed, he taught that with education and self-discipline, human goodness can be cultivated. With negative influences or neglect it can be wasted, but it remains an inherent part of human nature.

He also proposed the idea of The Four Sprouts, in which negative reactions can lead to positive outcomes because of human goodness. Feeling pity, for example, will grow to humanity, as feeling shame will grow to righteousness.

Mencius' writings eventually became the core philosophy of orthodox Confucianism.

Famous for Oratory

"Nothing is easier than self-deceit. For what each man wishes, that he also believes to be true."

✳   ✳   ✳   ✳

DEMOSTHENES, BORN IN Athens in 384 BCE, was considered the greatest of the Greek orators, and is famous for having incited the Athenians to fight against Phillip of Macedonia as well as Phillip's son Alexander the Great. His first taste of oratory came at the age of 20, when he successfully argued to gain the remainder of his family inheritance from his appointed guardians. For a number of years Demosthenes worked in the law and wrote speeches for lawsuits.

In his thirties, Demosthenes began to speak publicly; this is when he first began his political rhetoric. To strengthen his voice, he practiced speaking over the roar of waves at the coast with his mouth full of pebbles. Demosthenes' oratory was convincing: following the death of Phillip, he helped incite a rebellion against Alexander in 335 BCE. The rebellion was crushed, however, and while Demosthenes was spared, he'd become a marked man in the eyes of the Macedonians.

The following year, a number of Demosthenes' admirers in Athens suggested that the city honor him for his speeches by presenting him with a crown. The idea quickly became a political issue, and in 330 BCE, one of his supporters, Ctesiphon, was prosecuted for proposing the idea. In what became his most famous speech, *On the Crown*, Demosthenes attacked his political opponents and convinced them to release Ctesiphon.

When Alexander died, Demosthenes began to urge another revolt, but Alexander's successor quickly subdued the Athenians and condemned him and other rebels to death. Rather than be captured, Demosthenes took his own life on October 12, 322 BCE. He was 62 years old.

In Search of an Honest Man

"I am looking for an honest man" —*Diogenes often said this while carrying a lighted lamp through the streets of Athens during the daytime.*

* * * *

DIOGENES, BORN IN 412 BCE in the Greek colony Sinope, was a Greek philosopher and one of the founders of Cynicism, which says the purpose of life is to live in agreement with nature and rejecting possessions. He settled in Athens, and became a student of Antisthenes, an ascetic and the father of Cynicism. Antisthenes originally refused to take students, but Diogenes followed him everywhere he went until Antisthenes relented.

Diogenes infused his philosophical teaching with a sense of humor that was unique among the philosophers of the time. He thought that people rely too heavily on preconceived notions of the nature of evil. He believed in rejecting societal mores; as an ascetic, he lived in a large ceramic urn outside of a temple. Once, when he saw a peasant boy drink from his hands, Diogenes broke his only bowl.

Diogenes was famous for challenging the elites of his day. He once embarrassed Plato, who had defined a man as a "featherless biped." Diogenes presented a chicken at the Academy and declared "behold! I have brought you a man." Plato revised his definition, but publically thought Diogenes was mad.

Diogenes also is reported to have met Alexander the Great, was said to have seen Diogenes studying a pile of human bones. Alexander asked him what he was doing, and Diogenes responded that he was looking for the bones of the King's father, but "could not distinguish them from those of a slave."

Diogenes died in Corinth in 323 BCE.

Quotes on Sunlight from Diogenes and Others

"The sun too penetrates into privies, but is not polluted by them."

—DIOGENES

"A little rule, a little sway,
A sunbeam in a winter's day,
Is all the proud and might have
Between the cradle and the grave."

—JOHN DYER

"The sun, which passeth through pollutions and itself remains as pure as before."

—FRANCIS BACON

"An expression of it [beauty] can be a dustbin with a shaft or sunlight across it, or it can be a rose in the gutter."

—CHARLIE CHAPLIN

"I have seen the sunset, stained with mystic horrors."

—ARTHUR RIMBAUD

"Truth is as impossible to be soiled by any outward touch as the sunbeam."

—JOHN MILTON

A Seeker of Pleasure

He claimed: "Pleasure is the beginning and end of living happily."

✳ ✳ ✳ ✳

EPICURUS WAS BORN on the small Greek island of Samos in 341 BCE. His father was a schoolteacher, and the family was poor. He began developing his own ideas at a young age, having growing disillusioned with his teachers. After a number of years travelling, in about 306 BCE Epicurus established a school in Athens called The Garden, where he lived and taught for the remainder of his life. Here he developed and spread his philosophy of Epicureanism: the pursuit of pleasure.

His philosophy, which taught that the goal of life is pleasure, has since given rise to the use of the word *epicurean* to mean gourmet, but this is at odds with his original meaning. Epicurus considered pleasure to be attainable by living in contemplative moderation. He taught his students to shed anxieties and desires and enjoy the natural happiness that is found in the freedom from fear and absence of pain, called ataraxia and aponia, respectively.

Epicurus believed there are no gods that can harm humans, and likewise there is no afterlife. He taught that the things we actually need are easy to find, and those that make us suffer are easy to endure. According to him, one could only live a "pleasant" life by also living "wisely, well, and justly." Epicurus promoted egalitarianism at his school, accepting women and slaves, which was highly unusual at the time. His teachings have since influenced many great thinkers: among others, John Locke and Thomas Jefferson included his ideas about the pursuit of happiness in their own works.

"It is impossible to live pleasurably without living wisely, well, and justly, and impossible to live wisely, well, and justly without living pleasurably."

Euripides

Along with Sophocles and Aeschylus, Euripides was one of the three tragedians of ancient Greece whose works have survived. Euripides wrote more than ninety plays in his lifetime, 19 of which have survived.

✳ ✳ ✳ ✳

EURIPIDES WAS BORN in Salamis in 480 BCE. When he was a young boy, his father received an oracle that said Euripides would "win crowns of victory." His father assumed that meant he would be a great athlete, and sent him to train as one, but he also studied philosophy and the arts. Fulfilling the oracle, he won his first crown of victory in 441 BCE in the annual

Athenian festival of the arts, and would go on to win four more during his life.

Some of Euripides' most famous tragedies are *Medea*, *The Bacchae*, *Hippolytus*, and *Alcestis*. He pioneered the portrayal of heroes and gods as ordinary figures who were faced with extraordinary circumstances, which would influence later comic and romantic plays. Euripides also invented the style of focusing on the inner lives of his characters and thus exploring the workings of human psychology, which was entirely new to Greek theatre.

Euripides was distinctive among the ancient Athenian writers in the sympathy he extended to all of his characters, including women, which was unusual at the time. This practice often shocked his conservative audiences. Because of this, he was often compared to Socrates as one of the leaders of a corrupting movement of intellectual decadence. In 408 he chose voluntary exile but was invited to live and write at the court of Archelaus, the kind of Macedonia. He would live there until his death in 406 BCE.

Quotes from Euripides

"Those whom God wishes to destroy, he first makes mad."

"A sweet thing, for whatever time, to revisit in dreams the dear dead we have lost."

"God, these old men! How they pray for death."

"Today's today. Tomorrow we may be ourselves gone down the drain of Eternity."

"There is no benefit in the gifts of a bad man."

"We know the good, we apprehend it clearly, but we can't bring it to achievement."

"In this world second thoughts, it seems, are best."

"In a case of dissension, never dare to judge till you've heard the other side."

"Leave no stone unturned."

"A coward turns away, but a brave man's choice is danger."

"The day for honest men, the night for thieves."

"Slow but sure moves the might of the gods."

"A bad beginning makes a bad ending."

"Waste not fresh tears over old griefs."

"Every man is like the company he is wont to keep."

The First Historian

"Men trust their ears less than their eyes:" to Herodotus, seeing was believing.

* * * *

WHEN HERODOTUS PENNED his *Histories*, it was the first time a historian had ever approached the documentation of significant events in an investigative manner. Herodotus attempted to collect accounts of historical events from reliable witnesses, and practically invented the concept of using a primary source for a historical record. At the time, his approach represented a major shift from the time-honored Homeric tradition of passing down epic poems that recounted fantastic events. Because of his method, and the scope of his historical record of the ancient world, Herodotus is often called "the Father of History."

Nine Books

During Herodotus' travels, he collected accounts of historical events in the ancient world. His *Histories* are the major source of our understanding of the rise of the Persian Empire and the causes and outcome of the Greek and Persian Wars of the 5th century. He described the events leading up to the Trojan War and provided the primary account of the Battle of Thermopylae and other important battles of the Greco-Persian Wars.

Herodotus' wide-ranging *Histories* were not limited to war and politics. He also described the cultures of the ancient world, and gathered local folktales and ancient myths. In one, he recounts the tale of Arion, a musician who brought the *dithyramb*, an ancient hymn that honors Dionysus, to Corinth. Herodotus tells the story of how Arion was captured by pirates on his return from a musical competition in Sicily. Given the choice between suicide and being thrown into the sea, he asked permission to sing a final song, which, according to Herodotus, attracted a pod of dolphins. When he was thrown into the sea, one of the dolphins carried Arion to safety.

On his travels through Egypt, Herodotus reported on its geography and natural history, compiling lists of its local flora and fauna and describing the seasonal flooding of the Nile River. He listed its ancient kings and described the Great Pyramid and the Labyrinth of Egypt, as well as the funeral rites, religious practices and cuisine of Egypt.

The *Histories* were eventually divided into nine books, each named after one of the Greek muses for literature, science, and the arts.

Herodotus and His Shade

In ancient Greece, the only way for authors to publicize their works was to recite them at large festivals or gatherings. Herodotus presented his *Histories* at the Olympic Games; according to one account, by the historian Lucian, he read the entire history in one sitting to enthusiastic applause from the audience. But another historian claimed that Herodotus waited to begin his recitation until clouds had shaded the hot sun, but by then, the crowd had left. This event gave rise to the proverb "Herodotus and his shade" to refer to a missed opportunity or failure due to postponement.

Who Was Herodotus?

Ironically, very little is known about Herodotus' own life. He was born in the ancient Persian city Halicarnassus—modern day Bodrum, Turkey—on or about the year 484 BCE. By his own eyewitness accounts, Herodotus travelled extensively throughout the ancient world, first visiting Egypt, then through Tyre and eventually Babylon. No one knows where he eventually settled and died, although it may have been in Athens or Macedonia, sometime around 430 BCE.

Quotes from Herodotus

"In peace, children inter their parents; war violates the order of nature and causes parents to inter their children."

"If a man insisted always on being serious, and never allowed himself a bit of fun and relaxation, he would go mad or become unstable without knowing it."

"It is the gods' custom to bring low all things of surpassing greatness."

"Great deeds are usually wrought at great risks."

A Poet Lost to History

He's credited with writing the Iliad *and the* Odyssey—*but did he really exist?*

✳   ✳   ✳   ✳

THE ILIAD AND the *Odyssey* are the two major Greek epic poems Homer is credited with writing, and together they lay the foundation of Western literature. The *Iliad* describes the events at the close of the Trojan War, and the *Odyssey* chronicles Odysseus' ten-year journey home following the war.

The Iliad

The *Iliad* opens as the Trojan War is entering its tenth year. Following a dispute between Achilles, the Greek champion, and Agamemnon, the king of the Achaeans, Achilles refuses to fight for Agamemnon, and Zeus refuses to help as well.

Hector, the Trojan champion, attacks and drives the Achaeans back to their ships. Patroclus, Achilles' dearest companion, puts on his his armor and drives the Trojans back from the ships to their city walls, but is killed by Hector. Furious, Achilles reconciles with Agamemnon and charges into battle—against his mother's warning that if he does this he will die soon after. He routs the Trojans nearly single-handedly and kills Hector, dragging his body behind his chariot around the city.

Achilles returns to his camp, where he holds a funeral for Patroclus. Priam, Hector's father and the king of Troy, enters the camp to ransom his son's body. Achilles relents, and the Trojans hold an eleven-day funeral for Hector. As the epic closes, it is clear that although Troy is doomed, Achilles will not live to see it fall.

The Odyssey

Ten years after the fall of Troy, the Greek hero Odysseus still hasn't returned home to Ithaca. Since he is assumed to be dead, his home is overrun by rivals, who court his wife Penelope and feast on his food. The goddess Athena tells his son to look for his father at Pylos and Sparta, and she frees Odysseus from the goddess Calypso, who has imprisoned him as her lover for eight years.

Odysseus sails to the land of the Phaeacians, who give him shelter, and he tells them about his adventures following the Trojan war. During their journey, they encountered gods and monsters: the Cyclops trapped and devoured many of his men before Odysseus helped them escape; the goddess Circe turned his men briefly into pigs; they were nearly trapped by the seductive, deadly Sirens; and they narrowly avoided the sea monster Scylla and whirlpools of Charybdis. Eventually, his men angered Zeus and were killed in a storm.

After he tells his story, the Phaeacians ferry him home, where Odysseus disguises himself as a beggar. Penelope proposes a contest among the suitors: she agrees to marry whoever can string Odysseus' bow and shoot an arrow through twelve ox heads. Only Odysseus can, and he reveals his true identity and kills the suitors, aided by Athena. Then Odyssus and Penelope lovingly reunite at last.

The Homeric Question

The question of whether Homer ever truly existed has persisted among Classical scholars for centuries. There is no direct evidence that Homer was real, and the *Iliad* and *Odyssey* are reflective of the oral tradition of storytelling that was popular in ancient Greece. It's quite possible they are more likely the creation of many different oral poets rather than any single one.

Some scholars have noted the stylistic differences between the two works as additional evidence that the poet called Homer was probably a collection of various storytellers. Another aspect of the debate is the origin of the word "Homer." It could be a mistranslation of an ancient Mediterranean word for 'saga.' The matter may never be settled with certainty.

Quotes from Homer

Whoever he was or wasn't, the poet or poets we think of as Homer left a legacy of rich words that have resonates throughout Western culture.

"Whoever obeys the gods, to him they particularly listen."

—THE ILIAD

"A councilor ought not to sleep the whole night through, a man to whom the populace is entrusted, and who has many responsibilities."

—THE ILIAD

"The glorious gifts of the gods are not to be cast aside."

—THE ILIAD

"He lives not long who battles with the immortals."

—THE ILIAD

"A generation of man is like a generation of leaves: the wind scatters some leaves upon the ground, while others the burgeoning wood brings forth—and the season of spring comes on. So of men one generation springs forth and another ceases."

—THE ILIAD

"By their own follies they perished."

—THE ODYSSEY

"Look now how mortals are blaming the gods, for they say that evils come from us, but in fact they themselves have woes beyond their share because of their own follies."

—THE ODYSSEY

"There is nothing greater and better than this—when a husband and wife keep a household in oneness of mind, a great woe to their enemies and joy to their friends, and win high renown."

—THE ODYSSEY

"All strangers and beggars are from Zeus, and a gift, though small, is precious."

—THE ODYSSEY

"Nay, speak not comfortably to me of death, oh great Odysseus. Rather would I live on ground as the hireling of another, with a landless man who had no great livelihood, than bear sway among all the dead that be departed."

—THE ODYSSEY

"The gods, likening themselves to all kinds of strangers, go in various disguises from city to city, observing the wrongdoing and the righteousness of man."

—THE ODYSSEY

Which Caesar Was It?

Each quote below is attributed to either Julius Caesar or his successor Caesar Augustus (Octavian). Do you know who said what? We'll start you off with an easy one...

❊ ❊ ❊ ❊

1. I came, I saw, I conquered. (*Veni, vidi, vici.*)

a) Julius Caesar

b) Caesar Augustus

2. I love treason but hate a traitor.

a) Julius Caesar

b) Caesar Augustus

3. More haste, less speed.

a) Julius Caesar

b) Caesar Augustus

4. The die is cast. (*Iacta alea est.*)

a) Julius Caesar

b) Caesar Augustus

4. It is not these well-fed long-haired men that I fear, but the pale and the hungry-looking.

a) Julius Caesar

b) Caesar Augustus

5. I found Rome a city of bricks and left it a city of marble.

a) Julius Caesar

b) Caesar Augustus

6. All Gaul is divided into three parts.

a) Julius Caesar

b) Caesar Augustus

7. I wished my wife to be not so much as suspected.

a) Julius Caesar

b) Caesar Augustus

8. Men willingly believe what they wish.

a) Julius Caesar

b) Caesar Augustus

9. Young men, hear an old man to whom old men hearkened when he was young.

a) Julius Caesar

b) Caesar Augustus

10. Well done is quickly done.

a) Julius Caesar

b) Caesar Augustus

Answers: 1. a; 2. a; 3. b; 4. a; 5. b; 6. a; 7. a; 8. a. 9. b. 10. b.

Oppressor or Enlightened Leader?

Julius Caesar is one of the most recognized figures in all of human history. However, most people don't know as much about him as they think.

✳   ✳   ✳   ✳

CAESAR WAS NOT the first Roman emperor; indeed, he was never an emperor at all. He was a dictator, but in his time that word had a reasonable and legitimate political connotation. As history suggests, Caesar was able in many areas. He led men into battle with courage and skill and was also a brilliant administrator and politician who instituted reforms that benefited the common people of Rome.

Rising Out of Chaos

Caesar's birth in 100 B.C. (sometimes listed as 102 B.C.) coincided with great civil strife in Rome. Although his parents' status as nobles gave him advantages, Caesar's childhood was spent in a politically volatile Rome marked by personal hatreds and conniving. As an adult, he learned to be wary in his dealings with other powerful people. By the time Caesar was 20, a patrician named Sulla had been the Roman dictator for about 20 years. Although Caesar and Sulla were friends, Sulla later became enraged when Caesar refused to divorce his wife, Cornelia, who was the daughter of a man Sulla loathed (and murdered), Cinna. In order to save his neck, Caesar promptly left Rome for Asia.

When Sulla died in 78 B.C., Caesar returned to Rome and took up the practice of law. Caesar had everything necessary for success: He had received the best possible education, developed impressive oratorical skills, and made himself an outstanding writer. He also spent huge sums of money, most of which he had to borrow. The money went to bribes and sumptuous parties for the influential and bought Caesar access to power. Leading politicians looked on him favorably and rewarded him with a series of increasingly important political positions in Spain and Rome. Caesar's time in Spain was especially useful, as he used his position there to become very wealthy.

Coming Out on Top

In 59 B.C., Caesar, who was by now a general, made a successful bid for power in concert with Marcus Licinius Crassus, the richest man in Rome; and Pompey, another ambitious general who was known, to his immodest pleasure, as Pompey the Great. These three Type-A personalities ruled Rome as the First Triumvirate, with Caesar becoming first among equals as consul. Caesar had always been popular among the common people and with Rome's soldiers, and he aimed to cement that loyalty with reforms that would benefit them. Soon, Caesar was made governor of Gaul and spent the next 11 years conquering all of what is now France, with a couple of profitable trips to Britain for good measure. While on campaign, he wrote an account of his actions, called *Commentaries*, which is among the finest of all military literature.

Old Friends and New

To leave Rome, even for military glory, was always risky for any of the empire's leaders. While Caesar was abroad, Crassus was killed in battle. This void encouraged Pompey, who made it clear that Caesar was no longer welcome in Rome. Caesar and his army responded by crossing the Rubicon River in 49 B.C. to seize control of the city. (It was at this time that he reportedly said the proverb, "The die is cast.") Within a year of the civil war that followed, Caesar defeated Pompey. He also began a torrid affair with Egypt's Queen Cleopatra. After a few other actions against Rome's enemies, Caesar was acclaimed by all of Rome as a great hero. In turn, he pardoned all who had opposed him.

Hail, Caesar

Mindful of the fleeting nature of popularity, Caesar continued to promote a series of important reforms:

* Some of the land that had been held by wealthy families was distributed to common people desperate to make a living. As one might expect, this didn't go over well with the wealthy.

* Tax reforms insisted upon by Caesar forced the rich to pay their fair share. This innovation didn't win Caesar many new friends among the powerful.

* Retired soldiers were settled on land provided by the government. Because this land was in Rome's outlying territories, it became populated with a happy, well-trained cadre of

veterans meant to be Rome's first line of defense, if needed. Unemployed citizens were also given the opportunity to settle in these areas, where jobs were much more plentiful. This reduced the number of poor people in Rome and decreased the crime rate.

✳ As he had done earlier, Caesar made residents of the provinces, such as people living in Spain, citizens of Rome. This idea proved quite popular. Many years later, some of the Roman emperors actually came from Spain.

✳ Working people are happy people (so it's said). In a clever move, Caesar instituted a massive public works program that provided both jobs and a sense of pride among the citizens of Rome.

Beware the Ides of March

All these reforms notwithstanding, Caesar's enemies feared he would leverage his great popularity to destroy the Roman Republic and institute in its place an empire ruled by one man. So, in one of those moments of violence that turns the wheel of history, Caesar was assassinated by people he trusted on March 15, 44 B.C.—the Ides of March, for those of you who remember your Shakespeare. The civil war that followed was ultimately won by Caesar's nephew, Octavian, who changed his name to Caesar Augustus ... and who replaced the republic and instituted in its place an empire ruled by one man! Augustus was the first of a long succession of emperors who ruled virtually independent of the Roman Senate. It was the rulers who followed Caesar, then, and not Caesar himself, who proved the undoing of the system so cherished by Caesar's enemies.

In answer to the question as to what sort of death was the best, Julius Caesar reportedly replied, "A sudden death."

Lao Tzu

"Doing nothing is better than being busy doing nothing:" to Lao Tzu, it was better to empty the mind of bodily awareness, and be still.

✳   ✳   ✳   ✳

ORN SOMETIME IN the 6th century BCE during the Zhou Dynasty, Lao Tzu (or Laozi, "Old Master") founded the Chinese philosophy Taoism. Very little is known about Lao Tzu's life, but his teachings and philosophy have persisted for centuries and remain influential in China and throughout the modern world.

Life and Voyages

Most of what is known about Lao Tzu's life is apocryphal, and many legends surround the circumstances of his birth and life. According to legend, he was born after spending eight or eighty years in his mother's womb, and he lived to be 129 years old.

The *Shiji*, a biography of Lao Tzu written by Sima Qian in 145 BCE, provides much of what we know about him. According to the *Shiji*, Lao Tzu was born in the Henan Province, and had the family name Li. During the Zhou Dynasty, he was a historian and archivist at the royal court. It was around this time that he met Confucius, who found him fascinating. Lao Tzu on the other hand criticized what he perceived as the philosopher's arrogance.

Later in life, upon observing the decline of the Zhou Dynasty, Lao Tzu travelled west to live out his days as a hermit on the frontier. As he travelled through the Xiangu pass, a sentry named Yinxi asked him to write a book of his teachings. The resulting book is said to be the *Tao Te Ching*, or "Way of Virtue." Yinxi became his disciple and they left the pass to travel together.

The Tao

The *Tao Te Ching*, or more simply the *Tao* or the Way, is, along with the *Zhuangzi*, one of the two major works of Taoist philosophy. The *Tao* describes the teachings of Taoism with 81 short poems. The teachings are divided into descriptions of the philosophical and religious aspects of Taoism. The teachings emphasize *wu wei*, or "effortless action," simplicity, sincerity, and spontaneity. There are three basic virtues in Taoism, called the Three Treasures or the Three Jewels. In the Tao, they are described as compassion, frugality, and humility, although later interpretations took them to also mean *jing* (the essence of the physical body), *qi* (life force, including emotions), and *shen* (the spirit).

Lao Tzu highlighted the significance of nature in the Tao and preached that human lives would be enriched by a return to it. The work discusses the primitive state of all existence and heavily discusses the concept of naturalness at length. Lao promoted a limited government and urged humility and restraint in leadership, and urged detachment from desires and leading a simple life.

Taoism most heavily influenced the Han Dynasty, during which Lao Tzu was elevated to a nearly godlike status. This gave rise to the *Tianshi Dao* or "Way of the Celestial Masters' in the 2nd century CE. The movement eventually gained power in the Sichuan state during that time. Eventually, Lao Tzu came to be considered a personification of the *Tao*, which is described as natural, spontaneous, eternal, nameless, and indescribable.

Lao Tzu's influence is incredibly widespread, and is, with Confucianism, one of the foundations of Chinese philosophy, but the *Tao* also has heavily influenced many Western philosophers, political scientists and economists, and many of Lao Tzu's adages from the *Tao* have been adopted as maxims around the world.

Quotes from Lao Tzu

"When the people of the world all know beauty as beauty, there arises the recognition of ugliness. When they all know the good as good, there arises the recognition of evil."

"He who loves the world as his body may be entrusted with the empire."

"Manifest plainness. Embrace simplicity. Reduce selfishness. Have few desires."

"He who knows does not speak. He who speaks does not know."

"To know that you do not know is the best. To pretend to know when you do not know is a disease."

Livy

Without Livy, the rise of the Roman Republic and triumphs of its people may have been lost to history.

✳ ✳ ✳ ✳

LIVY WAS BORN in Patavium (modern-day Padua) around 59 BCE, and was formally educated there. He began writing brief philosophical and historical works at a young age. While little is known of his personal life, he did marry and had a small family. At the age of thirty, Livy travelled to Rome, where he would gain fame as a historian.

Livy's most famous work, *Ab Urbe Condita* (From the Foundation of the City), was a 142-volume history of the Roman Republic, covering a period of seven centuries from the founding of Rome through the collapse of the Republic and the beginning of the Imperial period and reign of Caesar Augustus. Only a fraction of the *Condita* survives, but the portion that does remain provides a fascinating picture of the rise of the Republic. In it, Livy described at length what he considered the downfall of the Roman character, and the work heavily emphasized a Stoic philosophy and ethical outlook. Livy believed that historical works should elevate as well as inform the reader.

The remainder of his work is mostly lost, although there are brief summaries of most of his writings. Livy was on familiar terms with the Emperor Octavian (Augustus), and is said to have encouraged the future Emperor Claudius to study history when he was young.

He returned to Patavium in his old age, and is believed to have died there in CE 17, a few years after the death of Augustus.

Quotes from Livy

"We can endure neither our vices nor the remedies for them."

"This above all makes history useful and desirable: it unfolds before our eyes a glorious record of exemplary actions."

"Shared danger is the strongest of bonds; it will keep men united in spite of mutual dislike and suspicion."

"From abundance springs satiety."

"Better late than never." (Potius sero quam numquam.)

"Favor and honor sometimes fall more fitly on those who do not desire them."

"Woe to the vanquished!"

"Those ills are easiest to bear with which we are most familiar."

"The result showed that fortune helps the brave."

"The populace is like the sea, motionless in itself, but stirred by every wind, even the lightest breeze."

"Good fortune and a good disposition are rarely given to the same man."

"We feel public misfortunes just so far as they affect our private circumstances, and nothing of this nature appeals more directly to us than the loss of money."

"The study of history is the best medicine for a sick mind; for in history you have a record of the infinite variety of human experience plainly set out for all to see; and in that record you can find for yourself and your country both examples and warnings."

Only the Good Die Young?

"Whom the gods love dies young."

✳ ✳ ✳ ✳

PERHAPS THE FIRST person to express an idea that would echo through the centuries all the way to rock 'n' roll artists of the late 20th century, Menander is widely recognized as one of the greatest writers of the Athens New Comedy movement. He won multiple awards for his works at the Lenaia, Athens' annual festival of the dramatic arts. While he wrote over 100 plays, only one has survived nearly complete; the rest are known only as fragments.

Menander was born around 340 BCE in Athens. The son of wealthy aristocrats, he was well-educated and exposed to the arts at an early age: his uncle, Alexis, was a poet during the Athens Middle Comedy period. Menander competed with other popular writers of his day in dramatic contests, which he won eight times. His chief rival, Philemon, won sometimes, but Menander thought of himself as the superior writer, and went so far as to taunt him whenever Philemon won a contest.

Nearly all of Menander's works were lost during the Middle Ages, and he was known only by fragments of his work until 1959, when an excavation in Egypt found a papyrus scroll containing his play *Dyskolos* along with portions of two others. *Dyskolos*, or "The Grouch," involves a youth named Sostratos, whom the god Pan enchants to fall in love with a peasant girl named Myrrhine. Her father is an old, cantankerous misanthrope, and a comedy of errors ensues. After many setbacks, Sostratos and Myrrhine are married.

Menander died in Piraeus in 290 BCE.

"The best of men cannot suspend their fate: The good die early, and the bad die late."

—DANIEL DEFOE, WRITING IN 1715

Ovid

One of the greatest of the Roman poets, he would live out his days exiled by the Emperor in a remote province on the Black Sea. The exact circumstances surrounding his exile are not clear, but Ovid wrote that it was for "a poem and a mistake."

✳ ✳ ✳ ✳

BORN PUBLIUS OVIDIUS Naso in Sulmo, Italy, in 43 BCE, Ovid was educated in rhetoric by Arellius Fuscus in Rome. His father wanted him to pursue a career as a lawyer, but following the death of his brother, Ovid abandoned the law and become a poet instead.

His first or many public recitations was when he was eighteen years old. He would go on to enjoy great success for the next 25 years, primarily writing poetry in elegiac style with erotic and romantic themes. Some of his better known works from this period include the *Amores*, a series of erotic poems written to a lover named Corinna, and the *Heroides*, love letters written by mythological heroines. He also wrote the *Ars Amatoria (Art of Love)*, a three-volume work about seduction that was intended to parody the style of didactic poetry that was popular at the time.

Ovid's most famous and perhaps most ambitious work is the *Metamorphoses*, completed in 8 CE. A fifteen-volume work, it covered the history of Greek and Roman mythology from the creation of the universe to the deification of Julius Caesar in 42 BCE. Ovid describes human beings being transformed into trees, constellations, animals, and flowers in the epic poem.

The same year, he was exiled by Augustus to Tomis, where he would spend the rest of his life. While there, he wrote two collections of poetry that described his depression and loneliness. Ovid died there in 17 or 18 CE.

Quotes from Ovid

"So I can't live either without you or with you."

"To be loved, be loveable."

"Nothing is stronger than habit."

"Time: the devourer of all things."

"You will be safest in the middle."

"Love is a thing full of anxious fears."

"The result justifies the deed."

"We take no pleasure in permitted joys. But what's forbidden is more keenly sought."

"We are ever striving after what is forbidden, and coveting what is denied us."

"Love will enter cloaked in friendship's name."

"Love is a kind of warfare."

"Water belongs to us all. Nature did not make the sun one person's property, nor air, nor water, cool and clear."

"So long as you are secure you will count many friends; if your life becomes clouded you will be alone."

Pindar

"Seek not, my soul, the life of the immortals; but enjoy to the full the resources that are within my reach."

✳ ✳ ✳ ✳

A GENUINE ROCK STAR of antiquity, Pindar was one of the most famous of the nine canonical lyric poets of ancient Greece. A large portion of his work was carefully preserved, which may be due to the high regard so many of his peers had for him.

Pindar is particularly celebrated for his *epinicia*, victory odes to notable figures and athletes of the day. One could say Pindar popularized the original athletic "fight song."

Life and Times

Pindar was born near the ancient Greek city of Thebes around the year 518. A noble, his family traced their lineage back to the city's founder Cadmus. He began producing poems fairly early on; his oldest existing ode dates from 498 BCE, written when he was just 20 years old. He continued to write poems until he was at least 72 years old, although the peak of his work is generally believed to have taken place from about 480 to 460 BCE.

Pindar travelled throughout the Greek world, visiting the royal courts in a number of city-states, which helped spread his reputation far and wide. He visited Syracuse, Delphi and Athens, among others, and wrote odes to many of these cities and their rulers. He became so highly regarded that when Alexander the Great invaded Greece, he ordered his army to spare Pindar's house in Thebes. Pindar had composed complimentary works about Alexander's father, King Alexander I of Macedon.

He is believed to have died in Argos in 443 or 438 BCE.

Epinicia, the Olympics, and Pherenikos

Pindar wrote many different kinds of works, including paeans, hymns for religious festivals, songs of praise and dancing, choral works, processionals and funeral lamentations. We know of many of these only as fragments, either because of ancient authors who quoted Pindar or from papyrus scraps found in Egypt.

45 epinicia have been preserved in their complete form, however, and these are the masterworks Pindar is best known for. While they were occasionally written to commemorate military victories, epinicia were typically written to celebrate athletic ones. Athletic games were extremely popular in ancient Greece, and Pindar was the master of the victory ode. An epinicion would traditionally be performed by a chorus in celebration of a victory. Pindar's epinicia are grouped into four books, one for each of the games of ancient Greece, the Olympian, Pythian, Isthmian and Nemean games.

His most famous is *Olympian Ode 1*, which celebrates Hieron, the ruler of Syracuse and winner of a horse race at the Olympic Games of 476 BCE. The epinicion praises Hieron for his wealth and hospitality, discusses the victory of his horse, Pherenikos, and talks about the fame and pleasure that came with being among the ranks of Olympic winners. The epinicion concludes by praising Hieron again offering hope that the ruler will win the chariot race as well, which was considered more illustrious than the single horse race (he didn't until 470, and Pindar celebrated that victory in his *Pythian Ode 1*).

Like many of his odes, his epinicia were complex in style, consisting of a series of triads, and they used the lyric Aeolian meter. They were packed with references to the ancestors of the victorious athlete, and often had allusions to the mythical gods and heroes that the athletic festivals were held to honor.

Quotes from Pindar

"The days that are still to come are the wisest witnesses."

"Words have a longer life than deeds."

"Not every truth is the better for showing its face undisguised; and often silence is the wisest thing for a man to heed."

A Foolish Mortal?

He was Nero's closest advisor and an influential essayist—but he would be accused of treachery and forced to commit suicide by Nero himself.

✳ ✳ ✳ ✳

SENECA THE YOUNGER was born Lucius Annaeus Seneca in Cordoba in 4 BCE and raised in Rome. His father was Seneca the Elder, a wealthy Roman equestrian and writer. Not much is known about Seneca's life until he became the advisor to the Emperor Nero in 54 CE. In the first few years in this role, Seneca, along with another advisor, Sextus Burrus, was able to heavily influence Nero and his rule. But they soon lost their sway over him. In 59, when Nero ordered the murder of his mother Agrippina during a power struggle, they went along with the plot.

Seneca wrote 12 essays on Stoic philosophy and morality that advocated living simply and in accordance with nature. His essays encourage the reader to accept suffering and death as normal parts of life. He also wrote at least ten tragedies; those that survived heavily influenced English theatre, including Shakespeare's tragedies *Hamlet* and *Titus Andronicus*.

According to the historian Dio, Seneca's actions were often at odds with his writing. Dio considered Seneca to be a hypocrite of the worst kind; one who railed against tyranny "while making himself the teacher of a tyrant."

Seneca retired to his country estate 62 after the death of Burrus. In 65, however, he was implicated in a plot to murder Nero. The Senate was growing unhappy with Nero's increasingly dictatorial leadership, and convinced Gaius Piso, a leading statesman, to lead a plot to seize power. The plot was uncovered and Nero ordered the conspirators, including Seneca, to commit suicide.

Quotes from Seneca

"What fools these mortals be."

"Once again prosperous and successful crime goes by the name of virtue; good men obey the bad, might is right and fear oppresses law."

"Of war men ask the outcome, not the cause."

"Authority founded on injustice is never of long duration."

"Who profits by a sin has done the sin."

"It is not the man who has too little, but the man who craves more, that is poor."

"For love of bustle is not industry—it is only the restlessness of a hunted mind."

"Live among men as if God beheld you; speak to God as if men were listening."

"If one doesn't know his mistakes, he won't want to correct them."

"That most knowing of persons—gossip."

"It is better, of course, to know useless things than to know nothing."

"Friendship is always helpful, but love sometimes even does harm."

Sophocles

Born in Attica in 496 BCE, Sophocles was one of the greatest playwrights of ancient Greece, and one of only three whose works have survived to this day. He wrote over 100 plays in his lifetime, but only seven remain in complete form: Ajax, Antigone, The Women of Trachis, Oedipus the King, Electra, Phioctetes, *and* Oedipus at Colonus.

✳   ✳   ✳   ✳

SOPHOCLES WAS THE son of a wealthy merchant, and was given a traditional aristocratic education, where he studied the arts. At the age of sixteen, he was selected to lead a boys' choir at a festival held to celebrate a military victory over the Persians. In 468 BCE, he defeated the preeminent poet Aeschylus in a competitive recitation, solidifying his reputation as a great writer. In 441 BCE, Euripides defeated Sophocles in the annual Athenian dramatic competition. Beginning with his first victory, however, Sophocles won the competition as many as twenty times.

He wrote approximately 120 plays during his lifetime. Sophocles was the first playwright to add a third actor to a play, which was a major development in dramatic theatre. Prior to his work the chorus played a larger role in plot exposition. Sophocles also didn't present his tragedies in trilogy format, which allowed him to pack all of the action into a single play, affording the possibility to heighten the drama.

He led a transformation of Greek tragedy from focusing on religion and morality to highlighting the fates and tribulations of individuals.

Some of his most famous characters are Oedipus, the mythical Greek king of Thebes; Antigone who defied a royal decree and put the will of the gods first; and Ajax, a warrior who fought in the Trojan War.

Sophocles died in 406 BCE in Athens.

Quotes from Sophocles

"Nobly to live, or else nobly to die, befits proud birth."

"Kindness begs kindness evermore."

"Men of ill judgment oft ignore the good that lies within their hands, till they have lost it."

"What dreadful knowledge of the truth can be when there's no help in truth!"

"The greatest griefs are those we cause ourselves."

"Time eases all things."

"I have nothing but contempt for the kind of governor who is afraid, for whatever reason, to follow the course he knows is best for the State."

"Nobody likes the man who brings bad news."

"Grief teaches the steadiest minds to waver."

"Wisdom outweighs any wealth."

"One word frees us of all the weight and pain of life: That word is love."

Terence

"I am human, therefore nothing relating to humanity is outside of my concern:" born in Carthage, North Africa, in either 195 or 185 BCE, Publius Terentius Afer was taken to Rome as the slave of the Roman Senator Terentius Lucanus, but later freed when the man became impressed with his intelligence and abilities. Terence went on to become a comedic playwright to whom many famous quotations are attributed.

✳　✳　✳　✳

TERENCE'S PLAYS BEGAN being performed in Rome some-time around 170 BCE. Like many Roman playwrights of his time, he adapted Greek plays to be performed before Roman audiences. Terence wrote six plays, all of which have survived in their complete form. Sometime around his 25th birthday, he would leave Rome, never to return. He may have traveled to Greece or returned to his native Carthage.

The fact that his plays were not lost, and that they were written in a simple, conversational style of writing made his plays very popular during the Middle Ages. In spite of the fact that his plays sometimes discussed subjects that were taboo or even heretical, the quality of his writing allowed his plays to escape the censure of the Church.

Terence's plays cover love triangles, dysfunctional family dynamics, and long-lost friends; one is written in part as a rebuke to Terence's critics. His popularity during the Middle Ages and after made him very influential during the neoclassical period of the 18th century. Thornton Wilder, a 20th century American writer, based his novel *The Woman of Andros* on Terence's play *Andria*.

Terence is considered a giant of Western literature due to his influence, and is often celebrated as the first poet of the African Diaspora in the West.

Quotes from Terence

"Moderation in all things. (Not anything in excess)."

"Obsequiousness begets friends, truth hatred."

"Lovers' rows make love whole again."

"Time heals all wounds."

"Extreme law is often extreme injustice."

"There is nothing so easy but that it becomes difficult when you do it reluctantly."

"While there's life, there's hope."

"Nothing has yet been said that's not been said before."

"What a difference there is between a wise person and a fool!"

"There are vicissitudes in all things."

"Fortune favors the brave."

"There are as many opinions as there are people: everyone has their own way of doing things."

He Said, "De calcaria in carbonarium…"

…a proverb that offers a choice between a kiln and a coal furnace. Less literally, you might say he was the originator of the phrase, "Out of the frying pan and into the fire."

✳ ✳ ✳ ✳

TERTULLIAN IS ONE of the most important figures in the early history of Christian literature. Born Quintus Septimius Florens Tertullianus in Carthage in 155 CE, he wrote the first major body of Latin Christian literature.

Having converted to Christianity around 197, he defended the early Christian church in over a dozen volumes of work and is considered by many to be the founder of Western Christian theology.

He is credited for being the first Latin writer to discuss the concept of the trinity, although he disagreed with contemporary doctrine regarding the Father, Son, and Holy Spirit being a single entity, instead considering them to be a group of three entities. He argued that each soul was created by God, rather than preexistent as Plato had stated. From this assertion, he concluded that the soul is naturally sinful but has within it the seeds of goodness. When this goodness awakens, he taught, the soul will naturally seek out God.

One of Tertullian's major teachings concerned whether Jesus was a man or a corporeal manifestation of the Holy Spirit. He argued that while Jesus did have a material existence, he was nevertheless a spirit, made out of nothing by the Word of God. This teaching would eventually be incorporated the Nicene Creed, which codified the theology and liturgy of the early Church.

Around 207, Tertullian apparently split with the Roman Church, and followed a Christian sect called Montanism, which believed in revelations that were not approved of by Rome. Despite this, he continued to write polemics against Gnostic theology and went on to be the predecessor of St Augustine.

Tertullian died sometime after 225.

Other Quotes from Tertullian

"One man's religion neither harms not helps another man."

"Truth does not blush."

"It is certainly no part of religion to compel religion."

"Truth persuades by teaching, but does not teach by persuading."

"Every country has its own language, yet the subjects of which the untutored soul speaks are the same everywhere."

Pop Quiz: Proverbs from Ancient Rome

Sometimes the wisest person around is "Anonymous." Match these Latin-language proverbs to the English forms we still hear and use today.

✳ ✳ ✳ ✳

1. Ad astra per aspera.

2. Bis dat qui cito dat.

3. Cave canem.

4. Caveat emptor.

5. De gustibus non disputandum.

6. Divide et impera.

7. Errare humanum est.

8. Flagrante delicto.

9. Habeas corpus.

10. In vino veritas.

11. Mater artium necessitas.

12. Pro bono publico.

13. Requiescat in pace.

14. Semper fidelis.

15. Vade in pace.

A. There's no accounting for taste.

B. You are to produce the person.

C. He gives twice who gives promptly.

D. Divide and rule.

E. For the public good.

F. To the stars through hardships.

G. Always faithful.

H. Red-handed

I. Let the buyer beware.

J. Necessity if the mother of invention.

K. Beware of the dog.

L. Rest in peace.

M. In wine, truth.

N. Go in peace.

O. To err is human.

Answers: 1. F; 2. C; 3. K; 4. I; 5. A; 6. D; 7. O; 8. H; 9. B; 10. M; 11. J; 12. E; 13. L; 14. G; 15. N.

Words from the White House

Washington's Farewell Address

The nation's first president sought to preserve political unity and to avoid long-term allegiance with any foreign power.

✳   ✳   ✳   ✳

BEFORE HE BECAME the nation's first president, George Washington led the Continental Army to victory in the Revolutionary War. Following this triumph, he could easily have assumed leadership of the country. His refusal to do so, retiring instead to his plantation home in Virginia, paved the way for civilian rather than military rule in the young nation.

It wasn't long, however, before Washington returned to public service in order to assist with the drafting of the Constitution in 1787. He then agreed to stand for office, and was unanimously chosen by the Electoral College (representatives from each state who cast official votes for president and vice president).

Almost as soon as Washington assumed the presidency in 1789, the country encountered its first international policy crisis, which was to split the nation into distinct political factions. France, having assisted America in its war for independence, was now in the midst of its own revolutionary war. The conflict escalated into war with Britain as well as Austria and Spain. Some American political leaders sympathized with the French revolutionary effort as a quest for liberty. Others, who hoped to restore positive relations with England, viewed the rebellion as a frightening descent into anarchy. This division helped carve the first political parties: the Federalists, who favored England, and the Republicans, who backed France.

In 1793, wishing above all to preserve national unity, Washington issued his Proclamation of Neutrality, stating that the country would not become involved in the war in Europe. It was this policy of nonintervention that would become his greatest political legacy, captured most notably in his Farewell Address of 1796:

"Observe good faith and justice towards all nations; cultivate peace and harmony with all ... In the execution of such a plan, nothing is more essential than that permanent, inveterate antipathies against particular nations, and passionate attachments for others, should be excluded; and that, in place of them, just and amicable feelings towards all should be cultivated."

The same address warned against the political divisions he saw developing stating that the nation must remain "indignantly frowning upon the first dawning of every attempt to alienate any portion of our country from the rest."

The Perennial Debate of Security vs. Liberty

In his attempts to protect the country from war, John Adams employed extreme measures that cost him his reputation.

❋　❋　❋　❋

JOHN ADAMS WAS born in Massachusetts in 1735, studied law at Harvard, and served in diplomatic roles during the Revolutionary War. After serving as the nation's first vice president under Washington, he was elected president in 1796.

When Adams took office, revolutionary France was at war with England. The United States struggled to remain neutral, but the French had begun to seize American trading ships bound for England. When Adams sent an envoy to negotiate a peace treaty, French officials demanded bribes before talks could proceed.

Outraged, Adams responded by building up the navy. By 1798 the nation was in a "quasi-war" at sea. Although war with France was never officially declared, the hostilities lasted for two years.

A Controversial Law

As part of his effort to limit French influence—and to silence his critics who supported the French Revolution—Adams signed into law the highly controversial Alien and Sedition Acts in 1798. The legislation extended the period required to become a naturalized citizen, allowed federal authorities to deport any foreigner they considered "dangerous," and made it a crime to publicly criticize the federal administration. Among those prosecuted for speaking against the government were several newspaper editors and a congressman.

In his annual message to Congress in 1799, Adams defended his legislative and military efforts to protect the nation, as seen in the quote that follows.

Adams was able to negotiate peace with France in 1800, but the extreme nature of the Alien and Sedition Acts damaged his reputation beyond repair, causing him to lose his bid for re-election.

"At a period like the present, when momentous changes are occurring and every hour is preparing new and great events in the political world, when a spirit of war is prevalent in almost every nation with whose affairs the interests of the United States have any connection, unsafe and precarious would be our situation were we to neglect the means of maintaining our just rights."

Other Quotes from Adams

"By my physical constitution I am but an ordinary man...Yet some great events, some cutting expressions, some mean hypocrisies, have at times thrown this assemblage of sloth, sleep, and littleless into rage like a lion."

—DIARY, 1779

"I must study politics and war that my sons may have liberty to study mathematics and philosophy. My sons ought to study mathematics and philosophy, geography, natural history, naval architecture, navigation, commerce, and agriculture, in order to give their children a right to study painting, poetry, music, architecture, statuary, tapestry, and porcelain."

—LETTER TO ABIGAIL ADAMS, 1780

"My country has in its wisdom contrived for me the most insignificant office that ever the invention of man contrived or his imagination conceived; and as I can do neither good nor evil, I must be borne away by others and meet the common fate."

—LETTER TO ABIGAIL ADAMS, 1793, ON THE VICE-PRESIDENCY

"I pray Heaven to bestow the best of blessings on this house and all that shall hereafter live in it. May none but honest and wise men ever rule under this roof."

—LETTER TO ABIGAIL ADAMS, 1800, REFERRING TO THE NEWLY-BUILT WHITE HOUSE

A Prolific Correspondent

Wife to one president, mother to another, Abigail Adams was the first First Lady to live in the White House, a prolific letter writer, and a thoughtful analyst of American politics.

✳ ✳ ✳ ✳

A BIGAIL ADAMS WAS born Abigail Smith in November 1744, daughter of a minister. Though she did not receive a formal education, she and her sisters read widely. She had a formidable intellect and a lively curiosity.

John and Abigail met when she was 17 and married a few years later. Their marriage was a close one. During the times when he was away due to business, politics, or war, she handled matters on the home front, and they corresponded frequently, leaving behind a large body of letters that cover a wide array of topics, from family life to politics to the revolution. They wrote over 1,000 letters to each other. Abigail often signed her letters, "Portia," the name of the wife of the Roman politician Brutus.

Adams greatly valued her opinions—though the fledgling republic did not heed Abigail's pleas to "remember the ladies" and grant them more education, independence, and property rights. Their letters provide historians a valuable look at the Revolution, and at the home front during the war. Later feminist scholars also admired Adams' calls for equality, and saw her as a foremother to later efforts for suffrage and equal rights.

During Adams' years in the presidency, Abigail was his hostess, first in Philadelphia and later in D.C., in the newly built White House. She continued to be one of her husband's greatest supporters and an influential advisor—so much so that her opponents derisively dubbed her "Mrs. President."

The presidency of John Adams had its controversies, especially the passage of the Alien and Sedition Acts. Adams lost the presidency to Thomas Jefferson in his bid for re-election, and they retired to their home in Massachusetts.

Abigail Adams passed away in 1818.

Quotes from Her Correspondence

"If we expect to inherit the blessings of our fathers, we should return a little more to their primitive simplicity of manners, and not sink into inglorious ease. We have too many high-sounding words, and too few actions that correspond with them."

—OCTOBER 16, 1774

"I wish I knew what mighty things were fabricating. If a form of government is to be established here, what one will be assumed? Will it be left to our Assemblies to choose one? And will not many

men have many minds? And shall we not run into dissensions among ourselves?

I am more and more convinced that man is a dangerous creature; and that power, whether vested in many or a few, is ever grasping, and, like the grave, cries, 'Give, give!' The great fish swallow up the small; and he who is most strenuous for the rights of the people, when vested with power, is as eager after the prerogatives of government. You tell me of degrees of perfection to which human nature is capable of arriving, and I believe it, but at the same time lament that our admiration should arise from the scarcity of the instances."

—27 NOVEMBER, 1775

"I long to hear that you have declared an independency. And, by the way, in the new code of laws which I suppose it will be necessary for you to make, I desire you would remember the ladies and be more generous and favorable to them than your ancestors. Do not put such unlimited power into the hands of the husbands. Remember, all men would be tyrants if they could. If particular care and attention is not paid to the ladies, we are determined to foment a rebellion, and will not hold ourselves bound by any laws in which we have no voice or representation.

That your sex are naturally tyrannical is a truth so thoroughly established as to admit of no dispute; but such of you as wish to be happy willingly give up the harsh title of master for the more tender and endearing one of friend."

—MARCH 31, 1776

"If you complain of neglect of education in sons, what shall I say with regard to daughters, who every day experience the want of it? With regard to the education of my own children, I find myself soon out of my depth, destitute and deficient in every part of education.

I most sincerely wish that some more liberal plan might be laid and executed for the benefit of the rising generation, and that our new Constitution may be distinguished for encouraging learning and virtue. If we mean to have heroes, statesmen, and philosophers, we should have learned women."

—AUGUST 14, 1776

Quotes from the First Ladies

"I little thought, when the war was finished, that any circumstances could possibly have happened, which would call the General into public life again."

—MARTHA WASHINGTON

"I am still determined to be cheerful and to be happy, in whatever situation I may be; for I have also learnt, from experience, that the greater part of our happiness or misery depends upon our dispositions, and not upon our circumstances. We carry the seeds of the one or the other about with us, in our minds, wheresoever we go."

—MARTHA WASHINGTON

"And now, dear sister, I must leave this house, or the retreating army will make me a prisoner in it, by filling up the road I am directed to take. When I shall again write you, or where I shall be tomorrow, I cannot tell!

—DOLLEY MADISON, WRITING DURING THE WAR OF 1812

"There is something in this great unsocial house which depresses my spirits beyond expression and makes it impossible for me to feel at home or to fancy that I have a home any where."

—LOUISA ADAMS

"If I get into the White House, I will neither keep house nor make butter.

—SARAH POLK

"It's all very well for those who like it, but I do not like this public life at all. I often wish the time would come when we would return to where I feel we best belong."

—ELIZA JOHNSON

"I know what's best for the President. I put him in the White House. He does well when he listens to me and poorly when he does not."

—FLORENCE HARDING

"The first lady is, and always has been, an unpaid public servant elected by one person, her husband.

—LADY BIRD JOHNSON

"I think it wasn't so much that the White House altered me in any essential way as that I found the resources with which to respond to a series of challenges. You never know what you can do until you have to do it. In the beginning, it was like going to a party you're terrified of, and finding out to your amazement that you're having a good time."

—BETTY FORD

"A leader takes people where they want to go. A great leader takes people where they don't necessarily want to go, but ought to be."

—ROSALYNN CARTER

"In 1981, when Ronnie and I moved to Washington, I never dreamed that our eight years there would be a time of so much emotion. But life in the White House is magnified: The highs were higher than I expected, and the lows were much lower."

—NANCY REAGAN

"That is the story of this country, the story that has brought me to this stage tonight, the story of generations of people who felt the lash of bondage, the shame of servitude, the sting of segregation, but who kept on striving and hoping and doing what needed to be done so that today, I wake up every morning in a house that was built by slaves—and I watch my daughters—two beautiful, intelligent, black young women—playing with their dogs on the White House lawn."

—MICHELLE OBAMA

A Call for Bipartisanship?

Having won the nation's first contested election, Thomas Jefferson tried, with limited success, to remake the government in his party's image.

❋   ❋   ❋   ❋

BORN IN 1743 TO a prominent family in Virginia, Thomas Jefferson was one of the primary founders of the new American republic, most notably penning the nation's Declaration of Independence.

Although he served as vice president under John Adams due to receiving the second-highest number of votes in the 1796 election, Jefferson and Adams were in fact political rivals. Jefferson, representing the Republican Party, favored small government and supported the French in their war with England, while Adams, a Federalist, took a more expansive approach to federal power and allied more closely with the British.

Thus the election of 1800, which pitted the two against each other, was the first contested election in American history. Moreover, the transfer of power from Adams to Jefferson was the first known occasion anywhere on which a leader peaceably ceded control to his adversary.

In the Inaugural

Jefferson's Inaugural Address appeared to acknowledge this graceful departure and promise an equally measured bipartisan approach to his presidency.

"Every difference of opinion is not a difference of principle. We have called by different names brethren of the same principle. We are all republicans—we are all federalists. If there be any among us who would wish to dissolve this Union or to change its republican form, let them stand undisturbed as monuments of the safety with which error of opinion may be tolerated where reason is left free to combat it."

Ironically, though his words were widely regarded as a message of moderation, Jefferson did not intend to promise unity between the two parties but rather to pay homage to the nation's history of republican government under a federal flag.

In fact, he worked throughout his presidency to dismantle the legacy of the Federalist government that preceded him. He slashed taxes, reduced the number of government employees, and scaled back the army and navy.

It was also under Jefferson, however, that the nation was able to double its size through the Louisiana Purchase. Although acquiring land was not an executive function specified in the

Constitution, Jefferson departed from his usual small-government stance to take advantage of Napoleon Bonaparte's shockingly low asking price of four cents per acre.

Despite his successful westward expansion, Jefferson's presidency ended on a low note. In an attempt to gain leverage over Britain and France, he persuaded Congress to prohibit all overseas shipping. The strategy proved economically disastrous for the United States, and did nothing to halt European aggression.

Other Quotes from Jefferson

"Ignorance is preferable to error; and he is less remote from the truth who believes nothing, than he who believes what is wrong."

—NOTES ON THE STATE OF VIRGINIA, 1781–1785

"I tremble for my country when I reflect that God is just."

—NOTES ON THE STATE OF VIRGINIA, 1781–1785

"The second office of the government is honorable and easy, the first is but a splendid misery."

—LETTER, 1797

The Monroe Doctrine

"The American continents, by the free and independent condition which they have assumed and maintain, are henceforth not to be considered as subjects for future colonization by any European power." Envisioning a country that covered the entire continent, James Monroe resisted both domestic and foreign threats to the nation's unity.

✳   ✳   ✳   ✳

A NATIVE OF VIRGINIA, James Monroe was Washington's lieutenant in the war for independence. He was elected to the Virginia House of Delegates and served in the Continental Congress that acted as the country's first national government. In addition to participating in the Virginia Convention that ratified the Constitution, he also became minister to France, governor of Virginia, secretary of state and secretary of war before being elected President in 1816.

Monroe's two terms in office were known as the "Era of Good Feelings," due to the absence of party strife after the collapse of the Federalists. But a number of bad feelings did surface, particularly over the issue of slavery, which began to split the remaining Republican Party in two.

The vision of America that Monroe most cherished was of a country that stretched across the continent, perhaps one day claiming the entire North American land mass. Having obtained Florida in 1819, he turned his attention to westward expansion. To this end, though a slave owner, he was willing to bargain to ensure continued territorial growth. The Missouri Compromise of 1820, which permitted slavery in Missouri, forbade the institution north and west of its southern border, and admitted Maine as a free state, was among the most famous acts of his administration devoted to preserving peace in the growing country.

How the Doctrine Came to Be

More famous still was the stance Monroe took against European nations seeking a foothold in the Americas. Between 1810 and 1822, several of Spain's colonies won their independence, forming the nations of Mexico, Venezuela, Ecuador and Peru. Monroe supported these victories as helping bring forth his vision of a New World of liberty breaking free from the Old World of oppression.

Concerned that Spain and its allies would try to reclaim these areas—and that they would go further and attempt to conquer parts of the United States—Monroe made a speech to Congress in 1823 describing a position that would later be known as the Monroe Doctrine.

In it, he stated that the Unites States would oppose any further attempts at colonization in the Americas and would refrain from involvement in European wars. He also warned Europe not to interfere with the newly independent nations.

By preventing further European involvement in the Americas, Monroe hoped to enhance the United States' power within the Western Hemisphere. Although he had no means of enforcing the Monroe Doctrine, it became an important policy tool in the years to come.

Jackson's Bank Veto Message

Andrew Jackson saw his campaign against the Second Bank of the United States as a battle for the common man against the privileged few.

* * * *

BORN TO SCOTCH-IRISH immigrants in a backwoods region of the Carolinas, Andrew Jackson was the first "self-made man" to reach the White House. With his Scottish Brogue accent and reputation for killing men in duels, he was an unlikely pick for a position previously reserved for gentlemen of distinguished heritage.

It was Jackson's command of the American forces in the most famous battle of his era, the successful defense of New Orleans in the War of 1812, that earned him nationwide acclaim and adoration. His status as a war hero nearly won him the presidency in 1824, but despite Jackson's greater share of the vote, the House of Representatives chose to give the office to John Quincy Adams. The ensuing outrage fueled his 1828 campaign, and he became the nation's seventh president the following year.

The central feature of Jackson's presidency was his crusade against the Second Bank of the United States. Although technically a private corporation, the bank wielded enormous power, functioning as a government-sponsored monopoly against which no state institutions could compete. Jackson, who favored small government and saw himself as the representative of the common man, viewed the bank as an unholy alliance between political favoritism and privileged economic interests.

The Bank's charter was set to expire in 1836, but its president Nicholas Biddle decided to petition for extension in 1832, thinking that in an election year Jackson would avoid drastic action. This turned out to be a major miscalculation, as Jackson's "Bank Veto Message" became the most famous statement of his administration.

Jackson crafted his message to appeal not to Congress but to the larger populace. For every section of the voting public, he had a complaint against the bank to suit their political perspective. The Bank, he said, did have some usefulness but not in its proposed form. He claimed it violated state's rights, was an elitist institution and catered to foreign interests.

In fact the message addressed so many different perspectives that it contradicted itself many times over. So incoherent was the argument that Biddle took it upon himself to distribute 30,000 copies of the statement, thinking it would discredit Jackson altogether.

Again, Biddle miscalculated. The public rallied to Jackson's cry, and he easily won his bid for reelection in 1832. Unfortunately, the veto contributed to a drastic economic downtown culminating in the Panic of 1837, but that problem was left to the succeeding administration.

"It is to be regretted that the rich and powerful too often bend the acts of government to their selfish purposes."

Pop Quiz: Which President Said It?

Do you know which quote was said by which president?

✳ ✳ ✳ ✳

1. "We believe that if men have the talent to invent new machines that put men out of work, they have the talent to put those men back to work."

a) John F. Kennedy

b) Bill Clinton

c) Donald Trump

2. "Yesterday, December 7th, 1941—a date which will live in infamy—the United States of America was suddenly and deliberately attacked by naval and air forces of the Empire of Japan."

a) Herbert Hoover

b) Franklin Delano Roosevelt

c) Harry Truman

3. "But there is one front and one battle where everyone in the United States—every man, woman, and child—is in action, and will be privileged to remain in action throughout this war. That front is right here at home, in our daily lives, and in our daily tasks."

a) Franklin Delano Roosevelt

b) Harry Truman

c) Woodrow Wilson

4. "It's a recession when your neighbor loses his job; it's a depression when you lose your own."

a) Andrew Jackson

b) Harry Truman

c) Bill Clinton

5. "Sure there are dishonest men in local government. But there are dishonest men in national government too."

a) Richard Nixon

b) Gerald Ford

c) Ronald Reagan

6. "Bear in mind this sacred principle, that though the will of the majority is in all cases to prevail...the minority possess their equal rights, which equal law must protect, and to violate would be oppression."

a) George Washington

b) Barack Obama

c) Thomas Jefferson

7. "The people are responsible for the character of their Congress. If that body be ignorant, reckless, and corrupt, it is because the people tolerate ignorance, recklessness, and corruption."

a) James Garfield

b) Grover Cleveland

c) George W. Bush

8. "When I go in for a physical, they no longer ask how old I am. They carbon date me."

a) George H. W. Bush

b) Benjamin Harrison

c) Ronald Reagan

Answers: 1. a; 2. b; 3. a; 4. b; 5. a; 6. c; 7. a; 8. c

Just A Few Remarks

In late 1863, President Abraham Lincoln received an invitation to make "a few appropriate remarks" at the November 19 dedication of a national cemetery at Gettysburg. Lincoln accepted the invitation.

✳   ✳   ✳   ✳

AFTER A LONG, slow procession to the brand-new cemetery south of the town of Gettysburg, Pennsylvania, Edward Everett, a famous and popular orator of the time, delivered an eloquent two-hour speech describing the Battle of Gettysburg and drawing lessons about it from European military history. After thundering applause from the thousands in attendance, President Lincoln rose, stepped to the front of the platform, and delivered his own brief tribute to those who fought and died there during the first three days of July 1863.

The Gettysburg Address

"Fourscore and seven years ago our fathers brought forth on this continent a new nation, conceived in liberty, and dedicated to the proposition that all men are created equal. Now we are engaged in a great civil war, testing whether that nation, or any nation so conceived and so dedicated can long endure. We are met on a great battlefield of that war. We have come to dedicate a portion of that field as a final resting place for those who gave their lives that that nation might live. It is altogether fitting and proper that we should do this. But, in a larger sense, we cannot dedicate—we cannot consecrate—we cannot hallow this ground. The brave men, living and dead, who struggled here have consecrated it far above our poor power to add or detract. The world will little note nor long remember what we say here, but it can never forget what they did here.

"It is for us, the living, rather, to be dedicated here to the unfinished work which they who fought here have thus far so nobly advanced. It is rather for us to be here dedicated to the great task remaining before us—that from these honored dead we take increased devotion to that cause for which they gave the last full measure of devotion; that we here highly resolve that these dead shall not have died in vain, that this nation, under God, shall have a new birth of freedom; and that government of the people, by the people, for the people, shall not perish from the earth."

The Aftermath

Applause interrupted the speech five times, and a tremendous ovation and three cheers followed its completion. Though Lincoln confided later that he felt the speech a "flat failure," Everett summed up the impact of the President's "few remarks" when he wrote him the next day: "I should be glad, if I could flatter myself that I came as near to the central idea of the occasion, in two hours, as you did in two minutes." This speech is likely Lincoln's most famous—it is engraved into the Lincoln Memorial on the Mall in Washington, D.C.

Other Quotes from Lincoln

"I have not permitted myself, gentlemen, to conclude that I am the best man in the country; but I am reminded in this connection of a story of an old Dutch farmer, who remarked to a companion once that it was not best to swap horses when crossing a stream."

—ABRAHAM LINCOLN, DURING THE PRESIDENTIAL CAMPAIGN OF 1864

"At what point shall we expect the approach of danger? By what means shall we fortify against it? Shall we expect some transatlantic military giant, to step the Ocean, and crush us at a blow? Never! All the armies of Europe, Asia and Africa combined, with all the treasure of the earth (our own excepted) in their military chest; with a Buonaparte [sic] for a commander, could not by force, take a drink from the Ohio, or make a track on the Blue Ridge, in a trial of a thousand years. At what point then is the approach of danger to be expected? I answer, if it ever reach us, it must spring up amongst us. It cannot come from abroad. If destruction be our lot, we must ourselves be its author and finisher. As a nation of freemen, we must live through all time, or die by suicide."

—ABRAHAM LINCOLN, 1838

The Emancipation Proclamation: Freeing the Slaves?

In late 1862, Lincoln needed to make a bold move to redefine the war and the reasons for fighting it. But not all slaves received their freedom as a result of the Emancipation Proclamation. Who was free, and who remained in servitude?

✳ ✳ ✳ ✳

FIVE DAYS AFTER the bloody Battle of Antietam in September 1862, President Abraham Lincoln issued a preliminary Emancipation Proclamation to his Cabinet. Scheduled to go into effect on January 1, 1863, the document was intended to apply only to states that were still in rebellion against the federal government on that date. In those states, any and all slaves would be freed from their masters for all time.

The Fine Print

Lincoln's plan caught everyone's attention, but it was not greeted with universal approval. The proclamation referred only to states (or parts of states) in rebellion, so slaves in the border states—Maryland, Kentucky, Missouri, and Delaware—or parts of Confederate states that were under Union occupation would remain in bondage. Radical Republicans who wanted to see an end to all slavery were angry, believing Lincoln had not gone far enough. Editorials in foreign and antigovernment domestic presses lambasted the President, pointing out that Lincoln had freed slaves only in areas where the federal government was no longer recognized nor accepted—where his authority had been rejected and the order would be ignored.

In Defense of Lincoln

In limiting the scope of emancipation, Lincoln believed he was acting within his constitutional powers to seize enemy resources—in this case, the enemy's slaves. He also remained within his powers by not acting against slavery in territory that remained loyal to the United States. The President recognized that he had to wait for legislation from Congress to end the practice of slavery in the Union itself.

It's All PR

Even though it freed no slaves immediately, the Emancipation Proclamation was a brilliant public relations move. With one stroke of his pen, Lincoln turned the war into one of liberation for the slaves, and he helped doom Confederate hopes for foreign recognition. No European country would dare to enter the war on the side defending enslavement. In addition, the possibility of slaves abandoning their owners and undermining what was left of the Southern economy was extremely appealing. The final January 1863 Emancipation Proclamation expanded on this idea by authorizing the government to enlist black soldiers and sailors. "In giving freedom to the slave, we assure freedom to the free," Lincoln declared. "We must disenthrall ourselves, and then we shall save our country."

Lincoln Defends Grant

During the Civil War (1861–65), after hearing complaints of General Ulysses S. Grant's hard-drinking ways, did Abraham Lincoln really say, "For heaven's sake, find out what he drinks, and make the rest drink it, too"?

✳   ✳   ✳   ✳

LINCOLN CERTAINLY HAD reason to make such a comment, and not the obvious one. His generals frustrated him, and he was always trying to kick their butts toward battle (preferably against the rebels rather than one another). Despite many Union advantages, the Confederacy habitually paddled the bluecoats until fighters such as Grant and Sherman put steel into the Union army's spine. What if jealous rivals were simply feeding a rumor mill?

There's an assumption that Grant was a drunkard to begin with. As a junior officer (1854), he did have a drinking problem and left the service because of it. In his Civil War return, he seemed to have learned his limits. Brigadier Grant made rapid gains in reputation, rank—and enemies. Numerous credible eyewitness accounts describe Grant as a moderate drinker, never intoxicated on the battlefield—something that can't be said of other leaders.

King George, the Joker

Don and Virginia Fehrenbacher, in *The Recollected Words of Abraham Lincoln*, write that the quote can be traced to an 1864 Democratic joke book and is likely a recycled witticism from King George II (1683–1760). When he received complaints from the British Court that General James Wolfe was a madman, the king replied, "Mad? Then I only hope he bites my other generals!"

A Square Deal

Theodore Roosevelt viewed the federal government as an arbiter between workers and business owners, protecting the rights of all.

✳ ✳ ✳ ✳

AFTER THE ASSASSINATION of President William McKinley, Theodore Roosevelt became the nation's youngest President just weeks before his 43rd birthday. Frail and sickly as a child of privilege growing up in New York City, he took it upon himself to develop a strong physique and character through what he termed the "strenuous life" of hard work and physical activity.

Roosevelt had a budding political career in New York before the Spanish-American War broke out in 1898. He seized the opportunity to organize a volunteer cavalry known as the Rough Riders, made up of a cross-section of American men that included ranch hands, Ivy League athletes, policemen and Native American scouts. The cavalry's fame helped him become governor of New York, and vice president soon after.

Upon McKinley's death, Roosevelt took to the presidency with the same energy he applied to all his pursuits. His approach to American industry, balancing the rights of workers with the needs of business owners, initiated the Progressive Era of reform that characterized the next two decades. Speaking at the New York State Fair in 1903, he described his administration's economic policies as a "square deal" that dispensed justice equally to all levels of American production.

The Panama Canal was another major accomplishment of the first years of his administration. The construction of the canal linking the Pacific and Atlantic oceans required not only an enormous feat of engineering but also the wresting of Panama from Colombia. Despite this political interference, the canal was widely viewed as a heroic achievement.

Roosevelt was the first President to be elected to the office after having assumed the title upon the death of his predecessor, and the first President to be awarded the Nobel Peace Prize (for negotiating a treaty ending the Russo-Japanese War). He is also remembered for his conservation efforts protecting the country's natural resources.

"We must treat each man on his worth and merits as a man. We must see that each is given a square deal, because he is entitled to no more and should receive no less."

Wild Child?

"If you can't say something good about someone, sit right here by me" was one of Alice Roosevelt Longworth's favorite maxims. She had it embroidered on a pillow that she kept in her study.

❋   ❋   ❋   ❋

THEODORE ROOSEVELT HAS six children, including Alice Lee Roosevelt, his daughter with his first wife. After her mother died and her father headed west, little Alice was taken care of by her father's sister Anna. When Theodore Roosevelt returned from his trip, Alice was three years old. The little girl had a wild streak from an early age and during her teenage years she took up smoking (which was quite unusual for women at the time). She was also known for her quick wit and sharp tongue. Alice married Nicholas Longworth (who would eventually rise to Speaker of the House) in the East Room of the White House in 1906. The marriage was amicable but distant, and both had affairs. When Alice did have a daughter, Paulina, 18 years after the marriage, it was obvious to most that the child's father was Senator William Borah of Idaho rather than Longworth. Both men adored the little girl, however. Alice Roosevelt Longworth died in 1980 at age 96.

"I can either run the country or control Alice—not both."

—THEODORE ROOSEVELT, WHEN QUESTIONED ABOUT HIS DAUGHTER'S ANTICS

A Return to Normalcy or an Introduction of Corruption?

Widely ranked among the worst Presidents in history, Harding was famous for making speeches that could be interpreted to support any number of positions.

❋   ❋   ❋   ❋

WARREN G. HARDING was a successful newspaper editor in Marion, Ohio, before his political career began. In 1899, he was elected to the Ohio senate, after which he became lieutenant governor and then a U.S. Senator. In the Senate, his attendance was spotty, which served him well by making him few enemies.

He was nominated to run for President by the Republican Party in 1920. He chose as his slogan "A return to normalcy," which referred to the fatigue the nation was experiencing in the aftermath of World War I and the major societal shifts inherent in women's suffrage and prohibition. During the campaign, Harding made no concrete promises, speaking only in generalities about stability and dignified government.

Presumably having tapped in to the reform-weary sentiment of the age, Harding won the election with a landslide victory of more than 60 percent. In his inaugural address, he continued to speak in vague terms about his goals and values. The Democratic politician William Gibbs McAdoo captured the perspective of Harding's critics by describing the President's speeches as "an army of pompous phrases moving across the landscape in search of an idea."

Harding's administration is remembered not for its accomplishments, few of which were attributable to the President, but for the scandals that took place while he was in office. In addition to the President's well-known affairs, one of which was with a German sympathizer while another produced an illegitimate child, several of the men in Harding's inner circle (known as the "Ohio gang") were found guilty of defrauding the government and sent to jail.

Although his secretary of commerce Herbert Hoover had urged Harding to expose the corruption before it became common knowledge, he feared the political repercussions and so remained silent. Harding did not live to see what would become of his friends, as he died from a heart attack in 1923.

"I speak for administrative efficiency, for lightened tax burdens, for sound commercial practices, for adequate credit facilities, for sympathetic concern for all agricultural problems, for the omission of unnecessary interference of Government with business, for an end to Government's experiment in business, and for more efficient business in Government administration."

—FROM HARDING'S INAUGURAL ADDRESS, 1921

"Never before, here or anywhere else, has a government been so completely fused with business."

—THE WALL STREET JOURNAL

FDR's Foresight

There's debate as to whether Franklin Delano Roosevelt coined the phrase "The only thing we have to fear is fear itself." Regardless of its origins, though, no one has uttered the words quite the way he did.

✳   ✳   ✳   ✳

THE FULL QUOTE is: "So, first of all, let me assert my firm belief that the only thing we have to fear is fear itself—nameless, unreasoning, unjustified terror which paralyzes needed efforts to convert retreat into advance." Thus said FDR, using his patrician New York diction, in the opening paragraph of his first inaugural address on March 4, 1933.

FDR was certainly a well-educated president, having studied at Groton, Harvard, and Columbia Law School. He was also an eloquent speaker who surrounded himself with talented speechwriters. Still, it appears that Roosevelt appropriated the famous line—and his potential sources include Michel de Montaigne, Francis Bacon, and Henry David Thoreau.

For his part, Roosevelt had good reason to address public fear. The United States floundered in the Great Depression. Russia had gone communist; millions there were dying as the result of famine. In Germany, defeated at great cost 15 years earlier,

Adolf Hitler had his country's young democracy on the ropes. On the positive side for the United States, it had recently dedicated Mt. Rushmore, and *King Kong* had just hit movie theaters. Small comfort, however, as Roosevelt was preparing Americans for draconian measures. Later in the speech, FDR proclaimed that if necessary he would put matters right with or without the cooperation of Congress, even if he had to seek a formal declaration of war upon "the emergency."

Although he was primarily referring to sweeping economic change, it seems Roosevelt also foresaw war. Most Americans preferred to let the Old World stew in its own tribal conflicts, but FDR saw that this might not be possible—and indeed, it was not.

Quotes on Fear

"The only thing I am afraid of is fear."

—ARTHUR WELLESLEY, DUKE OF WELLINGTON, 1831

"Any coward can fight a battle when he's sure of winning; but give me the man who has pluck to fight when he's sure of losing."

—GEORGE ELIOT, 1857

"Familiarity with danger makes a brave man braver, but less daring. Thus with seamen: he who goes the oftenest round Cape Horn goes the most circumspectly."

—HERMANN MELVILLE, 1850

"Cowards die many times before their deaths; The valiant never taste of death but once."

—WILLIAM SHAKESPEARE, *JULIUS CAESAR*

"Nothing is so much to be feared as fear."

—HENRY DAVID THOREAU, 1851

"Nothing is terrible except fear itself."

—FRANCIS BACON, 1623

Beer Time

In 1933, when newly elected president Franklin D. Roosevelt lifted the ban on alcohol, he famously said, "I think this would be a good time for a beer." For some states, however, Prohibition continued long after that proclamation.

✳ ✳ ✳ ✳

THE VOLSTEAD ACT, also known as the Prohibition Act of 1919, gave U.S. authorities power to enforce the 18th Amendment to the Constitution, which banned the sale, manufacture, and transportation of intoxicating beverages. These were defined as any drink containing more than 0.5 percent alcohol by volume. The 18th Amendment took effect in 1920 and heralded an American era forever associated with gangsters, bootleggers, and speakeasies.

The Prohibition movement evolved from the religion-based Temperance movement of the late 19th century, in part as a response to the explosion in the number of saloons around the time of World War I. A number of individual counties and states, particularly in the South, adopted their own local Prohibition laws prior to the national ban on alcohol in 1920. Prohibition quickly became unpopular, though, and created a nightmare for law-enforcement officials. In March 1933, shortly after he was elected president, Franklin Roosevelt amended the Volstead Act with the Cullen-Harrison Act, which allowed the manufacture and sale of "light" wines and 3.2 percent beer. In December of that year, he ratified the 21st Amendment to the Constitution, ending national Prohibition.

As well as being the first and only amendment to repeal a previous amendment to the Constitution, the 21st Amendment enabled individual states to use their own discretion in deciding when to repeal Prohibition. So, depending on where you lived, Prohibition may not have ended in 1933. Mississippi, the last dry state, did not repeal it until 1966.

Reshaping the Role of First Lady

As Franklin Delano Roosevelt was the longest-serving president, Eleanor was the longest-serving First Lady. She redefined the position and stayed politically active throughout her lifetime.

✳ ✳ ✳ ✳

ELEANOR ROOSEVELT, BORN Anna Eleanor Roosevelt, was one of the most influential First Ladies. A niece of Theodore Roosevelt and a distant cousin to Franklin, she grew up in a prominent family, though her parents died when she was young, casting a shadow over her childhood. Her marriage with Franklin had its difficulties, particularly in its early years. Eleanor struggled with an overbearing mother-in-law, finding out that Franklin had had an affair, and his bout with polio. The couple remained together, however, forging a political partnership. Eleanor urged him to remain politically active after the bout with polio. She herself was active in her husband's campaign for governor of New York, and his later campaigns for the presidency.

As First Lady, Roosevelt gave speeches, wrote columns, and advocated for women and civil rights, becoming a political powerhouse in her own right. At the time, her actions were considered quite controversial. After her husband's death, she remained active, serving as a delegate to the United Nations and later in the Kennedy administration as 1st Chair of the Presidential Commission on the Status of Women. She died in 1962 at the age of 78.

Did She Say It?

Roosevelt is often quoted as the originator of the phrase, "No one can make you feel inferior without your consent." Archivists, however, have not been able to track down a specific occasion on which she said those exact words. It may have been drawn from something Eleanor did say circa 1935 about inferiority, and it was attributed to her as early as 1940 and 1941.

Quotes from Eleanor Roosevelt

"Will people ever be wise enough to refuse to follow bad leaders or to take away the freedom of other people?"

—1939

"One of the best ways of enslaving a people is to keep them from education ... The second way of enslaving a people is to suppress the sources of information, not only by burning books but by controlling all the other ways in which ideas are transmitted."

—1943

"It isn't enough to talk about peace. One must believe in it. And it isn't enough to believe in it. One must work at it."

—1951

"To me who dreamed so much as a child, who made a dreamworld in which I was the heroine of an unending story, the lives of people around me continued to have a certain storybook quality. I learned something which has stood me in good stead many times — The most important thing in any relationship is not what you get but what you give."

—1960

"Life was meant to be lived, and curiosity must be kept alive. One must never, for whatever reason, turn his back on life."

—1960

"You gain strength, courage and confidence by every experience in which you really stop to look fear in the face. You are able to say to yourself, 'I have lived through this horror. I can take the next thing that comes along.' ... You must do the thing you think you cannot do."

—1960

The Military-Industrial Complex

A beloved military hero, President Eisenhower guided the nation peacefully through the early years of the Cold War—and coined the term "military industrial complex."

✳ ✳ ✳ ✳

WHEN DWIGHT DAVID Eisenhower accepted the Republican nomination for President in 1952, he was well known as the commanding general who led the Allied Forces to victory over Nazi Germany. His campaign slogan, "I like Ike," captured his appeal as a beloved war hero with humble roots in the tiny town of Abilene, Kansas, where he spent most of his childhood.

Despite his military background, Eisenhower's greatest achievements as President were in peacekeeping. Shortly after taking office in 1953, he assisted with the ceasefire of the Korean War, and remained committed to avoiding international conflict thereafter.

Maintaining peace proved no small feat as the Cold War between the U.S. and the Soviet Union intensified. With each of the two superpowers striving to increase its international influence, the Cold War pitted capitalism against communism in a bid for global dominance.

In this tense atmosphere, Eisenhower avoided direct military engagement with the Soviet Union. With both countries producing nuclear weapons, a full-scale war promised to be catastrophic. Yet while he did avoid formal military conflict, Eisenhower greatly expanded the use of covert operations to influence international politics. The Central Intelligence Agency became more than just an intelligence-gathering organization; it was granted the power to conduct secret activities that could not be traced to U.S. leaders. To control the threat of communism, the CIA utilized extreme measures, including espionage, bribery and, some historians have claimed, assassination.

Thinking Through the Road Ahead

Throughout his presidency, Eisenhower struggled to balance his desire to protect the country—and the world—from communism, with his commitment to peace. He believed that, in his words, "The only way to win World War III is to prevent it," through deterrents that included massive military armament, but he worried that a permanent and powerful military industry would have undue influence on future political decisions.

His farewell address to the nation before leaving office in 1961, in which he coined the term "military-industrial complex," captured the dilemma he saw the country facing as it attempted to prepare itself for war on a massive scale without turning that possibility into an inevitability.

"Only an alert and knowledgeable citizenry can compel the proper meshing of the huge industrial and military machinery of defense with our peaceful methods and goals, so that security and liberty may prosper together."

The Great Society

"We have the opportunity to move not only toward the rich society and the powerful society, but upward to the Great Society."

✳   ✳   ✳   ✳

LYNDON BAINES JOHNSON came from a long line of Texans, the earliest of which had helped to settle the state and fight for the Confederacy in the Civil War. It was during Johnson's studies at Southwest Texas State Teacher's College that he became interested in liberal reform, notably through his work as a student teacher in an impoverished Hispanic school.

Following graduation, he became a congressional aide, and then Texas director of the National Youth Administration, a federally-funded employment program. Aligning himself with President Franklin D. Roosevelt's New Deal, he became a U.S. congressman at just 28 years old, serving six terms in the House of Representatives before being elected to the Senate, where he remained for more than a decade.

Johnson had served five masterful years as the Senate majority leader before he ran in the Democratic presidential primary in 1960. He lost to John Fitzgerald Kennedy, who chose him as his running mate. As vice president, Johnson headed the space program, assisted with military policy, and headed the Equal Employment Opportunity committee, but overall wielded far less influence than he had in the Senate.

In November of 1963, Johnson ascended to the most powerful position in government. President Kennedy was shot by an assassin while visiting Dallas, Texas, and Johnson, who had accompanied him on the trip, was sworn in as President on the flight back to Washington.

LBJ's Presidency

Johnson's first acts as President were to push items that had been on Kennedy's legislative agenda: a new civil rights bill and a cut in federal income tax. Preparing to run in the 1964 election, he described in a commencement speech at the University of Michigan his vision of the "Great Society," in which poverty and rural injustice would be eradicated. After winning the election by the largest popular margin in history, he put in place many of his reforms including Medicare, education programs, and three more civil rights bills.

Foreign affairs, however, proved Johnson's undoing. As the conflict in Vietnam escalated, he committed money, firepower, and more than 500,000 troops to the failing and unpopular effort. The Vietnam War destroyed Johnson's standing, and he did not seek another term.

Our Long National Nightmare Is Over

Gerald R. Ford promised to bring closure to the era of unrest brought on by political corruption and the Vietnam War.

* * * *

GERALD RUDOLPH FORD was born in Omaha, Nebraska, and raised in Grand Rapids, Michigan. Popular and athletic in his youth, he attended the University of Michigan on a football scholarship. Upon graduation, he turned down offers from the National Football League to instead coach and attend law school at Yale University. After serving in the navy during World War II, he became a Republican congressman in the U.S. House of Representatives.

Ford remained in the House for 25 years, playing the part of the consummate insider who enjoyed the clubby culture of Capitol Hill as much as its power over national affairs. Through one such branch of the social scene, the Chowder and Marching Club, he came to know Richard M. Nixon, who at that time was also a member of the House.

As Nixon's political career led him eventually to the presidency, Ford became House minority leader, remaining loyal to Nixon in nearly all his votes. Even as the Watergate conspiracy began to come to light, Ford remained convinced of Nixon's innocence and continued as a strong supporter. He was rewarded for his devotion in 1973, when Nixon's vice president Spiro Agnew resigned after pleading no contest to charges of tax evasion. Ford was chosen as Agnew's replacement, receiving strong support from his friends in Congress.

Ascending to the Presidency

Ford only had eight months as vice president before Nixon became the first American President to resign from office. Nixon was embroiled in number of scandals and cover-ups and facing impeachment when he made the decision to step down. Addressing a nation that was suffering both from the administration's disgrace and the uneasy conclusion to the Vietnam War, Ford tried in his acceptance speech to assure Americans that the troubled era was ending, saying, "Our long national nightmare is over."

For his first 30 days, Ford was wildly popular. He put together a strong cabinet and made himself and his family available to the press. But in his first major acts as President – pardoning both Nixon and Vietnam draft dodgers – he destroyed that goodwill. His administration accomplished little in the ensuing two years, and he lost the 1976 election to Jimmy Carter.

Tear Down This Wall!

Initiating an end to the Cold War was one of the most significant accomplishments of Ronald Reagan's administration.

✳ ✳ ✳ ✳

RONALD WILSON REAGAN was born in Tampico, Illinois, the son of an alcoholic shoe salesman. Despite a rough childhood, he went from a job as a radio sportscaster to a successful Hollywood acting career. After narrating training films for the army during World War II, he took a position as a spokesman for General Electric and aligned himself with the Republican Party. By 1967, he was governor of California.

With Jimmy Carter's presidency crippled by economic woes and the ongoing Iran Hostage Crisis, Reagan easily unseated him in 1980. Although exit polls revealed that the outcome was more a rejection of Carter than a push for Reagan's conservative agenda, the president-elect interpreted the result as a call for a "Reagan Revolution" ending the liberal era of the 1960s and '70s. As soon as he was in office, he undertook a series of tax cuts and reductions in domestic spending, in addition to promoting increases in the military budget.

Reagan has been described as the "Teflon President," because, much like the coating that produces nonstick cookware, he always seemed to shake off tragedies and scandals without much damage. Only three months into his presidency, he was shot in an attempted assassination, but managed a full recovery. Later on, he battled colon cancer, leaving his vice president George H. W. Bush acting as President for eight days. Still, the public did not lose confidence in the oldest man to inhabit the White House. Even when Reagan was caught lying about having traded arms for hostages, and then illegally funneling the money received for the sale to Nicaraguan rebels, he enjoyed high approval ratings following his televised apology.

The Berlin Wall

One of Reagan's major initiatives was to combat communism worldwide. He delivered a speech in 1987 calling for the general secretary of the Communist Party of the Soviet Union, Mikhail Gorbachev, to tear down the wall separating East and West Berlin. While the speech probably had little impact on the eventual outcome of the Berlin Wall, Reagan's five summits with Gorbachev succeeded in achieving the first mutual agreement to reduce nuclear arsenals, signaling the beginning of the end of the Cold War.

"General Secretary Gorbachev, if you seek peace, if you seek prosperity for the Soviet Union and Eastern Europe, if you seek liberalization: Come here to this gate! Mr. Gorbachev, open this gate! Mr. Gorbachev, tear down this wall!"

Presidents on Government

Presidents have spoken extensively on government itself as an idea and an area of potential abuse.

✳   ✳   ✳   ✳

"Enlightened statesmen will not always be at the helm."

—JAMES MADISON

"While all other Sciences have advanced, that of Government is at a stand; little better understood; little better practiced now than three or four thousand years ago."

—JOHN ADAMS

"The other day, someone told me the difference between a democracy and a people's democracy. It's the same difference between a jacket and a straitjacket."

—RONALD REAGAN

"I agree with you, Mr. Chairman, that the working men are the basis of all governments, for the plain reason that they are the most numerous."

—ABRAHAM LINCOLN

"My brother Bob doesn't want to be in government — he promised Dad he'd go straight."

—JOHN F. KENNEDY

"The thing I enjoyed most were visits from children. They did not want public office."

—HERBERT HOOVER

"If a politician doesn't wanna get beat up, he shouldn't run for office. If a football player doesn't want to get tackled or want the risk of an occasional clip he shouldn't put the pads on."

—BILL CLINTON

"A government big enough to give you everything you want is a government big enough to take from you everything you have."

—GERALD FORD

"The chief duty of government is to keep the peace and stand out of the sunshine of the people."

—JAMES GARFIELD

"There are no good laws but such as repeal other laws."

—ANDREW JOHNSON, UNSURPRISINGLY NICKNAMED "SIR VETO"

"The spirit of resistance to government is so valuable on certain occasions, that I wish it to be always kept alive. It will often be exercised when wrong, but better so than not to be exercised at all. I like a little rebellion now and then. It is like a storm in the atmosphere."

—THOMAS JEFFERSON

"When we are sick, we want an uncommon doctor; when we have a construction job to do, we want an uncommon engineer, and when we are at war, we want an uncommon general. It is only when we get into politics that we are satisfied with the common man."

—HERBERT HOOVER

"Patriotism means to stand by the country. It does not mean to stand by the president."

—THEODORE ROOSEVELT

"A popular Government without popular information, or the means of acquiring it, is but a Prologue to a Farce or a Tragedy, or perhaps both."

—JAMES MADISON

"I have always said that my whole public life was an experiment to determine whether an intelligent people would sustain a man in acting sensibly on each proposition that arose, and in doing nothing for mere show or demagogical effect."

—JAMES GARFIELD

"If you think too much about being re-elected, it is very difficult to be worth re-electing."

—WOODROW WILSON

"I know no method to secure the repeal of bad or obnoxious laws so effective as their stringent execution."

—ULYSSES S. GRANT

"I met a very engaging young fellow who introduced himself to me as the mayor of the town, and added that he was a Socialist. I said, 'What does that mean? Does that mean that this town is socialistic?' 'No, sir,' he said; 'I have not deceived myself; the vote by which I was elected was about 20 per cent. socialistic and 80 per cent. protest.'"

—WOODROW WILSON

Presidential Oxymorons

Presidents are always in the public eye—and their words make it to the public's ears. Some sentiments come out a little less polished than others…

✳   ✳   ✳   ✳

O UR MOST FAMOUS foot-in-mouth president is George W. Bush, but his low-hanging fruit of malapropisms and unintended misstatements only stands out because of frequency. Other presidents made similar self-contradictory statements in the spirit of famous baseball player and manager Yogi Berra, or they simply stated the obvious as though it were stone-tablet truth. But sometimes, as Ronald Reagan accidentally pointed out, "Facts are stupid things."

Quotables

"When more and more people are thrown out of work, unemployment results."

—CALVIN COOLIDGE

"I have opinions of my own—strong opinions—but I don't always agree with them."

—GEORGE W. BUSH

"I have had many troubles, but the worst of them never came."

—JAMES GARFIELD

"Solutions are not the answer."

—RICHARD NIXON

"When a man is asked to make a speech, the first thing he has to decide is what to say."

—GERALD FORD

"I rise only to say that I do not intend to say anything."

—ULYSSES S. GRANT

In Times of War

A Pyrrhic Victory

Sometimes, victory can be almost as costly as defeat.

* * * *

PYRRHUS WAS AN ancient king, the ruler of a state called Epirus in what is now Greece, who was praised as a military leader. In early years, he fought in the complex, many-fronted wars that took place after Alexander the Great died and his empire began to unravel. Pyrrhus gained and lost land in Macedonia and other locations before turning his attention to the rising empire of Rome. At the invitation of the city of Tarentum, located in southern Italy, Pyrrhus crossed the Adriatic and went to war in 280 BCE.

A year later, he fought at the battle of Asculum. The battle was recounted by Plutarch, who states that Pyrrhus won (another chronicler, Cassius Dio, says the Romans did). But though the Romans lost 6,000 soldiers, Pyrrhus himself lost about 3,500, reportedly leading him to say in response to a congratulatory comment, "Another such victory over the Romans, and we are undone."

Pyrrhus continued to make war during his life, gaining and losing ground in Sicily, Italy, and Macedonia. He died, however, not in battle but in a street fight.

The Whites of Their Eyes

The famous saying, "Don't fire until you see the whites of their eyes," is often attributed to a Colonel in the American Revolutionary War. But the provenance of the phrase gets a little murky...

✳   ✳   ✳   ✳

IN JUNE 1775, two months after the start of the American Revolution, the vicious Battle of Bunker Hill erupted in Charlestown, Massachusetts, across the Charles River from Boston. This raises the first question...where did the fighting take place exactly?

The logical answer is on Bunker Hill. History books continue to cite that location more than 230 years after the fact—but they actually have it wrong.

Word has gotten around that British troops were planning an attack from Boston, Massachusetts, where they held complete control. On June 16, nearly 1,000 American militiamen led by Colonel William Prescott dug into the highest land in the area—a spot known as Bunker's Hill. But the commander thought better of the location and moved his troops a half mile closer to Boston, a lower elevation referred to as Breed's Hill. The soldiers quickly built a barrier of dirt that was 6 feet high, 80 feet across, and 160 feet long.

The next morning, British major general William Howe led more than 2,200 redcoats from Boston against the militiamen. But they were hampered by a lack of boats, lousy maps, and bad tides. While cannons fired against the patriots across the Charles River, Howe struggled to reach Charlestown itself. By mid-afternoon, his soldiers were finally ready to make their assault on Breed's Hill.

As the British advanced, someone on the American side, wanting the soldiers to get the most out of their gunpowder, famously yelled, "Don't fire until you see the whites of their eyes—then shoot low!" or "Don't one of you fire until you see the whites of their eyes." Many attribute this command to Colonel William Prescott. Others claimed that it was said first by Israel Putman, a General out of Connecticut—that when Prescott yelled it to his men, he was simply reiterating his own orders, and that other officers who had heard Putman also relayed the same command to their own men.

Whatever the case, it took the Brits three separate charges to eventually overtake the position and capture Charlestown. But they paid a high price, with more than a thousand deaths and injuries among the troops. The militia, which had grown to more than 2,500 soldiers, suffered close to 400 casualties. But the grit and determination of the Americans led Howe to never again fight a battle in Massachusetts.

An Overseas Origin?

Variants on the phrase may have been said earlier by other gunpowder-conserving commanders. It's said that Frederick the Great, the King of Prussia, or his officers said something similar in 1757: "By push of bayonets, no firing till you see the whites of their eyes." Another Prussian, Prince Charles, is quoted as saying, "Silent till you see the whites of their eyes," as far back as 1745. Whether Prescott or Putman had heard the phrase or came up with independently is lost to history.

General Washington

Before he was the nation's first president, Washington fought in the French and Indian War and was the commander-in-chief of the Continental Army. Here are some of his views on war from that pre-presidential time period.

✳   ✳   ✳   ✳

"Discipline is the soul of an army. It makes small numbers formidable; procures success to the weak, and esteem to all."

"Let us therefore animate and encourage each other, and show the whole world that a Freeman, contending for liberty on his own ground, is superior to any slavish mercenary on earth."

"The fate of unborn millions will now depend, under God, on the courage and conduct of this army. Our cruel and unrelenting enemy leaves us only the choice of brave resistance, or the most abject submission. We have, therefore, to resolve to conquer or die."

"To place any dependence upon militia is, assuredly, resting on a broken staff."

"Without a definitive naval force we can do nothing definitive. And with it, everything honorable and glorious."

I Have Not Yet Begun to Fight!

John Paul Jones was a naval hero of the Revolutionary War and a fascinating character.

✳ ✳ ✳ ✳

THE MAN WHO would become America's first naval hero was born in Scotland in 1747 as John Paul. Like many sailors of the day, he set to sea young, at the age of 13, and worked on several different British ships. Eventually he became captain of one. His fortunes foundered when he was accused of cruelty after a sailor he had flogged died. After an incident in which he killed another man in an argument (he claimed self-defense), he left for America, where a brother of his had lived. He also adopted the last name of "Jones."

In 1775, Jones volunteered to join the fledgling Continental Navy. He was first appointed first lieutenant of the USS *Alfred* before taking command of the USS *Providence*. In the early days of the war, Jones commanded several different ships, successfully harrying British merchant ships—and occasionally feuding with superiors. He gained public acclaim when the USS *Ranger* captured the HMS *Drake*, an incident that was seen as proof that the Continental Navy could stand up to Britain's established Royal Navy. (The acclaim came attached with some controversy, as Jones also had a conflict with his second-in-command; people accused Jones of trying to hog the glory of the capture.)

In 1779, Jones was aboard the USS *Bonhomme Richard*, part of a squadron that included the *Alliance* and *Pallas*. (Jones reportedly named the ship in honor of his friend Benjamin Franklin, who wrote the "Poor Richard" series.) In September 1779, the squadron encountered a large convoy of merchant ships escorted by the HMS *Serapis* and the *Countess of Scarborough*. During what became known as the Battle of Flamborough Head, the *Bonhomme Richard* engaged the *Serapis* in a long and grueling battle. During the fight, at a moment when the fight did not favor him and he was urged to surrender, Jones was said to utter his famous phrase, "I have not yet begun to fight." He managed to lock the *Bonhomme Richard* and *Serapis* together and boarded the British ship.

Some accounts add that at one point Jones was thought dead and his men wanted to surrender; when the British captain asked for confirmation that they would "strike their colors" (lower their flag in surrender), Jones rallied and proclaimed, "I have not yet thought of it, but I am determined to make you strike."

The *Bonhomme Richard* took heavy damage in the battle— much of it, ironically, from the *Alliance*, in broadsides meant for the *Serapis*—and ended up sinking, but only after the British surrendered. Jones and his sailors went to other vessels, and Jones himself took over the *Serapis* and sailed it to the neutral country of Holland.

After the war, Jones ended up entering Russian service in 1787, though various personal and professional conflicts marred his time there. He died in 1792 in Paris at the age of 45. Though he was buried in Paris, his body was later exhumed and returned to American soil in 1905, and he was re-interred in 1913 at the Naval Academy Chapel.

On the Hit Parade

During the Civil War, the feelings of civilians and soldiers in the North and South were captured in song. Lyrics of famous songs were sometimes altered to reflect what was going on at the time.

✳ ✳ ✳ ✳

MUSIC HAS THE ability to evoke a time or place more than just about anything. If filmmakers want to remind an audience of the '60s, they can use popular rock or soul songs of the time, just as the '20s can be invoked by playing ragtime. The Civil War era has its recognizable melodies, as well.

Northern Note-Worthies

Perhaps the most famous song to come out of the Civil War was written not by a soldier or a famous songwriter, but by a dedicated social activist named Julia Ward Howe. An ardent abolitionist living in Boston, Howe had attended a public review of infantry marching off to battle at the beginning of the conflict. With them, she sang what was becoming a very popular song of the time, "John Brown's Body," written by Vermont soldier Thomas Bishop. While many—including Howe—believed that "John Brown's Body" was a stirring tribute to the martyred abolitionist of Harpers Ferry, the song was actually a good-natured ribbing of Bishop's commanding officer, who also shared that common name. "John Brown's body lies a mouldering in the grave!" the song joyously declared.

Regardless of who the subject of the song was and how it was interpreted, the lyrics were somewhat macabre, perhaps too dark for the civilian public, and one of Howe's companions suggested that she try to compose some new lyrics for the popular tune. Always up to a challenge, Howe quickly developed lyrics whose power and potency are unquestionable: "The Battle Hymn of the Republic." Her words were published on the front page of *The Atlantic Monthly* and became an overnight sensation, spreading across the North like wildfire.

Southern Ditties

On the other side of the Mason-Dixon Line, lots of people were singing the regional anthem "Dixie," which, ironically enough, is generally attributed to a man from the Union state of Ohio named Daniel Decatur Emmett. The song, whose famous opening line declares, "I wish I was in the land of cotton," reflects the mood of the South in the years leading up to the Civil War. With pressure increasing from the Northern abolitionists and the impending inauguration of Abraham Lincoln, many in the South felt that their very way of life was under attack.

Emmett's first drafts of the song attempted to portray slavery in a positive light, eschewing the harsh and brutal aspects of the peculiar institution in an effort to counteract the waves of abolitionist literature coming from the North. During the war, soldiers often modified the lyrics to speak directly of current events. A Confederate version boasted: "Northern flags in South wind flutter / Send them back your fierce defiance! / Stamp upon the cursed alliance!" Union soldiers, on the other hand, sang the song with a mind for reclaiming what belonged to the United States: "Hurrah! Hurrah! The Stars and Stripes forever! / Hurrah! Hurrah! Our Union shall not sever!"

Bitter Ballads

While music could be a great tool for rallying support for each side's cause, it also reflected the bitterness and sorrow that the Civil War brought to the United States. Confederate Major James Randolph's "O I'm a Good Old Rebel" is a post-war lament and vicious condemnation of the victorious Union. "I can't take up my musket / and fight them now no more," the song spits, "but I ain't going to love them / now that is sartin sure."

Stephen Foster, the illustrious songwriter responsible for "Oh, Susannah," "My Old Kentucky Home," "Beautiful Dreamer," "Camptown Races," and "Old Folks at Home," composed a haunting ballad that echoed the cries of many Americans during those years: "Was My Brother in the Battle?" "He was ever brave and valiant, and I know he never fled / Was his name among the wounded or numbered with the dead?" Foster captured the terrible reality of the war, and the deep sorrow embedded in the lyrics is still palpable today.

Common Ground

Despite the differences between the soldiers of the North and South, they had still grown up in the same country, and their similarities led them to cherish a number of the same songs. "Lorena" was a song that wasn't partisan—it didn't take sides or taunt the opponent. In fact, it didn't make any kind of ideological pronouncements at all. It merely tugged at the heartstrings of all those who missed the ones they loved and the homes they left behind. The war itself is only mentioned fleetingly, as the impediment to the singer's love for his woman: "A duty, stern and pressing, broke / The tie which linked my soul with thee." In the end, it is clear that the stress of war has disillusioned the singer and that he can only hope to be rejoined with his beloved Lorena in the peace and purity of heaven. This stirring song swept through the ranks of both armies, a rare bit of common ground between two warring forces.

That Devil Forrest

A master tactician and a ruthless leader, Nathan Bedford Forrest saw his influence last long after the war ended.

✳ ✳ ✳ ✳

THE ESSENCE OF Confederate General Nathan Bedford Forrest's military strategy was to "get there first with the most men." It sounds elementary enough, but Forrest, who fought against many better-educated generals during the Civil War, won nearly all of his battles. It's said that during the war he came under fire 179 times and captured 31,000 prisoners.

Rising from the Ranks

Unlike many famous Civil War generals, Forrest wasn't a product of West Point. His education came from his own experience. His father died when Forrest was a teenager in northern Mississippi, so he left school to support his mother and eight siblings. Initially, he worked his family's farm, but he soon expanded into trading cotton, livestock, real estate, and slaves. By 1860, he ran a highly successful business and was the owner of a 3,000-acre plantation in Memphis, Tennessee.

At the outbreak of war, he enlisted in the Confederate army as a private, but he soon received permission to raise his own cavalry unit. Spending his own money, he outfitted a cavalry battalion of 600 and earned the rank of lieutenant colonel. Shortly thereafter, his exploits as a cavalry leader became the stuff of legend.

A Ruthless Reputation

A number of notorious tales surround Forrest. He had a reputation throughout most of the war for being tough and ruthless. This may be summed up in one of the most famous quotes attributed to him: "War means fighting, and fighting means killing."

One of Forrest's earliest exploits that started to build his reputation is his cavalry regiment's escape from besieged Fort Donelson in Tennessee. Ulysses Grant's army had won the day, and Confederate commanders were getting ready to surrender the fort to him the next morning. Forrest would have none of it, declaring, "I did not come here for the purpose of surrendering my command." A few officers planned to slip away, Forrest among them. He announced to his troops: "Boys, these people are talking about surrendering, and I am going out of this place before they do or bust hell wide open." His unit disappeared into the night.

While covering the Confederate retreat from the Battle of Shiloh two months later, Forrest was wounded. He was far ahead of his troops when he got shot, but he grabbed a Union soldier and used him as a shield to make his escape back to Confederate lines.

Raiding Behind Enemy Lines

When he recovered, Forrest was promoted to brigadier general and began a series of successful cavalry raids against Union supply lines. In one memorable raid into Tennessee in 1863, his regiment of fewer than 1,000 attacked a Union garrison twice that size at Murfreesboro. His horse soldiers trounced the 2,000 bluecoats there and captured all survivors, including Union commanding officer General Thomas T. Crittenden.

In an attempt to disrupt General Sherman's campaign on Atlanta, Forrest and his unit went behind enemy lines to attack a Union supply depot at Johnsonville, Tennessee. The Union forces were caught by surprise, and Forrest was able to destroy a gunboat fleet and several million dollars' worth of Union supplies. Sherman wrote to Grant, "That devil Forrest was down about Johnsonville and was making havoc about the gun-boats and transfers." Still, it had no effect on his maneuvers in Georgia. Years later in his memoirs, Sherman had to admit a grudging respect, calling the incident "a feat of arms which, I confess, excited my admiration."

The Fort Pillow Massacre

Forrest cemented his reputation as a ruthless general at Fort Pillow, Tennessee, in April 1864. He led a successful attack against the fort and offered fair treatment to the defenders if they surrendered. When Union commanders refused, Forrest's army brutally overran the fort and its defenders, reportedly shooting many men—primarily black soldiers—as they attempted to surrender. Forrest denied these accusations, but he later said, "The river was dyed with the blood of the slaughtered for 200 yards." The incident, which came to be known as the Fort Pillow Massacre, became a rallying cry for black Union soldiers.

This made Forrest a bit of a target himself, leading Sherman to wish that the army would "go out and follow Forrest to the death, if it cost 10,000 lives and breaks the Treasury." Four times Union generals sent forces out specifically to defeat Forrest; each time they failed. The second of these attempts led to the Battle of Brice's Crossroads in Mississippi, where Forrest's troops routed a federal force that was twice their size. He was finally beaten in the spring of 1865 and forced to surrender in Gainesville, Alabama, that May. This was after both General Lee and General Johnston had surrendered their own forces at Appomattox Court House and Durham Station.

A Lasting Legacy

After the war, Forrest returned to planting cotton and speculating on railroads. He certainly didn't abandon his Confederate ideals, though. Forrest, known as the Wizard of the Saddle during the war, became the first Grand Wizard of the Ku Klux Klan in 1867. The Klan formed to terrorize blacks, Northerners, and Republicans. Forrest died on October 29, 1877, at the age of 56.

Gallant Adventure at the Battle Of Mobile Bay

"Damn the torpedoes!" saves the day.

✳   ✳   ✳   ✳

THE LEGENDARY SAYING "Damn the torpedoes!" sounds like something that would have originated during the great sea battles of World War II. But that isn't the case. The speaker was Union Rear Admiral David G. Farragut, and he made the proclamation during one of the great sea battles of the Civil War, the Battle of Mobile Bay.

By the summer of 1864, Mobile Bay, Alabama, was the last major port still open against the Union blockade. The bay, which sits about 50 miles northeast of New Orleans on the

Gulf of Mexico, was protected by Fort Morgan, Fort Gaines, and Fort Powell. The bay itself was full of floating mines, which were then called torpedoes, as well as pilings and other obstructions. A narrow channel was the only relatively clear path through the bay, but it passed close to the guns of Fort Morgan.

Closing Down the Port

Mobile Bay was widely used by blockade runners to supply the Confederacy, so Union officials placed a priority on shutting it down. Admiral Farragut steamed to the bay with 14 wooden warships, 4 ironclad monitors, and 1,500 marines. When this force appeared, Confederate Admiral Franklin Buchanan moved his meager force of three wooden gunboats and one ironclad, the *Tennessee*, into the channel to confront them.

Farragut's leading ironclad, the *Tecumseh*, charged up the channel and positioned itself to take on the *Tennessee*. That maneuver swung the craft out of the safe zone, though, and it struck a mine. The explosion ripped the bottom of the ship—it sank in minutes. In the ensuing confusion, the rest of the Union line halted, making the federal ships sitting ducks for the Confederate cannons of Fort Morgan.

A Legend Is Born

That's when Farragut saw the chance to be a hero, or so some say. Legend has it that he lashed himself to the rigging of his flagship, the *Hartford*, and yelled out, "Damn the torpedoes! Full speed ahead!"

The rallying cry evidently worked, because the rest of the Union fleet sped into the harbor and neutralized the three wooden warships. Only the *Tennessee* remained. Its armor withstood cannon fire, so Farragut ordered his ships to ram the ironclad repeatedly. Eventually the ship's steering was wrecked, its smokestack was knocked off, and its gunport shutter chains were cut, making it impossible for the Confederates to return fire. After an hour of this battering, Admiral Buchanan, who had been wounded in the battle, raised the white flag.

It would take another two weeks to capture Fort Morgan, but the naval battle for Mobile Bay was over.

According to Robert E. Lee

"I shall carry with me to the grave the most grateful recollections of your kind consideration, & your name & fame will always be dear to me. Save in the defense of my native State, I never desire again to draw my sword."

—TO GENERAL WINFIELD SCOTT

"I can anticipate no greater calamity for the country than a dissolution of the Union. It would be an accumulation of all the evils we complain of, and I am willing to sacrifice everything but honor for its preservation."

"With all my devotion to the Union, and the feeling of loyalty and duty of an American citizen, I have not been able to make up my mind to raise my hand against my relative, my children, my home. I have, therefore, re-signed my commission in the Army."

—TO HIS SISTER, ANNE MARSHALL, IN 1861

"I am now considered such a monster, that I hesitate to darken with my shadow, the doors of those I love, lest I should bring upon them misfortune."

—ON HIS PUBLIC IMAGE SHORTLY AFTER HIS SURRENDER AT APPOMATTOX COURT HOUSE

"It is well that war is so terrible—we should grow too fond of it."

A Literary Look At The War

Walt Whitman, one of America's most famous writers, had unique experiences during the Civil War. He left behind his interpretation of the conflict in his poetry—and a poem with a phrase you still hear used today.

✳   ✳   ✳   ✳

WALT WHITMAN WAS born in 1819 and lived most of his life in New York. Early in his career, he worked as a printer, a journalist, and an occasional teacher. In the 1850s,

Whitman embarked on a path as a poet among transcendentalists, publishing the first version of *Leaves of Grass* in 1855. (He continued to add to and revise it throughout the rest of his life.) As the Civil War approached, Whitman believed it was more important to preserve the Union than to emancipate slaves. He hated both the fire-eaters of the South and the aggressive abolitionists of the North, feeling that extremists threatened the harmony of the Union. The South's greatest sin, Whitman felt, was secession, and the North's greatest virtue was devotion to the Union.

A Lasting Impression

The Civil War fascinated Whitman, and his experiences during the conflict transformed him as a writer: He left behind a catalog of colorful descriptions of both the political dispute and the conflict on the battlefield. For example, after the First Battle of Bull Run, he penned "Beat! Beat! Drums!" In this poem, Whitman calls on the drums and bugles to "scatter the congregations" and to take groom away from bride and "peaceful farmer [from] any peace" so they will serve in the war.

In the Thick of Things

In late 1862, Whitman learned through newspaper reports that his brother, George, was wounded in battle at Fredericksburg, Virginia. He immediately left New York for Virginia. While looking for his brother, he passed through a makeshift field hospital where he saw a heap of amputated human limbs and wondered if any of these belonged to his brother. He finally found George—all in one piece—with his regiment, recovering from a bullet wound that had pierced his cheek. Spending time with his brother and the war-hardened soldiers, Whitman was enraptured by the stories he heard. He also helped the young soldiers of the ranks bury the dead.

From the field in Virginia, Whitman decided to take up residence in the nation's capital and take a job copying material in the Army Paymaster's Office. He also volunteered as a nurse's assistant in the local hospitals, performing small acts of kindness to the wounded: reading to them, writing letters for them, and bringing them small gifts. It was this experience that inspired *Drum-Taps*, Whitman's collection of 43 poems that captures the emotional experiences of the war. These poems, such as "The Wound Dresser," show the nation's transformation from patriotic militarism to a sense of compassion and grief for the wounded and dead.

An Ode to Lincoln

Also among Whitman's most celebrated writings are those that define the commander in chief, Abraham Lincoln. While in Washington, D.C., Whitman lived within walking distance of the White House and crossed President Lincoln's path several times. He even attended the reception for his second inauguration, but he never actually met the President.

Although Whitman was unable to express his fondness for Lincoln in person, he left a written record of poetry that shows a great deal of respect and admiration for his President. He confirmed their common ideology, "We are afloat on the same stream—we are rooted in the same ground."

Whitman understood Lincoln's struggle and witnessed what the war did to him on a personal and physical level, writing that the president looked "worn and tired; the lines, indeed, of vast responsibilities, intricate question, and demands of life and death, cut deeper than ever upon his dark brown face; yet all the old goodness, tenderness, sadness, and canny shrewdness, underneath the furrows." He also complimented Lincoln's "purest, heartiest tenderness, and native western form of manliness."

After the Union victory and Lincoln's assassination, Whitman wrote what is probably his most famous ode to his fallen hero.

"O Captain! My Captain!"

O Captain! my Captain! our fearful trip is done;
The ship has weather'd every rack, the prize we sought is won;
The port is near, the bells I hear, the people all exulting,
While follow eyes the steady keel, the vessel grim and daring:
But O heart! heart! heart!
O the bleeding drops of red,
Where on the deck my Captain lies,
Fallen cold and dead.

O Captain! my Captain! rise up and hear the bells;
Rise up—for you the flag is flung—for you the bugle trills,
For you bouquets and ribbon'd wreaths—for you the shores a-crowding,
For you they call, the swaying mass, their eager faces turning;
Here Captain! dear father!
This arm beneath your head!
It is some dream that on the deck,
You've fallen cold and dead.

My Captain does not answer, his lips are pale and still,
My father does not feel my arm, he has no pulse nor will,
The ship is anchor'd safe and sound, its voyage closed and done,
From fearful trip the victor ship comes in with object won;
Exult O shores, and ring O bells!
But I with mournful tread,
Walk the deck my Captain lies,
Fallen cold and dead.

Pickett's Charge at the Battle of Gettysburg

"I was ordered to take a height, which I did, under the most withering fire I have ever known . . ."

—GENERAL GEORGE PICKETT, IN A LETTER TO HIS WIFE AFTER HIS ILL-FATED CHARGE

In what would go down in history as Pickett's Charge, the forces of Confederate General George Pickett led the march up Cemetery Ridge on the last day of the Battle of Gettysburg, Pennsylvania, in 1863. Nearly 12,000 soldiers marched more than a mile under heavy fire, and some managed to break through the Union line. However, lacking support behind and facing intense Union bombardment, they could not hold their ground; they retreated, having suffered horrific losses.

America's War Novel

"At times he regarded the wounded soldiers in an envious way. He conceived persons with torn bodies to be peculiarly happy. He wished that he, too, had a wound, a red badge of courage."

✳   ✳   ✳   ✳

THE CIVIL WAR ended in 1865, but its shadows lingered. Stephen Crane was born in 1871, years after the Civil War ended, and was not a veteran himself. However, his war novel *The Red Badge of Courage* was published in 1895 to critical acclaim.

Crane's protagonist was Henry Fleming, a private in the Union army, described often as "the youth." After fleeing from a battle, he suffers from shame, and acquits himself by returning to battle and even eventually acting as a standard-bearer. Crane's novel, unlike many previous war narratives, focused on Fleming's internal musings and realizations rather than an external record of actions.

Crane did research for his novels, including interviews with veterans. Fleming serves in a fictitious company, but details of the battles (and a short story Crane later wrote) seem to set the novel at a real battle, the Battle of Chancellorsville.

Some contemporary reviews praised the novel's realism, arguing that it could have been written by a veteran; other critics, including some veterans, were disparaging about Crane's lack of experience. Writer Ambrose Bierce, himself a veteran, was irate. However, the book became a bestseller in both the United States and England.

Crane's career after *The Red Badge of Courage* was not a long one. He did a tour of Civil War battlefields and wrote other short stories set during the war; he also served as a war correspondent during the Greco-Turkish and Spanish-American wars. In 1900, he died at the age of 28 of tuberculosis.

Excerpts from *The Red Badge of Courage*

"The youth was in a little trance of astonishment. So they were at last going to fight. On the morrow, perhaps, there would be a battle, and he would be in it. For a time he was obliged to labor to make himself believe. He could not accept with assurance an omen that he was about to mingle in one of those great affairs of the earth."

"He had, of course, dreamed of battles all his life—of vague and bloody conflicts that had thrilled him with their sweep and fire. In visions he had seen himself in many struggles. He had imagined peoples secure in the shadow of his eagle-eyed prowess. But awake he had regarded battles as crimson blotches on the pages of the past. He had put them as things of the bygone with his thought-images of heavy crowns and high castles. There was a portion of the world's history which he had regarded as the time of wars, but it, he thought, had been long gone over the horizon and had disappeared forever."

"In regard to his companions his mind wavered between two opinions, according to his mood. Sometimes he inclined to believing them all heroes. In fact, he usually admired in secret the superior development of the higher qualities in others. He could conceive of men going very insignificantly about the world bearing a load

of courage unseen, and although he had known many of his comrades through boyhood, he began to fear that his judgment of them had been blind. Then, in other moments, he flouted these theories, and assured him that his fellows were all privately wondering and quaking."

"Yet the youth smiled, for he saw that the world was a world for him, though many discovered it to be made of oaths and walking sticks. He had rid himself of the red sickness of battle."

Tall Tales About Napoleon

Napoleon Bonaparte, one of the most successful and brutal military leaders of all time, had a short fuse and was often shortsighted. But he was not, as is popularly believed, short in stature.

✳   ✳   ✳   ✳

Slighted by History

IT TURNS OUT that an error in arithmetic contributed to history's perception of Napoleon as a small man. The only known measurement of Bonaparte came from his autopsy, which reported a height of 5′2″. But it was not taken into account that this measurement was calculated in French units. Translating to slightly more than 168 centimeters, his height was actually 5′6″ by the English Imperial system. This was above average for a 19th-century Frenchman.

Another possible reason for this misconception is the fact that Napoleon kept himself surrounded by a group of relatively tall guardsmen. Napoleon was never seen in public without his "imperial guard." These soldiers averaged six feet in height and would have towered over Napoleon.

A Napoleon Complex

Napoleon wasn't short, but his temper was. Over time, the notion that the general's irascible, aggressive personality stemmed from his small size has been applied to any small-statured man who uses his temper to compensate for his height. This is referred to as a "Napoleon Complex," and though psychologists regard it as a negative social stereotype, it also proves to be a myth. In 2007, researchers at the University of Central Lancashire studied the effect of height on aggression in men. Using heart monitors to gauge reactions, scientists found that *taller* men were more likely to respond to provocation with aggressive behavior.

As Napoleon himself said, "History is the version of past events that people have decided to agree upon." It turns out that history cut Napoleon about four inches short.

The Significance of Waterloo

The Battle of Waterloo occurred near Brussels between French forces under Napoleon and combined British, Belgian, Dutch, German, and Prussian armies led by the British Duke of Wellington. The day began with Wellington and Napoleon facing each other across the field of battle after a night of heavy rain. The French leader delayed his attack until noon to allow the field to dry so that his artillery and cavalry could move more freely. French forces unsuccessfully attacked Wellington's center throughout the afternoon. Their early evening attack broke their opponent's center, but by then Prussian forces had assaulted the French flank, drawing critical resources away from the main fight. Wellington regrouped, drove the French back, and then advanced forcefully. Beset on two sides, the once-feared French army retreated. Over the preceding 20 years, Napoleon had established himself as one of the most powerful rulers and most successful military strategists since the days of the Roman Empire. His defeat at Waterloo ended once and for all his rule of France and his great influence over the affairs of Europe.

"Nothing except a battle lost can be half so melancholy as a battle won."

—ARTHUR WELLESLEY, DUKE OF WELLINGTON

The Maginot Line: Winning the Previous War

France built the Maginot Line in order to win another World War I. Unfortunately for the French, Germany did not plan to refight World War I.

✳   ✳   ✳   ✳

WHICH ILLUSTRIOUS GENERAL reportedly said, "The side which stays within its fortifications is beaten"?

Answer: Napoleon Bonaparte, Emperor of France

To understand why France built the Maginot Line, review the French World War I experience: France hosted nearly the entire Western Front, with six million soldiers killed, wounded, or captured. French generals concluded that modern defense was stronger than modern offense. "Next time," reasoned French generals, "we will inflict rather than suffer those losses."

From 1930 on, France spent vast sums blanketing its German and Luxembourg frontiers with a network of steel and concrete fortifications. A much lesser version extended along the Belgian frontier to the English Channel. People named it the Maginot Line for the French Minister of Defense who spearheaded it, André Maginot.

A Defensive Masterpiece

The Line was no modern Great Wall, but a series of mutually supportive fortifications. Let's tour a section to get a clear image. Picture a verdant hill topped by an armored observation post, studded with concrete bunkers and steel turrets, flanked by lesser forts and pillboxes. Interlocking fields of fire take excellent defensive advantage of all terrain. In places the concrete is ten feet thick. Out front are tank traps and wire. In the distance to each side you can see another hill with similar defenses; interval casemates lie between. Indoors, several stories of tunnels connect the various bastions like the roots of a gigantic tree. Ammunition elevators and railways move ammo to the guns and the wounded to a modern sickbay.

One thousand men defend this clean, modern fort complex, called an ouvrage. No more gas attacks; no more muddy, filthy trenches. Artillery can (and would, in one case) shell it all day without effect. The Maginot Line contained 44 large ouvrages, 58 small ouvrages, and 360 interval casemates.

A Huge Blow to France

German generals saw no reason to assail the Line: A quick and violent strike through the Netherlands and Belgium would enable Germany's mobile advance guard to bite deep into France north of the ouvrages, aided by close air support. The infantry, using standard tactics, would follow to occupy, consolidate, and control.

The strategy worked to perfection. On May 10, 1940, Germany tore into the Low Countries, quickly breaking into France well north of the ouvrages at Sedan. A minor German covering force tied down the 36 divisions defending the Line. Forty-six days later France surrendered.

All the Maginot Line did was encourage the Germans to find an easier place to invade.

The Charge of the Light Brigade

"Theirs not to reason why, Theirs but to do and die": the familiar phrase comes from Alfred, Lord Tennyson, writing of the disastrous Charge of the Light Brigade.

✳   ✳   ✳   ✳

MANY AMERICANS TODAY are probably hazy on the details of the Crimean War, and haven't read much Tennyson since high school. But the phrase about the lot of soldiers who "do and die" has stuck in the popular imagination.

The Crimean War took place in the mid-1850s. England, France, the declining Ottoman Empire, and Sardinia (then an independent kingdom) were fighting Russia. One major engagement of the war was the Siege of Sevastopol, which lasted for about a year, from September 1854 to September 1855. British, French, and Ottoman forces pushed through the Crimean peninsula, ultimately successfully.

An early battle in the larger Siege, the Battle of Balaklava took place in October 1854. During that battle, a confusion over orders led to the British Light Calvary Brigade suffering heavy losses when they charged against a well-fortified Russian position. The soldiers were valorized for their discipline and the damage they managed to inflict, even as they marched to slaughter. Of the 670 soldiers sent, more than 100 died, and another 160 were wounded.

Tennyson wrote and published the poem shortly after, one of several patriotic poems he published during the war.

1.

Half a league, half a league,
Half a league onward,
All in the valley of Death
Rode the six hundred.
"Forward, the Light Brigade!
"Charge for the guns!" he said:
Into the valley of Death
Rode the six hundred.

2.

"Forward, the Light Brigade!"
Was there a man dismay'd?
Not tho' the soldier knew
Someone had blunder'd:
Theirs not to make reply,
Theirs not to reason why,

Theirs but to do and die:
Into the valley of Death
Rode the six hundred.

3.

Cannon to right of them,
Cannon to left of them,
Cannon in front of them
Volley'd and thunder'd;
Storm'd at with shot and shell,
Boldly they rode and well,
Into the jaws of Death,
Into the mouth of Hell
Rode the six hundred.

4.

Flash'd all their sabres bare,
Flash'd as they turn'd in air,
Sabring the gunners there,
Charging an army, while
All the world wonder'd:
Plunged in the battery-smoke
Right thro' the line they broke;
Cossack and Russian
Reel'd from the sabre stroke
Shatter'd and sunder'd.
Then they rode back, but not
Not the six hundred.

5.

Cannon to right of them,
Cannon to left of them,
Cannon behind them
Volley'd and thunder'd;
Storm'd at with shot and shell,
While horse and hero fell,

They that had fought so well
Came thro' the jaws of Death
Back from the mouth of Hell,
All that was left of them,
Left of six hundred.

6.

When can their glory fade?
O the wild charge they made!
All the world wondered.
Honor the charge they made,
Honor the Light Brigade,
Noble six hundred.

Blitzkrieg

*"Man schlugen jemand mit der Faust und nicht mit gespreiz-
ten Fingern." ("One hits somebody with his fist and not with
fingers spread.")*

—GERMAN TACTICIAN GENERAL HANS GUDERIAN DESCRIBING THE BASIC CONCEPT OF
BLITZKRIEG WARFARE

✳   ✳   ✳   ✳

THE STATIC TRENCH warfare of World War I led to the
deaths of approximately ten million soldiers. Frontal
attacks over hundreds of yards, through open tracts of "no
man's land" strewn with barbed wire, offered defending soldiers
easy targets that were gunned down en masse. The appalling
loss of life during the Great War caused many military strategists to rethink how war was waged.

The Theory Behind Blitzkrieg

✳ The evolution of German military doctrine began in the
years following World War I. However, the new German
Army was severely limited in size and scope by restrictions
placed on Germany by the Treaty of Versailles. To circum-
vent the treaty's conditions, General Hans von Seeckt signed

a secret military alliance with the Russians, which allowed the Germans to test new weapons systems and tactics at Russian military sites.

* Prussian-born Heinz Guderian was instrumental in developing new armored-warfare tactics. Fluent in both English and French, he studied the theories advocated by military tacticians in Britain and France. As the head of the Inspectorate of Transport Troops, Guderian and his colleagues developed and tested new mechanized warfare strategies.

* Guderian advocated the elements of what would later be called Blitzkrieg in his book *Achtung—Panzer!* He believed an armored attack along a narrow front supported by airpower would have the best chances of success. In October 1937, Guderian wrote, "We believe that by attacking with tanks we can achieve a higher rate of movement than has been hitherto obtainable and . . . that we can keep moving once a breakthrough has been made."

The main elements of Guderian's new theory included:

* Deploying a large number of tanks.

* Utilizing motorized infantry that could move rapidly in conjunction with tanks.

* Coordinating air force attacks against the enemy front line and rear echelon with a focus on airfields, transportation links, and communication centers.

* Using self-propelled artillery.

* Establishing radio communication between frontline units and command centers to ensure the proper coordination between army and air force units.

* Surprising the enemy. Germany never openly declared war before invading any country during the war.

* The development of panzer divisions in combination with the new tactics enhanced the early successes of the German Army. Each panzer division was a self-contained unit consisting of tanks, mechanized infantry, self-propelled artillery, engineers, and antitank, antiaircraft, reconnaissance, and service personnel.

Putting Blitzkrieg Tactics to the Test

The first test of Germany's new military strategy occurred during the Spanish Civil War of 1936–39. Attacks by German tanks, fighter planes, and dive bombers were coordinated. Guderian later remarked the use of tanks in Spain was executed on too small a scale to make an accurate assessment of their effectiveness.

Hitler's desire to expand the territorial boundaries of the Third Reich forced his commanders into battle before they were fully provisioned for the Blitzkrieg-style assault they had hoped for. Only six newly formed panzer divisions were ready for battle when the Germans crossed the frontier into Poland in September 1939. The war in Poland was fought with predominantly unmotorized infantry and artillery. The panzer divisions that took part in the Polish invasion played, for the most part, a supplementary role to the conventional infantry divisions.

The real test for Guderian's new tactics came with the invasions of the Low Countries and France on May 10, 1940. Guderian's XIX Panzer Corps raced across France and captured the port cities of Boulogne and Calais on May 25 and 26. Dejected elements of the British Expeditionary Force and French Army were evacuated from Dunkirk beginning on May 26. General Erwin Rommel's 7th Panzer Division sped through France, reaching the English Channel on June 10. Nine days later he captured the vital port city of Cherbourg. Paris was occupied by June 14, and on June 25 the French capitulated.

Blitzkrieg tactics proved successful beyond all expectations when the Germans invaded Russia in June 1941. Within six months the German juggernaut had reached the outskirts of the capital city, Moscow. Unfortunately for the Germans, winter conditions, a calamitous lack of steady supplies, and inept leadership on the part of Hitler (who had dismissed some top generals and ignored the implications of a Russian counteroffensive), spelled the eventual defeat of the invading forces.

As a testament to Guderian's foresight, Allied commanders, including General George S. Patton, adapted Germany's mechanized tactics for their own use. Blitzkrieg-like elements have even found their way into more recent conflicts, including the American military's Operation Desert Storm.

Audie Murphy in His Own Words

A striking thing about Audie Murphy, the most decorated American soldier of World War II, was that his whole life was a series of battles. From a dirt-poor childhood to infantryman heroism in Europe to tumultuous personal struggles after the conflict, Murphy seemed ever in a desperate fight.

✳ ✳ ✳ ✳

BORN IN HUNT County, Texas, in 1924, Audie Murphy was the seventh of Emmett and Josie Murphy's 12 children. Tragedy struck the family early on. When Murphy was just 12, his father left. Four years later, his mother died. "Getting food for our stomachs and clothes for our backs," Murphy recalled, "was an ever-present problem." Three of his siblings went to an orphanage. Audie Murphy worked picking cotton, and to feed his family, he became an expert at shooting rabbits with a .22-caliber rifle. When the family gathered, he listened raptly to his uncles telling tales of valor during the Great War.

From Cook to Combat Hero

When war broke out, Murphy jumped at a chance to join the Marine Corps. But it rejected him. And no wonder—at 18, he was all of 5 feet 5 inches and 112 pounds. He enlisted in the regular army, which, after he swooned during a close-order drill, tried to make him a cook. "To reach for the stars," wrote Murphy, "and end up stirring a pot of C rations. I swore I would take the guardhouse first."

His ceaseless demands to see combat finally paid off in 1943. Murphy was sent to North Africa, then to the ferocious battle of Anzio in Italy, as part of Company B, 1st Battalion, 15th Infantry Regiment, 3rd Infantry Division.

His upbringing and outlook made him a natural soldier and combat leader. In battle, he preached that a "calm fury" was the best tactic. Under fire, he noted, "Things seem to slow down for me." He shrugged off malaria and a wound in the hip from a sniper's round. By the time his unit invaded southern France in August 1944, he'd earned his first medals and been field-promoted to second lieutenant, a rank he accepted only when assured he could stay with his unit.

In one battle, after taking out several machine-gun nests, he lost his best buddy when Germans feigning surrender shot his comrade down. In a fury, he killed the attackers, then turned their machine gun against other strong points. He was awarded the Distinguished Service Cross, the military's second-highest honor.

Murphy's greatest feat occurred on January 26, 1945, during bitterly cold fighting along the German border. His company of 18 was attacked by 6 Tiger tanks and more than 200 infantry. As his men fell back, Murphy jumped onto an abandoned tank destroyer whose gasoline was expected to blow any second. He grabbed its .50-caliber machine gun and sprayed bullets toward the Germans while radioing in artillery on himself.

"50 [yards] over!" he shouted on the field phone.

"50 over?" came the reply. "That's your own position."

"[Keep it coming!]," shouted Murphy.

After single-handedly breaking the attack and killing scores of Germans, he led the counterattack. His actions that day earned him the Medal of Honor. For other feats he was awarded two Silver Stars, two Bronze Stars, three Purple Hearts, the Legion of Merit, and two Croix de Guerre. Of his 37 medals, he sardonically noted soldiers ended up with a "Wooden Cross."

Haunted by War

When Germany surrendered, Murphy's men celebrated wildly, but he was desolate. Murphy wrote, "Like a horror film running backwards, images of the war flicker through my brain. The tank in the snow with smoldering bodies ..." Thereafter his psyche was stuck in the war. He exhibited the classic symptoms of post-traumatic stress syndrome, then called "shell shock." He wrote, "We have been so intent on death that we have forgotten life."

At home, after welcomes befitting an Achilles, he was wracked with nightmares. Murphy went to bed armed, sometimes waking up to fire his revolver at the wall. He'd twitch violently and freeze up. Insomnia led to a sleeping pill addiction. His first wife, actress Wanda Hendrix, divorced him. She said he once drew a gun on her. He married again, and with his second wife he had two sons, Terry and James.

Murphy fought his "demons" and helped others with theirs. Ahead of his time, he became an advocate of aid to veterans returning home with mental health woes. He also bought a house for his sister and found care for his three orphaned siblings.

On to the Silver Screen

After the war, Murphy worked as a rancher and horse breeder. He also wrote country and western songs, some of which were recorded by Roy Clark and Dean Martin. But Murphy channeled most of his pent-up energy into acting. He moved to Hollywood at the suggestion of James Cagney. Training as an actor, he spent penniless years there.

His fortunes changed in 1949 with the publication of his self-penned (with friend Dave McClure) best seller *To Hell and Back*, a terse, savagely honest account of his combat experience. Six years later, the book became a movie of the same name, starring none other than Audie Murphy as himself. The Universal movie grossed $10 million, a record that wasn't broken until Jaws.

Best at playing soldiers or outlaws, Murphy also impressed critics in John Huston's *The Red Badge of Courage*. He made a total of 44 films, most of which were Westerns. For his work on the big screen, Murphy was awarded a star on the Hollywood Walk of Fame.

On Memorial Day weekend in 1971, he died at 46 in a plane crash. The craft was manned by an unqualified pilot and had run into dense fog. Murphy was buried at Arlington National Cemetery. Today it's the second most-visited site at Arlington after JFK's grave.

We Shall Fight Them...

With the threat of a Nazi invasion looming just across the English Channel, Churchill delivered a rousing speech to Parliament that vowed resistance and promised an eventual victory.

✳ ✳ ✳ ✳

IN MAY 1940, Winston Churchill became the Prime Minister of England during one of its most perilous times in history. The Nazis had started World War II the previous September and already captured vast territories in Europe. In a series of coordinated attacks against Allied positions in the Battle of France, the Nazis had succeeded in splitting the French and British troops, and drove British troops nearly into the English Channel at Dunkirk. By early June the British Expeditionary Force had evacuated to southern England, leaving France entirely in German hands. Several armored Wehrmacht divisions were now stationed on the coast of Normandy, just across the Channel from Britain, and threatening an all-out invasion.

Morale in Britain was virtually nonexistent at the time, and many of the British people did not feel that Britain should be involved in the war with Germany. Churchill was faced with the huge task of having to deliver the news of the defeat to Parliament, warn that the threat of invasion was dire, and convince Parliament and the British people that war would be winnable. On May 13 he had already delivered a speech that said war was imminent, and that the only goal could be victory. Following the withdrawal, he would have to double down on this position in spite of the fact that the British Expeditionary Force had just suffered a crushing loss.

We Shall Fight on the Beaches

On June 4, Churchill addressed Parliament again, in the second of what would be three of his most stirring speeches. He began the speech with a frank report on the German attack and Allied retreat to Dunkirk. He described the resistance at Dunkirk at length; this resistance, which allowed the Allies enough time to withdraw, is now widely considered one of the greatest organized retreats in history. He freely admitted that the invasion of France was a "colossal military disaster," and that Hitler planned to invade the British Isles. While Britain was equipped to defend itself from such an invasion, he vowed that their war would not merely be a defensive one, but one that would eventually liberate France.

He finished his speech by returning to the threat of a German invasion, assuring the British people that in spite of the seriousness of the threat, Britain would never fall to the Nazis. The closing lines read:

"We shall go on to the end, we shall fight in France, we shall fight on the seas and oceans, we shall fight with growing confidence and growing strength in the air, we shall defend our Island, whatever the cost may be, we shall fight on the beaches, we shall fight on the landing grounds, we shall fight in the fields and in the streets, we shall fight in the hills; we shall never surrender, and even if, which I do not for a moment believe, this Island or a large part of it were subjugated and starving, then our Empire beyond the seas, armed and guarded by the British Fleet, would carry on the struggle, until, in God's good time, the New World, with all its power and might, steps forth to the rescue and the liberation of the old."

The speech was immediately heralded as historic, and moved a number of Members of Parliament to tears. In the third speech, delivered on June 18, following the surrender of France, he said that if the British Empire should last thousand years, "men will say this was their finest hour."

Churchill would lead Great Britain through WWII and the devastating Battle of Britain to eventual victory in 1945. He established close ties with the United States and cultivated a warm relationship with FDR, ensuring continued support for the duration of the war. Following the war, he resigned as Prime Minister and was leader of the opposition in Parliament for six years. He again served as Prime Minister from 1951–1955, when he retired from public life permanently. Churchill died on January 24, 1965.

So They Said

"Grant began by expressing a hope that the war would soon be over, and Lee replied by stating that he had for some time been anxious to stop the further effusion of blood, and he trusted that everything would now be done to restore harmony and conciliate the people of the South. He said the emancipation of the Negroes would be no hindrance to the restoring of relations between the two sections of the country, as it would probably not be the desire of the majority of the Southern people to restore slavery then, even if the question were left open to them."

—UNION GENERAL HORACE PORTER, ON THE SURRENDER AT APPOMATTOX COURT HOUSE

"You cannot make soldiers of slaves, nor slaves of soldiers... The day you make soldiers of them is the beginning of the end of the revolution. If slaves will make good soldiers our whole theory of slavery is wrong."

—CONFEDERATE GENERAL HOWELL COBB

"Future years will never know the seething hell and the black infernal background of countless minor scenes and interiors... of the Secession war; and it is best they should not—the real war will never get in the books."

—WALT WHITMAN

"General, if you put every [Union soldier] now on the other side of the Potomac on that field to approach me over the same line, I will kill them all before they reach my line."

—GENERAL JAMES LONGSTREET'S VOW TO ROBERT E. LEE AS COUNTLESS FEDERAL ASSAULTS WERE BEATEN BACK BY LONGSTREET'S FORCE AT FREDERICKSBURG

"By some strange operation of magic I seem to have become the power of the land."

—GEORGE MCCLELLAN, SHORTLY AFTER HE ASSUMED COMMAND OF UNION FORCES AROUND WASHINGTON IN 1861

"Will you pardon me for asking what the horses of your army have done since the battle of Antietam that fatigues anything?"

—ABRAHAM LINCOLN, TO GENERAL GEORGE MCCLELLAN, WHO HAD EXCUSED HIS LACK OF ACTION IN THE FALL OF 1862 DUE TO TIRED HORSES; MCCLELLAN WAS REMOVED FROM COMMAND SHORTLY THEREAFTER

"At early dawn, darkened by the threatening rain, Armistead, Garnett, Kemper and your Soldier held a heart-to-heart powwow. All three sent regards to you, and Old Lewis pulled a ring from his little finger and making me take it, said, 'Give this little token, George, please, to her of the sunset eyes, with my love, and tell her the "old man" says since he could not be the lucky dog he's mighty glad that you are.'"

—CONFEDERATE GENERAL GEORGE PICKETT TO HIS FIANCÉE ON THE DAY OF PICKETT'S CHARGE

"Lee's army will be your objective point. Wherever Lee goes, there you will go also."

—GENERAL ULYSSES S. GRANT TO GENERAL GEORGE MEADE, COMMANDER OF THE ARMY OF THE POTOMAC

"*Little did I conceive the greatness of the defeat, the magnitude of the disasters which it had entailed upon the United States or the interval that would elapse before another army set out from the banks of the Potomac onward to Richmond.*"

—WILLIAM HOWARD RUSSELL ON THE FIRST BATTLE OF BULL RUN

"*Our march yesterday was terribly severe. The sun was like a furnace, and the dust thick and suffocating. Many a poor fellow marched his last day yesterday. Several men fell dead on the road. Our boys have all come through so far, accepting the hardships as a matter of course, and remaining cheerful and obedient I assure you I feel proud of them.*"

—UNION COLONEL RUFUS R. DAWES

"*With malice toward none, with charity for all, with firmness in the right as God gives us to see the right, let us strive on to finish the work we are in, to bind up the nation's wounds, to care for him who shall have borne the battle and for his widow and his orphan, to do all which may achieve and cherish a just and lasting peace among ourselves and with all nations.*"

—ABRAHAM LINCOLN, SECOND INAUGURAL ADDRESS, 1865

Science and Nature

A Man Who Loved Nature

John Muir was perhaps the most influential conservationist in the history of the United States. A farmer, naturalist, and prolific writer, Muir's tireless efforts to protect America's natural resources led to the creation of the National Parks System. He is often called "John of the Mountains" or the "Father of the National Parks."

✳ ✳ ✳ ✳

JOHN MUIR WAS born in Scotland on April 21, 1838. When he was eleven, his family immigrated to the United States, settling in Wisconsin. Muir worked on his family farm until he attended the University of Wisconsin at 22. After three years, he left school to explore the northwest United States and Canada, supporting himself with odd jobs. In 1867, while he was working in a wagon wheel factory, he was injured and nearly lost his sight. Upon recovering, he determined to follow his dream of wandering the natural spaces of the nation.

At Home Outdoors

He first undertook a thousand-mile walk from Indianapolis to Florida. Muir sailed to Cuba, and then to New York, where he booked passage to San Francisco. It was in California that he would find his true home in the Sierra Nevada and Yosemite. Upon seeing Yosemite for the first time in 1868, he was overwhelmed by its pristine valley and soaring mountain peaks. Muir built a small cabin along Yosemite Creek, and lived there for the next two years. During this time, he explored Yosemite's high country, often alone, carrying nothing but a loaf of bread, a handful of tea, a tin cup, and a copy of Ralph Waldo Emerson's writings. He'd often spend the night sitting in his overcoat next to a campfire, reading Emerson. He was often visited by scientists, naturalists, and artists. In 1871, he was visited by Emerson himself. His hero offered him a teaching position at Harvard on the spot, but Muir declined, later saying he couldn't give up "God's big show" for a professorship.

Muir made four trips to Alaska and the Pacific Northwest over the next ten years, exploring Glacier Bay, Wrangel Island, and climbing Mount Rainer.

Activism and the National Parks

In 1874, Muir published a series of articles about the Sierra Nevada. These were the beginning of a vast collection of over 300 articles and 10 books about the natural world, conservation, and his travels. He married Louisa Strentzel in 1880, and raised a family with her in Martinez, California. But he never stopped travelling, visiting Australia, South America, Africa, Asia, and Europe, and returning many times to the Sierra Nevada.

In order to protect his beloved Yosemite and promote preservation of natural spaces, Muir co-founded the Sierra Club in 1892. The organization fought to protect the Park from grazing and prevent it from being reduced in size.

In 1889, a series of Muir's articles appeared in *Century* magazine that highlighted the devastation of the meadows and forests of Yosemite by sheep and cattle grazing. Working with *Century*'s editor Robert Underwood Johnson, Muir was able to convince Congress to create Yosemite National Park. Muir would eventually be involved in the creation of the Sequoia, Petrified Forest, Grand Canyon and Mount Rainer National Parks as well.

In 1901, he published *Our National Parks*, which prompted President Theodore Roosevelt to visit him in Yosemite. Upon entering the park, Roosevelt asked Muir to show him "the real Yosemite," and the two set off alone to hike through the back country. They talked late into the night, and slept under the stars at Glacier Point. The experience, and Muir's advocacy, convinced Roosevelt to create the National Parks Service and put Yosemite and other Parks under Federal protection.

Muir died in Los Angeles on Christmas Eve, 1914.

Quotes from John Muir

"Bears are made of the same dust as we, and breathe the same winds and drink of the same waters. A bear's days are warmed by the same sun, his dwellings are overdomed by the same blue sky, and his life turns and ebbs with heart-pulsings like ours and was poured from the same fountain."

"As far as the eye can reach it extends, a heaving, swelling sea of green as regular and continuous as that produced by the heaths of Scotland. The sculpture of the landscape is as striking in its main lines as in its lavish richness of detail; a grand congregation of massive heights with the river shining between, each carved into smooth, graceful folds without leaving a single rocky angle exposed, as if the delicate fluting and ridging fashioned out of metamorphic slates had been carefully sandpapered. The whole landscape showed design, like man's noblest sculptures. How wonderful the power of its beauty! Gazing awe-stricken, I might have left everything for it."

"A merry school of porpoises, a square mile of them, suddenly appear, tossing themselves into the air in abounding strength and hilarity, adding foam to the waves and making all the wilderness wilder. One cannot but feel sympathy with and be proud of these brave neighbors, fellow citizens in the commonwealth of the world, making a living like the rest of us. Our good ship also seemed like a thing of life, its great iron heart beating on through calm and storm, a truly noble spectacle. But think of the hearts of these whales, beating warm against the sea, day and night, through dark and light, on and on for centuries; how the red blood must rush and gurgle in and out, bucketfuls, barrelfuls at a beat!"

"Arriving by the Panama steamer, I stopped one day in San Francisco and then inquired for the nearest way out of town. 'But where do you want to go?' asked the man to whom I had applied for this important information. 'To any place that is wild,' I said."

99 Percent Perspiration

Thomas Alva Edison was one of the most prolific inventors in American history. Called "The Wizard of Menlo Park," Edison held over a thousand US Patents in his name, and had a profound impact on industry and life in the twentieth century. He also left some pretty good quotes on invention, hard work, and life.

✳ ✳ ✳ ✳

EDISON WAS BORN in Ohio in 1847. He developed hearing problems at a young age, either due to a case of scarlet fever or because he was struck by a train conductor when a laboratory he was working in on a boxcar set fire. He became a telegraph operator, working first for the Grand Trunk Railway and later for Western Union. He began his career as an inventor in 1877, and continued to be active in developing new commercial products right up until his death in 1931.

Phonograph

One of Edison's personal favorites among all of his inventions, the phonograph was also one of the first truly groundbreaking one. Edison's design used a needle that would vibrate when the user spoke into the receiver, causing it to make marks on a rotating drum wrapped in foil. Eventually, Edison would develop a phonograph that used discs and cylinders to allow music to be recorded—the forerunner of the record player. The first message Edison recorded was a recitation of the poem "Mary Had a Little Lamb." When he played it back, he and his staff were delighted by the invention's success.

Edison Light Bulb

Edison is probably best known for having invented the light bulb. This belief isn't precisely accurate, however: light bulbs had existed for several years before Edison's invention, but they were expensive, unreliable, and only lasted a few hours before they burned out. There was an ongoing race to perfect the electric light bulb when Edison took on the challenge.

His innovation was to create a vacuum inside the bulb, use a carbon filament, and reduce the voltage to make the bulb stable and long-lasting. His first success created a bulb that lasted for thirteen and a half hours. He later switched to using a carbonized bamboo filament. This bulb lasted over 1,200 hours.

Motion Picture

Edison's first motion picture device was similar to the design of his phonograph. $1/16$th inch pictures were arranged on a cylinder and viewed under a microscope as it rotated. Thanks to George Eastman's invention of 35mm celluloid film, Edison was able to develop the Strip Kinetograph. The film, cut into long strips that were perforated along the edges, moved past a shutter, and the viewer observed twenty-second films through a peephole. Later, Edison manufactured and marketed Thomas Arnat's Vitascope, which was the first movie projector.

Electric Power Grid

With the success of his light bulb, Edison realized that an electric distribution system was necessary to make it a commercially viable competitor with existing gas lighting utilities. In the 1880s he patented a system for distributing electricity and founded the Edison Illuminating Company. In January 1882, Edison's first steam-powered electric power station was turned on in London. It powered street lamps and a few houses close by. In September of that year his first generating station in the United States was switched on, providing 110 volts to 59 customers in lower Manhattan. And on January 19, 1883, the first incandescent electric streetlight system that used overhead wires was installed in Roselle, New Jersey.

Quotes from Thomas Edison

"To invent, you need a good imagination and a pile of junk."

"Sleep is like a drug. Take too much at a time and it makes you dopey. You lose time and opportunities."

"There is no substitute for hard work."

"Genius is one percent inspiration and ninety-nine percent perspiration."

"If there is such a thing as luck, then I must be the most unlucky fellow in the world. I've never once made a lucky strike in all my life. When I get after something that I need, I start finding everything in the world that I don't need—one damn thing after another. I find ninety-nine things that I don't need, and then comes number one hundred, and that—at the very last—turns out to be just what I had been looking for."

Famous, and Infamous, Words on Inventions

"Where a new invention promises to be useful, it ought to be tried."

—THOMAS JEFFERSON

"An amazing invention—but who would ever want to use one?"

—RUTHERFORD B. HAYES UPON MAKING A CALL FROM WASHINGTON TO PENNSYLVANIA WITH ALEXANDER GRAHAM BELL'S TELEPHONE, PATENTED ON MARCH 7, 1876

"Our inventions are wont to be pretty toys, which distract our attention from serious things. They are but improved means to an unimproved end."

—HENRY DAVID THOREAU

"Today we have ... the transmission of sight for the first time ... Human genius has now destroyed the impediment of distance ... in a manner hitherto unknown."

—HERBERT HOOVER DURING THE FIRST LONG-DISTANCE TRANSMISSION OF A LIVE PICTURE AND VOICE (APRIL 9, 1927)

"I've got hundreds of ideas stacked up—many of them worth more than the compact disc. But I haven't been able to work on them."

—JAMES T. RUSSELL

"But what is it good for?"

—ENGINEER AT THE ADVANCED COMPUTING SYSTEMS DIVISION OF IBM, COMMENTING ON THE MICROCHIP, 1968

"The concept is interesting and well-formed, but in order to earn better than a 'C,' the idea must be feasible."

—A YALE UNIVERSITY PROFESSOR, RESPONDING TO FUTURE FEDERAL EXPRESS FOUNDER FRED SMITH'S PAPER PROPOSING RELIABLE OVERNIGHT DELIVERY SERVICE

"There's a lunatic in the lobby who says he's invented a device for transmitting pictures over the air. Be careful, he may have a razor on him."

—EDITOR OF THE LONDON DAILY EXPRESS, COMMENTING ON A VISITOR

"Radio has no future"; "Heavier-than-air flying machines are impossible"; "X-rays will prove to be a hoax."

—ROYAL SOCIETY PRESIDENT WILLIAM THOMSON (LORD KELVIN), 1895, 1897

"There will never be a bigger plane built."

—A BOEING ENGINEER FOLLOWING THE FIRST FLIGHT OF THE 247, A TWIN-ENGINE PLANE BUILT TO CARRY TEN PEOPLE, 1933

"Name the greatest of all inventors—accident."

—MARK TWAIN

"Well-informed people know it is impossible to transmit their voices over wires, and even if it were possible, the thing would not have practical value."

—EDITORIAL IN *THE BOSTON POST*, 1865

E pur si muove

Galileo was one of the giants of modern science: he pioneered the use of the telescope to observe celestial bodies, advanced our understanding of physics, and famously demonstrated that objects of unequal weight fall at the same speed. He also publically contradicted the belief, popular at the time, that the Earth was the center of the universe—and was subjected to intense persecution because of it.

✳ ✳ ✳ ✳

Copernicanism vs. Heliocentrism

GALILEO WAS BORN in Florence, Italy in 1564. At the time, the official position of the Catholic Church, then a powerful political entity, was that the Earth was the center of the universe. This was based on several biblical references as well as the writings of Socrates and Ptolemy. In 1542 Nicolaus Copernicus had proposed a heliocentric model, in which the planets orbit the Sun. Without physical evidence, however, it was widely rejected by authorities and leading scientists.

In 1609, Galileo first heard about the invention of a telescope in Holland. Intrigued by this new invention, he set out to build his own, and with it to explore the cosmos. He observed and drew the mountains and craters of the Moon in great detail, discovered the moons of Jupiter, and observed the phases of Venus. In 1610 he published a catalogue of his discoveries, the *Sidereus Nuncius*, which made him famous throughout Europe.

And Yet It Moves

Armed with his discovery of the phases of Venus, which proved that Venus was orbiting the Sun, Galileo began to publicly advocate for a heliocentric system. This was seen as a direct challenge to the Church's authority, and in 1615 his writings were submitted to the Roman Inquisition. The Church presented various theological and mathematical arguments against the validity of heliocentrism. In spite of the fact that Galileo travelled to Rome to defend the theory, in 1616 the Inquisition declared heliocentrism not only "foolish and absurd in philosophy," but heretical to boot. The Pope ordered Galileo to abandon heliocentrism and stop defending the idea altogether.

For ten years, Galileo complied, avoiding the controversy. When a more liberal Pope came to power in 1632, he encouraged Galileo to publish an unbiased work about the arguments for and against heliocentrism. In the resulting work, *Dialogue Concerning the Two Chief World Systems*, Galileo instead openly advocated for heliocentrism. He was summoned to Rome and tried for heresy. He maintained his innocence throughout the six-month trial, until he was threatened with torture if he did not admit his guilt and recant his beliefs. He did recant, but reportedly whispered *"e pur sio muove,"* meaning "and yet it moves" in a final act of defiance.

House Arrest and Two New Sciences

Convicted of being "vehemently suspect of heresy," Galileo was sentenced to house arrest, under which he would remain for the rest of his life. He was also required to "abjure, curse and detest" the theory of heliocentrism.

While under house arrest, Galileo wrote one of his finest works, *Discourses and Mathematical Demonstrations Relating to Two New Sciences*. In it, he laid out his findings over the past thirty years of scientific study. The two new sciences were the motion of objects and strength of materials, and they laid the foundation for kinematics and material engineering.

In *The Two Sciences*, Galileo first proposed the idea that bodies of different mass fall at the same rate (this would be demonstrated by Apollo 15 astronauts on the Moon), as well as the behavior of bodies in motion, the principle relativity of motion, and the nature of infinity.

The Father of Modern Science died in 1642 at the age of 77. In 2016 the Juno spacecraft arrived at Jupiter, carrying a plaque in his honor.

"The proposition that the sun is the center and does not revolve about the earth is foolish, absurd, false in theology, and heretical."

—THE INQUISITION ON GALILEO'S THEORIES

Home Christmas

Lifelong innovators, the Orville and Wilbur Wright ushered the human race into the age of flight in 1903. Less than seventy years later, we would land on the moon.

✳ ✳ ✳ ✳

THE WRIGHT BROTHERS were raised in Dayton, Ohio, and were inseparable from a young age. They felt their personalities were perfectly complimentary; where Orville was an enthusiastic dreamer, Wilbur was steadier and dependable. In 1878, their father gave the brothers a toy helicopter made of bamboo, cork and paper, and powered by a rubber band. The boys played with the helicopter until it broke, at which point they built one themselves. Years later, they would describe this episode as the beginning of their interest in powered flight. In 1892, the brothers opened a bicycle shop in Dayton. This allowed them to hone their mechanical skills and fund their interest in building a powered flying machine. In 1899 they began experimenting with aeronautics.

Kitty Hawk

In 1900, the brothers began experimenting with gliders at Kitty Hawk. They chose the location because of the strong winds that blew in from the Atlantic and the soft landings afforded by the sandy beaches. They tested designs for powered flyers in a wind tunnel they built. By 1903 they were ready to test their first powered aircraft. On December 17, at 10:35 am, Orville piloted their propeller-driven biplane 120 feet, staying aloft for 12 seconds. They tested the plane three more times. On the last flight, Wilbur piloted the plane 852 feet in 59 seconds. They continued to improve their design over the next several years, eventually securing the first contract for an airplane with the US Army. Wilbur died of typhoid in 1912. Orville retired in 1915, and spent the rest of his life serving on the board of the National Advisory Committee on Aeronautics, the forerunner of NASA.

The Text of the Telegram

"Success. Four flights Thursday morning. All against twenty-one mile wind. Started from level with engine power alone. Average speed through air thirty-one miles. Longest fifty-nine seconds. Inform press. Home Christmas."

—TELEGRAM TO THE REVEREND MILTON WRIGHT, FROM KITTY HAWK, N.C.

The Secret to Success?

"If I were giving a young man advice in how he might succeed in life, I would say to him, pick out a good mother and father and begin life in Ohio."

—WILBUR WRIGHT

Eureka!

One of the greatest scientists of classical antiquity, Archimedes was a mathematician, astronomer, physicist, engineer, and inventor. He was far ahead of his time, and single-handedly had one of the most profound effects on scientific inquiry of anyone in the ancient world. Among other achievements, he created a system of exponential numbers, accurately estimated the value of pi, and discovered the spiral that bears his name.

✳   ✳   ✳   ✳

ARCHIMEDES WAS BORN in Syracuse, Sicily circa 287 BCE. He was the son of an astronomer named Phidias who estimated the size of the sun as twelve times larger than what was then commonly accepted knowledge. At a young age, Archimedes travelled to Egypt to study at the Library of Alexandria. Returning to Syracuse, where he would spend the rest of his life, befriending the king, Hiero II. He corresponded extensively with other mathematicians in the ancient world; much of what we know about him is from his letters. Archimedes also published at least nine treatises on geometry, mechanics, hydrostatics, and the cosmos.

The Turn of the Screw

A problem of moving water from a lower area to a higher one was a serious one at the time of Archimedes, as being able to do so would allow for more efficient irrigation systems and for the removal of bilge water from ships. Archimedes engineered the Archimedes Screw to solve the problem. The simple design places a screw within a cylinder, and could be hand-cranked. The design is still used in commercial and agricultural applications to this day.

The Eureka Moment

Archimedes is perhaps most famous for his discovery of a method to determine the volume of an irregularly-shaped object. King Hiero II had commissioned a crown be made for himself, and had supplied pure gold to a goldsmith for him to fashion it with. When he received the crown, Hiero was suspicious that the goldsmith had substituted silver for some of the gold, and asked Archimedes to come up with a way to find out if this was the case. This presented a problem: the density of the crown could not be determined without damaging it, and the volume could not be easily measured, as it was not a regularly shaped body like a sphere or a cube.

While bathing, Archimedes noticed that the level of water in the tub raised when he got in, and here he found his solution:

if submerged in water, the crown would displace an amount of water equal to its own volume. He leapt out of the tub, forgetting in his excitement to dress, and ran naked to the palace shouting "Eureka!" ("I have found it!")

The Siege of Syracuse

In 210 BCE, Roman forces besieged Syracuse, and Hiero asked Archimedes to assist in designing defenses for the city. He engineered the Claw of Archimedes, a long crane with a grappling hook affixed to one end. With it, the island city's defenders could grapple and capsize ships from behind the city walls. He also reportedly designed an ancient heat ray to attack ships: by polishing numerous brass or copper disks, defenders were said to have been able to reflect and concentrate the rays of the sun on the wooden Roman warships, setting them on fire.

Archimedes' war machines were only able to delay the Roman invasion, however. In 212, the Romans took the city of Syracuse. Despite orders be the Roman general that he be left unharmed, he was killed by a Roman soldier.

"Give me where to stand, and I will move the earth."

—ARCHIMEDES' STATEMENT ON WHAT HE COULD DO WITH LEVERS

First, Do No Harm

Prescribing plants as drugs, the extensive use of teaching texts, and even the modern conception of the physician as a scientist who trains by internship can be attributed to antiquity. Hippocrates, a Greek physician, is to this day heralded as "The Father of Medicine."

✳ ✳ ✳ ✳

HIPPOCRATES OF COS was a famous physician and teacher of medicine in the fifth century BC. He came to represent the ideal physician—devoted, kind, and skillful. He descended from a family of physicians that traced their roots back to the god Asklepios, and thus were called the "family of Asklepiads."

As the family expanded, it became a guild of physicians. Two schools developed from this group; Hippocrates headed the school on the island of Cos.

The Hippocratic Corpus

Supposedly, Hippocrates wrote a large body of work, known as the Hippocratic Corpus, which includes the famous Hippocratic Oath. Scholars have argued since ancient times as to how many (if any) of these treatises were actually written by Hippocrates himself. Rather than the work of a single author, this group of medical writings is now regarded as the work of many authors and traditions, which had their origins in fifth and fourth century BC medical literature.

When the librarians of Alexandria, Egypt, received any medical work, it appears that they classified it as having been authored by Hippocrates. It was the practice in ancient times to ascribe the works of an entire school to the founder, and students and disciples often wrote in the name of their master. Therefore, although Hippocrates himself may not have written any of this material, scholars still refer to the body of work as Hippocratic.

Diagnosis and Prognosis

Hippocratic medicine was concerned with prognosis, determining the likely course of an illness based on previous experience. Observation of the beginning and progress of the illness took into account the patient's appearance, noting especially breathing, sweating, excretion, and temperature. The physician looked for hollow, light-sensitive, or red eyes, cold ears, yellow skin color, and a tense face. He asked the patient about sleep, loose bowels, and appetite. The Corpus also discusses diagnosis at length. Diseases are described, classified by symptoms, and explained. Along with the descriptions go lists of suitable foods, herbal remedies, and treatments for disease. This work had elements of modern scientific method and practical applications for specific symptoms.

The Corpus also recognized the process of healing as a team endeavor, with the patient working to get well:

"Life is short and the Art (of medicine) long, the occasion urgent, experience deceptive, and decision difficult; yet not only must the physician be ready to do his duty but the patient, attendants, and circumstances must also cooperate if there is to be a cure.

The Hippocratic Oath

Perhaps the most famous part of the Hippocratic Corpus is the Hippocratic Oath. Many people think the words "First, do no harm," are part of it, but they are not. That phrase was popularized much later, in the 17th century. There is, however, a similar phrase in the Hippocratic Corpus, though not the oath itself, that says: "The physician ... must have two special objects in view with regard to disease, namely, to do good or to do no harm."

Still used today as a declaration of a doctor's moral responsibility, the oath is one of the world's first statements of medical ethics. One translation reads:

"I swear by Apollo, the Physician, and by Asklepios and Hygieia and Panaceia and all the gods and goddesses, making them my witnesses, that I will fulfill according to my ability and judgement this oath and this covenant:

To hold him who has taught me this art as equal to my parents and to live my life in partnership with him, and if he is in need of money to give him a share of mine, and to regard his offspring as equal to my brothers in male lineage and to teach them this art—if they desire to learn it—without fee and covenant; to give a share of precepts and oral instruction and all the other learning to my sons and to the sons of him who has instructed me and to pupils who have signed the covenant and have taken an oath according to the medical law, but to no one else.

I will apply dietetic measures for the benefit of the sick according to my ability and judgement; I will keep them from harm and injustice.

I will neither give a deadly drug to anybody if asked for it, nor will I make a suggestion to this effect. Similarly I will not give to a woman an abortive remedy. In purity and holiness I will guard my life and my art.

I will not use the knife, not even on sufferers from stone, but will withdraw in favor of such men as are engaged in this work.

Whatever houses I may visit, I will come for the benefit of the sick, remaining free of all intentional injustice, of all mischief, and in particular of sexual relations with both female and male persons, be they free or slaves.

What I may see or hear in the course of the treatment or even outside of the treatment in regard to the life of men, which on no account one must spread abroad, I will keep to myself holding such things shameful to be spoken about.

If I fulfill this oath and do not violate it, may it be granted to me to enjoy life and art, being honored with fame among all men for all time to come; if I transgress it and swear falsely, may the opposite of all this be my lot."

Shaping the Practice of Medicine

Peter Mere Latham was a physician who revolutionized the field of medical education. In the 19th century, he championed the idea that medical practitioners should also be teachers of clinical medicine.

✳ ✳ ✳ ✳

Physician to the Queen

LATHAM WAS BORN in 1761 to a medical family; his grandfather, John Latham, was the President of the Royal College of Physicians and the founder of the Medical Benevolent

Society. He followed in his grandfather's footsteps, becoming a medical resident at St Bartholomew's Hospital and attending Oxford University, where he received a Doctor of Medicine and joined the College of Physicians. Latham began working at a St. Bartholomew's as a resident physician in 1815, but he periodically returned to Oxford to deliver annual lectures. His reputation as a physician grew, and he would eventually go on to become the personal physician to Queen Victoria.

On Medical Education

In 1836, Latham published *Lectures on Subjects Connected with Clinical Medicine*, which primarily discussed diseases of the heart and pulmonary system. Latham's intent in publishing the book was to provide a medical manual for students, which was a fairly new idea at the time; until then, medical students primarily attended lectures given by physicians on medical topics. Latham's *Lectures* could therefore be considered the forerunner of medical college textbooks of today.

At that time the concept of a full-time professor and medical researcher also did not yet exist. Medical students would attend college and listen to lectures, but did not go through any kind of residency program before beginning their practice. There was also no uniform means of collecting or analyzing clinical data, and so the bulk of medical knowledge that was taught was based in existing and largely untested doctrine.

During his tenure at St Bartholomew's, Latham taught undergraduate medical courses, and he pioneered a number of educational techniques that are taken for granted today. Latham stressed the importance of what he called "self-learning" in clinical instruction, or observational learning. He believed that as a teacher he would be most effective if he presented his students with medical cases that they could then see with their own eyes, thereby building a foundation of experience that would serve them when they entered practice. He emphasized the value of lifelong learning, telling his students that "pathology is a study for your whole life." Latham believed that the essential purpose of learning was to gain a base of wisdom that could equip the clinician with keen problem-solving ability.

Latham was also a pioneer of the use of teaching aids. He encouraged his students to interact with patients, and said there were "a multitude of things" that could be learned at the patient's bedside. He had students attend postmortem autopsies and view pathological specimens, and thought that books and lectures should be used in medical education only sparingly and to supplement hands-on learning.

"The All-Pervading Poppy of Oblivion"

In spite of his extraordinary professional success and his contributions to the field of medical education, John Latham is not widely known, even to students of medicine or clinicians. William Bennett Bean, a 20th century internist and medical historian, described Latham's legacy as being "a classic victim of the all-pervading poppy of oblivion" due to his obscurity.

Latham retired from practicing medicine in 1865, and moved to Torquay, where he died in 1875.

Quotes from Latham

"The practice of physic is jostled by quacks on the one side, and by science on the other."

"The diagnosis of disease is often easy, often difficult, and sometimes impossible."

"We should always presume the disease to be curable, until its own nature prove it otherwise."

"It takes as much time and trouble to pull down a falsehood as to build up the truth."

"People in general have no notion of the sort and amount of evidence often needed to prove the simplest of fact."

Survival of a Quote

"Survival of the fittest," thought to summarize the theory of evolution, is actually a metaphor for natural selection that was not coined by Charles Darwin.

✳   ✳   ✳   ✳

A QUOTE MAY HAVE an original creator, but its evolution occurs independently of the person who said it first. "Survival of the fittest" has a definite creator: 19th-century economist Herbert Spencer. Yet after Spencer coined the phrase in *Principles of Biology* (1864), it took on a life if its own.

Spencer conjured the phrase as a reference to Charles Darwin's theory of natural selection, which Spencer had read about upon the 1859 release of *On the Origin of Species by Means of Natural Selection*. Darwin's theory was strictly biological: Given the preconditions of variation, replication, and heritability, traits favorable to a given environment are preserved over time (natural selection), and thus change occurs (evolution). By means of analogy, Spencer brought this concept into the economic realm to describe how the "fittest" societies evolve over time.

Despite popularizing the same phrase, Darwin and Spencer didn't use it in the same way. By "fittest" Darwin did not mean "best" but rather whatever trait allows an organism to survive and reproduce in a given environment, thereby increasing the frequency of said trait. Spencer, on the other hand, did intend fittest to mean "best," and he applied the idea to social evolution, not biology.

What Darwin meant by natural selection is best summarized by a quote that actually appeared in *On the Origin of Species*, from the first edition ad infinitum: "Any variation, however slight…if it be in any degree profitable to an individual of any species…will tend to the preservation of that individual, and will generally be inherited by its offspring."

So What Did Darwin Say?

Charles Darwin is one of the greatest biologists in history. His breakthrough insight that natural selection is the driver of evolution revolutionized biology and directly led to every major advance in the life sciences.

✳ ✳ ✳ ✳

DARWIN WAS BORN to a scientific family on February 12, 1809. His father Robert was a physician, and his grandfather Erasmus had theorized on evolution and the possibility of a single common ancestor for all life. Darwin was a capable student, but he preferred taking long walks in the countryside to the classroom. At 16 he attended medical school, but disliked the curriculum, although he enjoyed chemistry and zoology. He left medical school and enrolled in Cambridge in 1828, where he continued to pursue zoology, collecting beetles in his spare time.

The Voyage of the *Beagle*

After completing Cambridge, Darwin was offered a position as a naturalist on the HMS *Beagle*, a survey ship that would take a five-year voyage around the Southern Hemisphere. It was on this voyage that Darwin had his first inklings of what would become the Theory of Natural Selection. At Cape Verde, he observed ancient seashells on high cliffs far from the water. The ship's captain lent Darwin a copy of Charles Lyell's *Principles of Geology*, which argued that geologic change was the result of continual accumulation of minuscule changes over time.

In the Galapagos Islands, Darwin observed variations among tortoise shells from one island to the next, and saw that a number of similar finches had very different beaks that appeared related to their diet. The Galapagos animals were also clearly related to South American species, but had small differences. These observations laid the foundation for his discovery of natural selection.

On the Origin of Species

Darwin would spend the next twenty years variously presenting his findings from the voyage, writing books on geology, and assembling a comprehensive classification of barnacles. All the while, he was quietly writing about his theories on natural selection, but kept his discovery to himself; he was aware of the radical implications of the theory, and wanted to be absolutely certain it was airtight.

In 1858, however, his hand was forced when he received a letter from Alfred Russell Wallace describing his own very similar theories on natural selection. Their theories were jointly presented at the Linnaean Society on July 1, and in November 1859, Darwin's *On the Origin of Species* was published. The first printing of 1,250 copies sold out almost immediately, and the book sparked international interest. The *Origin* argued that all extant life on earth arose from a single common ancestor; that many more offspring are produced than can survive; and that slight variations among those offspring will allow some to have a better chance at survival.

Darwin eventually published six editions of the *Origin of Species;* many of the ideas associated with it, such as "survival of the fittest," did not appear until later editions; the word "evolved" appears only once in the first edition, and "evolution" was not added until the fifth. Although the theory was resisted by a few members of the scientific elite and the Church of England, the evidence for it was irrefutable, and it was soon widely accepted as fact. Darwin continued his work after the publication, writing two books on botany. In 1871 he published *The Descent of Man and Selection in Relation to Sex,* which demonstrated that humans are animals and laid out his theory of evolution by sexual selection.

"I see no good reasons why the views given in this volume should shock the religious sensibilities of anyone."

—CHARLES DARWIN, *THE ORIGIN OF SPECIES,* 1869

Thomas Henry Huxley

"To a person uninstructed in natural history, his country or seaside stroll is a walk through a gallery filled with wonderful works of art, nine-tenths of which have their faces turned to the wall."

✳ ✳ ✳ ✳

CALLED "DARWIN'S BULLDOG" for his staunch defense of his friend's theory of natural selection, Thomas Henry Huxley played a key role in the widespread acceptance of evolutionary theory during a series of famous debates.

Thomas Henry Huxley was born in Middlesex, England, in 1825. His father, a math teacher, was laid off when Huxley was ten, forcing him to give up formal schooling. The boy decided to educate himself, teaching himself German, Latin and Greek, and becoming an expert in physiology and zoology. A voracious reader, he also apprenticed with various physicians, and entered a school of anatomy beginning at age 16. At twenty, he passed his first exams at the University of London, and after two years, left to join the Royal Navy.

Huxley was assigned to the crew of the HMS *Rattlesnake* as the ship's doctor, and in 1846 the ship embarked on a four-year voyage to survey Australia and New Guinea. While there, he collected specimens of marine animals, and his findings were published by the Royal Society of London while he was still at sea. When he returned he was inducted into the Royal Society and became a Professor of Natural History.

Evolutionary Ideas in 1850

At the time of Huxley's induction to the Royal Society, a number of ideas about evolution had already been proposed. Jean-Baptiste Lamarck had proposed that acquired traits could be inherited in 1809; while the idea was incorrect, it was the first comprehensive theory of evolution. Prevailing wisdom was skeptical of evolution; the Church insisted that all organisms had been created in their current form, and while most understood that species could go extinct, many did not accept that one species could arise from another.

Huxley himself was initially doubtful of the veracity of evolutionary theories. He roundly rejected Lamarckism based on a lack of supporting evidence, and delivered a lecture at the Royal Society discussing his skepticism. Darwin contacted Huxley himself, and included him among the few scholars with whom he shared his theory of natural selection prior to making it public. Upon being shown Darwin's theory, Huxley famously exclaimed "how extremely stupid not to have thought of that!" When Darwin published *On the Origin of Species* in 1859, Huxley was convinced of the truth of evolution, and although he was privately undecided on natural selection, he publically defended the theory tenaciously.

Debate at Oxford

In 1860, Oxford University arranged a public debate on the merits of the theory of natural selection, attended by Huxley and a number of other prominent British scientists and theologians, including Samuel Wilberforce, a Bishop in the Church of England and a widely renowned public speaker. Huxley had already debated the paleontologist Richard Owen two days before.

Several speakers were called before Wilberforce, and when it was his turn, argued that Darwin's theory was not supported by the evidence, and noted that many of the leading scientific thinkers of the day were dismissive of it. Although he spoke at length, Wilberforce's argument is remembered mostly for only one remark, in which he asked Huxley whether it was on his grandmother's or grandmother's side that Huxley was descended from a monkey.

Huxley stood to defend natural selection, also speaking at length. At the end of his argument, he responded to

Wilberforce's question by saying he wouldn't be ashamed to be descended from a monkey, but that he was ashamed to be associated with a man like Wilberforce who used his oratory abilities to conceal the truth.

Louis Pasteur

"No, a thousand times no; there does not exist a category of science to which one can give the name applied science. There are science and the applications of science, bound together as the fruit to the tree which bears it."

✳   ✳   ✳   ✳

LOUIS PASTEUR'S CONTRIBUTIONS to modern biology are immense: he discovered pasteurization, vaccinations for anthrax and rabies, and microbial fermentation. His discoveries advanced the germ theory of disease, disproved the theory of spontaneous generation, and helped to found the study of bacteriology.

Pasteur was born in Dole, France, in 1822. Although he was an average student, he obtained a Bachelor of Arts in 1840, a Bachelor of Science in 1842, and a Doctorate at the École Normale in Paris in 1847. He spent the first several years of his career as a teacher and researcher in Dijon Lycée before becoming a chemistry professor at the University of Strasbourg. He married Marie Laurent, the daughter of the university's director, and together they had five children. Three survived to adulthood.

Chirality and Isomerism

In 1849, Pasteur was studying the chemical properties of tartaric acid, a crystal found in wine sediments, and comparing them to paratartaric acid, a synthetic compound which had the same chemical composition. The two behaved differently, however, and he determined to discover why. He passed polarized light through each crystal, and found that while tartaric acid rotated the light, paratartaric acid did not. In doing so he discovered the principles of molecular chirality and isomerism; the former describes compounds that are mirror images, and the latter the fact that compounds can have identical molecular formulas and different chemical structures.

Fermentation and Germ Theory

In 1856, a winemaker asked Pasteur his advice on preventing stored alcohol from going bad. Pasteur surmised that fermentation and spoiling are caused by microorganisms, and demonstrated that the presence of oxygen was not necessary for this to occur. He showed experimentally that wine soured when lactic acid was produced by bacterial contamination. Having established this, he then realized that by heating liquids could kill the majority of microorganisms that were present, preventing them from spoiling. He patented the process in 1865, calling it pasteurization.

His discovery that bacteria were responsible for fermentation and spoiling led him to suggest that the same microorganisms also caused human and animal diseases—now called the germ theory of disease. He proposed that protecting humans from bacteria could reduce disease, leading to the development of antiseptics.

Disproving Spontaneous Generation

For centuries, the prevailing wisdom held that living organisms arose spontaneously from nonliving matter; fleas were believed to appear from dust and maggots from dead flesh. Pasteur suspected that this was not the case when he observed that yeast did not grow on sterilized grapes. His assertion that spontaneous generation was incorrect sparked a furious debate, and the French Academy of Sciences proposed a cash prize for anyone who could prove or disprove the theory. Pasteur devised an experiment in which he boiled broth in swan-necked flasks. The necks of the flasks prevented airborne particles from reaching the broth. He also exposed a control set of boiled broth to the air. Nothing grew in the swan-necked flasks, but microorganisms did grow in the control set, demonstrating that spontaneous generation was incorrect.

Vaccination

Pasteur discovered the principle of vaccination almost by accident. While he was studying chicken cholera, his assistant inoculated a group of chickens with a culture of the disease that had spoiled. While the chickens became ill, they did not die. Pasteur attempted to re-infect the chickens, but discovered that the weakened culture had made them immune to cholera. Pasteur would go on to apply this principle to developing vaccinations for anthrax and rabies.

He founded the Pasteur Institute in 1887. In 1894, he suffered a stroke, and died the next year. He was buried at Notre Dame Cathedral.

"Louis Pasteur's theory of germs is ridiculous fiction."

—TOULOUSE PHYSIOLOGY PROFESSOR PIERRE PACHET, 1872

Building a Structure of Science

"Science is built up of facts, as a house is built of stones; but an accumulation of facts is no more a science than a heap of stones is a house."

Jules Henri Poincare was one of the great polymaths and scientific thinkers of the 19th century; his contributions to modern mathematics and physics are astonishing, and he single-handedly laid the groundwork for many of the discoveries that were made after his death.

✳ ✳ ✳ ✳

BORN IN NANCY, France in 1854, Poincare was an avid reader, and began reading popular science books at a young age before moving to more advanced texts. He had an incredible memory, and preferred linking the ideas he was reading in his head rather than learning by rote memorization. This skill would prove useful when he attended university lectures, as his poor eyesight kept him from being able to see what the professors were writing on the blackboard.

Upon graduation, he became a professor at the University of Paris, where he served for many years. He held positions in multiple departments, including astronomy, physics and mathematics. In 1880 he made the discovery that elliptic and automorphic functions were related to the same set of algebraic equations. He continued to do fundamental work through the 1880s in celestial mechanics and physics.

Poincare also helped to discover the theory of special relativity with Hendrik Lorentz and Albert Einstein. Einstein would later say that Poincare was one of the pioneers of the theory of relativity. In 1905 Poincare proposed the theory that gravitational waves emanated from bodies with mass, and propagated outward at the speed of light; this was later also predicted by Einstein based on general relativity.

He would continue to work in the field of mining even while he was making breakthrough discoveries in science and mathematics; in 1893 he became a chief engineer in the French Mining Corps, and was promoted to Inspector in 1910. He also worked to coordinate worldwide time in the French Bureau of Longitudes.

Poincare's contributions to modern science and mathematics were numerous and varied. He contributed to the special theory of relativity and quantum mechanics, Algebraic topology and geometry, electromagnetism, differential equations, to name just a few. He died on July 12, 1912, at the age of 58 in Paris.

The Three-Body Problem

Predicting the motions of a group of orbiting celestial bodies has been a problem since Sir Isaac Newton first published the *Principia* in 1687. The problem concerns how to correctly predict the individual motions of three or more bodies that are acting on one another gravitationally. Solving the problem would allow physicists to better understand the stability of the Solar System. In 1887, the King of Sweden established a prize for anyone who could solve the problem. Although Poincare was unable to solve the problem, he was still given the award for his work, which had considerably advanced understanding of celestial mechanics.

The Poincare Conjecture

Poincare is perhaps most famous for the mathematical conjecture named for him. It proposes that any circle made on its surface can be contracted to a single point: for example, a rubber band wrapped around the sphere can be slid down to a single point. This property is unique in 3-dimensional space to the sphere; it is not true for a disk (which has an edge) or a donut-shaped object, for example.

Poincare's conjecture asks whether the same holds true for a sphere in 4-dimensional space. The conjecture directed much of the next century's exploration in mathematics, and in particular the field of topology, which studies the properties of continuous space. The conjecture, proposed in 1904, was not solved until 2003, when Grigori Perelman showed that the same is true for a sphere in 4-dimensional space.

Celebrating Nature in Poetry

"The world is charged with the grandeur of God." Gerald Manley Hopkins was a 19th century English priest and poet. His poems were about nature and religion, and in an act that was particularly unusual for a priest of his time, Hopkins supported Darwin's theory of natural selection and assertion that humans were animals.

✳   ✳   ✳   ✳

Hopkins was born in 1844 in England, attended Oxford, and became a prolific poet. In 1866 he converted from Anglicanism to Catholicism, and became a priest in 1870, joining the Jesuit order. Hopkins' poetry was filled with detailed descriptions of nature, and he saw nature as the manifestation of God's glory. He wrote numerous sonnets celebrating the beauty of nature, and our place in it. His poems vary between fairly simple imagery and sweeping metaphysical observations of the divinity in all of the creatures found in nature. In "The Windhover," for example, he celebrates the relationship between a bird and the breeze.

A number of his poems are erotic in nature, and some display what are arguably homoerotic themes. He wrote several poems about his companion Digby Mackworth Dolben; after Dolben accidentally drowned, Hopkins wrote a number of elegiac poems about him. Late in life, he moved to Dublin, where he was a professor at University College Dublin. While there, he experienced intense isolation, far from his home, friends and family. During this time his poems took a darker turn, and in them he explored feelings of desolation and loneliness.

God's Grandeur

The world is charged with the grandeur of God.
It will flame out, like shining from shook foil;
It gathers to a greatness, like the ooze of oil
Crushed. Why do men then now not reck his rod?
Generations have trod, have trod, have trod;
And all is seared with trade; bleared, smeared with toil;
And wears man's smudge and shares man's smell: the soil
Is bare now, nor can foot feel, being shod.
And for all this, nature is never spent;
There lives the dearest freshness deep down things;
And though the last lights off the black West went
Oh, morning, at the brown brink eastward, springs—
Because the Holy Ghost over the bent
World broods with warm breast and with ah! bright wings.

Appreciative of God's Creation

"You will find something more in woods than books. Trees and stones will teach you that which you can never learn from masters."

✳ ✳ ✳ ✳

ST BERNARD OF Clairvaux was a French abbot, founder of speculative mysticism, and philosopher. He founded over 160 monasteries during his lifetime, left an enduring legacy on Christian thought, and was canonized in 1174.

St Bernard's contribution to Christian thought was the creation of medieval speculative mysticism, which taught that God's love was a mystical, ecstatic experience that could be experienced by any believer. The doctrine would be developed in the west over the next several hundred years, and influenced sweeping reforms when Pope Alexander III instituted canon law. Bernard developed a philosophy of mysticism that labored to connect it with rational theory, but he also wrote a number of philosophical treatises that had a strictly naturalist reflection on the state of the universe.

St Bernard argued that the universe is made up of beings that are the expression of God's creativity, and that they are perfectly ordered by God. He wrote that God gave each being its meaning for existence, and joined them all together into a perfect whole. Because God created the world, Bernard argued, all beings participate with god according to the nature given to them by God. This participation with God, he wrote, is divided into degrees, the lowest being simple existence, the middle being possession of life, and the highest being possession of reason. He rose to an influential position in the medieval Church, and played a pivotal role in exhorting the French to join the Second Crusade in 1144. He was an adviser to several popes, including Alexander III, and had miracles attributed to him. He died in 1153 and was buried at Clairvaux.

A Biographer and a Fisherman

"No man is born an angler:" although Walton wrote The Compleat Angler *in 1653, he continued to revise it for the next quarter century. Walton never claimed to be an expert at fly fishing himself, believing instead it was an art learned over the course of a lifetime.*

✳ ✳ ✳ ✳

A Lifelong Reader

IZAAK WALTON WAS born in Stafford, England, in 1594. In his teens he moved to London, where he attended Oxford for three years. Walton became a linen draper and ran a prosperous shop in London, but he loved reading and studying in his free time. He lived near St. Dunstan's Church, where he befriended the vicar and poet John Donne. When Donne's poems were published two years after his death, in 1633, Walton composed an elegy to accompany the volume. In 1640, he wrote his first of many biographies, *The Life and Death of Dr John Donne*, which accompanied a collection of Donne's sermons.

In 1644, following the Royalist defeat at Marston Moor during the English Civil Wars, Walton retired and returned to Staffordshire, where he would spend the remainder of his life reading, writing, fishing, and visiting a circle of clergymen who were friends of his. He published his second biography, *The Life of Sir Henry Wotton*, a poet and diplomat, in 1651. He would also write biographies of the Elizabethan bishop Richard Hooker in 1665 and of the poet George Herbert in 1670. The same year he published a collection of the four men's biographies.

The Compleat Angler

Walton is best known for *The Compleat Angler*, a discourse on the art of fishing. The book combines prose and verse, and quotes the 1613 book *The Secrets of Angling* by John Denny. The *Angler* opens with a description of a group of Londoners travelling to the Lea Valley in Hertfordshire on a fishing trip. The book is notable for its unpretentious nature; Walton himself never claimed to be an expert fly fisherman, and in fact the sections of the book on fly fishing (or "angling") were originally written by Thomas Barker, who wrote his own treatise on the topic in 1659.

In what is perhaps the book's most famous passage, Walton describes how one should handle live bait. His description is not technical so much as it is tender: he advises the reader to use the frog as if they loved him, and "harm him as little as you may possibly, that he may live the longer."

Much of the advice in the *Angler* is presented as a dialogue between the Londoners, whose main characters are a master fisherman, Piscator, and a student, Viator, although later editions changed Viator to Venator, a hunter, and added a falconer, Auceps. Piscator is not just a master fisherman, but also a pious and tranquil thinker, who enjoys friendship, good food, friendship and poetry. Their discussion is interspersed with songs and poems, anecdotes, quotes from classical literature and the Bible, meditations on virtue, and country folklore about fishing and rivers.

The book's unpretentious and friendly style made it hugely popular among anglers, and beginning in the 18th century, hundreds of editions have been published. The work has since become elevated from a simple sportsman's manual to an enthusiastic celebration of outdoor recreation and all things pastoral.

Walton died in 1683, and was buried in Winchester Cathedral.

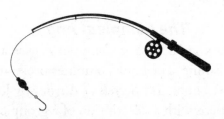

A Man of Discovery

"In completing one discovery we never fail to get an imperfect knowledge of others of which we could have no idea before, so that we cannot solve one doubt without creating several new ones."

Joseph Priestley was one of the founders of modern chemistry: he not only discovered oxygen and photosynthesis, but the next time you're enjoying soda water, you can thank him for that, too.

✳ ✳ ✳ ✳

JOSEPH PRIESTLEY WAS born in 1733 in Yorkshire, England, and was raised by a modest family of cloth-makers. As a Calvinist Dissenter to the Church of England, he was prevented from attending University in England, and instead enrolled in the Dissenters' Academy in Northhamptonshire in 1752. While there, he studied the sciences, philosophy, and literature, and gained a reputation as a stubborn freethinker. He eventually rejected his stern Calvinist upbringing, and co-founded Unitarianism in England.

Early Experiments on Electricity

In 1761, Priestley became a teacher at the Dissenting Academy in Warrington, where published a number of books on history and philosophy. While there, his interest in science grew, and he began writing a history of the study of electricity. In 1765, Benjamin Franklin visited Warrington, and encouraged Priestley to continue his work on electricity. In the *History and Present State of Electricity*, Priestley experiments in which he discovered that charcoal conducts electricity, described the inverse square law of electrical attraction, and observed the relationship between electricity and chemical reactions.

He also presented an argument that scientific progress was driven not by the theories proposed by a few men of genius, but rather on discoveries of "new facts" that anyone could make. He roundly rejected dogma and prejudice, arguing for individual inquiry instead. Based on the *History*, Priestley was inducted to the Royal Society of London in 1766.

Investigations in Chemistry and the Discovery of Oxygen

Priestley's discoveries about electricity encouraged him to begin experimenting in the field of Chemistry. Over the next twenty years, he published more than a dozen articles describing his experiments on gases and six volumes of his work *Experiments and Observations on Different Kinds of Air*. Prior to his work, chemists had identified three gases: air, fixed air (carbon dioxide), and inflammable air (hydrogen). Priestly discovered ten more: nitric oxide, nitrous oxide, nitrogen dioxide, ammonia, hydrogen chloride, sulfur dioxide, silicon tetrafluoride, carbon monoxide, nitrogen, and, most famously, oxygen.

In August 1774, while in his laboratory, Priestly heated red mercuric oxide, which gave off a colorless gas. He observed that a candle burned at a much greater intensity when it was exposed to the gas. "To complete the proof of the superior quality" of the gas, he placed a mouse in a sealed vessel filled with it. Had the vessel been filled with "common air," he wrote, it would have died within fifteen minutes. Instead, the mouse was still alive an hour later when Priestley removed it from the vessel, and "quite vigorous." Priestly called the gas "dephlogisticated air," based on the belief at the time that phlogiston was an airborne contaminant.

That October, Priestley met the French chemist Antoine Lavoisier in Paris, in one of the most important meetings in the history of modern science. Priestley described his experiments to Lavoisier, who not only successfully repeated his experiments, but spent the next five years intensively studying the gas. This would begin a scientific revolution in the field of chemistry that would ultimately overthrow the theory of phlogiston and lead to the advent of modern chemistry.

Exile to America

While still living in England, Priestley's support of the French and American Revolutions was labeled seditious by the government and the press. His home and laboratory were attacked and destroyed by a mob in 1791, and in 1794 he fled to the United States. He died there in 1804, and was buried in Philadelphia.

A Meditation on Nature and Death

"Go forth, under the open sky, and list to Nature's teachings:" William Cullen Bryant was an American poet, essayist, and editor of the New York Evening Post *for more than half a century. His poem "Thanatopsis" is a classic of American literature that celebrates both the grandeur of nature and the inevitability of death.*

✳   ✳   ✳   ✳

BRYANT WAS BORN in Massachusetts in 1794 to a family of Puritans. He read extensively as a young man, and also spent much of his time exploring the woods around his family's home. He began writing poetry at an early age, publishing his first poem in a Boston newspaper in 1807. He wrote his most famous poem, "Thanatopsis," around 1811; its sophistication in theme and verse were well beyond his years. He would go on to be a successful editor and published many other poems.

A Significant Poem

The poem was published in 1817 in the *North American Revie,* the first literary magazine in the United States. "Thanatopsis" advises that when one is saddened by the inevitability of death, they should look to the world and know that everyone who has ever lived, and everyone who ever will live, will soon join them in "the eternal resting-place." The work had a major impact on American literature, and marked a turning point at which American poetry came into its own right.

"Thanatopsis" was the first poem of its kind in that it did not emulate the style of neo-classical British poets such as Alexander Pope. It was so original that the senior editor of the *Review* initially doubted that Bryant had written it, saying that "no one on this side of the Atlantic" could write such poetry. The poem greatly inspired the development of American poetry for the next 200 years, and continues to be highly influential.

Thanatopsis

To him who in the love of Nature holds
Communion with her visible forms, she speaks
A various language; for his gayer hours
She has a voice of gladness, and a smile
And eloquence of beauty, and she glides
Into his darker musings, with a mild
And healing sympathy, that steals away
Their sharpness, ere he is aware. When thoughts
Of the last bitter hour come like a blight
Over thy spirit, and sad images
Of the stern agony, and shroud, and pall,
And breathless darkness, and the narrow house,
Make thee to shudder, and grow sick at heart;—
Go forth, under the open sky, and list
To Nature's teachings, while from all around—
Earth and her waters, and the depths of air—
Comes a still voice—
Yet a few days, and thee
The all-beholding sun shall see no more
In all his course; nor yet in the cold ground,
Where thy pale form was laid, with many tears,
Nor in the embrace of ocean, shall exist
Thy image. Earth, that nourished thee, shall claim
Thy growth, to be resolved to earth again,
And, lost each human trace, surrendering up
Thine individual being, shalt thou go

To mix for ever with the elements,
To be a brother to the insensible rock
And to the sluggish clod, which the rude swain
Turns with his share, and treads upon. The oak
Shall send his roots abroad, and pierce thy mould.

Yet not to thine eternal resting-place
Shalt thou retire alone, nor couldst thou wish
Couch more magnificent. Thou shalt lie down
With patriarchs of the infant world—with kings,
The powerful of the earth—the wise, the good,
Fair forms, and hoary seers of ages past,
All in one mighty sepulchre.   The hills
Rock-ribbed and ancient as the sun,—the vales
Stretching in pensive quietness between;
The venerable woods—rivers that move
In majesty, and the complaining brooks
That make the meadows green; and, poured round all,
Old Ocean's gray and melancholy waste,—
Are but the solemn decorations all
Of the great tomb of man. The golden sun,
The planets, all the infinite host of heaven,
Are shining on the sad abodes of death,
Through the still lapse of ages. All that tread
The globe are but a handful to the tribes
That slumber in its bosom.—Take the wings
Of morning, pierce the Barcan wilderness,
Or lose thyself in the continuous woods
Where rolls the Oregon, and hears no sound,
Save his own dashings—yet the dead are there:
And millions in those solitudes, since first
The flight of years began, have laid them down
In their last sleep—the dead reign there alone.

So shalt thou rest, and what if thou withdraw
In silence from the living, and no friend
Take note of thy departure? All that breathe

Will share thy destiny. The gay will laugh
When thou art gone, the solemn brood of care
Plod on, and each one as before will chase
His favorite phantom; yet all these shall leave
Their mirth and their employments, and shall come
And make their bed with thee. As the long train
Of ages glide away, the sons of men,
The youth in life's green spring, and he who goes
In the full strength of years, matron and maid,
The speechless babe, and the gray-headed man—
Shall one by one be gathered to thy side,
By those, who in their turn shall follow them.

So live, that when thy summons comes to join
The innumerable caravan, which moves
To that mysterious realm, where each shall take
His chamber in the silent halls of death,
Thou go not, like the quarry-slave at night,
Scourged to his dungeon, but, sustained and soothed
By an unfaltering trust, approach thy grave,
Like one who wraps the drapery of his couch
About him, and lies down to pleasant dreams.

Living Deliberately

Henry David Thoreau was a prolific nineteenth century American writer, naturalist, and philosopher. His most famous work is Walden, *a contemplation of the virtues of living simply and in accordance with nature.*

❋ ❋ ❋ ❋

THOREAU WAS BORN in Massachusetts in 1817, the son of a pencil maker. He studied philosophy and rhetoric at Harvard from 1833 to1837, and famously refused to pay the five dollar fee required to receive a Harvard diploma. After college, he befriended Ralph Waldo Emerson, who urged him to pursue philosophy and writing. In 1845 a mutual friend encouraged Thoreau to build a small hut in the woods near Walden Pond that would allow him enough solace to concentrate fully on his writing.

Walden

Thoreau built a small cabin on the shore of Walden Pond, which was in a second-growth forest on the Emerson's land, and moved in on July 4, 1845. He would live there for two years, two months and two days in an experiment in living simply, without any outside financial support. The cabin was ten feet by five feet, with a cot, fireplace, writing table, and three chairs for visitors. He planted a small garden, and did chores for the Emersons. His friends and family provided him with basic necessities beyond what he could grow and forage. Thoreau estimated that he spent less than thirty dollars over the course of the two years, or about $860 in today's money.

After leaving the cabin in the late summer of 1847, Thoreau moved back in with the Emersons, where he helped Lidian Emerson around the house while her husband was away in Europe. Thoreau worked intermittently over the next several years, during which time he worked continuously on a manuscript that described his experiences in the cabin. In 1854, he published *Walden, or Life in the Woods*, which was part memoir and part spiritual manifesto.

The book condenses his two years at Walden into one, and uses the passage of the seasons as a metaphor for personal development. Thoreau discusses the economy and logistics of the project in the first and longest chapter; in the second, he describes the places he considered moving to before settling on Walden, and says that he lives far from the post office, which represents society. Thoreau advises the reader to look for truth in nature as well as in literature in his chapters "Reading" and "Sounds," noting that he is never bored when he looks for pleasure in the sounds of birdsong, church-bells, and wildlife that ring around his cabin.

Walden contains meditations on the virtues of solitude as well as company. In the chapter "The Bean-Field," Thoreau rejoices in his work planting and maintaining a field of beans and discusses his delight in the environment. The next several chapters describe his comings and goings to the local village, where he takes his second bath, and where he is jailed for his refusal to pay taxes as a war resister and abolitionist. In the fall, he wanders the countryside, describes his neighbors, and extols the virtues of vegetarianism, abstinence from drinking, hard work and chastity. He describes Walden Pond in winter, and relates how fifty laborers came to the pond to cut ice blocks to ship to the South. The book concludes the following spring, describing the thundering melting of the pond, and as nature is reborn, so is Thoreau. He concludes *Walden* with an earnest appeal for nonconformity.

Walden has become an American classic, with its themes of simplicity, self-reliance, and a natural spirituality. Thoreau would continue to write prolifically until his death in 1862.

Quotes from Thoreau

"That man is the richest whose pleasures are cheapest."

—JOURNAL

"I think we should be men first, and subjects afterward. It is not desirable to cultivate a respect for the law, so much as for the right."

—CIVIL DISOBEDIENCE

"I came into this world, not chiefly to make this a good place to live in, but to live in it, be it good or bad."

—CIVIL DISOBEDIENCE

"I should not talk so much about myself if there were anybody else whom I knew so well."

—WALDEN

"To be awake is to be alive."

—WALDEN

"Public opinion is a weak tyrant compared with our own private opinion. What a man thinks of himself, that is which determines, or rather, indicates, his fate."

—WALDEN

"I went to the woods because I wished to live deliberately, to front only the essential facts of life, and see if I could not learn what it had to teach, and not, when I came to die, discover that I had not lived."

—WALDEN

"Heaven is under our feet as well as over our heads."

—WALDEN

"It is life near the bone where it is sweetest."

—WALDEN

Chief Seattle

Some of his most famous quotes about the sacredness of the Earth and the need for environmental stewardship may be falsely attributed to him.

✳   ✳   ✳   ✳

SEATTLE WAS A Native American chief of the Suquamish and Duwamish tribes of the Pacific Northwest. He was born around 1780, and quickly earned a reputation as a skilled warrior and healer. He was also known as a talented orator whose voice carried more than half a mile. He later became friends with Doc Maynard, one of the founders of the city of Seattle. He managed to keep his people out of the disastrous Battle of Seattle in 1856, in which a Native American raiding party attacked the city and were driven back by entrenched artillery.

When the United States government established a reservation for the various tribes of the region, Seattle, with the help of Doc Maynard, was able to keep his people from being moved there, and instead convinced the government to allow them to move to a reservation in Port Madison instead. Maynard also convinced the government to allow Seattle to take his father's longhouse from the traditional winter village of the Suquamish people on Agate Passage in the Puget Sound. Seattle lived on the Port Madison reservation for the rest of his life, although he often visited the city that bore his name. He died on June 7, 1866, and was buried on the reservation. This was more than a century before the speech attributed to him would be written.

The Speech

In or about 1854, Seattle did deliver a speech when the Governor of Washington State, Issac Stevens, visited Seattle. In 1887, a transcript of the speech composed from notes taken thirty years before was published in the *Seattle Sunday Star* by Henry A. Smith, but the location and details of the actual speech are uncertain. According to Smith, the Governor was visiting to discuss the terms of the sale or surrender of Suquamish and Duwamish land to white settlers, but in 1854 those lands were already considered to belong to the United States. Later versions of Seattle's speech appeared variously in histories of the region published in 1891 and 1929, and again in the memoir *Four Wagons West* by Roberta Frye Watt.

In the 1960s, the speech saw renewed popularity when a professor at the University of Texas named William Arrowsmith published a version that excised the flowery Victorian writing that Henry A. Smith had likely added. The speech that Seattle is famous for among contemporary environmentalists was actually composed by Ted Perry, a screenwriter who wrote the 1972 conservation movie *Home*, which was written for the Southern Baptist Radio and Television Commission. In a promotional poster for the movie, an image of Chief Seattle is superimposed with the text of the speech.

Perry combined elements of the speech as arranged by Professor Arrowsmith with an environmentally conscious message that Perry wrote himself, including the words "the earth does not belong to man; man belongs to the earth." Additionally, the movie's producer, John Stevens added the line "I am a savage and I do not understand" in order to make the speech palatable to a Southern Baptist audience.

The speech has been widely quoted in books and on television ever since, and shortened versions circulate on the internet, and probably will for a long time to come.

Excerpts from the Speech

"How can you buy or sell the sky, the warmth of the land? The idea is strange to us. If we do not own the freshness of the air and the sparkle of the water, how can you buy them?"

"Every part of the Earth is sacred to my people. Every shining pine needle, every sandy shore, every mist in the dark woods, every clear and humming insect is holy in the memory and experience of my people. The sap which courses through the trees carries the memory and experience of my people. The sap which courses through the trees carries the memories of the red man."

"What is man without the beasts? If all the beasts were gone, man would die from a great loneliness of the spirit. For whatever happens to the beasts, soon happens to man. All things are connected."

"Whatever befalls the Earth—befalls the sons of the Earth. Man did not weave the web of life—he is merely a strand in it. Whatever he does to the web, he does to himself."

Henry Van Dyke

"The first day of spring is one thing, and the first spring day is another. The difference between them is sometimes as great as one month."

A man of many talents, Henry Van Dyke was a nineteenth century American author, educator, clergyman, and diplomat, but he is best remembered for his poetry, which reflected his beliefs in extending sympathy to one's fellow person and living in company with nature.

✳   ✳   ✳   ✳

HENRY VAN DYKE was born in Germantown, Pennsylvania in 1852. His father was a Presbyterian minister who passed on his love of nature and fishing to his son. Van Dyke studied at Princeton University and graduated from Princeton Theological Seminary in 1877, where he later taught English literature. He became a Presbyterian clergy in 1879 and in 1883 he was appointed the pastor of the Brick Presbyterian Church in New York. While there, he started writing; he published his first book, *The Reality of Religion*, the following year. Over the next three years he worked on *The Story of the Psalms*, which combined his loves of scripture and poetry. In 1889 he published a literary criticism of the works of Alfred, Lord Tennyson, which established him as an important figure in the literary world.

A Natural Theology

While Van Dyke was a pastor in New York, he quickly gained a reputation as a talented preacher. His first widely recognized sermon, "The Voice of God," preached on hearing God in nature and reflected his lifelong love of the natural world. He incorporated his love of nature into his Christian theology, and it soon permeated much of his poetry as well. In his poem "God of the Open Air," Van Dyke celebrated "altars everywhere," and wrote that he prizes nature's creations "of dearest worth."

Public Service, Later Life, and Legacy

In 1908 Van Dyke lectured on American literature at the University of Paris. Woodrow Wilson had been a classmate of Van Dyke's, and in 1913 he appointed him the American Minister to the Netherlands and Luxembourg. He continued to write poetry for the remainder of his life, and also wrote nearly 90 short stories and several theological books. His short stories were published in six volumes as *The Works of Henry Van Dyke* in 1920. He died in 1933, and was buried in Princeton Cemetery.

Quotes on the Seasons

"If we had no winter, the spring would not be so pleasant: if we did not sometimes taste of adversity, prosperity would not be so welcome."

—ANNE BRADSTREET

"One swallow does not make a summer."

—ARISTOTLE

*"A little Madness in the Spring
Is Wholesome even for the King."*

—EMILY DICKINSON

*"There is no season such delight can bring,
As summer, autumn, winter, and the spring."*

—WILLIAM BROWNE

"No spring, nor summer beauty hath such grace, As I have seen in one autumnal face."

—JOHN DONNE

"There is a sumptuous variety about the New England weather that compels the stranger's admiration—and regret."

—MARK TWAIN

*"See, Winter comes to rule the varied year,
Sullen and sad."*

—JAMES THOMSON

"Daffodils, that come before the swallow dares, and take the winds of March with beauty."

—WILLIAM SHAKESPEARE

Ideas of a Nation

The Heart and Stomach of a King

When the threat of an invasion loomed, Elizabeth I rallied her troops with an unforgettable speech.

✳ ✳ ✳ ✳

QUEEN ELIZABETH I was born in 1533, the daughter of Henry VIII and Anne Boleyn. She ascended to the throne in 1558, following the death of her half-sister Mary I, and ruled England until her death in 1603. While she was Queen, Elizabeth instituted a number of Protestant reforms. Mary's widower husband, King Phillip II of Spain, who like Mary was a Catholic, declared Elizabeth a heretic and unlawful ruler of England, and supported a number of plots against her. Elizabeth retaliated by hiring privateers to raid Spanish ships in the Atlantic and supporting a Dutch revolt against the Spanish.

Phillip assembled a massive armada to invade England and overthrow Elizabeth. The Spanish Armada, made up of 130 ships, 8,000 sailors and 18,000 soldiers, set sail for England in May of 1588. 30,000 soldiers also massed in Flanders to await their arrival and support the invasion. The Armada was initially sighted off the coast of Cornwall in mid-July, and the next day the English fleet attacked. The two fleets engaged in several skirmishes over the next few weeks, and while neither side suffered significant losses initially, at the

Battle of Gravelines on August 1, the English were able to prevent the Armada from linking with the Army of Flanders.

The Speech at Tilbury

While the English navy had staved off the immediate danger by preventing the rendezvous between the Armada and the Army of Flanders, the Armada itself still posed a considerable threat, and an invasion by the Army of Flanders was still a possibility. 4,000 troops were stationed at the estuary of the River Thames, in Tilbury, on the southeast coast of England, in the event of an attempt to invade England by sailing up the river.

On August 8 (August 18 New Style), Queen Elizabeth went to Tilbury to rally the troops in what would become her most famous speech. By several accounts, she rode a white horse, and wore a plumed helmet and steel armor over a white velvet gown. She carried a baton made of silver and gold. She was flanked by the Earls of Essex and Leicester, and led by the Earl of Ormond, who carried her Sword of State. After riding among the troops, Elizabeth addressed them as her "loving people" and declared that she placed her trust and safety in the goodwill of her subjects. She said that she was prepared to die for her kingdom and her people, adding:

"I know I have the body but of a weak and feeble woman; but I have the heart and stomach of a king, and of a king of England too."

The invasion would never materialize; the English were not aware that the Spanish Armada was already retreating around Scotland and Ireland on their way back to Spain. On the west coast of Ireland, the Armada ran into storms that drove dozens of their ships aground. Fewer than 70 ships out of the original 130 would make it back to Spain.

Legacy

The victory over the Spanish Armada, and her speech at Tilbury, would make Elizabeth a heroine of the Protestant cause in Europe. She ruled for another fifteen years, and while her reign was not without its mistakes, she was grieved by many of her subjects when she died in 1603. Elizabeth remained a legendary symbol of national pride in the face of foreign threats through the 20th century.

"I will make you shorter by the head."

—REPORTEDLY SAID TO THE LEADERS OF HER COUNCIL WHEN THEY DISAGREED WITH A
PROPOSED COURSE OF ACTION

Better to Be Loved or Feared?

A 16th century diplomat, philosopher, humanist, and the author of one of the most influential books on political philosophy, Niccolo Machiavelli is considered the father of political science.

✳ ✳ ✳ ✳

NICCOLO DI BERNARDO dei Machiavelli was born in Florence, Italy in 1469, the son of an attorney. At the time of his birth, Italy was still divided into four competing city-states, and the powerful Medici family had ruled Florence for sixty years. During this tumultuous time in the country's history, various European powers, including France, Spain, Switzerland, and the Holy Roman Empire routinely invaded Italy and captured city-states as they vied for regional dominance.

In 1494, a rebellion established the Florentine Republic and expelled the Medici family. Machiavelli was appointed a diplomat of the Republic, and took several missions to the Vatican in Rome. His diplomatic experience to Rome and Spain would later influence his political philosophy in *The Prince*. In 1512, the Medici, with the support of the Vatican, recaptured Florence and abolished the Republic. Machiavelli was jailed for three weeks and tortured to discover if he had any role in the conspiracy of 1494. He denied any involvement, and was released, but forbidden from participating in politics.

Writing *The Prince*

Machiavelli returned to his country estate after his imprisonment, and immersed himself in writing and study. Initially a dark time in his career, Machiavelli's exile from politics would ultimately give him the time to develop his political philosophy and write the political treatises that would become *The Prince* and other works. *The Prince* has themes of self-determination in the face of the power of fate, and advances the political philosophy that ruthlessness and ambition are acceptable means to establish and maintain total authority. It is widely considered a manual for politicians on how to employ cunning and deceit in self-serving capacities, and gave rise to the pejorative term "Machiavellian" to describe someone who does so. The title character was likely inspired by Cesare Borgia, the illegitimate son of Pope Alexander VI whose ruthless fight for power Machiavelli witnessed firsthand while he was a diplomat in Rome.

The Prince discusses the politics of princedoms as well as republics, and the first part deals with "new" and "mixed" (parts of an older established state) princedoms. The second part of the book discusses the ways people can rise to power, according to Machiavelli. The first way is by their own virtue, which he sees as difficult, but resulting in a stable and respected position of power. The second is by the blessing of the existing regime, in which power is easier to attain but harder to keep. The third is by "criminal virtue," such as assassination or bribery; Machiavelli advises that if one wishes to attain power in this manner, they should execute their nefarious plans all at once, so that they do not run the risk of having to continually commit more wicked acts to maintain power. The fourth way one can come to power is by the selection of one's fellow citizens, either by those who want to command the people through the ruler, or by the people themselves.

Each has its own merits and pitfalls.

In addition to *The Prince*, Machiavelli wrote *The Discourses on Livy*, *On the Art of War*, a series of histories of Florence, and a number of poems and plays, including *The Mandrake*, a satirical criticism of the House of Medici. Machiavelli died in Florence on June 21, 1527, and was buried in the church of Santa Croce.

Quotes from Machiavelli

"From this arises the question whether it is better to be loved rather than feared, or feared rather than loved. It might perhaps be answered that we should wish to be both: but since love and fear can hardly exist together, if we must choose between them, it is far safer to be feared than loved."

"The chief foundations of all states, new as well as old or composite, are good laws and good arms."

"A prince should therefore have no other aim or thought, nor take up any other thing for his study, but war and its organization and discipline, for that is the only art that is necessary to one who commands."

"Among other evils which being unarmed brings you, it causes you to be despised."

"A prince being thus obliged to know well how to act as a beast must imitate the fox and the lion, for the lion cannot protect himself from traps, and the fox cannot defend himself from wolves. One must therefore be a fox to recognize traps, and a lion to frighten wolves."

"Where the willingness is great, the difficulties cannot be great."

L'etat, C'est Moi

King Louis XIV ruled France from 1643–1715, the longest reign of any monarch in European history. He is remembered for his belligerent foreign policy and his reforms—and for reportedly declaring, "I am the state."

✳   ✳   ✳   ✳

Louis XIV was born in Saint-Germaine, France, on September 5, 1638, the son of King Louis XIII. When he was four years old, his father died, and Louis XIV ascended to the throne. His godfather, Cardinal Jules Mazarin, became his tutor and chief minister. In 1648, the Parliament attempted to overthrow Mazarin and the Crown, but Mazarin's forces were victorious in 1653. Following Mazarin's death in 1661 Louis formally began his rule of France

Louis set about centralizing power and cementing his power. He established a number of reforms that improved France's taxation system, limited national borrowing, and cut the national deficit. He also exempted the nobility from having to pay taxes, which ensured their continued support of the Crown. Louis also created a number of institutes to promote the arts in French culture. He founded the Academie des Inscriptions et Belles-Lettres, a society that promotes the humanities, and constructed the Paris Observatory in 1672.

In the 1680s, Louis began efforts to establish a uniform religion in France. A devout Catholic, he persecuted the Protestant Huguenots, which culminated in the revocation of the Edict of Nantes in 1685. The Edict had protected the rights of the Huguenots, and a series of government repressions forced many to flee.

After 72 years as King of France, the longest rule in European history, Louis XIV died on September 1, 1715, at Versailles. His remains were exhumed and destroyed during the French Revolution.

"What is the throne? A bit of wood gilded and covered with velvet. I am the state."

—Napolean Bonaparte

Oliver Cromwell

Oliver Cromwell was an English politician and general who fought on the side of Parliament during the English Civil Wars, and became the Lord Protector of the British Isles during the Commonwealth.

✳ ✳ ✳ ✳

OLIVER CROMWELL WAS born in Huntington, England on April 25, 1599. He was raised to be intensely religious. Little is known of his early life; he was elected to Parliament in 1628 and again in 1640.

When the English Civil War broke out, Cromwell led a cavalry troop and was quickly promoted until he was one of the leaders of the Parliament's forces. At the battle of Marston Moor in 1644, Cromwell cemented his reputation as an outstanding commander when his forces routed the Royalist troops led by Prince Rupert. The following year he led his troops in defeating the Royalist forces at the battle of Naseby. In 1646 the Royalists surrendered. They launched another rebellion in 1648, but were swiftly defeated; following the second war, Cromwell agreed to the execution of the deposed king Charles I. In 1649, Scotland and Ireland rebelled against English rule. Cromwell invaded Ireland in a brutal campaign. His troops massacred civilians at Drogheda and Wexford in 1649. He defeated the Scottish army at the battle of Worcester in 1651, ending the war.

In 1653, Cromwell dissolved the House of Commons by force, and appointed himself Lord Protector of England, Ireland, Scotland and Wales. He united the four countries under one Parliament, although he dissolved it as well in 1655. Cromwell died on September 3, 1658, and shortly thereafter his government collapsed.

The monarchy was restored less than two years later.

Quotes from Cromwell

"A few honest men are better than numbers."

"The State, in choosing men to serve it, takes no notice of their opinions. If they be willing faithfully to serve it, that satisfies."

"I would have been glad to have lived under my woodside, and to have kept a flock of sheep, rather than to have undertaken this government."

"I had rather have a plain, russet-coated Captain, that knows what he fights for, and loves what he knows, than that you call a Gentleman and is nothing else."

"We declared our intentions to preserve monarchy, and they still are so, unless necessity enforce an alteration. It's granted the king has broken his trust, yet you are fearful to declare you will make no further addresses ... look on the people you represent, and break not your trust, and expose not the honest party of your kingdom, who have bled for you, and suffer not misery to fall upon them for want of courage and resolution in you, else the honest people may take such courses as nature dictates to them."

"I tell you we will cut off his head with the crown upon it."

"In every government there must be somewhat fundamental, somewhat like a Magna Charta, that should be standing and unalterable...that parliaments should not make themselves perpetual is a fundamental."

"Mr. Lely, I desire you would use all your skill to paint my picture truly like me, and not flatter me at all; but remark all these roughnesses, pimples, warts, and everything as you see me, otherwise I will never pay a farthing for it." (Attributed)

A Politician and an Inventor

"Treason doth never prosper: what's the reason? For if it prosper, none dare call it treason."

Sir John Harington was a poet, author, and politician, and the author of the above quote. But he is best remembered not for his epigrams on treason but for inventing the flush toilet.

✻　　✻　　✻　　✻

JOHN HARINGTON WAS born in Somerset, England on August 4, 1560. He was the godson of Elizabeth I, and was a member of her court. In 1584, when he attempted to translate an epic poem and began reciting risqué parts of it in Court, she banished him from her court, telling him he could not return until he had completed the entire translation. He completed the translation in 1591. While he was exiled from the court, he built a house, and in it he installed the first flushing toilet in history. He wrote a book about his invention titled *A New Discourse upon a Stale Subject*. The device consisted of a pan with an opening at the bottom that was sealed with a leather valve. A system of weights and levers poured water from a cistern above the pan that "flushed" the toilet. His invention did not become widely popular, and the chamber-pot continued to be the means by which most people relieved themselves indoors until the onset of the Industrial Revolution.

In 1599, Harington served in an army that invaded Ireland to put down a rebellion led by Hugh O'Neill, and sent intelligence reports back to the Queen about the progress the invasion was making. Following the death of Elizabeth, he remained in the Royal Court under King James, who granted him a knighthood. Harington died on November 12, 1612, and was buried near his home in Kelston.

The Quotable Nathan Hale

In 1776, Revolutionary War hero Nathan Hale was hanged by the British for espionage. Is it true that his last words were "I only regret that I have but one life to lose for my country"?

✳ ✳ ✳ ✳

THOSE ARE NOBLE words worthy of a brave Continental officer. No knowledgeable historian would call them inconsistent with Nathan Hale's character: He was a volunteer who dared a dangerous task, conducted himself like a gentleman after capture, and went bravely to the noose. His character isn't being questioned, but did he actually utter the immortal words for which he is known?

The evidence for the traditional quote comes from a British officer, Captain John Montresor, who told it to Hale's friend William Hull. The quote sounds paraphrased from Act IV of Joseph Addison's inspirational play *Cato*, one of Hale's favorites: "What pity is it, that we can die but once to serve our country!" (In addition to this quote, Patrick Henry's popular proclamation "Give me liberty or give me death" derives from Addison's play.)

Hale may have said the words, or something like them. Or Hull may have revised or misheard them, or Montresor may have gotten them wrong in the first place. There were only a few eyewitnesses, and versions didn't take long to begin wandering. Revolutionary-era media printed several variants on the theme, all of which make Hale sound like a valiant martyr.

What is beyond doubt: Hale was captured and legally executed as a spy. Before he died, he gave a rousing oration befitting a Yalie and a die-hard Continental patriot. This didn't stop his captors from putting him to death, but it did inspire them to tell the story, speak his name with respect (which British officers did not often do of their colonial counterparts), and describe him as a hero.

An Honest Man?

Sir Henry Wotton was an English poet, diplomat, and politician. He is best remembered for his quote regarding ambassadors: "An ambassador is an honest man sent to lie abroad for the commonwealth."

✳ ✳ ✳ ✳

SIR HENRY WOTTON was born in Kent, England on March 30, 1568. He was educated at Winchester College, at Oxford, and at Queen's College. While at Oxford, Wotton befriended Alericus Gentilis and John Donne. In 1589, he embarked on a journey through Europe that lasted for four years. On his return to England, he joined the bar, and began working as an intelligence minister. In 1602, while he was in Florence, he learned of a plot to kill James VI of Scotland. He disguised himself as an Italian and travelled under the assumed name "Ottavio Baldi" to deliver letters from the Duke of Tuscany to James to warn him. When James became King of England, Wotton became the Crown's ambassador to Venice.

Wotton established himself in Venice in 1604, and would spend the better part of two decades there. He worked closely with the Doge (Duke) of Venice in helping him resist aggression by the Holy Roman Empire. Around 1610, the saying that is famously attributed to Wotton was first uttered, and in 1611 Caspar Schoppe, a German scholar, wrote a book entitled *Ecclesiasticus*. In it he quoted Wotton on the topic of ambassadors. Sadly, Wotton temporarily fell out of favor of the King as a result.

Wotton served in the House of Commons twice, in 1614 and again in 1625. He retired in 1630, and died in 1639. He is buried at Eton College.

Speaking of Diplomats...

To call Secretary-General Dag Hammarskjöld (1905–61) an effective diplomat is a gross understatement. Upon Hammarskjöld's death, President John F. Kennedy remarked, "I realize now that in comparison to him, I am a small man. He was the greatest statesman of our century."

The son of Swedish prime minister Hjalmar Hammarskjöld, Dag Hammarskjöld was immersed in the political life at a young age. In a 1953 radio address, Hammarskjöld said, "From generations of soldiers and government officials on my father's side I inherited a belief that no life was more satisfactory than one of selfless service to your country or humanity."

After earning two degrees from Uppsala University, Hammarskjöld added a law degree and a doctoral degree in economics. The true embodiment of a Renaissance person, Hammarskjöld was well versed in the arts, literature, and history, and equally competent in physical pursuits such as gymnastics and skiing.

In 1930, Hammarskjöld entered public life in Sweden as a secretary to a governmental commission on unemployment. He rose through the ranks to become Sweden's UN delegate in 1949. In 1953, he was elected Secretary-General of the United Nations, a position to which he would be reelected in 1957.

Hammarskjöld received the Nobel Peace Prize posthumously in 1961 for a body of work that included the release of 15 American flyers held by the Chinese in 1955, efforts in the 1956 Middle East crisis between Egypt and Israel, and his final attempt at uniting warring factions in the Congo.

Not Just the Name of a Beer

"Let us contemplate our forefathers, and posterity, and resolve to maintain the rights bequeathed to us from the former, for the sake of the latter."

Samuel Adams, one of America's Founding Fathers, was an early resistor of British taxation, one of the leaders of the American Revolution, and a signer of the Declaration of Independence.

✳   ✳   ✳   ✳

SAMUEL ADAMS WAS born in Boston on September 27, 1722, in Boston. He graduated from Harvard College in 1743, and one of his first occupations, ironically, was as a tax collector. In the 1760s, Adams became influential in Boston's local government, where, in 1764, he began publically opposing British taxation for the first time.

When Britain, attempted to impose the Sugar Act on the colonies, Adams argued that Parliament had no constitutional basis by which to levy taxes on the colonies. In 1765, the Stamp Act was passed, inflaming anti-British sentiment that largely mirrored Adams' argument against the Sugar Act. In 1766, the Stamp Act was repealed because the colonists had made it effectively unenforceable. The next year, Parliament passed the Townshend Act, which established Customs Houses that taxed goods imported to America. Adams organized a boycott of the taxed goods, which eventually spread to Connecticut and Rhode Island. The British sent troops to enforce the tax.

Occupation and Tea Party

In October 1768, British troops landed in Boston. This marked a turning point for Adams, who, seeing Boston occupied, decided that independence from Britain was the only option for the colonies. He argued vehemently against the occupation in a series of letters and anonymous newspaper articles. Tensions between the British troops and the citizens of Boston came to a head in March 1770, when the troops killed five civilians in the Boston Massacre. Following the Massacre, Adams finally convinced the Governor and Army to withdraw the troops to a garrison outside the city.

In 1773, following a period of relative quiet in Boston, the Parliament passed the Tea Act, which effectively granted a monopoly to the British East India Tea Company in the colonies. The East India Tea Company was not subject to the duties imposed by the Townsend Act, which allowed them to undercut local merchants and drive them out of business. When the *Dartmouth*, a cargo ship carrying 342 chests of tea, arrived in Boston Harbor, Adams called for a mass meeting. The assembly demanded the *Dartmouth* be allowed to unload its cargo without paying the duty. Officials refused, and Adams incited a crowd to board the ship and dump the tea into the harbor in what would be called the Boston Tea Party.

The Revolution

Britain responded to the Boston Tea Party by closing Boston's harbor, restricting Town Meetings and removing elected officials for royal appointees. That September, Adams attended the First Continental Congress in Philadelphia. The Congress sent a petition to King George, but it had no effect, and so a Second Continental Congress was called. Adams served on several committees and played a significant role in maneuvering the Congress toward revolution. He tirelessly advocated that the Congress declare independence from Britain. When it did on July 4, 1776, Adams was the fifth delegate to sign the Declaration of Independence. During the War, Adams served on the Continental Congress, where he served on several committees involved in military affairs. He argued for paying reenlistment bonuses to soldiers in the Continental Army and fiercely opposed allowing Loyalists to remain in Boston.

Adams continued to serve in public life for twenty years following the Revolution, eventually serving as governor of Massachusetts until 1797. He died on October 2, 1803.

United We Stand, Divided We Fall

John Dickinson was an American writer, philosopher, and statesman who helped turn public sentiment against the Townshend Acts and spark the American Revolution. He co-authored the Articles of Confederation and helped draft the U.S. Constitution.

✳   ✳   ✳   ✳

JOHN DICKINSON WAS born in Maryland in 1732 to a well-to-do Quaker family. His family moved to Delaware when he was six years old. Dickinson's father became a judge there, and when he was 18, he followed in his footsteps, studying law in Philadelphia. In 1753, he sailed to England to study the court system for four years. While he was in London, Dickinson first learned of the philosophies of the

Enlightenment and arguments for individual rights. Dickinson returned to Philadelphia in 1757 and established a law practice. In 1760, he ran for and was elected to both the Delaware legislature and the Pennsylvania, as he held residency in both states. In 1764, he debated Benjamin Franklin on whether Pennsylvania should change from a commonwealth to a colony. He lost the debate, and his Pennsylvania assembly seat, as a result.

Seeds of Revolution

Following the French and Indian War, the British began taxing the colonies to recoup its losses and pay off its debts. In 1765, when Parliament enacted the stamp act, Dickinson was selected to represent Pennsylvania at the Stamp Act Congress (or First Congress of the Colonies) in New York City. At the Congress, Dickinson wrote the resolution opposing the Stamp Act. While Parliament relented, and repealed the Stamp Act in 1766, it soon followed with the Townshend Acts of 1767.

Dickinson began publishing a series of *Letters from a Farmer in Pennsylvania to the Inhabitants of the British Colonies*. The letters urged the colonists to engage in nonviolent resistance to the Townshend Acts, and cautions against prematurely resorting to revolutionary violence, urging that it be avoided until "the people are fully convinced" of its necessity. The letters were widely reprinted throughout the thirteen colonies between 1767 and 1768.

Circa 1768, Dickinson also wrote the lyrics of "The Liberty Song," using an existing tune. One of the later verses contains its most famous lyrics:

"Then join hand in hand, brave Americans all,
By uniting we stand, by dividing we fall."

(The sentiment dates back earlier, however—for example, early writer Aesop once wrote, "Union gives strength" in a fable about a bundle of sticks.)

Declaration of Independence

Dickinson attended both the First and Second Continental Congresses as a delegate from Pennsylvania. At the Second Congress, during the debate on the Declaration of Independence, Dickinson argued against declaring independence before the Congress had drafted the Articles of Confederation and found a foreign power with which to forge an alliance. Drawing on his Quaker background, he was also opposed to using violence if there was still a chance for peaceful negotiation. He abstained from the voting and refused to sign the Declaration, although he knew he could not remain a member of the Congress without signing.

He left, and joined the Pennsylvania militia as a brigadier general, but because of his opinions on Independence, he was unpopular, and he resigned his commission in December of 1776. In 1777, Dickinson freed his slaves. He was the only founding father to do so between 1776 and 1786.

Following the War, Dickinson served in the Congress of Confederation in 1779, and drafted the Articles of Confederation. He was elected president of Delaware in 1781 and president of Pennsylvania in 1782. In 1787, he represented Delaware at the Constitutional Convention in Philadelphia. During Thomas Jefferson's presidency, he often called on Dickinson for advice and counsel.

Dickinson died on February 14, 1808, and was buried at the Friends Meeting House graveyard in Wilmington, Delaware.

Give Me Liberty or Give Me Death

Patrick Henry was a politician who is known for his fiery rhetoric in support of the American Revolution.

✳   ✳   ✳   ✳

PATRICK HENRY WAS born in Virginia in on May 29, 1736. He was taught at a young boy by his uncle, an Anglican minister. When he was 1754, he married Sarah Shelton, and tried his hand at farming but was unsuccessful. In 1760 he passed the bar and began practicing law. In 1763 he gained fame while representing the county when a minister brought a lawsuit for back pay. The minister won his case, but Henry convinced the jury to award him a single penny in damages.

Henry was elected to the House of Burgesses in 1765. When the Stamp Act was passed that year, he spoke out against it. His speech against the Stamp Act was printed and distributed throughout the colonies, helping stoke public sentiment against British rule. In 1774, he met Samuel Adams at the Continental Congress in Philadelphia. At the Congress Henry called for the colonies to unite against British rule, saying "I am not a Virginian, but an American." In March 1775, at the Virginia Convention, he gave the speech he is best known for, a fiery call to arms:

"The gentlemen may cry, Peace, peace! But there is no peace. The war has actually begun! The next gale that sweeps from the north will bring to our ears the clash of resounding arms! Our brethren are already in the field! Why stand we here idle? What is it that the gentlemen wish? What would they have? Is life so dear or peace so sweet as to be purchased at the price of chains and slavery? Forbid it, Almighty God. I know not what course others may take, but as for me, give me liberty or give me death!"

A month later, the American Revolution began with the Battles of Lexington and Concord. During the conflict, he was elected governor of Virginia. He helped supply the Continental Army and sent Virginia troops to attack British forces.

Following the war, he opposed a centralized federal government. In 1787 he spoke out in the Virginia Statehouse against ratifying the Constitution, but it passed in spite of his efforts. In 1790 he retired from politics and returned to practicing law. He died on June 6, 1799.

Quotes on Liberty

"Abstract liberty, like other mere abstractions, is not to be found."

—EDMUND BURKE

"The basis of a democratic state is liberty."

—ARISTOTLE

"Our reliance is in the love of liberty which God has planted in us. Our defense is in the spirit which prized liberty as the heritage of all men, in all lands everywhere."

—ABRAHAM LINCOLN

"The greatest dangers to liberty lurk in insidious encroachment by men of zeal, well-meaning but without understanding."

—LOUIS BRANDEIS

"God grants liberty only to those who love it, and are always ready to guard and defend it."

—DANIEL WEBSTER

"The condition upon which God hath given liberty to man is eternal vigilance; which condition if he break, servitude is at once the consequence of his crime and the punishment of his guilt."

—JOHN PHILPOT CURRAN, 1790

"There is one safeguard known generally to the wise, which is an advantage and security to all, but especially to democracies as against despots. What is it? Distrust."

—DEMOSTHENES

"A republic, if you can keep it."

—ATTRIBUTED TO BENJAMIN FRANKLIN, 1787

"With a great price our ancestors obtained this freedom, but we were born free ... but that freedom can be retained only by that eternal vigilance which has always been its price."

—ELMER DAVIS, 1954

"While the people retain their virtue and vigilance, no administration, by any extreme of wickedness or folly can very seriously injure the government in the short space of four yearse."

—ABRAHAM LINCOLN, 1861

Seeking Liberty

"I had reasoned this out in my mind; there was one of two things I had a right to, liberty or death; if I could not have one, I would have the other, for no man should take me alive."

Harriet Tubman escaped from slavery, but returned to the South many times to lead more than 300 people to freedom. Called "Moses," she was one of the most vital conductors of the Underground Railroad, never once losing a passenger to slave-catchers. She fought in the Civil War, spying behind enemy lines and leading the raid at Combahee Ferry that liberated more than 700 slaves.

✳ ✳ ✳ ✳

HARRIET TUBMAN WAS born Araminta Harriet Ross around 1822 in Maryland to enslaved parents. She was one of nine children, but the slave owners split her family up, sending three of her sisters to faraway plantations when she was still young. When a Georgia slave trader attempted to buy her brother Moses, Tubman's father Rit resisted any more breakup of the family, and Moses stayed. Tubman's life was filled with violence from a young age; her masters beat and whipped her even as a child for minor infractions. When she was an adolescent, an overseer demanded she help him restrain another slave who had left the plantation without permission. She refused, and the overseer threw a heavy weight that struck her in the head. The injury would cause headaches, seizures and narcolepsy for the rest of her life. It also induced vivid dream states, which she considered religious visions. Harriet married John Tubman, a free African-American man, in 1844. They separated after she escaped.

Escape from Slavery and the Underground Railroad

In 1849, Tubman escaped slavery. Fearing that her family would be broken up following the death of the plantation's owner, she and two of her brothers fled. Her brothers had second thoughts, and Harriet brought them safely back to the plantation before fleeing to Philadelphia alone. On her 90-mile journey, she was assisted by the network of safe houses and guides called the Underground Railroad. Once she was relatively safe in the North, she vowed to return to rescue her family and other captive slaves. In December 1850, Tubman rescued her niece's daughters in her first of dozens of trips back to the South. That spring, she guided her brother Moses and two other men to freedom. That same year the Fugitive Slave Law was passed, which made it legal to capture escaped slaves in the North and return them to slavery. Northern law enforcement official were compelled to assist in capturing escaped slaves. As a result, Tubman extended the Underground Railroad all the way to Canada, where slavery was illegal.

Civil War

In 1858, Tubman met John Brown, who like her said he was called by God to destroy the institution of slavery. Tubman said she had a vision of meeting him before the encounter. Brown advocated using violence to that end, and Tubman helped him recruit volunteers for the raid on Harper's Ferry. The raid ended in failure, and when Brown was executed, Tubman said he had "done more in dying, than 100 men did in living."

When the Civil War began, Tubman initially served as a nurse and a cook in the Union Army, and later as a scout and spy behind enemy lines. She publically advocated for the Emancipation Proclamation, comparing slavery to a snake that had to be killed. In 1863, she led a raid by Union troops on several plantations along the Combahee River in South Carolina, freeing hundreds of slaves.

Following the war, she married Nelson Davis. She became active in the suffragist movement, speaking at the National Association of Afro-American Women in 1896. She died in 1913, surrounded by friends and family.

The Times That Try Men's Souls

Thomas Paine was a political writer whose pamphlet Common Sense *laid the foundations for the American Revolution and convinced the American colonists that the revolution was necessary. He also wrote several other influential treatises on subjects including the French Revolution and religion.*

* * * *

THOMAS PAINE WAS born in 1737 in England. His father was a Quaker and his mother was Anglican. He did not receive much schooling, but did learn to read and write. When he was 13 years old, he joined his father in his trade as a rope maker for ships. After living and working in England for most of his adult life, he sailed to America in 1774, arriving in Philadelphia. In America, he immediately began working in publishing, starting as an assistant editor of the *Pennsylvania Magazine.* He began writing his own articles, publishing them under assumed names. One of his earliest political articles attacked the institution of slavery, which he authored under the pseudonym "Justice & Humanity."

Common Sense

Paine had been in Philadelphia only five months when the Revolutionary War broke out at the battles of Lexington and Concord. He realized that the revolt could not merely be a rebellion against the taxes levied by Parliament, but should fight for complete independence from the British crown. He developed this position to a pamphlet fifty pages long that was printed on January 10, 1776. The pamphlet's title was *Common Sense.*

The pamphlet's rhetoric is designed to pressure the reader to choose a side and make a choice on the question of revolution against the Crown. *Common Sense* brilliantly forces the issue of complete independence from Great Britain, showing the reader that the only remedy against tyranny was freedom.

The incendiary pamphlet was widely reprinted and distributed throughout the thirteen colonies, and helped stoke revolutionary sentiment among the colonists. Because of it, recruitment by the Continental Army increased, and the colonies found themselves united for the cause of independence.

During the Revolution, Paine travelled with the Continental Army as an attaché to General Nathanael Greene. Between 1776 and 1783, he published a series of sixteen *Crisis Papers*, which encouraged the revolutionary soldiers to remain in the fight regardless of how dire the situation became, and to remember that they were fighting for the virtuous cause of liberty. The first of the *Crisis Papers*, published in December 1776, was read to the troops at Valley Forge to inspire them to persevere through the punishing winter.

After the Revolution

Following the war, Paine was appointed to the Committee for Foreign Affairs in 1777, and held the post until a scandal forced his resignation in 1779. He then served as clerk of the Pennsylvania General Assembly. While there, he wrote *Public Good* in 1780, which called for a Constitutional Convention to replace the Articles of Confederation.

In 1787, he returned to England, and began supporting the French Revolution. When he read an argument against the Revolution in April 1787, Paine wrote a response in 1791. *The Rights of Man* not only defended the Revolution but went on to and criticize the aristocracy and assail the tradition of inheritance. He was accused of treason and the book was banned, but by then he had already travelled to France.

He returned to America in 1802 at the invitation of President Thomas Jefferson, and lived there until his death in 1809.

Quotes from Thomas Paine

"Government, even in its best state, is but a necessary evil; in its worst state, an intolerable one."

—COMMON SENSE

"These are the times that try men's souls. The summer soldier and the sunshine patriot will, in this crisis, shrink from the service of their country; but he that stands it now, deserves the love and thanks of man and woman. Tyranny, like hell, is not easily conquered; yet we have this consolation with us, that the harder the conflict, the more glorious the triumph."

—COMMON SENSE

"What we obtain too cheap, we esteem too lightly."

—COMMON SENSE

"Those who expect to reap the blessings of freedom must, like men, undergo the fatigue of supporting it."

—THE CRISIS PAPERS

"Character is much easier kept than recovered."

—THE CRISIS PAPERS

"My country is the world and my religion is to do good."

—THE RIGHTS OF MAN

Extremism and Moderation

"Let our Republicanism, so focused and so dedicated, not be made fuzzy and futile by unthinking and stupid labels. I would remind you that extremism in the defense of liberty is no vice. And let me remind you also that moderation in the pursuit of justice is no virtue."

✳   ✳   ✳   ✳

KNOWN AS "MR. Conservative," Arizona Senator Barry Goldwater helped usher in a new era of right-wing Republicanism with his successful bid for the Republican presidential nomination in 1964. The quote above comes from his acceptance speech for the presidential nomination. Though he lost the election to incumbent President Lyndon B. Johnson, the rhetoric of Goldwater's campaign decisively split the conservative faction of the party from its more liberal Eastern bloc, paving the way for Ronald Reagan to win the presidency in 1980.

Goldwater pushed for reducing the size and power of the federal government in nearly all arenas but defense; he maintained that the communist threat necessitated a massive military buildup. His anti-communist stance was so extreme that he once joked about the nuclear bomb, "Let's lob one into the men's room at the Kremlin."

This tendency to speak off the cuff—he also told a panel of news reporters, "sometimes I think this country would be better off if we could just saw off the Eastern Seaboard and let it float out to sea"—contributed to Goldwater's election defeat. His opponents were able to paint him as an aggressive, impulsive reactionary who could lead the country into nuclear war. When his campaign featured the slogan, "In your heart, you know he's right," Johnson supporters successfully countered with, "In your guts, you know he's nuts."

"A thing moderately good is not so good as it ought to be. Moderation in temper is always a virtue; but moderation in principle is always a vice."

—THOMAS PAINE

William Pitt (the Younger)

"Necessity is the plea for every infringement of human freedom. It is the argument of tyrants; it is the creed of slaves."

At 24 years old, William Pitt became the youngest Prime Minister in English history. He led Britain against the French during the Napoleonic Wars and engineered the Acts of Union that established the United Kingdom of Great Britain and Ireland.

✳ ✳ ✳ ✳

W ILLIAM PITT WAS born in 1859 in Kent, the son of William Pitt (the Elder), a British statesman and cabinet member during the Seven Years' War. He attended Cambridge, and after his father died in 1778, he became a solicitor. In 1780, he joined Parliament and two years later became chancellor of the Exhcequer under Prime Minister Shelburne. When Shelburne's government dissolved, King George III called Pitt to form a government, but he declined. His rival, Charles Fox, led a coalition government as Prime Minister, and Pitt skillfully undermined it by bringing resolutions for parliamentary reform to the floor.

Prime Minister

In December 1783, a bill championed by Fox was defeated in the House of Lords, and George III, who was dissatisfied with him, immediately dissolved the coalition government and again invited Pitt to form a government as Prime Minister. When Parliament reconvened the following month, Pitt attempted to convince Fox to join his ministry, but he refused, and Parliament voted down the new government. Pitt, however, refused to resign, and eventually was able to convince enough of the members who had initially voted against his government to join him.

While Prime Minister, Pitt moved to enact a number of pieces of legislation, the first of which reorganized the British East India Tea Company. Others advanced his agenda of parliamentary reform and addressed the British national debt, which had ballooned to more than 240 million pounds—an astronomical figure in the 19th century—following the American Revolutionary War. Pitt instituted a series of taxes to begin paying down the debt.

War with France

In 1789, the French Revolution broke out, overthrowing the monarchy and establishing the French First Republic. In 1792, after several years of war in Europe between the French and various Monarchist coalitions, Pitt's government expelled the French ambassador and began military preparations. By 1794 Britain was engaged in all-out war with France, the bulk of which was waged by the Royal Navy on the high seas. The war with France was extremely expensive, and Pitt introduced the first income tax in the history of Britain. The Royal Navy was small when war broke out, and England was forced to enact the Quota System, a kind of regional draft, and Impressment, which forcibly recruited Englishmen into Naval service.

In 1798, the United Irishmen, led by Wolfe Tone, rebelled against British rule in Ireland. The rebellion spread throughout Ireland for several months, until British troops defeated the rebels at the battle of Vinegar Hill, and brutally suppressed civilian resistance. During the rebellion, France landed about 1,000 troops in Ireland; three months later they unsuccessfully attempted to land some 3,000 more. Fearing another rebellion in Ireland, Pitt designed the Acts of Union of 1800, which united the Kingdoms of Great Britain and Ireland and promised reforms to the treatment of Irish Catholics.

Pitt held two terms as Prime Minister, and served as Chancellor of the Exchequer until his death. He died in Surrey on January 23, 1806. He was forty-six years old, had never married and had no children. He was buried at Westminster Abbey.

A View of America from Outside

"They [the Americans] are the hope of this world. They may become its model."

A pragmatic economist, Anne Robert Jacques Turgot supported the American Revolution's ideals but opposed supporting them financially.

✳   ✳   ✳   ✳

A NNE ROBERT JACQUES Turgot was born in Paris on May 10, 1727, and entered the Seminary at Saint-Sulpice in 1743 and the Sorbonne in 1749. He was destined to join the priesthood, but in 1751, when he was about to be ordained, he abandoned the Church. He explained to his parents that he was a deist, which at the time was similar to an agnostic, and that he wouldn't be able to live a lie. He entered the bureaucracy in 1752 as a solicitor, and later a counselor magistrate to the Parliament that same year.

When Parliament was exiled in 1753 for defying the king, Turgot served with 39 other magistrates in the Royal Chamber as a member of the provisional government from 1753–54. During this time, he began accompanying Vincent de Gournay, who promoted physiocracy, an economic theory popular during the time that asserted that agriculture and land were the basis from which the wealth of nations was derived. In 1761, Louis XV appointed Turgot to the post of intendant of a region in southwest France. Turgot held this post for 13 years quite successfully.

While there, he wrote *Reflections on the Formation and Distribution of Wealth*. It is his best known work, and developed de Gournay's theories of physiocracy. Turgot argued for the division of society into three classes, the agricultural class, the artisan class, and the land-owning class. He also wrote that only the net profits from agriculture should be taxed, and called for removing restrictions to commerce and industry.

Revolutions Abroad and At Home

In 1774, Turgot was appointed Minister of the Navy, and held the post until 1776. While there, he vigorously opposed financial support of the American Revolution. Like many in France, he supported the goals of the Revolutionaries, and admired their commitment to a new, democratic form of government, and he also thought that the Americans would win the war. But ever the financial pragmatist, he argued that France could not afford to send financial support to the Americans. Others in government idealized American virtues and considered the Revolution a major step forward for mankind. Turgot argued that the colonists did not properly adopt the principles of physiocracy, and was appalled that they did not abolish slavery and required elected officials to swear a religious oath of office.

In 1776, Turgot attempted to push reforms in France. He introduced the Six Edicts to the French Court, which abolished certain taxes and offices. One of the Edicts, which abolished the use of *corvées*, unpaid laborers, by landowners, and another that abolished the powerful guilds, earned him the wrath of the privileged classes. Turgot soon found himself the target of an unrelenting attack by enemies in government. He attempted to appeal to the young king to support the reforms and protect him, but his enemies had successfully alienated him from the throne. His reforms were abandoned, and on May 12, 1776, Turgot was ordered to resign his position.

Turgot spent the remainder of his life immersed in studying science and literature, and in 1777 he was made the vice president of the Académie des Inscriptions et Belles-Lettres, a society dedicated to the humanities, but he never published anything again. He died in 1781 at the age of fifty-three.

A Lesser Known Revolutionary

"The freedom of the press is one of the great bulwarks of liberty, and can never be restrained but by despotic governments."

George Mason, an American Revolutionary, promoted the idea of inalienable rights, which influenced Thomas Jefferson when he wrote the Declaration of Independence. Mason later advocated for concepts that would lead to the adoption of the Bill of Rights.

✳ ✳ ✳ ✳

GEORGE MASON WAS born in Virginia on December 11, 1725. His father died when he was still a young boy, and his uncle, John Mercer, helped raise him. Mercer had a library with some 1,500 books in it, and the young Mason was a voracious reader. Mason was a neighbor of George Washington, and he soon developed an interest in local politics. In 1748, he unsuccessfully ran for election to the House of Burgess. In 1758, he successfully won election to the seat, and represented Fairfax County in the House.

The Revolution

In the 1760s, Mason grew to oppose the colonial policies of the British, and in particular the Stamp Act of 1765. Mason's argument against the Stamp Act was notable for its inclusion of anti-slavery views. He influenced the House of Burgess to support the boycott of British goods that would eventually be successful in repealing the Stamp Act. In 1775, as the possibility of a revolution loomed, Mason organized a Virginia militia that was independent of the British Army. At the outset of the American Revolution, George Washington was called to the Second Continental Congress following the battles of Lexington and Concord, and Mason took his place in the delegation to the Virginia Convention.

In 1776, the Virginia Convention convened to draw up a state Constitution, as the British authority in the state was all but through. The Convention directed Thomas Jefferson and other delegates to the Continental Congress to lobby for a full Declaration of Independence from the British Crown. The Convention also passed a full Declaration of Rights and got to work drafting the Constitution. Mason authored both almost single-handedly, and the first article of the Declaration of Rights was emulated by Jefferson when he drew up the Declaration of Independence two months later.

The Virginia Constitution

The Virginia Constitution was quickly adopted by most of the other states. It asserts the equality of all men and declared "inherent rights," including the freedom of "pursuing happiness and safety." It goes on to declare that power is derived from the people, and rejects the idea of privileged political classes such as Lords. The Constitution recommends the separation of powers, free elections, and restrictions of government power. Many of these restrictions, including freedom of the press, religion, protections against unwarranted search and seizure, trial by jury, and due process would later be adopted into the Bill of Rights in the United States Constitution.

Mason opposed the adoption of the Constitution at the Convention of 1787 on several grounds, including the fact that it did not abolish the slave trade—which Mason wrote was "disgraceful to mankind" despite the fact that he owned slaves himself. He also vehemently opposed the powers the Constitution granted to the Federal government, and argued that it did not go far enough to protect individual rights as the Virginia Constitution had done. He lobbied against ratification of the Constitution in Virginia, and refused to sign it himself. It passed, and Mason returned to Virginia. In 1791, the Congress ratified the Bill of Rights, which addressed many of Mason's concerns. He died in October the following year.

"The basis of our government being the opinion of the people, the very first object should be to keep that right; and were it left to me to decide whether we should have a government without newspapers, or newspapers without a government, I should not hesitate a moment to prefer the latter."

—THOMAS JEFFERSON, 1787

"Nothing can now be believed which is seen in a newspaper."

—ALSO THOMAS JEFERSON, 1807

My Country, Right or Wrong

Stephen Decatur was a commodore in the United States Navy who won a series of victories in the Tripoli War and War of 1812, and became the first American war hero after the Revolution.

✳ ✳ ✳ ✳

STEPHEN DECATUR WAS born in Maryland on January 5, 1779. His father had been a commodore in the U.S. Navy during the American Revolution, and Decatur followed his father's example, enlisting in 1798 as a midshipman. He directed the building of a number of U.S. ships, and became the youngest naval officer ever to reach the rank of captain in the Navy. He was famous for his natural leadership skills and his authentic concern for the sailors he was commanding. He won multiple victories against European powers during the Tripoli War, Quasi-War with France, and the War of 1812, helping establish the United States as a naval power in its own right.

During the War of 1812, his ship, the *United States*, encountered the British gunship *Macedonian*. In the ensuing battle, Decatur was seriously wounded by a flying splinter from the hull of the *United States*, but he continued to command his ship's attack. The *United States* quickly outgunned the *Macedonian* and captured it. Following the war, he became a member of the Navy Board of Commissioners.

In 1816, when giving a toast, Decatur reportedly proclaimed, "Our country! In her intercourse with foreign nations may she always be in the right; but our country, right or wrong." It was a quote that would resonate with Americans long afterward.

Decatur's career ended early when he became involved in a dispute with a rival officer, Commodore James Barron. Barron challenged Decatur to a duel, and killed him on March 22, 1820. He was buried in Philadelphia.

Right or Wrong?

"I can never join with my voice in the toast which I see in the papers attributed to one of our gallant naval heroes. I cannot ask of heaven success, even for my country, in a cause where she should be in the wrong ... My toast would be, may our country be always successful, but whether successful or otherwise, always right."

—JOHN QUINCY ADAMS, IN A LETTER TO HIS FATHER, 1816

"Be England what she will, With all her faults she is my country still."

—CHARLES CHURCHILL, 1764

"Our country right or wrong. When right, to be kept right; when wrong, to be put right."

—CARL SCHURZ, 1899

"'My country, right or wrong,' is a thing that no patriot would think of saying. It is like saying, 'My mother, drunk or sober.'"

—G.K. CHESTERON

Black Hawk

"You know the cause of our making war. It is known to all white men. They ought to be ashamed of it. "

Black Hawk led his people in the last fight to resist European encroachment on Native lands east of the Mississippi.

❋   ❋   ❋   ❋

MA-KA-TAI-ME-SHE-KIA-KIAK (BLACK SPARROW Hawk) was born in 1767 in a village in Illinois, near present-day Rock Island. The village was the summer retreat of the Sauk people; during the winter, they resided on the far side of the Mississippi for fur trapping and hunting. Black Hawk's father was a medicine man of the Sauk people. As a young man, he established himself as a war leader: at the age of 19 he led a band of 200 warriors in battle against the Osage. That same year, his father died in a battle with the Cherokee in Missouri, and Black Hawk inherited his medicine bundle, elevating his status among the Sauk people.

In the War of 1812, Black Hawk's Sauk band sent 200 warriors to fight on the side of the British. The United States had built Fort Madison in disputed territory in 1808; during the war, Black Hawk's band, along with other Native Americans allied with the British, besieged and captured the fort. Black Hawk and his band fought in several other battles during the War of 1812. Following the war, he signed a treaty in 1816 that ceded Sauk lands to the United States, although he later said he was not aware of this condition in the treaty.

Black Hawk War

Because of the treaty of 1816, Black Hawk and his people were forced to move to the west side of the Mississippi. Understandably angered by this development, in April 1832, a band of Sauks, with their allies the Kickapoos and Meskwakis, crossed the river into Illinois. Black Hawk hoped to avoid a direct military confrontation and peacefully resettle the Sauk summer grounds. The United States, however, assumed that the group was hostile and organized a militia. When Black Hawk sent a delegation to parley with US officials, the militia opened fire on them unprovoked.

Black Hawk responded by immediately counterattacking the militia, which was commanded by Major Isaiah Stillman. Notably, a young Abraham Lincoln was present at the battle as a member of the Illinois militia. Despite considerably outnumbering the Native force, the undisciplined militia panicked and fled in a disorganized retreat, and the engagement is named the Battle of Stillman's Run.

Black Hawk and his band were pursued into southern Wisconsin by US troops. During the War, warriors from other Native tribes conducted raids against unprotected forts and settlements in Illinois. In July, US troops found Black Hawk's band and attacked them successfully at the Battle of Wisconsin Heights. The Sauk retreated west toward the Mississippi, and the US troops again attacked twelve days later at the Battle of

Bad Axe, where they slaughtered men, women and children. Black Hawk escaped with several other leaders, but later surrendered and was imprisoned at Jefferson Barracks near St. Louis with eight other leaders.

President Andrew Jackson used the Black Hawk War as a pretext to harshly enforce the Indian Removal Bill, which he had signed in 1830, in all states east of the Mississippi. In April 1833, Jackson ordered Black Hawk and the other leaders be sent to Washington, DC, where with Jackson, and were again imprisoned for a few weeks at Fortress Monroe in Virginia before being sent back West. Their trip took them through several major cities, including Philadelphia, New York, and Detroit; they were met by large crowds wherever they were taken.

Following the tour, Black Hawk went to the Sauk tribal lands along the Iowa River, where he lived out the rest of his days in peace. He died there on October 3, 1838.

Speckled Snake

Speckled Snake was the chief of the Muscogee Creek people. He resisted Andrew Jackson's efforts to relocate his tribe west of the Mississippi river.

✳   ✳   ✳   ✳

SPECKLED SNAKE WAS the chief of the Muscogee people, a tribe in the Creek Confederacy of Nations who were originally located in areas of Tennessee, Georgia, Alabama, and Florida. Very little is known about Speckled Snake's early life or background, but he is famous for a speech he delivered to members of his tribe regarding relocation. In 1829, President Andrew Jackson was attempting to coerce the Muscogee people, as well as several other tribes in the southeastern United States, to abandon their tribal lands and move to reservations west of the Mississippi River.

A council of tribal chiefs of various peoples in the Creek Nation convened in July of 1829. A reporter from the Savannah *Mercury* was present at the meeting and reported what happened. President Jackson's ultimatum was delivered to the chiefs by a Tribal Agent. The chiefs responded with a "profound silence" that lasted for several minutes. Then, Speckled Snake, one of the oldest men in the room, rose to his feet, supported on either side by a younger warrior. He delivered a stirring argument against relocation. Speckled Snake noted that the Creek Nation peoples had always helped white settlers when they could, but once the whites were powerful enough, they began to forcibly encroach on Native lands, always wanting more.

During the Indian Removal of the 1830s, the Muscogee were forcibly relocated to Oklahoma.

The Speech

Brothers! I have listened to many talks from our great father. When he first came over the wide waters, he was but a little man, and wore a red coat. Our chiefs met him on the banks of the Savannah, and smoked with him the pipe of peace. He was then very little. His legs were cramped by sitting long in his big boat, and he begged for a little land to light his fire on. He said he had come over the wide waters to teach Indians new things, and to make them happy. He said he loved his red brothers; he was very kind.

The Muscogees gave the white man land, and kindled him a fire, that he might warm himself, and when his enemies, the pale faces of the South, made war on him, their young men drew the tomahawk, and protected his head from the scalping knife. But when the white man had warmed himself before the Indian's fire, and filled himself with their hominy, he became very large. With a step he bestrode the mountains, and his feet covered the plains and the valleys. His hands grasped the Eastern and the Western sea, and his head rested on the moon.

hen he became our great father. He loves his red children, and he said, "get a little farther, lest I tread on thee." With one foot he pushed the red man over the Oconee, and with the other he trampled down the graves of his fathers, and the forests where he had so long hunted the deer. But our great father still loved his red children; and he soon made to them another talk, he said "get a little farther, you are too near me." But there were some bad men among the Muscogees, then, as there are now. They lingered around the graves of their ancestors, till they were crushed beneath the heavy tread of our great father, their teeth pierced his feet, and made him angry. Yet he continued to love his red children, and when he found them too slow in moving, he sent his great guns before him to sweep his path.

Brothers! I have listened to a great many talks from our great father. But they always began and ended in this: "get a little further, you are too near me."

Brothers! Our great father says, "where we now are, our white brothers have always claimed the land." He speaks with a straight tongue, and cannot lie. But when he first came over the wide waters, while he was yet small, and stood before the great chief at the council on Yamacraw Bluff, he said, "give me a little land, which you can spare, and I will pay you for it."

Brothers! When our great father made us a talk, on a former occasion, and said, "get a little farther; go beyond the Oconee, the Ocmulgee, there is a pleasant country," he also said, "it shall be yours forever." I have listened to his present talk; he says the land where you now live is not yours—go beyond the Mississippi; there is game, and you may remain while the grass grows or the water runs. Brothers, will not our great father come there also? he loves his red children. He speaks with a straight tongue, and will not lie.

Brothers! Our great father says that our mad men have made his heart bleed, for the murder of one of his white children. Yet where are the red children he loves, once as numerous as the leaves of the forest? how many have been murdered by his war-riors; how many have been crushed beneath his own footsteps?

Brothers! Our great father says we must go beyond the Mississippi. We shall be there under his care, and experience his kindness. He is very good! We have felt it all before. Brothers! I have done.

The Melting Pot

The concept of America as a melting pot can be traced back through several people.

✳ ✳ ✳ ✳

An Early American Writer

J. HECTOR ST. John de Crevecoeur was an American writer of French origin whose writings about 18th-century American became a definitive account of the spirit of the young republic.

J. Hector St. John de Crevecoeur was born in Normandy, France, on December 31, 1735. When he was twenty years old, he travelled to Quebec, where he was a surveyor in the French militia during the French and Indian War. After the war, Crevecoeur moved to New York and applied for citizenship. He became a farmer there in 1770 and began keeping a journal of his life in America. In 1779, he returned to France to take care of his ailing father. In 1782, he wrote a collection of essays called *Letters from an American Farmer*. The essays described life on the American frontier and celebrated American ingenuity and simple living. *Letters* also extolled the idea of the American Dream as being available to everyone, and spoke of America as a place where anyone can become an American. He wrote: "Here [in America] individuals of all nations are melted into a new race of men, whose labors and posterity will one day cause great changes in the world."

Crevecoeur returned to New York in 1783, and lived there for most of that decade. *Letters* had made him popular in France, and he was appointed French consul to New York. In 1789, he visited France, and was caught amid the outbreak of the French Revolution. Fearing for his life, he went into hiding, and petitioned the American government for safe passage. James Monroe brought him the necessary papers, and he was able to leave. He returned to Normandy in his later years, and died there on November 12, 1813.

Updated for the 1900s

In 1908–1910, a play called *The Melting Pot* had great success in the United States; Theodore Roosevelt, then president, reportedly praised it. Its protagonist was a Jewish immigrant who had escaped pogroms in Europe to come to the United States. The play popularized the concept of the "melting pot" and included the lines, "America is God's crucible, the great melting pot where all the races of Europe are melting and re-forming."

Ironically, the author of the play was not himself American— Israel Zangwill was British.

John Brown

John Brown was a militant abolitionist who participated in the Bloody Kansas conflict and led a raid on Harpers Ferry in an attempt to spark an uprising against slavery in 1859.

✳ ✳ ✳ ✳

JOHN BROWN WAS born on May 9, 1800 in Torrington, Connecticut. His father, a Calvinist minister, taught him at a young age to support abolition. The lesson was seared into Brown's memory when he was twelve years old and witnessed the beating of a young African-American boy. Brown initially studied to be a minister, but instead became a tanner. His family moved around in his twenties and held different jobs.

In 1837, when the abolitionist Elijah Lovejoy was murdered, Brown swore to give his life to the abolitionist cause. He

founded the League of Gileadites, an armed group that protected African-Americans from slave catchers. In 1847 he met
with Frederick Douglass. When the Kansas-Nebraska Act
passed in 1854, Brown and five of his sons moved to Kansas to
fight in the conflict over whether the state would be free
or slave-owning territory. They killed five pro-slavery settlers
in 1856.

In 1858, Brown freed a group of slaves from a Missouri farm
and led them to freedom in Canada. He spent much of that
year and the spring and summer of 1859 making preparations
for the raid on Harpers Ferry. He gathered rifles, pikes and
ammunition, and organized a group of 21 men. He discussed
the raid with Harriet Tubman, who thought it was doomed to
failure. On October 16, 1859, Brown and his men attacked the
federal armory at Harpers Ferry and held it for two days before
they were overwhelmed by federal troops led by Robert E. Lee.

Brown was captured and convicted of treason. On December 2,
1859, he was executed. He became a symbol of the abolitionist
movement, and during the Civil War Union troops sang "John
Brown's Body" as they marched into battle.

Quotes by and about John Brown
"These men are all talk; What is needed is action—action!"

—1859

*"I am yet too young to understand that God is any respecter of
persons. I believe that to have interfered as I have done as I have
always freely admitted I have done in behalf of His despised poor,
was not wrong, but right. Now, if it is deemed necessary that I should
forfeit my life for the furtherance of the ends of justice, and mingle
my blood further with the blood of my children and with the blood
of millions in this slave country whose rights are disregarded by
wicked, cruel, and unjust enactments, I submit; so let it be done!"*

—HIS SPEECH TO THE COURT, 1859

*"But the question is, Did John Brown fail? He certainly did fail to get
out of Harpers Ferry before being beaten down by United States
soldiers; he did fail to save his own life, and to lead a liberating army*

into the mountains of Virginia. But he did not go to Harpers Ferry to save his life."

—FREDERICK DOUGLASS ON JOHN BROWN, 1881

"When John Brown stretched forth his arm the sky was cleared. The time for compromises was gone—the armed hosts of freedom stood face to face over the chasm of a broken Union—and the clash of arms was at hand. The South staked all upon getting possession of the Federal Government, and failing to do that, drew the sword of rebellion and thus made her own, and not Brown's, the lost cause of the century."

—FREDERICK DOUGLASS ON JOHN BROWN, 1881

The Union Was His Country

Henry Clay was major political figure in early nineteenth century America, helping push the nation into the War of 1812, orchestrating John Quincy Adam's presidency, and formulating the Missouri Compromise of 1820, the Tariff Compromise of 1833, and the Compromise of 1850.

✳ ✳ ✳ ✳

HENRY CLAY WAS born in Virginia on April 12, 1777. When he was three years old, he witnessed British troops ransack his family home, an experience that would shape his political views later in life. He studied law and was admitted to the Virginia bar in 1797. He moved to Kentucky to practice law, and married Lucretia Hart there in 1799. In 1803, Clay was elected to the Kentucky General Assembly. Three years later, he was appointed to the United States Senate, and in 1811 he was elected to the U.S. House of Representatives.

In the House, he quickly gained a reputation as a hawk, and urged the government to challenge Britain over its habit of conscripting American sailors into the Royal Navy. His influence was instrumental in pushing the United States into the War of 1812. At the end of the War, Clay helped negotiate the Treaty of Ghent. His efforts were critical in securing better terms than the British initially offered, and the resulting treaty established a lasting American independence from Britain.

The Great Compromiser

Over the course of his political career, Clay played a central role in negotiating compromises in several areas. In 1820, he helped negotiate the Missouri Compromise, which balanced the interests of slaveholding states with non-slave states as the country continued its western expansion, and helped stave off the imminent Civil War for several decades. In 1833 he was able to convince South Carolina not to secede when new American tariffs disproportionately affected agricultural states in the South. The Compromise Tariff reduced tariffs and averted a crisis. In 1850, when California was joining the Union, Clay helped negotiate the Great Compromise that allowed it to enter the Union as a non-slave state without adding an additional slave state. The bill also addressed the Fugitive Slave Law and abolished slavery in Washington, D.C.

In his 1848 speech, Clay proclaimed his allegiance not to any particular region of the United States but to the whole: "I have heard something said about allegiance to the South. I know no South, no North, no East, no West, to which I owe any allegiance... The Union, sir, is my country."

John Quincy Adams and Andrew Jackson

In the presidential election of 1824, three candidates ran: William Crawford, John Quincy Adams, and Andrew Jackson. When no candidate received enough electoral votes to win, the election, as directed by the Twelfth Amendment, went to the House of Representatives. Clay maneuvered the House to elect Adams, knowing that he would receive a Cabinet appointment in return.

Adams won, and Clay was made Secretary of State. Jackson was livid, and he blocked much of the new administration's legislation and publically disparaged Clay and Adams. In 1828 he won the presidency.

In 1832 Clay ran against Jackson. Democrats supported Jackson's National Bank and policies of Indian removal and nullification, which argued that any state could nullify a federal law it deemed unconstitutional. Clay opposed nullification and supported the Second Bank of the United States. Opposition to Jackson was split among three candidates, including Clay, and he won the election in a landslide. Clay also ran unsuccessfully for president again in 1844 and 1848. He remained in the Senate as the leader of the Whig party until his death on June 29, 1852. He was the first person ever laid in state in the Capitol rotunda. He is buried in Lexington, Kentucky.

"I would rather be right than be President."

—HENRY CLAY IN 1850

Frederick Douglass

"I appear this evening as a thief and a robber. I stole this head, these limbs, this body from my master, and ran off with them. "

After escaping from slavery, Frederick Douglass dedicated his life to fighting first for emancipation and later for women's suffrage. An orator, philosopher, and freedom fighter, he became the first African-American to hold high office in the U.S. government.

✳   ✳   ✳   ✳

FREDERICK DOUGLASS WAS born into slavery Maryland circa 1818. He lived with his maternal grandmother at first and later in the home of the plantation owner, who may have been his father. When he was 12 he was sent to Boston, where he learned to read and write. It was there that he began to read *The Columbian Orator*, a collection of political and philosophical essays, which shaped his views on freedom and human rights. At sixteen, Douglass was sent to work for Edward Covey, who had a reputation as a "slave-breaker." Covey whipped and beat Douglass mercilessly until one day, when he fought back, beating Covey, who never assaulted him again.

Escape and Abolitionism

In 1838, after two failed attempts, Douglass escaped to freedom with the help of Anna Murray, a free black woman from Baltimore. He made his way from Maryland to New York in less than a day. Murray met him there, and they married, settling in New Bedford, Massachusetts, a thriving community of free blacks. Douglass began to attend abolitionist meetings, and subscribed to *The Liberator*, William Lloyd Garrison's abolitionist newspaper. He began giving lectures on anti-slavery, and eventually spoke at the annual convention of the Massachusetts Anti-Slavery Society.

Garrison encouraged Douglass to write his autobiography; *Narrative of the Life of Frederick Douglass, an American Slave*, was published in 1845 and became a best seller. Following the publication, which made him a national figure, Douglass travelled to Europe to avoid recapture. He lived in Great Britain for two years, where he regularly spoke about the evils of slavery. After his supporters collected funds to buy his freedom, Douglass was able to return to the United States in 1847.

Women's Suffrage

Douglass began publishing several abolitionist newspapers of his own, the most famous of which is *The North Star*, whose motto was "Right is of no sex, truth is of no color, God is the Father of us all, and we are all brethren." In 1848, he attended the first convention on women's rights in Seneca Falls, where he spoke in favor of a resolution, proposed by Elizabeth Cady Stanton, which stated women's suffrage as a goal of the movement. Douglass said that the world would be improved if women were included in politics, and that he could not accept his right to vote as a black man if the right were not also extended to women. The resolution passed.

The Civil War and Reconstruction

During the Civil War, Douglass fought for the rights of black soldiers to join the Union Army, arguing that if the aim of the war was to end slavery, blacks must be allowed to fight. He also met with President Abraham Lincoln to discuss the treatment of black soldiers in the Union Army. In 1863, upon the Emancipation Proclamation, he criticized the fact that it only freed slaves in Confederate states. He also was publically disappointed that Lincoln did not support suffrage for black freedmen, and supported his opponent in the 1864 election.

Following the war, Douglass was appointed to a number of government positions, including diplomat to the Dominican Republic and president of the Freedmen's Savings Bank during Reconstruction. He praised President Ulysses Grant's signing of the 1871 Civil Rights Act, which was designed to combat the Ku Klux Klan and other white terror organizations in the South. In 1889, he was appointed consul-general to Haiti.

Frederick Douglass continued fighting for the rights of women and blacks until his death. On February 20, 1895, after attending a meeting of the National Council of Women, he died at his home. He is buried in Rochester, New York.

Quotes from Frederick Douglass

"They cannot degrade Frederick Douglass. The soul that is within me no man can degrade. I am not the one that is being degraded on account of this treatment, but those who are inflicting it upon me…"

"The man who is right is a majority. We, who have God and conscience on our side, have a majority against the universe."

"There is no conceivable reason why all colored people should not be treated according to the merits of each individual. It is not only the plain duty, but also the interest of us all, to have every colored man take the place for which he is best fitted by education, character, ability, manners, and culture. If others insist on keeping him in any lower and poorer place, it is not only his injury, but our universal loss."

"I have often been utterly astonished, since I came to the north, to find persons who could speak of the singing, among slaves, as evidence of their contentment and happiness. It is impossible to conceive of a greater mistake. Slaves sing most when they are most

unhappy. The songs of the slave represent the sorrows of his heart; and he is relieved by them, only as an aching heart is relieved by its tears. At least, such is my experience. I have often sung to drown my sorrow, but seldom to express my happiness. Crying for joy, and singing for joy, were alike uncommon to me while in the jaws of slavery. The singing of a man cast away upon a desolate island might be as appropriately considered as evidence of contentment and happiness, as the singing of a slave; the songs of the one and of the other are prompted by the same emotion."

"I make no pretension to patriotism. So long as my voice can be heard on this or the other side of the Atlantic, I will hold up America to the lightning scorn of moral indignation. In doing this, I shall feel myself discharging the duty of a true patriot; for he is a lover of his country who rebukes and does not excuse its sins. It is righteousness that exalteth a nation while sin is a reproach to any people."

"What, to the American slave, is your 4th of July? I answer: a day that reveals to him, more than all other days in the year, the gross injustice and cruelty to which he is the constant victim. To him, your celebration is a sham; your boasted liberty, an unholy license; your national greatness, swelling vanity; your sounds of rejoicing are empty and heartless; your denunciations of tyrants, brass fronted impudence; your shouts of liberty and equality, hollow mockery; your prayers and hymns, your sermons and thanksgivings, with all your religious parade, and solemnity, are, to him, mere bombast, fraud, deception, impiety, and hypocrisy—a thin veil to cover up crimes which would disgrace a nation of savages."

"You have seen how a man was made a slave; you shall see how a slave was made a man."

Ain't I a Woman?

Born into slavery, she became an orator and preacher.

＊　＊　＊　＊

SOJOURNER TRUTH WAS born Isabella Baumfree in New York circa 1797. Like her parents, she was enslaved, and when she was nine years old, Isabella was sold at auction, separating her from her family. She would be sold two more times before she escaped to freedom in 1826. New York emancipated slaves on July 4, 1827. When she learned that her five-year-old son had been illegally sold to a slave owner in Alabama, she sued him and won her son's freedom. This was the first time a black woman had successfully sued a white man in an American court.

In 1843, she changed her name to Sojourner Truth, became a Methodist, and began working for the cause of abolition. She lived in a community of abolitionists in Massachusetts, where she met leaders such as William Lloyd Garrison and Frederick Douglass. In 1850 she published *The Narrative of Sojourner Truth: A Northern Slave*. She began touring and giving speeches on slavery. In May 1851, while speaking at the Ohio Women's Rights Convention, she delivered the speech for which she would become famous. The speech was published in the *Anti-Slavery Bugle* and widely distributed.

Truth continued to work for equal rights for women and African-Americans her entire life. She died on November 26, 1883, and is buried near her home in Battle Creek, Michigan.

Ain't I a Woman?

The text of the speech reads:

Well, children, where there is so much racket there must be something out of kilter. I think that 'twixt the negroes of the South and the women at the North, all talking about rights, the white men will be in a fix pretty soon. But what's all this here talking about?

That man over there says that women need to be helped into carriages, and lifted over ditches, and to have the best place everywhere. Nobody ever helps me into carriages, or over mud-puddles, or gives me any best place! And ain't I a woman? Look at me! Look at my arm! I have ploughed and planted, and gathered into barns, and no man could head me! And ain't I a woman? I could work as much and eat as much as a man—when I could get it—and bear the lash as well! And ain't I a woman? I have borne thirteen children, and seen most all sold off to slavery, and when I cried out with my mother's grief, none but Jesus heard me! And ain't I a woman?

Then they talk about this thing in the head; what's this they call it? [Audience: "intellect"] That's it, honey. What's that got to do with women's rights or negroes' rights? If my cup won't hold but a pint, and yours holds a quart, wouldn't you be mean not to let me have my little half measure full?

Then that little man in black there, he says women can't have as much rights as men, 'cause Christ wasn't a woman! Where did your Christ come from? Where did your Christ come from? From God and a woman! Man had nothing to do with Him.

If the first woman God ever made was strong enough to turn the world upside down all alone, these women together ought to be able to turn it back , and get it right side up again! And now they is asking to do it, the men better let them.

Obliged to you for hearing me, and now old Sojourner ain't got nothing more to say.

The Little Woman

Harriet Beecher Stowe, a first-time novelist from Cincinnati, dramatized the problem of slavery for all to see in her novel Uncle Tom's Cabin.

✳   ✳   ✳   ✳

WHEN HARRIET BEECHER Stowe was introduced to President Abraham Lincoln, as the story goes, he said, "So, you're the little woman who wrote the book that started this great war." There's no question that few elements fueled the flames of hate across the country as much as *Uncle Tom's Cabin* did. Stowe's story of Tom, a saintly black slave, and the difficult life he and his fellow slaves endured, earned either praise or condemnation. Abolitionists across the North thought it was brilliant and oh-so-true. Southern critics, however, complained that it was inaccurate in how it portrayed plantation life.

Borrowing from Real Life

Stowe was a dedicated abolitionist who was more concerned about illustrating the evils of slavery than creating an accurate view of life on the plantation. Although she lived in Cincinnati for 18 years, just across the river from the slave state of Kentucky, she had little actual experience with Southern plantations. The information in most of her book was taken either from abolitionist literature or her own imagination. Stowe was researching a series of articles she intended to write when she heard about a slave woman who escaped from her masters in Kentucky across the frozen Ohio River. She immediately realized that she could use such a scene in a book. One of the most exciting parts of *Uncle Tom's Cabin* features Eliza, the slave heroine, escaping across the ice.

A Publishing Sensation

Uncle Tom's Cabin first appeared in 1851, serialized in the abolitionist newspaper *National Era*. Its popularity there led to the book's publication as a complete work the next year. It was an instant success, selling 10,000 copies in the first week and more than 300,000 by the end of its first year. *Uncle Tom's Cabin* had even greater popularity in Britain, where more than one million copies sold within a year. Stowe exposed the general public to an issue that most knew very little about. But the book didn't simply educate its readers—it also provoked heated debates in state and federal legislatures.

Interestingly, given today's negative meaning of the term "Uncle Tom," the character in Stowe's book demonstrated strength and traits that were quite heroic. In one instance, when ordered to whip a sickly female slave, Tom refuses and suffers the lash himself. He is ultimately killed by his wicked master, Simon Legree, because he will not betray two runaway slaves.

Not Controversial Enough?

As shocking as some found *Uncle Tom's Cabin*, many, particularly radical abolitionists, didn't think the book went far enough in denouncing slavery. Others, usually those who lived in the South, condemned the book as grossly exaggerated. One of Stowe's admirers was William Lloyd Garrison, the editor of abolitionist newspaper *The Liberator*. "I estimate the value of antislavery writing by the abuse it brings," he wrote to tell her. "Now all the defenders of slavery have let me alone and are abusing you."

I Will Be Heard!

William Lloyd Garrison was a journalist and one of the leaders of the antislavery movement in the mid-nineteenth century.

✳ ✳ ✳ ✳

WILLIAM LLOYD GARRISON was born Newburyport, Massachusetts on December 10, 1805. When he was thirteen, he became the apprentice of the editor of the *Newburyport Herald*, starting a life of journalism. He held several newspaper jobs during his teenage years. In 1826, he borrowed enough money to buy the *The Newburyport Essex Courant*, which he renamed the *Newburyport Free Press*. In 1828, Garrison moved to Boston. While he was working as an editor for a newspaper there, he met Benjamin Lundy, who convinced him of the necessity for abolition and offered him a position as an editor for the *Genius of Emancipation*, an antislavery paper.

In 1830, Garrison founded *The Liberator*, which slowly became one of the most prominent abolitionist newspapers in the country. In 1833, he founded the American Antislavery Society, but his refusal to go beyond simply writing about the evils of slavery caused a rift in the group, and several members left. Garrison also believed that the Union should be disbanded, arguing that the Constitution supported slavery. He and

Frederick Douglass made a series of anti-Union speeches in 1847. In 1854, when the Kansas-Nebraska Act was passed, Garrison criticized it as a terrible deal for the Union. During the Civil War, Garrison persisted in criticizing the U.S. Constitution, although he also supported Lincoln's policies.

Garrison died on May 24, 1879, and was buried in Boston.

Quotes from William Lloyd Garrison

"Our country is the world—our countrymen are all mankind."

"I cherish as strong a love for the land of my nativity as any man living. I am proud of her civil, political and religious institutions—of her high advancement in science, literature and the arts—of her general prosperity and grandeur. But I have some solemn accusations to bring against her."

"The compact which exists between the North and the South is a covenant with death and an agreement with hell."

"And now let me give the sentiment which has been, and ever will be, the governing passion of my soul: 'Liberty for each, for all, and forever!'"

"Tell a man whose house is on fire to give a moderate alarm; tell him to moderately rescue his wife from the hands of the ravisher; tell the mother to gradually extricate her babe from the fire into which it has fallen; —but urge me not to use moderation in a cause like the present. I am in earnest—I will not equivocate—I will not excuse—I will not retreat a single inch—and I will be heard!"

"Little boldness is needed to assail the opinions and practices of notoriously wicked men; but to rebuke great and good men for their conduct, and to impeach their discernment, is the highest effort of moral courage. "

"With reasonable men, I will reason; with humane men I will plead; but to tyrants I will give no quarter, nor waste arguments where they will certainly be lost."

"We may be personally defeated, but our principles never."

"You cannot possibly have a broader basis for any government than that which includes all the people, with all their rights in their hands, and with an equal power to maintain their rights."

An Abolitionist in the Senate

"Where Slavery is, there Liberty cannot be; and where Liberty is, there Slavery cannot be."

Charles Sumner, a Senator from Massachusetts from 1851–1874, was a leader of the Radical Republican faction that fought for the abolition of slavery and destruction of the Confederacy.

✳ ✳ ✳ ✳

CHARLES SUMNER WAS born on January 6, 1811, in Boston. His father Charles Sr. was an abolitionist and early advocate of school integration. Charles was the Clerk of the Massachusetts House of Representatives and practiced law. In 1825 he was elected Sherriff of Suffolk County. He taught his son from a young age that slavery was evil and that not only must enslaved African-Americans be given their freedom, but that they should have equal rights as whites. Sumner graduated from Harvard in 1834 and was admitted to the bar the same year. He travelled in Europe in 1837, and while in France he observed a group of black students at the Sorbonne who were treated as equals by their white classmates. The experience led him to realize that racial prejudice was a learned construct, and left him determined to return to America and work for the abolitionist cause.

Senator Sumner

In 1848, Sumner cofounded the Free Soil Party; the party's primary issue was opposing the expansion of slavery into new states as they joined the Union. In 1851, Sumner was elected to the United States Senate on the Free Soil ticket. In 1852, he delivered a speech to the floor of the Senate titled "Freedom National, Slavery Sectional" that criticized the Fugitive Slave Act, which had been passed as part of the Great Compromise of 1850.

He said then:

"Full well I know, sir, the difficulties of this discussion, arising from prejudices of opinion and from adverse conclusions, strong and sincere as my own. Full well I know that I am in a small minority, with few here to whom I may look for sympathy or support. Full well I know that I must utter things unwelcome to many in this body, which I cannot do without pain. Full well I know that the institution of slavery in our country, which I now proceed to consider, is as sensitive as it is powerful—possessing a power to shake the whole land with a sensitiveness that shrinks and trembles at the touch. But, while these things may properly prompt me to caution and reserve, they cannot change my duty, or my determination to perform it. For this I willingly forget myself, and all personal consequences. The favor and good-will of my fellow-citizens, of my brethren of the Senate, sir, —grateful to me as it justly is—I am ready, if required, to sacrifice. All that I am or may be, I freely offer to this cause."

In 1854, the Kansas-Nebraska Act made the issue of slavery in Kansas up to the settlers of the new state. Pro-slavery and anti-slavery forces—including John Brown—poured into Kansas to contest the issue. By October 1855, major violence had broken out across Kansas. Sumner gave a speech in May 1856 over two days that condemned the Kansas-Nebraska Act and demanded Kansas be admitted to the Union as a free state. He attacked the authors of the act, Steven A. Douglas and Samuel Butler, personally, saying, "The Senator from South Carolina has read many books of chivalry, and believes himself a chivalrous knight, with sentiments of honor and courage. Of course he has chosen a mistress to whom he has made his vows, and who, though ugly to others, is always lovely to him; though polluted in the sight of the world, is chaste in his sight I mean the harlot, Slavery. For her, his tongue is always profuse in words." The next day, Butler's cousin Preston Brooks attacked Sumner in the Senate chamber with a heavy cane, beating him unconscious.

Sumner's injuries were so extensive that he was unable to return to the Senate the following year. On his doctor's advice, he sailed to Europe to recover. While in Europe, he met with Alexis de Tocqueville, Harriet Beecher Stowe, and the French Prime Minister, among others. He returned to the United States in 1858 and resumed his duties in the Senate the following year.

Civil War

In 1861, Southern Senators withdrew from the Senate as the Civil War commenced. Sumner, the leader of the Radical Republican faction, repeatedly urged President Lincoln to free the slaves. In 1861 and 1862 the Republicans passed two acts that allowed the Union Army to free slaves who were captured from the Confederate Army. In 1861, Sumner spoke at the Massachusetts Republican Convention, and declared that the chief goal of the Union was to abolish slavery. At Sumner's urging, Lincoln signed the Emancipation Proclamation on January 1, 1863.Following the war, Sumner championed extending civil rights to African Americans, and moved for giving them the vote as well. He was argued for a broad form of Reconstruction that would promote mandatory education and redistribute Southern land to freed slaves.

Sumner continued to serve in the Senate until his death on March 11, 1874. He was laid in state in the U.S. Capitol rotunda, and buried in Cambridge, Massachusetts.

All Men and Women

"We hold these truths to be self-evident, that all men and women are created equal."

Elizabeth Cady Stanton was one of the founders of the women's rights movement. She called for the Seneca Falls Convention on women's rights, helped write the Convention's Declaration of Sentiments, and advocated for the vote as president of the National Woman Suffrage Association.

Elizabeth Cady was born in Johnstown, New York, on November 12, 1815. She attended Emma Willard's Troy Female Seminary, graduating in 1832. She often visited the home of her cousin Gerrit Smith, a social reformer and abolitionist, and their discussions shaped her early ideas about abolition, temperance, and equal rights for women. In 1840, Cady married Henry Stanton, himself a social reformer. She kept her own last name, and the couple removed the word "obey" from their marriage vows. On their honeymoon, they travelled to London to attend the World's Anti-Slavery Convention.

Seneca Falls and the Women's Rights Movement

At the Convention, the men in attendance voted to exclude the women from participating, and forced them to sit in a segregated section. Cady Stanton, along with other women in attendance, was outraged. She met with Lucretia Mott, and there the two discussed holding a worldwide convention on women's rights for the first time. Cady Stanton and Mott would remain friends and collaborators for the rest of their lives.

In 1848, their vision of a women's rights convention became reality at Seneca Falls, New York. At the convention, Cady Stanton pushed for the adoption of a resolution that declared obtaining suffrage for women was a key tenet of the women's rights movement. There was initial opposition to the resolution. Nevertheless she persisted, and with the support of Frederick Douglass and other attendees, it passed; "Resolved, That it is the duty of the women of this country to secure to themselves their sacred right to the elective franchise." She also helped draft the Declaration of Sentiments that laid out the goals of the movement.

Cady Stanton worked on the cause of abolishing slavery during the Civil War, and afterwards she continued to work for women's rights. In 1868, she began publishing the weekly newspaper *Revolution* with Susan B. Anthony, and co-founded the National Woman Suffrage Association (NWSA) with

Anthony in 1869. She became the organization's first president, and held the post for the next twenty years, when the NWSA merged with the American Woman Suffrage Association. Cady Stanton served as president of the joint organization, the National American Woman Suffrage Association, for two years.

Later Life and Work

Cady Stanton travelled regularly as a speaker on women's rights, including issues that went beyond suffrage: she advocated reforms of women's custody rights, birth control access, property and employment rights, and the right to divorce. She strongly advocated for a woman's right to ride a bicycle, and promoted the concept of the New Woman, who was independent and mobile.

She opposed the 14th and 15th Amendments on the grounds that they did not include women. This led to a major break in the women's rights movement between those suffragists who supported extending the vote to African American men first and women second, and those who advocated universal suffrage. She called for an amendment that would extend the vote to women, first at Seneca Falls and for the remainder of her life.

Between 1881 and 1886, she worked with Anthony and Matilda Joslyn Gage on the first three volumes of the *History of Woman Suffrage*, and in 1895 she published the first volume of *The Woman's Bible*. Cady Stanton had long held that organized religion helped to prevent women from obtaining equal rights. The second volume was published in 1898.

Elizabeth Cady Stanton died on October 26, 1902. Eighteen years later, on August 18, 1920, the 19th Amendment was passed, guaranteeing women the right to vote.

Resistant to Tyranny

"Cautious, careful people, always casting about to preserve their reputation and social standing, never can bring about a reform. Those who are really in earnest must be willing to be anything or nothing in the world's estimation."

✳ ✳ ✳ ✳

SUSAN B. ANTHONY was one of the leading figures of the women's rights movement in the 19th century. She co-founded the National American Woman Suffrage Association with Elizabeth Cady Stanton, and fought tirelessly her entire life to secure the vote for women.

Susan Brownell Anthony was born in Adams, Massachusetts on February 15, 1820. Her parents were Quakers, and they instilled in her a strong sense of morals and justice. From a young age, Anthony worked on social issues. In 1826, her family moved to Battenville, New York, and Anthony went to study at a Quaker boarding school near Philadelphia. Her father's mill went bankrupt in the 1830s, and after finishing school Anthony returned to Battenville, where she worked as a teacher. In the 1840s, her family moved to Rochester, New York, where they soon became involved in the movement to abolish slavery. Their farm in Rochester became a meeting place for abolitionists. In Rochester, Anthony secured a position as the headmistress of the girls' school at Canajoharie Academy.

Early Activism

Stanton left her job at the Academy in 1849 and dedicated herself more to causes of social reform. She was involved in the temperance movement, which organized against the production and sale of alcohol. The temperance movement was an important precursor to the women's rights movement; it was largely a movement of women, and often motivated by domestic abuse at the hands of drunken husbands. The temperance movement also showed women that there was significant political power in organizing a mass movement, even in spite of the fact that they were denied the vote.

In 1851, Anthony met Elizabeth Cady Stanton, who had been one of the organizers of the Seneca Falls Convention on women's rights. They would become lifelong friends and allies in the fight for universal suffrage. In 1852, they cofounded the Women's New York State Temperance Society, and were soon fighting for the vote. The pair cofounded the New York State Woman's Rights Committee, which campaigned for the right of women to own property and vote. In 1856, Anthony joined the American Anti-Slavery Society, and fought for the cause of abolition until the end of the Civil War.

Fighting for Suffrage

Following the War, Anthony concentrated on fighting for women's rights, and with Cady Stanton, she created the American Equal Rights Association in 1866. They began publishing *The Revolution*, a weekly newspaper that called for full and equal rights for women. In 1869, they founded the National Woman Suffrage Association, and Anthony travelled around the country speaking out for the women's right to vote. In 1872, she voted illegally in the presidentially election. She was arrested, and disputed the charges in court, but lost the case and was fined $100. She never paid the fine. At her trial, she quoted what she termed, "an old revolutionary maxim," saying, "Resistance to tyranny is obedience to God." (The saying is now often attributed to her, though it didn't originate with her.)

In 1881, she began writing the *History of Woman Suffrage*, with Cady Stanton and Matilda Joslin Gage. Several volumes were published over the next five years. In 1898, with the help of Ida Husted Harper, she wrote her autobiography, *The Life and Work of Susan B. Anthony: a Story of the Evolution of the Status of Women*.

In 1905, Anthony met President Theodore Roosevelt to lobby for a constitutional amendment that would extend the right to vote to women. She died the next year, on March 13, 1906, in Rochester, New York. 14 years later, on August 18, 1920, the 19th Amendment was passed, guaranteeing that right to women. In 1979, her portrait was minted on dollar coins; she was the first woman in history to be featured on US currency.

Quotes from Susan B. Anthony

"The men and women of the North are slaveholders, those of the South slaveowners. The guilt rests on the North equally with the South."

"I do not demand equal pay for any women save those who do equal work in value. Scorn to be coddled by your employers; make them understand that you are in their service as workers, not as women."

"Here, in the first paragraph of the Declaration, is the assertion of the natural right of all to the ballot; for how can 'the consent of the governed' be given, if the right to vote be denied?"

"The only chance women have for justice in this country is to violate the law, as I have done, and as I shall continue to do."

"I do not ask the clemency of the court. I came into it to get justice, having failed in this, I demand the full rigors of the law."

Let Woman Then Go On...

Lucretia Mott was an early social reformer, women's rights activist, and abolitionist, and one of the founders of the Free Religious Association and Swarthmore College.

✳ ✳ ✳ ✳

LUCRETIA MOTT (NEE Coffin) was born in Nantucket, Massachusetts on January 3, 1793 to Quaker parents. When she was 13 years old, she was sent to a Quaker boarding school in New York. Upon graduating, she remained there and began working as a teacher's assistant. She met James Mott while she was there, and the couple married in 1811 and moved to Philadelphia. In 1821, she was ordained as a Quaker minister, and was soon recognized for her outstanding oratory and fiery speeches.

When the Quakers split, she and James aligned with the progressive wing of the movement in 1827.

Mott was passionately opposed to slavery from an early age, and advocated divestment from products produced by slave labor. Because of this position she convinced her husband to leave the cotton trade in 1830. She became an early supporter of William Lloyd Garrison, a leading abolitionist, and worked with his American Anti-Slavery Society. Her outspoken opposition to the slave trade resulted in her regularly being threatened with physical violence, but she never wavered in her commitment to the abolitionist cause.

In 1840, Lucretia and James travelled to London to attend the World Anti-Slavery Convention as a delegate. The Convention voted to prevent women in attendance from being full participants in the proceedings, and required the female delegates to sit in a segregated section. The leaders of the Anti-Slavery movement wanted to prevent the cause of women's liberation from being associated with the worldwide movement for abolition. Mott met Elizabeth Cady Stanton at the Convention, and the two became friends and partners in the movement for women's rights.

Seneca Falls

At the World Anti-Slavery Convention, Mott and Stanton first discussed the idea of holding a convention on women's rights. In 1848, they organized the first such convention in history at Seneca Falls, New York. Stanton presented a resolution that declared the goal of the women's rights movement to secure the right to vote; Frederick Douglass spoke in favor of the resolution. Mott opposed it, believing that electoral politics in the United States were tarnished by the institution of slavery. Ultimately, however, she conceded that the right to vote must be extended to women, and the individual woman can choose whether or not to exercise that right. She was one of the signers of the Seneca Falls Declaration of Sentiments. She continued to work for the cause of women's rights for the remainder of her life, and in 1849 published the highly influential treatise Discourse on Woman. It read in part:

"Let woman then go on—not asking as favor, but claiming as right, the removal of all the hindrances to her elevation in the scale of being—let her receive encouragement for the proper cultivation of all her powers, so that she may enter profitably into the active business of life; employing her own hands, in ministering to her necessities, strengthening her physical being by proper exercise, and observance of the laws of health. Let her not be ambitious to display a fair hand, and to promenade the fashionable streets of our city, but rather, coveting earnestly the best gifts, let her strive to occupy such walks in society, as will befit her true dignity in all the relations of life. No fear that she will then transcend the proper limits of female delicacy. True modesty will be as fully preserved, in acting out those important vocations to which she may be called, as in the nursery or at the fireside, ministering to man's self-indulgence.

Then in the marriage union, the independence of the husband and wife will be equal, their dependence mutual, and their obligations reciprocal."

Later Work

In 1864, Mott and several other leading Quakers founded Swarthmore College in Philadelphia. Following the Civil War, Mott became the first president of the American Equal Rights Association, an organization that worked to secure voting rights for all citizens, including women and freed slaves. The organization split into two factions that disagreed on whether to prioritize women's suffrage or African-American suffrage, and while Mott resigned in 1868, she worked to reconcile the two factions. She also remained active in anti-war movements, and helped found the Universal Peace Union in 1866. In 1867 she co-founded the Free Religious Association, an interfaith organization dedicated to abolition.

Rapping on the Ballot Box

"Woman stock is rising in the market. I shall not live to see woman vote, but I'll come and rap on the ballot box."

Lydia Maria Child was a writer, antislavery activist, and feminist who wrote a number of abolitionist books that were highly influential in the lead-up to the American Civil War.

❋ ❋ ❋ '❋

LYDIA MARIA CHILD (née Francis) was born in Medford, Massachusetts on February 11, 1802. Her family was Unitarian and staunchly abolitionist. Her brother, a Unitarian minister and a professor at Harvard, was highly influential in her education, and helped expose her to works by Homer and Milton. She became a teacher at the Medford Seminary in 1824, and that year she wrote her first novel, *Hobomok*. In 1826 she founded the *Juvenile Miscellany*, a magazine for children. She married David Child, an editor, in 1828. When she met William Lloyd Garrison in 1831, she dedicated herself to the cause of abolition.

Child published *An Appeal in Favor of That Class of Americans Called Africans* in 1833. The book argued for equality of education and employment for African-Americans. The book was very controversial, and led to her magazine failing in 1834. But it also served to convince many people to join the abolitionist movement. She began editing the *National Anti-Slavery Standard* in 1841. Child and her husband moved to Wayland, Massachusetts in 1852. There she wrote several more books, including *The Freedmen's Book*, a compilation of the life stories of former slaves, in 1865, and *An Appeal for the Indians*, which called for justice for Native Americans. *An Appeal* helped encourage the creation of the U.S. Board of Indian Commissioners and President Grant's adoption of a Peace Policy towards Native Americans.

Despite her long history of advocacy, Child's most familiar words to us today are probably from her poetry for children; she was the writer of "Over the river and through the wood, to grandfather's house we go."

Lydia Maria Child died October 20, 1880, at her home in Wayland.

Quotes from Lydia Maria Child

"We first crush people to the earth, and then claim the right of trampling on them forever, because they are prostrate."

"They [the slaves] have stabbed themselves for freedom—jumped into the waves for freedom—starved for freedom—fought like very tigers for freedom! But they have been hung, and burned, and shot—and their tyrants have been their historians!"

"The nearer society approaches to divine order, the less separation will there be in the characters, duties, and pursuits of men and women. Women will not become less gentle and graceful, but men will become more so. Women will not neglect the care and education of their children, but men will find themselves ennobled and refined by sharing those duties with them; and will receive, in return, co-operation and sympathy in the discharge of various other duties, now deemed inappropriate to women. The more women become rational companions, partners in business and in thought, as well as in affection and amusement, the more highly will men appreciate home."

"I think we have reason to thank God for Abraham Lincoln. With all his deficiencies, it must be admitted that he has grown continually."

"Yours for the unshackled exercise of every faculty by every human being."

I Pledge Allegiance...

Francis Bellamy, a Christian socialist minister and writer, penned the U.S. Pledge of Allegiance in 1892.

✳   ✳   ✳   ✳

FRANCIS JULIUS BELLAMY was born on May 18, 1855 in Mount Morris, New York, to a deeply religious Baptist family. His family moved to Rome, New York when he was five years old, where his father became the minister of the First Baptist Church. Bellamy became a minister as well as a young man, and studied theology at the University of Rochester. After graduation, he travelled the Northeast to spread the Baptist ministry. He married Harriet Benton in 1881, and they had two sons, John and David. Bellamy unsuccessfully sought the nomination of the Prohibition Party during the 1882 election for Governor of New York. He later identified as a socialist.

The Pledge of Allegiance

Bellamy began working for the *Youth's Companion,* a magazine that promoted religion and patriotism, in 1891. The magazine featured contributions by luminaries of the day, including Mark Twain, Harriet Beecher Stowe, Booker T. Washington, and Jack London. Three years before he was hired, the magazine had started a campaign to sell American flags to public schools. James Upham, the head of marketing for the magazine, came up with the idea when he decided that American patriotic sentiment was diminished. Upham believed that it should be his life's goal to instill an appreciation for the ideals the country was founded on and a sense of nationalism in the youth of the day.

By 1892, the *Youth's Companion* had distributed more than 25,000 American flags to public schools across the nation. The demand for flags was fading, and Upham was looking for a way to revitalize it. That year was the 400th anniversary of Columbus' arrival in the Americas, and Upham conceived

of using it to give the flag movement a boost. The *Youth's Companion* called of a national day celebrating Columbus in schools all over the nation, during the World's Columbian Exposition in Chicago. A flag salute was to be part of the celebration. Upham asked Bellamy to write the pledge. As a socialist, he originally wanted to include the words "fraternity" and "equality" in the Pledge, but knowing that the committee on the celebration was opposed to equality for African-Americans and women, he decided against it.

The September 8, 1892 edition of the magazine published Bellamy's version of the Pledge, and he went to a national convention of school superintendents to promote the Columbus Day celebration. The convention was in favor of it, and put together a committee of educators to organize the program, with Bellamy as the chair. The program included a flag-raising ceremony followed by a recitation of the Pledge.

In 1942, the Pledge was formally recognized by the United States Congress, but changed Bellamy's words "my flag" to "the flag of the United States of America." The change was suggested because of the many immigrant children in public schools. In 1954, George MacPherson Docherty, the pastor of the New York Avenue Presbyterian Church, delivered a sermon as President Eisenhower sat in the first pew that urged adding the words "under God" to the Pledge. Eisenhower took his advice, and a bill to do so was introduced in Congress the next day.

Francis Bellamy died on August 28, 1931 in Tampa, Florida. He was buried in Rome, New York.

The Story Behind "America the Beautiful"

Katherine Lee Bates was an English professor at Wellesley College and a poet who wrote one of America's iconic patriotic ballads.

✳   ✳   ✳   ✳

KATHERINE LEE BATES was born in Massachusetts on August 12, 1889. Although her family was so poor that they had to move in with her mother's sister when she was twelve years old, her mother ensured that Bates received a good education. Bates attended Wellesley College, one of the few universities that accepted women at the time, and graduated in 1880. While she was an undergraduate one of her poems was published in the *Atlantic Monthly*. In 1888, she began teaching at Wellesley, and eventually became the chair of the college's English department. She became an expert on William Shakespeare, and in 1893 she wrote *The English Religious Drama*.

On a trip to Pike's Peak, Bates had her first ideas for the poem "America the Beautiful." It was first published in the July 1895 issue of *The Congregationalist*, though the original version of the text was a bit different than what we see today:

O beautiful for halcyon skies,
For amber waves of grain,
For purple mountain majesties
Above the enameled plain!
America! America!
God shed His grace on thee,
Till souls wax fair as earth and air
And music-hearted sea!

O beautiful for pilgrim feet
Whose stern, impassioned stress
A thoroughfare for freedom beat

Across the wilderness!
America! America!
God shed His grace on thee
Till paths be wrought through wilds of thought
By pilgrim foot and knee!

O beautiful for glory-tale
Of liberating strife,
When once or twice, for man's avail,
Men lavished precious life!
America! America!
God shed His grace on thee
Till selfish gain no longer stain,
The banner of the free!

O beautiful for patriot dream
That sees beyond the years
Thine alabaster cities gleam
Undimmed by human tears!
America! America!
God shed His grace on thee
Till nobler men keep once again
Thy whiter jubilee!

It quickly became popular, and was set to a tune by Samuel
Ward in 1910. Bates continued to write collections of poetry
and literary criticism, as well as travel writing about her visits
to Spain and England. One of her most notable collections of
poetry, *Yellow Clover: A Book of Remembrance*, was a collection
of sonnets for her intimate partner and lifelong companion
Katherine Coman, whose death in 1915 had left Bates heart-
broken. She retired from her professorship at Wellesley in
1925, and published her last collection of poems, *The Pilgrim
Ship*, in 1926.

Katharine Lee Bates died on March 28, 1929 in Wellesley,
Massachusetts.

The Current Lyrics

The current lyrics read:
O beautiful for spacious skies,
For amber waves of grain,
For purple mountain majesties
Above the fruited plain!
America! America!
God shed His grace on thee
And crown thy good with brotherhood
From sea to shining sea!

O beautiful for pilgrim feet,
Whose stern, impassioned stress
A thoroughfare for freedom beat
Across the wilderness!
America! America!
God mend thine every flaw,
Confirm thy soul in self-control,
Thy liberty in law!

O beautiful for heroes proved
In liberating strife,
Who more than self their country loved
And mercy more than life!
America! America!
May God thy gold refine,
Till all success be nobleness,
And every gain divine!

O beautiful for patriot dream
That sees beyond the years
Thine alabaster cities gleam
Undimmed by human tears!
America! America!
God shed His grace on thee
And crown thy good with brotherhood
From sea to shining sea!

William Hazlitt

"The love of liberty is the love of others; the love of power is the love of ourselves."

In unpretentious prose, William Hazlitt presented brilliant humanistic essays that explored the people and philosophy of early 19th century England.

✳ ✳ ✳ ✳

ILLIAM HAZLITT WAS born in Kent, England, on April 10, 1778. His family moved first to Ireland and then to America, where his father, a Unitarian minister, supported the revolution. When he was nine years old, his family returned to England. William was a quiet, reserved child, but he was also an avid reader. As a young man, he was not adept at conversation or writing, and in his early twenties he began painting. In 1802 he travelled to Paris and secured a job at the Louvre, but when war between England and France broke out in 1803, he had to return to England.

Despite his skill as a painter, Hazlitt began studying philosophy and metaphysics, and in 1805 he published his first book on the subject, *On the Principles of Human Action*, which gained him modest recognition as a competent philosopher. In 1808, he married Sarah Stoddart. He wrote several other essays, but none of them sold particularly well, and by 1811 he was bankrupt. He took a job lecturing on philosophy in London and began writing articles for the *Morning Chronicle* on literary and dramatic criticism. A collection of his articles, *A View of the English Stage*, was published in 1818 and earned him widespread recognition as a talented dramatic critic.

In 1817, he was a major contributor to the two-volume work *The Round Table*, a collection of 52 essays, 40 of which were written by him. That same year, he published the dramatic critical work *Characters of Shakespeare's Plays*, which was very well received and cemented his reputation as a critic. He became friends with contemporary writers such as Percy Bysshe Shelley and John Keats. His reputation as a sought-after lecturer grew, and he published collections of his lectures in *On the English Poets* in 1818 and *On the English Comic Writers* and *Lectures on the Dramatic Literature of the Age of Elizabeth* in 1819.

Divorce and Later Life

While his success as a critic was on the rise, Hazlitt's personal life was unraveling. In 1819 he and Sarah separated, and they divorced in 1822. He had a brief but disastrous affair with his landlord's daughter, and wrote about his experience in *Liber Amoris, the New Pygmalion* in 1823. He never stopped writing, however, and published his two best known works during this time. In 1821 he published *Table Talk*, a series of essays on art, aesthetics, and philosophy, and *The Plain Speaker*, a similar collection, in 1826.

In 1824, Hazlitt married a widow named Isabella Bridgwater in what may have been an arrangement of convenience. He wrote *The Spirit of the Age* in 1825; the book was a collection of 25 character sketches of notable philosophers, poets, and politicians of the day. He spent much the next year travelling in Europe, which he described in *Notes of a Journey in France and Italy* in 1826. He immersed himself in writing a four-volume biography of Napoleon, and partly due to this, and his general neglect, Bridgwater suddenly left him in 1827.

Hazlitt's final book recounted his long friendship with the painter James Northcote, and was published in 1830. He died in September of that year in Soho, London.

Don't Even Ask

When Civil War general William Tecumseh Sherman was mentioned as a possible Republican nominee for president in 1884, it is said that he rejected the notion, stating, "If nominated, I will not run. If elected, I will not serve." Although the intent of the quote is accurate, the words are wrong.

On March 31, 1968, when President Lyndon B. Johnson announced that he would not seek his party's nomination for a second full term as the nation's chief executive, his impending resignation was referred to a "Shermanesque statement."

President Johnson's words on that fateful evening, "I shall not seek, and I will not accept, the nomination of my party for another term as your president," were similar in intent to those used by William Tecumseh Sherman 84 years earlier. But what exactly did Sherman say when he turned down an invitation to run for the country's highest office? In addition to the dozen words inscribed above, some historians claim that Sherman was more concise and more adamant in his refusal to seek public office, declaring, "If nominated, I will not accept; if drafted, I will not run; if elected, I will not serve."

So where does the truth lie? According to the fourth edition of Sherman's memoirs, published in 1891, the general drafted a telegram to a colleague on June 5, 1884, in which he stated, "I will not accept if nominated and will not serve if elected." However, as early as 1871, Sherman had made his intent of not pursuing a political post perfectly clear. In an interview with *Harper's Magazine* on June 24 of that year, he said, "I never have been and never will be a candidate for president; that if nominated by either party I should peremptorily decline; and even if unanimously elected I should decline to serve."

He Stole My Line!

"That government is best which governs least" is commonly attributed to not one but three superstars of history: Thomas Jefferson, Thomas Paine, and Henry David Thoreau. Who in this grab bag of greats is the quote's true source?

That would be Henry David Thoreau, who wrote the words in *Civil Disobedience* (1849), his renowned essay about the necessity of individual resistance to unjust government. Thoreau wrote, "I heartily accept the motto—'That government is best which governs least'; and I should like to see it acted up to more rapidly and systematically." Thoreau was actually referencing another source, which is almost certainly the *United States Magazine and Democratic Review*, a political and literary journal that contained the words "The best government is that which governs least" in its first issue.

The quote is often attributed to Thomas Paine or Thomas Jefferson, who were both, like Thoreau, outspoken in defense of individual rights and limited government. The quote is not found in the writings of either man, and it is not clear why they are both reputed to be the progenitors. It is possible that these words, or something similar to them, were often spoken in conversations among the group of intellectuals to which both Paine and Jefferson belonged. If that's the case, Thoreau picked them up and wrote them down, thus ensuring their place in the towering tomes of famed quotes.

In *Civil Disobedience*, side by side with the "governs least" quote, is the first appearance of a similar yet more provocative passage that has also survived the test of time. Thoreau said, "It finally amounts to this, which I also believe—'That government is best which governs not at all'—and when men are prepared for it, that will be the government which they will have."

The Nez Percé War of 1877

For three months in 1877, Chief Joseph's 700 Nez Percé battled the U.S. Army as they retreated to Idaho. They were outnumbered by the 2,000-strong U.S. Army contingent, but they fought with great dignity and courage. Chief Joseph surrendered on October 5, 1877, in the Bear Paw Mountains in Montana. His surrender speech has lasted through the ages.

"I am tired of fighting... It is cold, and we have no blankets. The little children are freezing to death. My people, some of them, have run away to the hills, and have no blankets, no food. No one knows where they are—perhaps freezing to death. I want to have time to look for my children, and see how many of them I can find. Maybe I shall find them among the dead. Hear me, my chiefs! I am tired. My heart is sick and sad. From where the sun now stands I will fight no more forever."

—FROM CHIEF JOSEPH'S SURRENDER SPEECH

Herbert Spencer

"No one can be perfectly free till all are free; no one can be perfectly moral till all are moral; no one can be perfectly happy till all are happy."

A political theorist, philosopher, and biologist of Victorian England, Spencer enthusiastically supported evolution as the underlying force of all aspects of the physical world, from biological development to human society.

✳ ✳ ✳ ✳

HERBERT SPENCER WAS born in Derbyshire, England, on April 27, 1820. He had eight brothers and sisters, none of whom survived past childhood. As a young man he was a sick child, and never fully recovered from a series of chronic nervous breakdowns. Spencer's father George, originally a Methodist, converted to Quakerism, and served as secretary to the Derby Philosophical Society, which was founded by Charles Darwin's grandfather Erasmus. George Spencer passed his antiauthoritarian ideas and appreciation for empirical science on to his son.

As a young man, Spencer worked as a civil engineer on the railway, reading and writing articles for progressive journals in his spare time. In 1848 he secured a position as an assistant editor for *The Economist*, a weekly financial journal. While there, he interacted with many of the leading intellectuals of his day, including Thomas Huxley and John Tyndall. Spencer regularly published articles that discussed limiting the role of government in society. He advocated a laissez-faire economy, and supported abolishing national education and Poor Laws. In 1851, he published *Social Statistics* to rave reviews. He became close friends with George Eliot, whose office was across the street from his own; while they discussed marriage, they never married, but remained close friends and confidants all their lives.

In 1855, he wrote *Principles of Psychology*, which was controversial but also quietly influential. He was one of the first intellectuals to popularize the concept of evolution, and actually wrote about the theory seven years before Darwin wrote *On the Origin of Species*. Spencer's book, *A Developmental Hypothesis*, published in 1852, was not taken seriously primarily because it did not propose a system for natural selection, but in it, Spencer coined the phrase "survival of the fittest." (See page 145.)

Evolution and Social Darwinism

Spencer's ideas on evolution led him to the theory he is best remembered for, Social Darwinism. The idea applies the theory of natural selection to society, and argues that government-initiated social programs based in humanitarian efforts to help the needy were detrimental to society, as they interfered with the "natural order" of the survival of the fittest. Spencer argued that four concepts from developmental biology—growth, differentiation, integration, and adaptation—could be directly applied to understanding a growing society. He was not opposed to private charities, but believed that government programs would create families who were dependent on social programs.

Spencer was also opposed to intermarriage between Westerners and people from other cultures, notably the Japanese. He argued that mixing "divergent varieties" of people from "divergent modes of life" would produce people who were "adapted to neither." He said that immigration in general, and immigration in America in particular, would eventually give rise to "immense social mischief…and social disorganization."

Spencer was perhaps the most influential political philosopher of the Victorian era. He was the first philosopher to sell over a million copies of his books. His was hailed by contemporary philosophers and political thinkers, and his ideas continued to influence Western political thought for the rest of the 19th century. In the beginning of the 20th century, however, his reputation declined sharply.

Spencer died in 1903, and is buried at Highgate Cemetery near George Eliot.

Sitting Bull

"What treaty that the white man ever made with us have they kept? Not one."

Sitting Bull was one of the most famous Native American chiefs, and led one of the most tenacious resistance efforts against encroachment on Native lands by the United States.

✳ ✳ ✳ ✳

SITTING BULL WAS born in what is now South Dakota in 1831. His father, Returns Again, was a Hunkpapa Lakota warrior of high regard. Initially, Sitting Bull was called "Slow" because he did not show much talent for battle. When he was ten years old, he killed his first buffalo, and at fourteen he fought well in a battle against a rival tribe. Following the battle he was renamed Tatanka Iyotanka, or "Buffalo Who Sits Down." In his early twenties, he became the leader of the Lakota Strong Heart Society, the warrior class of the tribe. During the Dakota War of 1862–1864, Sitting Bull encountered American soldiers for the first time, leading the defense of a small village against an attack by 4,000 U.S. troops in the Battle of Killdeer Mountain.

Red Cloud's War

In 1866, Red Cloud, the leader of the Oglala Lakota, initiated a series of attacks on U.S. forts in Montana. During the war, which lasted for two years, Sitting Bull organized and led attacks against several forts and ambushed soldier and settler wagon trains and outposts in guerilla attacks. The Lakota were able to force the United States to offer a peace treaty in 1868. The Treaty of Fort Laramie guaranteed the Black Hills territory to the Lakota people, as well as all of the land west of the Missouri River in South Dakota and parts of surrounding territories. Sitting Bull did not think any part of the land should be ceded to whites, and he continued to sporadically attack forts in Missouri for the next several years.

The Great Sioux War

In the 1870s, gold was discovered in the Black Hills. Prospectors poured into the area, and the U.S. government abandoned the treaty and declared war on any Natives who resisted attempts to seize the land. During the fall of 1875, Natives from Lakota and other tribes arrived at Sitting Bull's camp. In June 1876 they held a ritual Sun Dance at the camp to prepare to defend their land. At the gathering, Sitting Bull danced for three days, during which time he had a vision in which the warriors defeated the Army.

Several days after the Sun Dance, a force led by General George Crook was attacked by Lakota warriors at Rosebud creek, forcing the Army to retreat after a long and bloody battle. A week later, General George Armstrong Custer encountered Sitting Bull's camp near the mouth of the Little Bighorn River. Not realizing the size of the force, Custer attacked. Sitting Bull led thousands of Lakota and Cheyenne warriors in a devastating counterattack that annihilated Custer's forces in an overwhelming victory. Custer was killed along with more than 250 of his men.

The United States responded to the defeat by flooding the Black Hills with troops, forcing many of the Lakota to surrender. In 1877, Sitting Bull led his band into Canada, where he remained for the next four years. In 1881 he returned to the Dakota Territory and was imprisoned for two years. In 1885 he joined Buffalo Bill's Wild West Show, but he soon grew disillusioned with the performance and returned to the Lakota land, where he lived in a cabin on the Grand River.

In 1889, the government grew fearful that Sitting Bull would join the burgeoning Ghost Dance movement, a spiritual movement that preached a return of Native lands to the Lakota. They sent police to arrest Sitting Bull on December 15, 1890. When Sitting Bull resisted, the police shot him in the head and chest, killing him.

"When I was a boy the Sioux owned the world; the sun rose and set on their land; they sent ten thousand men to battle. Where are the warriors today? Who slew them? Where are our lands? Who owns them?"

The Plessy v. Ferguson Dissent

John Marshall Harlan served as an associate justice on the United States Supreme Court for more than thirty years. A complicated figure who supported the Union but opposed Emancipation, Harlan was the only justice to dissent on Plessy v. Ferguson, *the decision that upheld "separate but equal" racial segregation.*

✳ ✳ ✳ ✳

JOHN MARSHALL HARLAN was born in Kentucky on June 1, 1833. His father, James Harlan, practiced law and served in the House of Representatives from 1835–1839. Harlan was named after Supreme Court Justice John Marshall. He graduated from college in 1850 and studied law, passing the Kentucky bar in 1853. He practiced law at his father's practice. During the Civil War, although he supported slavery, Harlan joined the Union Army and served as a colonel during the war.

In 1863, he resigned his commission in the Army and won election as the State's Attorney General on the Union Party ticket. In 1871 and 1875, he ran unsuccessfully for governor of Kentucky as the Republican nominee. In 1876, he helped Rutherford B, Hayes secure the Republican nomination for the presidential election.

Supreme Court

Hayes appointed Harlan to the Supreme Court in 1877. During his tenure on the Court, Harlan gained a reputation for writing dissenting opinions on major cases. He was the sole dissenter on the *Civil Rights Cases* decision, which struck down the 1875 Civil Rights Act as unconstitutional. Harlan wrote that the decision to strike down the Act, which banned racial discrimination by private citizens, was overly narrow, and that striking down the Act would violate sections of the Fourteenth Amendment.

In 1890, Louisiana passed a law that required railroads to have separate cars for whites and African-American riders. A group of New Orleans residents decided to challenge the law, and Homer Plessy volunteered to be arrested in order to instigate a test case. He bought a first-class ticket and boarded a "whites only" car. He was arrested and tried in Orleans Parish. Plessy lawyers argued that the law violated the Thirteenth and Fourteenth Amendments. Plessy lost the trial in Orleans Parish and the appeal to the Louisiana Supreme Court, and his lawyers appealed to the Supreme Court.

In *Plessy v. Ferguson*, the Supreme Court ruled that the Louisiana law did not violate the Fourteenth Amendment, laying the foundation for more than sixty years of "separate but equal" laws in the South. *Plessy* would not be overturned until *Brown v. Board of Education* in 1954. In Plessy, Harlan was again the lone dissenter to the judgment. He argued that the Constitution did not recognize one class of citizens to be dominant over another, and that everyone is equal under the law. He also presciently wrote that the Court's decision would one day be as infamous as the *Dred Scott v. Stanford* decision of 1857.

Harlan also dissented in *Hawaii v. Mankichi* in 1903, in which the Court ruled that constitutional protections did not automatically extend to people living in US Territories. He dissented again in 1905, when the Court struck down a New York law that established a maximum number of hours for a work week. Harlan remained on the Court until he died on October 14, 1911, in Washington, DC. His grandson, John Marshall Harlan II, served as an associate justice on the Supreme Court from 1955–1971.

Excerpts from the Dissent

"If a white man and a black man choose to occupy the same public conveyance on a public highway, it is their right to do so, and no government, proceeding alone on grounds of race, can prevent it without infringing the personal liberty of each."

"The white race deems itself to be the dominant race in this country. And so it is, in prestige, in achievements, in education, in wealth, and in power. So, I doubt not, it will continue to be for all time, if it remains true to its great heritage and holds fast to the principles of constitutional liberty. But in the view of the Constitution, in the eye of the law, there is in this country no superior, dominant, ruling class of citizens. There is no caste here. Our Constitution in color-blind and neither knows nor tolerates classes among citizens. In respect of civil rights, all citizens are equal before the law."

"If evils will result from the commingling of the two races upon public highways established for the benefit of all, they will infinitely less than those that will surely come from state legislation regulating

the enjoyment of civil rights upon the basis of race. We boast of the freedom enjoyed by our people above all other peoples. But it is difficult to reconcile that boast with the state of the law which, practically, puts the brand of servitude and degradation upon a large class of our fellow citizens, our equals before the law. The thin disguise of "equal" accommodations for passengers in railroad coaches will not mislead anyone, nor atone for the wrong this day done."

Give Me Your Tired, Your Poor...

A talented poet, Emma Lazarus is best known for her work "The New Colossus," which is displayed on the foundation of the Statue of Liberty.

❋ ❋ ❋ ❋

EMMA LAZARUS WAS born in New York City on July 22, 1849. She had six brothers and sisters; her parents Moses and Esther Lazarus were descended from a family that had lived in New York since before the American Revolution. Her family was affluent, having amassed a fortune in the sugar refining business, and owned a mansion in Rhode Island. Lazarus received a classical education and became interested in poetry at a young age. In 1866, her father published her poetry in *Poems and Translations Written between the Ages of Fourteen and Seventeen*. When she was nineteen, Lazarus sent some of her poems to Ralph Waldo Emerson, one of the most famous writers of the time. He was impressed enough that he agreed to privately tutor her.

Lazarus developed a widespread reputation for her writing while during her lifetime, and became friends with other well-known writers of the 19th century, such as Robert Browning and Henry James. She published dozens of poems in popular magazines such as *Lippincott's* and *The Century*. She published several books of poetry, including *Admetus and Other Poems*, in 1871, and *Songs of a Semite* in 1882. She also wrote a novel and two plays and translated the works of German poets into English. Lazarus was also a leading literary critic, and argued that a new American aesthetic, unique from European literary style, was beginning to take form, and cited Walt Whitman, Harriet Beecher Stowe, and others as representative of this new aesthetic.

Lazarus was also an advocate for the rights of Jewish people in America and abroad. In the 1880s she was speaking against anti-Semitism and aiding Jewish refugees who were immigrating to the United States. She helped establish the Hebrew Technical Institute, which provided vocational training for new arrivals, and supported creating a Jewish homeland in Palestine.

The New Colossus

Lazarus is today best known for her poem "The New Colossus," which she wrote in 1883. When France presented the Statue of Liberty to America to stand in New York harbor, New York needed to raise enough money to build the pedestal the statue would stand on. Lazarus donated the poem to a fundraising auction. She was initially opposed to the idea, but when she was told the statue would be a momentous sight to immigrants arriving in New York harbor, she agreed. The poem speaks directly to those immigrants, welcoming them from faraway lands to the United States, the "Land of Exiles."

The poem was read at the auction, but forgotten for several years after, until Lazarus' friend Georgina Schuyler found the poem and led an effort to have it and Lazarus memorialized. In 1903, a plaque displaying the poem was installed on the Statue's base. The poem fundamentally changed the symbolism of the Statue: originally it was meant to be a tribute to the principles of international democracy, but afterwards, the Statue became a welcoming symbol that greeted immigrants and refugees arriving in America.

Emma Lazarus died in New York on November 19, 1887, when she was just thirty-eight years old. She is buried in Brooklyn's Beth-Olom Cemetery.

The New Colossus

Not like the brazen giant of Greek fame,
With conquering limbs astride from land to land;
Here at our sea-washed, sunset gates shall stand
A mighty woman with a torch, whose flame
Is the imprisoned lightning, and her name
Mother of Exiles. From her beacon-hand
Glows world-wide welcome; her mild eyes command
The air-bridged harbor that twin cities frame.
"Keep, ancient lands, your storied pomp!" cries she
With silent lips. "Give me your tired, your poor,
Your huddled masses yearning to breathe free,
The wretched refuse of your teeming shore.
Send these, the homeless, tempest-tost to me,
I lift my lamp beside the golden door!"

Henry Cabot Lodge

"If a man is going to be an American at all let him be so without any qualifying adjectives."

Henry Cabot Lodge was a Republican Senator from 1893–1924 and longtime friend and advisor to Theodore Roosevelt. Following World War I, he successfully blocked the United States from participating in the newly created League of Nations.

✳ ✳ ✳ ✳

HENRY CABOT LODGE was born May 12, 1850, in Beverly, Massachusetts, and grew up in the Beacon Hill area of Boston. He graduated from Harvard College in 1872 and attended law school there, graduating in 1874 and passing the bar in 1875. In 1876, he was one of the first students to be granted a doctorate in history at Harvard. He remained there for three years as a history professor, and continued to write and edit works on American history for the rest of his life. In 1880, he was elected to the Massachusetts House of Representatives, and to the United States House of

Representatives in 1887. In 1893, he was elected to the Senate as a Republican.

During the Spanish-American War, Lodge strongly supported U.S. intervention in Cuba, arguing that the United States had a moral obligation to support the "Cubans in their struggle for freedom." He also was in favor of the U.S. invasion of the Philippines, and following the war, argued in favor of annexing them. He also advocated strengthening the U.S. Navy and expanding American influence in foreign affairs.

A close friend of Theodore Roosevelt, he supported his decision to support James Blaine in the 1884 presidential election even as many republicans—dubbed "Mugwumps"—were defecting to Democratic candidate Grover Cleveland. Cleveland won the election, but Lodge's support for Blaine cemented his political standing in the Republican Party. When Roosevelt broke with the Republicans and ran as a Progressive Party candidate in 1912, Lodge supported Taft, the Republican incumbent. Woodrow Wilson won the election, and Roosevelt and Lodge reconciled soon after.

The League of Nations

In 1917 the United States entered World War I, and Lodge was in support of the war effort, and attacked pacifists for undermining the nation's security. He also accused Wilson of allowing the nation to be underprepared for the imminent war. In 1916 he gave a speech at the League to Enforce Peace in which he backed the idea of an international peacekeeping apparatus. Following the war, Wilson and Senate Democrats wanted the United States to join the League of Nations.

Lodge was tepidly in favor of joining, but not without reservations that he felt would help maintain American sovereignty. He believed it was unwise to enter into an international agreement that would allow the League to compel the United States to enter a war without the approval of the Congress. In 1919, Republicans regained control of the Senate, and

Lodge was made the chairman of the Senate Foreign Relations Committee. This placed him in a position that allowed him to direct the opposition to the adoption of the Treaty of Versailles, which contained the covenant that established the League of Nations. He took a two-pronged approach: first he delayed the debate on the Treaty in order to allow enthusiasm to die down, and then he introduced the Lodge Reservations, a series of amendments that would require passage by Congress before the United States would abide by League decisions. President Wilson refused to accept the Lodge Reservations, and the Treaty was defeated in the Senate. When Warren G. Harding was elected in 1920, it was considered a vindication of Lodge's opposition to the Treaty.

Lodge on Immigration

There was a tide of nativist and anti-immigration sentiment in the 1890s and early 1900s; an Immigration Restriction League was formed to agitate against unskilled immigrants, and against immigrants who came from countries perceived as "less American." Italian-American immigrants in particular were seen as unable to assimilate and a threat to America's future. Lodge took part in this anti-immigration sentiment. After an incident where eleven Italian-Americans were lynched by a mob in New Orleans, he called for new restrictions on Italian-American immigrants.

In an 1888 speech he said, "Let every man honor and love the land of his birth and the race from which he springs and keep their memory green. It is a pious and honorable duty. But let us have done with British-Americans and Irish-Americans and German-Americans, and so on, and all be Americans ... If a man is going to be an American at all let him be so without any qualifying adjectives; and if he is going to be something else, let him drop the word American from his personal description."

Henry Cabot Lodge died on November 9, 1924, and was buried in Cambridge.

By and For the Working People

Samuel Gompers was one of the most significant leaders of the early labor movement. He cofounded and was the first president of the American Federation of Labor.

* * * *

S AMUEL GOMPERS WAS born in London on January 27, 1850 to a very poor family. He attended a free Jewish school when he was six years old, where he learned to read and write. When he was thirteen, his family immigrated to the United States, settling in New York City. Gompers began working with his father as a cigar-maker. They joined the Cigar-Makers' Union, and Gompers quickly rose to a leadership position in the organization. He built the Union into a successful organization despite the advent of technological advances that could threaten cigar-makers' jobs.

In 1881, Gompers helped organize an informal association of several unions in order to promote collective bargaining across trades. In 1886, the loose affiliation was formally organized into the American Federation of Labor (AFL). Gompers became its president, and was the first leader of a national union who encouraged using strikes as an effective weapon to put pressure on employers.

Gompers was vehemently opposed to the Socialist faction within the AFL, believing that they acted toward political ends rather than toward securing conditions from employers. An immigrant himself, he opposed open immigration from Europe for fear that it would lower wages in the United States. He supported the U.S. invasion of Cuba during the Spanish Civil War, believing that it would improve conditions of cigar-makers there.

After a long illness, Gompers died on December 13, 1824, in San Antonio, Texas.

Quotes from Samuel Gompers

"What does labor want? We want more schoolhouses and less jails; more books and less arsenals; more learning and less vice; more leisure and less greed; more justice and less revenge; in fact, more of the opportunities to cultivate our better natures."

"No lasting gain has ever come from compulsion. If we seek to force, we but tear apart that which united, is invincible. There is no way whereby our labor movement may be assured sustained progress in determining its policies and its plans other than sincere democratic deliberation until a unanimous decision is reached. This may seem a cumbrous, slow method to the impatient, but the impatient are more concerned for immediate triumph than for the education of constructive development."

"[The labor movement is] a movement of the working people, for the working people, by the working people, governed by ourselves, with its policies determined by ourselves..."

"The trade union movement represents the organized economic power of the workers... It is in reality the most potent and the most direct social insurance the workers can establish."

A Dedicated Organizer

"While there is a lower class I am in it, while there is a criminal element I am of it; while there is a soul in prison, I am not free."

Eugene Debs was a labor organizer, activist, founder of the Industrial Workers of the World, and the Socialist Party's candidate for U.S. president five times from 1900–1920.

❋ ❋ ❋ ❋

EUGENE DEBS WAS born on November 5, 1855 in Terre Haute, Indiana, to French immigrants. His father owned a textile mill. When he was 14, Debs dropped out of school to work in railroad shops on the Vandalia Railroad. He eventually became a locomotive fireman, and when he was twenty years old, helped to organize a local chapter of the Brotherhood of Locomotive Firemen, a workers' organization that offered benefits to locomotive firemen's families. He was the associate editor of the *Firemen's Magazine* in 1878 and was elected the national secretary and treasurer of the Brotherhood in 1880. Debs was elected to the Indiana legislature in 1885.

From the beginning, Debs was a dedicated advocate of organizing labor by industry rather than by craft; he wanted to organize all railroad workers into one comprehensive union, rather than have them divided into smaller unions based on their role in operating the railroad. His efforts to join the various railroad craft-based brotherhoods were initially unsuccessful, but in 1893 he was elected president of the American Railway Union, which had been organized in February of that year. The ARU was able to bring railroad workers from the different brotherhoods together into the first industrial union in the United States.

The Pullman Strike

The ARU gained national recognition in 1894, when it conducted a strike of railroad workers against unilateral wage cuts by the Great Northern Railway. The strike lasted 18 days and forced the company to agree to arbitration of the wage cuts, and the arbitrators found in favor of the strikers. It was the first major victory of an industrial union. Inspired by this success, railroad workers on other lines began to organize for higher wages. On May 11, 1894, the worker of the Pullman Palace Car Company went on strike without authorization from the leadership of the ARU.

The Pullman Company ran a company-owned town on the outskirts of Chicago; Pullman's workers were required to live in his town and shop at his stores. Debs opposed the strike at first, but when he learned of the workers' conditions and the fact that their wages went right back to the company, he endorsed it. The company refused to arbitrate the strike, and on June 26, railroad workers across the company began refusing to work on any trains that had Pullman cars. On July 2, President Grover Cleveland ordered 20,000 troops to Chicago in order to suppress the strike. Along with other leaders of the ARU, Debs was arrested and imprisoned for six months. While the ARU leadership was in prison, the Pullman company, backed by the troops, crushed the strike.

Socialism

Debs passed the time in prison reading, and came across the works of Karl Marx and other writers who were critical of capitalism. He began to view the labor movement with a new class consciousness, and in 1897 he announced that he was a socialist and founded the Socialist Party of America. In 1905 he founded the Industrial Workers of the World, with the motto "one big union," that attempted to unite all unions into one. He later left the group as it grew increasingly radical. Debs ran for president on the Socialist ticket five times; in 1904 he received more than 400,000 votes. In 1918 he was convicted of sedition and had his citizenship revoked. In 1920, he received his highest popular vote—more than 900,000—while he was in prison for criticizing the government's prosecution of radicals under the Espionage Act.

Debs died on October 20, 1926. His book *Walls and Bars* was published the following year.

Seeking the Best Possible

"My temperament and habit had always kept me rather in the middle of the road; in politics as well as in social reform I had been for 'the best possible.'"

Jane Addams was a social reformer, feminist and pacifist who founded Hull House, one of the first settlement houses in America in 1889. She was the first female president of the National Conference of Social Work, and won the Nobel Peace Prize in 1931.

✳ ✳ ✳ ✳

J ANE ADDAMS WAS born in Cedarville, Illinois on September 6, 1860. Her father was a businessman and Illinois State Senator, and was personal friends with Abraham Lincoln. As a child, Addams suffered from tuberculosis that left her with a curved spine, which made it difficult for her to play with other children. She would have lifelong health problems as a result. As a teenager, she read Charles Dickens, and his books inspired a desire to work among the poor. She studied at Rockford Female Seminary, graduating in 1881. That same year her father died, and she inherited $50,000 (about $1.2 million today). Addams attended medical school in Philadelphia, but illness prevented her from completing her degree. In 1887, she travelled with her close friend Ellen Gates Starr to London, where she visited Toynbee Hall. Toynbee was a settlement house; these establishments brought middle-class volunteers to live and work among the poor, providing day care, education, and healthcare. Addams and Starr resolved to start a settlement house in Chicago.

Hull House

In 1889, Addams and Starr opened Hull House on Chicago's near west side. It was one of the first settlement houses in North America. The settlement was named for the building's original owner, and Addams and Starr organized it to provide services to immigrants and poor residents of the surrounding tenements. The organization eventually grew to more than ten buildings. Hull House provided child care, a public kitchen, educational classes, an art gallery, a summer camp, and social programs. Hull House built the first public playground in the city, and established a theatre group that has been credited as the founder of the American "Little Theatre" Movement.

Addams and Starr also provided emergency medical services when doctors were not available, often volunteering as midwives and nurses. Hull House also was one of the first organizations that sheltered victims of domestic violence. Hull House advocated for the people it served, leading efforts to pass legislation at all levels of government on child welfare, women's suffrage and healthcare and immigration reform.

Other Work

Addams served on the Chicago Board of Education beginning in 1905, chairing the Board's School Management Committee. In 1910, she was elected the first female president of the National Conference of Social Work, and the next year she established the National Federation of Settlements, which she led for more than twenty years. At the outbreak of World War I, Addams became the chair of the Women's Peace Party, and spoke regularly on pacifism. In 1915, she attended the International Congress of Women at the Hague with social reformers Emily Greene Balch and Alice Hamilton. From 1919 to 1929 she was president of the 1919 to 1929. She shared the Nobel Peace Prize in 1931 for her work promoting pacifism.

Many of the Hull House buildings were torn down when the University of Illinois at Chicago was built in 1963. The original Hull House remains on Halsted Avenue on the near west side, and is now a museum. Jane Addams died on May 21, 1935, in Chicago, Illinois.

Contested Conventions and Smoke-Filled Rooms

Harry Micajah Daugherty was an influential Republican politician and Attorney General. Although he was only elected to public office once, and served briefly, he played a significant role in other candidacies, notably securing the nomination for Warren G. Harding in the 1920 election. He also left behind a quote that is dragged out today whenever there might be a contested convention…

✳   ✳   ✳   ✳

H ARRY MICAJAH DAUGHERTY was born in Ohio on January 26, 1860. His father, a farmer, died of diphtheria when he was four years old, and he was forced to start working at a young age to help support the family. His mother wanted Daugherty to become a Methodist minister, but he had no interest in that path. He attended the University of Michigan law school beginning in 1878, despite the fact that he had no undergraduate degree. While he was in law school, he made money by gambling; he won a large amount of money betting on the 1880 presidential election. He and his brother were also successful at sports gambling, in part because they tapped telegraph wires to get the results of sports matches ahead of bookmakers. When Daugherty graduated from law school in 1881, he returned to Ohio to begin practicing law. He gained a reputation for helping his clients by using political contacts.

The Political Fixer

In 1883, Daugherty was a delegate to the Ohio State Republican Convention. While there, he assisted Joseph Foraker, a judge, in securing the party's nomination in the 1883 race for governor. Although Foraker lost the 1883 race, he was elected governor in 1885, and returned his friend's favor by helping him get elected as chairman to the Fayette County Republican Central Committee. Daugherty had a brief career as an elected official, serving two terms in the Ohio State Legislature form 1890–1894. In 1893, he moved his law practice to Columbus, Ohio, and was very successful representing corporations in litigation.

Daugherty unsuccessfully ran for Ohio Attorney General in 1895 and Governor in 1897, and decided he was better suited to run other candidate's campaigns than seek public office himself. In 1896, the Ohio Republicans split into two factions when Daugherty's old friend Foraker ran for John Sherman's senate seat. Seeing that Foraker had less support than Sherman, Daugherty abandoned his friend rather than be on the losing side, and threw his support behind Sherman.

The Election of 1920

In 1899 Daugherty first met Warren G. Harding, who ran for Lieutenant Governor in 1902. He managed Harding's successful 1914 campaign for Senate and his campaign for president in 1920. Daugherty was one of the bosses of the Ohio Republican Party by 1920, and his position allowed him to propel Harding to the nomination after the convention was deadlocked on selecting a candidate.

At the time, the *The New York Times* reported that Daugherty had said that the nomination would be decided when, "some 12 or 15 men, worn out and bleary eyed for lack of sleep, will sit down about 2 o'clock in the morning around the table in a smoke-filled room in some hotel and decide the nomination." Indeed, in a room at the Blackstone Hotel in Chicago, Daugherty managed to secure the nomination on the tenth ballot.

When Harding named Daugherty Attorney General, public opinion was firmly against him, and he was nearly impeached in 1922. He was dogged by rumors of political corruption, and in 1924 when he refused to launch a Justice Department investigation into potential misconduct by officials in the Harding administration, President Calvin Coolidge fired him. In 1927 Daugherty went on trial twice for charges of fraud and graft while he was Attorney General. Both trials resulted in hung juries. He returned to Ohio to practice law, maintaining his innocence. In 1932, he co-authored *The Inside Story of the Harding Tragedy*, which defended himself and the former president.

Law and…Disorder?

"The confrontation was not created by the police. The confrontation was created by the people who charged the police. Gentlemen, get the thing straight, once and for all. The policeman isn't there to create disorder. The policeman is there to preserve disorder."

✳   ✳   ✳   ✳

CHICAGO MAYOR RICHARD J. Daley's infamous slip of the tongue served to capture the chaos of the Democratic National Convention in 1968. During the four-day event, anti-Vietnam War protesters filled the parks and streets of Chicago, despite Daley's refusal to grant them permits. Police responded with such violence that a government-funded study later described their actions as a "police riot."

The convention took place during a year of extreme unrest. The assassination of Martin Luther King, Jr. led to riots across the county, the Vietnamese Tet Offensive struck a major blow against public confidence in the American war effort, and the assassination of Robert Kennedy left the Democratic Party without one of its leading anti-war candidates. Vice President Hubert Humphrey, who appeared poised to win the nomination, announced just before the convention that he stood with President Lyndon Johnson in support of the war.

Daley knew that protests were likely and was determined to keep control of the city. He assembled close to 12,000 police officers, 7,500 Illinois National Guardsmen, 7,500 Army troops, and 1,000 secret service agents. Clashes between police and protesters started the night before the convention and continued over several days. During the most violent encounter known as the "Battle of Michigan Avenue," police beat people indiscriminately, injuring reporters and bystanders as well as protesters.

Between the bloody street scenes and the fractious and unruly convention, the events in Chicago helped turn the political tide toward Republican presidential candidate Richard Nixon and his promise to restore "law and order."

Blood, Sweat, and Tears

When he became prime minister during his nation's darkest hours of World War II, Winston Churchill told Parliament: "I would say to the House, as I said to those who have joined this government: 'I have nothing to offer but blood and toil, tears and sweat.'" But that's not the first time the phrase had been used.

✳   ✳   ✳   ✳

WINSTON POURED A defiant dash of mustard on the last part, bracing listeners for the lousy war news to come. Perhaps it was a preemptive strike against the inevitable second-guessing that would surely result; it simply wouldn't do to raise hopes that he knew he could not possibly fulfill. He made good on his offer: Britain got all the blood, toil, tears, and sweat it could want, and Winston's words gained fame.

The error lies not in the quote itself but in denying Churchill credit for having uttered the words. By the same token, however, people are wrong to assume that he invented the phrase. Churchill likely borrowed from Henry James's 1886 novel *The Bostonians*, which contains a similar line. Another source could have been Theodore Roosevelt, who used this reference in at least one oration: "The credit belongs to the man who is actually in the arena, whose face is marred by dust and sweat and blood...."

Borrowed from the Best

Roosevelt may have used it in other contexts as well. If that's where Churchill got it, he at least had an excellent source. The prime minister was a generation younger than Roosevelt and had probably read some of his speeches. Perhaps he remembered the reference when it came time to compose this vital address to Parliament. Maybe Churchill was even hoping the reference would stir the heart of Teddy's younger cousin, Franklin D. Roosevelt, then president of the United States—which is where Britain's greatest hope for victory lay.

Patriotism Is Not Enough

Edith Cavell was a World War I nurse, humanitarian and spy. She assisted Allied soldiers in escaping German-occupied Belgium. She was captured and executed, and faced the firing squad courageously. Her death made her an icon of the Allied cause.

✳   ✳   ✳   ✳

EDITH CAVELL WAS born on December 4, 1865, in a village in Norwich, near London. Her father, an Anglican priest, had a significant influence on her deep religious faith. Cavell was educated at Norwich High School for Girls, and worked for several years as a governess in London and Brussels. In 1895, she began training to be a nurse at London Hospital, completing her studies in 1900. She worked in a number of hospitals in London until 1907, when she was recruited to be the matron of a new nursing school in Brussels. In 1910 she began publishing *L'infirmiere (The Infirmary)*, one of the first professional nursing journals. Cavell taught nursing in various hospitals in Belgium and worked to improve nursing standards of care.

The First World War

In 1914, while Cavell was in England, World War I began. She returned to Belgium to work at her hospital, which became a hub for the Red Cross. Germany invaded Belgium that year and imposed strict martial law on Brussels. When the Allies withdrew from Belgium, hundreds of British soldiers were left behind, trapped in Brussels. Cavell began assisting them, hiding them in the hospital and in safe houses around Brussels. She was able to organize a network of sympathetic Belgians who helped the soldiers escape to Holland. She also continued her nursing duties, and treated wounded soldiers from both the German and Allied armies. The martial law outlawed "aiding the enemy," and threatened strict punishments. Nevertheless, she persisted in helping Allied soldiers despite the danger.

In 1915, German authorities began to suspect Cavell of helping Allied soldiers escape to Holland. In addition to organizing the network, she was also outspoken about the injustice of war and the occupation of Brussels. In August she was arrested and interned at St. Gilles prison. During her brief trial, she neither denied the charges nor attempted to defend her actions, saying only that she felt she was compelled to assist anyone in need, regardless of their nationality. The military tribunal found her guilty of treason and sentenced her to death. The sentence was roundly criticized as being overly harsh, especially because she freely admitted her actions, and had saved the lives German as well as Allied soldiers.

The U.S. minister to Belgium, Brand Whitlock, along with the Spanish ambassador, petitioned the German High Command to commute Cavell's death sentence. He warned them that executing a nurse would damage their international reputation. Count Harrach responded that he would prefer to see Cavell executed than see any German harmed, and that he only regretted he did not have more English women to shoot.

Cavell was kept in solitary confinement in the weeks leading up to her execution, and was permitted few visitors. The night before she was executed, Reverend Stirling Gahan, and Anglican chaplain, visited her in her cell, and recorded her iconic statement regarding patriotism: "Patriotism is not enough. I must have no hatred or bitterness towards anyone."

Edith Cavell was executed by firing squad on the morning of October 12, 1915. She became an icon of the British war effort, and her execution was widely used in propaganda efforts.

Let Me Finish!

Software magnate Ross Perot had a relatively low national profile until he decided that he might like to be president of the United States in 1992.

❉   ❉   ❉   ❉

DISMISSED BY MANY as merely an eccentric, self-made Texas billionaire, Ross Perot created a political storm in the 1992 presidential election by mounting the most serious challenge to the two-party political establishment in modern history. In June '92, Perot led the polls with 39 percent compared with 31 percent for incumbent Republican George H. W. Bush and 25 percent for Democrat Bill Clinton. Come November, Perot secured 18.9 percent of the popular vote, making him the most successful third-party candidate since Theodore Roosevelt in 1912. Considering his colorful background and unpredictable temperament, Perot would indeed have made an unusual choice for president.

The Myth of Perot

The future candidate was born in Texarkana in 1930 to a Texas horse trader and cotton dealer. Many of the details about his early life have been embellished over the years, not least by the man himself, so it can be tricky deciphering fact from fiction. One popular story has it that, as a boy, Perot delivered newspapers on horseback through a dangerous neighborhood of Texarkana so he could escape any potential muggers. When an unauthorized biography of the Texan was published in 1990, the author claimed that Perot in fact rode a bicycle rather than a horse. For six months, Perot barraged the author and his editor with witness accounts supporting the horse story, demanding a retraction. (He never received one.)

Perot graduated from the U.S. Naval Academy at Annapolis. He was unhappy with what he saw as the Navy's stifling bureaucracy and the immoral behavior of his comrades, but he served his four-year obligation. Working in sales at IBM proved more to the young Perot's liking, and he quickly became one of the company's top salespeople. In 1962, he fulfilled his annual sales quota as early as January. This accomplishment, he claims, caused IBM to force him to sit idly for the next six months because the company didn't want its sales representatives earning more than their managers. This may be another myth, however, as his former colleagues refute these claims, saying that sales reps were actively encouraged to sell more than 100 percent of their quotas and thus earn more commission.

The Birth of EDS

Perot began the road to fortune in 1962 by founding Electronic Data Systems, or EDS, a company that provided computer systems to other companies without their own machines by outsourcing idle time on still other companies' computers. When he sold the company to General Motors in 1984, the deal made Perot a billionaire and GM's largest stockholder until the company bought him out two years later.

Popular myth has it that Perot launched EDS with a mere $1,000 in the form of a check from his wife, Margot. Even Perot himself acknowledges that this claim isn't entirely accurate. The $1,000 check merely covered the registration fee for the new corporation, not the entire start-up costs. Still, Perot propelled the Texarkana-based company to incredible growth, despite some highly unusual business practices.

Under Perot, EDS employees were required to sign an agreement whereby, if they were fired or quit within two years, they had to repay the company $9,000 to cover their training expenses. Men had to wear dark suits with white shirts and a tie and always keep their hair cut short. Facial hair was banned, and recruiters were allegedly directed not to hire any man with a weak handshake in case he turned out to be a homosexual. Perot also decried marital infidelity, which he was known to punish by firing. While women made up 44 percent of the

EDS workforce, only 5 percent of senior personnel were female. This was in part because Perot preferred hiring former military men for key positions.

Conspiracy Theories

Perot's affinity for the military extended to supporting covert operations. In 1978, when two EDS executives working in Iran were arrested by revolutionary forces there, Perot recruited a retired U.S. Army officer to lead a group of volunteers in a secret mission to break them out. That story formed the basis of Ken Follett's thriller *On Wings of Eagles*. Perot also helped fund Oliver North's arms-for-hostages deal that came to light in the Iran-Contra scandal of 1986.

A renowned conspiracy theorist, Perot believed that U.S. government officials were actively involved in covering up the existence of American POWs still being held in Vietnam after that war ended. In 1985, he offered the Vietnamese $10 million for every American released, and in 1987, he traveled to Hanoi in order to directly negotiate with the Vietnamese authorities. At no time, however, did Perot reveal any evidence to support his claims. It was Perot's allegations of another conspiracy (this time aimed at him personally) that many political commentators believe were very costly to him in the 1992 election.

Politics as Usual

Despite leading the polls in June, Perot dropped out of the race in July. Just as suddenly, he resumed his bid on October 1. In an appearance on *60 Minutes* the week before the election, Perot made unsubstantiated claims that he dropped out of the race because the Republican Party had threatened to release compromising photos of his daughter prior to her wedding.

Perot's strong showing in the '92 vote meant that he qualified for federal funding for the 1996 election. But this time, running on the Reform Party ticket, Perot didn't fare quite as well at the polls. Many attribute this to his debate with Vice President Al Gore on CNN's *Larry King Live*. Perot's repeated requests to "let me finish" turned him into a figure of fun and ultimately signaled his political demise.

Since that time, Ross Perot has mostly kept a low political profile. In terms of business, after he was bought out by GM, Perot and his associates founded Perot Systems, an information technology company that rose to join the Fortune 1000. In 2009, the computer company Dell agreed to buy it for $3.9 billion in cash. That wouldn't be considered a bad way to finish in anyone's book.

"I don't have any experience in running up a $4 trillion debt. I don't have any experience in gridlock government, where nobody takes responsibility for anything and everybody blames everybody else."

Raging Against the Machine

"There's a time when the operation of the machine becomes so odious, makes you so sick at heart that you can't take part. You can't even passively take part. And you've got to put your bodies upon the gears and upon the wheels, upon the levers, upon all the apparatus, and you've got to make it stop. And you've got to indicate to the people who run it, to the people who own it, that unless you're free the machine will be prevented from working at all!"

✳   ✳   ✳   ✳

MARIO SAVIO WAS one of the student leaders at the University of California at Berkeley who organized massive demonstrations to protest the school's restrictions on political activity on campus. Over several months beginning in September of 1964, the students held a series of rallies and sit-ins that persuaded the university to ease its restrictions and also sparked the larger student protest movement of the 1960s.

The Berkeley student protests became known as the Free Speech Movement. Initially, student political groups resisted the administration's rules by setting up tables to offer political literature in prohibited areas. The situation escalated when eight participants were suspended and, soon after, one was arrested by campus police. Student supporters quickly surrounded the police car, resulting in a standoff that lasted more than 32 hours.

Savio's speech preceded a sit-in during which some 1,000 protesters occupied the university's administration building. More than 600 policemen were dispatched and more than 800 people were arrested. The following day, a crowd of 5,000 rallied in support of the students' cause.

The administration ultimately capitulated. Berkeley and many other university campuses soon became major sites of political activity, especially for protests against the Vietnam War.

Addressing the Problem of the Color Line

"The problem of the twentieth century is the problem of the color line."

W.E.B. Du Bois was a historian, author, activist, and one of the leaders of the struggle to obtain civil rights for African-Americans during the first half of the 20th century. He co-founded the National Association for the Advancement of Colored People.

✳ ✳ ✳ ✳

WILLIAM EDWARD BURGHARDT Du Bois was born in Great Barrington, Massachusetts, on February 23, 1868, in Great Barrington, Massachusetts. He was able to attend school with white classmates, and his white teachers supported his academic studies. In 1885, he was accepted to Fisk University, a historically black college in Nashville, Tennessee. It was while he was in Nashville that Du Bois had his first encounters with Jim Crow laws and found himself treated as a second-class citizen.

While he was at Fisk, he began developing a deep awareness of the viciousness of American racism. After graduating from Fisk with a bachelor's degree, he attended Harvard College from 1888–1890, where he graduated *cum laude* with a bachelor's in history. He supported himself with scholarships and summer jobs while he studied. He began a graduate program in sociology at Harvard in 1891, and traveled to the University of Berlin to study at Humboldt-Universität. While he was in Germany, Du Bois was exposed to progressive political views and studied with some of the most prominent sociologists of the time. In 1895, he became the first African-American to receive a Ph.D. from Harvard.

Writing and Activism

In 1894, Du Bois accepted a teaching position at Wilberforce University in Ohio. While there, he married Nina Gomer in 1896. That summer, he accepted a year-long research appointment at the University of Pennsylvania. While there, he conducted sociological field work in the poor African-American neighborhoods of Philadelphia. In 1899, Du Bois published his findings in the first sociological case study of the African-American community, titled *The Philadelphia Negro: A Social Study*. His study found that racial segregation was a highly negative factor in social outcomes in African-American communities. In *The Philadelphia Negro*, Du Bois coined the term "the talented tenth," which he used to describe the probability of one in ten African-American men becoming leaders of their community.

Du Bois published *Strivings of the Negro People* in 1897, an article that argued against Frederick Douglass' assertion that African-Americans should integrate into white society. Instead, he wrote, African-Americans should embrace their roots while striving to secure a place in American society. That same year, he accepted a position at Atlanta University. While there, he produced dozens of academic papers and began hosting the annual Atlanta Conference of Negro Problems. He gained national prominence when he spoke out against Booker T. Washington's Atlanta Compromise. The Atlanta Compromise proposed that African-Americans in the South should submit to white rule, provided they were guaranteed education and economic opportunities. Dubois argued that African-Americans were guaranteed equal rights by the Fourteenth Amendment, and should fight for them.

In 1903, Du Bois wrote *The Souls of Black Folk*, a collection of essays on race. In it, he argues that African-Americans in the South deserve the right to vote, education, and equal treatment before the law. He also discusses his opposition to the Atlanta Compromise, and the Black experience in America. Although Du Bois was not the first to use the term "color line" to refer to segregation (it dates back to at least 1881, when it was used by Frederick Douglass), the essays in this book did emphasize the term and bring it to prominence.

Du Bois co-founded the co-founded the National Association for the Advancement of Colored People in 1909, and edited *The Crisis*, its monthly publication. The NAACP challenged Jim Crow laws with test cases in the courts, and organized political opposition to segregation in marches. By 1920, the organization had nearly 90,000 members.

W.E.B. Du Bois died on August 27, 1963, in Accra, Ghana. The next day, Dr. Martin Luther King Jr. delivered the iconic "I Have a Dream" speech at the March on Washington.

Calling for Nonviolence and Change

"Nonviolence is the first article of my faith. It is also the last article of my creed."

Mahatma Gandhi was the leader of India's independence movement, and pioneered the use of nonviolent civil disobedience to challenge powerful governments. His philosophy would influence many important movements in the 20th century, including the American Civil Rights Movement.

✳ ✳ ✳ ✳

MOHANDAS KARAMCHAND GANDHI was born in Kathiawar, India, on October 2, 1869. At age 13 he was married to Kasturba Makanji, and was a shy teenager. His family encouraged him to enter the legal profession, and in 1888 he travelled to London to study the law. When he returned to India in 1891, he initially struggled in his legal practice, and in 1893 he obtained a one year contract to work as a lawyer in South Africa. Upon arriving there, he was disgusted by the extreme racial segregation he witnessed.

Political Awakening

On June 7, 1893, while he was travelling by train, a white South African objected to him riding in the first-class railcar, and demanded he move to the rear of the train. Gandhi refused, and was thrown off the train at the next station. The next year, he founded the Natal Indian Congress to fight segregation. At the end of his contract, he remained in South Africa to organize against racial injustice. His legal practice expanded while he was there. During World War I, he organized an all-Indian ambulance corps for the British, believing that it would advance the cause of Indian self-determination. While in South Africa, he began studying world religions. In 1906, Gandhi organized his first *Satyagraha*, or "truth and firmness," a

campaign of civil disobedience to protest the South African government's treatment of Indians. Hundreds of protestors, including Gandhi, were imprisoned. In 1913, Gandhi was able to negotiate concessions from the government, including recognition of Hindu marriages. He returned to India in 1915.

Fight for Independence

Upon his return, Gandhi founded an ashram, or hermitage, that was receptive to all castes, which was unusual at the time. He lived as an ascetic, devoting himself to prayer, meditation, and fasting, and wore only a simple shawl and loincloth. In 1919, the Rowlatt Act was passed, which permitted authorities to imprison Indians without trial. Gandhi organized a Satyagraha campaign of peaceful demonstrations. On April 13, British troops opened fire on a peaceful crowd, slaughtering nearly 1,000 people. Gandhi assumed leadership of the Indian National Congress and called for a general strike. He was arrested in 1922 and pled guilty to sedition. He was released in 1924.

The Salt Satyagraha

In 1930, Gandhi organized a Satyagraha to protest the British monopoly on salt in India. He led a few dozen followers on a 240 mile march across Indian to the Arabian Sea. There, he made salt from evaporated seawater in a symbolic act of defiance. The Salt Satyagraha sparked a wave of civil disobedience across India, and more than 60,000 people were imprisoned for similar acts. The 1930 protests elevated Gandhi to a worldwide figure, and he was named *Time Magazine's* Man of the Year while he was still imprisoned for his act.

Independence

In 1931 Gandhi was released from prison, and negotiated to end the Salt Satyagraha in exchange for the release of thousands of political prisoners. He attended the London Round Table Conference to attempt to press for home rule, but was unable to secure concessions from the British. He returned to India, and was imprisoned again in 1932 by Viceroy Willingdon. He was eventually released, and left the Indian National Congress in 1934.

After Britain's influence was diminished following World War II, the Indian National Congress and the Muslim League jointly negotiated with Parliament for independence. Gandhi promoted a united India, but the final plan partitioned the subcontinent into two states: Muslim Pakistan and Hindu India. A wave of terrible violence swept the subcontinent, with attacks and reprisals between Muslims and Hindus leaving hundreds dead. Gandhi appealed for peace and expressed sympathy for Muslims, which enraged many Hindus who came to view him as a traitor.

On January 30, 1948, Nathuram Godse, a Hindu extremist who was angry at Gandhi's promotion of tolerance toward Muslims, shot him while he was on his way to a prayer meeting, killing him.

Culture

Casablanca

Nearly seven decades after its initial release, Casablanca (1942) remains one of the most popular and critically acclaimed motion pictures ever made. But was the line, "Play it again, Sam," actually spoken in the film?

※ ※ ※ ※

What Almost Was

THE STORY, DESPITE its World War II backdrop, is really one for the ages, a thrilling tale of lost love and personal sacrifice to which everyone can relate. And the casting couldn't have been better. Humphrey Bogart as disillusioned nightclub owner Rick Blaine and a radiant Ingrid Bergman as his former love, Ilsa, are simply riveting to watch. Add Claude Rains as the corrupt but endearing Captain Louis Renault; Paul Henreid as Victor Laszlo, Ilsa's resistance-fighter husband; and Dooley Wilson as Sam, the nightclub's resident pianist, and you have an almost perfect picture—which is a miracle, really, considering *Casablanca*'s chaotic creation.

Based on an unproduced play titled *Everybody Comes to Rick's* written by Murray Burnett and Joan Alison, *Casablanca* came very close to bearing absolutely no resemblance to the beloved film everyone knows today. Early in the process, it was rumored that Ronald Reagan was being considered for the role of Rick, and Warner Bros. wanted Hedy Lamarr to play Ilsa. But she was unavailable for loan-out from MGM, which kept her off the picture. Most startling of all, the movie's signature song, "As Time Goes By," was almost cut from the picture.

Luckily, the fates intervened and *Casablanca*, which was directed by Michael Curtiz, came to star Bogart and Bergman. But the filming was anything but easy. Howard Koch, one of the writers, described the movie as "conceived in sin and born in travail." Several key roles had yet to be cast when production began, and the script was in various stages of completion even as shooting began. Indeed, much of the script was written on the fly, with pages often delivered in the morning for that day's filming.

But perhaps most surprisingly of all, the cast didn't know how the movie would end until the final scene was filmed.

Studio Rush

Many of the problems were the result of Warner Bros.' decision to rush the film into production to capitalize on America's recent involvement in World War II. In fact, had the play upon which the movie was based been evaluated by studio readers just a few weeks earlier than it was, there was a very good chance it would have been rejected due to lack of interest.

But once approved, Warner Bros. went all in on *Casablanca*. The film's final budget came in at around $950,000. Bogart, who was red hot following *The Maltese Falcon* (1941), received $3,500 per week, while Bergman received $3,125 per week. The highest-paid actors were Conrad Veidt and Claude Rains, who received $5,000 weekly to play Major Strasser and Captain Renault, respectively. The lowest paid main performer was Wilson, who received just $500 per week. On top of it all, the studio ponied up a then-record $20,000 for the screen rights to *Everybody Comes to Rick's*.

Propelled by a tremendous wave of patriotism among American filmgoers, the studio's investment paid off in spades.

Warner Bros. had originally intended to release the film in 1943 but rushed it to select theaters just 18 days after Allied troops reclaimed the real-life Casablanca from the Germans in November 1942. The film received more free publicity when Franklin Roosevelt, Winston Churchill, and Josef Stalin held a summit in Casablanca that just happened to coincide with the film's general release on January 23, 1943.

Award Winner

Casablanca was also a hit at the Academy Awards, winning Oscars for Best Screenplay, Best Picture, and Best Director. No one was more surprised than Curtiz, who didn't even have a speech prepared.

Today, *Casablanca* remains a perennial favorite. In 1989, it was selected for preservation in the Library of Congress's National Film Registry, and in 1998, it was named the second greatest movie ever made (behind *Citizen Kane*) by the American Film Institute.

Play It

And no, the line, "Play it again, Sam," doesn't appear in quite that form. At various points, both Ilsa and Rick urge Sam to "Play it," but not to play it again. That hasn't stopped others from using the line: Woody Allen had a Broadway play and movie titled *Play It Again, Sam* that references *Casablanca* frequently. And of course that wasn't the only famous quote from the movie, which also included these immortal lines:

"Of all the gin joints, in all the town, in all the world, she walks into mine."

"I think this is the beginning of a beautiful friendship."

"We'll always have Paris."

"Here's looking at you, kid."

"You'll regret it. Maybe not today. Maybe not tomorrow, but soon and for the rest of your life."

In Conclusion...

Speaking of movies, here's a chance to prove your movie mettle. Match these last lines to the movies they ended.

✳ ✳ ✳ ✳

1. "...All right, Mr. DeMille, I'm ready for my close-up."

2. "Eliza? Where the devil are my slippers?"

3. "Hey, Stella! Hey, Stella!"

4. "I do wish we could chat longer, but I'm having an old friend for dinner. Bye."

5. "I'm not a cabdriver. I'm a coffeepot."

6. "Life is a state of mind."

7. "Love means never having to say you're sorry."

8. "Mein Fuehrer, I can walk!"

9. "Oh, no! It wasn't the airplanes. It was Beauty killed the Beast."

10. "Shut up and deal."

11. "...Tara! Home. I'll go home, and I'll think of some way to get him back! After all, tomorrow is another day!"

12. "The greatest trick the Devil ever pulled was convincing the world he didn't exist. Like that, he's gone."

13. "The horror. The horror."

14. "Wanna dance, or would you rather just suck face?"

15. "Well, nobody's perfect."

16. "You know somethin', Utivich? I think this might just be my masterpiece."

17. "You know, they're totally irrational and crazy and

absurd and—but uh, I guess we keep going through it ...
because ... most of us need the eggs."

18. "You're still here? It's over! Go home. Go!"

Answer Choices

A. *Annie Hall* (1977)

B. *The Apartment* (1960)

C. *Apocalypse Now* (1979)

D. *Arsenic and Old Lace* (1944)

E. *Being There* (1979)

F. *Dr. Strangelove* (1964)

G. *Ferris Bueller's Day Off* (1986)

H. *Gone with the Wind* (1939)

I. *Inglourious Basterds* (2009)

J. *King Kong* (1933)

K. *Love Story* (1970)

L. *My Fair Lady* (1964)

M. *On Golden Pond* (1981)

N. *The Silence of the Lambs* (1991)

O. *Some Like It Hot* (1959)

P. *A Streetcar Named Desire* (1951)

Q. *Sunset Boulevard* (1950)

R. *The Usual Suspects* (1995)

Answer Key: 1. Q; 2. L; 3. P; 4. N; 5. D; 6. E; 7. K; 8. F; 9. J;
10. B; 11. H; 12. R; 13. C; 14. M; 15. O; 16. I; 17. A; 18. G.

Writing from the Bottom

"My place in society was at the bottom. Here life offered nothing but sordidness and wretchedness, both of the flesh and the spirit; for here flesh and spirit were alike starved and tormented."

—*Jack London, "What Life Means to Me," from* Revolution and Other Essays *(1910)*

✳   ✳   ✳   ✳

WRITER JACK LONDON was born in San Francisco in 1876. His family was quite poor, and by age ten, London was selling newspapers to bring in money. He held various other jobs for the next decade—he worked at a cannery, then as a window washer, then as a security guard. He even worked on a whaling boat in the Pacific at one time.

At age 19, he took a year-long course that covered everything most students learn in four years of high school. He then enrolled at the University of California at Berkeley. He had studied there for a year before the Klondike gold rush began. London went to the Klondike, but he did not find any gold—and he contracted scurvy.

After he retuned from the Klondike, he began writing essays, short stories, news articles, and novels. His pieces at times appeared in such publications as the *Overland Monthly* and the *Atlantic Monthly*. In 1900, London married Bess Maddern, and they had two daughters before divorcing in 1904. During these years, London continued to write, covering the Russo-Japanese War and the 1906 San Francisco earthquake.

Jack London died of kidney disease in 1916. *The Call of the Wild* (1903), *The Sea Wolf* (1904), and *White Fang* (1906) are classic Jack London titles.

"I would rather that my spark burn out in a brilliant blaze than it should be stifled by dry-rot."

The Wright Stuff

"Every great architect is—necessarily—a great poet. He must be a great original interpreter of his time, his day, his age." That quote is attributed to Wisconsin native Frank Lloyd Wright, perhaps the greatest and most influential American architect of all time. In a life that spanned more than 92 years, Wright would experience paramount professional and creative success and satisfaction. He would also endure horrific personal heartache and strife.

✳ ✳ ✳ ✳

The Student Becomes the Master

ANOTHER QUOTE: "FORM follows function—that has been misunderstood. Form and function should be one, joined in a spiritual union."

In Richland Center, Wisconsin, Frank *Lincoln* Wright was born on June 8, 1867; he later changed his middle name after his parents divorced. Frank studied engineering at the University of Wisconsin-Madison for two semesters before moving to Chicago to try his hand at architecture.

After six years of absorbing the style and lessons of his mentor, architect Louis Sullivan, Frank embarked on his own path. Early in his career, he and his wife Catherine lived in Oak Park, a suburb of Chicago, where he built a studio adjacent to their home. During his Oak Park studio days, he worked on more than 125 commissions and developed into a supremely confident visionary. Frank championed an open concept style of "prairie" homes, characterized by their low, horizontal lines. Some of his designs from that period included the Avery Coonley house, the Darwin Martin house, the Ward Willits house, and the Robie house.

Some of his early non-residential masterpieces included the Larkin Building in Buffalo, New York, and the Unity Temple in Oak Park. He became a strong proponent for "organic architecture" in which a building's design flows cohesively with the nature around it.

Adultery! Exile!

"Early in life I had to choose between honest arrogance and hypocritical humility. I chose the former and have seen no reason to change."

Frank was master of his professional domain, but his domestic life was decidedly messy. Though married with enough children to fill...well, a house...Wright fell in love with the wife of a client for whom he was designing a home. The society that had praised and admired the architect now condemned him as an adulterer. Shunned by peers, Frank and his mistress Mamah Cheney ditched their families in 1909 and fled to Europe.

When the lovers returned to America more than a year later, they settled down in Spring Green, Wisconsin, where Frank had spent childhood summers with relatives. There Frank designed a retreat so the couple could live away from the judgment and gossip of others. He built his famous Taliesin home on a hill overlooking the valley of the Wisconsin River.

Unfortunately, Taliesin would not prove to be the sanctuary that Frank had intended. Tragedy struck in 1914 while Frank was in Chicago overseeing a construction project. Julian Carlton, a disgruntled former servant, set fire to Taliesin. Mamah, her two visiting children, and four others tried to escape the flames, but an ax-wielding Julian blocked the only exit. He murdered seven people that day. This event devastated Frank's world.

Haunted! Cursed!

"I believe in God, only I spell it Nature."

Haunted by his loss, Frank threw himself into his work, completing the Midway Garden commission in Chicago and spending several years in Tokyo, building the impressive Imperial Hotel. When the Great Kanto Earthquake of 1923 ravaged

Tokyo, Frank's Imperial Hotel was one of the few buildings left standing. He also took comfort in the arms of sculptor, and alleged morphine addict, Miriam Noel. She resided with him at the newly built Taliesin II.

Frank's legal wife Catherine finally granted him a divorce in 1922, and the next year he engaged in an ill-advised marriage to Miriam. She left him by 1924. While still married to Miriam, Frank became enamored with Olga (Olgivanna) Milanoff Hinzenberg, a ballet dancer 33 years his junior. In another juicy scandal, Olgivanna and her daughter Svetlana dashed overseas to be with Frank at Taliesin. Her Russian architect hubby tried to have Frank arrested in violation of the Mann Act (a law that banned trafficking women across state lines), but the charges didn't stick. In 1925, Olgivanna gave birth out of wedlock to Frank's seventh child. That same year, the Taliesin home fell victim to a second fire, this time an accident. Rumors ignited that Frank and the home were cursed.

Rebuilding a Life

"The longer I live, the more beautiful life becomes."

The resilient architect finally married his live-in love Olgivanna on August 25, 1928. He rebuilt Taliesin a third time. Taliesin III, deemed a National Historic Landmark in 1976, still stands today. It is open for public tours and has been described as Wright's "autobiography in wood and stone."

The next several decades would be highlighted by some of Wright's greatest professional triumphs. This included the machine-inspired and beautifully curved Administration Building of the S. C. Johnson & Son Company in Racine, Wisconsin. There were also his less flashy Usonian houses for the middle class. He designed his Fallingwater masterpiece, a breathtaking house built on a waterfall. In 1943, he was commissioned to design the Guggenheim Museum.

His designs live on all over the world.

"Let's Play Two!"

During the 1950s and '60s, Ernie Banks was one of the most feared hitters and skilled fielders in Major League Baseball. But it was his sunny disposition and abiding love of the game that earned him the undying respect of Chicagoans on both the North and South sides.

✳ ✳ ✳ ✳

ERNIE BANKS IS without a doubt the most beloved player ever to appear on the Chicago Cubs roster. Known as Mr. Cub, this hard-hitting shortstop and first baseman was one of the league's dominant power hitters during the 1950s and 1960s, often racking up more dingers than the better-known hitting legends of the era such as Mickey Mantle, Willie Mays, and Hank Aaron.

Banks became the Chicago team's first African American player in 1953 after spending a few years on a Negro League barnstorming club. He quickly earned the starting shortstop position in Chicago as well as the begrudging respect of pitchers around the nation. In 1955, he led the league in home runs and smacked a first-time-ever five grand slams—a single-season record that would stand for 30 years.

Over the next five seasons, he banged out more round-trippers than any player in the majors. Lean and wiry, he did not have the typical physique of a power hitter, but like Hank Aaron, he had remarkably strong and quick wrists, which allowed him to wield his bat like a whip and make mincemeat of such legendary pitchers as Sandy Koufax and Don Drysdale.

Though his fielding was erratic in his first few seasons, the young slugger worked tirelessly to hone his glove skills. He eventually became one of the most proficient infielders in the game, winning the Gold Glove Award in 1960. A few years earlier, he had won back-to-back Most Valuable Player (MVP) awards, as well. The MVP honors are particularly notable because he was playing for a perennially losing team. During the '50s, the Cubs never finished better than fifth place, and it was unheard of for the MVP to go to a player on a team that wasn't at least contending for the pennant.

Banks played his entire career from 1953 to 1971 in a Cubs uniform. His affiliation with the most lovable losers in baseball history also granted him another ignominious record in the baseball annals—most games played (2,528) without a single post-season appearance. Most of us would find it unbearable to be trapped in such a paradox—to be one of the league's best players shackled to one of the league's worst teams. But Banks never bellyached, never lamented, and never uttered a word of frustration. Rather, he always displayed a remarkably cheery, grateful, and humble persona and took the field each day as if he were a rookie reporting for his first big-league game. On perfect Chicago summer days, Banks would often use his famous pregame slogan "Let's play two!" For long-suffering Cubs fans, his combination of prowess and passion for the game made him a beacon of hope during long, dark years.

Banks hung up his spikes after the 1971 season, but he remained with the club as a coach. In the second month of Banks's second season after retirement, Cubs manager Whitey Lockman was ejected from a game after an argument with an umpire, and Banks helmed the club for the remaining inning and a half of play in the Cubs' victory, making him the first African American to manage a Major League Baseball team during a game. Banks was elected to the Baseball Hall of Fame in 1977, his jersey number was retired in 1982 (the first Cubs jersey to be so honored), and he has been, and will always remain, a defining figure in the history of the Chicago Cubs.

* The Wrigley Field nickname "the Friendly Confines" is closely associated with Ernie Banks. Some believe he coined the phrase; all agree he popularized it.

"Yes, Virginia"

As the 19th century drew to a close, New York's Sun *penny newspaper answered a query from a little girl, and in so doing, created a holiday tradition that continues to the present day.*

✳   ✳   ✳   ✳

Virginia o'hanlon, an Upper West Side resident who had just celebrated her eighth birthday in 1897, was so delighted by her presents that she began to wonder what she might receive at Christmas. "[As] a child, I just existed from July to December, wondering what Santa Claus would bring me," O'Hanlon later revealed. "I think I was a brat." She worried whether Santa Claus even existed at all, because school friends had been saying otherwise. Virginia's father ducked the issue by telling her to ask the newspaper because "if you see it in the *Sun*, it's so." Ah, those were less cynical times!

Beloved Reply

An unsigned September 21, 1897, *Sun* editorial (written by Francis Pharcellus Church) was entitled "Is There a Santa Claus?" It touched a nerve with the public. "Virginia," the piece begins, "your little friends are wrong." And later: "Yes, Virginia, there is a Santa Claus. He exists as certainly as love and generosity and devotion exist."

Readers asked for seasonal reprints of the editorial. By 1902, the *Sun* grudgingly noted, "This year requests for its reproduction have been so numerous that we yield." In 1924, the paper ran it as the lead editorial in the Christmas Eve edition, and the paper began routinely republishing the piece every Christmas season. Even after the *Sun* folded in 1950, other newspapers kept the custom going.

Santa's Legacies

Virginia O'Hanlon, who grew up to become an educator, received correspondence about the letter throughout her life.

In 1998, PBS's *Antiques Roadshow* authenticated and appraised Virginia's original letter at $20,000-$30,000. Over a century later, the newspaperman's impassioned reply to a small child's question remains one of the most cherished Christmas messages ever published.

"Yes, Virginia" Editorial, New York's *Sun* newspaper, September 21, 1897

VIRGINIA, your little friends are wrong. They have been affected by the skepticism of a skeptical age. They do not believe except they see. They think that nothing can be which is not comprehensible by their little minds. All minds, Virginia, whether they be men's or children's, are little. In this great universe of ours man is a mere insect, an ant, in his intellect, as compared with the boundless world about him, as measured by the intelligence capable of grasping the whole of truth and knowledge.

Yes, VIRGINIA, there is a Santa Claus. He exists as certainly as love and generosity and devotion exist, and you know that they abound and give to your life its highest beauty and joy. Alas! how dreary would be the world if there were no Santa Claus. It would be as dreary as if there were no VIRGINIAS. There would be no childlike faith then, no poetry, no romance to make tolerable this existence. We should have no enjoyment, except in sense and sight. The eternal light with which childhood fills the world would be extinguished.

Not believe in Santa Claus! You might as well not believe in fairies! You might get your papa to hire men to watch in all the chimneys on Christmas Eve to catch Santa Claus, but even if they did not see Santa Claus coming down, what would that prove? Nobody sees Santa Claus, but that is no sign that there is no Santa Claus. The most real things in the world are those that neither children nor men can see. Did you ever see fairies dancing on the lawn? Of course not, but that's no proof that they are not there. Nobody can conceive or imagine all the wonders there are unseen and unseeable in the world.

You may tear apart the baby's rattle and see what makes the noise inside, but there is a veil covering the unseen world which not the strongest man, nor even the united strength of all the strongest men that ever lived, could tear apart. Only faith, fancy, poetry, love, romance, can push aside that curtain and view and picture the supernal beauty and glory beyond. Is it all real? Ah, VIRGINIA, in all this world there is nothing else real and abiding.

No Santa Claus! Thank God! he lives, and he lives forever. A thousand years from now, Virginia, nay, ten times ten thousand years from now, he will continue to make glad the heart of childhood.

Out of This World!

The original Star Trek series brought us two popular quotes: Captain James Kirk's "Beam me up, Scotty," and Dr. Leonard "Bones" McCoy's "Damn-it, Jim, I'm a doctor, not a ..." But any Trekkie worth his or her dilithium crystals knows that neither quote is exact.

✳   ✳   ✳   ✳

A Universe of One-Liners

CAPTAIN KIRK SAID a lot of things in the original series (when he wasn't busy smooching space women), but he never said, "Beam me up, Scotty." He did, however, utter a number of variations on that statement over the course of the series and in subsequent movies. These included: "Beam me up," "Beam us up, Scotty," "Beam them out of there, Scotty," and "Scotty, beam me up." It's a minor point, to be sure, but one of great importance to the legions of die-hard *Star Trek* fans.

The quote most often attributed to Dr. McCoy has had its variations, too. Most people put a "Damn-it" in front of the line, but Bones never uttered that expletive in the TV series (a product of the 1960s, *Star Trek* was almost devoid of curse words). However, the doctor did mutter, "Damn-it, Jim!" and "Damn-it, Spock!" on a number of occasions in various *Star Trek* movies.

The "I'm a doctor, not a . . ." routine was used a couple of times during the original series, most evidently in the episode titled "The Devil in the Dark," in which Captain Kirk orders Dr. McCoy to attend to an injured Horta, a creature that is essentially a sentient rock. McCoy's response is typical of his character: "I'm a doctor, not a bricklayer!" Bones made similar sarcastic comments whenever he was required to perform a task that was outside his expertise. In the case of the Horta, he did as he was instructed and ably patched up the wounded creature with cement.

Knowing a good quote when it hears one, the *Star Trek* franchise used Dr. McCoy's popular catchphrase throughout later series and motion pictures. For example, the holographic doctor in *Star Trek: Voyager* (played by Robert Picardo) used the phrase on a couple of occasions. And so did others. In one episode in which Picardo's doctor asks another holographic physician for help after their ship has been taken over by Romulans, the second doctor replies, "I'm a doctor, not a commando!"

Likewise, in the series *Star Trek: Deep Space Nine* (the episode titled "Trials and Tribble-ations"), when Dr. Bashir (Alexander Siddiq) is asked about events in the 23rd century, he quips, "I'm a doctor, not a historian."

There are additional variations of the "I'm a doctor, not a . . ." statement. In the movie *Star Trek: First Contact*, a holographic doctor says, "I'm a doctor, not a doorstop." And in the video game *Star Trek: Bridge Commander*, players who try to engage engineer Brex in too much chitchat are eventually scolded with, "Damn-it, Jim! I'm an engineer, not a conversationalist!"

Long-Lasting Legacy

Star Trek has given viewers much over the 40-plus years it has been around, including innovative scientific concepts that are actually starting to become reality. Its influence even reached NASA, which named its prototype space shuttle *Enterprise*, after the starship featured in the show.

The Great Debates

Abraham Lincoln and Stephen Douglas may have defined the art, but the debating team at Wiley College opened eyes that had previously been glued shut.

✳   ✳   ✳   ✳

THERE IS PERHAPS nothing more satisfying than a true come-from-behind story. Most people can identify in some way with the plight of the downtrodden, the ignored, the oppressed—the true underdogs of our world. When members of that camp are somehow able to rise above, to take on the omnipotent powers that be and to win, it triggers a feeling deep down inside us that anything is indeed possible. During the Great Depression, such a Cinderella story was set into motion at Marshall, Texas. After it had played itself out, racial stereotypes about intellect would be forever turned upside down, and a group of previously unknown college students would come to national prominence.

Seeds Take Root

Noted African American poet and educator Melvin B. Tolson (1898–1966) believed strongly that all people should stand up for their rights.

Given the era and Tolson's skin color, such a mindset was forward thinking and controversial. But this was simply the way that Tolson, an English professor at all-black Wiley College from 1924 to 1947, operated. Nothing, it seemed, could stand in his way for long.

In addition to his teaching duties, Tolson wrote poetry and novels, directed plays, and even coached football. By living his life with such a can-do attitude, Tolson deconstructed racial stereotypes and gained considerable fame throughout the Southwest. Poet/playwright Langston Hughes wrote of him, "Melvin Tolson is the most famous Negro professor in the Southwest. Students all over that part of the world speak of him, revere him, remember him, and love him."

Many also strived to emulate him. When Tolson formed a debating team to help his students build up their confidence, the teacher wasn't lacking for applicants. Using radical techniques of his own design, Tolson taught his debaters how to become formidable opponents. He drilled them repeatedly on the finer points of physical gesturing and appropriate pauses, effectively showing them the importance of skillful acting during debate. He also taught them to pre-guess their opponent's strategy, and he wrote specific rebuttals for them to study before each event. Such preparedness promised that his students would always have a counterpunch at the ready.

Thumping the Competition

In most contests, a certain amount of time is required before a rookie participant can get up to speed. Perhaps owing to the intense training rendered by Tolson, this was *never* the case for the Wiley Debating Team. Beginning with its very first debate, the group continually mowed opponents down, one by one; it then set its sights on its next "victim." Slowly but steadily, the debaters' notoriety grew. From 1929 until 1939, the Wiley team proved to be wily indeed. Debating 75 total times, the team lost only one competition. Lying in its wake were such noted African American schools as Tuskegee, Howard, and Fisk universities. But, by far Wiley's greatest moment came in 1935 when the-little-team-that-could vanquished the vaunted University of Southern California, the reigning national debating champ. This upset victory proved far and away that capability rests where you find it.

Hollywood Takes Notice

This celebrated debate proved so powerful that Hollywood later immortalized it in *The Great Debaters* (2007). With Denzel Washington cast as Professor Tolson (in addition to directing the film), the movie substituted Harvard University for USC, but otherwise the plot was the same. Much like David versus Goliath, the young debaters cut their champion opponents down to size and scored a major strike against racial prejudice for their efforts. Not too many tales, real or imagined, work out better than that.

The Vast Wasteland of TV

If you've ever referred to TV as a vast wasteland, thank Newton Minow. If your response when you hear the name is to ask who that is, read on.

✳ ✳ ✳ ✳

SPEAKING TO THE National Association of Broadcasters in 1961, Federal Communications Council Chairman Newton N. Minow told television executives to improve the educational and social value of their programming or risk losing the license to broadcast.

At the time of Minow's speech, there were only three major networks. The percentage of households with television sets had grown during the 1950s from 9 percent to almost 90 percent. The predominant formats on television were Westerns, sitcoms, and game shows, with news and educational programming claiming only a small share of airtime.

The Federal Communications Commission was charged with ensuring that public airwaves be used for the "public interest, convenience, and necessity." Minow accused broadcasters of failing to fulfill this obligation by concerning themselves only with ratings and not with "the service of the people and the cause of freedom."

The executives took notice, introducing more nonfiction and public affairs programming and using dramas to address relevant social issues like poverty and health care. By the end of the decade, educational programming had taken a major leap forward, with the number of educational stations quadrupling and the newly formed Public Broadcasting Service featuring groundbreaking children's shows like *Sesame Street*.

"I invite each of you to sit down in front of your television set when your station goes on the air and stay there, for a day, without a book, without a magazine, without a newspaper, without a profit and loss sheet or a rating book to distract you. Keep your eyes glued to that set until the station signs off. I can assure you that what you will observe is a vast wasteland."

Picasso True to His Word

"Give me a museum and I'll fill it."

✳   ✳   ✳   ✳

MANY PAINTERS, SCULPTORS, and artists achieve their greatest fame after taking their last breath. Not so with Pablo Picasso, whose works and influence revolutionized world art in the first half of the 20th Century. The charismatic Spanish artist did more than fill a single museum. His tens of thousands of paintings, sculptures, drawings and ceramic masterpieces truly defined an era.

Along with Georges Braque, Picasso is considered the cofounder of Cubism. No matter what one called his style or creations, though, there is no doubt Picasso left an indelible stamp on what art would become. He is credited with inventing Collage, and had a strong pull toward Symbolism and Surrealism at various points in his life.

"I do not seek," Picasso once said. "I find." He was not referring to fame, but fame is one thing Picasso surely found— whether or not he was looking for it. His following and the awe he inspired in his fans were seemingly limitless. Art lovers from all corners of the world were drawn to his works. Les Demoiselles d'Avignon (1907), Three Musicians (1921) and Girl Before a Mirror (1932), painted at vastly different times in his life, are just a few of his countless works that cemented Picasso's legacy among the most accomplished, gifted and prolific artists of all time.

Some referred to Picasso as a magician. His greatest trick, in that vein, might have been making the walls separating an art connoisseur from a novice art enthusiast disappear. Those in both categories, after all, can recognize a Picasso.

He Conjured Angels— and Masterpieces

"I saw the angel in the marble and carved until I set him free."

✳ ✳ ✳ ✳

ONE OF THE greatest sculptors, painters and architects in the history of humankind was also an acclaimed poet. In fact, the words of Michelangelo di Lodovico Buonarroti Simoni were often another form of his 15th and 16th Century art.

When he spoke of setting angels free from marble blocks, a case could certainly be made that he was speaking literally. After all, the man whose works defined the Italian Renaissance period sculpted the "Angel" (1494–95) that kneels in the Basilica of San Domenico in Bologna, Italy, and of course the "David" (1501–04)—one of the most legendary pieces of art ever crafted.

However, Michelangelo spent great portion of his almost 90 years of life thinking of bigger principles than the art itself. And that's saying something, considering his epic sculptures and paintings that adorn the Sistine Chapel and countless museums around the globe. He penned hundreds of poems and sonnets later in life, and his description of freeing angels from marble certainly was meant to express a belief about the vast beauty that can often be culled from the ordinary.

"In every block of marble," Michelangelo explained, "I see a statue as plain as though it stood before me, shaped and perfect in attitude and action. I have only to hew away the rough walls that imprison the lovely apparition to reveal it to the other eyes as mine see it."

Quotes about Marble, Monuments, and More

"Architecture, sculpture, painting, music, and poetry, may truly be called the efflorescence of civilized life."

—HERBERT SPENCER

"I would much rather have men ask why I have no statue, than why I have one."

—CATO THE ELDER

"Others, I take it, will work better with breathing bronze and drawing living faces from marble; others will plead at law with greater eloquence, or measure the pathways of the sky, or forecast the rising stars. Be it your concern, Roman, to rule the nations under law (this is your proper skill), and establish the way of peace."

—VIRGIL, THE AENEID

"Life is made up of marble and mud."

—NATHANIEL HAWTHORNE

"Not marble, nor the gilded monuments of princes, shall outlive this powerful rime."

—WILLIAM SHAKESPEARE, "SONNET 55"

"A man's truest monument must be a man."

—MINOT JUDSON SAVAGE

Mad, Bad, and Dangerous to Know

Lord Byron: Famous. Infamous. All of the Above.

✳ ✳ ✳ ✳

LORD BYRON'S RESUME included some must-reads of the early 19th Century. Narrative poems *Don Juan* and *Childe Harold's Pilgrimage* were among them, as was the shorter lyric work "She Walks in Beauty." George Gordon Byron, his name by birth in 1788, had a passion for politics, a way with words and an accompanying intellect that some—most notably Lord Byron himself—considered legendary.

His social resume was legend as well, in ways that put Byron in the company of some of the most reviled figures in world history. Suffice it to say that his legacy during what was considered the Romantic Movement included "romances" that no one but Byron smiled upon. "Mad, bad and dangerous to know" is how Lady Caroline Lamb described her former lover.

His well-known affair with the married Lamb outraged those in his native Great Britain, but might not have been his signature misstep. He is said to have fathered a child with his half-sister, after having earlier confessed romantic feelings toward distant cousins. His affairs crossed both genders and seemingly knew no bounds.

In addition to his work in Great Britain's House of Lords and his many political writings, Byron also gained fame for, well, being famous. He was truly one of the first "superstar" figures to grow popular in ways that seemed to transcend his achievements. His wife, Annabella, termed the craze "Byromania." Lord Byron embraced it, but later fled in a self-imposed exile from his homeland. After falling ill, he died in Greece at age 36.

Quotes from Lord Byron

"I'll publish right or wrong: Fools are my theme, let satire be my song."

—*English Bards and Scotch Reviewers*

*"I live not in myself, but I become
Portion of that around me."*

—*Childe Harold's Pilgrimage*

"Roll on, thou deep and dark blue ocean—roll!"

—*Childe Harold's Pilgrimage*

"I awoke one morning and found myself famous."

—after the publication of cantos from *Childe Harold's Pilgrimage*

"My great comfort is, that the temporary celebrity I have wrung from the world has been in the very teeth of all opinions and prejudices. I have flattered no ruling powers; I have never concealed a single thought that tempted me."

—Letter

*"She walks in beauty, like the night
Of cloudless climes and starry skies."*

—"She Walks in Beauty"

*"Oh God! it is a fearful thing
To see the human soul take wing
In any shape, in any mood."*

—"The Prisoner of Chillon"

*"So, we'll go no more a roving
So late into the night,
Though the heart be still as loving,
And the moon be still as bright."*

—"So, We'll Go No More A-Roving"

"Pleasure's a sin, and sometimes sin's a pleasure."

—*Don Juan*

*"Let us have wine and women, mirth and laughter,
Sermons and soda water the day after."*

—*Don Juan*

The Intersection of Music and Poetry

"Music is the universal language of mankind—poetry their universal pastime and delight."

Henry Wadsworth Longfellow provided both to his legions of fans as one of the most popular and accomplished artists of the 19th Century.

✳ ✳ ✳ ✳

MAKE NO MISTAKE about it. Longfellow was a poet—a beloved one. His poetry, however, held music to which songwriters might well aspire. He would often consider the subject of his verse for days while deciding on the meter and style in which he would bring the subject to life. Frequently, the result was something that soared beyond poetic. His writing was melodic.

Longfellow was born in Portland, Maine, in 1807 and proved an exceptional student. He was a voracious reader, became fluent in Latin and published his first poem at age 13 in the *Portland Gazette*. He pursued collegiate studies in Maine and Massachusetts, all the while submitting writings and poetry to literary magazines across the country. During a three-year European tour as a young man, he taught himself several languages and spent time getting to know author Washington Irving. Upon his return, he took up teaching Spanish, French and Italian at his alma mater, Maine's Bowdoin College.

Poetry Drove Him

Teaching was a start for Longfellow. Poetry, however, was his passion. Certainly, he worked at it. He witnessed writer Washington Irving's legendary work ethic first-hand and had always been a committed perfectionist as a student. Words came naturally to this legendary linguist, though, and once Longfellow began experiencing life's trials he built up a world of material from which he captivated the attention of the literary world.

Longfellow married former classmate Mary Storer Potter of Portland, Maine, in 1831. On his second trip to Europe, though, in 1835, he was devastated when Storer died from complications of a miscarriage. He spent a year grieving in Germany and Switzerland before returning to the U.S., taking a job at Harvard in 1836 and publishing his first collection of poems five years later.

By the mid-1850s, having become a national figure through his popular collections, Longfellow retired from teaching to focus on his poetry. A student of history who was deeply concerned about national issues, Longfellow turned actual events into melodic poems, sometimes weaving fictional characters among factual circumstance. *Hiawatha,* a lengthy poem about Native American trials, and *The Courtship of Miles Standish and Other Poems* were immensely successful. The subsequent *Paul Revere's Ride* hinted at a coming conflict—the Civil War—and also earned great acclaim.

Another Tragic Turn

It was a few months into the war, in 1861, when Longfellow lost a second wife. Frances Longfellow, his wife of 18 years and mother of his six children, spilled wax on her dress and was badly burned in the ensuing fire. She died despite Henry's frantic efforts to save her. Longfellow went two years without publishing, but his worldwide popularity never waned. His works were being translated all over the world.

Longfellow was a literary beacon in Romanticism, but his writings were not limited to one movement. They covered many themes. Longfellow managed to combine his love for European literature and thought with his devotion to American themes, history and hope. In doing so, he became the most beloved American poet of the 19th Century long before his death in 1882. Long after it as well.

> *"Lives of great men all remind us*
> *We can make our lives sublime.*
> *And, departing, leave behind us.*
> *Footprints on the sands of time."*
>
> —HENRY WADWSWORTH LONGFELLOW, "A PSALM OF LIFE"

Malory Pens 'Authoritative' Arthurian Tale

"Whoso pulleth out this sword of this stone and anvil, is rightwise king born all of England."

✳   ✳   ✳   ✳

THE LEGEND OF King Arthur and his Knights of the Round Table existed long before Thomas Malory came along. Malory was said to have been an otherwise nondescript country manor lord who inherited an estate in Northampton Shire in 1434, when he was in his mid-20s.

When he gained acclaim, it was for all the wrong reasons. Mallory became something of a rabble rouser, organizing attacks and thievery on the Duke of Buckingham and Combe Abbey, from which he and his gang stole livestock and valuables. He ended up in jail for much of his young adult life, and would likely have died with little legacy if not for his vision and gift in putting pen to paper.

The Arthurian legend lived among scattered sources prior to Malory, most notably in the form of a 14th Century French poem and two anonymous British writings. Working from these but inserting his own deft touches and vivid imagination, Malory—largely while imprisoned—wrote 21 books covering eight romances. It was the first long-form, English-language version of the legend of Arthur, Lancelot, Guinevere, et al.

The first printed edition of Malory's work came out in 1485, published by William Caxton, and was named *Le Morte*

D'arthur. It came out at a time when rebellions and strife were the norm in England, and many thought the virtues of loyalty and integrity had gone by the wayside. Malory gained acclaim for comparing the nobility of the Arthurian characters to that of those who ruled at the time.

Butler Sets Table on When to Eat Oysters

"It is unseasonable and unwholesome in all months that have not an 'r' in their name to eat an oyster."

✳ ✳ ✳ ✳

WHEN WILLIAM BUTLER, a contemporary of Shakespeare and physician to King James I, set forth this "pearl" of wisdom for oyster consumption in 1599, the Cambridge man could never have imagined how long the rule would govern culinary choices worldwide.

Evidence is scattered about Butler's connection to the quote, but it appeared in a 1599 British cookbook written by Henry Buttes and dedicated to Lady Anne Bacon. Oysters, it said, were considered "venerious"—most likely meaning spawning— during the non-R, warmer-weather months of the year.

Over subsequent decades in kitchens, restaurants, and oyster fisheries, the rule has been argued, adhered to, and broken. Most agree there are two reasons some prefer to avoid eating oysters during the warmer months. Spawning is one of them. It starts when the temperatures heat up in May. Oyster flesh tends to become milkier during this time.

Back in Butler's day, there was also a concern about storage. With no refrigeration, it was more difficult to keep oysters—or seafood of any kind—from going bad in the heat unless it went straight from the sea to the table. The "R" months were a lot safer for ensuring a bad oyster didn't leave one sick for days.

Butler might have smiled to know that New York City enacted a law in 1715 banning collection from oyster beds once the water warmed up in May. They wanted to make sure the spawning season replenished the beds to avoid a scarcity. The law stayed on the books until 1807. Butler might have chuckled, too, to know that some in the NYC oyster business began referring to August as "Orgust."

Donne Blazed New Trails in Poetry

He wrote of love and dwelled on death. And it was in the latter that John Donne, in due time, became known and respected as one of the most fascinating and talented poets to ever put pen to parchment.

✳   ✳   ✳   ✳

JOHN DONNE WAS born in London in 1573 to a Roman Catholic family that refused to attend Anglican services at a time when that practice, called Recusancy, was illegal. He was adventurous and at times reckless as a young man, with weaknesses for women and literature. The latter served him well as he grew in poetry and prose, though his first attempts at earning educational degrees were denied because he refused to renounce his Catholic faith. Eventually, he did and was ordained in the Church of England. He served as Dean of St. Paul's Cathedral from 1621 until his death 10 years later.

Donne's writings ranked him among the foremost Metaphysical poets. His style was gripping and sensual, with many of his early works focusing on themes of love and death. From one of his best-known love poems, "A Valediction: Forbidding Mourning," comes:

"Such wilt thou be to me, who must
Like th' other foot obliquely run;
Thy firmness makes my circle just,
And makes me end, where I begun."

Later in his career, he wrote more forebodingly of ruin and peril, never letting go of his love for metaphor or fascination with death as a theme. From "The First Anniversary:"

"And new philosophy calls all in doubt,
The element of fire is quite put out;
The sun is lost, and th'earth, and no man's wit
Can well direct him where to look for it."

Tragic Loss and a Turn to God

Though Donne gained a faithful following among a group that adored his work, his life was a tough one. While serving as chief secretary to Sir Thomas Egerton in his mid-20s, he fell in love with and secretly married Egerton's niece, Anne More. Both Egerton and Anne's father were opposed. When they found out, Donne was fired and imprisoned, and had to fight to keep his marriage from being annulled.

Anne bore her husband 12 children over their 16 years of marriage. Two were stillborn, including one in 1617 that preceded Anne's death five days later. Donne went into deep mourning, writing "17th Holy Sonnet" for his departed love and a defense of his own suicide—a work that was never published and a suicide that was, fortunately, never carried out.

Over his final years, particularly after receiving his Anglican orders, Donne wrote poetry and prose that frequently called on Christ's sacrifice on the cross. His verse in "Divine Meditations 18" calls out an unworthiness to look upon his Lord:

"O Saviour, as thou hang'st upon the tree;
I turn my back to thee, but to receive
Corrections, till thy mercies bid thee leave."

In Time, Popularity Soared

Though he made a mark during his lifetime, it was not until long after his death that Donne became almost universally recognized as one of the greats. Many in the 18th and 19th Centuries dismissed his work as crude in both content and meter. By the late 1800s, however, minds opened and Donne was not only accepted, but celebrated. Helping his cause was the fact the likes of Robert Browning, T.S. Eliot and William Butler Yeats praised the way he combined intellect and passion in his works.

His work and phrasing inspired recent writers too. "Meditation 17," found in *Devotions upon Emergent Occasions*, contains the paragraph:

"No man is an island, entire of itself; every man is a piece of the continent, a part of the main. If a clod be washed away by the sea, Europe is the less, as well as if a promontory were, as well as if a manor of thy friend's or of thine own were: any man's death diminishes me, because I am involved in mankind, and therefore never send to know for whom the bells tolls; it tolls for thee."

From that meditation, the phrase "No man is an island," has provided countless song titles and lyrics and *For Whom the Bell Tolls* was the title of an Ernest Hemingway novel.

Memorable First Lines from John Donne

"Go and catch a falling star."

—"SONG (GO AND CATCH A FALLING STAR)"

"For God's sake hold your tongue, and let me love."

—"THE CANONIZATION"

"Batter my heart, three-person'd God."

—"BATTER MY HEART, THREE-PERSON'D GOD"

"Death, be not proud, though some have called thee Mighty and dreadful, for thou art not so."

—"DEATH, BE NOT PROUD"

"I am a little world made cunningly Of elements, and an angelic sprite."

—"HOLY SONNET NO. 5"

Master of Haiku

"My poetry is like a stove in the summer or a fan in the winter. It runs against the popular tastes and has no practical use." So said Matsuo Basho—but he was perceived by others as a master of the art.

✳ ✳ ✳ ✳

MATSUO BASHO DID not invent the haiku, though he did become a master of the art. In fact, the form of poetry was not called haiku in his day, but rather *hokku*. Basho, born near Ueno in 1644, was the only one of his siblings to show an interest in literature over farming. He moved to Kyoto and began studying Chinese Poetry and Taoism under a well-respected local poet. Basho began writing in a style called *haikai no renga*. It was a style constructed in a series of related verses, the opening verse known as *hokku*.

Writers soon began composing these three-line verses, consisting of five, seven and five syllables, and frequently calling on imagery from nature, as standalone poems. Basho mastered the style that would come to be called haiku. He published several under different names until 1680, when a student gave him basho trees as a gift. Thereafter, he was Basho.

Trials shaped his life and his writings. A fire that destroyed his home and most of his city in the early 1680s may have contributed to a period in his life when he shut himself off from the world and remained in a hut. However, he embraced Buddhist philosophies and eventually made a conscious decision to embrace the world around him, rather than shunning it. Many of his best writings came from his subsequent travel.

The Long Road

Though Basho wrote many of his poems in what is now Tokyo, it was a journey he took on foot in 1689 that led to his most famous work, *Oku no Hosomichi*, or *Narrow Road to the Interior*.

Before the journey, he had created his own form of poetry called *haibun*. It was a hybrid style that combined haiku with prose and was perfect for chronicling a progression or journey. That's precisely what Basho set out on.

Over a five-month span of 1689, Basho and his apprentice, Sora, traveled 1,200 miles on foot. They headed north from Tokyo, through the uplands and lowlands of the northern province of Tohuku, and then southwest along the Sea of Japan to the central city of Ogaki. It was a journey that inspired his greatest writings, and one that his disciples follow still today in an effort to walk in his footsteps.

Every year, thousands of people make pilgrimages to Basho's Trail, to his birthplace and to his burial shrine. A linguist born and raised in Kyoto, the late Helen Tanizaki, once said, "Everyone I went to school with could recite at least one of Basho's poems by heart. He was the first writer we read in any exciting or serious way."

Basho's Legacy

Though he was certainly respected in his time as a beautiful poet for his simple and natural style, Basho gained even wider acclaim after his death at age 50. Recall that haiku was not a widespread form at the time. Throughout the 18th Century, he was celebrated as a pioneer of the haiku form that became revered for its beauty.

His works became widely translated in the 1900s, when his influence continued to climb. He was an inspiration to American writers like Ezra Pound and even many U.S. "Beat Generation" poets in the 1950s and '60s for his simplicity and use of imagery and embracing of the world around him.

"He who creates three to five haiku poems during a lifetime is a haiku poet. He who attains to complete ten is a master."

Swift Brought Out the Child in Readers

"Books, the children of the brain."

* * * *

THOUGH HIS MOST famous work, *Gulliver's Travels*, was written later in his life, Jonathan Swift never lost the ability to tap into a reader's child-like imagination. The Irish satirist did so with a unique style that led some to begin calling the deadpan and ironic satire used by subsequent authors as "Swiftian." Swift likely would have found that ironic in itself, considering he published his early works under pseudo-names like MB Drapier, Lemuel Gulliver and Isaac Bickerstaff.

Born in 1667, Swift became an Anglican priest in the late 17th Century and graduated from essays and short manuscripts to books. He quickly became renowned for his biting political satire, including the anonymously released *A Tale of a Tub* and *The Battle of the Books*.

After moving to London as a secretary under Sir William Temple, Swift became editor of the Tory newspaper, *The Examiner*, where he grew his reputation as a literary thorn in the side of the Whigs. He also fell in love with the young daughter of Temple's housekeeper, and remained in love with Esther Johnson until her death in 1728.

Swift moved back to his hometown of Dublin and became Dean at St. Patrick's Cathedral in 1713. It was there that he began writing *Gulliver*, which he finished in 1726. The book, which recounts political events that Swift experienced throughout his life, was a rousing success in Swift's day and throughout the following centuries.

Swift lost the ability to speak after suffering a stroke in 1742 and died three years later.

Quotes from Jonathan Swift

"Satire is a sort of glass, wherein beholders do generally discover everybody's face but their own."

"And surely one of the best rules in conversation is, never to say a thing which any of the company can reasonably wish had been left unsaid..."

"Falsehood flies, and truth comes limping after it, so that when men come to be undeceived, it is too late; the jest is over, and the tale hath had its effect: like a man, who hath thought of a good repartee when the discourse is changed, or the company parted; or like a physician, who hath found out an infallible medicine, after the patient is dead."

"I love good creditable acquaintance; I love to be the worst of the company."

"Reasoning will never make a man correct an ill opinion, which by reasoning he never acquired ..."

"Every man desires to live long, but no man would be old."

"I never wonder to see men wicked, but I often wonder to see them not ashamed."

"He was a bold man that first ate an oyster."

"'Tis an old maxim in the schools,
That flattery's the food of fools;
Yet now and then your men of wit
Will condescend to take a bit."

Of Letters and Inoculation

"Satire should, like a polished razor keen, wound with a touch that's scarcely felt or seen."

✳   ✳   ✳   ✳

SOME CONSIDERED HER one of the very early feminists. Others called her writing "masculine," though agreeing that she stood up for women of her generation and of great inequality between the genders. What no one disputes is this: Lady Mary Wortley Montagu could write with the best of them.

Her letters and poems took eloquent jabs at those with whom she disagreed—those who vouched for social norms that favored men. In her "Epistle from Mrs. Yonge to Her Husband," she speaks for a wife accused of adultery by an adulterous husband:

"Defrauded Servants are from Service free,
A wounded Slave regains his Liberty.
For Wives ill us'd no remedy remains,
To daily Racks condemn'd, and to eternal Chains."

An Aristocrat and a Writer

Mary was born in 1869, and within a year her father became the Earl of Kingston. She was fascinated by literature from an early age. At a time when formal education was not typically lavished upon women, she used the library in her father's mansion to self-teach. She taught herself Latin, a language almost exclusively taught to boys. And she could not stay away from great writing. In putting her own pen to parchment, she called herself a poet but wrote in virtually every genre, from sonnets to songs to countless letters.

She eloped with Edward Wortley Montagu in 1712, largely to avoid the man her father wanted her to marry, Irish heir Clotworthy Skeffington. Four years after their marriage and one year after Lady Mary had overcome a bout with smallpox, Edward was appointed as British ambassador to Turkey and they moved to Istanbul.

Lady Mary's time in the Ottoman Empire became famous for two things. Her *Letters from Turkey* (or *Turkish Embassy Letters*), probably her best-known writings, espoused the merits of women in literature and called out a different experience than readers might have encountered from male writers who had traveled to the same places. She pored over the letters, putting her heart and soul into them, clearly intending them for a publication that occurred after her death.

The other lasting legacy Lady Mary brought back from Turkey involved smallpox. In addition to her own experience, the disease had taken the life of her brother in 1713. In Turkey, she witnessed women inoculating children, which was not common practice in Western Europe. She wrote about it in many of her letters and had her son, Edward, vaccinated shortly before he turned 5.

Upon her return to England, Lady Mary pushed for the introductions of those inoculations in Western medicine, touting their benefit and criticizing English doctors who either refused to inoculate or did so incorrectly. She met a great deal of opposition, but is credited with bringing smallpox vaccines into popular use.

Letters to her daughter, Lady Bute, later in her life covered a range of social issues and inspired following generations of young women. Lady Mary had left England in 1739, citing health reasons although it became known that she took up living with Italian Count Francesco Algarotti. She received word of her husband Edward's death in 1861 and returned to England from Venice. She died herself in 1862, within a year of her return.

You Are What You Eat

Though not a chef, Anthelme Brillat-Savarin was the foremost food writer of his time. He touted cooking as a science, and his ideas about diet and obesity remain relevant to this day.

✳   ✳   ✳   ✳

HAD THERE BEEN a Food Network in the late 18th and early 19th Centuries, it's a safe bet Anthelme Brillat-Savarin would have hosted his own show. And that's saying something, considering he was not a chef at all, but rather a French attorney and politician. Brillat-Savarin was born in Belley, a river town in Eastern France, in 1755. He followed his father into the law business, ventured into politics and in 1792 was elected mayor of his hometown. One of his deep beliefs was in the merit of capital punishment, a controversial cause about which he wrote and delivered speeches.

Brillat-Savarin's tour as mayor lasted just one year. Some in Paris saw him as a counter-revolutionary and seized his property. A bounty was placed on his head toward the end of the French Revolution, sending Brillat-Savarin to Switzerland, The Netherlands and eventually to the newly-formed United States. He lived in Boston, Philadelphia, New York and Hartford, making his way by teaching French and violin lessons. He was actually playing first violin in New York's John Street Orchestra for a time.

A Foodie at Heart

For all his many talents, however, Brillat-Savarin was more inspired by food than perhaps anything else. His parents were both good cooks, and two of his brothers were gourmets. Brillat-Savarin was welcomed back to France in 1796 and soon gained a lifelong position in the Court of Cassation. While in Paris, Brillat-Savarin could focus on his writing, and that writing ventured well beyond the bounds of politics and law.

His most famous work held the long French title *Physiologie du Goût, ou Méditations de Gastronomie Transcendante; ouvrage théorique, historique et à l'ordre du jour, dédié aux Gastronomes parisiens, par un Professeur, membre de plusieurs sociétés littéraires et savantes.* It has been translated, and shortened, to *The Physiology of Taste* or *The Philosopher in the Kitchen.* It was published anonymously in December 1825, two months before Brillat-Savarin's death.

One of Brillat-Savarin's tenets was that food was, quite objectively, good or bad. That is, a person's reaction to a dish did not indicate anything at all about the quality of the dish. The dish was either of good, medium or poor quality to begin with. One's reaction to it reflected on the person, not the food itself.

And when it came to those dishes, Brillat-Savarin's belief that "you are what you eat" was in many ways a foreshadowing to what became known as the Atkins diet in modern times. He espoused a diet low in carbohydrates for weight loss and better health. He advised readers to stay clear of starches and flour-based dishes, claiming that they lead to greater rates of obesity. "All animals that live on farinaceous food grow fat willy-nilly," he wrote, "and man is no exception to the universal law."

Brillat-Savarin, who never married, died at age 70. He remains an inspiration to several food writers, TV personalities and critics of today. The dishes he loved were usually not lavish ones, but rather simple ones. His legacy also lives on in a cheese (Brillat-Savarin) and a cake (gateau Savarin) named in his honor.

Quotes from Brillat-Savarin

"Tell me what you eat, and I will tell you what you are."

"A dessert without cheese is like a beautiful woman with only one eye."

"A meal without wine is like a day without sunshine."

A Man of the People

Tragedy, both endured and witnessed, shaped William Wordsworth's concern with the "common man" in his writings.

✳ ✳ ✳ ✳

IN 1778, WHEN he was just 8 years old, William Wordsworth lost his mother. He lost his father while in grade school. A young orphan, he was easily recognizable among his four siblings as the one who, from an early age, began expressing his views in verse. And if tragedy breeds great art, William certainly had enough to nudge him along his way.

After studying at St. John's College in Cambridge, Wordsworth set out on a walking tour of Europe. He experienced the

French Revolution first-hand, and witnessing the strife of others deeply impacted his writing. That writing was about to become published poetry, beginning with the collections *An Evening Walk* and *Descriptive Sketches* in 1793.

The tragedies of William's childhood and his experiences away from home compelled Wordsworth to a focus on the "common man," and "common speech," in his writings. He disagreed with those who considered lyric poetry a lesser art than epic poetry, a belief he expressed in his own works and by producing appealing, accessible art.

Wordsworth married childhood friend Mary Hutchinson in 1802 and fathered five children with her. Two of their children died in 1812. That, too, shaped his writing focus, as did a friendship he forged with famed poet Samuel Taylor Coleridge. They co-wrote, in 1798, the well-known *Lyrical Ballads*.

His most famous work, *The Prelude*, was published posthumously in 1850, the year Wordsworth died, and is considered the preeminent example of English Romanticism. It was a classic he worked on throughout much of his life.

Wisdom from Wordsworth

"That best portion of a good man's life,
His little, nameless, unremembered, acts
Of kindness and of love. "

—"LINES COMPOSED A FEW MILES ABOVE TINTERN ABBEY"

"I have said that poetry is the spontaneous overflow of powerful feelings; it takes its origin from emotion recollected in tranquility."

—PREFACE TO *LYRICAL BALLADS*

"The world is too much with us; late and soon,
Getting and spending, we lay waste our powers;—
Little we see in Nature that is ours;
We have given our hearts away, a sordid boon!"

—"THE WORLD IS TOO MUCH WITH US"

"The child is father of the man."

—"MY HEART LEAPS UP"

"Our birth is but a sleep and a forgetting:
The Soul that rises with us, our life's Star,
Hath had elsewhere its setting,
And cometh from afar:
Not in entire forgetfulness,
And not in utter nakedness,
But trailing clouds of glory do we come
From God, who is our home:
Heaven lies about us in our infancy!
Shades of the prison-house begin to close
Upon the growing Boy,
But he beholds the light, and whence it flows,
He sees it in his joy."

—"ODE. INTIMATIONS OF IMMORTALITY FROM RECOLLECTIONS OF EARLY CHILDHOOD"

"I wandered lonely as a cloud
That floats on high o'er vales and hills,
When all at once I saw a crowd,
A host, of golden daffodils."

—"I WANDERED LONELY AS A CLOUD"

Universally Acknowledged Truths

"It is a truth universally acknowledged, that a single man in possession of a good fortune must be in want of a wife."

Though she herself never married, Jane Austen—through her six timeless novels—challenged the norms for love and marriage in the early 19th Century. Along the way, she captured the hearts of countless readers who continue to devour her words to this day.

✳ ✳ ✳ ✳

JANE AUSTEN WAS born in England in 1775, at a time when formal schooling was not the norm for young girls. However, her parents sent her and sister Cassandra to Oxford, and encouraged Jane's creative side through books and writing materials. Jane was further educated by her father and brothers in a close family that routinely acted out plays in their barn as a form of entertainment.

Family was first for Austen, who had six brothers along with her older sister (and eventually 33 nieces and nephews), and much of the information known about her life comes from the letters she wrote to her family members. In those letters, she often wrote about themes that were also focal points in her books. Among them: love, marriage, equality, and prejudice.

From an early age, Austen used irony to educate and entertain. She began writing poems and stories for her family before she was even in her teen years. She finished a satirical novel called *Love and Friendship,* parodying popular writings of the day, at age 14. Sometimes her sister, Cassandra, provided watercolor images to go along with the prose. There was not only a budding author in the Austen home, but one who had commentary to express on the social norms of the day.

Pride and Prejudice

Austin wrote *First Impressions* just before the turn of the century, and it almost became her first published novel. She was not aware at the time of her father's efforts to have it published. He sent it to Thomas Cadell, a London-based publisher, but Cadell is said to have rejected the work without even opening the package.

Austen continued writing, oblivious to her first "rejected" manuscript, and in 1811 her brother Henry helped get *Sense and Sensibility* to publisher Thomas Egerton. It was first published anonymously, and its success nudged Egerton toward publishing what would be considered Austen's masterpiece two years later. *Pride and Prejudice* was a revised version of *First Impressions,* and before 1813 was over it was coming out in a second edition.

Two of the books themes appear in the title, but love and marriage were also central to the classic. Though Jane never married, at least two men in her past shaped the way she viewed the institution. Around age 20, she spent considerable time with a young man named Tom Lefroy and wrote to her sister of a love she had developed for him. His family, however, did what they could to keep them apart. They were not interested in a marriage between their son and Jane, particularly as Tom was studying law in London.

Years later, in December 1802, Jane received a marriage proposal from Harris Bigg-Wither, a longtime friend. It could have been the kind of marriage women of that day dreamed of. Bigg-Wither was a man of means, and stood to inherit a sizeable real estate sum. Jane accepted the proposal, but rescinded the very next day after realizing she did not feel love for her once childhood friend.

Austen parodied traditional thinking about marriage when her character, Charlotte Lucas, says, "'I am not romantic, you know. I never was. I ask only a comfortable home; and considering Mr. Collins's character, connections, and situation in life, I am convinced that my chance of happiness with him is as fair as most people can boast on entering the marriage state."

"'For what do we live, but to make sport for our neighbours, and laugh at them in our turn?"

—*Pride and Prejudice*

'Twas a Poem for the Ages

"'Twas the night before Christmas when all through the house,
Not a creature was stirring, not even a mouse.
One Clement Clark Moore wrote verse without a care,
That credit for his classic one day would be there."

✳   ✳   ✳   ✳

ON CHRISTMAS EVE 1822, the last thing on Clement Clark Moore's mind was receiving "credit" for a poem he penned for his children for recitation. After all, Moore was well accomplished long before writing the verses he called "A Visit from St. Nicholas." Like his father before him, the New York native was a high honors graduate of Columbia College, and went on to earn a Master's Degree from Columbia University.

Moore was a family man, with wife Catharine Elizabeth and nine children, and a religious man who donated a large portion of his inheritance to a seminary. He was an educator and an accomplished writer who penned books and poetry.

However, nothing reached the masses quite like that St. Nicholas story. It was published anonymously in 1823, the year after he wrote it, and took off like a Christmas Eve reindeer. It began appearing in newspapers and magazines across the country.

It was not until 1844, though, that Moore first took credit for his work when it appeared in his collection, *Poems*. Some attribute what became commonly known (by its first line) as "'Twas the Night Before Christmas" to Henry Livingston, Jr., rather than Moore, in a debate that carries on to this day. Livingston also wrote poems for children, but made no mention in his lifetime of having penned "A Visit from St. Nicholas."

The Night Before Christmas

'Twas the night before Christmas, when all through the house
Not a creature was stirring, not even a mouse;
The stockings were hung by the chimney with care,
In hopes that St. Nicholas soon would be there;

The children were nestled all snug in their beds;
While visions of sugar-plums danced in their heads;
And mamma in her 'kerchief, and I in my cap,
Had just settled our brains for a long winter's nap,

When out on the lawn there arose such a clatter,
I sprang from my bed to see what was the matter.
Away to the window I flew like a flash,
Tore open the shutters and threw up the sash.

The moon on the breast of the new-fallen snow,
Gave a lustre of midday to objects below,
When what to my wondering eyes did appear,
But a miniature sleigh and eight tiny rein-deer,

With a little old driver so lively and quick,
I knew in a moment he must be St. Nick.
More rapid than eagles his coursers they came,
And he whistled, and shouted, and called them by name:

"Now, *Dasher!* now, *Dancer!* now *Prancer* and *Vixen!*
On, *Comet!* on, *Cupid!* on, *Donner* and *Blitzen!*
To the top of the porch! to the top of the wall!
Now dash away! dash away! dash away all!"

As leaves that before the wild hurricane fly,
When they meet with an obstacle, mount to the sky;
So up to the housetop the coursers they flew
With the sleigh full of toys, and St. Nicholas too—

And then, in a twinkling, I heard on the roof
The prancing and pawing of each little hoof.
As I drew in my head, and was turning around,
Down the chimney St. Nicholas came with a bound.

He was dressed all in fur, from his head to his foot,
And his clothes were all tarnished with ashes and soot;
A bundle of toys he had flung on his back,
And he looked like a pedler just opening his pack.

His eyes—how they twinkled! his dimples, how merry!
His cheeks were like roses, his nose like a cherry!
His droll little mouth was drawn up like a bow,
And the beard on his chin was as white as the snow;

The stump of a pipe he held tight in his teeth,
And the smoke, it encircled his head like a wreath;
He had a broad face and a little round belly
That shook when he laughed, like a bowl full of jelly.

He was chubby and plump, a right jolly old elf,
And I laughed when I saw him, in spite of myself;
A wink of his eye and a twist of his head
Soon gave me to know I had nothing to dread;

He spoke not a word, but went straight to his work,
And filled all the stockings; then turned with a jerk,
And laying his finger aside of his nose,
And giving a nod, up the chimney he rose;

He sprang to his sleigh, to his team gave a whistle,
And away they all flew like the down of a thistle.
But I heard him exclaim, ere he drove out of sight—
"Happy Christmas to all, and to all a good night!"

Children's Poem Twinkles into Famed Nursery Rhyme

Born as a poem, "Twinkle, Twinkle Little Star" became a nursery song that many generations of children passed on to many generations thereafter. It remains one of the most popular nursey rhymes and lullabies to this day.

✳   ✳   ✳   ✳

BRITISH SISTERS JANE and Ann Taylor had written other children's poems before they penned "The Star" (its original name) in 1806. *Original Poems for Infant Minds*, for example, was a collection they published two years earlier. Jane, also an engraver and novelist, enjoyed a prolific career in literature. "Taylor's capacity to reveal the inner life as a thing is, it could be asserted, unrivaled in English literature before Dickens," contemporary critic Stuart Curran wrote of Jane.

Before older sister (by a year and a half) Ann went off to get married, their collaborations produced rhymes that children loved. None was bigger than "The Star." It was a poem in a collection called *Rhymes for the Nursery*. However, when someone began singing it to the tune of the 1761 French song, "Ah! vous dirai-je, maman," magic happened.

The melody has also become commonplace in "Baa, Baa Black Sheep" and "The Alphabet Song," but the imagery and story of a night traveler finding his way by the light of a star sets the Taylor sisters' verses in a class of their own.

Jane lived to be only 40 years old, dying of breast cancer in 1824. Ann, who also wrote a great deal of prose during her lifetime and was a literary critic, wrote an autobiography before her death at age 84 in 1866.

Keats Made Every Word Count

"'Beauty is truth, truth beauty,'—that is all Ye know on earth, and all ye need to know."

Though he lived to be just 25 and published only 54 poems, there has never been another like John Keats. He is remembered as one of the greats from the Romantic era, turning a painful life into some of the most beautiful verse ever written.

✳ ✳ ✳ ✳

IF NOT FOR the glorious words he wrote, the life of John Keats might be remembered as a tragic one. Born in England in 1795, he lost his father tragically at age 8. Thomas Keats was returning home after having visited John at school when he cracked his skull in a horse riding accident and died the next day. John and his three siblings lost their mother to tuberculosis six years later. Their grandmother appointed Richard Abbey as legal guardian, but Abbey squandered away the family money and never told John of an inheritance that could have changed his life.

Such pain certainly shaped Keats' early writing. Struggling financially, he decided to pursue a career in medicine that never materialized. Literature, however, was always a solace to him.

He was an avid reader from a young age and wrote his first poem, "An Imitation of Spenser," at age 19. He became greatly depressed, and shortly after receiving a license to practice apothecary and surgery he declared that he was dedicating his career to writing poetry.

Taking a Political Turn

Keats' beautiful use of imagery, masterful turns of phrase and biting, ironic wit were staples of his work. He met and befriended Leigh Hunt, publisher of *The Examiner*, in a twist that would also come to define Keats' path. Hunt was a radical whose writing landed him in prison in 1813 when he was accused of libeling Prince Regent.

Keats' support of Hunt was unwavering, earning him many of the same enemies Hunt had amassed. Keats penned a sonnet, "Written on the Day that Mr. Leigh Hunt Left Prison," and continued to write daringly about politics, in addition to his wide assortment of other topics.

He published his first volume of poems in 1817 and then committed to writing 40 lines a day toward a work he titled "Endymion," based on the Greek myth of the same name. The final version was 4,000 lines long.

Critical acclaim was elusive for Keats, even though fans of his work had never read the likes of him. Some of the criticism from the establishment was political in nature. Others had a hard time following his unorthodox style and structure. It wasn't until after his death that Keats became widely renowned as one of the true greats.

More Tragedy

Love was also a theme for Keats, who appears to have held such feelings for two women in his life. He met Isabella Jones in 1817 and published "Isabella" the following year. It recounts the story of a woman who falls for a man beneath her social standing, shunning the man her family wants her to marry.

Keats also befriended a woman named Frances "Fanny" Brawne in 1818 and became intimate with her. However, their relationship never had a chance once John returned from a walking tour of Northern England and Scotland that year to tend to his sick brother, Tom, who later died of tuberculosis.

John himself developed symptoms of the disease in 1819. Shortly after publication of his last volume of poetry, he moved to Italy to live with his close friend, painter Joseph Severn, seeking warmer climes on the advice of a doctor. He weathered great pain in his final years, dying in February of 1821.

Keats on Poetry

Keats wrote of his ideas on poetry in letters to various friends.

"If poetry comes not as naturally as leaves to a tree it had better not come at all."

"Poetry should be great and unobtrusive, a thing which enters into one's soul, and does not startle or amaze with itself, but with its subject."

"I would sooner fail than not be among the greatest."

Shelley Unleashed a Monster

She wrote: "I beheld the wretch—the miserable monster whom I had created."

A prolific and important writer and key figure in a famed literary circle, Mary Shelley is best known for creating a monster. Frankenstein, published in 1818, would prove to be her greatest legacy, one that lives on to this day.

❋ ❋ ❋ ❋

INSPIRATION FLOWED ALL around a young Mary Shelley, born Mary Godwin in London in 1797, even though her mother died 11 days after her birth due to labor complications. Her father, William Godwin, was a philosopher, writer and firm believer in education. His connections among the high thinkers of London became Mary's connections, too. Samuel Taylor Coleridge once recited a poem in the Godwin's living room. Scientists Humphry Davy and William Nicholson, early experimenters with galvanic electricity, were also counted among their friends and would wind up having an impact on the *Frankenstein* story, Shelley's most famous.

Mary's personal life was nothing if not complicated. She had a broken relationship with her stepmother, who married William when Mary was 4. She was raised largely by her older sister, Fanny, and was close with her stepsister Claire Clairmont, who wound up pregnant with the child of famed poet Lord Byron. Mary herself fell in love with Percy Shelley, whose wife was pregnant at the time he and Mary ran off together. It wasn't until after his wife's suicide in 1816 that Percy and Mary wed.

A Life of Literature

Percy had been estranged from his own family, who considered him a radical, and later became estranged from Mary's father William over financial matters. So Mary, Percy and Claire spent years either traveling or in self-imposed "exile." As always, they surrounded themselves with literature.

They accompanied Lord Byron on a trip to Lake Geneva, Switzerland, in 1816. Byron suggested they all share a ghost story. After struggling at first to come up with one, Mary conjured the tale of a doctor who, in a failed effort to play God and create life, built a monster that frighteningly came to life. Percy encouraged her to expand on the story and worked with her over the next two years as she penned *Frankenstein; or, The Modern Prometheus*. Mary Shelley was well-published and appreciated for her writing both in her own time and even more so after her death in February of 1851, but *Frankenstein* would become her legacy.

There was some debate over its authorship in the early years, as it was published anonymously and many credited Percy Shelley as its author. Mary takes proper credit for the work in subsequent editions, writing in the 1831 edition, "How I, then a young girl, came to think of, and to dilate upon, so very hideous an idea?" While the extent of Percy's contributions is not entirely agreed upon, there is no disagreement about the profound impact *Frankenstein* has had in almost two centuries since its publication.

The Frankenstein monster remains one of the most widely recognized characters in the horror genre, and dozens of films, TV programs and works of literature have used the character or versions of the character to induce fear, drama and even laughs. From *The Bride of Frankenstein* (1931) to *The Curse of Frankenstein* (1957) to Mel Brooks' classic and hilarious *Young Frankenstein* (1974), Shelley's lakeside "ghost story" has—just like its monstrous character—truly taken on a life of its own.

Delacroix Brought Literature to Life

"Painting is only a bridge linking the painter's mind with that of the viewer."

The leader of the French Romantic movement, Eugene Delacroix also shaped Impressionism and Symbolism. His passion for his paintings and murals was unrivaled as he brought the works of many famous authors and poets to life.

✳   ✳   ✳   ✳

BORN INTO A prominent family near Paris in 1798, Eugene Delacroix lost both parents at an early age. He was largely raised by his older sister Henriette, whose husband was a French ambassador. His brother-in-law's connections afforded Delacroix several advantages when it came to schooling, but his art was still mainly self-taught. He learned more from studying the Louvre than he ever did in the classroom.

His first paintings were nothing like the classic teachings of his main instructor, Pierre Guérin, but a more free and colorful style that would later come to establish him as the preeminent French Romanticist. His first major work, *The Barque of Dante* (1822), was much talked-about (with considerable opposition) for its imagery, loosely based on Dante's *Inferno*, and the fact it broke away from French Neo-Classicism.

Critics Were Everywhere

Falling in and out of favor with the traditional French art community became a common theme through Delacroix's life. From his sometimes exotic topics to his unconventional use of color to his dramatic brushstrokes, he broke the mold. Sometimes it was to the delight of critics; sometimes to their chagrin. Always, however, it was true to the passion Delacroix had for his art.

Delacroix identified with the works of William Shakespeare, Lord Byron, and Walter Scott, among other authors and poets, and brought their writings to life in his art. His take on a Byron play in the 1827 painting *Death of Sardanapalus* sent him falling out of favor with many in the art and literary community at the time. It depicts the death of an Assyrian king, and shows the king's guards carrying out a graphic slaughter of his servants, animals and concubines.

Byron's play depicts no such orders of a massacre, and many felt Delacroix took perhaps too many liberties with his imagination. The negative reception sent Delacroix into a period where he experimented with many different types of subjects ranging from oriental scenes to animals to exotic nudes.

He painted his most influential and popular piece in 1830. *Liberty Leading the People* portrayed the will and strength of Parisians, carrying weapons and marching forward under the red, white and blue flag. The French government purchased the painting, displaying it until some felt it glorified liberty too much and it was taken down.

Liberty Leading the People returned to prominence following the French Revolution of 1848, when Napoleon III put it on display. The painting has spent most of its life in the Louvre, and it earned Delacroix several prominent commissions over the last half of his life to paint murals for numerous public buildings in France, including the ceiling of a gallery in the Louvre and the Chapel of Holy Angels in the Church of Saint-Sulpice.

Delacroix took a trip to Africa in 1832, after the French had conquered Algeria, and what he saw there further shaped his work. He was fascinated by Morocco and Islamic Africa. *Women of Algiers in their Apartment* (1834) and *Jewish Wedding in Morocco* (1837) were two of the prominent works coming out of the trip.

Known as one of the most versatile painters of his time, Delacroix lived to see his influence recognized when 36 of his works were showcased at the Universal Exposition of 1855. He and Jean-Auguste-Dominique Ingres were honored as France's two greatest living artists. Delacroix died eight years later, in 1863.

"The first virtue of a painting is to be a feast for the eyes."

Hugo's Mastery Spanned Genres, Political Stances

"A library implies an act of faith which generations, still in darkness hid, sign in their night in witness of the dawn."

One of the greatest French writers in history, Hugo is world renowned for two works that were published more than 30 years apart, The Hunchback of Notre-Dame *and* Les Miserables. *Hugo was also an accomplished poet and artist whose work reflected changing political landscapes in his homeland.*

✳ ✳ ✳ ✳

Politics were a tug-of-war in France in the 19th Century, and so it was in the Hugo home. Victor was born in 1802 to a Napoleon-supporting father, Leopold, and a mother, Sophie, who sided with Catholic and royal political beliefs. His parents' opposing political views certainly shaped Victor's childhood, during which Napoleon became emperor of France (1804) and the monarchy was restored when Napoleon fell 10 years later.

Hugo's brilliance as a writer was apparent from an early age, when his political views leaned toward those of his mother. He was just 20 when his first collection of poetry was published, earning him a pension from Louis XVIII. So devoted was Victor to his mother, in fact, that he waited until after her death in 1821 to marry his childhood friend, Adele Foucher, because his mother was opposed to it. The couple had five children, including a son who died as an infant.

As he grew older, Hugo's political leanings trended away from the establishment. He truly became a voice of the people, and his writings began to summon change. *The Hunchback of Notre-Dame*, for example, in addition to becoming one of the classic books of its time, prompted the City of Paris to give Notre Dame Cathedral a long-overdue restoration so it could welcome its new throngs of visitors.

A young Hugo aspired to write like famed Romanticism figure Chateaubriand, but Victor surpassed even that lofty goal. Mallarmé, a poet and literary critic, argued that Hugo "divided all French literature into two epochs—before and after Hugo."

Tacking Social Injustice

The Hunchback of Notre-Dame furthered Hugo's fame in 1831, but it would not even be known as his masterpiece by the time his prolific career ended. That honor would go to *Les Miserables*, published in 1862, following a tumultuous political career Hugo undertook earlier in his life.

He spoke on behalf of King Louis-Philippe in 1845, was elected to Parliament as a conservative three years later and ultimately broke with the conservatives to speak out for the end of poverty and injustice among the French people. He spoke out for social reform and for the abolishment of the death penalty. In 1851, when Napoleon III claimed power, Hugo proclaimed him a traitor to France and went into exile.

It was under those circumstances that *Les Miserables* came to be. After he worked on it for the better part of two decades, it was released in 1862 and sold out in hours. It became an instant favorite among the French people, while the establishment was predictably critical. *Les Miserables* became one of the most influential classics in literary history, and remains a favorite today.

Hugo, also an accomplished artist who somewhat quietly produced more than 4,000 drawings, was hailed as a national hero upon his return to Paris in 1870. He lived in his homeland until his death after a bout with pneumonia in 1885. One of the largest parades in French history was held to celebrate his 79th birthday, and his funeral attracted more than two million—more than the population of Paris at the time.

Wisdom from *Les Miserables*

"The supreme happiness in life is the conviction that we are loved."

"Great grief is a divine and terrible radiance which transfigures the wretched."

"Would you realize what Revolution is, call it Progress; and would you realize what Progress is, call it tomorrow."

"Great blunders are often made, like large ropes, out of a multitude of fibers."

Poe Alters Landscape of American Literature

Eccentric at best, misunderstood at worst, and recognized as one of the first American writers to gain worldwide acclaim, Edgar Allan Poe contributed to the growth of several genres during his brief 40 years of life. His 1845 poem, "The Raven," remains a classic.

✳ ✳ ✳ ✳

O NCE UPON A midnight dreary," the well-known opening line of "The Raven," could easily describe the early life of Poe. Poe was born in Boston to two struggling actors in 1809. His father abandoned the family when Edgar was 1 and his mother died the following year. Sent to Richmond to live with John and Frances Allan (and to take their name), the orphaned Poe tangled with both his foster father and his life in general.

Poe attended the University of Virginia for one semester, enlisted in the U.S. Army under a phony name and could not make it as a West Point cadet. He wanted to be a writer at a time when no one, particularly no one in the U.S., made authoring a fulltime job. The odds were stacked against Poe, but he was game to try.

Poe, who was 26 when he fell in love with his 13-year-old cousin, Virginia Clemm, whom he married in 1836. He had enjoyed varying degrees of success with poetry and prose early in his career until making a concerted effort to produce a masterpiece with his poem, "The Raven," in 1845. The tale of a talking raven visiting a mourning narrator resonated with readers due to its themes of love and loss, and its struggle between wanting to hold onto painful sorrow and trying to forget it.

Poe's life would feature more such sorrow. His wife died in 1847, and his drinking and depression worsened. Both have been discussed as possible causes, among others, for his own death two years later. Though he never reaped a rich bounty for his literature during his life, Poe is credited with inventing detective fiction, with spurring others toward science fiction, and with popularizing the short story.

The Raven, First Verse

Once upon a midnight dreary,
 while I pondered, weak and weary,
Over many a quaint and curious volume of forgotten lore—
While I nodded, nearly napping,
suddenly there came a tapping,
As of some one gently rapping,
rapping at my chamber door.
"'Tis some visitor," I muttered,
"tapping at my chamber door—
Only this and nothing more."

On Striving, Seeking and Finding

The most popular of the Victorian Era poets in Great Britain, Lord Alfred Tennyson did not seek the limelight but found fame nonetheless. "Ulysses," one of his most famous poems, had a lasting legacy that produced the motto for the 2012 Summer Olympic Games in London.

✳   ✳   ✳   ✳

B Y THE TIME he was 18 years old in 1827, Alfred Tennyson needed to get away. His father drank heavily and suffered from mental breakdowns. One brother was an opium addict and another had to be committed to an asylum. Alfred found his outlet from the chaos in literature, left for Trinity College in Cambridge and teamed up with his brother Charles on a published collection, *Poems by Two Brothers*.

One of those brothers would go on to become the preeminent Victorian Era poet. Alfred's talent was unmistakable from an early age. Though his shyness kept him from expressing himself well publicly, he clearly had a lot to say, along with a mastery of language that connected with all who read him. After just two years in Cambridge, Tennyson won the Chancellor's Gold Medal for "Timbuktu," one of his first pieces written there.

His second volume of *Poems,* in 1842, included his classic "Ulysses," in which he writes in blank verse of the character in Homer's *Odyssey.* The death of one of Tennyson's closest friends compelled him to write it in 1833, and many have found inspiration in its last lines. The poem culminates with, "To Strive, to seek, to find, and not to yield." It was adopted as the motto of the Summer Olympic Games in London in 2012.

Tennyson succeeded William Wordsworth as Poet Laureate in 1850 and held the post longer than anyone in history, until his death in 1892.

Ulysses

It little profits that an idle king,
By this still hearth, among these barren crags,
Match'd with an aged wife, I mete and dole
Unequal laws unto a savage race,
That hoard, and sleep, and feed, and know not me.
I cannot rest from travel: I will drink
Life to the lees: All times I have enjoy'd
Greatly, have suffer'd greatly, both with those
That loved me, and alone, on shore, and when
Thro' scudding drifts the rainy Hyades
Vext the dim sea: I am become a name;
For always roaming with a hungry heart
Much have I seen and known; cities of men
And manners, climates, councils, governments,
Myself not least, but honour'd of them all;
And drunk delight of battle with my peers,
Far on the ringing plains of windy Troy.
I am a part of all that I have met;
Yet all experience is an arch wherethro'

Gleams that untravell'd world whose margin fades
For ever and forever when I move.
How dull it is to pause, to make an end,
To rust unburnish'd, not to shine in use!
As tho' to breathe were life! Life piled on life
Were all too little, and of one to me
Little remains: but every hour is saved
From that eternal silence, something more,
A bringer of new things; and vile it were
For some three suns to store and hoard myself,
And this gray spirit yearning in desire
To follow knowledge like a sinking star,
Beyond the utmost bound of human thought.

This is my son, mine own Telemachus,
To whom I leave the sceptre and the isle,—
Well-loved of me, discerning to fulfil
This labour, by slow prudence to make mild
A rugged people, and thro' soft degrees
Subdue them to the useful and the good.
Most blameless is he, centred in the sphere
Of common duties, decent not to fail
In offices of tenderness, and pay
Meet adoration to my household gods,
When I am gone. He works his work, I mine.

There lies the port; the vessel puffs her sail:
There gloom the dark, broad seas. My mariners,
Souls that have toil'd, and wrought, and thought with me—
That ever with a frolic welcome took
The thunder and the sunshine, and opposed
Free hearts, free foreheads—you and I are old;
Old age hath yet his honour and his toil;
Death closes all: but something ere the end,
Some work of noble note, may yet be done,
Not unbecoming men that strove with Gods.
The lights begin to twinkle from the rocks:

The long day wanes: the slow moon climbs: the deep
Moans round with many voices. Come, my friends,
'T is not too late to seek a newer world.
Push off, and sitting well in order smite
The sounding furrows; for my purpose holds
To sail beyond the sunset, and the baths
Of all the western stars, until I die.
It may be that the gulfs will wash us down:
It may be we shall touch the Happy Isles,
And see the great Achilles, whom we knew.
Tho' much is taken, much abides; and tho'
We are not now that strength which in old days
Moved earth and heaven, that which we are, we are;
One equal temper of heroic hearts,
Made weak by time and fate, but strong in will
To strive, to seek, to find, and not to yield.

The World of Voguing

When most people hear the word vogue, they think of Madonna's hit 1990 song and music video of the same name. However, the song is actually based on a dance with a rich history and with moves far more complex than suggested by Madonna's call to "strike a pose, there's nothing to it."

* * * *

The Movement Begins

THE ROOTS OF voguing may travel as far back as late 19th-century Chicago, where underground gay communities hosted elaborate drag balls. For the most part, these balls were only held on New Year's Eve and Halloween, when the participants could legitimize their drag. Other theories argue that voguing got its start in Harlem during the 1920s Harlem Renaissance, when black gays hosted costume balls.

Whatever the precise genealogy of voguing, it emerged as a distinct art form during the mid- to late-1970s, in the poor

African American and Latino gay communities of Harlem. While the youths of Harlem were organizing themselves into gangs, the voguing community had a different idea. Instead of gangs, they formed voguing "houses." Each house was presided over by a "mother," and the different houses competed in voguing competitions called "balls."

Strike a Pose

The essence of voguing is that the performer flawlessly fuses together several diverse components of a dance, all while walking down a runway dressed up as a specific persona. The vogue dance varies from community to community, but it generally combines elements of jazz, gymnastics, bodybuilding, ballet, break-dancing, and karate. Complex hand and arm movements are incorporated as part of the "pose," which imitates traditional runway poses. The term voguing came as a reference to the fashion magazine *Vogue*.

Inseparable from the dance is the persona. Voguers are asked to perform in a given category, such as "businessman," "femme queen," or "school girl." Essential to the success of the performance is "realness"—the voguer must convincingly look and act like a businessman, for instance, from clothing to accessories to gesture. Voguers are rewarded with trophies and cash prizes.

Many voguers lived in poverty and made money illegally. They were often discriminated against for their sexual orientation and cast to society's edges. The different ballroom houses fostered a sense of community, and many voguers became skilled and devoted dancers. The underground ballroom scene had its own lingo, its own rules, and, above all else, its own dance.

The Underground Goes Overground

As the voguing movement became more popular, members of the Harlem houses would sometimes visit the midtown clubs of mainstream Manhattan. By the late 1980s, professional voguers were hired at trendy midtown hot spots, and some clubs hosted "vogue night" every week.

The process seemed complete in 1989 when the ballroom scene's most famous houses staged a competitive ball at a celebrity-studded AIDS fund-raising event in Manhattan. That same year, top voguers were sent to vogue down the Paris runways. A 1989 *Time* magazine article declared, "At the hottest clubs in Manhattan, on MTV and at Paris fashion shows, the ultra-hip are into voguing."

And then, in 1990, documentary filmmaker Jennie Livingston released *Paris Is Burning*, a documentary about underground ball culture that was seven years in the making. The film was critically acclaimed and spawned an avalanche of academic controversy that deserves a genre of its own.

Movie critics and academics alike were intrigued by the socially subversive nature of voguing as presented in Livingston's film. They argued that by dressing as movie stars and fashion models, the socially marginalized voguers were actually mocking the power given these roles by society. Others vehemently disagreed with this interpretation, pointing out that the vogue competitors did not mock but rather emulated and admired these roles, thus paying homage to the very power structures that kept them down. A central part of the ballroom philosophy was that one can feel beautiful by looking beautiful; by imitating power, one can have it—at least for those few shining moments out on the runway. Voguing was thus simultaneously an act of control and escapism. Venus Xtravaganza, one of the film's stars, expressed her desire to be a "spoiled, rich white girl."

Ironic Consequences

Voguing's 15 minutes of fame did embody a puzzling irony: An underground culture that sought to imitate the mainstream was made mainstream by a documentary that sought to represent the underground. Yet, once Madonna's song hit the airwaves and Livingston's movie graced the big screen, the media's new proprietorship of voguing quickly proved that, in fact, the voguers themselves could never hope to become the spoiled, rich white girls that they dressed up to be. Madonna made millions off her song, and so did MTV. Within two years of the release of *Paris Is Burning*, all but two of the subjects featured in the film sued for a portion of the film's profits. Their case was denied. Within five years of the film's release, five of those in the film were dead. Venus Xtravaganza, a prostitute, was murdered by one of her clients.

The fear that the documentary carnivorously absorbed voguing into the mainstream is arguably the least of the concerns of the voguing community itself. Ballroom houses continue to thrive, having sprung up in Los Angeles, Chicago, and even in Indiana and Kentucky. The ballroom community is alive and well, proving once again that subcultures continue to exist, even if they aren't featured on MTV.

John Ruskin

"Remember that the most beautiful things in the world are the most useless; peacocks and lilies for instance."

A leading Victorian art critic, John Ruskin emphasized the connection between nature, art, and society, and is widely considered a forerunner of modern ideas concerning sustainability and the environment.

✳ ✳ ✳ ✳

JOHN RUSKIN WAS born in London on February 8, 1819 to a merchant family; his father had made a fortune in the wine trade. Ruskin was an only child and homeschooled; his father's extensive collection of watercolor paintings influenced him at an early age. He also travelled extensively as a child with his family, which further developed his ideas on nature and society. He attended Oxford for five years, where he won the Newdigate Prize for his poetry. He also worked for much of his time at Oxford on an extensive, though unfinished, dissertation on the painter JMW Turner, a Romanticist landscape painter.

Art Criticism

He began publishing short essays on art criticism in the 1830s, and in 1843 he published the first of what would become the five-volume series *Modern Painters*. The work drew on Ruskin's amateur fascination with botany and geology, and the first volume dealt extensively with the themes of Nature in Turner's paintings, defending what he considered the "truths" of his work, examining tone, color, space, earth, water, and vegetation in turn. Ruskin would continue working on *Modern Painters* until the fifth volume was published in 1860.

Ruskin wrote his art criticism in a plain style of prose that both vividly described the works he was discussing and made his writing accessible to a wide audience. In doing so, he introduced the possibility of art appreciation to a many newly wealthy members of the commercial and professional classes. He urged young painters to seek the meanings of art in Nature, "rejecting nothing, selecting nothing, and scorning nothing."

Following the publication of the first volume of *Modern Painters*, Ruskin turned his attention to architecture; in 1849, following his honeymoon with Effie Gray touring Gothic churches in northern France, he wrote *The Seven Lamps of Architecture*, in which he argued for seven moral principles that should guide architecture. His respect for original style in architecture would inspire the architecture conservation movement of the 20th century. In 1851, he published the first volume of *The Stones of Venice*. The book is primarily a history of the architecture of that city, but it also argues that art and architecture are the manifestation of the social conditions that produce them. He said, "All great art is the work of the whole living creature, body, and soul, and chiefly of the soul."

In 1851, his marriage fell apart, and Ruskin began travelling extensively. He published more volumes of *Modern Painters* and *The Stones of Venice*, and in 1858 he began teaching painting to the daughters of Maria La Touche. He became infatuated with Rose La Touche, who was a child at the time, and when she turned 18 he asked her to marry him. She put him off for three years, until she finally refused in 1872. She died following a long illness in 1875, and Ruskin fell into a deep depression marked by severe breakdowns.

Ruskin was appointed a Professor of Fine Art at Oxford in 1870, and while there he wrote and published *Fors Clavigera*, a monthly magazine of cultural theory. While there, he published *Fiction Fair & Foul*, a discussion of English writers, and *The Storm-Cloud of the Nineteenth Century*, which studied the effects of industrial pollution on weather patterns. Between 1885 and 1889 he wrote *Praeterita*, his autobiography, but never finished it.

He died on January 20, 1900.

Quotes by Ruskin

"Let us reform our schools, and we shall find little reform needed in our prisons."

"That country is the richest which nourishes the greatest number of noble and happy human beings."

"Give a little love to a child, and you get a great deal back."

Misunderstood Blake
One of the Greats

During his lifetime, many thought Blake to be insane. Though appreciated by precious few until after his death, the British poet, painter and engraver is now universally recognized for his talent and vision.

❋ ❋ ❋ ❋

WILLIAM BLAKE WROTE, "To see a World in a Grain of Sand/And a Heaven in a Wild Flower/Hold Infinity in the palm of your hand/And Eternity in an hour." The poem itself ("Auguries of Innocence"), published posthumously, juxtaposes innocence with evil and itself and can be seen as a metaphor for Blake's misunderstood life.

Born in London in 1757, he began engraving early in his life. He also showed an aptitude for painting and poetry, and offered a number of prophesies in his work. During his time, he was considered irrational at best and raving mad at worst. It wasn't until after his death when scholars began to universally recognize the vision in his works. William Rossetti, a 19th Century scholar, called him a glorious luminary.

Blake married Catherine Sophie Boucher in 1782, the same year he met her. He taught her to read, write and engrave, passions that allowed Blake to make their living. He published *Poetical Sketches*, his first collection of poems, the following year.

His works were influenced by both the French and American Revolutions. Blake also espoused what were then considered radical thoughts about religion and sexuality via his poetic and artistic imagery. He claimed to have seen visions, and his art reflected prophesies through religious imagery that only furthered the notion of his madness.

Blake's influence took off following his death in 1827, as biographers, scholars and artists began to see him as a counterculture icon. Beat poets writing more than 100 years after his death viewed Blake as an inspiration.

Quotes from Blake

"Can I see another's woe,
And not be in sorrow too?
Can I see another's grief,
And not seek for kind relief?"

—SONGS OF INNOCENCE, "ON ANOTHER'S SORROW"

"Poetry fettered fetters the human race. Nations are destroyed, or flourish, in proportion as their poetry, painting, and music are destroyed or flourish!"

"'Love seeketh not itself to please,
Nor for itself hath any care,
But for another gives its ease,
And builds a Heaven in Hell's despair.'

So sung a little Clod of Clay
Trodden with the cattle's feet,
But a Pebble of the brook
Warbled out these metres meet:
'Love seeketh only self to please,
To bind another to its delight,
Joys in another's loss of ease,
And builds a Hell in Heaven's despite.'"

—"THE CLOD AND THE PEBBLE"

"I was angry with my friend;
I told my wrath, my wrath did end.
I was angry with my foe:
I told it not, my wrath did grow."

—"THE POISON TREE"

Bronte and Sisters Broke New Ground

"Reader, I married him."

Charlotte Bronte was one of three sisters from England who turned the literary world—belonging almost exclusively to men at that time—on its head. Charlotte's Jane Eyre became one of the most popular works not only of its time, but over generations to come.

✳   ✳   ✳   ✳

THE FAMED BRONTE sisters—Charlotte, Emily and Anne—were born in Yorkshire between 1816 and 1820 to parents who encouraged schooling and the use of imagination. Their mother died of cancer when Charlotte was 5 and two of their other sisters died young, leaving Charlotte to take up a motherly role herself from a young age.

The trio lost themselves in books and their own writing. Charlotte also began working as a governess, and her experience trying to oversee one poorly behaved young boy served as inspiration for John Reed's character in the opening scenes of *Jane Eyre*.

In 1846, Charlotte, Emily and Anne put out their debut publication under pen names. It was a collection of their poems, with authoring credits going to Currer, Ellis and Acton Bell. They maintained the first initials of their actual names, but used gender-neutral monikers to avoid the critical lambasting they feared might come to women.

The next year, each published a solo work under the same pen names. For Charlotte, *Jane Eyre* was a revision of an initial manuscript she had titled *The Professor*. The story of a governess who eventually falls in love with her boss achieved early success and has remained popular among generations of readers.

Her sisters found individual success, too—Emily with *Wuthering Heights* and Anne with *Agnes Grey*, all released in 1847. Their actual identities were revealed the following year.

Charlotte married the Rev. A.B. Nicholls in 1854. Later that year, while pregnant, Charlotte became ill with pneumonia, and both she and the baby died.

Eliot: A Brilliant Enigma

One of the leading Victorian Era authors and 19th Century intellectuals, George Eliot—the pen name of Mary Ann Evans—was celebrated for her writing but often derided for everything from her behavior to her appearance. Through it all, her social criticism and insight left a lasting impact.

✳ ✳ ✳ ✳

MARY ANN EVANS, who wrote under the pen name George Eliot in an effort to be taken more seriously in a time when female authors were generally pigeon-holed as romance writers, was born in a rural English setting in 1819. Because she was not considered an attractive girl (a stigma that, sadly, followed her throughout her life), her father felt it was even more important for her to get an education and sent her off to schools until she was 16. It was then that Mary's mother died, so she returned to home to care for her father's house. By that time, she had already proven to be a tireless reader and a talented young writer.

She also had begun to doubt the religious principles of her upbringing. When a move near Coventry at age 21 put her in contact with the free-thinking Charles and Cara Bray, the foundation for her writings began to take shape. The Brays regularly hosted debates in their home among some of the most progressive thinkers of the time, and Mary was engrossed. Charles Bray also stepped up to publish some of Evans' first writings in the local newspaper.

Mary Becomes George

Mary's father died in 1849, and after doing some traveling through Europe she settled in London in 1850 intent on becoming a writer. She took an editor job at a radical journal, *The Westminster Review*, contributing several articles and essays to the publication.

Her pen name, adopted in the early 1850s, is said to be a nod to George Lewes, a critic with whom she became intimate and lived with despite the fact he was married. It was one of many "scandalous" episodes that earned George Eliot great social disapproval.

Eliot's seven novels focused largely, but not exclusively, on social issues and politics. Her first, *Adam Bede* in 1859, met with great success. In *Felix Holt, the Radical* in 1866, Eliot took readers into a small-town pub to meet the book's characters and get to know about their work habits without describing them in a work setting. "One way of getting an idea of our fellow-countrymen's miseries," she wrote, "is to go and look at their pleasures."

Her most acclaimed work was *Middlemarch* in 1872. Her realism and insightful commentary, told overtly or through her characters, stood out among Victorian Era authors. Sometimes overshadowing her brilliant literature, however, were the scandals of her relationships. Her sexuality and open, out-of-marriage relationships were unusual enough for the era. Her homeliness also seemed to be a fascination for critics. It added up to an unconventional career for Eliot, who did enjoy considerable success in her lifetime and became revered as one of the greats as later generations passed.

There was one more name change for George. In May of 1880, she became Mary Ann Cross when she married John Cross. Even wedding vows would not calm the scandal, however. Quite the contrary, in fact: Cross was 20 years younger than Mary, a difference many viewed in an even less favorable light than adultery.

Mary had been battling kidney disease, and later that year contracted a throat infection. She died on December 22, 1880.

Quotes from Eliot

"If we had a keen vision of all that is ordinary in human life, it would be like hearing the grass grow or the squirrel's heart beat, and we should die of that roar which is the other side of silence."

—*MIDDLEMARCH*

"If youth is the season of hope, it is often so only in the sense that our elders are hopeful about us."

—*MIDDLEMARCH*

"We hand folks over to God's mercy, and show none ourselves."

—*ADAM BEDE*

"If art does not enlarge men's sympathies, it does nothing morally."

—*LETTER*

Johnson Known for 'Anthem,' NAACP Leadership

"Out from the gloomy past, till now we stand at last
Where the white gleam of our bright star is cast."

✳ ✳ ✳ ✳

JAMES WELDON JOHNSON was born in 1871 in Jacksonville, Florida, and his mother taught him to love both learning and music. She was a musician and public school teacher, and James went off to Atlanta University convinced he could help the African-American community through a career in education as well.

During the summer after his freshman year, he went to rural Georgia on a volunteer trip to teach the descendants of former slaves to read and write. He said the experience shaped everything he did through the remainder of his career.

Johnson became a school principal in Jacksonville after his graduation, but that was just the beginning. In 1900, to celebrate the birthday of Abraham Lincoln, he wrote a song called "Lift Every Voice." It was performed by 500 Jacksonville school children and became immediately popular in the black community—so much so that it came to be known as the "Negro National Anthem."

Johnson went on to a decorated career as a lawyer, diplomat, song writer and civil rights leader. He is perhaps best known for his leadership of the National Association for the Advancement of Colored People (NAACP). He started working for the group in 1917, and three years later became the first African-American selected to run the NAACP as its secretary.

Johnson also served as U.S. Consul to Venezuela under President Theodore Roosevelt. He died in 1938.

Lyrics

Lift every voice and sing
Till earth and heaven ring,
Ring with the harmonies of Liberty;
Let our rejoicing rise,
High as the list'ning skies,
Let it resound loud as the rolling sea.
Sing a song full of the faith that the dark past has taught us,
Sing a song full of the hope that the present has brought us,
Facing the rising sun of our new day begun,
Let us march on till victory is won.

Stony the road we trod,
Bitter the chastening rod,
Felt in the days when hope unborn had died;
Yet with a steady beat,
Have not our weary feet
Come to the place for which our fathers sighed
We have come over a way that with tears has been watered,
We have come treading our path through the blood of the
slaughtered,
Out from the gloomy past, till now we stand at last
Where the white gleam of our bright star is cast.

God of our weary years,
God of our silent tears,
Thou who hast brought us thus far on the way;
Thou who has by Thy might
Led us into the light,
Keep us forever in the path, we pray.
Lest, our feet stray from the places, our God, where we met
Thee,
Lest, our hearts, drunk with the wine of the world, we forget
Thee,
Shadowed beneath Thy hand, may we forever stand,
True to our God, true to our native land.

All the News That's Fit to Print

At a time when some newspapers were chasing readers with salacious stories, Adolf Simon Ochs proved that an honest, accurate and trustworthy approach could be every bit as successful. The standard he set leading two newspapers, including The New York Times, *made him one of the most respected men in the business.*

✳ ✳ ✳ ✳

OCHS LEARNED EARLY in his life the importance of sticking to his principles. His parents, Jewish immigrants who fled Germany for Tennessee, chose opposite sides in the United States Civil War. His mother, Bertha, sided with the Confederacy, but his father, Julius, opted to serve the Union army. Their differences did not divide the couple or their family.

Adolf, the oldest of six children, was born in 1958. At age 11, he left school and went to work at the *Knoxville Chronicle* to bring in extra money for his family. There, he assisted editor William Rule, who became a mentor. Ochs learned printing and reporting, calling the gig his high school and his university. He learned his lessons well, showing interest, aptitude and a tireless work ethic.

At age 19, he took his skills to the *Chattanooga Times*. When the paper began to fail later that year, Ochs borrowed $250 and purchased controlling interest in the operation. As its publisher, he declared that the paper would be "clean, dignified and trustworthy." He shunned the temptation to chase salacious stories in an effort to drive sales, as several other were doing at a competitive time in the industry.

Ochs wanted to draw a clean line between news reporting and editorial opinion. The former was the staple of his operation; the latter would be clearly identified. In this way, the *Chattanooga Times* made a name for itself as an honest, reliable source of the news. And Ochs' paper thrived, becoming one of the most successful in the south.

Off to the Big Apple

The formula worked so well the first time, Ochs tried it again in 1896, borrowing money to purchase a newspaper. This time, it was *The New York Times*. He and his wife, Effie (the daughter of a Cincinnati rabbi), were off to the big city.

The Times, the longtime leader of the New York City newspaper industry, had fallen on rough years against two rival city papers run by William Randolph Hearst and Joseph Pulitzer. Those papers, which embraced salacious stories, cost one cent; *The Times* charged three. Not surprisingly, readership was on the decline.

Under Ochs' leadership, though, the tide turned. While some were advising him to raise the price to cover a rough year of losses in 1897, Ochs decided to drop the price to one cent and stick to the principles of honest, unbiased, trustworthy journalism. He put the phrase, "All the News That's Fit to Print" on the masthead. By the 1920s, readership soared from less than 10,000 to some 780,000.

While Ochs brought *The Times* back to its rightful place as one of the nation's most respected sources of news, he also made an impact on the architectural landscape of the two cities in which he operated papers. In 1904, he moved *The Times* to Longacre Square in Manhattan. It would later be renamed Times Square. And in 1928, he constructed a temple dedicated to his parents in Chattanooga.

Ochs died while on a trip to Chattanooga in 1935. His only daughter, Iphigene Bertha Ochs, was married to Arthur Hays Sulzberger. Saulzberger followed Ochs as publisher of *The Times* from 1935 until 1961.

'America's Composer' Kept Country Singing

Irving Berlin was born in Russia, but he might be the most important songwriter in American history. From show tunes to anthems, this prolific music man penned some of the most popular songs ever written.

✳ ✳ ✳ ✳

THE AUTHOR OF America's unofficial soundtrack was born Israel Baline in Tyumen, Russia, in 1888. It was not a great time to grow up Jewish in Russia, so his family fled to New York City to escape persecution when he was a young boy. They settled on the lower east side and Israel, whose father was a cantor in the synagogue, began hanging out with a singing beggar and belting out tunes in the streets. A modest start indeed.

Eventually, some of the local restaurants and cafes hired him for pennies to entertain their guests. He also earned a gig touting certain acts at burgeoning vaudeville venue Tony Pastor's Music Hall. His big break, though, came when he was hired as a singing waiter at Pelham Café in Chinatown in 1906. The 18-year-old was drawing a following, and he collaborated with pianist "Nick" Nicholson on his first published recording, "Marie from Sunny Italy" in 1907.

The record featured a typo that would change the teenager's life. His name appeared as "I. Berlin." Rather than explain, he decided to stick with Irving Berlin. Soon, the name would become synonymous with some of the most popular songs of the early 20th Century.

On His Way

Berlin started turning heads as a lyricist. Between 1908 and '11, he put words to the music of several composers. One of his first such efforts, "Sadie Salome, Go Home," sold more than 200,000 copies in 1909. Two years later, writing prolifically for the Waterson & Snyder music publishing company, he wrote what would become the all-time classic "Alexander's Ragtime Band and earned the nickname "King of Tin Pan Alley."

Berlin wrote melodies, too, despite being adequate at best as an untrained, self-taught pianist. And he began churning out tunes that would become standards, as well as several musicals.

Berlin married Dorothy Goetz in 1912, but his new bride contracted typhoid fever and died only a few months after their honeymoon. Berlin was devastated when he wrote "When I Lost You," one of his most popular ballads.

Berlin's father was opposed to Postal Telegraph Cable Company heiress Ellin Mackay, whom he met in 1925, so the two eloped. News of their marriage made the front page of *The New York Times.*

If Mackay was big news in New York, Berlin was keeping an entire nation singing. Among the most well-known of the 1,500-plus songs on his resume were "What'll I Do," "White Christmas," "Blue Skies," "Easter Parade" and an arrangement of "God Bless America" that Kate Smith turned into a national anthem of sorts in 1938.

Berlin also hit it big with musicals and motion pictures. Among them: *Puttin' on the Ritz* (1929), *Alexander's Ragtime Band* (1938), *Annie Get Your Gun* (1946) and *Easter Parade* (1948), along with three Fred Astaire and Ginger Rogers films.

Annie Get Your Gun starred Ethel Merman and featured the hit songs "There's No Business Like Show Business" and "Anything You Can Do I Can Do Better," songs that became engrained in the minds and vocal chords of the nation. Indeed, for Berlin, there was no business like the entertainment business. He was nominated for nine Academy Awards during his 101-year life, including seven in the music category. He won that Oscar in 1943 with "White Christmas."

Yeats Wrote of Ireland, but for the World

Nobel Prize winner W.B. Yeats wrote passionately of his homeland but truly impacted literature worldwide with his poetry. It's not something he necessarily intended to do. Reflecting decades of political turmoil through his verse, Yeats remains popular and relevant some eight decades after his death.

❋   ❋   ❋   ❋

WILLIAM BUTLER YEATS was born in Dublin in 1865, the son of well-known painter John Butler Yeats. A family of means, they were members of the Anglo-Irish landowning class —a group that tended to consider itself English though living in Ireland. However, Yeats carved his own path as he grew up and became involved in the Celtic Revival movement, shunning English influences in favor of Irish heritage despite having lived in London for 14 years during his childhood.

Yeats first had his poetry published in 1885 in the *Dublin University Review,* around the time he developed an interest in mysticism and the occult that would thread their way through his writings throughout his career. That same year, he met and befriended John O'Leary, an Irish patriot who had been imprisoned for revolutionary activities as a Celtic Revivalist. O'Leary advised like-minded Irishmen to stick to their roots and embrace the Irish spirit in their writing, and Yeats was all in.

"When I first wrote, I went here and there for my subjects as my reading led me, and preferred to all other countries Arcadia and the India of romance," he once explained. "But presently I convinced myself...that I should never go for the scenery of a poem to any country but my own, and I think that I shall hold to that conviction to the end."

His poem "Easter 1916" addresses an unsuccessful uprising, and contains the much-quoted lines, "Too long a sacrifice / Can make a stone of the heart" and "All changed, changed utterly: / A terrible beauty is born."

Off to London

Yeats continued to write beautifully of his Irish homeland and the Irish spirit after moving with his family to London in 1886. It was there that he met and fell in love with Maud Gonne, known both for her beauty and for her fervent nationalist political views. She greatly influenced Yeats' poetry though she turned down his marriage proposals and wound up marrying another man.

While he remained unmarried until he was in his 50s, Yeats embraced and mastered many poetic techniques, relying on traditional forms as his foundation, and had a way of bringing imagery from the ordinary to life and captivate a growing following of readers. A member of groups and clubs dedicated to poetry, politics, the theater, and also the occult, Yeats blended his wide range of interests in his writing.

The Wind among the Reeds (1899) was the culmination of his 19th Century work. His first three volumes of the 20th Century—*In the Seven Woods* (1903), *The Green Helmet and Other Poems* (1910), and *Responsibilities* (1914)—Yeats took a marked turn toward a simpler, more conversational style. While maintaining a high level and volume of writing throughout his life, Yeats also stayed very involved in politics (he was appointed a senator of the Irish Free State in 1922) and also ran the Abbey Theatre of Ireland for many years.

Yeats was 51 when he married Georgie Hyde Lees, half his age, in 1916. The couple had two children, Anne and Michael. Yeats was awarded the Nobel Prize in literature in 1923 "for his always inspired poetry, which in a highly artistic form gives expression to the spirit of a whole nation."

Many of Yeats' lines have been both quotes and repurposed as titles of books, movies, and so forth. Some of his most famous lines come from "The Second Coming," published in a 1921 collection: "Things fall apart; the center cannot hold; / Mere anarchy is loosed upon the world." And "The best lack all conviction, while the worst / Are full of passionate intensity."

The poem "A Prayer for My Daughter" contains "That is no country for old men," while "The Circus Animals' Desertion" contains the phrase, "I must lie down where all ladders start, / in the foul rag-and-bone shop of the heart."

In one of his later poems, "Among School Children," Yeats writes reflectively on his life, closing with: "O body swayed to music, O brightening glance / How can we know the dancer from the dance?" Yeats died at age 73 in 1939.

Melville Gave Us a Whale of a Tale

"We cannot live only for ourselves. A thousand fibers connect us with our fellow men."

✳   ✳   ✳   ✳

HERMAN MELVILLE WAS a crossroads in 1850. The 31-year-old New Yorker had enjoyed success with his debut novel, *Typee*, a few years earlier but was struggling to produce a manuscript he had promised about a whaler on the South Seas. He had buried an older brother and married Elizabeth Shaw a few years earlier. He was writing, but his efforts lacked inspiration.

Then along came the summer of 1850. Melville and a group of writers embarked on a climb of Monument Mountain in Massachusetts. It was there he met New Englander Nathanial Hawthorne, of *The Scarlet Letter* fame, and the two quickly became close. In fact, Melville bought a farm in Massachusetts and moved his family there so he and Hawthorne could be neighbors.

The vigor having returned to his craft, Melville finished what started out as *The Whale* and became *Moby Dick*. The tale of

Ishmael, Ahab and a great white whale became one of the true American classics. The *Oxford Companion to English Literature* calls the book "the closest approach the United States has had to a national prose epic."

The fibers that connected Melville with his fellow man—Hawthorne, in this case—came along at just the right time. Melville continued writing until just a few years before his death in 1891. He turned away from the novel in favor of poetry in his later years.

Though he gained popularity in the mid-19th Century, it was not until 20–30 years after his death that Melville enjoyed a critical revival as his works were revisited and his name ascended near the top of the list of great American writers.

Lines to Remember from *Moby Dick*

"Call me Ishmael."

"I have no objection to any person's religion, be it what it may, so long as that person does not kill or insult any other person, because that other person don't believe it also. But when a man's religion becomes really frantic; when it is a positive torment to him; and, in fine, makes this earth of ours an uncomfortable inn to lodge in; then I think it high time to take that individual aside and argue the point with him."

"The White Whale swam before him as the monomaniac incarnation of all those malicious agencies which some deep men feel eating in them, till they are left living on with half a heart and half a lung. That intangible malignity which has been from the beginning; to whose dominion even the modern Christians ascribe one-half of the worlds; which the ancient Ophites of the east reverenced in their statue devil;—Ahab did not fall down and worship it like them; but deliriously transferring its idea to the abhorred white whale, he pitted himself, all mutilated, against it. All that most maddens and torments; all that stirs up the lees of things; all truth with malice in it; all that cracks the sinews and cakes the brain; all the subtle demonisms of life and thought; all evil, to crazy Ahab, were visibly personified, and made practically assailable in Moby Dick. He piled upon the whale's white hump the sum of all the general rage and hate felt by

his whole race from Adam down; and then, as if his chest had been a mortar, he burst his hot heart's shell upon it."

"There is no steady unretracing progress in this life; we do not advance through fixed gradations, and at the last one pause:— through infancy's unconscious spell, boyhood's thoughtless faith, adolescence' doubt (the common doom), then scepticism, then disbelief, resting at last in manhood's pondering repose of If. But once gone through, we trace the round again; and are infants, boys, and men, and Ifs eternally. Where lies the final harbor, whence we unmoor no more?"

"It is not down in any map; true places never are."

"Towards thee I roll, thou all-destroying but unconquering whale; to the last I grapple with thee; from hell's heart I stab at thee; for hate's sake I spit my last breath at thee."

Flaubert Insisted on Perfectionism, Realism

French novelist and playwright Gustave Flaubert was the ultimate perfectionist. His search for the perfect word, the perfect sentence and the perfect story resulted in one of the great novels of the 19th Century, Madame Bovary.

✳ ✳ ✳ ✳

WHILE OTHERS WERE churning out novels at a pace of one per year, Gustave Flaubert was thoroughly researching every subject and idea he considered, painstakingly deliberating over every word and rewriting until he was thoroughly satisfied with everything he put on paper. Frequently, that satisfaction was hard to come by.

As a result, his library might not compare to those of his contemporaries, but his impact was enormous. The controversial *Madame Bovary*, his first published novel in 1857, is considered a classic, and his contributions to Romanticism and Realism have been lauded by writers and critics through the generations.

Early Interest

The son of a surgeon, Flaubert was born in 1821 in Northern France. Some say he began writing as early as 8. He was also a voracious reader, showing a particularly keen interest in Shakespeare.

His initial career interest was law, but Flaubert suffered an attack of epilepsy while studying in Paris in 1844 and decided it was time to pursue his dream of becoming a writer. The following year he began working on the acclaimed *Sentimental Education*, a novel about the romantic life of a young man during the French Revolution, though it was not published until 1869.

His first published novel, in 1857, became an all-time classic and provided a glimpse into the meticulous style of Flaubert. "Human speech is like a cracked kettle on which we tap crude rhythms for bears to dance to," one of his characters in Madame Bovary explains, "while we long to make music that will melt the stars." That was Flaubert in a nutshell. He wanted each word to be "le mot juste," the perfect word. He avoided clichés at every cost and labored over everything he wrote.

A Classic

His precise writing style was debated by his contemporaries and emulated by many who followed. *Madame Bovary* created a stir for its subject matter—the adulterous wife of a doctor trying to escape her empty life—and Flaubert was charged with obscenity and hurting public morality. He won his case, however, being cleared of the charges.

It was also the style of the novel that set the literary world on its ear. Meticulously written over the course of five years, it has been described as the perfect work of fiction. It was published in six installments and became the most influential French novel of the 1800s. Given that it sometimes took him weeks to produce a single page, it's no surprise that additional Flaubert classics did not start flying off the shelves. He truly labored over his craft. It would be five years before he published *Salammbo,* and another seven before the already-started *Sentimental Education* was published.

The aim was perfection, and for that Flaubert is celebrated as perhaps the most thoughtful writer ever to put pen to paper. Flaubert may have had only one or two love interests in his life: an older woman, Elisa Schlésinger, he met in his early travels; and the poet Louise Colet, to whom he wrote a series of letters. He battled epilepsy throughout his adult life and died at age 59 in 1880.

Schliemann Finds His Treasure in Troy

"I have gazed on the face of Agamemnon."

Clinging to the words of Homer and on a mission to find the ancient city of Troy, German archaeologist Heinrich Schliemann struck gold in what is modern-day Turkey. Though his methods were questioned, he is credited with uncovering the ruins of a land some thought was forever lost.

✳ ✳ ✳ ✳

HEINRICH SCHLIEMANN WAS the son of a Lutheran minister in Germany and one of nine children. From an early age, he showed a keen interest in history and literature. In fact, he claimed that he verbalized his passion for discovering and excavating the lost city of Troy began at age 8, stemming from his early love of Homer's *Iliad* and *Odyssey.*

Schliemann began his career as a tradesman and proved to be a quick learner. He spent a year in Amsterdam and not only learned Dutch, but Spanish, Italian and Portuguese as well. He added Russian to his repertoire while on assignment in St. Petersburg, and later picked up Latin, English, French and other languages.

His quick mind helped Schliemann amass great wealth in various endeavors. He moved to California in 1851, during the gold rush, and started a banking business reselling gold dust. He sold the business a year later and moved to Russia, eventually making a small fortune reselling elements required to make ammunition to the Russian government during the Crimean War.

Schliemann had a knack for being in the right place at the right time when it came to business, and so it was with his lifelong passion of discovering the site of the Trojan War —a city that had been abandoned in 500 AD and lost through the ages.

The Quest

Schliemann used some of his wealth to study Ancient Greek and Latin in Paris. In 1868, he took a trip to Ithaka, a Greek island, to search for the palace of Ulysses. From there he set out on his quest to find Troy, clutching a copy of Homer's *Iliad* and little else on his journey.

British archeologist Frank Calvert had already begun excavations in the Troas region of what is now Turkey. Calvert identified Hisarlik as the 15th Century site that was built on the ruins of Troy. It was a hill upon which Schliemann stood and declared, "I was fully convinced that it was here that ancient Troy had stood."

Schliemann had what Calvert did not—the funds to execute an archaeological dig. What many agree he did not have was the expertise to manage a dig professionally. While the discovery of the ancient city under several layers of ruins gained Schliemann worldwide acclaim, the destruction wreaked upon many of the artifacts also earned him great scorn from the archaeological community.

Schliemann declared the artifacts "Priam's Treasure" and even had his young wife, Sophia, dress up in the gold and jewelry. More controversy would follow, as artifacts he dug up from the layer he called Troy proved to be from a period earlier than the Trojan War. Many concluded that Schliemann actually destroyed relics from what was Troy in getting to ruins that predated the ancient city that consumed him all his life.

Schliemann continued to excavate (including three subsequent excavations of Troy) until 1890, when he fell ill and died at age 68. He was buried in a mausoleum in Athens shaped like an ancient Greek temple. Despite the controversy surrounding his discovery, Schliemann remains a largely celebrated figure for unearthing the ancient city.

Procter Poured Soul into Poetry

Her writings about "the lost chord" from the 1800s still resonate with readers today.

✳ ✳ ✳ ✳

THOUGH TUBERCULOSIS TOOK her life at an early age, Adelaide Anne Procter accomplished much, and helped a great many, during her 38 years. Born in London in 1825 to a poet, Bryan Procter, and his wife Anne, she grew up as an acquaintance to a number of great poets, writers and literary thinkers. She loved reading and showed an early gift for writing, publishing her first poem while still in her teen years.

Not wanting to take advantage of Charles Dickens' friendship with her father, Procter began submitting poems to his publication, *Household Words*, under the pen name Miss Berwick. Dickens loved her submissions and published many of them, giving his large audience access to Procter's brilliant writing. One of her pieces, "A Lost Chord," would be set to music in 1877 as "The Lost Chord" by Arthur Sullivan and became a huge musical success.

A turning point in her life came in 1851, when she converted to Catholicism. She became extremely devout in her belief and had long been interested in philanthropic causes.

Her writing through the remainder of her life reflected this, as Procter wrote about the impoverished, the homeless and the downtrodden.

She took on women's equality issues at a time when such topics were generally repressed. She became Queen Victoria's favorite poet.

It was not just in her writing that Procter showed her devotion to such issues. She was a prominent advocate for Catholic widows and orphans through the Providence Row Night Refuge and a leader in a society pushing for the employment of women.

The Lost Chord

1.

Seated one day at the organ,
I was weary and ill at ease,
And my fingers wandered idly
Over the noisy keys;
I know not what I was playing,
Or what I was dreaming then,
But I struck one chord of music,
Like the sound of a great Amen,
Like the sound of a great Amen.

2.

It flooded the crimson twilight,
Like the close of an angel's psalm,
And it lay on my fevered spirit,
With a touch of infinite calm,
It quieted pain and sorrow,
Like love overcoming strife,
It seemed the harmonious echo
From our discordant life,

3.

It linked all the perplexed meanings
Into one perfect peace,
And trembled away into silence,
As if it were loth to cease;
I have sought but I seek it vainly,
That one lost chord divine,
Which came from the soul of the organ,
And entered into mine.

4.

It may be that death's bright angel
Will speak in that chord again;
It may be that only in Heav'n
I shall hear that great Amen.
It may be that death's bright angel
Will speak in that chord again;
It may be that only in Heav'n
I shall hear that great Amen.

From Cotton Field To Mansion

Born to former slaves and hit hard by fate, this ambitious woman became a cosmetics queen and devoted herself to African-American affairs.

✳ ✳ ✳ ✳

DECADES BEFORE OPRAH Winfrey arrived on the scene, an African-American woman built a business empire that made her immensely wealthy. Like Oprah, she used much of that wealth in the service of good causes. But Madame C. J. Walker did this at a time when segregation was the law of much of the land, and economic opportunities for African-Americans—let alone African-American women—were practically nonexistent.

"There Is No Royal, Flower-Strewn Road to Success"

A Louisiana native, Madame was born to former slaves in 1867 and named Sarah Breedlove. She had a crushingly hard early life, picking cotton as a little girl, and finding herself orphaned by the time she was seven. Sarah married at 14, and by 20 she was a widow with a young daughter.

Sarah moved to St. Louis, where she labored as a laundress and cook. A mysterious scalp ailment that left her bald inspired her to develop a restorative compound she dubbed "Madam Walker's Wonderful Hair Grower" (she'd taken the name "Madame C. J. Walker" after marrying a man named Charles Walker). A carefully recruited network of African-American saleswomen distributed the product door-to-door and helped make Madame's enterprise a huge success.

Philanthropist

In 1910, Walker established a factory in Indianapolis to manufacture the hair grower and other cosmetics. By 1917, Walker's company had assets of a million dollars—a huge sum at the time and an unprecedented achievement for someone of her background.

Walker built a townhouse in New York City's Harlem neighborhood and a magnificent estate, Villa Lewaro, in suburban Westchester County. But Madame Walker was a philanthropist as well as an entrepreneur. She gave generous financial support to organizations devoted to improving the lives of her fellow African-Americans—including the newly founded National Association for the Advancement of Colored People (NAACP).

Her influence went beyond just giving money: She traveled to the White House as part of a delegation protesting lynching in the South, and she regularly hosted the leading African-American intellectuals and activists of the day.

Madame Walker died on May 25, 1919. In her own words, "There is no royal, flower-strewn road to success, and what success I have obtained is the result of many sleepless nights and real hard work."

Pop Quiz: Which Mythical Land?

Dorothy, the Tin Man, and Toto are deeply familiar characters. So are Alice, the White Rabbit, and the Cheshire Cat. Oz and Wonderland have entertained children—and adults—for generations.

Each quote below comes from either L. Frank Baum's The Wonderful Wizard of Oz *or Lewis Carroll's* Alice in Wonderland. *Do you know which quote is associated with which fantastic fiction world?*

✳   ✳   ✳   ✳

1. "If you drink much from a bottle marked 'poison' it is almost certain to disagree with you, sooner or later."

a) Oz

b) Wonderland

2. "No matter how dreary and gray our homes are, we people of flesh and blood would rather live there than in any other country, be it ever so beautiful. There is no place like home."

a) Oz

b) Wonderland

3. "There is no living thing that is not afraid when it faces danger. The true courage is in facing danger when you are afraid, and that kind of courage you have in plenty."

a) Oz

b) Wonderland

4. "Curiouser and curiouser!"

a) Oz

b) Wonderland

5. "When I used to read fairy-tales, I fancied that kind of thing never happened, and now here I am in the middle of one! There ought to be a book written about me, that there ought! And when I grow up, I'll write one."

a) Oz

b) Wonderland

6. "You people with hearts," he said, "have something to guide you, and need never do wrong; but I have no heart, and so I must be very careful."

a) Oz

b) Wonderland

7. "I have always thought myself very big and terrible; yet such little things as flowers came near to killing me, and such small animals as mice have saved my life.'

a) Oz

b) Wonderland

8. "Everything's got a moral, if only you can find it."

a) Oz

b) Wonderland

Answer key: 1. b; 2. a; 3. a; 4. b; 5. b; 6. a; 7. a; 8. b

Carroll Created a 'Wonderland' for the World

The author of Alice's Adventures in Wonderland *broke new ground for the use of imagination in literature. His masterpieces, which also include* Through the Looking-Glass and What Alice Found There, *remain staples for children and adults everywhere.*

✳ ✳ ✳ ✳

CHARLES L. DODGSON, born in Cheshire, England, in 1832, suffered from a bad stutter. The oldest of 11 children and a whiz in math, writing, poetry and just about everything else under the academic sun just could not get the words out of his mouth sometimes—except, that is, when he was talking to children. Curiouser and curiouser!

Fortunately, the author better known by his pen name Lewis Carroll was in his comfort zone around the little ones. He loved to entertain children with his stories, and one Alice Liddell, daughter of famed author, dean and schoolmaster Henry George Liddell, was the inspiration who changed the course of children's literature.

Carroll spent countless hours telling Alice fantastic stories, and one day while on a picnic with Alice and her two sisters he is said to have recited the first-ever telling of the story that would become, in 1865, *Alice's Adventures in Wonderland.* Alice urged Carroll to write the story down for her, and the rest is history.

The success of the book, which brought the world characters like the Hatter, White Rabbit, Cheshire Cat and Queen of Hearts, prompted Carroll to follow up with the 1871 sequel *Through the Looking-Glass and What Alice Found There. Alice* became the most popular children's book in England by the time of Carroll's death in 1898, and by the early 1900s it had become one of the most popular in the world.

Yellow Brick Road Led
Baum to Fame

Lyman Frank Baum grew up far from Kansas in New York State, but he taught readers all over the world that there was no place like home. Baum began writing for children in his 40s and produced an all-time classic in The Wonderful Wizard of Oz.

✳ ✳ ✳ ✳

THERE WAS LITTLE to indicate that Lyman Frank Baum would write one of the most beloved children's books of all time. Born to a barrel factory owner in Chittenango, New York in 1856, he did not earn his high school degree and decided to pursue acting and stage writing before settling on careers in journalism and eventually business.

Baum married Maud Gage, the daughter of famed suffragist Matilda Joslyn Gage, in 1882 and enjoyed telling imaginative stories to his four sons. He enjoyed it so much, in fact, that in his 40s he decided to try to make a living at authoring for children. His first publications, *Mother Goose in Prose* and *Father Goose, His Book*, did well, but they would soon become afterthoughts compared to what happened in 1900.

Dorothy, Toto, the Munchkins, and the evil Wicked Witch of the West captured the imagination of readers everywhere when he published *The Wonderful Wizard of Oz*. Baum intended the book to be a fairy tale for "children today," he wrote in the intro. It wound up being a fairy tale for every generation of children—and adults—ever since.

Baum moved his family to Hollywood in 1910 to begin turning his tales into movies. His *Oz* stories first came out in short films. The blockbuster movie *The Wizard of Oz* came out in 1939, 20 years after his death, ensuring that Baum's characters would keep capturing the attention of audiences around the world.

How Did Dorothy Get Home?

One change from book to movie concerns the famous line: in the book, Dorothy does say, "There is no place like home," early in the book, in a conversation with the Scarecrow. When she wishes to go home at the end of the book, however, she claps her shoes together and says, "Take me home to Aunt Em!" In the movie, she repeats, "There's no place like home," at the comparable point, and that phrasing has stuck in the public imagination.

Morris Elevated Design to Highest Art

"If you want a golden rule that will fit everybody, this is it: Have nothing in your houses that you do not know to be useful, or believe to be beautiful."

From home design to literature to politics, William Morris operated with a discerning eye and an exquisite touch. Associated with the Pre-Raphaelite Brotherhood and the English Arts and Crafts movement, he campaigned for Great Britain's 19th Century socialist movement.

✳ ✳ ✳ ✳

WILLIAM MORRIS WAS born in 1834 in Essex, England, the son of a prominent financier. As a child, he was a voracious reader and was also interested in gardening, practicing on his family's sprawling grounds. His early ambitions were architecture and painting. Morris attended Oxford, where he became inspired by the medieval architecture. He was drawn to middle age values like chivalry and community.

Morris met lifelong friend and collaborator Edward Burne-Jones while both were in their first year at Oxford. Along with other aspiring young artists and thinkers like Richard Watson Dixon and Charles Faulkner, their "brotherhood" would meet regularly to debate, recite Shakespeare and discuss politics and art.

Morris took an architectural apprenticeship in London after earning his BA but began to tire of architecture. He met and became close friends with Dante Gabriel Rossetti, one of the most prominent pre-Raphaelite painters, and through Rossetti also became acquainted with others producing what he considered to be world-changing art.

Around the same time he was deciding to give up architecture for painting and poetry, Morris met Jane Burden at a theater performance and, in 1859, married her despite her working-class upbringing. He commissioned an architect friend, Philip Webb, to build them a home in Kent. Morris wanted a modern home that was "medieval in spirit." Webb obliged, and Morris and his wife moved into Red House in 1860.

Passion for Design

Red House proved to be the inspiration for what Morris would become—one of the foremost names in textile design. With help from his friends, he spent the better part of two years decorating and furnishing the home. Their gifts for design were obvious, so they decided in 1861 to turn their passion into a business: Morris, Marshall, Faulkner & Co. They began producing furniture, tableware, embroidery, stained glass, tiles and other home furnishings. Morris could not find any wallpaper he liked, so wallpaper design became another staple of the business.

The impact of their business extended far beyond Red House. Homes and churches all over England began turning to Morris and his colleagues, who started calling themselves "The Firm." They showcased their work at the 1862 International Exhibition in South Kensington and soon found themselves in high demand. Their designs continued to influence décor in homes and churches well into the 20th Century.

Morris left no stone unturned in the design industry, which he considered art. He took up dyeing and weaving textiles, coming up with new designs and eschewing chemical dyes in favor of organic ones. He became politically active, at one point embracing Marxism and founding the Socialist League in 1884.

While most of his greatest contributions came in the area of home design and décor, Morris continued to paint and write throughout his life. He published several collections of poetry and fiction, translated ancient and medieval works and founded the Kelmscott Press in 1891. Its 1896 edition of the *Works of Geoffrey Chaucer*—put out the year Morris died—is widely recognized as a masterpiece in book design.

American Whistler an Aesthetic Movement Leader

James McNeill Whistler subscribed to the credo "art for art's sake," and combined many of his favorite styles into one all his own. His work impacted multiple generations of artists both in Europe and the United States.

✳ ✳ ✳ ✳

THE SON OF a successful Massachusetts railroad engineer, Whistler grew up in a mansion in Springfield and moved to St. Petersburg, Russia, in 1842, when Nicholas I of Russia hired his father to engineer a railroad from St. Petersburg to Moscow. James was 8 years old at the time, and already a world traveler.

He would later spend some time living with his sister and her husband, a doctor who also painted, in London, where he picked up an interest in art. He began reading about artists and their styles and pondered it as a career. Whistler returned to the U.S. when his father died of cholera in 1849, and two years later enrolled in the U.S. Military Academy at West Point.

While others were working toward careers in the sciences or as military officers, Whistler excelled in drawing classes but had little passion for some of the other subjects. He failed chemistry and, in 1854, was dismissed from the school. He decided to go to Paris to pursue a career in the arts.

Société des Trois

Whistler was already fluent in French from his years in Russia when he moved to Paris in 1855. There, he enrolled at the Academie Gleyre under Charles Gleyre, who would tutor the likes of Monet and Renoir in subsequent years. Whistler also spent countless hours self-teaching, responding to works in the Louvre and expending his artistic horizons through friendships with others passionate about art.

Two contemporaries, Henri Fantin-Latour and Alphonse Legros, joined Whistler in his devotion to the styles of Rembrandt and Courbet, among others. They began calling themselves the Société des Trois. Whistler painted his first self-portrait in a Rembrandtesque style in 1858, *Portrait of Whistler with Hat*.

It was five years later when Whistler attained international acclaim with *Symphony No. 1, The White Girl*. It was rejected by the Royal Academy and the Salon, but earned a spot as a major attraction at the popular Salon des Refusés in 1863. The painting depicts a woman in a white dress standing on a white polar bear skin in front of a white curtain with a lily in her hand. The model is said to have been his mistress.

Whistler subscribed to the credo, "art for art's sake." He frequently named his paintings in abstract terms for that very reason. He appreciated the beauty of nature, but he felt it was there to be interpreted. An artist's rendering of nature, that is, elevated the natural beauty itself. In his artist's eye, nature was not meant to be reproduced on a canvas in the same way it existed on its own.

Whistler invented a unique signature for his paintings: his initials within a styled butterfly. Rather than place it as a separate mark from the subject of the work, he used the butterfly as a part of the composition.

In 1888, Whistler married the widow of architect E. W. Godwin, Beatrice Godwin. Ten years later, he became a charter member and first president of the International Society of Sculptors, Painters and Gravers. Whistler died in London in 1903, known as a leader in the Aesthetic movement and as one whose ideas helped spawn what became known as modern art.

Whistler on Art

"Industry in art is a necessity—not a virtue—and any evidence of the same, in the production, is a blemish, not a quality; a proof, not of achievement, but of absolutely insufficient work, for work alone will efface the footsteps of work."

"If the man who paints only the tree, or flower, or other surface he sees before him were an artist, the king of artists would be the photographer. It is for the artist to do something beyond this: in portrait painting to put on canvas something more than the face the model wears for that one day: to paint the man, in short, as well as his features; in arrangement of colours to treat a flower as his key, not as his model."

"Nature contains the elements, in colour and form, of all pictures, as the keyboard contains the notes of all music. But the artist is born to pick, and choose, and group with science, these elements, that the result may be beautiful—as the musician gathers his notes, and forms his chords, until he bring forth from chaos glorious harmony. To say to the painter, that Nature is to be taken as she is, is to say to the player, that he may sit on the piano. That Nature is always right, is an assertion, artistically, as untrue, as it is one whose truth is universally taken for granted. Nature is very rarely right, to such an extent even, that it might almost be said that Nature is usually wrong: that is to say, the condition of things that shall bring about the perfection of harmony worthy a picture is rare, and not common at all."

"To say of a picture, as is often said in its praise, that it shows great and earnest labor, is to say that it is incomplete and unfit for view."

Renoir and the Roots of Impressionism

"I have a predilection for painting that lends joyousness to a wall."

A modest upbringing did not foretell the impact Renoir would have on art. From copying designs onto dishware, he went on to become one of the key figures in the growth of Impressionism and one of the most well-known painters in history.

✳ ✳ ✳ ✳

THERE WAS LITTLE reason to believe that a young Pierre-Auguste Renoir, born in Limoges, France in 1841, would grow up to inspire a revolutionary movement in art and have his work purchased by the Louvre. His parents were a tailor and a seamstress and Pierre-Auguste was their sixth child. Two of his older siblings died as young children. A move near Paris when Pierre-Auguste was still a preschooler set the stage for a young, inquisitive boy to discover art.

Renoir took an apprenticeship to a porcelain painter during his teenage years, copying designs onto plates and other dishware. He signed up for free drawing classes at a local school, spent countless hours copying works in the Louvre and took on odd jobs as a decorative painter to earn money to live on.

He entered the famed l'Ecole des Beaux-Arts in 1862, grateful for a chance to study under Charles Gleyre. It was at Gleyre's studio that he met and became friends with Frédéric Bazille, Claude Monet and Alfred Sisley, a group that would influence the direction of his work.

Impressionism

Renoir had works accepted to the annual Paris Salon exhibit in 1864 and 1865. His debut Salon painting was *La Esmeralda*, inspired by a character in Victor Hugo's *Notre-Dame de Paris*. Even with some notoriety, however, Renoir spent considerable time living from studio to studio with his circle of artist friends. At times, he could not scrounge up enough money to buy paint.

Renoir was drafted into France's army in 1870 during their war with Germany, but he fell ill and never saw any action. In 1874, he and a group of friends decided to showcase their own paintings in Paris. While their first such exhibit did not meet with the kind of success they had hoped for, history documents its importance as the first-ever Impressionism exhibition.

Renoir's works, and those of his like-minded contemporaries, featured bright palettes and striking light. Impressionism gave viewers a look at the subjects of the paintings as if they had just caught a glimpse. Renoir became known for the warmth he portrayed in his subjects and for using different types of brushstrokes to create a unique feel.

A wealthy couple, publisher Georges Charpentier and his wife Marguérite, took a keen interest both in Renoir's works and in his company, bringing him into their social circles and, in the process, earning him numerous commissions. He began to earn wide acclaim with works like *Madame Charpentier and her Children*, *Dance in the Country*, *Dance in the City* and *Dance at Bougival*.

Renoir married longtime girlfriend and frequent model for his paintings Aline Charigot in 1890. The couple had two sons, Jean in 1894 and Claude in 1901. Renoir was crippled by rheumatism that disfigured his hands and a stroke later in his life. He continued to paint for the remainder of his days, however, and lived just long enough to see the Louvre purchase one of his paintings within a year of his death in 1919. Some of Renoir's paintings have sold for more than $70 million U.S. in recent years.

"I'm like the children at school; the clean page has to be filled with good writing, and splash—a mess! I'm still making messes and I'm forty years old."

James Helped Characterize the New World

If, as he said, "it takes a great deal of history to produce a little literature," Henry James must have hoarded history like few before or since. Over a long and prolific writing career, he elevated the short story as an art form and gave the world a compelling snapshot of life in America.

✳   ✳   ✳   ✳

THE SON AND namesake of a prominent lecturer and younger brother of philosopher William James, Henry was born in New York in 1843. While William was outgoing, Henry was more introverted: a bookworm, some said. Both boys were taken overseas to learn under governesses and tutors as young children, though they also spent considerable time in Manhattan. Subsequent years in Rhode Island and Boston gave Henry an awareness and love of New England that would later be reflected in his writing.

Extremely bright, James enrolled in Harvard Law School at age 19 but spent only one year there. Law was not his passion. Books were. He occupied his time reading authors like Nathaniel Hawthorne and Charles Augustin Sainte-Beuve, and writing his own tales as well. By 1865, the prestigious *Atlantic Monthly* was publishing his stories. The editor, William Dean Howells, became a friend of Henry's and together they are credited for ushering in the era of American Realism.

Transatlantic Experience

Steeped in an understanding of Europe that few young American writers could match thanks to his childhood experiences, James continued to travel abroad, visiting England, France and Italy in 1869. By this time, the 26-year-old was already recognized among the best short story writers in the United States.

He returned to Massachusetts and finished his first novel, *Watch and Ward*, though he called *Roderick Hudson* his debut five years later. Beginning with the latter, James made his mark by writing about America, and the innocence of the "New World" compared to the corruption of the "Old." *Roderick Hudson* depicted an American sculptor struggling with his artistic passions and personal relationships while in Italy.

Through books like *Roderick Hudson*, *The American* and *Daisy Miller* over the next few years, readers all over the world were immersed in the American spirit and to life in the United States and to the adventures of American characters abroad. James also wrote about social form in 1880s novels *The Bostonians* and *The Princess Casamassima*.

Over 51 years of writing, James produced 20 novels, more than 100 short stories, a dozen plays and countless quantities of reviews, travel pieces and articles. More than perhaps anyone before him, he elevated the stature of the short story, gripping readers with fascinating tales and accessible characters, while also showing the kind of craftsmanship that also ranked him among the great American novelists.

James penned three of his most masterful novels later in his life, producing *The Ambassadors*, *The Wings of the Dove* and *The Golden Bowl* in the first few years of the 20th Century. He had been living in Europe for more than 20 years by this time. James returned to New York in 1905 for the first time in more than a quarter century and edited a New York edition of his selected works.

James spent most of his final years in England. He became a British subject in 1915, received the Order of Merit from King George V in 1916 and died just weeks later in London.

"The only obligation to which in advance we may hold a novel without incurring the accusation of being arbitrary, is that it be interesting."

A Man of Quips

"Advertising is the art of convincing people to spend money they don't have for something they don't need."

✳   ✳   ✳   ✳

WILL ROGERS POSSESSED many gifts. Perhaps the greatest was his ability to use humor to connect with people. It helped him become, seemingly without his even trying, one of the most popular actor/stage performer/cowboy/political commentator/newspaper men of his era, and a national treasure to all who experienced him.

Will Rogers became a household name in his native Oklahoma for his rope tricks, vaudeville and circus acts and cowboy shenanigans that ultimately found their way to the big screen on both silent films and talking pictures. He found humor in the ordinary and expressed his unique views of the world in a manner that connected with the common man.

Rogers' commentary on politics, in particular, had American simultaneously laughing and thinking.

"Once a man holds public office," Rogers once said, "he is absolutely no good for honest work." And of his own political affiliations, Rogers quipped, "I'm not a member of any organized political party. I'm a Democrat."

Rogers actually launched a mock presidential campaign in 1928, promising only one thing if he won—his immediate resignation. He connected with the "common man" in ways that no actual political candidate ever could. His writings were among the most read commentaries and humor pieces in print, and his quips became popular talk around dining room tables nationwide.

Rogers became a spokesman for the aviation industry later in his career. He was killed along with famed pilot Wiley Post, a fellow Oklahoman, when their aircraft went down in an Alaska lagoon in 1935. Rogers was honored with his picture on a U.S. Post Office stamp in 1948.

Pop Quiz: Advertising

Match each advertising slogan to its company.

✳ ✳ ✳ ✳

1. A little dab'll do ya!

2. Be all that you can be.

3. Between love and madness lies obsession.

4. Breakfast of Champions.

5. Do what tastes right.

6. Eat fresh.

7. Give me a break, give me a break, break me off a piece of that (item)

8. Good to the last drop.

9. Have it your way.

10. I'm lovin' it.

11. Improving home improvement.

12. It keeps going and going and going.

13. More saving. More doing.

14. So easy a caveman can do it.

15. Taking care of business.

16. The best part of waking up is…

17. Think outside the bun.

18. We do chicken right!

19. It takes a tough man to make a tender chicken.

20. You can't top the copper top.

Answer Choices

A. Calvin Klein

B. Kit-Kat

C. Burger King

D. Lowe's

E. Brylcreem

F. Wendy's

G. Home Depot

H. Office Depot

I. Taco Bell

J. Energizer

K. KFC

L. U. S. Army

M. Perdue

N. Wheaties

O. GEICO

P. Maxwell House

Q. Folgers

R. Duracell

S. McDonald's

T. Subway

Answer key: 1. E; 2. L; 3. A; 4. N; 5. F; 6. T; 7. B; 8. P; 9. C; 10. S; 11. D; 12. J; 13. G; 14. O; 15. H; 16. Q; 17. I; 18. K; 19. M; 20. R

Doyle Introduces World to Its Detective

How did Arthur Conan Doyle manage to give up a medical career to write about a detective and his trusty sidekick? It's elementary, my dear Watson.

✳   ✳   ✳   ✳

ARTHUR CONAN DOYLE had two passions in his life. One was writing. The other was Spiritualism, a faith he adopted after giving up his Roman Catholic upbringing. The combination of the two served the author well, but it took some time to get there.

Doyle's father was an alcoholic; his mother a delightful story-teller with whom Doyle was attached at the hip. He cried when he was sent away from his native Scotland in 1868, at age 9, to attend a Jesuit prep school in England that practiced violent corporal punishment. He wrote regular letters to his mother, and eventually amassed a captivated audience of fellow students with his brilliantly told tales.

Doyle graduated from Stonyhurst College in 1876 and, rather than follow in his father's footsteps into art, surprised his family by deciding to attend medical school. While he would eventually abandon that field, it was during his med school experience that a stroke of good fortune had him meet Dr. Joseph Bell, an observant and deductive professor who would inspire one of literature's most famous characters.

Sherlock Holmes Is Born

Before turned Dr. Bell into his most iconic hero, Detective Sherlock Holmes, Doyle relinquished his Catholic faith in favor of Spiritualism—a belief system based on contact with spirits of the dead—and earned his medical degree in 1881. He took on jobs in the medical field, including his first on a boat from England to Africa, and later opened a private practice.

However, his passion for storytelling and his desire to spread the doctrine of Spiritualism led him toward a career in writing.

He married Louisa Hawkins, who would bear him two children, in 1885. The following year, he started writing a mystery novel first titled *A Tangled Skein*. It would be renamed *A Study in Scarlet* two years later and published in *Beeton's Christmas Annual*. The two protagonists, originally bearing different names, were Detective Holmes and his loyal assistant Dr. Watson by the time the story reached print in 1888 and gave Doyle's literary career the boost it needed.

While Doyle also published several works that showcased his fascination with spirits and the paranormal, he stuck with the Holmes story as his bread and butter. Some 60 stories featuring Holmes and Watson would dominate his career and become some of the most beloved books in the world. Doyle even tried to kill off Holmes in 1893, drawing the ire of readers, but he brought him back in the popular *The Hound of Baskervilles* in 1901—one of the most revered of the many classic Holmes stories.

Louisa Doyle contracted tuberculosis in the 1890s and finally died in her husband's arms in 1906. One year later, after pulling himself out of a debilitating depression, Doyle married Jean Leckie, who bore him three more children.

The author brought Holmes and Watson to the stage in a play called *The Speckled Band* that debuted in London in 1910. He used a good portion of the money he earned from all things Holmes to fund his missionary work and published many writings on Spiritualism.

A doctor diagnosed Doyle with *angina pectoris* in 1929, but he ignored the warnings and left on a psychic tour through The Netherlands. He was so ill on his return that he had to be carried, and was bedridden until his death on July 7, 1930.

Famous Sayings from Sherlock Holmes

Incidentally, Holmes never said "Elementary, my dear Watson," in those exact words, at least in the books. He does say "Elementary," and call his compatriot "My dear Watson." But the habit of stringing those two phrases together belongs to later works based on Arthur Conan Doyle's detective. Here are some things that are pulled directly from Doyle:

"I consider that a man's brain originally is like a little empty attic, and you have to stock it with such furniture as you choose. A fool takes in all the lumber of every sort that he comes across, so that the knowledge which might be useful to him gets crowded out, or at best is jumbled up with a lot of other things, so that he has a difficulty in laying his hands upon it. Now the skillful workman is very careful indeed as to what he takes into his brain-attic. He will have nothing but the tools which may help him in doing his work, but of these he has a large assortment, and all in the most perfect order."

—*A STUDY IN SCARLET*

"How often have I said to you that when you have eliminated the impossible, whatever remains, however improbable, **must be the truth?"**

—*THE SIGN OF FOUR*

"It is a capital mistake to theorize before one has data. Insensibly one begins to twist facts to suit theories, instead of theories to suit facts."

—**"A SCANDAL IN BOHEMIA"**

"Is there any other point to which you would wish to draw my attention?"

"To the curious incident of the dog in the night-time."

"The dog did nothing in the night-time."

"That was the curious incident," remarked Sherlock Holmes.

—**"SILVER BLAZE"**

"Come, Watson, come!" he cried. *"The game is afoot. Not a word! Into your clothes and come!"*

—**"THE ADVENTURE OF THE ABBEY GRANGE"**

Thayer Hits Grand Slam with 'Casey'

The Mighty Casey might have struck out, but Ernest Lawrence Thayer hit one out of the park with perhaps the most famous sports poem of all time.

✳   ✳   ✳   ✳

THE OUTLOOK TURNED out brilliant for young Ernest on that day,
He penned a poem that, in sports, has truly led the way.
The Harvard grad—a comic—grabbed the nation with a tale,
That decades later strikes a heartfelt chord still without fail.

Massachusetts native Ernest Thayer served as editor of the *Harvard Lampoon* while graduating from honors from the Ivy League college. He was a prolific comedy writer and aspiring journalist who was hired by the *San Francisco Examiner* as a humor columnist in 1886.

Anything he covered for the newspaper, however, paled in comparison to a whimsical baseball poem he crafted on June 3, 1888. The National League was a mere 12 years old. The American League of Major League Baseball was 12 years away from its inception. However, Thayer tapped into a national connection to the sport in beautiful rhyme when he wrote a balled he called "Casey."

The star of the fictional "Mudville" baseball team, awaiting his turn to come to the plate and be a hero, amazingly gets that chance with two outs in the ninth inning. To the crowd's chagrin, however, the Mighty Casey strikes out to end the game:

"Oh, somewhere in this favoured land the sun is shining bright
The band is playing somewhere,
and somewhere hearts are light;
And somewhere men are laughing,

and somewhere children shout,
But there is no joy in Mudville—mighty Casey has struck out."

The first public reciting of the poem took place on Thayer's
25th birthday. The young writer went on to publish several
other comic poems on both coasts. He never matched the
popularity of "Casey," which became known as "Casey at the
Bat," nor did he ever reveal whom, if anyone, inspired the
poem. It lives on as perhaps the most revered sports poem in
American history.

Hit the Ball as Far as I Could

Recognition for a man who often found himself overshadowed.

✳   ✳   ✳   ✳

LARRY DOBY MUST have resigned himself to finishing second. In 1947, he made his debut for the Cleveland Indians,
becoming the second African-American to play major-league
baseball in the 20th century. Three decades later, Doby became
the second black man to manage a major-league team. (Frank
Robinson was the first, for the Cleveland Indians in 1975.) Yet,
Doby never publicly complained about being a bridesmaid. He
handled his role as a secondary baseball pioneer with dignity
and grace, advancing the cause for other African-Americans
who would succeed him.

Doby starred in the Negro Leagues from 1942 to 1947, though
he did lose some of that time to service in World War II. His
abilities as a hard-hitting second baseman caught the attention
of Cleveland Indians owner Bill Veeck, who was aggressively
seeking black talent for his major-league team in 1947. In the
early days of July, Veeck arranged to purchase Doby's contract
from the Newark Eagles. Veeck paid $15,000 to Eagles owner
Effa Manley for Doby, who was hitting .414 at the time.

Jackie Robinson had broken the game's color barrier only
11 weeks earlier, making his Brooklyn Dodgers debut on April

15. Unlike Robinson, Doby did not receive the benefit of playing minor-league ball, which would have allowed him to make a gradual transition to the majors. Instead, Veeck brought Doby directly from the Negro Leagues to the Indians.

Veeck also laid out some ground rules. "He sat me down and told me some of the do's and don'ts," Doby recalled. "Don't even turn around at a bad call at the plate, and no dissertations with opposing players—either of those might start a race riot."

On July 5, Veeck personally escorted Doby to Comiskey Park, where the Indians were playing the Chicago White Sox. Doby didn't start the game but would immediately find himself tested. Pinch-hitting in the seventh inning with two men on base, Doby struck out, swinging and missing badly. It didn't matter. In the larger scheme, Doby had arrived—second overall, but the first black player in American League history.

Over the years, historians have carefully examined the racism that Jackie Robinson faced from teammates, opponents, and fans during his early days in the majors. But the similar obstacles that Doby faced have not received nearly as much scrutiny. Like Robinson, Doby heard insults from opposing players and taunts from fans who didn't want a black man sharing the diamond with his white counterparts. Most of Doby's teammates showed him a cold indifference, but a few were outright nasty and rude. Some even refused to shake Doby's hand before his first game. On one occasion, an opposing player spit on Doby as he slid into second base, but he chose not to retaliate. "I couldn't react to [prejudicial] situations from a physical standpoint," Doby once said. "My reaction was to hit the ball as far as I could."

Doby's debut season did not unfold as dramatically as Robinson's did. While Robinson played well enough to win Rookie of the Year and helped the Dodgers advance to the World Series, Doby played sparingly and flailed at the plate, hitting only .156 in 32 at-bats. But Doby rebounded in 1948.

He became the Indians' regular center fielder, hit .301 with 14 home runs, and helped Cleveland clinch the AL pennant.

Although baseball's color barrier had delayed his major-league career, Doby diligently overcame the late start. By the time his career ended, he had qualified for seven All-Star teams, led the American League in home runs twice, and finished second in the MVP voting in 1954. In 1978, he was hired again by Veeck, this time to manage the White Sox.

Doby didn't always end up in second place. He was the first African-American to lead his league in home runs, the first to hit a homer in the World Series, and the first to be on a Series-winning team (the Indians in 1948). Coupled with his performance in the Negro Leagues, Doby's many pioneering accomplishments helped earn him election and induction to the Baseball Hall of Fame in 1998. Always a man of great strength and dignity, Doby passed away in 2003 at the age of 79.

Chapter 7

Places

Stevenson Took Readers on Quite a Journey

"For my part, I travel not to go anywhere, but to go. I travel for travel's sake. The great affair is to move."

✳   ✳   ✳   ✳

ROBERT LOUIS STEVENSON was born in Edinburgh, Scotland, in 1850, but he would not stay in any one place for long. Travel became a way of life for this novelist and poet, inspiring much of his lasting body of work.

It was expected that, like his father and a long line of male descendants before him, Stevenson might go into the lighthouse engineering business. He had other ideas. He was often ill as a youngster, spending countless hours reading from his bed. He also spent summers with his maternal grandfather, a philosophy professor who loved storytelling. Stevenson switched his focus from engineering to law at the University of Edinburgh, but his passion was writing. It was a passion he took on the road. It started with articles about his travels through Europe, particularly France, where in 1876 he met and fell in love with an older, married woman named Fanny Vandegrift Osbourne.

His first two books, *An Inland Voyage* (1878) and *Travels with a Donkey in the Cevennes* (1879), were based on those trips to

France. Fanny, who had decided to return to her California home to stay with her husband, beckoned Stevenson in 1879. The trip—a steerage ride across the Atlantic followed by an emigrant cross-country train ride, just about killed the author. He made it to Monterey, at last, and married Fanny after her divorce.

He continued to inspire readers with tales of his vast travels, but his two masterpieces spanned different genres. *Treasure Island* (1883) resulted from an imaginary treasure map he drew with his step-son, while the novella *Strange Case of Dr. Jekyll and Mr. Hyde* (1886) followed a dream that woke him up screaming.

Stevenson's illnesses eventually caught up with him. He died of a brain hemorrhage in 1894 at a mere 44 years old.

Quotes from Stevenson

"To travel hopefully is a better thing than to arrive."

"The untented Kosmos my abode,
I pass, a willful stranger;
My mistress still the open road
And the bright eyes of danger."

"But we are all travellers in what John Bunyan calls the wilderness of this world—all, too, travellers with a donkey: and the best that we ind in our travels is an honest friend. He is a fortunate voyager who finds many. We travel, indeed, to find them. They are the end and the reward of life. They keep us worthy of ourselves; and when we are alone, we are only nearer to the absent."

"The road lay under chestnuts, and though I saw a hamlet or two below me in the vale, and many lone houses of the chestnut farmers, it was a very solitary march all afternoon; and the evening began early underneath the trees. But I heard the voice of a woman singing some sad, old, endless ballad not far off. It seemed to be about love and a bel amoureux, her handsome sweetheart; and I wished I could have taken up the strain and answered her, as I went on upon my invisible woodland way."

Sell a Country?

"Sell a country! Why not sell the air, the clouds and the great sea, as well as the earth? Did not the Great Spirit make them all for the use of his children?"

Tecumseh became a legend not only for his brave leadership in battle, but for the words he shared with a nation in turmoil. The Shawnee chief inspired his people and fought many brave battles before being killed in the Battle of the Thames in 1813.

* * * *

TECUMSEH WAS BORN in Ohio in 1768. His father, Puckshinwau, was a Shawnee war chief, though Tecumseh would far surpass him in battle and political influence. He was just 6 when his father was killed in the French and Indian War, and the son was not far from carrying on the family tradition. Tecumseh stood out as a warrior, even as a teenager. He joined the American Indian Confederacy under Mohawk chief Joseph Brant, and learned that a union of tribes was best suited to thwarting encroachment on their territories, a stance he would rally behind as he became a chief himself.

His mother took the family to Missouri after the death of his father, and Tecumseh and his older brother Chiksika participated in a series of successful raids against settlements in Kentucky and Tennessee.

By 1800, Tecumseh was a prominent Shawnee chief and a leader among his people. His bravery and keen intellect made him well-equipped to head up the efforts to fight those who were looking to slaughter Native Americans.

He envisioned a confederacy of tribes, united in their efforts to protect their people and their lands. When other tribal chiefs signed treaties giving up their land to white frontiersman, Tecumseh argued that they should have their thumbs cut off.

Fighting for Their Lives

Tecumseh and his people were fighting for their lives, quite literally, in the early 1800s. One of his younger brothers, Lalawethica, experienced a series of visions that promised a land of religious deliverance for Native Americans, changed his name to Tenskwatawa and began preaching the good news to his people. Tecumseh was reluctant to believe until the summer of 1806, when his brother correctly predicted a solar eclipse. With that, the chief was swayed.

There was still the matter of preserving their lives and land, however. Tecumseh and his brother moved their settlement to present-day Indiana in 1808, to the confluence of the Tippecanoe and Wabash rivers. Tecumseh stepped up his efforts to unite tribes as one confederacy against the invading white man. They traveled throughout the Midwest, preaching the absurdity of selling or signing away Indian land—land that the "Great Spirit" had given to their people. He was only partially successful.

While several tribes of Native Americans did have degrees of success defending themselves and their land against invaders, bad news was on the horizon. Tecumseh was on a southern trip, trying to recruit the Creeks to join him, when American forces marched against his settlement in November of 1811, burning residences and depleting the food supply.

The War of 1812 followed. Tecumseh went north, to Michigan, and fought valiantly in helping British troops capture Detroit. At one point, Tecumseh led a group of 400 men who charged out of the woods, then circled back around and did it again to make it appear as though there were twice as many forces under his lead. The maneuver worked, prompting the opposing general to surrender. However, Tecumseh was killed at the Battle of the Thames in 1813. He remains a revered figure in Native American lore for his bravery, intellect, oratory skills, and desire to bring unity among the tribes.

All Around America

"Whatever America hopes to bring to pass in the world must first come to pass in the heart of America."

—DWIGHT EISENHOWER

"In thinking of America, I sometimes find myself admiring her bright blue sky—her grand old woods—her fertile fields—her beautiful rivers—her mighty lakes, and star-crowned mountains. But my rapture is soon checked, my joy is soon turned to mourning. When I remember that all is cursed with the infernal spirit of slaveholding, robbery and wrong, —when I remember that with the waters of her noblest rivers, the tears of my brethren are borne to the ocean, disregarded and forgotten, and that her most fertile fields drink daily of the warm blood of my outraged sisters, I am filled with unutterable loathing."

—FREDERICK DOUGLASS

"It is from the blues that all that may be called American music derives its most distinctive characteristic."

—JAMES WELDON JOHNSON

"One of the brightest gems in the New England weather is the dazzling uncertainty of it."

—MARK TWAIN

"Twenty-one years later I read over the notes of that day's experience and the picture of the Grand Canyon from this point is once more before me. I did not know when writing the notes that this was the grandest view that can be obtained of the region from Fremont's Peak to the Gulf of California, but I did realize that the scene before me was awful, sublime, and glorious—awful in profound depths, sublime in massive and strange forms, and glorious in colors."

—JOHN WESLEY POWELL

"Let America be America again.
Let it be the dream it used to be.
Let it be the pioneer on the plain
Seeking a home where he himself is free.

(America never was America to me.)"

—LANGSTON HUGHES

"The past few days when I've been at that window upstairs, I've thought a bit of the 'shining city upon a hill.' The phrase comes from John Winthrop, who wrote it to describe the America he imagined. What he imagined was important because he was an early Pilgrim, an early freedom man. He journeyed here on what today we'd call a little wooden boat; and like the other Pilgrims, he was looking for a home that would be free.

I've spoken of the shining city all my political life, but I don't know if I ever quite communicated what I saw when I said it. But in my mind it was a tall, proud city built on rocks stronger than oceans, wind-swept, God-blessed, and teeming with people of all kinds living in harmony and peace; a city with free ports that hummed with commerce and creativity. And if there had to be city walls, the walls had doors and the doors were open to anyone with the will and the heart to get here."

—RONALD REAGAN

"New England is a finished place ... It is the first old civilization, the first permanent civilization in America."

—BERNARD DE VOTO

"Up in the mountains of New Hampshire, God Almighty has hung out a sign to show that there He makes men."

—DANIEL WEBSTER

"I doubt if the texture of Southern life is any more grotesque than that of the rest of the nation, but it does seem evident that the Southern writer is particularly adept at recognizing the grotesque."

—FLANNERY O'CONNOR

"Just an old sweet song
Keeps Georgia on my mind."

—"GEORGIA ON MY MIND," STUART GORRELL AND HOAGY CARMICHAEL

"I am in love with Montana. For other states I have admiration, respect, recognition, even some affection, but with Montana it is love, and it's difficult to analyze love when you're in it."

—JOHN STEINBECK

"It seemed like a matter of minutes when we began rolling in the foothills before Oakland and suddenly reached a height and saw stretched out ahead of us the fabulous white city of San Francisco on her eleven mystic hills with the blue Pacific and its advancing wall of potato-patch fog beyond, and smoke and goldenness of the late afternoon of time."

—JACK KEROUAC

"To the lover of pure wildness Alaska is one of the most wonderful countries in the world."

—JOHN MUIR

"God has a special providence for fools, drunks, and the United States of America."

—OTTO VON BISMARCK

Sandburg Turned Industry into Verse

"Hog Butcher for the World / Tool Maker, Stacker of Wheat / Player with Railroads and the Nation's Freight Handler / Stormy, husky, brawling / City of the Big Shoulders."

✻ ✻ ✻ ✻

CARL SANDBURG HAILED from Galesburg, Illinois, the son of Swedish immigrants to the United States. The family struggled, so Carl left school in his early teen-age years to lay bricks, wash dishes and tackle several other odd jobs to bring in a few extra dimes. At 17, he hit the road for Kansas with little more than the clothes on his back. When life as a hobo wore on him, he enlisted and spent eight months in Puerto Rico during the Spanish-American War.

Sandburg, though, was neither a soldier nor a brick-layer. He was a writer—a revelation that would come out after he worked to put himself through Lombard College just after the turn of the century. He left in 1903 without a degree, but the encouragement he received there to pursue his writing inspired him to give it a go.

He published a pamphlet called "Reckless Ecstasy" in 1904. He then took a job as a newspaper and advertising writer in Milwaukee, where he met his wife, Lillian (Paula) Steichen. He assisted Milwaukee's first Socialist mayor from 1910–12. And it was a move to Chicago to write for the *Daily News* that truly turned his career.

A member of Chicago's literary renaissance along with Ben Hecht, Theodore Dreiser, Sherwood Anderson and Edgar Lee Master, Sandburg reached the masses writing about the city and its industry. His *Chicago Poems* of 1916 included "Chicago," which gave the town its "big shoulders" nickname. Two years later, his *Cornhuskers* collection led to a Pulitzer Prize. More than three decades later, he added a second Pulitzer for his *Complete Poems* (1950).

Sandburg wrote for children and adults, he wrote plenty about Abraham Lincoln, and he never lost the passion for capturing life in the Midwest right up until his death at 89 in 1967.

Serenading the Windy City

Over the years, dozens and dozens of songs have been written that feature or mention Chicago, and many have become national or even international hits. Some simply use Chicago as a big city backdrop, while others glorify a unique aspect of the city's character or capture a significant moment in its turbulent history.

* * * *

* **"Chicago (That Toddling Town)":** Composer Fred Fisher got his start in the music business in Chicago and went on to become a major figure in New York City's Tin Pan Alley. His Midwestern roots showed through, however, in "Chicago (That Toddling Town)," his most enduring song. The swinging tune, which paints Chicago as a raucous party town, became a hit in the 1920s and has been recorded by the likes of Frank Sinatra, Duke Ellington, and Benny Goodman.

✳ **"My Kind of Town":** In the 1964 film *Robin and the Seven Hoods*, Frank Sinatra and his Rat Pack buddies played Prohibition-era gangsters, and Frank debuted "My Kind of Town." Written by Jimmy Van Heusen and Sammy Cahn, the Oscar-nominated song, which mentions such landmarks as the Wrigley Building and the Stockyards, became a staple of Sinatra's repertoire.

✳ **"Chicago":** Written by Graham Nash in 1970 and popularized by the group Crosby, Stills, Nash, and Young, "Chicago" is a moving plea that calls on its audience to take political action. The song brings attention to the plight of the Chicago Seven, the young political activists who were tried for inciting a riot at the 1968 Democratic National Convention.

✳ **"Lake Shore Drive":** Aliotta, Haynes, and Jeremiah are a little-known folk group from the hinterlands of Wisconsin who likely would not be remembered if it weren't for their fondness for the distinctive Chicago thoroughfare called Lake Shore Drive. The trio wrote and recorded a raggy piano number that perfectly conveys the experience of driving down the eight-lane concrete ribbon that follows almost the entire length of the city's shoreline.

✳ **"The Lincoln Park Pirates":** Singer-songwriter Steve Goodman was considered by many to be the Windy City's unofficial court composer for such songs as "Daley's Gone," his heartfelt homage to the city's best-known mayor, and the witty and tender "A Dying Cub Fan's Last Request." In "Lincoln Park Pirates," he sends a blistering shot across the bow of the Lincoln Towing Company, Chicago's most notorious enforcer of private parking lot restrictions. Reminiscent of a sea shanty, the tune blasts the reviled auto impounders for their exorbitant fees and well-known habit of damaging the cars in their custody.

* **"Bad, Bad Leroy Brown":** Jim Croce was a radio sensation in the early 1970s who was known for his distinctive pop tunes and evocative love songs. One of his most enduring numbers is "Bad, Bad Leroy Brown," a streetwise boogie number about a tough guy from Chicago's South Side who gets his comeuppance when he tries to move in on another man's wife.

* **"The Night Chicago Died":** Paper Lace was a forgettable British pop band from the 1970s that scored a major hit in the States with "The Night Chicago Died." The insipid tune tells the fictional story of a shoot-out between Chicago police and the henchmen of bootlegger Al Capone. It is often cited as one of the worst songs of the 1970s.

* **"Sweet Home Chicago":** One of a handful of songs written and recorded by legendary bluesman Robert Johnson, "Sweet Home Chicago" has become a staple in the blues canon and was given a huge boost in popularity when it was featured in the 1980 film *The Blues Brothers*.

Horace Greeley's Gripe

Did this 1800s news mogul and presidential hopeful coin the phrase "Go West, young man"? Greeley was certainly the most prominent person to say it in a memorable way.

* * * *

HORACE GREELEY WAS a self-made newspaperman, social critic, and advocate who built the influential *New York Tribune* into a mighty voice for change. He opposed monopolies, the death penalty, and slavery, and he advocated homestead land grants and egalitarianism. In a *Tribune* editorial dated July 13, 1865, Greeley wrote, "Washington is not a place to live in. The rents are high, the food is bad, the dust is disgusting and the morals are deplorable. Go West, young man, go West and grow up with the country."

Although he was a solid advocate for Western settlement, Greeley was attempting to speak to a different issue. He was addressing disgruntled civil servants in D.C. who had complained at length about low pay and high living costs in their city of employment. What Greeley meant was, "If you don't like it here, go somewhere else."

A number of historians credit the phrase to John B. Soule, writing in the *Terre Haute Express* in 1851. That credit lacks one key component: a specific date. If we're sure someone said or wrote something, we usually know exactly when. With Soule, we do not, so a firm credit becomes problematic. He probably did say it, but just as likely, so did others before and after. In the 1800s, many thousands sought their fortunes out West. In effect, "Go West" was the era's equivalent of saying, "Apply to college."

Greeley's own story ended less optimistically. He ran against Ulysses S. Grant for president, was soundly defeated, lost his mind and his newspaper, and died insane. His assessment of Washington, D.C., however, has in many ways endured the test of time.

Gunfight at the O.K. Corral

"You're looking for a fight and now you can have it."

—WYATT EARP, TO THE CLANTONS AND MCLAURYS

ON OCTOBER 26, 1881, the most famous gunfight in the history of the American West occurred in the silver mining town of Tombstone, Arizona. Lasting about 30 seconds, the shoot-out left three members of the Clanton-McLaury gang dead and three members of the Earp/Holliday faction wounded. Only one man was left unscathed—Wyatt Earp, who also was the last survivor of the fight when he died in Los Angeles, California, in 1929. Western movie stars Tom Mix and William S. Hart were pallbearers at his funeral.

The following men took part in the O.K. Corral gunfight:

Ike Clanton (1847–87), left before the shooting started
Frank McLaury (1848–81), shot to death
Tom McLaury (1853–81), shot to death
Billy Clanton (1862–81), shot to death
John H. "Doc" Holliday (1851–87), wounded on the hip
Virgil Earp (1843–1905), shot in the leg
Morgan Earp (1851–82), shot in the shoulders
Wyatt Earp (1848–1929), not wounded

Good Guys?

Popular sentiment casts Holliday and the Earps as "the good guys," but others see Clanton and the McLaurys as victims of an outrageous abuse of power. Though Clanton and the McLaurys were accused of being illegally armed, Wyatt Earp and Doc Holliday were not officers of the law at the time either, so they were illegally armed as well. Sheriff Behan witnessed the shoot-out and arrested Holliday and the Earps. A month later a Tombstone judge ruled that the homicides were justified.

Talkin' About Texas

"Just to think about old Texas
Makes a fellow proud, gee whiz!
How could anybody blame us
When you know how big she is?"

—Jennie Lee Blanton

"Each year El Paso gets more sunny days—over 300—than any other U.S. city."

—Jerome Pohlen, author, Oddball Texas

"Texas could get along without the United States, but the United States cannot, except with great hazard, exist without Texas."

—Sam Houston

"Fraudulent debtors in the United States skipped away from their creditors during the night, and chalked on their shutters the three cabalistic letters 'G.T.T.'—'Gone to Texas.'"

—NEVIN O. WINTER, DESCRIBING SOME OF THE EARLY AMERICAN PIONEERS TO TEXAS

"Texas is the number-one bird-watching destination in the United States, and the Rio Grande Valley is the number-one bird-watching area in Texas. Some 465 species of birds, including 34 species found nowhere else in the country, have been spotted in Texas. Most can be found in the Rio Grande Valley."

—JUNE NAYLOR, AUTHOR, *OFF THE BEATEN PATH—TEXAS*

"These Texians are the most independent people under the whole canopy of heaven."

—J. FRANK DOBIE, WRITER AND FOLKLORIST

"Most people who are real Texans by birth or at least by attitude know that a 'Mexican breakfast' consists of a cup of black coffee and a cigarette."

—CLAY REYNOLDS, NOVELIST

"On the eighth day God created Texas."

—ANONYMOUS

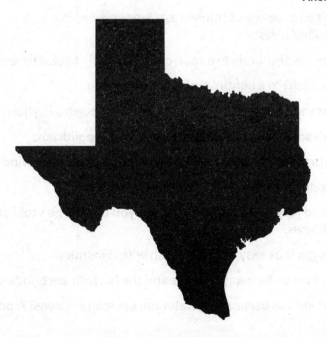

That's Just Like...

To talk like a real Texan, one has to get a handle on the art of crafting clever "rhetorical tropes." Heck, it's not as hard as it sounds—it's only comparative similes and metaphors. What are those? Simple: catchy statements that describe something as *being* or being *equal to* something else in some way. Here are some examples.

* He's so scared his skin jumped up and crawled all over him.

* That woman's so old the spring has gone out of her chicken.

* They're bad enough to be locked up under the jail.

* He's so big, you could split him in half and still have enough for two people.

* She had calluses from pattin' herself on her own back.

* He'd fight a rattlesnake and spot it the first bite.

* They're as brave as the first man who ate an oyster.

* It's so cold the wolves are eatin' the sheep for the wool.

* That's as cold as an ex-wife's heart.

* That dog looks as confused as a woodpecker in a petrified forest.

* If you put his brain in a sparrow, it would fly backwards.

* It's deader 'n a lightin' bug in a milk pitcher.

* That's as hard as pushin' a wet noodle through a keyhole.

* She's so dishonest she'd play cards with a politician.

* My brother's so drunk that he couldn't tell wet from windy.

* If brains were bacon, she wouldn't even sizzle.

* He's so ignorant that when he tells you howdy, he's told you all he knows.

* This job is as easy as catchin' fish with dynamite.

* She lives so far away that her and the horizon are buddies.

* That kid's as useless as a water bucket without a well rope.

Stanley and Livingstone

Whether or not the famous words were really spoken, the two men really did meet in the heart of the "Dark Continent."

* * * *

DR. DAVID LIVINGSTONE first went to Africa from Scotland to win Christian converts. Finding little success, Livingstone reinvented himself as an explorer. Although an intrepid seeker of knowledge, he proved a lousy expedition chief. After his 1858 Zambezi Expedition flopped, Livingstone had a difficult time finding donors willing to fund his expeditions. Regardless, he set out in search of the Holy Grail of 1800s African exploration—the Nile River's source.

Livingstone never did find the source of the Nile, though he did discover the source of the Congo River. In 1866, Livingstone took sick in the wilds of south-central Africa and lost touch with civilization for nearly six years. As a publicity stunt, the *New York Herald* newspaper sent journalist Henry Morton Stanley on a Livingstone hunt. In 1871, Stanley found Livingstone near Lake Tanganyika and (supposedly) greeted him with the famous question, "Dr. Livingstone, I presume?" They became colleagues and friends.

Stanley (1841–1904) outlived Livingstone (1813–73) by 30 years. One of Stanley's last wishes was to be buried next to Livingstone in London's Westminster Abbey, but the British government refused permission.

Stanley and the Congo

Don't expect the Congolese to build Stanley any monuments—he helped midwife the so-called "Congo Free State" (today the Democratic Republic of the Congo). The Congo Free State became the poster child for bad colonialism.

Stanley got a lot of press when he found Dr. Livingstone. This attracted interest from Belgium's King Leopold II, who contracted Stanley to explore, build roads, and make deals with native leaders. Leopold thus established a personal fief in the Congo, and from 1877 to 1885 he secured access to rubber and copper—materials that were vital to European industry. Leopold's thugs wrung forth every ounce of both, infamously severing the hands of any Congolese who failed to meet the rubber quota.

No one can know how many Congolese died under Leopold, but estimates run to millions. The Congo achieved independence from Belgium in 1960, but this naturally wealthy nation has endured despotic kleptocracies ever since.

"We went into the heart of Africa self-invited; therein lies our fault."

—HENRY MORTON STANLEY

Snow On and Snow Forth

Canadians are known as good communicators on the world stage: polite and articulate. We'll let you be the judge based on the following quotes and quips. If you don't like them, then "Fuddle-duddle" to you!

✳ ✳ ✳ ✳

"If some countries have too much history, we have too much geography."

—ECCENTRIC CANADIAN PRIME MINISTER WILLIAM LYON MACKENZIE KING, REMARKING ON THE COUNTRY'S IMMENSE SIZE IN 1936

"Fuddle-duddle."

—PRIME MINISTER PIERRE ELIOT TRUDEAU, SAID ON THE FLOOR OF THE HOUSE OF COMMONS IN 1971. OTHERS REPORTEDLY HEARD THE F-BOMB.

"If the national mental illness of the United States is megalomania, that of Canada is paranoid schizophrenia."

—CANADIAN WRITER MARGARET ATWOOD

"A Canadian is someone who knows how to make love in a canoe."

—CANADIAN WRITER PIERRE BERTON

"Patriotism is not dying for one's country, it is living for one's country. And for humanity. Perhaps that is not as romantic, but it's better."

—AGNES MACPHAIL, FIRST FEMALE MEMBER OF PARLIAMENT

"The Americans are our best friends whether we like it or not."

—ROBERT THOMPSON, LEADER OF THE SOCIAL CREDIT PARTY OF CANADA

"Living next to [the United States] is in some ways like sleeping with an elephant. No matter how friendly or even-tempered is the beast, if I can call it that, one is affected by every twitch and grunt."

—PRIME MINISTER PIERRE ELIOT TRUDEAU

"They told me I was going to have the tallest, darkest leading man in Hollywood."

—CANADIAN-BORN ACTRESS FAY WRAY, REFERRING TO HER GIANT COSTAR IN THE 1933 MOVIE KING KONG

"I am so excited about Canadians ruling the world."

—PRIME MINISTER JOHN DIEFENBAKER

"When fortune empties her chamber pot on your head, smile and say 'We are going to have a summer shower.'"

—JOHN A. MACDONALD, CANADA'S FIRST PRIME MINISTER, IN 1875

"Ladies and gentlemen, please forgive me, but that man [pointing to a political opponent] makes me sick."

—PRIME MINISTER JOHN A. MACDONALD, WHOSE CHRONIC ALCOHOLISM CAUSED HIM TO VOMIT IN THE CANADIAN HOUSE OF COMMONS ON MORE THAN ONE OCCASION

"No longer can a hero of a romantic novel be described as standing 'six foot in his stocking feet' and 'without an ounce of superfluous fat on him.' Nor will he be able to thrash a villain 'within an inch of his life'—although the villain will no doubt try for his 0.45359 kilograms of flesh. Naturally, a miss will be as good as 1.609 kilometres."

—MAURICE DE SOISSONS, COMMENTING ON CANADA'S ADOPTION OF THE METRIC SYSTEM IN A 1970 ISSUE OF CHATELAINE MAGAZINE

"I am rather inclined to believe that this is the land God gave to Cain."

—JACQUES CARTIER'S FIRST DESCRIPTION OF THE CANADIAN EAST COAST, IN 1534

"Character, like a photograph, develops in darkness."

—Turkish-born Canadian photographer Yousuf Karsh

"You know that these two nations have been at war over a few acres of snow."

—French satirist Voltaire, describing the spoils of battle in the French/British conflict over Canada in 1759

"Whatever women do, they must do twice as well as men to be thought half as good. Luckily, this is not difficult."

—Charlotte Whitton, mayor of Ottawa and Canada's first female mayor, in 1963

"Never retract, never explain, never apologize. Get the thing done and let them howl."

—Nellie McClung, early Canadian feminist, in 1915.

A Teller of the Tallest Tales

"A traveler has a right to relate and embellish his adventures as he pleases, and it is very impolite to refuse that deference and applause they deserve."

✳ ✳ ✳ ✳

THE TALL TALE is a genre all its own. The sky is truly the limit—or perhaps no limit at all—when embellishment is the norm.

Rudolf Eric Raspe did not set out to make a name writing tall tales. German born (1736) and trained in law, he started as a clerk in a university library and began his publishing career in poetry. He published works of his own and also wrote translations.

His paper on the bones and teeth of elephants and other animals, published in the 59th volume of *Philosophical Transactions*, earned Raspe election to the Royal Society of London as a fellow. He wrote prolifically on many subjects and befriended several esteemed thinkers, exchanging letters with the likes of Benjamin Franklin.

After being banished from the Royal Society for "breaches of trust" and while working as a mining expert for Sir John Sinclair, Raspe concocted a fictional German nobleman named Baron Munchausen. *Baron Munchhausen's Narrative of his Marvellous Travels and Campaigns in Russia* was published anonymously in 1785. The zany tales were a combination of Raspe's own experiences, crazy stories heard in his own travels and certainly some influences from other authors like Swift's *Gulliver's Travels*.

The stories opposed the Enlightenment era concept of rationalism, taking readers on a journey in completely irrational and comical directions. Raspe eventually got credit for his authorship of the tall tales, which stand as some of the most well known in literary history. Raspe died in 1794.

A Bit of an Adventure

Here's just a taste of Munchhausen's adventures...in this episode, he encounters both a lion and a crocodile in short succession.

"Near the banks of a large piece of water, which had engaged my attention, I thought I heard a rustling noise behind; on turning about I was almost petrified (as who would not be?) at the sight of a lion, which was evidently approaching with the intention of satisfying his appetite with my poor carcase, and that without asking my consent. What was to be done in this horrible dilemma? I had not even a moment for reflection; my piece was only charged with swan-shot, and I had no other about me: however, though I could have no idea of killing such an animal with that weak kind of ammunition, yet I had some hopes of frightening him by the report, and perhaps of wounding him also. I immediately let fly, without waiting till he was within reach, and the report did but enrage him, for he now quickened his pace, and seemed to approach me full speed: I attempted to escape, but that only added (if an addition could be made) to my distress; for the moment I turned about I found a large crocodile, with his mouth extended almost ready to receive me. On my right hand was the piece of water before mentioned, and on my left a deep precipice, said to have, as I have since learned, a receptacle at the bottom for venomous creatures; in short I gave myself up as lost, for the lion was now upon his hind-legs, just in the act of seizing me; I fell involuntarily to the ground with fear, and, as it afterwards appeared, he sprang over me. I lay some time in a situation which no language can describe, expecting to feel his teeth or talons in some part of me every moment: after waiting in this prostrate situation a few seconds I heard a violent but unusual noise, different from any sound that had ever before assailed my ears; nor is it at all to be wondered at, when I inform you from whence it proceeded: after listening for some time, I ventured to raise my head and look round, when, to my unspeakable joy, I perceived the lion had, by the eagerness with which he sprung at me, jumped forward, as I fell, into the crocodile's mouth! which, as before observed, was wide open; the head of the one stuck in the throat of the other! and they were struggling to extricate themselves! I fortunately recollected my *couteau de chasse*, which was by my side; with this instrument I severed the lion's head at one blow, and the body fell at my feet! I then, with the butt-end of my fowling-piece, rammed the head farther into the throat of the crocodile, and destroyed him by suffocation, for he could neither gorge nor eject it."

New York Quotables

"It'll be a great place if they ever finish it."

—O. HENRY

"If you live in New York, even if you're Catholic, you're Jewish."

—LENNY BRUCE

"The wise people are in New York because the foolish went there first, that's the way the wise men make a living."

—FINLEY PETER DUNNE

"Everybody ought to have a lower East Side in their life."

—Irving Berlin

"Living in New York is like being at some terrible late-night party. You're tired, you've had a headache since you arrived, but you can't leave because then you'd miss the party."

—Simon Hoggart

"When it's 100 degrees in New York, it's 72 in Los Angeles. When it's 30 degrees in New York, in Los Angeles it's still 72. However, there are 6 million interesting people in New York, and only 72 in Los Angeles."

—Neil Simon

"There is something distinctive about living in New York; over eight million other people are doing it."

—Don Herold

"If you're not in New York, you're camping out."

—Thomas E. Dewey

"New York is large, glamorous, easy-going, kindly and incurious, but above all it is a crucible—because it is large enough to be incurious."

—Ford Madox Ford

"The city is an addiction."

—Timothy Leary

"The only real advantage of New York is that all its inhabitants ascend to heaven right after their deaths, having served their full term in hell right on Manhattan Island."

—Barnard Bulletin

""It's a fickle town, a tough town. They getcha, boy. They don't let you escape with minor scratches and bruises. They put scars on you here."

—Reggie Jackson

"It isn't like the rest of the country—it is like a nation itself—more tolerant than the rest in a curious way. Littleness gets swallowed up here. All the viciousness that makes other cities vicious is sucked up and absorbed in New York."

—John Steinbeck

A Small Step in a Strange Place

"That's one small step for [a] man, one giant leap for mankind."

✳ ✳ ✳ ✳

AS HE STEPPED off the ladder of the Apollo 11 lunar module and onto the moon's surface, becoming the first man to walk on the moon, Neil Armstrong paused to acknowledge the NASA space program's tremendous accomplishment. He had prepared the statement in advance and intended to say "one small step for a man," but the excitement of the moment caused him to unintentionally omit the article.

The Apollo 11 mission fulfilled the goal President John F. Kennedy had set eight years earlier, when he told Congress, "I believe that this nation should commit itself to achieving the goal, before this decade is out, of landing a man on the moon and returning him safely to the Earth." Kennedy's ambition was to upstage the Soviet Union's space flight successes, which had included launching the Sputnik satellite into orbit and sending the first man into space.

Although Cold War rivalry was a major factor in expanding NASA's agenda, the two countries later pooled their resources for a number of space projects. The International Space Station, a multinational earth-orbiting research facility, is one such successful collaboration.

Chapter 8

The Human Condition

Is That a Cigar in Your Pocket?

Did Freud really say, "Sometimes a cigar is just a cigar," or does our subconscious just wish he had?

※ ※ ※ ※

THANKS TO SIGMUND Freud, penis envy and Oedipal complexes are common fodder for awkward conversations the world over. The Austrian psychiatrist, considered "the father of psychoanalysis," made popular the idea that your mind can hide its true desires, which are revealed only if you examine dreams and other subconscious thoughts for symbolism.

What a relief to hear that Freud, the ultimate overthinker, might have admitted that sometimes an object has no hidden meaning. In most retellings, this apocryphal anecdote occurs during a lecture on one of his pet topics, such as phallic imagery. An audience member cheekily asks what Freud's omnipresent cigars represent (wink, wink), causing the doctor to pronounce, "Sometimes a cigar is just a cigar."

Although Freud's fondness for cigars is well documented—he smoked 20 a day—there is no record he ever wrote or uttered the phrase. It is not included in his official papers, personal letters, or memoirs, nor is it mentioned in his daughter's biography. Even the curators of the Freud Museum in London can't verify it.

The quotation has a long history in comedy and is often linked with cigar-wagging Groucho Marx doing an imitation of Freud. On the other hand, folklorists relate the saying to Rudyard Kipling's poem *The Betrothed*, which reads, "And a woman is only a woman, but a good cigar is a smoke."

But Freud might have said, if he had been the type to say such things, "Sometimes a pithy saying is just a pithy saying."

Nature Abhors a Vaccuum

Benedict de Spinoza was one of the most important Western philosophers of the 17th century. He contributed to numerous areas of philosophy, and he combined influences from numerous historical figures and great philosophers from classical antiquity and his contemporaries.

✳   ✳   ✳   ✳

BENEDICT DE SPINOZA was born in Amsterdam on November 24, 1632. His family was of Sephardic Jewish descent, having settled in Amsterdam after fleeing the Portuguese Inquisition of 1536. In addition to speaking Portuguese at home, Spinoza learned Dutch, Spanish, Hebrew, and Latin. He attended a Torah yeshiva as a child, and when he was seventeen he began working for his father's import business. Three years later he began studying Latin with Franciscus Enden. Enden introduced the young man to modern philosophy and progressive political and scientific ideas, including the works of Descartes. In his mid-twenties, he grew disillusioned with Judaism, and when he made his ideas known, he was excommunicated by the congregation of his Temple. He spent the rest of his life developing his philosophy.

Spinoza's best known work is his treatise *Ethics*, which he wrote in 1664–65 and published in 1667. In it he argued for an ethics that grows out of a system of metaphysics that identifies God with Nature. Rather than being the removed creator and ruler of the universe, Spinoza argued that God was Nature itself, and that Nature is an infinite and deterministic system. He wrote that humans could only find happiness by seeking a rational understanding of the Natural system.

Spinoza's ideas were controversial for his time. In 1670 he moved to The Hague, where he worked on scientific essays and a political treatise. On February 20, 1677, he died at his home in The Hague.

Quotes from Spinoza

"Nature abhors a vacuum."

"Beauty, my dear Sir, is not so much a quality of the object beheld, as an effect in him who beholds it. If our sight were longer or shorter, or if our constitution were different, what now appears beautiful to us would seem misshapen, and what we now think misshapen we should regard as beautiful."

"Nature is satisfied with little; and if she is, I am also."

"A free man thinks of death least of all things; and his wisdom is a meditation not of death but of life."

"Nature offers nothing that can be called this man's rather than another's; but, under nature, everything belongs to all—that is, they have authority to claim it for themselves."

Living Life Forwards

"It is perfectly true, as the philosophers say, that life must be understood backwards. But they forget the other proposition, that it must be lived forwards."

To Kierkegaard, truth was subjective, Christianity was personal, and God was infinite. His work influenced Western thought well into the 20th century.

✳ ✳ ✳ ✳

SØREN KIERKEGAARD WAS born in Copenhagen, Denmark on May 5, 1813, to a well-to-do family. Kierkegaard read extensively as a young man, exploring both classical and contemporary philosophy as well as plays. He often wandered the streets of Copenhagen, lost in thought. In 1830 he began attending the School of Civic Virtue, and later studied theology at the University of Copenhagen. He began keeping journals while in university, and they grew to some 7,000 pages by the end of his life. His journals provide a great deal of insight about the development of Kierkegaard's philosophy, although he also published widely. He successfully defended his dissertation in 1841, which discussed irony as it related to the works of Socrates.

Philosophy and Early Writing

In 1842, Kierkegaard wrote the first of many treatises on religion, *De Ombinus Dubitandum Est*, "Everything Must be Doubted." In it he discussed the existential problems that arise from the Cartesian system of applying rational skepticism to all things. Kierkegaard followed *Omnibus* with two other books that explored these themes, *Philosophical Fragments* and *Concluding Unscientific Postscript*. In 1843, he anonymously published his first work, *Either/Or*, a two-volume magnum opus on the development of human consciousness. He argues that consciousness begins as a form that is essentially hedonistic, and develops into one that values ethics and morality. The work is presented as two views of life: the first is the aesthetic view, which values beauty and seduction, and the second is the ethical view, which values critical discourse and moral responsibility. *Either/Or* established Kierkegaard's reputation as a writer and philosopher.

Existentialism and Christendom

Kierkegaard continued to publish anonymously during the 1840s, writing a series of "Upbuilding Discourses" that began as two essays and eventually grew to eighteen over the course of a decade. The *Discourses* are written to help improve (or "upbuild") the reader's thinking rather than tear it down, and deal with ethics, morality, love, and religion. He published *Fear and Trembling* and *Repetition* in 1843; in them, he laid the foundations of Existentialist thought. Although Kierkegaard never used the word "existentialism" in his work, he is considered one of the founders of the movement. He argued that human experience, and by extension truth, was inherently subjective, in sharp contrast to the objectivity of mathematics and science. Kierkegaard thought that objective study was too removed from the human experience to be able to approach truth. He used the "Knight of Faith" to illustrate his ideas in these works. This individual is one whose faith in himself and God grants him the freedom to act independently from the world.

In *Works of Love*, published in 1847, he explores the concept of *agape* love. Agape, or charitable love, which stems from the ancient Greeks, was considered the highest form of love, as compared to erotic love and familial love. *Works of Love* relies heavily on Existentialist arguments to make its case. In his later years, Kierkegaard attacked the Lutheran Church in his writing. He criticized Bishop Jacob Peter Mynster after his death, arguing that his ideas about Christianity were incorrect, and that Mynster's theology did not ask enough from Christians. Mynster had been lauded as a "truth-witness" following his death, and Kierkegaard vehemently contested the characterization. He published his criticism in a series of pamphlets called *The Moment*.

Kierkegaard collapsed in the street in October 1855. He lingered in a hospital bed for a month before dying inNovember.

Quotes from Kierkegaard

"What the age needs is not a genius—it has had geniuses enough, but a martyr, who in order to teach men to obey would himself be obedient unto death. What the age needs is awakening. And therefore someday, not only my writings but my whole life, all the intriguing mystery of the machine will be studied and studied. I never forget how God helps me and it is therefore my last wish that everything may be to his honour."

"But on the other hand, the understanding, reflection, is also a gift of God. What shall one do with it, how dispose of it if one is not to use it? And if one then uses it in fear and trembling not for one's own advantage but to serve the truth, if one uses it that way in fear and trembling and furthermore believing that it still is God who determines the issue in its eternal significance, venturing to trust in him, and with unconditional obedience yielding to what he makes use of it: is this not fear of God and serving God the way a person of reflection can, in the somewhat different way than the spontaneously immediate person, but perhaps more ardently."

An American Philosopher

A leader of the American Transcendentalist movement, poet and philosopher Ralph Waldo Emerson is perhaps best known for his essay "Self Reliance."

✳   ✳   ✳   ✳

RALPH WALDO EMERSON was born in Boston on May 25, 1803. His father was a Unitarian minister. Emerson graduated from Harvard College in 1821 and attended the Harvard School of Divinity in 1824. In 1826, he travelled to South Carolina and Florida, where he first witnessed slavery, an experience that would stay with him his entire life.

In 1829, he was ordained a Unitarian minister and married Ellen Tucker the same year. When she died in 1831 of tuberculosis two years later, Emerson was distraught, and had a crisis of faith that resulted in his resignation from the ministry.

Emerson travelled to Europe for a year, and while he was there he met William Wordsworth, Samuel Taylor Coleridge and other writers. Upon his return to America, he began giving talks about spirituality and living ethically, and published many of these lectures as essays. In 1834 he moved to Concord, and married Lydia Jackson the next year. In Concord he began spending time with a group of intellectuals that included Henry David Thoreau and Margaret Fuller.

The Transcendentalists

Emerson's circle of friends eventually became known as the American Transcendentalists. They espoused a belief that one can move past, or transcend, the physical senses to acquire a deeper spiritual experience of the world. They believed that God was not a remote, enigmatic deity, but one who could be understood by introspection and exploration of one's place in the natural world. Emerson's essays began to reflect this philosophy. In 1836 he published "Nature," which laid out the foundations of transcendentalism. In it, he divided nature into four functions: Beauty, Commodity, Discipline, and Language. He followed this essay with "The American Scholar," which encouraged American writers to create their own literary style instead of attempting to imitate European modes of writing.

Emerson soon became one of the leading figures of the Transcendentalist movement. He founded *The Dial*, a literary magazine, and published dozens of essays in the 1840s. One of his best known essays, "Self-Reliance," was published in 1841. It presented a discussion on one of his recurrent themes: the importance of resisting conformity and "foolish consistency," and the necessity of following one's own ideas. During the 1840s Emerson also wrote "Friendship" and "Experience," two well-known essays.

Later Work

By 1860, Emerson's work began showing a more moderate philosophy that spoke of the importance of balancing individual nonconformity with social responsibility, which he discussed in "The Conduct of Life," published that year. In it, he tackled some of the difficult problems of the day, including the question of slavery. He argued that the Civil War would be necessary to ensure a rebirth of the nation, writing that "wars, fires, and plagues" destroy old institutions and allow society to recreate itself. He drew on the natural cycle of destruction preceding creation to support his position. He began advocating for the abolition of slavery in his lecture circuit in the 1860s.

Following the Civil War, Emerson toured less, and began to be referred to as "the Sage of Concord." He continued to write during the 1870s, publishing "Society and Solitude," and later *Parnassus*, a collection of poetry.

Emerson died on April 27, 1882, in Concord.

Quotes from Emerson

"Slavery is disheartening; but Nature is not so helpless but it can rid itself of every last wrong. But the spasms of nature are centuries and ages and will tax the faith of shortlived men. Slowly, slowly the Avenger comes, but comes surely. "

"There are two classes of poets—the poets by education and practice, these we respect; and poets by nature, these we love."

"I read your piece on Plato. Holmes, when you strike at a king, you must kill him."

"People seem not to see that their opinion of the world is also a confession of character."

"Respect the child. Be not too much his parent. Trespass not on his solitude."

"Sometimes a scream is better than a thesis."

"Let me never fall into the vulgar mistake of dreaming that I am persecuted whenever I am contradicted."

"In every work of genius we recognize our own rejected thoughts: they come back to us with a certain alienated majesty."

"A foolish consistency is the hobgoblin of little minds, adored by little statesmen and philosophers and divines."

"To be great is to be misunderstood."

The First Autobiographer

Who wrote the first autobiography? Saint Augustine of Hippo, way back in the fourth century A.D. And just what was it that made Augustine's story so memorable that he wanted to share it with the world? We'll tell you.

✳   ✳   ✳   ✳

AUGUSTINE WAS BORN in present-day Algeria, in Africa. As a young man, he joined the Manichean religion, which was a spiritual movement from the Middle East that blended elements of Christianity with Buddhism and other ancient religions of the East. In his late twenties, Augustine became disillusioned with the Manichean philosophy, and he was baptized into the Christian church at age thirty-three. This was a great relief to his mother Monica, who had tried to raise him as a Christian and had long pleaded with him to convert. She later joined him in the Catholic sainthood.

About ten years after Augustine's conversion, he wrote his autobiography as a series of thirteen books, collectively called the *Confessions*. While his greatest achievements were still ahead of him, the *Confessions* detail Augustine's childhood and wayward youth, then address his conversion to the Christian path. About his youth, he famously wrote, "As a youth, I prayed, 'Give me chastity and continence, but not right now.'"

As he grew older, Augustine was not noted for his tolerance— he mercilessly sought to stamp out competing Christian sects, for example—but he was quite the *bon vivant* in his youth. He enjoyed plays and other entertainment, fine living, and the fairer sex. He fathered a child by his live-in girlfriend, a concubine who was sent off to a monastery shortly before Augustine became a Christian. Augustine never told his readers her name, but he treasured their son, Adeodatus, until the boy's untimely death at age sixteen.

Augustine's own personality comes through clearly in his writings. He worried about everything, found fault with himself even after he converted to Christianity, and constantly dissected his motives and beliefs. After finishing his autobiography, Augustine became a bishop and wrote *The City of God*, a classic work of Catholic philosophy. He died at age seventy-six, and thanks to his autobiographical works, we know all about the life he lived.

A Star of the Renaissance

"Obstacles cannot crush me. Every obstacle yields to stern resolve. He who is fixed to a star does not change his mind."

Painter, inventor, mathematician, and scientist, Leonardo da Vinci was the embodiment of the "Renaissance Man." His work almost single-handedly shifted the course of Western civilization, and his influence resonates to this day.

✳ ✳ ✳ ✳

LEONARDO DA VINCI was born in Vinci, Italy, on April 15, 1452. He was apprenticed to Andrea del Verrocchio, one of the most famous painters of the day. There he learned not only painting and drawing, but also studied drafting, carpentry, metallurgy, and chemistry. According to legend, when da Vinci painted *The Baptism of Christ* in 1472, Verrocchio stopped painting, declaring that he could never be as good as da Vinci.

Although he was a prolific painter, only fifteen of da Vinci's paintings are known to have survived. One of these is *The Last Supper*, which he completed in 1498. The original painting is mostly destroyed, although numerous copies have been made. Da Vinci's *Mona Lisa*, which he completed in 1507, is perhaps the most recognized painting in the world. The painting is a brilliant example of the technique of *sfumato*, in which the background is softened by shading tones together.

Many more of his sketches and drawings are extant. Perhaps the best known of these is the *Vitruvian Man*, which shows the proportions of the human figure.

In addition to his painting, da Vinci's ideas for inventions were various and brilliant. His sketches show plans for a prototypical helicopter, hydraulic pumps, and mechanical devices. His *Treatise on Painting*, printed posthumously, included many of his anatomical drawings. He also kept dozens of notebooks that he filled with his drawings and ideas.

Da Vinci died on May 2, 1519 in France.

A Wide Enough World?

Aaron Burr served honorably in the Revolutionary War, served as Attorney General of New York, and was Vice President of the United States, yet he is remembered for killing Alexander Hamilton in a duel.

✳   ✳   ✳   ✳

ARON BURR WAS born on February 6, 1756 in Newark, New Jersey. His parents died when he was a boy, and he was raised by his uncle. When he was thirteen he began attending the College of New Jersey, and finished in only three years, after which he began attending law school. When the Revolutionary War broke out, Burr left school to join the Continental Army, serving with the division commanded by Benedict Arnold. He attained the rank of major, and was transferred to serve with George Washington. Following the War, he returned to law school, and passed the Bar in 1782. He practiced in Albany, New York, and became the New York State Attorney General in 1789.

He was elected to the United States Senate in 1791, defeating Alexander Hamilton's father-in-law. He lost his reelection, and blamed Hamilton for spreading rumors about him, costing him the election. In the presidential election of 1800, he ran against

Thomas Jefferson. They received the same number of electoral votes, and the U.S. House of Representatives elected Jefferson. Hamilton helped organize the opposition to Burr, who was incensed. When he ran for Governor of New York, he again lost, and again blamed Hamilton. He challenged Hamilton to a duel, and on July 11, 1804, he shot Hamilton, killing him. Later he reflected, "Had I read Sterne more and Voltaire less, I should have known the world was wide enough for Hamilton and me," opposing Laurence Sterne, the author of the sprawling *The Life and Opinions of Tristram Shandy, Gentleman*, against the more strident Voltaire.

A scandal in 1807 that resulted in his being tried and acquitted for treason ultimately left him ruined. He died on September 14, 1836, on Staten Island, New York.

He Thought and Was

A mathematician, philosopher, and scientist, Descartes almost single-handedly invented modern Western philosophy.

✳ ✳ ✳ ✳

RENÉ DESCARTES WAS born in a small town in central France on March 31, 1596; the town has since been named after him. He was raised by his maternal grandmother until he was eight years old, when he was sent to a Jesuit boarding school until he was fifteen. There, he studied rhetoric, natural philosophy, ethics, and astronomy. He attended the University of Poitiers, where he studied law. He is widely credited with being the architect of modern Western philosophy; his ideas were radical for their time. Descartes believed that all ideas that preceded him should be cleared away, as they were preconceived and inherited. Instead, he declared the starting place for determining the new philosophy to be simply the statement "I exist." From this statement he deduced the quote he is most famous for: "I think, therefore I am." (In Latin, "Cogito, ergo sum," in French, "Je pense, donc je suis.")

In saying so, he echoed St. Augustine, 1,200 years earlier: "Of this last doubt, I cannot doubt: that I doubt," and an even earlier statement by Aristotle: "To be conscious that we are perceiving or thinking is to be conscious of our own existence." Neither of those fit so easily on a T-shirt, though!

Descartes contended that all truths—natural, philosophical physical, and metaphysical—were ultimately linked as parts of a greater, complete Truth. This was, to some degree, an extension of the ideas that had been proposed by Frances Bacon early on in the 17th century. Descartes' most famous treatises are perhaps *Meditations on First Philosophy* and *Principles of Philosophy*, in which he developed many of the ideas he would become famous for. These works continue to be standards in philosophy studies the world over. He also developed the Cartesian coordinate system of geometry, which is still used today and is the foundation of much of modern mathematics.

Descartes died on February 11, 1650, in Stockholm, Sweden.

Thomas à Kempis

"Man proposes, but God disposes."

His Imitation of Christ *is second only to the Bible in popularity among Christians.*

✳   ✳   ✳   ✳

THOMAS À KEMPIS was born Thomas Haemerkin in Kempen, Germany, in 1380 to artisan parents. His name "Kempis" comes from the German "von Kempen," in reference to his hometown. Kempis' father was most likely a metal smith; his original surname meant "little hammer." At thirteen, he was sent to school in Holland. While he was there, he met followers of the Modern Devotion movement called the Brethren of the Common Life. Modern Devotionists preached spiritual renewal through the practice of piety, humility, and simple living. The Brethren had a profound impact on Thomas.

In 1399, he left school and travelled to Zwolle to visit his brother Jan at the Monastery of St. Agnes. In 1406, he would become ordained at St. Agnes and became a sub-prior at the Monastery in 1429.

The Imitation of Christ

Kempis wrote the work he is best known for between the years 1418 and 1427. The Imitation of Christ was immediately popular, and was copied over by hand hundreds of times before 1650; 750 hand-copied manuscripts of the book are known. The Imitation is comprised of four sections that deal with spiritual life, the interior life, interior consolation, and the Eucharist.

Kempis advocated withdrawing from the world and contemplating Christ's teachings in quiet solitude. This was divergent from many of the teachings that were popular in the early 15th century, which espoused a more active imitation of Jesus. Saint Augustine and Saint Francis had advocated an outward imitation of Jesus that stressed poverty and preaching the gospel. Kempis' work, which drew heavily on the teachings of the Modern Devotion movement, was the first major work to propose an alternate path to salvation.

The Imitation may be one of the most reprinted books in history. There are more than a thousand editions of The Imitation in the British Museum alone, and a collection of 400 more editions were donated to the city of Cologne in 1838. There are more than 500 editions written in Latin and another 900 written in French. The immense popularity of the book has not faded even today, and it remains the most popular book on Christian spirituality after the Bible itself.

In The Imitation, Kempis emphasized the importance of solitude and silence, and wrote that in quiet meditation, all the "allurements" of the world drop away, leaving one with an undisturbed conscience. He discussed themes of inner peace and a pure heart, and said that God will defend those who have a clear conscience and a humble demeanor. The Imitation contains a long dialogue between Jesus and a disciple. Jesus tells the disciple the world offers only things that provide fleeting happiness, but these are sought enthusiastically, while God offers eternal happiness, and men are indifferent to it. He says the salvation lies in submitting to God's will and not worrying about the future. In the final section of the book, Kempis wrote that the Eucharist is the means by which spiritual grace is received and the soul is replenished.

Kempis spent the rest of his life copying the Bible and reflecting in quiet meditation at the Monastery of St. Agnes. He died in 1471 and was buried in Utrecht, near the Monastery.

"First keep the peace within yourself, then you can also bring peace to others."

Nasty, Brutish, and Short

Without government, Hobbes argued, humans would be at one another's throats in an instant.

* * * *

THOMAS HOBBES WAS born in Westport on April 5, 1588. He was raised by his uncle, and received an excellent education. Hobbes studied Latin and Greek, and when he was fourteen he enrolled in Oxford, graduating in 1608. He became the private tutor of William Cavendish, the son of the Earl of Devonshire. Through his association with the Cavendishes, Hobbes was introduced to intellectual circles that discussed the politics of the day. His student became a member of Parliament in 1614, and Hobbes often sat in on debates. In 1640, he wrote a treatise defending King Charles I and supporting the Royalist faction. The work was published as his first book, *The Elements of Law, Natural and Politic*. The conflict between the Royalists and Parliamentarians ultimately led to all-out war in 1642. Hobbes left England out of fear for his safety, and lived in France until 1651.

The Political Philosopher

While in Paris, Hobbes wrote a series of comments on Descartes' *Discourse and Optics*. He disagreed with Descartes on the primacy of the mind, and argued that motion was the basis of nature, society, and the mind. Descartes responded, and the two began publishing replies to one another's arguments, which were added to Descartes' *Meditations on First Philosophy* in 1641. This exchange laid the groundwork for Hobbes' developing political ideas. When Hobbes and Descartes met in 1648, the meeting was tepid, and although they respected one another as intellectuals, they did not enjoy one another's company.

Hobbes published his first work on politics, *De Cive* ("On the Citizen") in 1642. In it, he presented the first indications of the political philosophy that he would become known for in *Leviathan. De Cive* discusses Hobbes' ideas about the "natural condition" of humanity and talks about the necessity of a stable government for a functioning society. The work is divided into three sections: Liberty, Empire, and Religion. Hobbes had originally intended *De Cive* to be the third book in a trilogy of works on human knowledge, but the impending English Civil War led him to rush the work to publication in order to address the growing political unrest there.

Leviathan

In Paris, while the Civil Wars were raging in England, Hobbes began writing *Leviathan*, which would become one of the most important books on political philosophy in Western thought. In it he argued that the social contract, in which members of the social order agree to accept certain rules and duties to maintain it, is a natural evolution of human society. Hobbes also argued that an absolute ruler, with the power of the biblical monster Leviathan, was necessary to protect the people from their own shortcomings. Without such control, Hobbes thought society would descend into anarchy, a "war of all against all."

In the state of nature, he argued, there were "No arts; no letters; no society; and which is worst of all, continual fear and danger of violet death; and the life of man, solitary, poor, nasty, brutish, and short."

Hobbes' argument is methodical: he begins by describing human nature as completely selfish, and argues that the natural condition of humans is one of amorality and fear, giving rise to perpetual warfare. He then concludes that only a powerful government can keep a society from descending into chaos.

He returned to England after the Civil Wars, where he continued to write. He completed the *Elements of Philosophy* trilogy in 1658. Thomas Hobbes died on December 4, 1679.

Conquering with Glory

Le Cid broke all the rules of theatre when it was produced, and with it, Pierre Corneille created an entirely new genre that would become classical French tragedy.

✳ ✳ ✳ ✳

PIERRE CORNEILLE WAS born in Rouen, France on June 6, 1606 to an affluent family. Nearly all the men in his family were lawyers. Pierre was educated by Jesuits and became licensed in law in 1628. He worked as in the department of forests and waterways in his twenties. By then he'd already written his first play, a comedy called *Melite*, performed in his hometown in 1629 and in Paris the following year. He wrote a series of comedies throughout the 1630s, and his talent as a playwright caught the attention of the powerful Cardinal de Richelieu, who included him in his Society of the Five Authors. The Cardinal provided the Society with ideas and outlines for plays, and they wrote them.

Le Cid

Around this time there was a growing movement to approach tragic theater by employing what were called "classical unities."

The approach required unity of time, place, and action, which essentially meant that a play should take place in one act over the course of a single day, in one location, and deal with a single event. This idea was couched in a misreading of Aristotle's writings about the nature of tragedy. Corneille wrote the experimental tragedy *Médée* in this form in 1635. In 1637 he wrote *Le Cid*. It would come to be considered the most significant play in the history of French Theatre.

The play centers on Don Rodrigue from the legend of El Cid, a Spanish nobleman in medieval Spain. His name derives from the Moors' name for him, which meant The Lord. In the play, Rodrigue is in love with a woman named Chimène, and they plan to marry. But when Chimène's father insults Rodrigue's, he is forced to challenge her father to a duel, and kills him. Chimène, despite her love for Rodrigue, demands justice from the King. But when the Moors invade, Rodrigue leads the Spanish to victory, redeeming him in the eyes of the King and earning him the title Le Cid. Chimène asks that one of the King's knights duel Rodrigue for honor, and he agrees. Rodrigue disarms the knight, and Chimène agrees to marry him in a year. Rodrigue then sets out to invade the territory of the Moors.

A line from the play speaks to Corneille's risk in writing the play: "To conquer without risk is to triumph without glory." Fortunately for Corneille, *Le Cid* was an instant popular success, and touched off a war of polemics among Corneille's supporters and rivals. Jean Chapelain, a theatre critic of the time, wrote a review of the play that argued for the "regular" style of French tragedy and criticized Le Cid as implausible, but nonetheless commended its beauty. The play is considered the true birth of the French period of classical tragedy during the 17th century.

Cornielle continued to write roughly one play per year until 1674, when his final play, *Surena*, was written, but they did not enjoy the same level of success as *Le Cid*. Other playwrights were beginning to be popular, including Jean Racine. In 1670 Racine and Cornielle were each tasked with writing a play about the Roman general Titus and his affair with Berenice of Cilicia. Racine's was considered the better version, and remains the more famous play.

Cornielle retired from the theatre after writing *Surena*. He died in Paris in 1684.

Reigning or Serving

In Paradise Lost, *John Milton created what is widely considered the greatest epic poem of the English language. In* Paradise Regained, *he explored the temptation of Christ.*

❋　❋　❋　❋

JOHN MILTON WAS born in London on December 9, 1608. His parents, John and Sara Milton, were Protestants; his father had been disowned by Milton's grandfather for converting from Catholicism. Milton was a middle child, with an older sister and a younger brother. He attended St. Paul's School, where he learned several languages. At Christ's College in Cambridge, Milton earned a Bachelor of Arts in 1629 and a Master of Arts in 1632. He then spent six years in independent study, during which time he began writing poetry and essays. In 1638, he travelled to Europe, and visited Galileo, who was under house arrest for his espousal of the heliocentric model of the universe. As the Civil War loomed in England, he returned home.

Milton married Mary Powell in 1642. When they separated for a number of years, he wrote a series of essays advocating for legalizing divorce called *The Divorce Tracts*. They reconciled, and had four children together.

In 1652 Mary died, and the same year Milton lost his sight. (His poem "On His Blindness" from this time period contains one of his most oft-quoted lines: "They also serve who only stand and wait.") He married Katherine Woodcock in 1656, but she died after just two years of marriage.

A Puritan, Milton was opposed to the Royalists and the Anglican Church, and he supported Oliver Cromwell and the Parliamentarians during the English Civil Wars. He wrote pamphlets on freedom of the press and likely attended the execution of Charles I after the second Civil War. He wrote publications for Cromwell's government when Cromwell assumed power. In 1649 he wrote *The Tenure of Kings and Magistrates*, which asserted the right of the people to overthrow monarchs, and *Iconoclasts*, which explicitly defended the execution of Charles I. In 1652 Milton wrote *The First Defense*, a polemic that supported the Parliament's government, and in 1654 he wrote *The Second Defense*, which supported Cromwell's rule of England.

Cromwell died in 1658, and the following year his government collapsed. In spite of the restoration of the monarchy, Milton obstinately continued to espouse his support of the Commonwealth. He wrote *A Treatise of Civil Power* in 1659, in which he attacked a state-sponsored Church. When Charles II assumed the throne in 1660, Milton went into hiding. His books were burned and a warrant was issued for his arrest. When a general pardon was issued, he came out of hiding and was briefly imprisoned, but powerful friends managed to secure his release.

Paradise Lost

Milton married Elizabeth Minsull after he was released from prison, and spent the next ten years living in London. During this time he worked on *Paradise Lost*, which he published in 1667. The work is a ten-volume, free-verse epic poem that relates the story of Adam and Eve, their temptation by Satan, and their expulsion from the Garden of Eden. *Paradise Lost* is considered Milton's greatest work as well as the most significant epic poem ever written in the English language. It is interpreted as a civil war between the forces of Heaven and Hell, and contains the famous line: "Better to reign in hell, than serve in heaven." Curiously, Milton takes the side of Heaven and the supreme monarch in the poem, which runs contrary to his lifelong opposition to the Crown. In 1671, he published *Paradise Regained*, an epic poem that tells the story of the temptation of Jesus by Satan, and *Samson Agonistes*.

John Milton died in London on November 8, 1674.

John Locke

"It is one thing to show a man that he is in error, and another to put him in possession of the truth."

John Locke was one of the most significant philosophers in 17th century England. His ideas about government revolutionized Western ideas about politics, and influenced the revolutions of the 18th century.

❋ ❋ ❋ ❋

JOHN LOCKE WAS born on August 29, 1632, in Somerset, England. His parents were Puritans and Locke was raised in that faith. His father was a lawyer, and Locke received an excellent education. He attended Westminster School in London, and enrolled in Christ Church, Oxford, in 1652, where he studied metaphysics, Latin, and Greek. He graduated in 1656, returning in 1658 for a Master of Arts. Following graduate school, he took on a teaching job at Oxford. Some years later Locke would receive a bachelor's of medicine from Oxford as well. He was inducted into the Royal Society in 1668.

Locke's landmark work, *Two Treatises of Government*, was published anonymously in 1689. His ideas about the Natural Rights of Man and the social contract were groundbreaking at the time, and laid the foundations for much of the philosophy of the 18th century. This work significantly influenced Thomas

Jefferson, John Adams, and many of the other leaders of the American Revolution, and also inspired the French Revolution.

After an attempt on the life of King Charles II that became known as the Rye House Plot, Locke fell out of the good graces of the government, in spite of the fact that he was most likely not involved. He was forced to flee to Holland. While there, he wrote *An Essay Concerning Human Understanding*, which was as groundbreaking as his *Two Treatises*. The work spanned four volumes and explored the nature of human knowledge. Following the Glorious Revolution of 1688, Locke was able to return to England. He spent his final years in Essex, where he died on October 28, 1704.

Quotes from Locke

"To love truth for truth's sake is the principal part of human perfection in this world, and the seed-plot of all other virtues."

"New opinions are always suspected, and usually opposed, without any other reason but because they are not already common."

"I have always thought the actions of men the best interpreters of their thoughts."

"No man's knowledge here can go beyond his experience."

"He that uses his words loosely and unsteadily will either not be minded or not understood."

"Religion, which should most distinguish us from the beasts, and ought most particularly elevate us, as rational creatures, above brutes, is that wherein men often appear most irrational, and more senseless than beasts."

"The end of law is not to abolish or restrain, but to preserve and enlarge freedom. For in all the states of created beings, capable of laws, where there is no law there is no freedom."

"Wherever Law ends, Tyranny begins."

"Thus parents, by humouring and cockering them when little, corrupt the principles of nature in their children, and wonder afterwards to taste the bitter waters, when they themselves have poison'd the fountain."

Aphra Behn

"Variety is the soul of pleasure."

Aphra Behn was one of the first women to be a successful professional writer. She inspired generations of women writers, among them Virginia Woolf. And if, as she wrote, "variety is the soul of pleasure," she led a varied and enjoyable life.

✳   ✳   ✳   ✳

APHRA BEHN (NÉE Johnson) was born near Canterbury, England, in about 1640, although the exact date of her birth is unknown. Possibly due to deliberate obfuscation by Behn herself, the circumstances of her origins and early life are unclear, and there are several conflicting accounts of her parentage. Behn claimed that her father was a barber named John Amis, but other accounts variously report her parent's surname as Cooper or Johnson. She is believed to have spent some of her time in Dutch Guiana in South America, and during the journey her father reportedly died, leaving Behn and her mother to remain there for some months. Behn claimed that her experiences in Guiana were the inspiration for the novel she is best remembered for, *Oroonoko*.

Life and Writing

In 1664, after returning to England, she married Johann Behn, a Dutch or German merchant. He died soon after they were married, but Behn kept his last name for the remainder of her life. During the English Civil Wars, she was a supporter of the Royalists, and following the Restoration of Charles II, she dedicated her play *The Rover II* to the Duke of York, one of the staunchest Royalists. In 1665, her affiliation to the king led Thomas Killigrew, a playwright and member of the court, to recruit her as a spy during the Second Anglo-Dutch War. Behn was sent to Antwerp to gather intelligence and turn Thomas Scot, a member of the group of English exiles who were fomenting a plot against the king.

Behn was either paid very late or not at all for her intelligence work, and was soon forced to pawn her jewelry to meet her expenses. But her debts were mounting faster than she could pay them, and she was eventually thrown into debtor's prison. In order to raise money to pay, she began writing plays for the King's Company and the Duke's Company, the two playhouses that had been established at the start of the Restoration. Behn's first play, *The Forc'd Marriage*, was completed in 1670, and the next year she wrote *The Dutch Lover*.

Behn's plays were largely successful, and she became acquainted with many of the other writers of the day, including John Dryden and Elizabeth Barry. In 1688, she published *Oroonoko*, one of the first English novels, and almost certainly the first one written by a woman. The novel tells the story of an African prince who is in love with a woman named Imoinda. The king also falls in love with Imoinda, and takes her as one of his wives, although she has already secretly married Oroonoko. The king finds out and sells Imoinda into slavery, but tells Oroonoko she has been executed. Later, Oroonoko is kidnapped and sold into slavery in Dutch Guiana by an Englishman. There he is reunited with Imoinda, and the two lead a failed slave revolt. Facing capture, Imoinda asks Oroonoko to kill her. He does, and is himself killed.

Oroonoko remains Behn's best-remembered work, but she also completed a total of nineteen plays, several novels and numerous works of poetry. She continued writing until she died, on April 16, 1689. She is buried in Westminster Abbey.

From Her Plays

"Money speaks sense in a language all nations understand."

"Patience is a flatterer, sir, and an ass, sir."

"There's no sinner like a young saint."

"Each moment of the happy lover's hour is worth an age of dull and common life."

A Seeker of Truth

"Truth often suffers more by the heat of its defenders than from the arguments of its opposers."

William Penn founded the colony of Pennsylvania as a refuge of religious freedom for religious observers of all denominations and beliefs.

✳   ✳   ✳   ✳

WILLIAM PENN WAS born on October 14, 1644 in London. His father served in the Royal Navy and his family was well-do-to. His father supported the restoration of Charles II and personally brought Charles back to England from exile. For his support, he was granted a knighthood and appointed Commissioner of the Navy. Penn studied theology and the law at Oxford, but he was expelled for espousing his newly acquired Quaker beliefs. He was sent to Ireland by his father to manage his family's landholdings, but while there he was arrested for attending a Quaker meeting. His father's influence got him out of jail, and he was immediately recalled to England.

The Activist Quaker

Beginning in 1668, Penn started publishing essays about his religious ideas. He wrote *The Sandy Foundation Shaken*, which argued against a number of fundamental doctrines of Anglicanism, and was imprisoned in the Tower of London for the work. While he was in the Tower, he wrote *No Cross, No Crown*, which argued for believers to revert to a version of early Christianity that emphasized self-sacrifice and spirituality. Although he was released in 1669, he continued to preach the Quaker tenets of self-sacrifice and social reform, and was arrested repeatedly for his actions. He made a number of missionary trips to Germany at this time. In 1672, he married Gulielma Maria Springett, a fellow Quaker. The couple had three children.

Pennsylvania

Conditions for the Quakers were deteriorating rapidly by the 1670s; they refused to stop preaching their doctrines, and the government continued repressing them. Through his contacts, Penn was able to appeal to King Charles II to allow the Quakers to resettle in the American colonies. The Quakers purchased land in New Jersey, and Penn petitioned the King to increase the Quaker's land west of the Delaware River. The king owed roughly 16,000 pounds sterling (over 2 million pounds today) to Penn's father for his support during the English Civil Wars, and to repay them he granted Penn's request in 1681, giving him a charter for more than 45,000 square miles, making Penn the largest landowner in the New World.

Penn named the new colony "Sylvania," or "The Wooded Land," but the King changed the name to Pennsylvania in honor of Penn's father. Penn moved there in 1682 with a group of Quakers, and they quickly established a new government. In *Letter to the Free Society of Traders*, written in 1683, Penn describes the development of the new colony. Pennsylvania's constitution explicitly granted religious freedom to everyone, regardless of denomination, and was the first colony in America to do so. Penn also ensured that the constitution limited his own powers, and drastically reduced the number of crimes that were punishable by death to only murder and treason; English law had more than 200 capital crimes.

Penn returned several times to England to see to financial and other matters. He had difficulty administering Pennsylvania, and at one point was nearly swindled out of his ownership of the colony by a crooked business manager. Despite his setbacks Pennsylvania's population grew rapidly, and Philadelphia was quickly becoming an intellectual center of the colonies.

William Penn died in Berkshire, England, on July 30, 1718.

Amazing Grace, How Sweet the Sound

Once a slave trader, John Newton had a religious conversion that turned him into an abolitionist and led him to write the famous hymn "Amazing Grace."

* * * *

JOHN NEWTON IN London on August 4, 1725. His father was a shipmaster, and when he was eleven years old he started going to sea with his father. He accompanied his father on voyages six times. When he was eighteen, Newton was captured by a press gang and forced to serve in the Royal Navy aboard the HMS *Harwich*.

During his service, he was transferred to the *Pegasus*, whose crew disliked him and left him with a slave dealer on the West Coast of Africa. He was kept in bondage until 1748, when he was rescued by a man his father had hired to find him. During the return voyage to England, the ship was caught in a terrible storm of the coast of Ireland. Nearly drowning, he called out to God to save him, and when he survived, he credited divine intervention.

Newton began to study the Bible on the remainder of the journey to Britain, and on March 19, 1748, he converted to evangelical Christianity. He continued to work in the slave trade, but as he gained sympathy for the enslaved Africans due to his own experiences, he eventually left the slave trade for good in 1755 and became ordained as a minister in 1764.

In 1779, he wrote "Amazing Grace" about his personal experience with Christianity. The hymn would become one of the most recognized Christian songs in the English-speaking world.

"I am not what I ought to be—ah, how imperfect and deficient! I am not what I wish to be—I abhor what is evil, and I would cleave to what is good! I am not what I hope to be—soon, soon shall I put off mortality, and with mortality all sin and imperfection. Yet, though I am not what I ought to be, nor what I wish to be, nor what I hope to be, I can truly say, I am not what I once was; a slave to sin and Satan; and I can heartily join with the apostle, and acknowledge, 'By the grace of God I am what I am.'"

—JOHN NEWTON

George Berkeley

"He who says there is no such thing as an honest man, you may be sure is himself a knave."

George Berkeley was an Irish philosopher, bishop, and scientist who developed a theory of empiricism that declared everything, with the exception of the spiritual world, only exists as far as it can be perceived by the senses.

✳ ✳ ✳ ✳

GEORGE BERKELEY WAS born in Kilkenny, Ireland, on March 12, 1685. He received a formal education, attending Kilkenny College in 1696 and going on to receive a bachelor's of arts from Trinity College in Dublin in 1704. He began developing his theories about empiricism while at Trinity, and studied time and vision, which resulted in his developing the hypothesis that he would later call "immaterialism." In 1707, he published his first treatise, *Arithmetic and Miscellaneous Mathematics*. Berkeley was elected a Fellow at Trinity that year, and began revising the theories he had developed earlier.

Berkeley's major contribution to Western philosophy was his theory of immaterialism, in which he asserted that a thing exists only if it is perceived. To be, he argued, means to be perceived. Furthermore, he declared his hypothesis that there is nothing of material substance in the world, only that which is perceived by the senses of the observer.

The idea was revolutionary for its time, and influenced many of the philosophers of 18th century England. Berkeley published *An Essay Towards a New Theory of Vision* in 1709, which built on his theory of immaterialism, arguing that the things we see are not objects themselves, but only light and color with which we construct objects in the mind. He further developed this theory in his *Treatise Concerning the Principles of Human Knowledge* in 1710, in which he argued that our perception of the world is largely relative.

Jonathan Edwards

"A little, wretched, despicable creature; a worm, a mere nothing, and less than nothing; a vile insect that has risen up in contempt against the majesty of Heaven and earth."

A believer in the "outpouring of the spirit," Edwards was a revivalist minister who preached that mankind needed to be born again in God in order to find salvation.

✳ ✳ ✳ ✳

JONATHAN EDWARDS WAS born in East Windsor, Connecticut on October 5, 1703. His father was a Puritan evangelical minister, and Edwards was raised studying theology, the bible, and classical philosophy form a young age. He attended Yale College from 1716–1720, and was accepted to Yale's graduate school in 1721. He continued studying theology and philosophy at Yale, as well as comparative religions such as Deism, Anglicanism, and others. He was also exposed to empiricist and rationalist philosophy. Edwards wrote extensively about natural philosophy and metaphysics while he was at Yale. He believed that the aesthetics of an entity were an essential part that underlay its overall harmony.

The Great Awakening

In 1726, Edwards became the pastor of his grandfather's church outside of Boston. He married Sarah Pierpoint in 1727;

the couple would have ten children together. In the 1730s, the First Great Awakening, a Protestant revivalist movement that swept the American colonies, began. The movement was characterized by fiery sermons that evoked a deeply emotional spirituality in the listeners. The Great Awakening abandoned the rituals and hierarchy that had marked the Protestant church until then, and promoted a far more personal form of Christianity that emphasized introspection and personal ethics.

In 1738, Edwards published *A Faithful Narrative of the Surprising Work of God*, which depicted the events of the Awakening in his own church. The work would become a model for revivalists in the colonies and Great Britain. It also made him well known as a talented revivalist preacher. Edwards' sermons and writing emphasized the wickedness and immorality of humankind, spoke vividly of the reality of Hell, and preached the necessity of being "born again" in God. His work had millenarian themes that addressed the Second Coming of Christ, and he believed that history could be construed as a steady fulfillment of God's promises in scripture.

Edwards also addressed critics of the revivalist movement. Edwards wrote several more books in the 1740s, including *The Distinguishing Marks of a Work of the Spirit of God*, *Some Thoughts Concerning the Present Revival*, and *A Treatise Concerning Religious Affections*. In these works he established the framework of revivalist thought and pioneered a new philosophy of love for one's fellow man.

In 1750, Edwards lost his position as pastor when he tried to enforce stricter rules on his congregation. He was opposed about the church's policy of allowing anyone to join, as he felt it allowed nonbelievers and hypocrites to become members of the church. The rejection of his harsh views is often considered a turning point in the history of the American church because it represented the complete break from the theology of the New England Way of strict Puritanism as established by the original settlers. Edwards travelled to western Massachusetts as a missionary to Mohawk and Mahican people. While there, he wrote several of his major works, including one that explored the concept of free will, which he argued was determined by one's grace or sinfulness, and another that defended the idea of original sin. In 1757, he returned to the East Coast, and became president of the College of New Jersey, which would later become Princeton. He died after only a few months there due to complications from a smallpox inoculation, and is buried on the Princeton grounds.

All the Good You Can

John Wesley's methodical study of scripture and approach to Christian life would grow to be one of the largest Protestant denominations in England and Europe.

✳   ✳   ✳   ✳

JOHN WESLEY WAS born in northern England in on June 28, 1703. He had fourteen brothers and sisters. His father, Samuel, was a poet and clergyman. Wesley was taught to read at a young age, and his parents taught him classical languages and biblical scripture. Twice a day, his mother would test him on his studies, and once a week she would engage in one-on-one spiritual lessons with Wesley and each of his siblings. When he was five, he was nearly killed when the family rectory caught fire, but was saved when a parishioner pulled him to safety from an upper window. The experience left a lifelong impression on Wesley, and was later cited as evidence that there was a divine plan for him.

When Wesley was eleven, he was sent to boarding school in London, and in 1720 he began attending Christ Church at Oxford. He became a fellow at Oxford when he was twenty three and was ordained in 1728. In 1729 he and his brother Charles co-founded the "Holy Club" at Oxford, a group of students and fellows who met for prayer and engaged in methodical Bible studies. The members also provided food to the poor, taught orphans how to read, and visited convicts in prison. The term "Holy Club," along with the term "Methodist," was originally a derogatory taunt bestowed on the members by other students at Oxford.

Wesley and his brother travelled to America as to do missionary work, preaching in Savannah, Georgia. On their voyage, they met members of the Moravian Church, one of the oldest Protestant denominations in the world. Moravians preached love, unity, and liberty as their guiding tenets, and Wesley was impressed with their piety and faith. After two years in Georgia, where the brothers' mission to spread the Gospel among Native Americans was largely unsuccessful, Wesley returned to London. There, he joined a Moravian church, and remained with them for about a year.

Conversion and Founding of Methodism

On May 24, 1738, while he was attending a Moravian meeting in Aldersgate Street in London, Wesley had a deeply spiritual experience. As one of the congregants read from Martin Luther, he had an intense emotional reaction to a passage describing how faith in Christ allows God to change a person's heart. The experience led him to begin preaching a message of personal salvation through faith in Christ. The Aldersgate Experience, as it came to be known, was a pivotal moment that led to the founding of the Methodist Church, and Aldersgate Day is still celebrated in the Methodist religion.

Wesley worked with the Moravian Church initially, and studied at their headquarters in Germany in 1738. He soon took to preaching open-air sermons, finding that it allowed him to spread his message to people who did not regularly attend church services. He left the Moravians in 1739 over a disagreement regarding prayer, and founded the Methodist Society that year. He and the Methodists quickly drew the ire of the Anglican Church, and as it refused to ordain Wesley's ministers, he did so himself, a practice that helped grow the Methodist movement rapidly.

Wesley continued spreading Methodism with open-air preaching and ordination of lay ministers for the next fifty years. He died in London on March 2, 1791.

John Wesley's Rule (Maybe)

The words that became known as "John Wesley's Rule" are:

"Do all the good you can,
By all the means you can,
In all the ways you can,
In all the places you can,
At all the times you can,
To all the people you can,
As long as ever you can."

There is however, considerable doubt as to whether Wesley said this himself. An exact match is not found in his writings, although some similar sentiments were. The words remain associated with him and the Methodist Church. Whoever said them first, they're probably not bad words to live by!

Born Free

"Man is born free, and everywhere he is in chains."

Rousseau's political ideas helped kickstart the Enlightenment, influenced the American and French Revolutions, and reverberate through society to this day.

✳ ✳ ✳ ✳

JEAN-JACQUES ROUSSEAU WAS born in Geneva, Switzerland, on June 28, 1712. His mother died when he was an infant, and his father abandoned the child when he was ten years old. He was raised by his aunt and uncle until he left Geneva in 1738. He travelled through Europe for a few years, settling in Paris in 1742.

For eleven months in 1743 he served as a secretary to the French ambassador to Venice, and while there he fell in love with Italian opera. But he was often paid late, if at all, and he soon left the post, taking with him a deep mistrust of government and bureaucracy. He returned to Paris, broke and with few job prospects. He fell in love with Therese Levasseur, and they had four children together, but Rousseau coerced her to give them up to an orphanage to newborns as he had no interest in raising them.

In 1750 Rousseau entered an essay competition at the Academie de Dijon. The competition posed the question as to whether the restoration of arts and sciences had contributed to the "purification of morals." Rousseau submitted the essay *Discourse on the Arts and Sciences*, which took first place and made him instantly famous. *Discourse* argues that the arts and sciences ultimately ruin human morality. In it, Rousseau first presented the philosophy that he would espouse his entire life: that civilization has a destructive effect on human beings.

The Social Contract

In 1754 Rousseau returned to Geneva, where he joined the Calvinist religion. He wrote the *Discourse on Inequality* in 1755 in response to another competition by the Academie de Dijon. This essay did not win, but in it Rousseau developed the arguments of his 1750 essay. *Inequality* argues that man is essentially good in his natural state, as he existed before civilization arose, and that society is artificial and corrupt, and that it only results in promoting unhappiness. The essay draws the conclusion that material progress actually destroys any possibility of sincere relationships, and gives rise to jealousy and suspicion. Rousseau further argued that private property is the basis of all inequality.

During the 1750s, Rousseau also wrote novels and composed music. His novel *Julie, ou la nouvelle Heloise*, an epistolary novel that references the letters of Heloise and Abelard, was published in 1761 and was immensely popular. In 1762, he published what would become his most famous philosophical treatise, *The Social Contract*. The book explores the relationship of man to society. Breaking with his earlier writings, in the *Contract* Rousseau argued that the natural state of man is a brutish one that lacks any morality, and only society can give rise to ethical actors. In nature, he argued, each individual is in constant competition for resources with everyone else. Only by joining with one another to collectively address threats can humans be successful; this arrangement is society, or the social contract.

The Social Contract served as the inspiration for many of the political movements of the second half of the 18th century. The work dismisses the divine right of monarchs, arguing that the people are sovereign and have the right to govern themselves. This idea would inspire the American and French Revolutions, and continues to be the dominant political philosophy in Western thought to this day.

Rousseau died on July 2, 1778, at his friend's chateau in Ermenonville, France.

"To renounce liberty is to renounce being a man, to surrender the rights of humanity and even its duties."

Comedy or Tragedy

With his book The Castle of Otranto, *Horace Walpole invented the genre of the gothic horror novel more than a century before Steven King appeared on the scene.*

✳   ✳   ✳   ✳

HORACE (ORIGINALLY HORATIO) Walpole was born on September 24, 1717 in London. His father was the Prime Minister Sir Robert Walpole. Horace was educated at Eton and at King's College in Cambridge. In 1739, he travelled through France and Italy with his schoolmate Thomas Gray.

They would remain close friends for the rest of their lives. When he returned to England in 1741, he began serving in Parliament, attending debates for nearly thirty years. Walpole never married.

In 1747, Walpole inherited an estate at Twickenham, and he built a large Gothic revival villa there that he named Strawberry Hill. The villa, with battlements, turrets, and cloisters, was a forerunner of the Gothic revival style of the 19th century. He filled the villa with a collection of curious and antiquarian objects that lent the interior a fairy-tale quality. He amassed a large library and set up a printing press on the grounds, which he used to publish works including his own writing and Gray's *Odes* in 1757. Strawberry Hill was open to tourists during his lifetime, and the villa's name eventually became synonymous with Gothic revival architecture.

The Castle of Ontrato

In 1765, Walpole wrote *The Castle of Ontrato* and initially published it anonymously. The novel is widely recognized as having established the genre of gothic fiction that would become extremely popular throughout the 18th and 19th centuries, and it inspired later writers such as Edgar Allen Poe, Bram Stoker, and Ann Radcliffe.

The book opens in Ontrato on the wedding day of Conrad, the son of Lord Manfred, to Isabella. On the day of the wedding, Conrad is crushed by a gigantic helmet that mysteriously falls on him. Manfred is terrified that the ominous event signals that an ancient prophecy that signaled the end of his line is coming true, and he leaves his wife and tries to marry Isabella himself. Isabella flees with the help of a peasant named Theodore. Manfred has Theodore locked in a tower and pursues Isabella, who is hiding in an underground church. Theodore escapes with the help of Manfred's daughter, Matilda, and in a series of mistaken identities, Manfred accidentally kills Matilda. Theodore marries Isabella and becomes the king of Ontrato.

Ontrato was the first novel to use a number of devices that would become standard set-pieces in Gothic fiction, including strange noises, doors opening for no reason, and a heroine fleeing from an evil male figure.

Walpole wrote a number of other novels, including *The Mysterious Mother* in 1768, a tragedy that dealt with themes of incest. He wrote an amateur historical book the same year called *Doubts on the Life and Reign of King Richard the Third*. He also wrote a four-volume study of art history, *Anecdotes of Painting in England*, which was completed in 1771. Walpole's letters, of which there are more than four thousand, are a comprehensive picture of the history and tastes of 18th century England. His letters were published over fifty years in 48 volumes. They include one line that seemed to have been a favorite of his and which is still quoted today: ""This world is a comedy to those that think, a tragedy to those that feel."

Horace Walpole died in London on March 2, 1797.

The Innocent and the Guilty

"It is better that ten guilty persons escape than one innocent suffer."

William Blackstone's writings on the law were so influential that they are still cited in Supreme Court decisions nearly three hundred years later.

✳ ✳ ✳ ✳

WILLIAM BLACKSTONE WAS born July 10, 1723 in London. He was educated by his uncle Thomas Bigg, a surgeon, and attended Oxford beginning in 1738. In 1744 he became a fellow at Oxford and the next year he was admitted to the bar. He had moderate success as a barrister, and in 1750 he earned a Doctor of Civil Law degree. Three years later, he retired from practicing law in order to focus on teaching at Oxford.

Student of Common Law

Blackstone's interest lay primarily in the study of common law—that branch of the law that is developed by judges and courts, rather than legislative statues and executive orders. His lectures on English common law were the first ever to be delivered in a university. Blackstone presented the subject as a uniformly logical system of applying precedent, and glossed over its more archaic aspects in order to promote his belief that English law was the manifestation of 18th century wisdom. His lectures were hugely popular and earned him a very comfortable living.

Blackstone's first lecture, *A Discourse on the Study of Law,* was delivered in 1758. The lecture was so popular that its first printing was sold out almost immediately. *A Discourse* emphasized the importance of widely promoting the academic study of English law as a safeguard against its practice falling under the control of a select few members of society.

While his lectures earned him praise and respect among the aristocracy, Blackstone had difficulty with the politics at the University of Oxford, and found himself generally unpopular there. He was the target of an anonymous pamphlet that was very critical of him in 1758, resulting in a nervous breakdown, and in 1759 he lost an election for Vice Warden.

Soon after, he left Oxford and moved to London, where Prince George III sponsored him so that he could continue his writing and lectures. In 1761 he was elected to Parliament where he served for nine years. That same year he married to Sarah Clitherow. In 1763 Blackstone was appointed the solicitor general to the Crown.

Commentaries on the Laws of England

Between 1765–1769, Blackstone published his four-volume work *Commentaries on the Laws of England,* a magnum opus on the study of common law. Each volume deals with a different aspect of English law: the rights of persons, the rights of things, private wrongs, and public wrongs. One of the hallmarks of the work is its plain language, which makes it accessible to the layperson as well as the academic reader. The *Commentaries* became the seminal work on English law, establishing a concrete system of jurisprudence that had a thoughtful respectability about it.

The *Commentaries* laid the groundwork for the development of the American legal system as well. America's Founding Fathers were all very familiar with the work, and the Declaration of Independence, the Federalist Papers, and many of the early decisions by the John Marshall Supreme Court drew heavily on the *Commentaries* for guidance. They were so influential that they are regularly cited as legal precedent in decisions by the United States Supreme Court to this day.

In 1770, Blackstone was appointed a judge on the Court of Common Pleas, and served without particular distinction for ten years. He died on February 14, 1780, in Berkshire.

James Boswell

"He who praises everybody, praises nobody."

James Boswell was a close friend of Samuel Johnson, and wrote a biography of him that is widely considered the greatest biography of the 18th century. Nearly a century after Boswell died, his journals were published, revealing him to be one of the greatest diarists of the English language.

✳ ✳ ✳ ✳

JAMES BOSWELL WAS born on October 18, 1740, in Edinburgh, Scotland. His father was a magistrate, and Boswell received a private education at home. Beginning in 1753 he attended the University of Edinburgh, where he studied the arts. In 1758 he began studying the law, and attended the University of Glasgow, where he attended lectures by Adam Smith. He passed his civil law examination in 1762, and his father allowed him to move to London. That year, he began keeping a journal. In his journals, which he kept for the rest of his life, Boswell's skill as a writer is clear. He relates his experiences as if they were unfolding while he wrote them down; his colleagues and friends appear almost like characters in a novel.

When he was twenty-two years old, Boswell met Samuel Johnson, who was already a well-established poet, essayist, and literary critic of considerable fame. The two struck up a friendship that would last until Johnson's death on December 13, 1784. Boswell wrote a biography of Johnson that was published in 1791 to immediate critical acclaim. It related the life and works of Johnson, but also incorporated conversations Boswell had had with him. The biography also included many personal details about Johnson, which was highly unusual at the time. It is still considered one of the greatest biographies ever written.

Boswell died in London on May 19, 1795.

A Writer of Aphorisms

Johann Kaspar Lavater contributed to physiognomy, a pseudoscientific movement that believed you actually can judge a book by its cover.

✻ ✻ ✻ ✻

JOHANN KASPAR LAVATER was born in Zürich on November 15, 1741, and formally educated at the Zürich Gymnasium. He was ordained in 1760 and began serving as the pastor of St. Peter's Church. Lavater is best known for his revival and popularization of physiognomy, a belief that had originally been espoused by ancient Greeks but fallen out of favor after the Middle Ages. Physiognomy proposed that a person's character can be judged by their outward appearance and, in particular, their face. Aristotle originally proposed the idea in his *Prior Analytics,* and the idea was popular during the Middle Ages. Chaucer mentioned the subject in his *Canterbury Tales.* Henry

VIII outlawed the subject in 1530, however, as a fraud practiced by "beggars and vagabonds."

Lavater revived interest when he published his four-volume *Essays on Physiognomy* in 1775. He collaborated on the book with Goethe, and the famous writer lent credence to the study that made it quite popular in Europe. Lavater later incorporated physiognomy in his religious beliefs, and he and Goethe eventually had a falling out over Lavater's religious zeal. Lavater's ideas fell out of favor toward the end of his life.

Lavater also published a biography of Pontius Pilate in 1785 and the *Secret Journal of a Self Observer* in 1795. His 1788 book *Aphorisms on Man* contains several quotes that wear a bit better than his belief in physiognomy. They include: "He who, when called upon to speak a disagreeable truth, tells it boldly and has done is both bolder and milder than he who nibbles in a low voice and never ceases nibbling," and "Say not you know another entirely, till you have divided an inheritance with him."

In 1799, France invaded Switzerland. That year, Lavater enraged a French grenadier, who shot him. More than a year later, Lavater died of his wounds on January 2, 1801.

An Observer of People

"If you enquire what the people are like here, I must answer, 'The same as everywhere!'"

An incredibly prolific writer, Goethe produced what is considered the greatest masterpiece in the history of German literature.

✳ ✳ ✳ ✳

JOHANN WOLFGANG VON Goethe was born in Frankfurt, Germany, on August 28, 1749. His family was upper-middle class. Goethe's father, a lawyer, educated him until he was sixteen, when he went to Leipzig to study the law as well.

While he was at law school he began writing poetry and plays. Because of a long illness, his studies were put on hold; he finished law school in 1771. In 1772 Goethe wrote his first major play, *Gotz von Berlichingen*. Two years later he completed the novel *The Sorrows of Young Werther*. Both were well-received and established Goethe's reputation as a writer and the leader of the "Romantic Revolt," a literary movement that was occurring in Germany.

The Duke of Weimar invited Goethe to join his court in 1775, and he served there as the director of the Ministries of Finance, Agriculture and Mines for the next ten years. The two became good friends, and the Duke invited numerous other artists and writers to his court. Goethe, however, found that his administrative duties were interfering with his literary endeavors, and he left the court in 1786, travelling to Italy to pursue his art.

When he returned to Germany, the Duke appointed him the director of the Weimar State Theatre and granted him a generous stipend that allowed Goethe to focus on writing.

Faust

Goethe married his mistress, with whom he'd had a son seventeen years earlier, in 1806. His literary success brought him fame throughout Germany and Europe, and Napoleon was among his admirers. Goethe produced more than 140 volumes of work in his lifetime, but his most famous work is perhaps *Faust*. The tragic play was completed in two parts; the first was finished in 1808 and the second in 1832.

The play is generally considered the greatest work of German literature. It is a retelling of a classic German legend: Faust, a successful and talented scholar, is God's favorite human being, and is attempting to learn all there is that can be known. Mephistopheles, a demon, makes a wager with God that he can turn Faust away from God. God accepts the bet, and Mephistopheles pays Faust a visit.

Faust's studies have stalled, and the demon makes him an offer: he will do anything Faust wants while he is alive, but when he dies he must serve Mephistopheles in Hell. Faust agrees. The demon helps him seduce a woman named Gretchen, but when Gretchen accidentally kills her mother, her brother challenges Faust, who, with the demon's help, kills him. Gretchen, who has had a child with Faust, drowns the baby and is imprisoned for murder. Faust attempts to free her, but she refuses to go with him, and he flees. In part two, Faust awakens in a field, having forgotten the events of part one. He has a series of adventures in which Mephistopheles helps him become a powerful figure. When he dies, Mephistopheles attempts to claim his soul, but he is rescued by angels, who carry him to heaven.

In addition to his numerous works for the stage, Goethe wrote many novels, including *Egemont* in 1788, *Pandora* in 1810, and *Wilhelm Meister's Journeys* in 1829. He also published short stories, collections of poetry, and even scientific treatises such as *The Theory of Colors*, written in 1810. Goethe died on March 22, 1832, already considered one of the greatest writers in German history.

Telling Human Stories

"There are only two or three human stories, and they go on repeating themselves as fiercely as if they had never happened before."

Cather's lyrical descriptions of life on the Great Plains are a cornerstone of American literature. She won a Pulitzer Prize in 1923 for her novel One of Ours, *set in Nebraska during World War I.*

✳ ✳ ✳ ✳

WILLA CATHER WAS born on December 7, 1873, in Back Creek Virginia. When she was ten years old, her family moved to Nebraska, and settled in Red Cloud the following year. Cather was initially uncomfortable in the wide-open spaces of the Great Plains, but after a year, she developed a deep love of the land. Red Cloud would feature in much of her later writing, and her passion for the terrain would become the core of much of her writing. In 1895, she began attending the University of Nebraska, and while there she began writing for the *Nebraska State Journal* and the *Lincoln Courier*. When she graduated, Cather moved back east, and became the editor for *McClure's Magazine* in New York. She met Edith Lewis in the early 1900s, and the two moved in together in 1908 and lived together for the rest of Cather's life. Neither married, and there is speculation that they were life partners as well as lovers.

The Great Plains Trilogy

In 1913, Cather published her first novel, *O Pioneers!* The book (the source of the quote that begins this essay) is set in Nebraska and celebrates the spirit of Swedish farmers who settled the Great Plains: "the history of every country begins the heart of a man or a woman." She would follow *Pioneers* with *The Song of the Lark,* published in 1915, and *My Antonia* in 1918. The latter two novels feature fiercely independent female protagonists. Both are Bohemian immigrants who settled the Great Plains. Much of the imagery of the Great Plains trilogy was drawn from Cather's own childhood. The fertile land of the American West as much a character as the protagonists. The trilogy moves through the settling and development of the American west as well as the beginnings of equality that American women were fighting for at the time.

In *Death Comes for the Archbishop,* Cather again tells the story of settlers, who are this time French missionaries travelling to Colorado. The book was very well received and reinforced Cather's reputation as a great American novelist. In 1922, she wrote *One of Ours,* for which she received the Pulitzer Prize the following year. The novel tells the story of Claude Wheeler, who struggles with malaise while growing up in Nebraska. When World War I begins, he enlists in the Army, believing he has found a purpose for this life. He dies in the trenches during a German attack.

One of Ours is based in part on Cather's cousin Grosvenor Cather, who was killed in 1918 in France, and earned the Silver Star and Distinguished Service Cross for his actions in World War I. Cather visited French battlefields and interviewed veterans and wounded soldiers while she was writing the novel, which gave it a deep realism that resonated with readers.

In 1931, her novel *Shadows on the Rock* was the most popular novel in the United States. Cather published her last collection of short stories, *Obscure Destinies*, in 1932. She published the novel *Lucy Gayheart* in 1935 to wide acclaim. In 1940, while staying on Grand Manan Island with Lewis, she completed her final novel, *Sapphira and the Slave Girl*.

Cather died at the home she shared with Edith Lewis on April 24, 1947. She and Lewis are buried together in New Hampshire.

"Only solitary men know the full joys of friendship. Others have their family; but to a solitary and an exile his friends are everything."

—SHADOWS ON THE ROCK

A View of History

"History…is indeed little more than the register of the crimes, follies, and misfortunes of mankind."

Gibbon was an English historian whose History of the Decline and Fall of the Roman Empire *would be one of the first major works of history published in the 18th century about classical antiquity.*

✳ ✳ ✳ ✳

EDWARD GIBBON WAS born May 8, 1737, in Surrey, England. His grandfather had made a fortune as a merchant, and Gibbon's family was wealthy. He was often very ill as a child, and his mother neglected him. His aunt Catherine cared for him, and when he was ten years old his mother died and Catherine raised him from then on. As a young boy, he was an eager reader, and in 1749 he was sent to Westminster School. His poor health forced him to withdraw, and he had some home schooling from private tutors, but the majority of his education was found through books. By the time he was fourteen, he already knew he wanted to be a historian. His self-sufficiency as a scholar, which he developed at a young age, would remain with him his entire life; his magnum opus was completed without consulting any other scholars and was entirely the product of his own research.

When Gibbon's health improved in 1752, his father sent him to Oxford. He found himself largely left to his own devices there, and after reading about Catholic theology, converted to Catholicism in 1753. Because of the law of the time, this disqualified from most avenues of employment, and his enraged father sent him to stay with a Calvinist minister. While there, he studied Latin and French literature, and was eventually readmitted to the Protestant faith. At this point he quietly lost interest in religion.

Scholar of the Roman Empire

In 1763, Gibbon travelled to Paris, where he spent time with a number of French philosophers. In 1764 he travelled to Rome for the first time, where he was taken with the Coliseum and ruins of the ancient civilization. While touring the ruins of the Roman Capitol, on October 16, 1764, Gibbon was suddenly inspired to write a comprehensive history of the decline and fall of the city. It was only some years later that he would expand his study to the entire empire.

In 1770, Gibbon's father died, and Gibbon began studying Roman history as his primary occupation. He joined a London intellectual group known simply as "The Club" in 1775, where he made the acquaintance of Dr. Samuel Johnson, one of the most distinguished scholars of the time. In 1776, Gibbon published Volume I of *The History of the Decline and Fall of the Roman Empire*. The entire work would be published over a period of thirteen years, span six volumes, and cover the historical period from 98 CE to 1590. The first volume also traces the rise of Christianity, which Gibbon discussed with a fair amount of skepticism.

The first half of *The Decline and Fall* deals with a period of about 300 years of European history, up to about 500 CE. The second half covers the next millennium. It is the first major historical work that relies heavily on primary sources, and laid the groundwork for later historical studies. The exhaustive nature of the work and degree of research Gibbon put into it have made it one of the greatest works of modern historical inquiry.

Following the completion of *The Decline and Fall*, Gibbon was elected to the Royal Society. In 1790, he turned his attention to writing his memoirs. He died in London on January 16, 1794.

Letters of Advice

An influential 18th century English politician, Stanhope wrote Chesterfield's Letters to his illegitimate son, which were collected and published posthumously. The collection of more than four hundred letters provides a glimpse of the life and concerns of a nobleman of the day.

✳   ✳   ✳   ✳

PHILLIP DORMER STANHOPE was born on September 22, 1694, the son of the 3rd Earl of Chesterfield and Lady Elizabeth Savile. He attended Cambridge, graduating when he was nineteen. That same year he became a Member of Parliament, in spite of the fact that he was too young to serve. In 1728, Stanhope became the British Ambassador to The Hague. He was knighted in 1730, when he was made the Lord Steward of the Royal Household, a rank equivalent to a member of the Cabinet. He politically opposed the Prime Minister Robert Walpole, and as a result, was prevented from holding public office until 1744. That year he was named the Lord Lieutenant of Ireland, a position he held for two years. He was named the North Secretary of State in 1746, and remained in that position until 1748.

Stanhope had an illegitimate son, and as he could not be directly involved in the boy's upbringing, he wrote hundreds of letters to him over a thirty-year period. The letters were written to provide his son with proper morals, manners, and education. Stanhope composed them in French and Latin as well as English, and discussed literature, history, and politics. Stanhope's letters were collected and published by his son's widow in 1774. Stanhope died on March 24, 1773.

What Stanhope Said

Ironically, one of Stanhope's pieces of advice to his son was, "Advice is seldom welcome; and those who want it the most always like it the least." So was Stanhope's advice to his son worth taking? We've included some selected excerpts so you can decide.

"Be wiser than other people if you can; but do not tell them so. "

"The knowledge of the world is only to be acquired in the world, and not in a closet."

"An injury is much sooner forgotten than an insult."

"There is time enough for everything, in the course of the day, if you do but one thing at once; but there is not time enough in the year, if you will do two things at a time."

"The world is a country which nobody ever yet knew by description; one must travel through it one's self to be acquainted with it."

"I recommend you to take care of the minutes: for hours will take care of themselves."

"Speak of the moderns without contempt, and of the ancients without idolatry."

"Never seem wiser, nor more learned, than the people you are with. Wear your learning, like your watch, in a private pocket: and do not pull it out and strike it; merely to show that you have one."

"In my mind, there is nothing so illiberal and so ill-bred, as audible laughter... I am sure that since I have had the full use of my reason, nobody has ever heard me laugh."

"Little minds mistake little objects for great ones, and lavish away upon the former that time and attention which only the latter deserve. To such mistakes we owe the numerous and frivolous tribe of insect-mongers, shell-mongers, and pursuers and driers of butter-flies, etc. The strong mind distinguishes, not only between the useful and the useless, but likewise between the useful and the curious."

"Let this be one invariable rule of your conduct—never to show the least symptom of resentment, which you cannot, to a certain degree, gratify; but always to smile, where you cannot strike."

"I wish to God that you had as much pleasure in following my advice, as I have in giving it to you."

Trying to Learn from History

"What experience and history teach is this—that people and governments never have learned anything from history, or acted on principles deduced from it."

Hegel's dialectics would become one of the most influential ideas in Western philosophy for the next hundred years.

❈ ❈ ❈ ❈

GEORG WILHELM FRIEDRICH Hegel was born in Stuttgart, Germany, on August 27, 1770. His father Georg was a civil servant, and his mother Maria was the daughter of a member of the Württemberg court. Maria taught him Latin as a child, and instilled in Hegel a lifelong love of learning. He attended an elite preparatory school before attending the Seminary at the University of Tübinge at his father's urging. While he was there he became interested in philosophy, and instead of joining the clergy, as his father had wanted, he became a private tutor and continued to study philosophy in his spare time.

Dialectics

Hegel's father died in 1799, leaving him with a modest inheritance that allowed him to spend more time working on developing his ideas about philosophy. Hegel's theories were based on the transcendental idealism of Immanuel Kant and the progressive political ideology of Rousseau, but ultimately reject Kant as overly restraining. He developed a new philosophy that attempted to create a systematic means of understanding world history. Hegel's ideas would become the philosophy that is known as *dialectics*, or the juxtaposition of two opposing arguments.

In 1801 Hegel published his first book, an examination of the relationship between religion and philosophy in which he rejected mysticism and argued for a rational basis of attempting to understand the self. He began giving lectures on logic and metaphysics, and in 1802 he began publishing a journal on philosophy with his friend and colleague Friedrich Schelling. Hegel's position as a lecturer was unpaid, and in 1806 he found his financial situation increasingly perilous. Under pressure to publish, he worked that year on what would become his magnum opus, *The Phenomenology of Spirit*, which was published in 1807. In it, he lays out his three-part philosophy of dialectics.

Dialectics was not new at the time—the notion had existed at least since Aristotle—but Hegel brought a modern understanding to the concept and applied it as a method for dissecting nature and history. Hegel's dialectics consist of three developmental parts: the thesis, or original state of things, which gives rise to the antithesis, or the reaction and contradiction to the thesis, and the synthesis, in which the thesis and antithesis are resolved. Hegel himself did not use these terms, preferring the abstract, negative, and concrete to describe the relationship, but thesis/antithesis remains the popular idea.

One of the major aspects that set Hegel's dialectics apart from the classical understanding of the idea was that it was not a concrete set of principles that describe the world as it is a methodology for attempting to understand it. Experiences, to Hegel, are valuable empirical data for observing the unfolding of the natural world and human history. He believed that the "totality" of experience is the sum of a series of experiences rather than something couched in an "absolute mind."

Hegel continued teaching, first at a school in Nuremberg from 1808–1815, and then as the chair of the philosophy department at the University of Berlin from 1816–1829. During this time he wrote the *Encyclopedia of the Philosophical Sciences*, *Elements of the Philosophy of Right*, and the *Philosophy of Spirit*,

Hegel died on November 14, 1831 in Berlin. The legacy of his philosophy reverberated through the centuries, influencing British Idealism, existentialism, Marxism and fascism. Philosophers continue to advance Hegel's ideas to this day.

Writer of American Classics

"A tart temper never mellows with age, and a sharp tongue is the only edge tool that grows keener with constant use."

Named for one of America's Founding Fathers, Washington Irving would write some of the first great American legends.

✳ ✳ ✳ ✳

WASHINGTON IRVING WAS born in Manhattan, New York on April 3, 1783. The week he was born, the news of the colonists' victory in the American Revolution reached New York, and his mother named him after George Washington. When he was six years old, he was taken to see Washington's inauguration as President, and shortly after he met Washington. Irving was privately educated, but had little interest in his lessons; by the time he was fourteen years old, he was regularly playing hooky to go to the theatre instead.

Sleepy Hollow and Rip Van Winkle

In 1798, a wave of yellow fever swept New York City, and Irving was sent to the country to stay with relatives in Tarrytown, New York. While he was there, he visited the small village of Sleepy Hollow, a Dutch settlement, and learned the local tall tales and ghost stories. He also visited the Catskill Mountains, which he would later write had a "witching effect" on his imagination. The Catskills would become the setting for the story "Rip Van Winkle," which contains the quote that opens this essay.

When he returned to Manhattan, he began submitting articles about the theatre to his older brother's magazine, the *Morning Chronicle*. He wrote under the pseudonym Jonathan Oldstyle, and his articles were very popular and gained him some fame throughout the east coast. Irving travelled to Europe from 1804–1806, and upon returning he began studying law. He freely admitted in later years that he was not a very good student, and he just barely passed the bar exam in 1806. He continued writing, publishing the humorous magazine *Salamagundi* with his brother William. In 1809 he wrote a satirical history of the city of New York under the moniker Diedrick Knickerbocker, which was well received. He briefly served in the military during the War of 1812.

In 1815, he travelled to England, where he would publish his most famous stories. Over the course of two years, 1819–1820, he wrote a series of short stories that were serially published and collected in *The Sketch Book of Geoffrey Crayon, Gent.* He wrote "The Legend of Sleepy Hollow" and "Rip Van Winkle" under his Knickerbocker pen-name.

Geoffrey Crayon was the first literary work by an American that enjoyed widespread success in England and Europe, and it made Irving an international star. The book also furthered the esteem of American authors in England and Europe. In 1822, Irving wrote *Bracebridge Hall*, and followed it with *Tales* of a *Traveller* in 1824. He was invited to Madrid by the U.S. Minister to Spain, and spent two years there researching *A History of the Life and Voyages of Christopher Columbus*, which was published in 1828. The next year he wrote *Chronicle of the Conquest of Grenada*, and in 1832 he published *Tales of the Alhambra*.

Irving returned to the United States in 1832, and explored the territories along the frontier, a journey that would become *A Tour on the Prairies* in 1835. He served a second term as minister to Spain in the 1840s, and then moved to an estate at Sunnyside, New York. He wrote a series of biographies and historical works during the next twenty years, including a five-volume biography of George Washington. Irving died at his home on November 28, 1859.

Going Ahead

The frontiersman, soldier, and U.S. Representative Davy Crockett was a larger-than-life figure whose legend has made him one of the great American folk heroes.

✳ ✳ ✳ ✳

DAVY CROCKETT WAS born in Greene County, Tennessee on August 17, 1786. When he was eight years old, his father, John, taught him how to shoot a rifle, and he regularly accompanied his brothers when they went hunting. When he was thirteen, his father sent him to school. But after attending school for only a few days, he got into a fight with the school bully. Afraid to go home, as he might have been punished, and afraid to return to school, as he might face revenge, Crockett ran away from home. He spent the next two years wandering and living in the woods, where he honed his skills hunting and trapping. When he was fifteen, he finally returned home. He married Mary Finley the day before his twentieth birthday, and had three children with her. When she died, he married the widow Elizabeth Patton.

Creek War and War of 1812

Crockett's exploits as a frontiersman were part of a carefully crafted image, but his status as a folk hero was firmly based in real events of his life. In 1813, during the Creek War, a group of warriors in the Red Stick Creek faction attacked Fort Mims, overwhelming the defenders and massacring almost everyone in the fort. This became a rallying cry to mobilize settler militias throughout the Southeastern United States. Crockett joined the Tennessee Militia under John Coffee, which marched into Alabama. He spent most of his time with the Militia as a scout, preferring to hunt game for the troops rather than take part in raids on Creek encampments. He served with the Militia until Christmas Eve, 1813.

When Andrew Jackson requested the help of the Tennessee Militia in attacking British forces in Florida during the War of 1812, Crockett reenlisted in September 1814. The Militia followed the main column of troops into Florida, but saw little action because they were mostly in the rear of the American forces. Crockett and his fellow militiamen spent most of their time hunting and foraging for food. He returned to Tennessee in December.

U.S. Congressman

In 1821, Crockett was elected to the Tennessee State House of Representatives, and held his seat until 1823. In 1825, he ran for the U.S. Congress unsuccessfully, but won as election to Congress the following year. He won a seat in Congress the following year, and began his term on March 4, 1827. Crockett was reelected in 1829 and opposed the Indian Removal Act of 1830, being the only Congressman from Tennessee to do so. In 1831 the Cherokee chief John Ross sent Crockett a personal letter thanking him for his vote. Crockett was defeated in the 1831 election, in part because of his vote on the Act. In 1833 he ran again, this time successfully, but failed to be reelected in 1835. In 1834 he published his autobiography, *A Narrative of the Life of David Crockett,*

Written by Himself. The epigraph of the book described Crockett's philosophy:

"I leave this rule for others when I'm dead,
Be always sure you're right—THEN GO AHEAD!"

The Alamo

After losing the 1835 election, Crockett's lost interest in serving in government. His attention turned to Texas, where there was growing talk of revolution among settlers of American origin. Crockett raised a company of 30 volunteers and arrived in Texas in January 1836. They made their way to San Antonio and by February 8, they were at the Alamo. On February 23, the Mexican Army arrived and besieged the defenders. Crockett and the other defenders of the Alamo held out until March 6, when the Mexican Army attacked. The defenders were able to repulse the first two waves, but the third breached the wall. Davy Crockett and the other defenders were killed.

The Autobiography's Beginning

The beginning of the first chapter gives a flavor of the autobiography:

"As the public seem to feel some interest in the history of an individual so humble as I am, and as that history can be so well known to no person living as to myself, I have, after so long a time, and under many pressing solicitations from my friends and acquaintances, at last determined to put my own hand to it, and lay before the world a narrative on which they may at least rely as being true. And seeking no ornament or colouring for a plain, simple tale of truth, I throw aside all hypocritical and fawning apologies, and, according to my own maxim, just 'go ahead.' Where I am not known, I might, perhaps, gain some little credit by having thrown around this volume some of the flowers of learning; but where I am known, the vile cheatery would soon be detected, and like the foolish jackdaw, that with a *borrowed* tail attempted to play the peacock, I should be justly robbed of my pilfered ornaments, and sent forth to strut without a tail for the balance of my time."

Arthur Schopenhauer

"Every man takes the limits of his own field of vision for the limits of the world."

Schopenhauer argued that the individual can choose to do what they want, but they cannot choose what they want to do.

✳   ✳   ✳   ✳

ARTHUR SCHOPENHAUER WAS born on February 22, 1788 in Danzig (present-day Gda sk). His father Heinrich was a wealthy merchant, and his mother would become a famous writer. In 1793, Danzig was annexed by the Kingdom of Prussia, and the family moved to Hamburg. Schopenhauer was given an excellent education. When his father died in 1805, he had to work for two years as a merchant; his mother and sister moved to Weimar, where his mother opened a literary *salon* and befriended other writers such as Goethe and Christoph Wieland. In 1809, Schopenhauer was able to finally attend the University of Göttingen, where he studied the natural sciences before switching to the humanities. He immersed himself in the works of Plato and Immanuel Kant. In 1811, Schopenhauer began attending the Univerity of Berlin, and earned a doctorate in philosophy from the University of Jena in 1813.

The Young Philosopher

Schopenhauer spent the winter of 1814 in Weimar, where he met Goethe at his mother's *salon*. A historian named Friedrich Majer introduced Schopenhauer to the Hindu Vedas and Upanisads. This was a pivotal moment in Schopenhauer's philosophical development. He would later cite the Vedas, along with Plato and Kant's writings, as the foundation upon which he built his own philosophical ideas. In spite of a strained relationship with his mother, her status as a best-selling novelist allowed Schopenhauer access to her publishing house, and helped him get several of his early works published. The following spring, he left Weimar and moved to Dresden, where he wrote *On Vision and Colors* in 1816 in support of Goethe's 1810 treatise *The Theory of Colors*.

The World as Will and Representation

In 1814, Schopenhauer had begun working on what would become his masterwork: *The World as Will and Representation*, published in 1819. The work consists of four volumes that comprehensively address the theory of knowledge and develop a philosophy of the natural world. Schopenhauer rejected the philosophy of Immanuel Kant, asserting that the world as we understand it is only a representation of the real world and not the world in its true essence. One can know themselves in two ways: externally, or as they appear, and internally, as part of what Schopenhauer saw as the essence of all things in the universe, and referred to as the Will, or, very simply, the will to live.

The Will, he argues, is the essence of everything, and exists independently of space and time, of purpose and causation. It manifests beginning in the inorganic reactions in nature, through living organisms in nature, and ultimately to humanity's rational actions. At the end of this ascension is only death, the apex of the Will. Schopenhauer argued that the ascension of the Will is fraught with misery and suffering, and only by denying it can one transcend suffering. The first two books deal extensively with this philosophy; the second two and discussed the meaning of aesthetics and ethics. Schopenhauer contended that all ethics are based on two impulses: the affirmation or denial of the Will.

Schopenhauer's work did not receive a great deal of attention when it was published, but it would be hugely significant, and influenced the work of Freud, Nietzsche, Tolstoy, Jung, and Camus, among many others. After lecturing briefly at the University of Berlin beginning in 1820, he retired to Frankfurt in 1833, where he would remain for the next 28 years. He died on September 21, 1860.

Convincing Customers

"Any color that he wants as long as it is black."

Henry Ford's innovative use of the assembly line to manufacture the Model T ford made automobiles widely affordable for the first time, significantly impacting the industry and landscape of 20th century America.

* * * *

HENRY FORD WAS born on his parents' farm near Dearborn, Michigan, on July 30, 1863. He was a very inquisitive child, and always trying to figure out how things worked. On his thirteenth birthday, his father gave him a pocket watch. Ford immediately took the watch apart and put it back together. His father's friends and neighbors soon heard about his abilities, and they were soon asking young Henry to fix their watches when they stopped working. When he was 16 years old, feeling unfulfilled by farm work, he left home and went to Detroit, where he got a job working as a machinist's apprentice at a shipyard. While there, he learned how to build and repair steam engines along with bookkeeping.

In 1888, he married Clara Bryant, and for a few years he went back to farming to support his young family. In 1891, he secured a job as an engineer at the Edison Illuminating Company, and within two years he was promoted to a chief engineer at the company. His promotion allowed him enough money to begin experimenting with gasoline-powered horseless carriages. He successfully constructed his first model, the Ford Quadricycle, in 1896. In a meeting with company executives, he presented his plans to Thomas Edison, who encouraged him to keep working on his design.

The Ford Motor Company

Ford continued improving his horseless carriage, and in 1903 he founded the Ford Motor Company with his old friend

Alexander Malcomson and a group of investors that included the Dodge brothers. On October 1, 1908, the company introduced the Model T, which had a simple design that made it both easy to repair and inexpensive to buy. The car was soon everywhere. Sales were steadily increasing, and for the next several years, the Ford Motor Company posted profit gains of 100%. In his autobiography, he writes of this time:

"Therefore in 1909 I announced one morning, without any previous warning, that in the future we were going to build only one model, that the model was going to be 'Model T,' and that the chassis would be exactly the same for all cars, and I remarked: 'Any customer can have a car painted any colour that he wants so long as it is black.'

I cannot say that any one agreed with me."

In 1913, in order to increase efficiency in manufacturing the Model T, he introduced the moving assembly line to his factories. The system was conceived of by a group of production executives at the company, and it made it possible to produce Model Ts at an astonishing rate. It also allowed the company to reduce the price of the car, making it widely accessible. Ford introduced a wage of five dollars a day in 1914 along with profit sharing for long-term employees, which attracted highly skilled mechanics to his assembly lines and ensured low worker turnover. In 1926 he reduced the company's work week from six days to five.

Political Beliefs

Ford was strongly opposed to unions, believing they curtailed worker productivity. He also, for several years, employed a "Social Department" that intruded on his employee's private lives, investigating their behavior away from work before they could be approved for profit sharing. These were not the only areas in which his views were controversial; Ford was also a vehement anti-Semite. He went so far as to publish an anti-Semitic newspaper called *The Dearborn Independent* and a four-volume collection of anti-Semitic conspiracy theories called *The International Jew*. He was praised by Heinrich Himmler and Adolf Hitler, who based his production of the Volkswagen on Ford's Model T.

Henry Ford died on April 7, 1947, near his home in Dearborn, Michigan.

Douglas Jerrold

"Some people are so fond of ill luck that they run halfway to meet it."

He wrote of ill luck, but Douglas Jerrold was one of the most prolific literary figures and humorists in Victorian London.

✳ ✳ ✳ ✳

OUGLAS JERROLD WAS born in London on January 3, 1803, and raised on the Isle of Sheppey in Kent. His father Samuel was an actor, and Douglas occasionally joined him in stage productions. During the War of 1812, Jerrold joined the Royal Navy in 1813, serving until 1815 on a ship of the line called the *Namur*. His captain Francis Austen was Jane Austen's brother. He saw almost no action, but gained a lifelong love for the sea.

In 1816, following the War, Jerrold's father moved the family back to London, where his son was hired as an apprentice to a printer. In 1819, he was hired as a typesetter for the *Sunday Monitor*. His poetry started being published around this time in magazines, and following a critical review of an opera, he was hired to contribute to the newspaper on a regular basis.

The Playwright

When he was fourteen, Jerrold wrote a comedy called *More Frightened than Hurt*; it was performed in 1821 at Sadler's Wells Theater in the Islington borough of London. The play was well received, and he was hired to write plays by the Coburg Theater, now called The Old Vic, near Waterloo Station in London. He married Mary Swan in 1824 and continued working for the Coburg until 1829. That same year, he wrote *Black-Eyed Susan*, which dealt with the impressments gangs of the Royal Navy. The play was performed at the Surrey Theatre in London, and it made him famous. England was recovering from the Napoleonic Wars and class tensions were extremely high. Thus the political climate was ripe for a play that was critical of the upper classes, and *Black-Eyed Susan* was immensely popular and enjoyed enormous success.

In 1830, based on his reputation from *Black-Eyed Susan*, Jerrold was hired by Drury Lane, one of the premiere theaters in London, to produce a play. On 1832, *The Bride of Ludgate* opened there to critical acclaim. He became the managing director of the Strand Theater in 1836, and while there, he produced *The Painter of Ghent*. It was his only tragedy, and he starred in the play, but it did not do well, and he soon left the Strand. He continued acting, and in 1851 he appeared in *Not So Bad as We Seem* alongside Charles Dickens. His final piece, *Heart of Gold*, was produced in 1854.

During these years he continued working as a journalist. He was a regular contributor to multiple magazines and newspapers. He is perhaps best remembered for his articles in *Punch*, the English satirical magazine. His first article appeared in the second edition of *Punch*, and his column appeared in every subsequent edition until Jerrold's death. He wrote under numerous different pen names. During the Great Exhibition of 1851 in Hyde Park, Jerrold described the plate-glass and cast-iron exhibition hall as "a palace of crystal" in an article for *Punch*. The name stuck, and the building was called The Crystal Palace until it was destroyed in a fire in 1936. Jerrold also edited several newspapers and magazines, including *Lloyd's Weekly Newspaper*. The publication was struggling when he took over as editor, and he almost single-handedly increased circulation until it was one of the most popular newspapers of the day.

Writing on Concealment and Guilt

"No man, for any considerable period, can wear one face to himself, and another to the multitude, without finally getting bewildered as to which may be true."

Nathaniel Hawthorne's novel The Scarlet Letter *is one of the great works of classic American literature.*

✳ ✳ ✳ ✳

NATHANIEL HAWTHORNE WAS born on the Fourth of July, 1804, in Salem, Massachusetts. Hawthorne's family was descended from some of the earliest Puritan settlers of Salem; more than 150 years before his birth, his ancestor John Hathorne was one of the judges who presided over the Salem Witch Trials in the 17th century. When he learned this, the author changed his name to "Hawthorne" in order to distance himself from his ancestors.

Hawthorne's father died at sea when Nathaniel was only four years old. When he broke his leg as a boy, he was bedridden for several months, and during this time he developed a love of reading and decided he would become a writer. Hawthorne studied at Bowdoin College from 1821–1825, where he became friends with Henry Wadsworth Longfellow as well as other writers.

After graduation, Hawthorne returned to Salem, where he began writing. He published *Fanshawe*, his first novel, in 1828, to positive reviews. He began publishing short stories in literary journals, and these were collected in *Twice-Told Tales* in 1837. In 1838 he was engaged to Sophia Peabody, a transcendentalist, and they married in 1842. The two stayed briefly at the Brook Farm, a transcendentalist commune, where he met Ralph Waldo Emerson and Henry David Thoreau. Hawthorne's early writing did not provide for a steady income, and so he worked at the Boston Custom House weighing salt and coal.

The Scarlet Letter

In 1846, Hawthorne was hired as a surveyor at the Salem Custom House, which gave his family some financial security, but also interfered with his writing. Following the election of Zachary Taylor, Hawthorne, a Democrat, lost this politically-connected appointment. He initially protested his dismissal in a letter to the *Boston Daily Advertiser*, but soon found that his dismissal allowed him the free time to work on his writing again. His next novel, *The Scarlet Letter*, published in 1850, would catapult him to fame, be one of the first mass produced books in the United States, and become a classic of American literature.

The novel draws on Hawthorne's own Puritan roots, and is set in Puritan Boston in the 17th century. It opens with the protagonist, Hester Prynne, being punished for the crime of adultery. She is made to stand on a platform in the town square, and must wear a scarlet "A" on her dress. He husband, who was thought to have been lost at sea, is at the edge of the crowd, and he swears to find the father of Hester's illegitimate child. Hester refuses to reveal the name of the father to the authorities or to her husband, and goes to raise her daughter, Pearl, on the outskirts of town. Years later, her husband discovers that the Reverend Dimmesdale is Pearl's father. The quote above refers to Dimmesdale, who suffers psychologically from his guilt. Eventually Dimmesdale admits his guilt to the town and dies in Hester's arms. Hester is later buried near his grave, and they share a single tombstone with a scarlet letter A on it.

The novel's themes of guilt, repentance, and dignity in the face of repression made it one of the most influential American works of the 19th century. Hawthorne would write several more novels in his lifetime, as well as multiple collections of short stories. He was held in very high esteem by many of his peers, including Edgar Allan Poe, who called him "an indisputable genius." Hawthorne died in his sleep on May 19, 1864, at Plymouth, New Hampshire.

John Stuart Mill

"It is better to be Socrates dissatisfied than a pig satisfied."

Promoting the happiness of all sentient beings was the highest form of ethics, according to Mill.

✳ ✳ ✳ ✳

JOHN STUART MILL was born in London on May 20, 1806. His father, a philosopher and historian, played a large role in his early education. Mill began learning Greek when he was three years old, and Latin when he was eight. By the time he was a teenager, Mill had a strong background in world history, logic, and economic theory. When he was fourteen, he travelled to France for a year, and stayed at the home of the mechanical engineer Samuel Bentham. On his return, his father used his connections at the British East India Company to secure a job for him. Eventually Mill would replace his father as a chief examiner at the company.

Mill suffered a nervous breakdown and fell into a deep depression in 1826. The "mental crisis," as he would later describe it, was brought on by the demands his father placed on him, but it would have a beneficial outcome. While he was struggling with his depression, Mill began to reconsider the validity of some of the philosophy his father and Samuel Bentham had taught him. He began reading the poetry of William Wordsworth, which he found relaxing, and as he came out of his depression he left much of his old ideas behind.

Harriet Taylor and Major Works

In 1830 he became friends with Harriet Taylor, a philosopher and feminist writer. They collaborated on many of the works Mill would go on to publish under his own name. The two exchanged essays on women's rights, marriage, and philosophy. When Taylor's husband died in 1851, she and Mill married. They continued to work together until she died in 1858.

Harriet's daughter Helen continued to work with Mill for fifteen years following her mother's death.

In 1830, John Herschel published a work on natural philosophy that argued that laws were self-evident truths. Several luminaries continued to expand on his work for the next decade. In 1843 Mill published his first major work, *A System of Logic*, which opposed Herschel's work, arguing that laws could be deduced by inductive logic and observation.

Mill's next major work, *On Liberty*, would not be published until 1859. It was Mill's landmark work, arguing for individual freedom from the government and society. Mills argued that people should not be constrained in their behavior or beliefs by either the law or social mores. Four years later, he would follow it with *Utilitarianism*, which was published initially as a series of essays. It would be his most famous work. *Utilitarianism* discusses much of Bentham's philosophy, and in it he offers his "greatest happiness principle." This argues that one's actions should be designed to promote the happiness of as many sentient beings as possible. The "rightness" of an action can be measured by the amount of happiness it produces. Any code of ethics that arose from such a standard would be easy to internalize, and therefore naturally spread itself.

In 1869, Mill wrote *The Subjection of Women*, in which he argues for women's suffrage and equal education. This was a very controversial position for a man to take at the time, and he was subjected to some ridicule because of it. While he was initially in favor of a free market, he also supported labor unions and farming cooperatives as his philosophy began to take on a more socialist inclination, perhaps in part due to Harriet Taylor's influence.

Mill died on May 8, 1873 in Avignon, France.

"The best state for human nature is that in which, while no one is poor, no one desired to be richer, nor has any reason to fear being thrust back by the efforts of others to push themselves forward."

Oliver Wendell Holmes

"I find the great thing in this world is not so much where we stand, as in what direction we are moving: To reach the port of heaven, we must sail sometimes with the wind and sometimes against it—but we must sail, and not drift, nor lie at anchor."

✳ ✳ ✳ ✳

OLIVER HOLMES WENDALL was a physician, professor, inventor, poet, and father of a Supreme Court Justice, who left behind an extensive body of work.

Oliver Wendell Holmes was born on August 29, 1809, in Cambridge, Massachusetts. He spent much of his spare time as a boy reading the books in his father's extensive library. He received a formal education at Phillips Academy, and graduated from Harvard in 1829. Holmes studied the law and medicine, but he is remembered for his poetry. In 1830, he published one of his most famous poems, "Old Ironsides," an ode to the USS *Constitution*. The ship was one of the six original frigates in the United States Navy, and Holmes' poem helped prevent it from being decommissioned. The *Constitution* is currently the oldest working naval vessel in the world.

Holmes would become a member of the Fireside Poets, a group of 19th-century New England poets that included Henry Wadsworth Longfellow and William Cullen Bryant. In addition to poetry, Holmes published the first of several collections of essays in 1858 titled *The Autocrat of the Breakfast-Table*, the source of the quote above. The essays originally appeared in *The Atlantic Monthly* and discuss a range of topics with a stereotypical "Yankee" outlook. Holmes' essays popularized a variety of terms that are part of the American lexicon, including "Boston Brahmin" and "anesthesia." Holmes also wrote three novels, published two collections of poetry, a biography of Ralph Waldo Emerson, and a travelogue of Europe.

Holmes died in his sleep on October 7, 1794, and is buried in Cambridge.

More from Oliver Wendall Holmes

"For there we loved, and where we love is home,
Home that our feet may leave, but not our hearts,"

—"HOMESICK IN HEAVEN"

"You can never be too cautious in your prognosis, in the view of the
great uncertainty of the course of any disease not long watched,
and the many unexpected turns it may take. I think I am not the first
to utter the following caution : —Beware how you take away hope
from any human being."

—ADDRESS TO MEDICAL GRADUATES AT HARVARD

"Build thee more stately mansions, O my soul,
As the swift seasons roll!
Leave thy low-vaulted past!
Let each new temple, nobler than the last,
Shut thee from heaven with a dome more vast,
Till thou at length art free,
Leaving thine outgrown shell by life's unresting sea!"

—"THE CHAMBERED NAUTILUS"

"Oh, better that her shattered bulk should sink beneath the wave;
Her thunders shook the mighty deep, and there should be her grave;
Nail to the mast her holy flag, set every threadbare sail
And give her to the god of storms, the lightning and the gale!"

—"OLD IRONSIDES"

"The world's great men have not commonly been great scholars, nor
its great scholars great men."

—THE AUTOCRAT OF THE BREAKFAST TABLE

"Knowledge and timber shouldn't be much used, till they
are seasoned."

—THE AUTOCRAT OF THE BREAKFAST TABLE

Thinking on Genius

"Genius will not live and thrive without training, but it does not the less reward the watering pot and pruning knife."

A feminist, transcendentalist, journalist, and revolutionary Margaret Fuller wrote the first feminist book in the United States.

✳ ✳ ✳ ✳

MARGARET FULLER WAS born in Cambridge, Massachusetts, on May 23, 1810. Her father, a lawyer and politician, began educating her at a young age, and Fuller was literate by the age of four. He did not allow him to read the kind of novellas and books on etiquette that were typically given to girls of the day, instead teaching her Latin and giving her the classics to read. Her father was rather overbearing, and his insistence on precision in Fuller's lessons gave her nightmares and caused her to sleepwalk.

Fuller attended school beginning in 1821, and when she was fourteen she was sent to Boston to attend a boarding school for young women. Upon finishing she returned to her family home in Cambridge, where she continued studying classical philosophy, several languages, and literature. In 1833, her family moved to rural Groton, Massachusetts, where Fuller was isolated and had to manage the household when her mother fell ill. She published her first piece of literary criticism in the *Western Messenger*. in 1835. Her father died in October of that year, which devastated Fuller.

Transcendentalism and Writing

Fuller visited Ralph Waldo Emerson in 1836 and secured a job that year teaching in Boston, and later in Providence, Rhode Island. In 1839 she returned to Boston and began hosting discussion groups with prominent women from New England. These "Conversations" would continue until 1844, and Fuller intended them to supplant the education so many women were denied at the time, and covered natural philosophy, history, literature and the arts.

In 1839 Fuller also co-founded a transcendentalist journal, *The Dial*, with Ralph Waldo Emerson. She began editing the journal in 1840, and quickly became widely recognized as one of the leaders of the movement. She regularly visited Brook Farm, a transcendentalist community nine miles outside of Boston. In 1844, she travelled through the Midwest, and wrote *Summer on the Lake* about her journey. The book met some acclaim, and Horace Greeley, the editor of the *New York Tribune*, invited her to join the newspaper as a literary critic.

Woman in the Nineteenth Century

In 1845, Fuller wrote one of her best-known works, *Woman in the Nineteenth Century*. The book was the first major feminist work published in the United States. It originally appeared in serial format in *The Dial* as *The Great Lawsuit: Man vs. Men, Woman vs. Women*. In it, she argued that the European heritage of the United States has prevented America from ever reaching true equality, and that its treatment of Native Americans and African Americans was a result of this inherited immorality. She argues for the practice of divine love to right these wrongs. Fuller says that only be elevating women to be the equals of men can this kind of divine love be truly achieved. She defines four kinds of marriage, which she ranks from least to best: the shared household, mutual idolatry, intellectual companionship, and religious union. These ideas blend transcendentalist philosophy with feminism in a landmark work.

In 1846, the *Tribune* sent Fuller to Europe as a correspondent. She travelled to Italy, where she met Giovanni Angelo. In 1848, they had a son together, and the next year they took part in a rebellion that attempted to establish a Roman Republic. The rebellion failed, and they fled to Florence before boarding a ship to New York. The ship ran aground during a storm on July 19, 1850. Their bodies were never recovered.

Martin Farquhar Tupper

"Error is a hardy plant: it flourisheth in every soil."

One of the most prolific writers of 19th century England, Martin Tupper died in obscurity, but his legacy in English literature outlived him, and influenced later writers ranging from Henry Wadsworth Longfellow to Karl Marx.

✳ ✳ ✳ ✳

MARTIN FARQUHAR TUPPER was born in London on July 17, 1810. His father, for whom he was named, was a physician. Following a number of years at the Charter House, Tupper went to Christ Church at Oxford. He graduated with a Bachelor's of Arts in 1832, and then received a Master's in 1835. He passed the Bar the same year, although he never practiced law. Instead, he began his writing career, contributing to periodicals. Some years later, he completed his studies with a Doctorate of Civil Law in 1847.

Literary Career

Tupper wrote the first essay of several that would eventually become *Proverbial Philosophy* in 1837. These were a collection of instructive pamphlets that discussed etiquette and social mores, and the source of the quote above. It was moderately successful in England. It did not initially sell in America, although after several revisions it began gaining in popularity, eventually selling close to a million copies there. The prose of *Proverbial Philosophy* was simple and broadly accessible, which contributed to its success.

Tupper was a prolific writer, and he followed that work with a new collection of essays, novel, or short stories nearly every year after. He began with a collection of essays and sonnets that celebrated seventy well-known men and women in 1839. In 1841 he wrote *An Author's Mind*, which contained the outlines of ideas for some thirty books that he hadn't written.

He followed this in 1844 with three collections of short stories that were meant as parables regarding vice. His writing touched on numerous subjects, including Christianity, English patriotism, poetry, biographies, and prose works.

In *Stephan Langton*, he recounted the events leading up to the Magna Carta and the dispute between King John and Pope Innocent III in one of the first historical novels written in English. In 1845 he was inducted into the Royal Society, and presented with a gold medal by the King of Prussia for his work in science and literature. In 1886 he published an autobiography, in which he recounted his early upbringing and experiences as an author.

Personal Life and Later Work

Tupper had a widespread reputation as a friendly, kind man. He married Isabella Devis, his first cousin, in 1835, and the couple had eight children together. He is reported to have been concerned with humanitarian issues of the day, as evidenced by his support of the Student Volunteer Movement for Foreign Missions, and early student exchange program that recruited college and university students for missionary service abroad. The organization helped promote warm relations between Britain and the United States. Tupper also reportedly encouraged literature by African writers, although he has been criticized for an 1850 ballad, "The Anglo-Saxon Race," in which he wrote "the world is for the Anglo Saxon race."

Tuller's writing diminished towards the end of his life, and with the exception of his autobiography, he published very little in his later years, eventually falling into some obscurity as his popularity waned. He retired to a small estate in Surrey, and died at his home there in November of 1889.

More from *Proverbial Philosophy*

"Well-timed silence hath more eloquence than speech."

"A good book is the best of friends, the same today and forever."

"Error is a hardy plant; it flourisheth in every soil;
In the heart of the wise and good, alike with the wicked and foolish;
For there is no error so crooked, but it hath in it some lines of truth;
Nor is any poison so deadly, that it serveth not some
wholesome use."

"Wait, thou child of hope, for Time shall teach thee all things."

"If the mind is wearied by study, or the body worn with sickness, It
is well to lie fallow for a while, in the vacancy of sheer amusement;
But when thou prosprest in health, and thine intellect can soar
untired, To seek uninstructive pleasure is to slumber on the couch
of indolence."

An Influential Editor

"The illusion that times that were are better than those that are,
has probably pervaded all ages."

Horace Greeley founded and edited the New York Tribune,
one of the best-known and most widely circulated American
newspapers of the 19th century.

✳   ✳   ✳   ✳

HORACE GREELEY WAS born on his family's farm near
Amherst, New York, on February 3, 1811. For the first
twenty minutes of his life, he could not breathe. His parents
were farmers of modest means, and they had to move multiple
times during Horace's childhood. He attended public school
as a boy, and was an excellent student. Several of his parents'
neighbors, seeing his brilliance, offered to pay for Greeley to
attend private school, but his parents refused to accept charity.
Greeley, meanwhile, read every book he could find, and one of
his neighbors had an extensive library that he visited frequently.

When he was eleven years old, he ran away from home to try
to become a printer's apprentice, but he was not old enough.
Four years later, he tried again, and was hired by the *Northern
Spectator*, a newspaper in Vermont. While he worked there, he
spent nearly all of his free time reading books from the town's

public library. In 1830, he moved to Erie, Pennsylvania, where his family was living. He stayed there for only a year before leaving again.

The *New York Tribune*

In 1831, Greeley moved to New York City, finding work as a journalist and editor for a number of different newspapers there. He met Mary Cheney the same year, and they were married in 1836. In 1834, he began publishing the *New Yorker*, although it folded during the economic crisis of 1837. In 1841, he founded a daily newspaper, the *New York Tribune*. It initially had only six hundred subscribers, but it would eventually grow to have the highest circulation of any newspaper in the country. Greeley came up with the novel idea of selling weekly submissions that were mailed all over the nation. The newspaper reflected Greeley's belief that young men should seek their fortune by settling the American West: "Turn your face to the great West, and there build up a home and fortune."

The *Tribune* was unique in that it was the first newspaper whose reporting was truly national, rather than simply local; this helped boost its nationwide circulation and esteem. It was the first newspaper to hire a full-time correspondent to cover politics in Washington, D.C. Other newspapers soon copied this innovation. The newspaper gave Greeley a national platform for his political beliefs; it soon was vocally anti-slavery and opposed the admission of new slave states into the Union. Greeley also took the radical step of being the first newspaper to hire a woman, Margaret Fuller, as a literary critic. She joined the *Tribune* in 1844.

In 1924, the Tribune merged with the *New York Herald* to become the *New York Herald-Tribune*, which folded in 1966 after more than 120 years of publication.

Politics and Later Life

In 1848, Greeley served in the U.S. House of Representatives following the resignation of David Jackson for election fraud.

Greeley's term was brief—he did not seek reelection and only served three months— but while he was there he used the *Tribune* to launch investigations of Congress, which incensed many. In 1854, he broke with the Whigs to found the Republican party. He supported Lincoln and used the newspaper to call for the abolition of slavery during the Civil War. In 1872, he ran for President as the Republican party's candidate, but lost to Ulysses S Grant in a landslide. His wife died five days before the election, and on November 29, Greeley died as well. He is buried in Brooklyn.

A Prolific and Steady Writer

"A small daily task, if it be really daily, will beat the labors of a spasmodic Hercules."

Trollope's six-volume series Chronicles of Barsetshire, which related the social and political happenings in the fictional county, were praised in his time for their realism, and are still revered as romantic descriptions of Victorian England.

✳ ✳ ✳ ✳

ANTHONY TROLLOPE WAS born in London on April 24, 1815. His father was a barrister of some affluence, and Trollope attended high-class public schools. Following school, he was hired as a junior clerk at the London General Post Office, a position that he hated, but in 1841 he was transferred to Ireland to work as a postal surveyor, and he enjoyed the social life he found there. In 1844, he married Rose Heseltine, and the two began living in Tipperary, Ireland. Trollope began writing in the late 1840s.

The *Chronicles of Barsetshire*

Trollope wrote four novels set in Ireland during his time there. Two were set during the Irish Potato Famine, and the third also dealt with the repercussions of the Famine. The third, published in 1848, was a lighthearted story about romantic exploits of different social classes. The novels were not very well received. In 1851, he was recalled to England to conduct a survey of rural mail routes. One of the mailboxes he had installed, in Guernsey in 1852, is still standing.

During this time he came up with the idea for the first novel in the *Chronicles of Barsetshire*, called *The Warden*. Published in 1855, it tells the story of a caretaker at an old people's home, who comes under criticism for turning a profit from the home. *The Warden* was well-received, and publishers encouraged Trollope to write more books in the same style. The resulting *Barsetshire* series would eventually include six books about the people who lived in the fictional county: *Barchester Towers*, published in 1857, *Doctor Thorne* in 1858, *Framley Parsonage* in 1861, *The Small House at Allington* in 1864, and *The Last Chronicle of Barset* in 1867. The books are variously humorous and dramatic. *Doctor Thorne* describes the social structure of Victorian England, of which landowners occupied the higher levels. *The Last Chronicle* is the saddest novel in the series, and tells the story of a scholar named Mr. Crawley, who is destitute and lonely.

Later Work

In 1867, Trollope resigned from his position at the Post Office, and ran unsuccessfully for Parliament the following year. In addition to the *Barsetshire* series, he wrote eighteen more novels, many of which were first published in serial form. He was said to write at a rate of one thousand words per hour, and completed most of his writing before breakfast. In his *Autobiography*, he wrote of his commitment to staying on task and delivering his work on time:

"There was no day on which it was my positive duty to write for the publishers, as it was my duty to write reports for the Post Office. I was free to be idle if I pleased. But as I had made up my mind to undertake this second profession, I found it to be expedient to bind myself by certain self-imposed laws.

When I have commenced a new book, I have always prepared a diary, divided into weeks, and carried it on for the period which I have allowed myself for the completion of the work. In this I have entered, day by day, the number of pages I have written, so that if at any time I have slipped into idleness for a day or two, the record of that idleness has been there, staring me in the face, and demanding of me increased labour, so that the deficiency might be supplied."

His autobiography is also the source of the quote that begins the essay; the same basic sentiment is expressed in *The Last Chronicle of Barset*, when he writes, "It's dogged as does it. It ain't thinking about it."

Some of his notable works include *Orley Farm*, published in 1862, and *Can You Forgive Her?* Published in 1865, this was his first politically-themed novel, as well as the first in another series about the fictional Duke of Omnium and his family line.

Trollope published forty-seven novels in all. In 1875, he wrote *The Way We Live Now*, his longest novel and the last significant Victorian novel to be published in serial form. He retired to a small village in Sussex in his final years. Trollope died in London on December 6, 1882.

"Always remember that when you go into an attorney's office door, you will have to pay for it, first or last."

—*THE LAST CHRONICLE OF BARSET*

Writing of All Things Beautiful

Alexander's poignant Christian hymns, written more than a century ago, still resonate with churchgoers all over the world.

✳   ✳   ✳   ✳

CECIL FRANCES ALEXANDER (née Humphreys) was born in Dublin in April, 1818. She displayed a talent for poetry when she was fifteen years old, when she composed her first

Christian hymn. By adulthood, she had a reputation as a talented hymn writer, publishing *Verses for Holy Seasons* in 1846, *The Lord of the Forest and His Vassals* in 1847, and *Hymns for Little Children* in 1848. The third collection included some of her most famous works, several of which are still popular to this day, including "All Things Bright and Beautiful," the Christmas Carol "Once in Royal David's City", and "There Is a Green Hill Far Away." In 1850, Frances married Reverend William Alexander and moved to Derry in present-day Northern Ireland. There she began working in parochial education. She established the Derry Diocesan Institution for the Education of the Deaf and Dumb, funding the school with profits from the sales of *Hymns for Little Children*.

In 1855, the couple moved to County Donegal, and in 1867 they returned to Derry when William was appointed Bishop of Derry and Archbishop of Armagh. William also published several collections of poetry. Cecil died on October 12, 1895, and is buried in Derry. A collection of her hymns and poems was published posthumously. Her hymns remain some of the most popular among Irish Protestants and Christians around the world.

All Things Bright and Beautiful

All things bright and beautiful,
all creatures great and small,
all things wise and wonderful,
the Lord God made them all.

Each little flower that opens,
each little bird that sings,
he made their glowing colors,
he made their tiny wings.

The purple-headed mountain,
the river running by,
the sunset, and the morning
that brightens up the sky.

Facing Facts

"It is as fatal as it is cowardly to blink facts because they are not to our taste."

John Tyndall's discoveries— of the Greenhouse Effect, magnetism, and more— are still applicable today, and he was a tireless promoter of the cause of science.

❋　❋　❋　❋

JOHN TYNDALL WAS born in County Carlow, Ireland, on August 2, 1820. His family was poor, but he was able to have a basic education, and pursued a career as a surveyor following his schooling. In 1847, after performing surveys of England and Ireland for eight years, he became interested in the sciences. Tyndall had saved enough money from his work to be able to afford to attend the University of Marburg, Germany, from 1848 to 1850, earning a Ph.D. there. After he earned his degree, however, he had difficulty finding work for the first few years, until he was able to secure a position in 1853 at the Royal Institution in London as a professor of natural philosophy.

Scientific Study

Tyndall began studying magnetism and magnetic polarity, and pursued this research until 1856. His work on magnetism attracted the attention of other physicists of the day, and in 1852 he was inducted as a Fellow of the Royal Society. While he was at the Royal Institution, he became friends with the brilliant physicist and chemist Michael Faraday. Faraday was already extremely popular because of his entertaining and enlightening lectures. Tyndall would eventually be appointed to the chair held by Faraday upon his mentor's retirement.

Faraday had encouraged Tyndall in his successful study of magnetism, but in the late 1850s, the protégé would embark on his own area of novel research: the effects of heat and light energy (called radiant energy) on vapors and gases in the air. He was able to show experimentally that the heat in the Earth's atmosphere was caused by the ability of the gases present in the air to absorb radiant energy. He invented a device called a thermopile that converted radiant energy to electricity, which allowed him to make accurate measurements of air temperature when various gases were present. He correctly measured the radiant energy absorption potential of several atmospheric gases in 1859. His work was the first to prove the existence of the Greenhouse Effect.

In order to make his measurements as accurate as possible, Tyndall needed to ensure that there were no microscopic dust particles present in the air sample he was measuring. In the 1860s he hit upon the idea of shining intense light at the air sample; if dust particles were present, the light would be scattered. This effect, which he first described, is now called Tyndall Scattering. His work led to many other discoveries that are still relevant: in 1862 he determined a means of measuring the amount of carbon dioxide in a patient's breath, and this is still used to monitor anesthetized patients in hospitals today.

Science Education

Tyndall was also a dedicated promoter of scientific inquiry. He regularly gave public lectures on scientific topics to lay audiences at the Royal Society. On a tour of the United States, during which he delivered dozens of lectures, he was praised for his ability to not only teach science accurately, but in a manner that made it entertaining and captivated his audiences. He wrote multiple books on science, and eventually grew to be one of the most famous physicists of his day. He often wrote and spoke about the importance of science education and how teaching was the noblest profession he could think of. He was a vocal supporter of Darwin's theory of Natural Selection, and worked against the influence of religion on science.

Tyndall died on December 4, 1893.

A Solitary Philosopher

"To know how to grow old is the masterwork of wisdom, and one of the most difficult chapters in the great art of living."

Henri Frédéric Amiel was not well known during his lifetime, but he kept a private journal of his thoughts and ideas. When it was published after his death, the world learned of his brilliance.

✳ ✳ ✳ ✳

HENRI FRÉDÉRIC AMIEL was born on September 27, 1821, in Geneva. His ancestors were originally of French origin, but were members of the Huguenot religious minority who were persecuted following King Henry IV's Edict of Nantes in 1598. Having fled France rather than convert to Catholicism, they were driven to Switzerland. Ameil's parents when he was still a young man. He began travelling, and met with many of the intellectual luminaries of his day, before settling in Berlin, where he engaged in the study of the history of German philosophy.

Study and *Journal Intime*

In 1849, Amiel was appointed to a position at the Academy of Geneva as a professor of aesthetics, as a subtopic of the study of philosophy. He held the post for six years, until he transferred over to the study of moral philosophy. While he was able to engage in his studies unmolested, the appointment was not without political ramifications. His university position was given to him by friends in the Democratic Party of Switzerland, and as they were at odds with the Aristocratic Party, which was the dominant political force at the time, Amiel was unable to secure the kind of patronage that would have allowed him to publish in the leading journals of the time and gain recognition for his ideas during his life.

Amiel wrote more than a dozen essays on moral philosophy, aesthetics, and history. His essays were as wide-ranging as they were insightful. Amiel discussed the contemporary Swiss literary movement in an 1849 essay. He wrote a metaphysical essay called *The Part of the Dream* in 1863, and he composed a short history of Charles the Bold, a fifteenth-century Duke of Burgundy, in 1876. None met with any real acclaim, and Amiel generally considered himself to be a failure as a writer and a philosopher.

But one of his books would meet widespread acclaim following his death: the *Journal Intime*, Amiel's personal journal. Although he also wrote several volumes of poetry along with his historical and philosophical studies, the *Journal* is the only book that was ever published under his authorship to any acclaim. It gained a reputation across Europe and was eventually translated into English by the British novelist Mary Augusta Ward in 1885.

The *Journal* is a fairly short work, but it revealed an intensely self-conscious and thoughtful mind. He discusses literature, including his disdain for Victor Hugo, and talks about music, religion, ethics, the weather from day to day, and education. He discusses the nature of friendship and the meaning of life and death. In just over two hundred pages, the *Journal* paints an intimate portrait of Amiel. He is a complex figure, at once devoutly religious and deeply skeptical, a conservative Protestant who is also interested in Buddhist ideas, very pragmatic and at the same time a romantic.

Amiel died in Geneva on May 11, 1881.

Quotes from the *Journal*

"An error is the more dangerous the more truth it contains."

"Charm: the quality in others that makes us more satisfied with ourselves."

"Spite is anger which is afraid to show itself, it is an impotent fury conscious of its impotence."

"To repel one's cross is to make it heavier."

Turning Experience into Writing

"Man grows used to everything, the scoundrel!"

Fyodor Dostoyevsky's life experiences—the murder of his father, his exile in Siberia—provided many of the themes that would make him one of the greatest Russian novelists in history.

* * * *

FYODOR MIKHAILOVICH DOSTOEVSKY was born on November 11, 1821, in Moscow. He was educated as a young man at a military engineering school, but he did not enjoy the curriculum and spent much of his time reading fiction. While he was away at school, his father was murdered by serfs working on his estate. This experience would later influence his writing, with murder being a central aspect of his works. After serving for two years in the army, Dostoyevsky began writing. His first novel, *Poor Folk*, was published in 1846 to great critical acclaim. The same year he wrote *The Double*, a novella about a man with a split personality. Although he continued publishing short stories, it would be twenty years before he published another novel.

Revolution and Exile

In 1846, Dostoyevsky became involved with the Petrashevsky Circle, a literary discussion group with progressive political views. The group was opposed to the Tsarist regime and system of Russian serfdom. In 1849, members of the group including Dostoyevsky were arrested, found guilty of sedition, and sentenced to death. They were stood in front of a firing squad, and at the last moment a message from the Tsar arrived which commuted their sentence. The Tsar had in fact never intended to execute them, but used the mock execution to frighten the prisoners before they were sent to a prison camp in Siberia. The experience would haunt Dostoyevsky for the rest of his life, and mock execution appeared in his later works.

While in exile in Siberia, he experienced terrible, cruel living conditions that caused him to reexamine his ideals. Shackled for the entire imprisonment, and sharing a filthy, vermin-infested barracks with other prisoners, he endured four years of hard labor. Following an epileptic seizure, he had a spiritual reawakening in which he decided that the Russian people would be responsible for the spiritual salvation of the world. During this time he also came up with his belief that suffering was a necessary means to salvation. This belief would become one of the central themes of much of his later writing.

Literary Works

Following his release from the camp, Dostoyevsky served four more years in the army and received a pardon from the Tsar. In 1866 he published *Crime and Punishment* (the source of the quote above), which relates the story of a student who brutally murders a pawn-broker and attempts to justify his crime to himself and to his lover, Sonya. He is eventually caught and serves eight years in Siberia, where he finds redemption and salvation with her help. *Crime and Punishment* was Dostoyevsky's first great masterpiece, and became an instant sensation that remains one of the Russian classics. He followed it with *The Idiot* in 1869, *Demons* in 1872, and *The Brothers Karamazov* in 1880. *The Brothers Karamazov* was Dostoyevsky's final novel, and is his longest work. It is widely considered his magnum opus. *Karamazov* explores themes of Christianity, philosophy, morality and belief. It is arranged into 12 books that tell the story of the Karamazov family and the death of the family patriarch. In the book's most famous chapter, "The Grand Inquisitor," Ivan Karamazov, a nonbeliever, recites a poem of the same name to his brother, a monk. The poem tells of the Second Coming of Christ during the Spanish Inquisition, and uses this parable to explore the ideas of free will and human nature.

Only a few months after *The Brothers Karamazov* was published, Dostoyevsky died, on February 9, 1881.

Schoolboy Wisdom

"He never wants anything but what's right and fair; only when you come to settle what's right and fair, it's everything that he wants and nothing that you want."

Thomas Hughes was a 19th-century English politician and author who is best known for his semi-autobiographical novel, Tom Brown's Schooldays.

✳   ✳   ✳   ✳

T HOMAS HUGHES WAS born on October 20, 1822, in Oxfordshire, England. He was the son of a clergyman, and attended Rugby School, the setting for his famous novel. He attended Oriel College, Oxford, graduating in 1845. In 1848, he began practicing law and became a judge in 1882. He served in Parliament from 1865–1874. Hughes was notable for his progressive political views. He was involved in the early Christian Socialism movement, which advocated extending the teachings of Jesus to government reforms that helped the poor. In 1854, he cofounded the Working Men's College, which promoted the Christian Socialist's ideas regarding education and served as its principal from 1872–1883. Hughes supported the formation of some of the first trade unions in England. He was involved in the co-operative movement and served as the president of the Co-operative Congress in 1869.

Hughes is best known for his semiautobiographical novel, *Tom Brown's Schooldays,* which was published in 1857 and is the source of the quote above. The book established the genre of British school novels, in which fictional schools from Greyfairs to Hogwarts became famous. *Schooldays* was instantly popular and was translated into several languages during the 19th century. Hughes followed it with *Tom Brown at Oxford* in 1861, which had less success. He also wrote a number of nonfiction works, including travelogues, political treatises, and a biography of Alfred the Great.

Little Deeds

Julia Fletcher Carney was a poet and educator who is best remembered for her poem, "Little Things."

❋   ❋   ❋   ❋

JULIA FLETCHER CARNEY was born in Lancaster, Massachusetts, on April 6, 1823. She was a naturally gifted writer from a young age. Her mother thought this was not a worthwhile skill and discouraged her writing. When Fletcher was eight, she contracted scarlet fever. During her long recuperation, her neighbors and the local library provided her with books to read. She read voraciously, and the books of prose and poetry inspired her to continue writing. When she was fourteen, Fletcher's poems and articles began being published by local newspapers. In 1840 she moved to Philadelphia, where she lived with her sister and taught at a private school.

In 1844 she moved to Boston, where she taught primary school until she married Thomas Johnson Carney in 1849. The couple moved around the East Coast for several years before heading west, where they settled on the prairie. Four of their children died during this time. Carney continued writing, although her writing moved away from poetry and focused more on essays on social reform. When Thomas died in 1871, she returned to Illinois with her children, only five of whom survived to adulthood.

Carney's poem, "Little Things," for which she is best known, was written in 1845. She initially did not give it a title. It was published in an edition of the McGuffey Reader, a textbook that was popular in primary education in the 19th century.

"Little Things"

Little drops of water,
Little grains of sand,
Make the mighty ocean

And the pleasant land.
So the little moments,
Humble though they be,
Make the mighty ages
Of Eternity.

So the little errors
Lead the soul away
From the paths of virtue
Far in sin to stray.

Little deeds of kindness,
Little words of love,
Help to make earth happy
Like the Heaven above.

The Laureate of the Nursery

William Brighty Rands wrote many of the famous nursery rhymes that have been passed down from the Victorian era, and was dubbed "The Laureate of the Nursery" by his contemporaries.

✳ ✳ ✳ ✳

WILLIAM BRIGHTY RANDS was born on Christmas Eve, 1823, in Chelsea, England. According to some accounts his father was a shopkeeper, and to others a candle maker. In either case, his family was not well off, and Rands did not receive much formal education. He read as many books as he could, usually standing at second-hand bookstores. He taught himself Latin and Greek as a young man, and later Spanish and French as well. He held various jobs, including working in a warehouse, in a theatre, and as a clerk in a barrister's office.

Career and Nursery Rhymes

In 1857, having taught himself stenography, he began working at the House of Commons as a reporter for Messrs. Gurney & Co. He was a talented reporter, and received a note of thanks for his efficiency from a committee of the House. He kept this position until August 1875, when poor health forced him to resign. During these years, he wrote prose and poetry in his spare time. In 1855 he was already writing for the *Illustrated Times*, and he continued to write a column for the magazine for young men on etiquette until 1871. He also was a regular contributor to several literary journals, including *Good Words*, *St. Paul's Magazine*, and *Boy's Paper*.

Rands wrote articles under the pennames Matthew Browne, T. Talker, and Henry Holbeach for the *Contemporary Review*, beginning in December 1869 with an article on morality. He wrote literary reviews for the *Pall Mall Gazette* and was a regular contributor to many other magazines and newspapers. In 1878 he founded a London newspaper called the *Citizen*. He also occasionally delivered sermons at a chapel in Brixton, and also composed hymns for the church service. He published several books of poetry; the first, titled *Chain of Lilies and Other Poems*, was published in 1857, although in later years he expressed dissatisfaction with the collection.

Although Rands was a prolific journalist, he is best remembered for his nursery rhymes, which he wrote dozens of. His nursery rhymes were collected in *Lilliput Lyrics*, which was published posthumously in 1899. The collection includes "Lilliput Levee," in which he wrote what might be considered the procrastinator's creed: "Never do today what you can / Put off to tomorrow."

Rands wrote the poem "Beautiful World," which was published in *Lilliput Lectures* in 1871, and it is considered one of his best. Though the poem is only ten lines long, it succinctly and brilliantly relates the human condition. The poem opens by describing how daunted one can feel by their smallness as compared to the size and wonder of the whole Earth. But it draws the simple, elegant close: "You are more than the Earth, though you are such a dot: You can love and think, and the Earth cannot!"

Rands also wrote a series of fanciful, allegorical fairy tales for children, publishing a new one every Christmas for a number of years. These were reprinted posthumously in the collection *Lilliput Legends*. He also wrote a two volume historical work in 1869, *Chaucer's England*, under the penname Matthew Browne.

William Bright Rands died on April 23, 1882, in London. He was fifty-eight years old.

Following Ideals

"Ideals are like stars; you will not succeed in touching them with your hands. But like the seafaring man on the desert of waters, you choose them as your guides, and following them you will reach your destiny."

A German-American revolutionary, politician, journalist and social reformer, Carl Shurz was the first German immigrant elected to the U.S. Senate, where he fought for higher moral standards in government.

❋　❋　❋　❋

CARL SCHURZ WAS born on March 2, 1829, near Cologne, in what was then Prussia. He attended school for only a few years, as his family was too poor to pay for his education, and he was forced to drop out before he graduated. Later, he was able to pass an equivalence examination that allowed him to enroll in the University of Bonn. While he was there he became involved in the German Nationalist revolution of 1848, publishing a nationalist newspaper with his friend Gottfried Kinkel. In 1849 he joined the armed struggle for German independence and fought in a number of battles against the Prussian Army as an artillery officer. When the German forces were defeated at the siege of Rastatt later that year, Schurz was able to escape, making his way to Zürich. He returned to Prussia in 1850, where he helped Kinkel escape from prison. The pair made their way to Great Britain, where Schurz made a living as a German teacher. He married Margarethe Meyer in 1852, and together they immigrated to America. Margarethe would later establish the kindergarten system in the United States.

The couple arrived in Philadelphia in July, but eventually settled in Wisconsin, where Schurz almost immediately became involved in local politics. He joined the Republican Party and began doing anti-slavery organizing. In 1857, he ran unsuccessfully for Lieutenant Governor, and in 1858 he volunteered for Abraham Lincoln's Senate campaign.

The Civil War

In 1862, Schurz was commissioned as a brigadier general in the Union Army and took command of a division. In August of 1862 he led troops at the Second Battle of Bull Run. He was promoted to major general and the following year he led the Union Army's Ninth Corps he fought at Chancellorsville, Gettysburg, and Chattanooga. His Ninth Corps was routed by Stonewall Jackson's troops at Chancellorsville, and they again retreated at the battle of Gettysburg, leading the press to criticize German-American units in the Union Army. In the final months of the war, Schurz served with General Sherman's Army during the March to the Sea.

Following the war, he toured the Southern states on behalf of President Andrew Johnson. Schurz was a staunch advocate for the rights of African-Americans, and he delivered a report to the President that recommended allowing Southern states to rejoin the Union with full rights. Johnson disagreed, and ignored his report.

Schurz and his wife moved to Detroit in 1866, where he became the editor of the *Detroit Post*. In 1867, they moved again, to St. Louis, where he became editor of the *St. Louis Westliche Post*. While in Missouri, he had his first and only electoral victory in 1869, and served as a U.S. Senator until 1875. He fought political corruption and opposed federal troops enforcing Reconstruction-era laws or extending full rights to African-Americans. In 1872, breaking with President Ulysses S. Grant on these and other issues, he founded the Liberal Republican Party, which opposed a second term for the President. He returned to the Party to support Rutherford B. Hayes, and was granted an appointment as Secretary of the Interior, where he served from 1877–1881.

Following his career in public service, Schurz returned to journalism, editing the *New York Evening Post* and *The Nation*. He died on May 14, 1906 in New York City.

Making a Living, and a Legacy

"Resolved to take Fate by the throat and shake a living out of her."

Louisa May Alcott was a prolific writer whose novel Little Women, *loosely based on her and her sisters' upbringing, has become one of the classics of American literature.*

✳ ✳ ✳ ✳

LOUISA MAY ALCOTT was born on November 29, 1832, in the Germantown section of Philadelphia. Her father, Bronson Alcott, was a teacher and her mother, Abby May, was a social worker. Bronson Alcott was a transcendentalist, and Louisa grew up among leaders of that movement, including Ralph Waldo Emerson and Henry David Thoreau. Alcott was educated primarily by her father, who ran an experimental school in Boston; she attended it for some time and was also educated at home.

While her father had altruistic ideals, his transcendentalist utopian community, The Fruitlands, was a failure, and her family struggled to make ends meet. (Alcott wrote at one point, "My definition [of a philosopher] is of a man up in a balloon, with his family and friends holding the ropes which confine him to earth and trying to haul him down.") Alcott worked as a teacher, seamstress, and domestic servant to help support her family. Writing soon became a creative outlet for Alcott. Her first book, *Flower Fables*, a collection of short stories she had originally written for Ralph Waldo Emerson's daughter, was published when she was seventeen.

The Civil War and *Little Women*

Alcott was raised in a socially progressive environment. Her parents, like almost all transcendentalists, were opposed to slavery. In 1847, her home became a station on the Underground Railroad when her family housed a fugitive slave for one week. Alcott read the Seneca Falls Declaration of Sentiments in 1848, and became the first woman to register to vote in Concord, Massachusetts. Her writing reflected her feminist ideas, depicting imaginative, self-reliant female protagonists, who, like Alcott herself, had to shake a living out of Fate. When the Civil War broke out, she volunteered as a nurse, but contracted typhoid and had to return home. In 1863 she wrote of her experiences in *Hospital Sketches*, which brought her acclaim. She began writing stories for *The Atlantic Monthly*. In 1868, she wrote *Little Women* in part to help support her family financially.

Little Women tells the story of four sisters, Meg, Jo, Beth, and Amy March, and is largely based on recollections of Alcott's own childhood. The character Jo is based on Alcott. The sisters' New England family is not affluent, but has a generally optimistic view of life. The book follows the sisters as they grow up and grapple with the challenges of adult life, including employment and marriage. The book was immediately successful, and allowed Alcott to settle her family's debts. In 1870, Alcott embarked on a European tour to promote the book, which was published as *Good Wives* in the United Kingdom. She followed it with two sequels: *Little Men* in 1871 and *Jo's Boys* in 1886.

She also wrote eleven unrelated novels under her own name and four more under a pseudonym. She published a collection of short stories in six volumes between 1872–1882.

Other than her trip to Europe and occasional visits to New York City, Alcott spent the remained of her life between Boston and Concord. She never married, and cared for her parents. Late in life, she adopted her niece, also named Louisa May after her. Her mother died after a long illness in 1877, and her father died ten years later.

Alcott died on March 6, 1888, in Boston. She is buried in Sleepy Hollow Cemetery in Boston, on a hillside known as Authors' Ridge, where Nathaniel Hawthorne, Emerson, and Henry David Thoreau are also buried.

Charlotte Perkins Gilman

"There is no female mind. The brain is not an organ of sex. As well speak of a female liver."

Feminist, intellectual, and writer, Gilman wrote the iconic short story "The Yellow Wallpaper" to call attention to the treatment of women.

✳ ✳ ✳ ✳

CHARLOTTE PERKINS GILMAN was born in Hartford, Connecticut on July 3, 1860. Her father abandoned the family when Charlotte was still a baby, leaving her mother destitute and forcing her to raise the children on her own. The family often stayed with Charlotte's great-aunts; among them were Harriet Beecher Stowe, the author of *Uncle Tom's Cabin*, and Isabella Beecher Hooker, a prominent suffragist and women's rights activist.

Having to constantly move around had an impact on Gilman's education; she attended seven different schools over just four years, and stopped going when she was fifteen years old. Her mother, devastated by the abandonment by Gilman's father, did not allow her children to make close friendships, leaving Gilman isolated and lonely. Gilman made up for her loneliness by spending much of her free time at the local public library, where she read about classical antiquity. When she was eighteen, she enrolled in the Rhode Island School of Design, where she studied painting.

In 1884 Gilman married Charles Stetson, an artist, although she had originally rejected his proposal based on the intuition that he was not the right person for her. They had a daughter together named Katherine. Gilman experienced severe postpartum depression following the birth of Katherine, and found her depression dismissed as hysteria, which was common at the time. This experience would be the inspiration for her best-known short story, "The Yellow Wallpaper." She divorced Stetson in 1894.

Writing and Activism

Gilman wrote multiple short stories and novellas, but the most famous one by far is "The Yellow Wallpaper," which was published in 1892 in *The New England Magazine*. The story discusses a woman who has been shut in a room by her husband because of concerns about her health, and slowly descends into mental illness as a result. Her husband, who is also her physician, decides he knows what is best for her, in spite of the fact that he continues to prescribe a treatment that is in fact the opposite of what would help her. Having nothing else to pass the time with, the protagonist becomes obsessed with the room's yellow wallpaper. "The Yellow Wallpaper" was based on Gilman's own experience with depression and the "rest cure" that was prescribed to her; she sent a copy of the story to the doctor who had treated her.

"The Yellow Wallpaper" is considered a landmark work of women's fiction. It presents themes that deal with the role of women in a patriarchal society. At the time, women's autonomy was severely curtailed by social customs, and they were widely considered to suffer from "hysteria" and "nerves," which served to undermine their independence. Gilman wrote the story in order to try to have an impact on this.

Gilman's writing also included other short stories and a collection of satirical poems, but she also wrote nonfiction. She gained a reputation as a brilliant lecturer and intellectual. She wrote *Women and Economics*, the source of the quote that begins the essay, in 1898; in it, she called for economic independence for women. She followed this work in 1903 with *The Home: Its Work and Influence* and *Does a Man Support His Wife?* in 1915. She also published *The Forerunner*, a feminist magazine, from 1909 to 1916.

In 1935, Gilman discovered that she had inoperable breast cancer. She committed suicide on August 17 of that year.

Rabindranath Tagore

"The truth comes as conqueror only because we have lost the art of receiving it as guest."

Rabindranath Tagore was an Indian poet and musician who had a major impact on Indian art and literature in the 19th century. In 1913 he became the first non-European person to be awarded a Nobel Prize for Literature.

❊   ❊   ❊   ❊

RABINDRANATH TAGORE WAS born May 7, 1861, the youngest son of Debendranath Tagore. His father was the leader of the Brahmo Samaj, a Hindu sect in 19th-century in Bengal, in northeast India. The sect was focused on reviving what it saw as the fundamentals of Hinduism as they were described in the *Upanishads*. Tagore was educated at home by his father, and when he was seventeen years old he was sent to England to receive a formal education, although he did not complete his studies there.

When he returned to India, he managed the family estates. This experience brought him into close contact with many of the laborers who were employed by his family, and this led to him becoming interested in social reforms. He founded a school at Shantiniketan where he attempted to incorporate the ideals of Brahmo Samaj into the educational program. For a number of years, Tagore was active in the Indian Home Rule movement, and was close friends with Mahatma Gandhi.

Literary Success

Tagore had begun writing poetry when he was only eight years old, and released his first collection of poetry when he was sixteen. The collection, which he released under the pseudonym *Bh nusimha*, was initially thought to be long-lost poetry from antiquity. In the 1870s he began publishing short stories under his own name, and he quickly enjoyed critical success. He became known in the West when his poems were translated into English, and he soon began traveling through Europe on lecture circuits. As his fame grew in the beginning of the twentieth century, Tagore met with many other luminaries of the day, including Albert Einstein, Ezra Pound, William Butler Yeats, and George Bernard Shaw. He toured South America, the United States, Asia and the Soviet Union.

Tagore had a very significant impact on the Bengal Renaissance, writing hundreds of poems in over fifty volumes, eight novels, more than eighty short stories, and composing more than two thousand songs. He also was a prolific artist, and made dozens of drawings and paintings. In 1913, he became the first non-European to receive the Nobel Prize for Literature for his collection *Gitanjali: Song Offerings*, published the previous year.

Political Views

Tagore was opposed to imperialism, and supported Indian independence. He worked with Gandhi to promote the cause, and discussed his political views in *Manast*, which he wrote when he was still in his twenties. In 1915, King George V bestowed a knighthood on Tagore. In 1919, following the Jallianwala Bagh massacre, in which British troops killed as many as a thousand unarmed civilians, Tagore renounced his knighthood in protest. He preferred to promote education as the remedy to British colonialism rather than support all-out revolution. This view drew the ire of many Indian nationalists, and he was nearly assassinated during a trip to San Francisco in 1916. He wrote several popular nationalist songs in support of independence.

Tagore continued writing until his final days. He wrote short stories in 1940 and 1941, as well as poetry that is considered some of his finest work, in spite of the fact that his health was failing and he was suffering from chronic pain. He died at home on August 7, 1941.

"In this playhouse of infinite forms I have had my play, and here have I caught sight of him that is formless."

Stories with Twists

"It was beautiful and simple as all truly great swindles are."

William Sydney Porter, known popularly by his penname O. Henry, was one of the great American writers of the early 20th century. He was the first well-known writer to discuss the lives of lower-class New Yorkers, and his parable "The Gift of the Magi" is considered a classic American short story.

✳   ✳   ✳   ✳

WILLIAM SYDNEY PORTER was born on September 11, 1862 in Greensboro, North Carolina. He attended school for only a few years, but was an avid reader, and would read anything he could get his hands on. When he was nineteen, Porter began working in his uncle's drugstore, and in 1881 he became a licensed pharmacist. At twenty, he moved to Austin, Texas, working variously as a ranch hand, pharmacist and a bank teller. He also began writing in his spare time. In 1887, he eloped with Athol Estes, whose parents objected to their marriage because she had tuberculosis. Porter began working as a draftsman for the Texas General Land Office that year, a position that afforded him a comfortable salary. The couple had a son who died in childbirth in 1888, and a daughter, Margaret, in 1889. Athol encouraged her husband's interest in writing; in 1894 he wrote *Bexar Scrip No. 2692*, and began contributing to a humorous magazine called *The Rolling Stone*.

The Fugitive Becomes O. Henry

In 1894, Porter was indicted for embezzling bank funds. His father-in-law posted his bail, and Porter fled to New Orleans and then to Honduras. While he was living there, he became friends with the train robber Al Jennings; he would later write a book about Jennings. While he was a fugitive, Porter wrote *Cabbages and Kings*, a novel about a fictional South American country called The Republic of Anchuria. He coined the term "banana republic" in this book, which was published in 1904.

When Porter learned that his wife had become seriously ill, and was near death, he returned to Texas in early 1897. He turned himself in, and his father-in-law again posted his bail so he could be by her side. Athol died that July; the following February Porter was found guilty of embezzlement and imprisoned in Ohio. As a licensed pharmacist, he worked and stayed in the hospital wing of the prison, where he wrote over a dozen short stories, published under pseudonyms. The most popular one was O. Henry.

When he got out of prison in 1902, Porter moved to New York City, where he wrote a story a week for the *New York World Sunday Magazine* as O. Henry. He published collections of his stories every year between 1906 and 1910. His stories were set in New York City and showed the everyday lives of the city's denizens. In Porter's most famous story, "The Gift of the Magi," an impoverished couple sells their cherished possessions to be able to afford gifts for one another. He secretly pawns his watch in order to buy combs for her, and she secretly sells her hair to buy a watch chain for him. When they realize what has happened, the couple finds that one another's love is the best gift of all.

The source of the quote that begins the essay comes from " The Octopus Marooned" in *The Gentle Grafter*. In it, a man relates a past piece of graft, in which he and a partner bought all the saloons in a city isolated by a flood and raised prices:

"Well, sir, it took Bird City just ten minutes to realize that it was in a cage. We expected trouble; but there wasn't any. The citizens saw that we had 'em. The nearest railroad was thirty miles away; and it would be two weeks at least before the river would be fordable. So they began to cuss, amiable, and throw down dollars on the bar till it sounded like a selection on the xylophone.

"There was about 1,500 grown-up adults in Bird City that had arrived at years of indiscretion; and the majority of 'em required from three to twenty drinks a day to make life endurable. The Blue Snake was the only place where they could get 'em till the flood subsided. It was beautiful and simple as all truly great swindles are."

Unfortunately for the man, after his partner drinks a bit too much of their own wares, he got loquacious—and accidentally convinces the town to commit to temperance.

Porter's short stories often had surprise endings and coincidences, and he was a master of irony. He died on June 5, 1910, in New York City, but collections of his short stories continued to be published for decades after his death.

Jules Renard

"There are moments when everything goes well; don't be frightened, it won't last."

A 19th century French author, Jules Renard was acclaimed for his use of irony and cruel circumstances to present comical situations in his writing. His journals provided insight into the life of a Parisian writer in the late 19th and early 20th centuries.

J ULES RENARD WAS born on February 22, 1864, in Chalons-du-Maine, France. His father, François Renard, was a laborer who was working on construction of a railroad when he was born. Renard was raised in Nièvre, in central France. His family was of modest means, and Renard's childhood was neither happy nor easy; he would later describe it as "a great ruddy silence." He did not attend formal school, but developed a love of reading at an early age. In 1885, he joined the French military, serving in Bourges for one year.

Work and Legacy

Renard married Marie Morneau in April 1888. The couple moved to Paris that same year and Renard began publishing articles in various Paris newspapers. He wrote prodigiously, publishing short stories, plays, and several novels. He would eventually publish twenty novels between 1888 and 1919, including *Two Fables Without a Moral* in 1893, *The Winemaker in his Vineyard* in 1894, *Les Phillipe* in 1907, and *Ragotte* in 1909. He also wrote seven plays and a posthumously published journal, the source of the quote that begins the essay, as well as the quip: "I am not sincere even when I am saying that I am not sincere."

Renard's best-known work is *Poil de Carrotte* (Carrot Head), published in 1894. *Poil de Carrotte* is a semiautobiographical novel that tells the story of young François Lepic, a redheaded child whose parents are cruel to him. Lepic's father does not care about him one way or the other, and his mother openly hates him. Lepic is subjected to daily humiliations, but uses cunning and wit to maintain his dignity and survive the adult world. The book is notable for its wit and irony, and became a classic of French literature. In 1900 Renard adapted *Poil de Carrotte* into a play with the help of Andre Antoine, a groundbreaking theatre director.

In 1904, Renard was elected mayor of Chitry, his hometown. In 1907 he was inducted into the Goncourt Literary Society, or Academie Goncourt, with the help of his friend Octave Mirbeau. The Goncourt Society was founded in 1903 as an alternative to the French Academy, the preeminent literary society in Paris at the time. The Goncourt Society awards an annual prize for fiction in several categories, and Renard's appointment solidified his status as a literary celebrity in Paris. In 1925, Renard's private journal, which spanned the years 1887 to 1910, was published. It is widely considered a masterwork of introspection and humor, and provides insights into the literary scene in Paris at the turn of the 20th century.

Renard's work inspired many other writers of the early 20th century; in particular Somerset Maugham decided to publish his own journals as *The Writer's Notebook* after reading Renard's journals. In the introduction, Maugham praised Renard as the inspiration for the work.

Renard died in on May 22, 1910, in Paris.

Hopefully Not a Bore

"A bore is a man who, when you ask him how he is, tells you."

Bert Leston Taylor was a poet, journalist, and humorist. He wrote a column for the Chicago Tribune *that helped catapult the newspaper to national acclaim during the Chicago Renaissance of the early 20th century.*

✳ ✳ ✳ ✳

BERT LESTON TAYLOR was born November 13, 1866, in Goshen Massachusetts. When he was a boy, his family moved to New York, where Taylor attended public school. He studied law at New York University in 1881–82 but found it unrewarding and decided to pursue a career in journalism instead. Taylor founded a magazine, *The Aerolite*, but it was unsuccessful. He moved around the country, working for newspapers in Vermont, New Hampshire, and Minnesota.

In 1899 Taylor and his wife, Emma Bonner, moved to Chicago, where he began writing a column for the *Chicago Journal*. In 1901, he was hired by the *Chicago Tribune*, where he wrote a column titled "A Line o' Type or Two." Taylor wrote the column until 1903, when his family moved to Connecticut, where he became a contributing editor to the humorous magazine *Puck*.

Without Taylor's column, the *Tribune* was losing readership, and they made him a very lucrative offer to lure him back. He returned in 1909, and continued writing for the newspaper, which he would do for the rest of his life. His writing was sharp and satirical, and he used a polished style that helped elevate the journalistic standards of the early 20th century.

He died in Chicago on March 19, 1921.

Becoming Indispensable

"What another would have done as well as you, do not do it. What another would have said as well as you, do not say it; written as well, do not write it. Be faithful to that which exists nowhere but in yourself—and thus make yourself indispensable."

A French humanist, philosopher and writer, André Gide received the Nobel Prize for Literature in 1947 for his many works on the human condition.

✳ ✳ ✳ ✳

ANDRÉ PAUL GUILLAUME Gide was born in Paris, France, on November 22, 1869, an only child. He was sent to boarding school in Paris, but ill health soon forced him to return home. He was home-schooled by his governess and private tutors. In 1887 he returned to the École Alsacienne where he studied for his baccalaureate examination, which he passed in 1889. He published his first work, an autobiographical work titled *The Notebooks of André Walter*. It was written in the first person, which Gide would use regularly in his later writing.

Early Work and Sexuality

In 1891, Gide began attending Stéphane Mallarmé's "Tuesday Evenings," where he was exposed to the French Symbolist movement, an art movement that had origins in the gothic component of Romanticism. Gide wrote several books in the Symbolist style, including *Narcissus* in 1891 and *The Lovers' Attempt* in 1893. He travelled to North Africa in 1893, and his exposure to a very different set of ethical and moral standards helped him rebel against the strict Victorian mores he felt constrained by in France.

Part of this rebellion was a growing acceptance of his homosexuality. He wrote "Fruits of the Earth," a lyrical poem that discusses his release from the fear of sin and his acknowledgment that he had to follow his impulses. Upon returning to France in 1894, however, he felt once again smothered by the strict conventions of Europe. He went back to North Africa that year, and met Oscar Wilde and Alfred Douglas, who advised him to accept his sexuality.

In 1895, Gide returned to France when his mother died. That fall, he married his cousin Madeleine, although they never consummated the marriage. At the turn of the century he began to gain recognition as a talented literary critic. In 1908 he founded *The New France Review*, a literary journal that featured many of the leading writers for the next thirty years. During World War I, he volunteered for the Red Cross, in Paris, and following the war he returned home and began writing.

Travels and Later Works

Gide had begun keeping a journal as a young man, and he began writing his autobiography in 1916. In 1918, he wrote *Corydon*, a defense of homosexuality that showed he had finally reconciled himself with his sexuality. The publication was a disaster, however, as many of his colleagues and even his closest friends publically disavowed him. He and his wife became estranged, and he found himself largely isolated.

Beginning in 1925, Gide travelled extensively, and published books about several of the places he visited, including French Equatorial Africa and the U.S.S.R. In his books *Return from the U.S.S.R.* and *Afterthoughts* on the U.S.S.R. he expressed disillusionment in the Soviet system. His 1926 novel *The Counterfeiters* explores the corrupting influences on a group of schoolboys.

In 1938, his wife fell ill, and they reconciled before she died. In 1942, Gide returned to North Africa, where he wrote *Theseus*, which examined the value of the past and of tradition. In 1947 Oxford conferred a Doctor of Letters on Gide, and the same year he received the Nobel Prize for Literature. In 1950 he published the final volume of his *Journal*, which spanned more than sixty years of his life. He died on February 19, 1951 in Paris.

"Sin is whatever obscures the soul."

The "Great Man" Theory of History

"The history of the world is but the biography of great men."

Thomas Carlyle was one of the great Scottish philosophers of the 19th century. His major works include a biography of Frederick the Great and a history of the French Revolution, and he conceived of the (later much disputed) idea of the historical Hero figure as the catalyst for major events.

✳   ✳   ✳   ✳

THOMAS CARLYLE WAS born in Galloway, Scotland, on December 4, 1795. His father, a strict Calvinist, educated him as a young man and had a significant impact on his philosophical development. In 1809, Carlyle enrolled in the University of Edinburgh, intending to study theology and later to join the clergy. While at Edinburgh, however, he became interested in studying mathematics and education. He became interested in the works of Goethe, and translated his novel

Wilhelm Meister's Apprenticeship into English. As his interests shifted, Carlyle ultimately abandoned his plans to go into the ministry, choosing instead to become a writer.

In 1826, Carlyle married Jane Welsh, who had been introduced to him by a mutual friend. While they remained married until Carlyle's death, they fought regularly. Their relationship is one of the most famous of any two literary figures; it is chronicled by thousands of letters they wrote one another. While they were very much in love with each other, they were regularly on bad terms and fought often. After a number of years, they became increasingly estranged from one another. The couple first lived in rural Scotland, but later moved to London, where they hosted social parties for fellow literary figures and intellectuals.

The French Revolution and Other Work

In the mid-1830s, Carlyle began to publish his essays in *Fraser's Magazine* to some success, but he ultimately became famous for his book *The French Revolution: A History*, published in 1837. The three-volume work was unique for its dramatic prose and bringing together multiple perspectives on the Revolution. The *History* is a passionate account of the Revolution, and much of it is written in the present tense, which adds an air of immediacy to the work. Carlyle began exploring his ideas regarding the role of "heroes" in historical events in the *History*. He believed that these individuals were necessary to take charge of the societal forces that will lead to progress and revolutions.

He would explore these ideas in his later books. *On Heroes, Hero-Worship, and the Heroic in History* was published in 1841; it was a litany of "heroic" figures through history, ranging from Odin and Muhammad to Oliver Cromwell and Rousseau. In *Past and Present*, published in 1843, he examines medieval history and discusses 19th century British society, arguing that the ruling class must become heroic in order to elevate England and help guide the nation. He also wrote lengthy biographies of Cromwell and Frederick the Great, both of whom he considered examples of the historical hero who took extraordinary action when historical circumstances warranted it. These biographies took an immense toll on Carlyle; he often referred to his experience writing the biography of Frederick the Great as his "Thirteen Years' War."

In a devastating blow to Carlyle, his wife Jane died unexpectedly in 1866. He partially retired, splitting his time between Edinburgh and London, and did produce another major historical work. He wrote *Reminiscences of Jane Welsh Carlyle* during his later years; the work was published posthumously. Following a long period of mourning his wife, Carlyle died in London on February 5, 1881, and was buried beside his parents in his boyhood home in Scotland.

"A well-written Life is almost as rare as a well-spent one."

—Thomas Carlyle

"I can see that the Lady has a genius for ruling, whilst I have a genius for not being ruled."

—Jane Welsh Carlyle

"A positive engagement to marry a certain person at a certain time, at all haps and hazards, I have always considered the most ridiculous thing on earth."

—Jane Welsh Carlyle

The Original Mid-Life Crisis?

"In the middle of the journey of our life I came to myself in a dark wood where the straight way was lost."

Dante's Divine Comedy, *a masterpiece of world literature, is considered the greatest piece of literature ever to be composed in the Italian language.*

✳   ✳   ✳   ✳

DANTE ALIGHIERI WAS born in about 1265 in the Republic of Florence. His family's involvement in the politics of the Florentine Republic would later feature in Dante's *Divine Comedy*. His mother died when he was a very young child. When he was a teenager, he was set up in an arranged marriage to Gemma Donati, but he was already in love with Beatrice Portinari. She would be a major influence on Dante. He met her when she was nine years old, and Dante later wrote that he fell in love at first sight. Beatrice died suddenly in 1290, and Dante wrote *The New Life*, his first book of poetry, in which he described his love for her.

Dante began studying philosophy and the politics of Florence; the city at the time was the center of a political struggle between the Holy Roman Empire and Florentine Republicans. Dante was appointed to a position as a civil servant, but in 1302 he fell into disfavor with the power faction allied to the Pope, and was exiled. He travelled to Bologna in 1304, where he began envisioning *The Divine Comedy*. In 1306, he was banished from Bologna along with other exiles from Florence, and settled in Padua.

The Divine Comedy

In 1312 Dante travelled to Pisa, where a new Holy Roman Emperor was named that same year. He began working on *The Divine Comedy* in earnest that year, and finished the *Inferno*, the first part of the epic poem, in 1314. He settled in Ravenna in

1317 and spent the next four years working on the second and third parts, *Purgatorio* and *Paradiso*.

The Divine Comedy describes a journey through Hell, Purgatory, and Heaven. The poem is presented from the first person and takes place over the course of Good Friday through the Wednesday after Easter in the year 1300. Dante is guided by the Roman poet Virgil through Hell and Purgatory, and through heaven by Beatrice.

Each of the realms is divided into ten sections: there are nine circles of Hell, plus Satan's realm; nine rings of Purgatory, plus the Garden of Eden; and nine levels of Heaven, plus God's realm. Each circle of Hell is reserved for a different type of sinner, and each consisting of different torments. Each level of Purgatory likewise has different kinds of suffering. As he is guided through Heaven by Beatrice, he meets revered characters from Christian history, such as King Solomon, St Thomas Aquinas, and Dante's own ancestors. The *Divine Comedy* ends as Dante encounters the Holy Trinity of God.

The *Comedy* was intended to be both a warning against immoral behavior and a commentary on the political factions that had exiled him from Florence in 1300. It remains the preeminent work of literature ever written in the Italian language, and it helped elevate the Tuscan dialect to the standardized version of Italian.

Dante completed *The Divine Comedy* in 1320. He died there in September of the following year when he was on his way back to Ravenna following a diplomatic mission to Venice. While no manuscript of his own survives, hundreds of copies of the *Comedy* from the 14th and 15th centuries do.

"All hope abandon, ye who enter here!"

Winning a Victory for Humanity

"Be ashamed to die until you have won some victory for humanity."

Born into poverty and largely self-taught, Horace Mann revolutionized the public education system in the United States in the early 19th century.

✻   ✻   ✻   ✻

H ORACE MANN WAS born on May 4, 1796 in Franklin, Massachusetts. His family was extremely poor, and Mann was able to attend school for less than two months a year while he was growing up. He learned to read and write, and spent most of his free time at the town library, where he read almost every book they had. When he was twenty, Mann was admitted to Brown University, where he became interested in political science, social reform, and education. At his graduation, he delivered a commencement address that stressed the importance of education and philanthropy for further advancing the human race.

Political Career

After graduating, Mann passed the Massachusetts Bar and practiced law for a number of years. In 1827, he ran successfully for the State House of Representatives, where he served until 1833. In 1835, he was elected to the State Senate, and was made the President of the Senate in 1836. His primary goals as a legislator were the improvement of Massachusetts' infrastructure and the building of railroad lines and canals to advance commercial opportunities and modernize the rural areas of the state. The educational system of Massachusetts, which had been established in 1647, was struggling, and Mann was one of the leaders of an education reform movement. In 1837, he helped create the Massachusetts State Board of Education, and served as its general secretary. It was one of the first such institutions in the United States.

The Board was not well funded, but Mann was an effective leader. In 1838 he began publishing the *Common School Journal*, one of the first periodicals about public education in the nation. The *Journal* promoted his ideas about educational reform, and provided advice to teachers. After visiting Europe to learn more about public education systems, he promoted a version of public education based on the Prussian school system.

Mann's Educational Principles

Mann began developing a set of educational principles that, while controversial at the time, became extremely influential in public school in the 19th century. His six principles maintained that Citizens cannot be both ignorant and free; the public should finance, control and maintain education; public schools should welcome children from varying socioeconomic backgrounds; public education must not favor one religion over another; education should promote the tenets of a free society; and teachers should be highly trained professionals. In order to fulfill the sixth principle, Mann promoted the establishment of "Normal School" where teachers could be trained to follow these guidelines. The first of these schools was established in 1839 in Lexington.

Mann's principles ignited a fierce controversy and drew the ire of both sides of the political spectrum. The clergy was incensed over the removal of religion from the classroom, and many politicians believed the government should not have so much control over local schools. But Mann ultimately prevailed when his methods were borne out by the improved outcomes at Massachusetts public schools. His efforts are now widely recognized as having spurred the genesis of the modern public education system.

In 1848, Mann was elected to the U.S. House of Representatives in 1848, serving until 1853, when he became the president of Antioch College in Ohio. He died on August 2, 1859.

A Fine and Private Place

A poet and Member of Parliament, Andrew Marvell was known during his life for his crafty political maneuvers following the Restoration. A collection of his poems was published posthumously and remains among the best English poetry of the 17th century.

✳ ✳ ✳ ✳

ANDREW MARVELL WAS born in Yorkshire on March 31, 1621. He attended the Hull Grammar School, and in 1633 he went to Trinity College, Cambridge. His first poems were published in the *Musa Cantabrigiensis* when Marvell was only sixteen. He received his bachelor's of arts in 1638, and remained in residence at Cambridge until 1640. He travelled through Europe from 1642 to 1646 while the English Civil Wars were raging. Returning to England following Cromwell's victory, he wrote the bulk of his poetry in the 1650s. Marvell wrote the poem he is best remembered for, "To His Coy Mistress," in this period, although it would not be published until after his death. It remains one of the best examples of the metaphysical poetry of the time, which emphasized the spoken quality of the verse over its lyrical value. It contains the oft-quoted lines, "The grave's a fine and private place, / But none, I think, do there embrace."

In 1653 he befriended John Milton, who secured him a job as the Assistant Latin Secretary to the Council of State. In 1659, Marvell was elected to Parliament. Following the Restoration of the English monarchy, Marvell managed to convince the Crown not to execute Milton, who had published a number of articles denouncing the monarchy and supporting Cromwell. Marvell wrote a poem for the introduction of Milton's *Paradise Lost* in 1667.

Marvell died on 16 August, 1678. His *Miscellaneous Poems* were printed posthumously in 1681.

"Let us roll all our strength and all
Our sweetness up into one ball,
And tear our pleasures with rough strife
Through the iron gates of life:
Thus, though we cannot make our sun
Stand still, yet we will make him run."

A Wish after Death

"When I am dead, my dearest, sing no sad songs for me."

✳   ✳   ✳   ✳

CHRISTINA GEORGINA ROSSETTI was born in London on December 5, 1830, to a family of poets and artists. She showed an early talent, dictating her first story to her mother when she was a child. Her parents educated her at home, and she was an avid reader. Her parents' circle of friends included many Italian artists and writers, who often visited the home. Christina attended school briefly until a nervous breakdown forced her to leave at fourteen. When she was eighteen she became engaged to the painter James Collinson, but they broke off the engagement when he converted to Roman Catholicism.

Rossetti began writing poetry when she was twelve, and began writing experimental verse in 1847. She published her first poems in 1848 in *The Anatheum,* a literary journal. She contributed regularly to several other literary journals of the time, and published her first collection of poetry, *Goblin Market and Other Poems,* in 1862. "Song" comes from that collection and is still quoted today after funerals and memorials.

The collection was very well received and established her reputation as the best female poet in Europe at the time, earning praise from Tennyson and other leading poets.

Rosetti published eight collections of poetry and nursery rhymes during her lifetime, as well as two works of prose and several nonfiction works. Her wide circle of friends included many of the famous writers of the day, including Charles Dodgson (Lewis Carroll) and Elizabeth Jennings. Rossetti died on December 29, 1894.

"Song"

When I am dead, my dearest,
Sing no sad songs for me;
Plant thou no roses at my head,
Nor shady cypress tree:
Be the green grass above me
With showers and dewdrops wet;
And if thou wilt, remember,
And if thou wilt, forget.
I shall not see the shadows,
I shall not feel the rain;
I shall not hear the nightingale
Sing on, as if in pain:
And dreaming through the twilight
That doth not rise nor set,
Haply I may remember,
And haply may forget.

Chapter 9

Love and Marriage

Whither Thou Goest

A popular wedding reading actually comes from the words the Biblical figure of Ruth spoke to her mother-in-law Naomi.

✳   ✳   ✳   ✳

RUTH WAS A gentile woman, a Moabite to be exact. The Moabites were descendents of Abraham's nephew Lot. Lot escaped the destruction of the cities of Sodom and Gomorrah by fleeing to a tiny town called Zoar and then to the mountains, living in caves with his two daughters. Afraid there was no hope for carrying on their family line because of their isolation, Lot's daughters impregnated themselves by their dad after getting him drunk on a couple of occasions. The eldest daughter named her son Moab, which may literally mean "from father." And while that reality may mess with our moral sensibilities, it is nonetheless where the Moabite people came from.

The most notable thing about Ruth, historically speaking, is that her name appears in the genealogy of Christ, as recorded in Matthew 1. Some might be surprised at the presence of gentile blood in the lineage of Jesus, but even more surprising, perhaps, is that Rahab is listed too. Rahab was Ruth's second mother-in-law, a gentile woman who had been assimilated into the Israelite community after her career ended as a prostitute in the city of Jericho. Because she had helped the Israelite spies hide from Jericho's authorities, Rahab was rewarded by being spared when God caused the city walls to collapse. She married a man named Salmon and gave birth to Boaz, who became Ruth's second husband. This distinction of being included in Christ's ancestry—an honor accorded to both Ruth and Rahab—seems to clearly underscore God's divine intention to extend his grace and mercy to Jew and gentile alike.

Ruth's own story is one of loyalty and love; romantic and heartwarming, it comes complete with tragic beginning and happy ending. The most famous passage in the book is still used in some wedding ceremonies today: "Where you go, I will go; where you lodge, I will lodge; your people shall be my people, and your God my God" (1:16). This is not, however, Ruth's wedding vow to her second husband, Boaz, but her pledge of loyalty to stay with her first mother-in-law, Naomi, whose widowhood forced her to return home to Israel from the land of Moab.

Though Ruth had also been widowed when her own husband (Naomi's son) died, Ruth chose to cling to Naomi rather than remain with her own people. Her gift of devotion and love to Naomi went far beyond anything Naomi could have expected or even hoped. Ultimately, Ruth's marriage to Boaz is the fairy-tale ending of the story. Boaz nobly "redeems" Ruth and Naomi from poverty and reestablishes Naomi's family heritage (as well as her joy) through Obed, the first son born to Boaz and Ruth. The rest is history, and the four-chapter book bearing Ruth's name can be read in one sitting.

African Wedding Customs

There's an African proverb that says, "A man without a wife is like a vase without flowers."

❊   ❊   ❊   ❊

M ARRIAGE IN NEARLY every corner of Africa is considered an integral part of life, and many wedding rituals there have survived centuries. Because the African diaspora is so vast, traditions vary from region to region. The beauty of some of the rituals has enticed various Western couples with African roots to incorporate them into their own weddings.

Ethiopia

Many African weddings begin with the paperwork, so to speak. Since a lot of marriages are still arranged (or at least seen as political moves), dowries are paid, and multiple meetings may take place between the bride's and the groom's family. This is the case for certain tribes in Ethiopia, where once the marriage has been approved and the dowry paid, the men in the groom's party go to the house of the bride for a mock standoff. The women "guard" the house, and the men must sing and entertain the women for passage.

Kenya

Kenya's Swahili Muslims give weddings a lot of attention. For a full week surrounding the big day, participants live it up with singing, dancing, and feasting. But the men and the women party separately, which pleases both groups looking for a little time away from each other. After the public ceremony, the bride goes off with the women again, this time to learn more about how to be a proper wife before the marriage begins. The women wear their best jewelry to this party and sport fancy hairdos for the occasion, which includes live music and lots of good food.

Namibia

If you're a member of the Himba people and happen to be a bride, sleep with one eye open. Members of the community kidnap a bride before the ceremony and dress her in a ceremonial leather headdress. Once the ceremony is complete, the bride is brought into the groom's house where the family tells her what her responsibilities will be as the wife. After that, they anoint her with butterfat from cows, which shows that she has been accepted into the family. Gee, thanks!

Nigeria

In this West African country, brides stay sequestered in a special hut before the wedding. The groom must bring tobacco and chickens to all the guests that have gathered outside. Once they're satiated, the groom is allowed to come inside, and the marriage is official. The next day, a goat is slaughtered, and the blood is poured over the threshold. Then, refreshingly, the bride's mother asks her daughter if she's pleased with her husband. If she is, a party commences with lots of food and dancing. Guests at the party pay a penny to see the bride's face and give her sandalwood to rub on her body. (It should also be noted that ceremonies with Western influences are gaining in popularity in Nigeria, too.)

Senegal

To propose in Senegal, you'll need some money and some kola nuts. A hopeful groom's family sends these items to the bride's family. If the family accepts the proposal, the kola nuts (which were once used in the making of Coca-Cola) are distributed to friends and family as a way of announcing the marriage. Before the wedding day, the groom's family throws a big party for the bride-to-be, welcoming her into their circle. When it's time for the ceremony, the groom's house is used, and guests bring gifts of spices, rice, and beverages, among other things. With the money she collects, the bride is expected to buy cooking utensils, which she takes with her to her new husband's home.

Old Lovers

Writing plays during Shakespeare's time must have been a daunting task. John Webster managed quite successfully, becoming known for his dark stories and brilliant dialogue.

✳ ✳ ✳ ✳

JOHN WEBSTER WAS the greatest playwright of the Shakespeare Era not named William Shakespeare. And there's no dishonor in that. Best known for his dark tragedies despite an ability to write gripping comedies equally well, Webster wrote in the early 1600s. Some of his plays, like many of Shakespeare's, are still performed today.

Wrote 19th Century playwright and critic Algernon Charles Swineburne about the Shakespearean Age: "The crowning gift of imagination, the power to make us realize that thus and not otherwise it was, that thus and not otherwise it must have been, was given—except by exceptional fits and starts—to none of the poets of their time but only to Shakespeare and to Webster."

Webster's most lasting contributions to the genre were tragedies *The White Devil* and *The Duchess of Malfi*. The former first reached the stage in 1612 and the latter some two years later. They attained moderate success at the time but advanced in critical stature during the 20th Century. Their macabre tone had the likes of T.S. Eliot contending that Webster could always see "the skull beneath the skin."

On Relationships

In another of his famous plays, *Westward Ho* (circa 1605), one of the characters claims that "old soldiers, sweetheart, are surest, and old lovers are soundest." The end of the line has been oft quoted as a form of relationship advice through the years—especially by those with a few years of experience on their resumes.

The play itself was a "city comedy" and satire about life in London at a time when the city was evolving from its walled, medieval character to a more modern and progressive place. It became the subject of "counter satire" when George Chapman, Ben Jonson, and John Marston published *Eastward Ho*, which featured enough overt anti-Scottish sentiment that King James I was offended and had Chapman and Jonson arrested. Both plays derive their titles from the shouts of the boatmen who carried passengers from one side of the Thames to the other.

Webster certainly did not take personal advice from his own character's line. Old lovers may be soundest, but he married 17-year-old Sara Peniall in 1606. Not much more is known about his personal life. In fact, the dates of his birth and death have been debated.

What is known is that he collaborated with prolific writer Thomas Dekker on the writing of *Westward Ho*, and that it was performed at least a year or two before it was actually published. After Chapman, Jonson, and Marston countered with *Eastward Ho*, Webster and Dekker returned the favor with *Northward Ho*, completing a satirical trilogy that predated the impactful tragedies Webster would go on to write.

In addition to the lasting line about old lovers and the fact *The White Devil* and *The Duchess of Malfi* continue to be performed in theaters, Webster has lived on via modern cultural references. He has been portrayed in documentaries about the Shakespearean Era, and *The White Devil* and *The Duchess of Malfi* were mentioned in the 1983 song "My White Devil" by English rock group Echo & The Bunnymen.

To My Dear and Loving Husband

Anne Bradstreet's lines to her husband from centuries ago still resonate with people in love today.

✳   ✳   ✳   ✳

ANNE BRADSTREET WAS an early American poet—from the days before the United States even existed! She was born in 1612 in England to a Puritan family. Anne, her husband Simon, and Anne's parents arrived in America in 1630 and settled in Massachusetts.

Anne's responsibilities were many: she and her husband raised eight children, in a less than comfortable colonial setting. At one point her family's home burned down, leaving them homeless, and Bradstreet suffered from ill health. But she found time to write poetry—about her life, about her relationship with God, about her religious and emotional struggles.

In 1647, her brother -in-law took her manuscript of poetry to London, where it was published as *The Tenth Muse Lately Sprung Up in America*. The author was listed as "a Gentlewoman of those Parts".

Bradstreet wrote multiple poems to and about her husband and children. Perhaps the most famous is "To My Dear and Loving Husband," still read at weddings today.

If ever two were one, then surely we.
If ever man were lov'd by wife, then thee;
If ever wife was happy in a man,
Compare with me ye women if you can.
I prize thy love more than whole Mines of Gold,
Or all the riches that the East doth hold.
My love is such that Rivers cannot quench,
Nor ought but love from thee, give recompence.
Thy love is such I can no way repay,
The heavens reward thee manifold I pray.
Then while we live, in love lets so persevere,
That when we live no more, we may live ever.

Writing of Life and Love

"It is easier to be a lover than a husband, for the same reason that it is more difficult to be witty every day, than to say bright things from time to time."

French writer Honoré de Balzac wrote of life, influenced Realism, and had an interesting grand romance of his own.

✳   ✳   ✳   ✳

Honoré de Balzac was born in France in 1799. A prolific novelist, playwright, and essayist, he was an early writer in the Realism movement, which attempted to depict humans realistically: as fascinating, dynamic, sometimes flawed individuals. His magnum opus, *La Comedie humaine*, was a series of linked novels, stories, and essays depicting French society.

Balzac's own marriage could come from a story. He entered into a correspondence with a woman who wrote him a letter in response to one of his works. The first letter was sent anonymously, but it so intrigued Balzac that he put out an advertisement to try to encourage the writer to contact him again—sort of an early version of Craiglist's missed connections! The writer, a married Polish noblewoman named Ewelina Hańska, did respond, and they began a correspondence that would last 15 years. After Hańska was widowed in 1841, she and Balzac pursued a romantic relationship. The road to marriage was circuitous due to financial setbacks and various objections from outside. In 1850, the couple married. Balzac, in poor health, died only five months later. Victor Hugo acted as the eulogist at his funeral.

Balzac left behind a rich legacy of works, a number of unfinished and planned works, and a fascinating life story.

Quotes from Balzac

"Marriage is a fight to the death, before which the wedded couple ask a blessing from heaven, because it is the rashest of all undertakings to swear eternal love; the fight at once commences and victory, that is to say liberty, remains in the hands of the cleverer of the two."

— *Physiologie du Mariage*

"The most virtuous women have in them something that is never chaste."

—*Physiologie du Mariage*

"Love is the most melodious of all harmonies and the sentiment of love is innate."

— *Physiologie du Mariage*

"The more a man judges, the less he loves."

— *Physiologie du Mariage*

"Our heart is a treasury; if you pour out all its wealth at once, you are bankrupt. We show no more mercy to the affection that reveals its utmost extent than we do to another kind of prodigal who has not a penny left."

— *LE PÈRE GORIOT*

"Girls are apt to imagine noble and enchanting and totally imaginary figures in their own minds; they have fanciful extravagant ideas about men, and sentiment, and life; and then they innocently endow somebody or other with all the perfections for their daydreams, and put their trust in him."

—*A WOMAN OF THIRTY*

"Love has its own instinct, finding the way to the heart, as the feeblest insect finds the way to its flower, with a will which nothing can dismay nor turn aside."

—*A WOMAN OF THIRTY*

One Happiness in Life

"There is only one happiness in life, to love and be loved."

✳ ✳ ✳ ✳

AMANTINE-LUCILE-AURORE DUPIN WAS born in Paris, France, in 1804. She lived a fascinating, free-spirited life. In 1822, she married Casimir Dudevant, and they had two children together. In 1831, though, she left her husband; they were legally separated in 1835. In 1831, she also published her first stories, collaborations with a romantic liaison, Jules Sandeau, signed Jules Sand. In 1832, she published her first novel, *Indiana*, under the pen name George Sand.

Sand wrote multiple novels, specializing in pastoral novels about the countryside, and other works, including plays and essays. She was also known for her lifestyle: she wore men's clothes and went to places to which women usually didn't, and she had a string of lovers, including Frédéric Chopin.

Sand died at the age of 71.

Quotes from George Sand

"Life resembles a novel more often than novels resemble life."

—*METELLA*

"Immodest creature, you do not want a woman who will accept your faults, you want the one who pretends you are faultless – one who will caress the hand that strikes her and kiss the lips that lie to her."

—*LETTER*

"In the stormy days of our youth, we imagine that solitude is a sure refuge from the assaults of life, a certain balm for the wounds of battle. This is a serious mistake, and experience teaches us that, if we cannot live in peace with our fellow-men, neither romantic raptures nor aesthetic enjoyment will ever fill the abyss gaping at the bottom of our hearts."

—*WINTER IN MAJORCA*

"Life in common among people who love each other is the ideal of happiness."

—*HISTOIRE DE MA VIE*

"Art for the sake of art itself is an idle sentence. Art for the sake of truth, for the sake of what is beautiful and good — that is the creed I seek."

—*LETTER*

Love Amongst the Poets

Victorian Poets Robert Browning and Elizabeth Barrett Browning shared a common love for writing, and each other.

✳ ✳ ✳ ✳

ELIZABETH MOULTON-BARRETT WAS born in 1806. She wrote poetry from a young age, possibly as young as 4 years old. A manuscript poem from the time when she was six or eight still exists. She was a prodigious reader and writer, and her love of writing was encouraged by her parents, who compiled her collections. She persisted in writing despite chronic health problems, and began publishing her poetry, as well as translations and essays.

Her 1844 collection, *Poems*, garnered popular attention. One of her admirers was Robert Browning. Born in 1812, he was himself a poet and playwright—though her popularity at the time outstripped his.

They courted in secret because they feared her father's disapproval. Indeed, when they married privately, he was upset and disinherited his daughter, and the couple decamped to Italy. They remained in Italy throughout their marriage and the birth of their son, Pen. In 1850 Barrett Browning published *Sonnets from the Portuguese*, which includes Sonnet 43 with its famous opening lines, "How do I love thee? Let me count the ways." Her marriage is also seen to have influenced *Aurora Leigh*, an epic poem about a female writer balancing writing and love.

Though Robert Browning penned the famous quote, "Grow old along with me! / The best is yet to be" in the poem "Rabbi Ben Ezra," one of his dramatic monologues, the couple did not have that opportunity. Elizabeth passed away in 1861 at the age of 55, after a period of ill health; Robert died in 1889.

Here are some of her sonnets on romantic love.

Sonnet 14

If thou must love me, let it be for nought
Except for love's sake only. Do not say
"I love her for her smile —her look —her way
Of speaking gently,—for a trick of thought
That falls in well with mine, and certes brought
A sense of pleasant ease on such a day"
For these things in themselves, Beloved, may
Be changed, or change for thee,—and love, so wrought,
May be unwrought so. Neither love me for
Thine own dear pity's wiping my cheeks dry,—
A creature might forget to weep, who bore
Thy comfort long, and lose thy love thereby!
But love me for love's sake, that evermore
Thou may'st love on, through love's eternity.

Sonnet 22

When our two souls stand up erect and strong,
Face to face, silent, drawing nigh and nigher,
Until the lengthening wings break into fire
At either curvèd point,—what bitter wrong
Can the earth do to us, that we should not long
Be here contented? Think. In mounting higher,
The angels would press on us and aspire
To drop some golden orb of perfect song
Into our deep, dear silence. Let us stay
Rather on earth, Belovèd,—where the unfit
Contrarious moods of men recoil away
And isolate pure spirits, and permit
A place to stand and love in for a day,
With darkness and the death-hour rounding it.

Sonnet 43

How do I love thee? Let me count the ways.
I love thee to the depth and breadth and height
My soul can reach, when feeling out of sight
For the ends of Being and ideal Grace.
I love thee to the level of everyday's
Most quiet need, by sun and candlelight.
I love thee freely, as men strive for Right;
I love thee purely, as they turn from Praise.
I love thee with the passion put to use
In my old griefs, and with my childhood's faith.
I love thee with a love I seemed to lose
With my lost saints,—I love thee with the breath,
Smiles, tears, of all my life!—and, if God choose,
I shall but love thee better after death.

Who Really Discovered the 'Way to a Man's Heart'?

Fanny Fern has been credited with coining the phrase that lets women know—conventionally speaking, of course—the way to a man's heart. However, the saying may have originated in Great Britain a few years earlier.

✳ ✳ ✳ ✳

YEARS BEFORE MEDICAL science developed alternate ways to access the human body's blood-pumping mechanism, it was determined—quite probably by a woman—that the best way to reach a man's heart is through his stomach. Independent research over many decades has been unable to verify this with 100% certainty, although there is empirical evidence suggesting its truth.

Fanny Fern, an American children's author, humor writer, and newspaper columnist in the 19th Century, is most widely credited with proclaiming that the way to a man's heart is through his stomach. However, instances of the reference, or at least very close approximations, have been uncovered in literature that predates Fern.

The *Oxford Dictionary of Proverbs*, for example, cites John Adams as the author of an 1814 letter that said, "The shortest road to men's hearts is down their throats." Fern was not quite 3 years old at the time, so presumably had no impact on Adams' observation.

Dinah Mulock, on the other hand, was a contemporary of Fern's when she authored the quote, "The way to an Englishman's heart is through his stomach," although clearly men from other nations also react well to a delicious, home-cooked meal.

Fern Made a Name

Whether or not she first penned the famous saying, Fern enjoyed many significant accomplishments through her writing career. She was born Sara Payson Willis in Portland, Maine. Her father was a newspaper owner and two of her siblings also went on to achieve fame. Older brother Nathaniel Parker Willis grew up to be a renowned journalist and magazine owner (*Home Journal*), while her younger brother Richard Storrs Willis became a musician and wrote the melody for "It Came Upon the Midnight Clear."

Sara chose the pen name Fanny Fern because it conjured the childhood memory of her mother picking ferns. She eventually stuck with it outside of her writing endeavors as well.

Fern was a skilled and prolific writer who first made her name writing magazine articles and later authored books. Her first, *Fern Leaves,* was published in 1853 and became a bestseller. It sold 46,000 copies in its first four months on bookshelves, giving her enough wealth to purchase a home in Brooklyn.

By 1855, she was a *New York Ledger* columnist making $100 a week—an unheard-of sum for a journalist in that day, particularly a female one. Her column ran every week from January 1856 until two days after her death, following a six-year battle with cancer, in October 1872. During her great career, she also co-founded an organization for women writers and artists and was an ardent suffrage advocate.

Whether or not Fern first coined the phrase, she certainly used it at least once in her volumes of copy. By the mid-1800s, it had become an oft-cited maxim, appearing in New Hampshire and Virginia newspapers in the 1830s, in multiple books in the 1840s, and in countless tales from those days forward.

It can be argued that Fern either mastered the art of reaching a man's heart in this manner, or colossally failed at it. She herself was married three times.

A Satirical Look at Love

"Remember, it's as easy to marry a rich woman as a poor woman."

✳ ✳ ✳ ✳

MARRIAGE IN WILLIAM Makepeace Thackeray's day was quite often an exercise in social advancement. Men were expected to marry within their "class." For women, especially, marriage was a chance to set the stage for a good life. Love was frequently well down the list of priorities for finding a good— or at least suitable—spouse.

In *The History of Pendennis: His Fortunes and Misfortunes, His Friends and His Greatest Enemy* (1849), Thackeray offers the tale of the rural-born Arthur Pendennis, who moves to London in search of his place in society. His father has died, and Arthur is navigating two schools of thought in choosing a wife. His mother wants him to shirk the superficial pursuit of social standing and marry her ward, Laura Bell.

Meanwhile, the uncle Arthur reveres would rather see him marry a wealthy woman, reciting the aforementioned quote. After all, Major Pendennis assures, it's a "devilish deal pleasanter to sit down to a good dinner, than to a scrag of mutton in lodgings."

The plot was no stretch for Thackeray. He was born in Calcutta, India, in 1811 and lost his own father when he was 5 years old. He was sent to England for schooling, attending the Charterhouse School and Trinity College in Cambridge before embarking on his successful writing career. Thackeray had published an all-time classic satire of high societal greed and snobbery in his most popular work, *Vanity Fair*, in 1848.

Quotes from Thackeray
"I think I could be a good woman if I had five thousand a year."

—*VANITY FAIR*

"Let the man who has to make his fortune in life remember this maxim. Attacking is his only secret. Dare, and the world always yields: or, if it beat you sometimes, dare again, and it will succumb."

—*THE LUCK OF BARRY LYNDON*

"The world is a looking-glass, and gives back to every man the reflection of his own face. Frown at it, and it will in turn look sourly upon you; laugh at it and with it, and it is a jolly kind companion; and so let all young persons take their choice."

—*VANITY FAIR*

"This I set down as a positive truth. A woman with fair opportunities, and without a positive hump, may marry whom she likes."

—*VANITY FAIR*

"Some cynical Frenchman has said that there are two parties to a love-transaction: the one who loves and the other who condescends to be so treated."

—*VANITY FAIR*

"Mother is the name for God in the lips and hearts of little children."

—*VANITY FAIR*

'It is best to love wisely, no doubt; but to love foolishly is better than not to be able to love at all. Some of us can't: and are proud of our impotence, too."

—*THE HISTORY OF PENDERRIS*

Tolstoy Lived One of his Most Famous Lines

"Happy families are all alike; every unhappy family is unhappy in its own way."

The opening line of Anna Karenina is one of the most famous in all of literature. Its author, Leo Tolstoy, knew a thing or two about happiness and its opposite as it pertained to family life.

✳ ✳ ✳ ✳

RUSSIAN COUNT LEV Nikolayevich Tolstoy was unquestionably one of the greatest writers of all time. He would be in that category were it only for timeless classics *War and Peace* and *Anna Karenina*. That he gave the world other great novels, along with brilliant short stories, novellas, essays and plays during his 80-plus years of life (1828–1910) confirms his place among the very best who ever put one word after the next.

In love and happiness, however, Tolstoy had his struggles. The great artists often do, and the greatest ones turn their toils into wisdom for the ages.

In 1862, Tolstoy married Sophia Andreevna Behrs. He was 34 at the time; she was 18. Tolstoy is alleged to have given Sophia his diaries, recounting his previous sexual experience and past relationships, and the fact that one of his parents' servants had borne him a child. Though this got their marriage off to something of a rocky start, the couple was by all accounts happy in the early years.

Over the years, Leo and Sophia had 13 children. Five of them died during childhood. While Leo wrote, Sophia served as his proofreader and assistant, and she copied his manuscripts by hand. She also helped with the finances his work brought in. Sophia, however, had interests of her own that went unrealized. She wanted to pursue photography and music, but Leo seemed to have little interest.

Road Turns Rocky

Tolstoy Biographer A.N. Wilson described their marriage as one of the most miserable in the history of literature. Leah Bendavid-Val, who authored *Song Without Words: The Photographs and Diaries of Countess Sophia Tolstoy*, called it "love-hate." They were "very emotional, very passionate," Leah Bendavid-Val explained, "and their love was full and passionate and deep and rich—and so was their hatred. And unfortunately, the hatred seems to have won out in the end."

By the time Tolstoy opened *Anna Karenina* (1877) with the famous line proclaiming "all happy families are alike; each unhappy family is unhappy in its own way," his had long since fallen into the latter category. Critics note that the point of the line was to note that happy home lives tend to share certain qualities. In his, there were holes.

Verbal communication might have been one of the missing traits. Both Leo and Sophia embracing the written word as they did, they spelled out many of their thoughts to each other in their diaries rather than engaging in conversation. Leah Bendavid-Val pointed out that many of these revelations were things they did not dare say aloud in the presence of the other.

Sophia did not agree with some of Leo's beliefs as time wore on, particularly as those beliefs grew more radical toward the end of his life. She also became concerned that he had written a new will, and allegedly went searching for it. When he overheard her in his study, he grew outraged and decided to leave her. He boarded a train, became ill with pneumonia, and died shortly thereafter at age 82.

Wallace: In Praise of Motherhood

"Would that never storms assailed it,
Rainbows ever gently curled
For the hand that rocks the cradle
Is the hand that rules the world."

✳ ✳ ✳ ✳

WILLIAM ROSS WALLACE, a Kentucky-born poet with Scottish roots, lived and wrote in the 1800s. It was a time when child-raising was almost exclusively the domain of women, and his most famous poem remains a beautiful tribute to mothers everywhere.

"The Hand that Rocks the Cradle Is the Hand that Rules the World" was published in 1865, some 20 years into his writing career. Wallace's father, a minister, died when William was an infant, perhaps further sealing the bond between William and his mother. Wallace did his undergraduate studies at Indiana University and Hanover College, also in Indiana, and returned to his native Kentucky for law school.

His friend, Edgar Allen Poe, called Wallace "one of the very noblest of American poets." Wallace started his career as a lawyer in New York City before deciding to focus on his writing pursuits. He wrote for several magazines and newspapers, including the *New York Ledger* and *Louisville Daily Journal*.

Several of Wallace's poems gained acclaim, beginning in the 1840s, but none had the staying power of his heartfelt homage to motherhood. Each of its four stanzas concludes with line, "For the hand that rocks the cradle / Is the hand that rules the world." It has become an oft-quoted line in praise of mothers.

In 1992 *The Hand that Rocks the Cradle* also became a psychological thriller on the big screen. The latter, Wallace probably could have done without.

Arnold: Conflicted on Love

Thoughtful, intellectual, and serious, Matthew Arnold spent half his career writing poetry and the other half writing prose. The Englishman can be something of an acquired taste for some, but his legacy is unmistakable.

❋ ❋ ❋ ❋

AFTER BEGINNING HIS career as a teacher of the classics at the same school where his father once served as headmaster, Matthew Arnold took a job as a government school inspector. It was not what the aspiring poet wanted to do, ultimately, but it allowed him to travel his native England. Those experiences, combined with his passion for the pen, launched Arnold into the public eye—first as a poet and later as a masterful author of critical essays.

Arnold was a serious thinker, and his poetry reflects his intellectual, meditative nature. He wrote what he called "modern" poems. Some labeled him a sage writer—one who instructs and advises on social issues of the time, sometimes in a chastising manner.

His first three volumes of poetry, published between 1849 and '53, contain most of his lasting poetic works before virtually abandoning the art in favor of prose. However, one of his classics on love, "Dover Beach," was not published until 1867, some 16 years after it was written.

Though its most famous line ("Ah, love, let us be true to one another!") is sometimes uttered in a loving tone, the poem actually contradicts the positive message of another of his poems, "The Buried Life." In "Dover Beach," Arnold sends out a cry amid great darkness, writing of fighting, struggle, and confusion.

Dover Beach

The sea is calm tonight.
The tide is full, the moon lies fair
Upon the straits; on the French coast the light
Gleams and is gone; the cliffs of England stand,
Glimmering and vast, out in the tranquil bay.
Come to the window, sweet is the night-air!
Only, from the long line of spray
Where the sea meets the moon-blanched land,
Listen! you hear the grating roar
Of pebbles which the waves draw back, and fling,
At their return, up the high strand,
Begin, and cease, and then again begin,
With tremulous cadence slow, and bring
The eternal note of sadness in.

Sophocles long ago
Heard it on the Ægean, and it brought

Into his mind the turbid ebb and flow
Of human misery; we
Find also in the sound a thought,
Hearing it by this distant northern sea.

The Sea of Faith
Was once, too, at the full, and round earth's shore
Lay like the folds of a bright girdle furled.
But now I only hear
Its melancholy, long, withdrawing roar,
Retreating, to the breath
Of the night-wind, down the vast edges drear
And naked shingles of the world.

Ah, love, let us be true
To one another! for the world, which seems
To lie before us like a land of dreams,
So various, so beautiful, so new,
Hath really neither joy, nor love, nor light,
Nor certitude, nor peace, nor help for pain;
And we are here as on a darkling plain
Swept with confused alarms of struggle and flight,
Where ignorant armies clash by night.

Madame de Stael

Given a platform among the elites and intellectuals, Madame de Stael became one of the most important female figures of her time. Loathed by Napoleon and embraced by those who opposed him, she wrote and spoke of war, politics, and love.

✳ ✳ ✳ ✳

ANNE LOUISE GERMAINE de Stael, born Anne Louise Germaine Necker in Paris in 1766, had an important seat at the table almost from the outset. Her father, Jacques Necker, was a prominent Swiss banker who led national finance for King Louis XVI. Her mother hosted a very prominent salon in

Paris, where intellectuals gathered to discuss current events and share literature, tell stories, recite poetry and sing songs.

Surrounded by some of the brightest minds of the day, Anne Louise was afforded opportunities that most young girls could only dream about. She embraced them with vigor, developing strong political opinions, a love for literature, and a deep desire to be involved in the issues. As she grew up, she made sure she was part of the conversation.

On the arrangement of parents, Anne married Baron Eric de Stael-Holstein, the Swedish ambassador to Paris, in 1786. She was 20 and he was 36, and by all accounts—including her own—the relationship was never one of mutual love. They separated in 1797, though they remained married until the baron died in 1802.

To and From Paris, with Love

King Louis XVI and Marie Antoinette had a falling out with her father in the final days of the French monarchy, and Jacques was dismissed in 1789. It was the beginning of the French Revolution, and the Swedish embassy in Paris offered the family diplomatic asylum. Jacques and his family later took refuge at Lake Geneva, Switzerland.

Anne's writings, novels and literary criticism, favored dissent against the monarchy and developed a wide following. For obvious reasons, they were not popular among the establishment. She, too, fled. She returned to Paris in 1794, resumed hosting salons and continued to gain fame. It was in 1796 that Madame de Stael published "A Treatise on the Influence of the Passions," which included the lasting lines:

"Love is the whole history of a woman's life, it is but an episode in a man's."

The text truly came to define Madame de Stael's romantic life. She took an interest in men of stature and intellect throughout her life, but admitted that "I always loved my lovers more than they loved me." No one knew about her second marriage until after her death in 1817. It was to Albert Jean Michel de Rocca, 23 years her junior, and spanned the final six years of her life.

It was said that her one "true" love was novelist and politician Benjamin Constant, but they never married. And there were questions about the paternity of at least two of the four children she bore during her life.

One thing is certain: When Napoleon Bonaparte took power in 1799, it did not take long for him to begin viewing her as a nuisance at best—and a national threat at worst. Madame de Stael was seen as someone who taught people how to think for themselves, and the French leader was more interested in followers than thinkers.

Madame de Stael fled to Austria, Russia, Finland, Sweden and England between 1812 and '14, when Napoleon's fall prompted her return to Paris.

Her health began failing and she died at age 51.

Quotes from Madame de Stael

"A man must know how to defy opinion; a woman how to submit to it."

—*Delphine*

"We cease loving ourselves if no one loves us."

—*Sophie*

"Love is the emblem of eternity; it confounds all notion of time; effaces all memory of a beginning, all fear of an end: we fancy that we have always possessed what we love, so difficult is it to imagine how we could have lived without it."

—*Corinne*

Quotes from a Humorist

Jerome K. Jerome was a writer and humorist. Born in England in 1859, he became most famous for his travelogue, Three Men in a Boat (To Say Nothing of the Dog.) *But he also had a number of quotes on love worth remembering.*

✳   ✳   ✳   ✳

"Nothing—so it seems to me ... is more beautiful than the love that has weathered the storms of life. ... The love of the young for the young, that is the beginning of life. But the love of the old for the old, that is the beginning of—of things longer."

—"THE PASSING OF THE THIRD FLOOR BACK"

"Love is like the measles; we all have to go through it. Also like the measles, we take it only once ... No, we never sicken with love twice. Cupid spends no second arrow on the same heart."

—"ON BEING IN LOVE"

"A boy's love comes from a full heart; a man's is more often the result of a full stomach. Indeed, a man's sluggish current may not be called love, compared with the rushing fountain that wells up when a boy's heart is struck with the heavenly rod. If you would taste love, drink of the pure stream that youth pours out at your feet. Do not wait till it has become a muddy river before you stoop to catch its waves."

—"ON BEING IN LOVE"

"Love is too pure a light to burn long among the noisome gases that we breathe, but before it is choked out we may use it as a torch to ignite the cozy fire of affection."

—"ON BEING IN LOVE"

"Let your boat of life be light, packed with only what you need—a homely home and simple pleasures, one or two friends, worth the name, someone to love and someone to love you, a cat, a dog, and a pipe or two, enough to eat and enough to wear, and a little more than enough to drink; for thirst is a dangerous thing."

—THREE MEN IN A BOAT

Wedding Chatter

"Who, being loved, is poor?"

—OSCAR WILDE

"When you fish for love, bait with your heart, not your brain."

—MARK TWAIN

"If you want to be loved, love and be lovable."

—ATTRIBUTED TO MULTIPLE SOURCES

"Do not marry a man to reform him. That is what reform schools are for."

—MAE WEST

"Marriage is an alliance entered into by a man who can't sleep with the window shut, and a woman who can't sleep with the window open."

—GEORGE BERNARD SHAW

"Passion makes the world go round. Love just makes it a safer place."

—ICE T

"My most brilliant achievement was my ability to be able to persuade my wife to marry me."

—WINSTON CHURCHILL

"A happy home is one in which each spouse grants the possibility that the other may be right, though neither believes it."

—DON FRASER

"Life without love is like a tree without blossoms or fruit."

—KAHLIL GIBRAN

"Love comforteth like sunshine after rain."

—WILLIAM SHAKESPEARE

"Sometimes I wonder if men and women really suit each other. Perhaps they should live next door and just visit now and then."

—KATHARINE HEPBURN

Chapter 10

Popular Sayings

The Quintessential '60s Phrase

"Turn on, tune in, and drop out."

✳ ✳ ✳ ✳

THIS CATCHPHRASE OF 1960s counterculture came from psychologist Timothy Leary. Along with his close friend Richard Alpert (later known as Ram Dass), he helped inspire the "hippie" generation to abandon traditional social mores in favor of spiritual exploration and personal expression.

Leary coined the phrase shortly after he and Alpert were dismissed from the faculty at Harvard University, where they had been conducting controversial experiments that involved giving graduate students the hallucinatory drug psilocybin. Their interest in incorporating LSD into their research, coupled with the revelation that some undergraduates had access to their drugs, proved too much for university officials. Both psilocybin and LSD were, however, legal at the time.

Leary went on to become a popular speaker and icon of the counterculture movement. He brought the phrase "turn on, tune in, drop out" to prominence at San Francisco's 1967 Human Be-In, a gathering of some 20,000 people in Golden Gate Park. The event focused on themes like ecological awareness, and a rejection of consumerism. Featured musicians included Jefferson Airplane and the Grateful Dead.

The Be-In helped anoint San Francisco as the center of the emerging hippie culture. The movement continued to flourish there during that year's "Summer of Love."

Bridesmaids and Brides

You'd think the origin of the phrase "Always a bridesmaid, never a bride" might come from a wedding planner, a romantic comedy, or a lifestyle magazine. It actually came from a set of advertisements for…mouthwash?

✳ ✳ ✳ ✳

YES, IT'S TRUE. The phrase "Often a bridesmaid but never a bride" comes from a commercial for Listerine that first appeared in 1925 and ran for more than ten years. The antiseptic, invented in 1879, had been sold many for other antiseptic purposes before that point—sterilizing items and cleaning—but this ad campaign focused on a relatively new use: fighting bad breath. Your average person in the '20s might not have heard about the term halitosis before, but it would surely, the ads warned, doom them to singlehood.

The print ads showed a series of pensive, melancholy women who were saddened by witnessing happiness instead of experiencing it. "Edna's case was a really pathetic one," Listerine proclaimed. She was "always a bridesmaid but never a bride."

Another ad related the desperate case of Eleanor, pictured as a pretty woman dressed in a bridesmaid's outfit, leaning sadly against a wall: "Men were attracted to her, but their interest quickly turned to indifference. Poor girl! She hadn't the remotest idea why they dropped her so quickly…and even her best friend wouldn't tell her."

Listerine, which claimed to stop bad breath "4 times better than any tooth paste," was the answer to '20s spinsterhood—or at least it claimed to be. Nor were women the only people targeted as victims of halitosis. Comparable ads directed at men included the line, "'Can I be happy with him in spite of that?' one maiden asked herself."

Whether those who used Listerine before every date, as the ad recommended, did find love, we don't know. But Listerine's sales did spike greatly. From that angle—and the angle of providing a memorable catchphrase to generations to come—the ad campaign was a great success.

P. T. Barnum's Giant Sucker

P. T. Barnum, the consummate huckster, supposedly laughed at the audiences he tricked, saying, "There's a sucker born every minute." But have we misjudged America's Greatest Showman?

✳ ✳ ✳ ✳

THE PHRASE—WHICH SUGGESTS that every scam, no matter how obvious, will find a gullible mark—has been attributed to several late-19th-century sources, including con man Joseph "Paper Collar Joe" Bessimer and humorist Mark Twain. Most often, it is attributed to P. T. Barnum.

What a Circus!

Phineas Taylor Barnum (1810–91) both amused and appalled audiences with his collections of freaks, oddities, and wonders. Writer Herman Melville boldly declared him "sole heir to all ... lean men, fat women, dwarfs, two-headed cows, amphibious sea-maidens, large-eyed owls, small-eyed mice, rabbit-eating anacondas, bugs, monkeys and mummies." In the name of entertainment, he promoted "humbugs"—obvious hoaxes designed to delight and entertain, such as the "Feejee Mermaid" and a woman whom he claimed was George Washington's 161-year-old nanny.

Barnum insisted that people enjoyed being fooled so long as they got "several times their money's worth." Though it seems likely that such a showman would utter this dismissive phrase, Barnum's acquaintances denied it upon inquiry from his biographer, saying that Barnum actually treasured and respected his patrons.

Start of the Punchline

The true story behind the phrase can be traced to George Hull, a businessman from Binghamton, New York. In 1868, Hull (a fervent atheist) argued with a fundamentalist preacher who insisted the Bible be taken literally, including Genesis 6:4 ("There were giants in the earth in those days"). Hull purchased an enormous slab of gypsum and hired a stonecutter to carve it into a ten-foot-tall statue of a giant with lifelike details such as toenails, fingernails, and pores. The statue was stained with sulfuric acid and ink and shipped to a farm near Cardiff, New York, where it was then buried.

A year later, Hull hired workers to dig a well near the spot where the statue was buried. As he intended, the workers discovered the statue and were excited by their find. (Six months earlier, fossils had been unearthed—with much publicity—at a nearby farm.) Hull had the workers excavate the statue, and then he charged people to see the Cardiff Giant, as it had become known.

Hull sold his statue for nearly $40,000 to a group of exhibitors headed by David Hannum. Barnum became interested in the find and offered to rent it for $50,000, but Hannum refused. Rather than make a higher offer, Barnum built his own Cardiff Giant, declaring that Hannum had sold him the giant after all and that Hannum's was the forgery. Newspapers widely publicized Barnum's story, causing audiences to flock to Barnum while Hannum bitterly declared, "There's a sucker born every minute," in reference to the duped crowds.

Careful What You Sue For

Hannum sued Barnum for calling his giant a sham. At trial, Hull admitted that the original giant was a hoax. The judge ruled in Barnum's favor, saying that it is not a crime to call a fake a fake.

Afterward, one of Barnum's competitors, Adam Forepaugh, mistakenly attributed (or intentionally misattributed) Hannum's phrase to Barnum. The consummate show-man didn't deny saying it; in fact, he went so far as to thank Forepaugh for the publicity.

Snoopy's Opus

In 1965, Charles M. Schulz's comic strip Peanuts *featured Snoopy writing his first line as a novelist: "It was a dark and stormy night." Although Snoopy made the phrase famous, it's a misconception that it had never been used before.*

✳ ✳ ✳ ✳

THE LINE BECAME famous as the worst possible way to open a novel and epitomized an amateur style of writing. That said, a number of published novels have actually opened with that very line.

English novelist Edward George Bulwer-Lytton's 1830 novel *Paul Clifford* contains this startling first line: "It was a dark and stormy night; the rain fell in torrents, except at occasional intervals, when it was checked by a violent gust of wind which swept up the streets (for it is in London that our scene lies), rattling along the housetops, and fiercely agitating the scanty flame of the lamps that struggled against the darkness."

Whoa. Type that into Microsoft Word, and the Office Assistant will immediately draw your attention to the fact that the line is "too long…and may be hard to follow." No kidding.

In 1982, the English department at San Jose State University began the Bulwer-Lytton Fiction Contest to "celebrate" decidedly bad opening lines. Each year, it "challenges entrants to compose the opening sentence to the worst of all possible novels." (Another of Bulwer-Lytton's lines is "The pen is mightier than the sword.")

Popular Prose

The *Paul Clifford* author wasn't the only person to begin a novel with those same seven words. Madeleine L'Engle's 1962 science-fantasy novel, *A Wrinkle in Time*, opens with the line, and Ray Bradbury used it for comic effect in his 2004 mystery, *Let's All Kill Constance* (he followed it with "Is that one way to catch your reader?"). Even Snoopy himself tapped out variations on the line, including "It was a dark and stormy noon" and this opener for another would-be novel: "He was a dark and stormy knight."

Famous Giants

Sir Isaac Newton saw further by standing on the shoulders of giants. Most attribute this apt image to the famed physicist himself, but Newton was quoting the less famous giants who came before him.

✳ ✳ ✳ ✳

IN FEBRUARY 1676, Sir Isaac Newton wrote in a letter to his friend Robert Hooke, "If I have seen further it is by standing on ye shoulders of giants." Since then, the line has been quoted and re-quoted as prized testament to the modesty inherent in the scientific method: Even Newton knows he's nothing without the accumulated knowledge of yesteryear.

Yet Newton's quote is an adaptation of past pronouncements, all delivered by scholars of old. One of the earliest known references to the metaphor comes from scholar John of Salisbury, who wrote in 1159 that fellow scholar Bernard of Chartres "used to say we are like dwarfs on the shoulders of giants."

The quote became better known in the early 17th century, when famous scholar Robert Burton re-quoted less famous scholar Didacus Stella: "I say with Didacus Stella, a dwarf standing on the shoulders of a giant may see farther than the giant himself."

It was not until Newton became associated with the phrase that it gained fame outside of scholarly circles. His version is actually relatively immodest, as he takes out the bit about the dwarf. Yet he never actually claimed to be the quote's originator. Rather, the credit to Newton perfectly demonstrates how quotes become memorable in the first place: by being attributed to famous people. Sociologist Robert Merton, who wrote an entire book on the quote's history, sagely observes that it "became Newton's own, not because he deliberately made it so but because admirers of Newton made it so."

Hell's Belles

Comparing the furor and fires of Hades to the content of a woman's contempt has long been addressed by the adage "Hell hath no fury like a woman scorned." Not only is the message misquoted, but its author has long been mislabeled.

✳ ✳ ✳ ✳

FEW SCRIBES HAVE described the complexities of the female persona with the delicacy and decorum of William Shakespeare. However, he did not liken the disdain of man's better half to the luminous flares of the devil's lair. The credit for that comparison should be given to English author, playwright, and poet William Congreve, who scripted the lines "Heaven has no rage like love to hatred turned, nor hell a fury like a woman scorned" in the lone tragedy he penned during his career, *The Mourning Bride*. Congreve, whose comedies are still popularly featured on stages worldwide, died unaware that a line from a largely unsuccessful work would live forever in the light of day—albeit in an abridged and inauthentic form.

Its inaccurate usage was best exemplified during the 1991 confirmation hearings regarding Clarence Thomas's nomination to the Supreme Court. During the proceedings, Anita Hill, a university professor and former attorney and advisor to Thomas, accused the nominee of sexual harassment and sexual impropriety, an imputation that shocked the nation. Thomas denied any wrongdoing, pointing the finger at Hill herself. Senate Judiciary Committee chair Joseph Biden summarized Hill's testimony by saying, "After being spurned, she took up the role in the way Shakespeare used the phrase 'hell hath no fury like,' and that's what's being implied here." Fortunately, Alan Simpson, an obviously literate senator from Wyoming, stepped forward and corrected his colleague, informing the assembly of the actual author and the correct quote.

"Married in haste, we repent in leisure."

—FROM CONGREVE'S *THE OLD BACHELOR*

"Musick has Charms to sooth a savage Breast."

—FROM CONGREVE'S *THE MOURNING BRIDE*, OFTEN MISQUOTED AS *"BEAST"*

Hollywood Heresy

Credit Hollywood, not Notre Dame football coach Knute Rockne, with the emotional plea "Win one for the Gipper."

✳ ✳ ✳ ✳

THE OFT-REPEATED LINE is from the movie *Knute Rockne: All American*, which was released in 1940. In the famous football flick, Rockne tells his troops that their teammate George Gipp's dying words were: "Rock, sometime when the team is up against it and the breaks are beating the boys, tell them to go out there with all they've got and win just one for the Gipper." No one really knows what Gipp and his coach talked about in the days before the star player's death. Gipp died in 1920, and Rockne met his own tragic fate in a plane crash in 1931, so neither man was in a position to refute the scriptwriter's soliloquy.

What is known is this: Rockne didn't get around to using Gipp's request as a motivating muscle until 1928, a full eight years after George died. According to Francis Wallace, the newspaper reporter who was responsible for dubbing the team the "Fighting Irish," Rockne made his famous speech to his underdog charges before a game against Army at Yankee Stadium on November 10, 1928. Wallace reported that Rockne rose before the assembled throng and said, "The day before he died, George Gipp asked me to wait until the situation seemed hopeless and then ask a Notre Dame team to go out and beat Army for him. This is the day, and you are the team." Although that does evoke the spirit of "win one for the Gipper," in reality those words are a Hollywood embellishment.

The quote gained new life when Ronald Reagan, who played the role of Gipp in the Hollywood homily about Rockne, used the catchphrase as a rallying cry during the 1988 Republican Convention.

"Oh, the Humanity!"

On May 6, 1937, when the luxury German airship Hindenburg burst into flames midair, 36 people lost their lives.

✳   ✳   ✳   ✳

WHEN THE ZEPPELIN Company completed the 242-ton *Hindenburg* in 1936, the airship had the distinction of being the largest ever made. At 804 feet long and 135 feet wide, the dirigible was approximately four times larger than modern Goodyear blimps and managed a top speed of more than 80 miles per hour. On May 3, 1937, 36 passengers and a crew of 61 boarded the airship in Frankfurt, Germany, for the first transatlantic flight of the season. The craft's landing on May 6 at New Jersey's Lakehurst Naval Air Station was delayed for several hours because of a storm. When weather conditions finally improved, the *Hindenburg* began its widely publicized and highly anticipated approach for landing.

When the craft was about 200 feet above the ground, horrified onlookers noticed a small burst of flame on the ship's upper fin. Less than half a minute later, the flame had ignited

the *Hindenburg's* 7 million cubic feet of hydrogen. Some passengers jumped from the windows, others fell, and the rest were trapped in the burning craft. Herbert Morrison, reporting for radio station WLS in Chicago, uttered the words "Oh, the humanity!" as he watched the fiery vessel hit the ground. The recording remains one of the most famous in broadcast history.

Most modern playbacks mislead: They play his voice too fast (making him sound more rattled than he was). They also suggest it was broadcast live (it wasn't) and combined with video (nope). The episode vaulted him into a very successful broadcasting career.

Despite the speed at which the airship incinerated, only 35 of the 97 passengers and crew onboard died in the disaster, along with one member of the 200-strong ground crew. The cause of the fire has never been explained with certainty, though it is believed to have been a result of the highly combustible varnish used to treat the fabric on the outside of the *Hindenburg*. Other theories have cited foreign sabotage, sparks from static electricity, and lightning strikes.

The Hindenburg incident was by no means the only major airship catastrophe; it was simply the highest-profile one. Airships were proving too fragile for passenger use, even as early passenger airlines were gaining the dominant role they hold today. Today numerous countries and firms (famously, Goodyear) operate airships for advertising or observation purposes—especially at football games.

What Do You Mean by That?

Up for Grabs

This phrase, which means that something is available to anyone who wants it, is a fairly recent expression, dating back to the Great Depression, when restaurants saved every scrap of excess food. The leftovers were put into bags and set at the end of the counter, where any person in need could take one without suffering the indignity of having to beg.

Mad as a Hatter

The Mad Hatter was popularized in Lewis Carroll's *Alice's Adventures in Wonderland*, but Carroll did not coin the phrase. Making hats had already been linked with madness. During the early days of processing felt to use in hatmaking, the toxic substance mercury was used, which resulted in many industry workers developing mental or neurological disturbances. From this unfortunate situation, the phrase "mad as a hatter" came to indicate anyone who had gone insane.

Crocodile Tears

When someone is said to be crying "crocodile tears," they are feigning sorrow. This phrase actually does come from crocodiles and specifically refers to a peculiarity in which crocodiles shed tears while eating. This is caused by food pressing against the roof of the animal's mouth, which activates the lachrymal glands that secrete tears, making crocodiles appear to be crying without really being sad at all.

It's Greek to Me

This phrase, used by someone to indicate that he or she doesn't understand a word of what's being said, is really a quotation from the first act of William Shakespeare's *Julius Caesar*. The character Casca, one of the plotters who participates in Caesar's assassination, describes overhearing Cicero, who was speaking in Greek to deter eavesdroppers. The ploy obviously worked.

How Cool Are Cucumbers?

In his poem "A New Song of New Similes," eighteenth-century English author John Gay wrote, "I'd be... cool as a cucumber could see the rest of womankind." Not at all unwittingly, Gay coined a phrase that has become part of our collective consciousness. But are cucumbers really all that cool?

✳ ✳ ✳ ✳

L ET'S TURN BACK the clock a few hundred years. Imagine you're in India, the supposed birthplace of the cucumber. It's about one hundred degrees in the shade. You've just polished off a dish of delectable but fiery hot vindaloo chicken, and now it feels like steam is shooting out of your ears and nostrils, like you're a character in a Warner Brothers cartoon. Instinctively, you reach for a glass of ice water. But wait! In your dizzy, sweaty haste, you've forgotten that refrigeration—and Warner Brothers cartoons, for that matter—won't be invented for centuries.

There is no ice water! How do you extinguish the fire that rages in your mouth? That's right: You reach for a few slices of cool cucumber, and they really hit the spot.

While there's no reason to believe that its physical temperature is lower than that of any other vegetable, the cucumber's mild flavor and watery flesh give it a refreshing quality that has made it a favorite warm-weather ingredient in cooling salads, relishes, and yogurt sauces for generations. It should come as no surprise that the cucumber hails from the same family of plants (*Cucurbiticeae*) as the watermelon.

But there is evidence to suggest that cucumbers can keep you "cool" in other ways. The cucumber's skin is a source of fiber, and several studies have shown that a high-fiber diet may help to lower your blood pressure, a benefit for those who share some of the personality traits of certain steam-shooting cartoon characters. And when applied directly to the skin, the ascorbic acid (vitamin C) and caffeic acid found in the cucumber can help soothe and seemingly cool irritations and reduce swelling.

You may have heard of another, nondietary use for cucumbers: Rock stars have been known to stuff them into their pants to enhance a certain physical feature. The "prop" couldn't be sillier, but they think it makes them look cool.

What Does Humble Pie Taste Like?

Which would you rather swallow: your pride or a mouthful of deer gizzard? Original recipes for humble pie included the heart, liver, and other internal organs of a deer, or even a cow or a boar. Talk about your awful offal!

✳ ✳ ✳ ✳

THE TERM "HUMBLE pie" derives from "umble pie," which dates back roughly to fourteenth-century England. The term "numbles," then later "umbles," referred to those aforementioned, um, select bits of a deer carcass. Umble pie was eaten by servants, whose lords feasted on the more palatable cuts of venison or whatever beast was being served. If meat was on the menu and you were eating umble pie, you were likely to be in a lower position in society. The transition from the original term to the pun "humble pie" was an easy one, given that some English dialects silence the "h" at the beginning of words.

For some reason, modern recipes for humble pie do exist, although these call, mercifully, for cuts of beef or other meat. Others are dessert pies with sweet fillings that inspire humility only when you're in the presence of a bathroom scale.

So the next time you've done somebody wrong, just apologize, take your lumps, wait for time to heal the wound, and consider yourself fortunate. It's better to spend "thirty days in the hole," to quote the 1970s British supergroup Humble Pie, than to eat a boar's intestines.

A Moon of Green Cheese

The notion that the moon is made of green cheese is less a myth than a rumor that never quite got a foothold in society. When it comes up in conversation, it's usually in a tongue-in-cheek sort of way, rather than as a serious discussion. There may be some people who believe the moon is indeed made of cheese— they're probably the same folks who would agree to put a down payment on the London Bridge.

✳   ✳   ✳   ✳

S AYING "THE MOON is made of green cheese" is roughly equivalent to saying the word "gullible" is not in the dictionary. The phrase began as an innocuous line in John Heywood's *Proverbs*, which was printed in 1546. It was utilized by writers of the period as an ironic and colorful way of saying a person would believe anything—no matter how blatantly false it might be. In its original context, "green" referred not to the color of the supposed cheese, but to its age. To say something is green is to say it is young and unripe.

More than 460 years later, the phrase has many colloquial uses. It is often substituted for any statement known to the general public as false. Individuals now proudly claim that the moon is made of cheese, albeit facetiously, as evidence of their willingness to support an unpopular belief. And, of course, it is still used as a sarcastic be-all-end-all in a debate, a classic and comical way of saying a person is simple-minded: "If you believe [insert contested belief here], you probably believe the moon is made of cheese."

NASA appears to enjoy perpetuating the green cheese rumor. On April Fools' Day in 2002, the space-travel agency published a satellite photo of the moon that "proved" its make-up to be dairy. (The image showed an expiration date printed inside one of the moon's many craters.) No word on whether someone tried to take a bite out of a moon rock.

Is It Really Darkest
Before the Dawn?

Someone once said: "It's always darkest before the dawn. So if you're going to steal the neighbor's newspaper, that's the time to do it."

✳ ✳ ✳ ✳

IF WE'RE TALKING about metaphors and not about stealing newspapers, it does appear darkest just before the dawn. That is to say, a bad situation often seems worst right before it gets better. English dramatist John Webster conveyed this notion in his tragic 1614 play *The Duchess of Malfi*. In Act IV, Bosola says to the Duchess: "Leave this vain sorrow. Things being at the worst, begin to mend."

As a proverb, "It's always darkest before the dawn" has been around for centuries in various incarnations. Original credit usually goes to seventeenth-century British scholar and preacher Thomas Fuller. In *A Pisgah-Sight of Palestine* (1650), he wrote: "It is always darkest just before the day dawneth."

Today the old saying is still used in reference to just about every type of bad situation, from war to our own personal lives. Is it any wonder, then, that the phrase has inspired so many country crooners? Dwight Yoakam, Emmylou Harris, Dave Evans, and the Stanley Brothers have all recorded renditions of a song called "The Darkest Hour Is Just Before Dawn." So if you're feeling as brokenhearted, dejected, and bereft as a Nashville lover scorned, this could be the tune to add to your collection.

However, when you've run out of tissues and you're ready to look at this issue from a purely unemotional and scientific point of view, no, it is not literally darkest just before the dawn. The best time to don those night-vision goggles and swipe your neighbor's paper? Figure somewhere around midnight—not 12:00 AM, but the actual halfway point between sunset and sunrise. Of course, that doesn't account for factors like glowing full moons and very bright streetlamps, so be sure to wear a ski mask.

Did Mother Goose Write Her Own Nursery Rhymes?

Should we even point out that geese can't write? Nah, why bother?

✳ ✳ ✳ ✳

MOTHER GOOSE MADE her first appearance in literary history way back in 1650 with a bit part in a French book called *La Muse Historique*. The author gave Mother Goose—or *Mere Oye*, as she's called in French—a passing reference in a single line that translates to "like a Mother Goose story." Hardly an auspicious debut for a character who would eventually become so venerable.

But Mother Goose didn't have to wait too long for her big break. Roughly fifty years later, French lawyer and poet Charles Perrault took her name and made it famous. During the reign of Louis XIV, Perrault served as a poet laureate, producing odes to commemorate events in the life of the Sun King. He also wrote love poems, memoirs, essays, short stories, and a book of tales called *Histoires ou contes du temps pass, avec des moralités (Histories or Tales of Past Times, with Morals)*. The frontispiece of the book carried an engraving of an old woman and the words *Contes de la Mere l'Oye*, which, as you've probably figured out, means "Tales of Mother Goose." Later editions replaced Perrault's original title with the more memorable *Tales of Mother Goose*.

Perrault's stories were fairy tales, not the rhymes with which we associate Mother Goose today. His work included stories about Sleeping Beauty, Little Red Riding Hood, Cinderella, Puss 'n Boots, and others. Perrault published these stories in 1697, more than a century before the Brothers Grimm gathered versions of many of the same folk stories from the German countryside for their own book of fairy tales.

How did Mother Goose get her current association with juvenile poems like "Humpty Dumpty"? In the 1760s, another author, John Newbery, wrote a book of nursery rhymes and called it *Mother Goose's Melody: or Sonnets for the Cradle*, which was published on both sides of the Atlantic. In America, a printer in Boston distributed it. Perhaps that's why, a century later, some folks tried to claim that Mother Goose was a Bostonian matron named Elizabeth Goose, who was related to the printer. As you now know, this claim was just a fairy tale.

The Owl and the Pussy-Cat

Edward Lear was an illustrator and poet whose works are some of the best-known from the 19th century English writers. His nonsense poetry was very popular, and he made the limerick a well-known style of verse.

❋ ❋ ❋ ❋

EDWARD LEAR WAS born in London on May 13, 1812, to a middle-class family. He had twenty brothers and sisters. His parents could not afford to raise all of the children. When he was four years old, his oldest sister Ann, who was twenty-five, took him to live with her and became his mother figure. Lear was frequently ill as a child and had poor health his entire life. He suffered from epilepsy and had seizures that left him with feelings of guilt and shame well into adulthood. His various illnesses caused him frequent periods of deep depression that he called "The Morbids."

Lear is remembered for his brilliant and witty nonsense poetry, the most famous of which is "The Owl and the Pussy-Cat." The poem was published in an 1871 collection called *Nonsense Songs, Stories, Botany and Alphabets* and begins:

"The Owl and the Pussy-cat went to sea
In a beautiful pea green boat,
They took some honey, and plenty of money,
Wrapped up in a five pound note."

Lear's poetry was a celebration of words, both real and imaginary. His best-known invention is the word "runcible," which he incorporated into several of his poems. The word has no fixed meaning, and Lear himself never was clear on what the definition might be.

Lear was one of the first major writers to use limericks widely, and is responsible for their popularity. He was also a gifted artist who illustrated his and other books of poetry, and published several travelogues with beautiful illustrations of Greece and Italy. Lear died on January 29, 1888, in Italy.

"There was an Old Man with a beard,
Who said, "It is just as I feared!—
Two Owls and a Hen,
Four Larks and a Wren,
Have all built their nests in my beard!"

The Fat Lady Singing

Who was the fat lady and why was she singing?

✳ ✳ ✳ ✳

YOGI BERRA, THE Hall of Fame catcher for the New York Yankees, was as famous for his verbal foibles as for his baseball skills. Here's Yogi on memory: "This is like *deja vu* all over again." On economics: "A nickel isn't worth a dime today." On making tough choices: "When you come to a fork in the road, take it."

"It ain't over until the fat lady sings" sounds like it would be a Yogism, especially since he coined this similar gem: "It ain't over till it's over."

But this isn't the case. "It ain't over until the fat lady sings" made its way into popular usage in the 1970s. Though it's most often called upon to describe sporting events, this pearl of wisdom has also been applied to other forms of competition—like when a beaming Bill Clinton showed up to a 1992 election party in Arkansas wearing a T-shirt that sported the phrase "The Fat Lady Sang." (Knowing William Jefferson Clinton's reputation, onlookers would've been excused for wondering whether or not the phrase really was just a figure of speech.)

But even though the term is a recent creation, pinpointing its origin is surprisingly difficult. The *Washington Post* has suggested one theory, attributing the saying to a San Antonio sportswriter by the name of Dan Cook. According to the *Post*, it was overheard and picked up by Dick Motta, then the coach of the Washington Bullets, who used it throughout the Bullets' 1978 run to the NBA championship. (The fat lady sang for the Bullets in 1997, when their name was changed to the Wizards.)

Another Theory

The second (and less likely) theory refers to the American singer Kate Smith, a portly soprano who reached prominence in the 1930s and 1940s. Ms. Smith—known to Yankees fans today as the voice singing "God Bless America" during the seventh-inning stretch—was in great demand at ribbon-cutting ceremonies, political conventions, World Series games, and the like, often closing these events with her version of the Irving Berlin standard. Is Smith the "fat lady"? It's an intriguing possibility, but it's pretty unlikely. For one, she didn't *always* cap her appearances with "God Bless America."

Regardless of its origin, the phrase now evokes an image of the opera—or at least a caricature of that pompous art form. American sports fans don't exactly have a reputation for being culturally sophisticated; the closest some of them get to the art world is painting their faces before the big game. When they think of opera, they envision an enormous woman, usually wearing a horned helmet, belting out the final notes before the curtain falls.

This image—probably drawn from the character of Brünnhilde in Wagner's *Ring Cycle*—has become shorthand for opera in the non-opera world. And even though Wagner's opera might not end until the fat lady sings, the curtain falls for most of us well before then. That's because we fall asleep sometime during the first act.

What Is "Auld Lang Syne" Anyway?

It's been called the most popular song to which nobody knows the words. And with lyrics like "And gie's a hand o thine," who can blame us? Fortunately, most people aren't in any condition to care when it's sung during the first minutes of January 1.

✳   ✳   ✳   ✳

THE TITLE AND the other odd words are from the old Lallans Scots-English dialect. "Auld lang syne" translates literally to "old long since" and is generally taken to mean "times long past"—"the good old days," in other words.

We know the song because the famous Scottish poet Robert Burns wrote it down in 1788. Burns claimed that he heard it from an old man, but historians believe that the poet tweaked the song substantially and possibly added new verses, so books credit the words to him. The first verse and chorus go like this:

Should auld acquaintance be forgot,
And never brought to mind?
Should auld acquaintance be forgot,
And auld lang syne?

For auld lang syne, my dear,
For auld lang syne,
We'll take a cup o' kindness yet,
For auld lang syne!

The lyrics are up for interpretation, of course, but the gist is something like this: The first verse poses the question—should we forget old friends and times long past? The chorus says no—we friends will enjoy each other's company again, for old time's sake.

Some interpret the rest of the song as a story of two separated friends. Following this view, the second verse is a description of old friends drinking at the same time, many miles apart.

The third and fourth verses describe the two friends wandering the countryside looking for each other. For example, the song says, "We twa hae run about the braes/And pou'd the gowans fine" ("We two have run about the hills and picked the daisies"). In the final verse, they reunite and have a drink.

The old man whom Burns supposedly encountered likely sang "Auld Lang Syne" to another tune. It's not clear when its lyrics were paired up with its current melody, but it may have been as early as 1796, when it was published in a collection of Scottish songs.

There's evidence that the song was associated with New Year's Eve as early as the nineteenth century, both in America and England. But it is Canadian bandleader Guy Lombardo who is credited with really popularizing the pairing. He had heard Scottish immigrants singing the song when he was a boy in London, Ontario, in the early nineteen hundreds; later, he made it one of his band's standards. In 1929, he included it in a New Year's Eve radio broadcast, and for the next forty years, he played it every New Year's Eve—first on the radio and later on television. All the while, folks have been mumbling everything past the first line.

Let Them Eat Cake

Did she or didn't she?

✳ ✳ ✳ ✳

QUEEN OF FRANCE Marie Antoinette may not have been a very nice person, and she may have made many foolish or unkind statements, but she almost surely never said the sentence that most people associate with her: "Let them eat cake." We know this because the phrase appears in Jean-Jacques Rousseau's *Confessions*, which was completed in 1769. Rousseau attributed the unsympathetic remark—supposedly said in response to the French people starving—to a "young princess," but the phrase had been ascribed to various other sovereigns for decades before Marie arrived in France in 1770.

While it is possible that Marie was familiar with *Confessions*, as it was published 20 years before the French Revolution began, it is highly doubtful that she actually read it—she wasn't exactly known as an intellectual. A more likely scenario is that someone on the side of the Revolution read Rousseau's work, decided the arrogant remark sounded like something the queen would say, and simply started spreading the rumor.

Like a Good Neighbor, Barry Manilow Was There

You might not think you know any Barry Manilow music—but even if you're not a fan, you very likely do.

✳ ✳ ✳ ✳

SPECIFICALLY, EVEN IF you've never heard "Copacabana" or "Mandy" (and we're taking those claims with a grain of salt), you've almost certainly heard a State Farm commercial with the jingle, "Like a good neighbor, State Farm is there." And Barry Manilow was responsible for that jingle.

Manilow, born in 1943, was working in the advertising world as a jingle writer in the late '60s and throughout the '70s. The ad agency Needham, Harper & Steers, now known as DDB Chicago, was responsible for the 1971 State Farm campaign. Manilow wrote and performed the jingle that has stuck in our heads for decades. And that wasn't the only jingle that Manilow worked on—he also wrote the music for Band-aid's "I am stuck on Band-aid brand, 'cause Band-aid's stuck on me." (Donald Wood was responsible for the lyrics.) He also sang on commercials for other companies, including Kentucky Fried Chicken and Pepsi.

In 2009, Manilow received an honorary Clio award in recognition of his earlier work. The awards are given to honor achievements in advertising and design.

An Apple a Day

You know how the phrase ends. But where did it come from? And does it work?

✳ ✳ ✳ ✳

"AN APPLE A day keeps the doctor away." If you guess that the origin of the phrase has something to do with advertising, perhaps on behalf of the powerful apple lobby, you'd... be wrong. We can't pinpoint an exact origin for this phrase, but some version of it dates back to at least the 1800s. An 1866 magazine lists a Welsh proverb: "Eat an apple on going to bed, And you'll keep the doctor from earning his bread." A 1913 book of folklore lists the version we have today.

Apples are definitely healthy. They contain phytonutrients, polyphenols, and flavonoids that are good for regulating blood sugar. They contain good quantities of fiber and Vitamin C. Some studies point to cardiovascular benefits such as reducing cholesterol level. One study found that regularly eating apples (along with pears) could reduce stroke risk.

In 2013, a study published in the *British Medical Journal*, titled "A statin a day keeps the doctor away: comparative proverb assessment modelling study" examined the results of giving the participants either an apple or a statin (a medication that lowers lipid levels) a day. Compared to the statin, the apple didn't come off badly—and it didn't have the side effects! In short, eating an apple a day may not be a guarantee that the doctor will stay away, it can provide health benefits. If you like apples, chomp away, and thank the Welsh for giving you a reason!

Noli Equi Dentes Inspicere Donati

So wrote Saint Jerome. Run that through Google Translate, and you get a statement we still use today.

✳ ✳ ✳ ✳

ST. JEROME WAS born in Italy between 340 and 350. Born Eusebius Sophronius Hieronymus, he went to Rome to study and there learned Latin and Greek. After a few years of study, he set out to travel for a time. Although he had become baptized during his years in Rome, he became more diligent about his faith during his travels. He worked on essays, commentaries, correspondence, and translations, including a well-known translation of the Bible.

In "On the Epistle to the Ephesians," he uses the Latin phrase above. Roughly, it translates to, "Don't look a gift horse in the mouth." In the 1500s, the phrase was included in playwright and proverb-collector John Heywood's work as "No man ought to looke a geuen hors in the mouth."

Why would you be looking at a horse's mouth anyway? Specifically you'd be looking at its teeth; among other changes, a horse's teeth grow more prominent with age as its gums recedes. Basically, the proverb warns against looking too closely at a gift and becoming ungrateful—whether or not a horse is a bit "long in the tooth," it's a free horse. Who'd turn one down?

Little-Published de Rojas Provides Wisdom for the Ages

"When one door closes, fortune will usually open another." It's not only the most famous quote attributed to Fernando de Rojas. It's one of the most lasting and resonant nuggets of wisdom across the centuries.

✳ ✳ ✳ ✳

FERNANDO DE ROJAS has only one work on his authoring resume, but it was a dandy. *La Celestina*, also known as the *Tragicomedy of Calisto and Melibea*, is considered the first Spanish prose masterpiece and the most influential work of the early Renaissance in Spain. Written entirely in dialogue, it was published in 1499, serving as the bridge between the Medieval and Renaissance periods in Spanish literature.

The main character, Celestina, serves as a go-between for two young lovers in a tale that ends tragically for both. Celestina's ironic humor carries the story, complementing the theme of how humans struggle in vain while fate conspires against them.

Rojas was born to Jewish parents in Spain in 1465. He began working on *La Celestina* while studying at the University of Salamanca. Rojas received a law degree and worked briefly as a mayor of Talavera. It is widely believed that *La Celestina* is the only book he ever wrote, although he is credited with contributing a time-tested piece of wisdom in the observation, "When one door closes, fortune will usually open another."

Variations of the quote have helped countless people—over centuries—cope with lost opportunities or bad breaks in their lives. Rojas certainly saw the doors to parenthood open in his life. He and wife Leonor had four sons and three daughters. Rojas died in 1541.

Henry IV Provided a Promise Worth Stealing

"A chicken in every pot." It might not sound like much of a promise, but when Henry IV offered it up during his reign over France between 1589 and 1610, he had no idea world leaders would still be "borrowing" the phrase centuries later.

✳   ✳   ✳   ✳

H ENRY IV, OR Henry of Navarre, served as King of Navarre from 1572 until his death in 1610. A direct descendant of Louis IX of France, he was called to serve as King of France when his brother-in-law and distant cousin, Henry III, died in 1589. Henry ruled at a time when there was great religious dissent between Catholics and Protestants, and his own religious tolerance was unique for the time. As a result, those on both sides resented him. He was the subject of no less than a dozen assassination attempts, the final one successful.

Although he grew to be endeared after his death, coming to be remembered as "Good King Henry," Henry had a soft spot for his subjects during his living years as well. He wanted all of France—Catholic, Protestant or otherwise—to be prosperous. It was reputed that one of his greatest wishes was that each of his peasants would enjoy "a chicken in his pot every Sunday."

Over the years, that phrase came to be a rallying cry for politicians trying to attach themselves to prosperous times. It was attributed to four consecutive U.S. presidents between 1920 and 1936.

Though often linked to Herbert Hoover, there is no evidence that Hoover ever spoke the phrase. It was used in a 1928 Republican campaign advertisement, denoting Republican prosperity that provided "a chicken in every pot. And a car in every backyard, to boot."

Duke's Satire Lives On

When a situation becomes more complex, or perhaps when there's an uncomfortable pause in the telling of a story, it might be a great time for a narrator to jump in. "The plot thickens," the narrator might say, not knowing that he or she is quoting a 17th century duke.

✳ ✳ ✳ ✳

GEORGE VILLIERS WAS the son and namesake of the 1st Duke of Buckingham. His father was assassinated when George was just seven months old, elevating George as the 2nd Duke of Buckingham at an age when he was too young to rule. That would come in due time, as would his fighting for the King in the English Civil War in the 1640s and a career as a statesman. Those, however, are secondary in this venue to his work as a satirist and playwright.

Villiers was lampooning John Dryden, the Poet Laureate at the time, when he authored *The Rehearsal*. The 1671 stage production was a play within a play—a mockery of the process of putting on a play. At one point, the fictitious playwright looks over the proceedings and says, "Ay, now the plot thickens very much upon us."

The Rehearsal was a success for Villiers—enough so that it was reprinted as an English drama and even made it into collections of Dryden's work. Later in Dryden's career, critics used the "plot thickens" phrase to mock another of his stories.

In the decades and centuries since, the phrase has been used to indicate added complexity in a story or situation. And it's a safe bet that more than 99 percent of the time (readers of this book excluded), those uttering the words have no idea who brought them into our lexicon.

Russians Our First 'Frenemies'

The word "frenemy" is more than 60 years old, tracing its origins to a Nevada newspaper article about the United States and its relationship with Russia. It has enjoyed renewed popularity in an era when combining words has become commonplace.

❋ ❋ ❋ ❋

I F "FRENEMY" SEEMS like a word that might inspire a teen Disney movie (*Frenemies*, 2012), or perhaps episodes of *Glee* or *Sex and the City*, it has. We live in an era when blended words can help one stay below the Twitter character limit and make for quicker text messaging, and "frenemy" has certainly helped the causes.

However, it might come as a surprise that the word is more than 60 years old. Walter Winchell, a newspaper gossip columnist and radio commentator, was writing a piece for the *Nevada State Journal* in 1953 about United States relations with the Soviet Union. In it, he asked rhetorically, "Howz about calling the Russians our Frienemies?"

Disregard the use of the word "howz," if you will, and consider that the last word of his question has lived on well after Winchell's death in 1972. It turned out to be one of many "Winchellisms" for which he is remembered.

More commonly spelled "frenemy" (without the "i" used by Winchell), the word was added to the *Oxford English Dictionary* in 2008. Its definition: "A person with whom one is friendly, despite a fundamental dislike or rivalry; a person who combines the characteristics of a friend and an enemy."

"In appearance, at least, he being on all occasions glad to be at friendship with me, though we hate one another, and know it on both sides."

—SAMUEL PEPYS, WRITING IN 1668, PROVES THAT THE CONCEPT OF FRENEMIES LONG PREDATES THE TERM

Dennis Took Theatre by Storm

English playwright John Dennis struggled to make an impact with his productions, but he managed to contribute greatly to theatre with a noise-making prop. And, it turns out, his lasting impact came with the turn of a phrase.

✳   ✳   ✳   ✳

ORN IN LONDON in 1658, John Dennis inherited a large sum of money as a young adult and was thus afforded the ability to dedicate his career to literature and the theatre, though he was accomplished at neither. He wrote plays spanning the 17th and 18th centuries and also worked as a critic, publishing several essays on poetry, opera, Shakespeare, and other topics of the day.

One of his plays, *Appius and Virginia*, earned a run at the Drury Lane Theatre in London in 1709 but was cancelled after just three nights. During those performances, though, Dennis had managed to improve on a prop that produced thunder sound effects. It was essentially a metal bowl filled with lead balls that were rattled around to sound like thunder. Dennis replaced the lead balls with metal ones for a more realistic sound.

Shortly after his play was cancelled, Dennis was sitting in the crowd for a performance of *Macbeth* when he heard "his" effect being used. "That's my thunder, by God!" he is purported to have said. "The villains will not play my play but they steal my thunder."

From its literal meaning at the time, the phrase "steal my thunder" has come to represent one's figurative robbing of credit or limelight from the person deserving of it. It wound up being Dennis' most lasting contribution.

Alain Rene Lesage: Just the Facts

French novelist and playwright Alain-Rene Lesage contributed several successful works to the world of literature and the theatre, but it was a keen observation he made that has been quoted by (and wrongly attributed to) political figures who followed him. "Facts," he said, "are stubborn things."

✳ ✳ ✳ ✳

ALAIN-RENE LESAGE PRECEDED the more modern "alternative facts" debate by more than three centuries, but he could easily have been in the middle of 21st Century politics when he said, "Facts are stubborn things."

Lesage enjoyed success in the early part of the 18th Century with novels like *The Devil upon Two Sticks* and *Gil Blas* and the stage comedy *Turcaret*. He lived to be almost 80 and was known as a captivating storyteller, though he was hard of hearing and had to use an ear horn. His assessment of the stubbornness of facts resonated with fellow writers —and at least one famous U.S. founding father.

John Adams, successfully defending British soldiers who had fired upon the crowd during the Boston Massacre in 1770, claimed, "Facts are stubborn things; and whatever may be our wishes, our inclinations, or the dictates of our passion, they cannot alter the state of facts and evidence."

Many began crediting Adams with the saying—one of many famous phrases incorrectly attributed to U.S. founding fathers, who were actually quite adept at using already-spoken wisdom to further their cause in building a country.

Burke Called for Forces of Good to Unite

"When bad men combine, the good must associate; else they will fall one by one, an unpitied sacrifice in a contemptible struggle."

Over time, this Edmund Burke quote evolved to the more concise version, "The only thing necessary for evil to win is for good men to do nothing."

✳ ✳ ✳ ✳

EDMUND BURKE IS considered by many to be the father of British Conservatism. An Irish statesman born in Dublin in 1729, he served for 20 years (1774–94) in the British House of Commons as a Whig and was one of the foremost political theorists of his day. He was also a great orator and writer, and his contributions to political thought and philosophy on all pressing matters of the day helped shape the direction of politics in Great Britain.

Though Burke offered words of wisdom on the power of government, taxation and the revolution in the U.S. colonies, the French Revolution, and foreign affairs elsewhere in the world, one of his most lasting contributions came in his 1770 essay, *Thoughts on the Cause of the Present Discontents*. In it, Burke wrote that "When bad men combine, the good must associate; else they will fall one by one, an unpitied sacrifice in a contemptible struggle."

It was a philosophy he held dear in his political life, and one that found its way into the lexicon of other politicians and spokesmen who followed him. Most often nowadays the sentiment is quoted as "The only thing necessary for evil to win is for good men to do nothing," which Burke did not write but clearly inspired.

Quotes by Burke

"Laws, like houses, lean on one another."

"There is, however, a limit at which forebearance ceases to be a virtue."

"It is a general popular error to suppose the loudest complainers for the publick to be the most anxious for its welfare."

"Toleration is good for all, or it is good for none."

"Certainly, Gentlemen, it ought to be the happiness and glory of a representative to live in the strictest union, the closest correspondence, and the most unreserved communication with his constituents. Their wishes ought to have great weight with him; heir opinions high respect; their business unremitted attention. It is his duty to sacrifice his repose, his pleasure, his satisfactions, to theirs,— and above all, ever, and in all cases, to prefer their interest to his own. But his unbiased opinion, his mature judgment, his enlightened conscience, he ought not to sacrifice to you, to any man, or to any set of men living. These he does not derive from your pleasure,—no, nor from the law and the Constitution. They are a trust from Providence, for the abuse of which he is deeply answerable. Your representative owes you, not his industry only, but his judgment; and he betrays instead of serving you if he sacrifices it to your opinion."

"In doing good, we are generally cold, and languid, and sluggish; and of all things afraid of being too much in the right. But the works of malice and injustice are quite in another style. They are finished with a bold, masterly hand; touched as they are with the spirit of those vehement passions that call forth all our energies, whenever we oppress and persecute."

"Whenever a separation is made between liberty and justice, neither, in my opinion, is safe."

"Neither the few nor the many have a right to act merely by their will, in any matter connected with duty, trust, engagement, or obligation."

"The tyranny of a multitude is a multiplied tyranny."

"All who have ever written on government are unanimous, that among a people generally corrupt, liberty cannot long exist."

"The people never give up their liberties but under some delusion."

Burns Gave Scotland a Poetic Voice

Robert Burns longed to be the national poet of Scotland, and he got his wish. This leader of the Romantic Movement inspired early liberals and socialists and remains a celebrated figure in his homeland.

✳ ✳ ✳ ✳

BORN A TENANT farmer in Alloway, Scotland, in 1759, Burns was not cut out for the grueling labor of the fields. He much preferred literature and love. Inspired by the likes of Milton and Shakespeare, he spent countless hours writing poetry in his youth.

Burns fathered several children out of wedlock while in his 20s, the first with his mother's servant. As tumultuous as his family life became, however, Burns was in his comfort zone with a pen and parchment.

One of his early poems, "To a Mouse" (1785), is said to have occurred to him when he accidentally destroyed a mouse's winter nest while plowing a field. It contains a line that has been reused and reworked in speech and literature many times through the years. "The best-laid schemes o' mice an' men gang aft agley," Burns wrote, setting the stage for writers like John Steinbeck to chronicle how the most thought-out plans often go awry.

Burns' first major published volume, *Poems, Chiefly in the Scottish Dialect* (1786), received great praise among critics and was acclaimed across many classes—a rare feat in those days. His widespread appeal was built on both his gifts and his subject matter.

Burns celebrated farm life, traditional Scottish culture, regional experiences, class differences, politics, and religion with an openness and beauty that was easily embraced. He also gained a great following in song, co-publishing (with James Johnson) a collection of traditional Scottish music, *The Scots Musical Museum*. It contains perhaps the most celebrated of Burns' folk songs, "Auld Lang Syne."

Marriage and a National Honor

That Burns had an eye on becoming his nation's poet was all but spelled out in his 1787 "The Answer." In it, he writes: "Ev'n then a wise (I mind its power) / Shall strongly heave my breast / That I for poor auld Scotland's sake / Some useful plan, or book could make / Or sing a sang at least."

He married Jean Amour in 1788. The couple had nine children, though only three survived infancy. Three years later, he moved his family to Dumfries, took up work as a tax collector and wrote "Tam O'Shanter," considered a classic of narrative poetry.

Burns was well on his way to national reverence in his homeland. He was asked to write lyrics for *The Melodies of Scotland* and contributed more than 100 songs to the volume, stamping himself among the greatest lyricists in history. By putting words to traditional Scottish folk tunes while preserving the time-tested melodies, Burns again reached across the classes and took a place among the most beloved Scotsmen in history.

Scottish television channel STV conducted a poll of its viewers and online users in 2009 in which Burns was voted the greatest Scot of all time, beating out William Wallace and Sir Alexander Fleming. Though suffered from a heart condition and lived to be only 37, the "Ayrshire Ploughman" is still celebrated every year on his birthday (January 25) in Scotland. The annual "Burns suppers" across the country typically culminate with a rendition of "Auld Lang Syne."

Schlegel Both Critic and Philosopher

Friedrich von Schlegel, best known as a literary critic and poet, has also earned considerable study among philosophers through the generations. He and his brother, August Wilhelm, hold distinction as leaders of the Romantic Movement in Germany.

✳ ✳ ✳ ✳

FRIEDRICH VON SCHLEGEL once said that "the historian is a prophet in reverse." In his case, however, the historians had a little more work to do than in many circumstances. That is, undermining the role history played in any evaluation of Schlegel would be doing a disservice to the growth his legacy has undergone since his death in 1829.

Schlegel was born in 1772, the son of a Lutheran pastor in Hanover, Germany. He studied law, but by age 21 he dedicated himself to literature and moved to Jena to work with his like-minded brother, August. While there, he befriended many great thinkers and literary minds and wound up giving lectures at the local university.

Schlegel published his first two books in the late 1770s, exploring the ancient Greeks and Romans, particularly their early poetry. He and August also co-founded a magazine called *Athenaeum*, contributing articles and essays that can be credited with sparking the Romantic Movement in Germany.

Friedrich pushed boundaries in his idealistic, freedom-celebrating writing and philosophies.

New Thinking, New Religion

Schlegel continued to publish and lecture after moving to Paris in 1802. His topics ranged from Oriental philosophy to language in India. On the latter subject, he offered that Sanskrit contained too many vocabulary and grammar similarities to

Latin, German and other European languages to have been coincidence—a finding that came to be further explored and commonly accepted by researchers who followed.

In 1808, the same year he published those findings, Schlegel and his wife Dorothea (whom he had married four years earlier) converted to Catholicism. He became less embracing of political and religious freedom after joining the Catholic Church, a switch that showed in his writings and lectures over the final 20 years of his life.

Schlegel spent most of those last 20 years in Vienna. There, his work took on a more diplomatic tone than a young Schlegel ever showed during his "Romantic phase." It has been criticized by many and studied in depth. Famed French literary theorist Maurice Blanchot offered harsh criticism of Schlegel's later works, writing:

"[A]s a young man he is an atheist, a radical, and an individualist…Some years pass: the same Schlegel, converted to Catholicism, a diplomat and journalist in the service of Metternich, surrounded by monks and pious men of society, is no longer anything but a fat philistine of unctuous speech, lazy, empty, his mind on food, and incapable of remembering the young man who had written: 'A single absolute law: the free spirit always triumphs over nature.' Which is the real one? Is the later Schlegel the truth of the first?"

Here again, the historian gets to play prophet in reverse. As drastic a change as Schlegel made in his later years (even starting a Catholic magazine that drew the ire of his brother), he is most remembered for his brilliant mind and early daring.

If not the unquestioned founder of the German Romantic School, Schlegel was the loudest force behind its growth. His ideas shaped German literature and 19th Century thinking. On that, "reverse prophets" can agree.

The Golden Age

"Yellow-colored objects appear to be gold."

—ARISTOTLE

"Do not hold as gold all that shines as gold."

—ALAIN DE LILLE

"Hyt is not al gold that glareth."

—GEOFFREY CHAUCER

"But al thing which that shineth as the gold / Nis nat gold, as that I have herd it told."

—GEOFFREY CHAUCER

"All that glisters is not gold."

—WILLIAM SHAKESPEARE

"All, as they say, that glitters, is not gold."

—JOHN DRYDEN

"All that is gold does not glitter."

—J.R.R. TOLKIEN

"Well, all that glitters isn't gold, I know you've heard that story told."

—NEIL YOUNG

Perry's Heroic Victory Spawns Evolving Message

"We have met the enemy and they are ours. Two ships, two brigs, one schooner and one sloop."

✳ ✳ ✳ ✳

FOR A CONSIDERABLE time, Oliver Hazard Perry must have thought he was cursed. The lifelong naval man who enjoyed great success in battle had taken ill aboard the *Revenge* in 1810. He and his crew had also weathered battle damage and storms, and in January 1811 the ship was lost off the coast of Rhode

Island. Oliver was commissioned to Lake Erie in the War of 1812 and given precious little manpower to fight the British.

Against all odds and flying a homemade battle flag that urged "Don't give up the ship," Perry deftly, and contentiously, earned one of the most stunning victories of the war. It marked the first time that an entire British naval squadron had ever surrendered.

Perry relayed news of the victory with the famous words that sent a country into celebration. "We have met the enemy and they are ours," he reported to Gen. William Henry Harrison. The quote remains one of the most famous in U.S. Naval history and is commemorated—along with the flag—at the U.S. Naval Academy in Annapolis, Maryland.

Over the years, the quote has also morphed into a warning that has nothing to do with Perry or his great victory. "We have met the enemy and he is us" was first used on a 1970 poster that promoted Earth Day. The idea, of course, was to point out the environmental damage that humans can cause. That version of the quote has also been used in comic strips and applied to other causes, and has become well-known in its own right.

Howitt Famously Cautions against Seduction

"'Will you walk into my parlour?' said the Spider to the Fly,
'Tis the prettiest little parlour that ever you did spy..."

✳   ✳   ✳   ✳

ENGLISH POET MARY Howitt did much of her writing in collaboration with her husband, William Howitt. The couple was so inseparable, in fact, their friends used to call them "William and Mary" with something of a royal flair. However, the 1829 publication of "The Spider and the Fly" gave Mary a fame and distinction all her own.

The first line of the poem draws readers in as the Spider lures the Fly into his lair using flattery to seduce. The Fly ultimately gives in, and pays the ultimate price. Howitt ends the poem with an overt warning to "dear little children," urging them never to give in when aempter uses such charm to seduce.

From literature to film to modern video games (of all things), the opening of the poem has stood the test of time as one of the most quoted lines ever. Lewis Carroll parodied the first line in *Alice's Adventures in Wonderland* in the "Lobster Quadrille," which utilizes the same rhyming scheme.

The Rolling Stones released "The Spider and the Fly" as a single in 1965, and The Cure made reference to the poem in their 1989 song "Lullaby." The poem has been animated for TV and the big screen, and the opening line uttered in virtually every format imaginable.

Howitt wrote prolifically into her 80s. She died in Rome in 1888, less than two months before she would have turned 90.

The Spider and the Fly

Will you walk into my parlour, said a Spider to a Fly;
'Tis the prettiest little parlour that ever you did spy.
The way into my parlour is up a winding stair,
And I have many pretty things to shew when you get there.
Oh, no, no! said the little Fly; to ask me is in vain:
For who goes up that winding stair shall ne'er come
down again.

"I'm sure you must be weary, dear, with soaring up so high;
Will you rest upon my little bed?" said the spider to the fly.
"There are pretty curtains drawn around, the sheets are fine
and thin,
And if you like to rest while, I'll snugly tuck you in."
"O no, no," said the little fly, "for I've often heard it said,
They NEVER, NEVER WAKE again, who sleep upon
YOUR bed."

Said the cunning Spider to the Fly, Dear friend, what can I do
To prove the warm affection I have ever felt tor you?
I have within my parlour great store of all that's nice:
I'm sure you're very welcome; will you please to take a slice!
Oh, no, no! said the little Fly; kind sir, that cannot be;
For I know what's in your pantry, and I do not wish to see.

Sweet creature, said the Spider, you're witty and you're wise;
How handsome are your gaudy wings, how brilliant your eyes!
I have a little looking-glass upon my parlour-shelf;
If you'll step in one moment, dear, you shall behold yourself.
Oh, thank you, gentle sir, she said, for what you're pleased
to say;
And wishing you good morning now, I'll call another day.

The Spider turn'd him round again, and went into his den,
For well he knew that silly Fly would soon come back again.
And then he wore a tiny web, in a little corner sly,
And set his table ready for to dine upon the Fly;
And went out to his door again, and merrily did sing,
Come hither, pretty little Fly, with the gold and silver wing;
Your robes are green and purple; there's a crest upon your head;
Your eyes are like the diamond bright, but mine are dull as lead."

Alas, alas! how very soon this silly little Fly,
Hearing his wily flattering words, came slowly fluttering by.
With humming wings she hung aloft, then nearer and
nearer drew.
Thinking only of her crested head and gold and purple hue:
Thinking only of her brilliant wings, poor silly thing! at last,
Up jump'd the cruel Spider, and firmly held her fast!
He dragg'd her up his winding stair, into his dismal den,
Within his little parlour; but she ne'er came down again.

And now, my pretty maidens, who may this story hear,
To silly, idle, flattering words, I pray you ne'er give ear;
Unto an evil counsellor close heart, and ear, and eye,
And learn a lesson from this tale of the Spider and the Fly.

Andersen the Unquestioned Father of Fairy Tales

Denmark's Hans Christian Andersen was more than a children's writer. He was a poet, playwright and novelist, although he is most remembered for several magical fairy tales that have stood the test of time.

✳ ✳ ✳ ✳

*T*HE EMPEROR'S NEW *Clothes, The Ugly Duckling, The Little Mermaid, The Princess and the Pea* and *Thumbelina* were just a few of the classic fairy tales Hans Christian Andersen gave to children—and parents—over several generations. The Danish author did not set out to become perhaps the best-known children's author of all time, but it's what he accomplished with a unique style and captivating story lines that have resonated for almost two centuries, and counting.

Andersen was born in 1805 and grew up in relative poverty. His mother was a washerwoman and his father a shoemaker who died when Hans was 11, but not before instilling in his son a love for storytelling. Hans was tall and awkward as a youth, often drawing uncomfortable laughs when telling stories, dancing or reciting plays in an attempt to entertain. He said he planned to become famous someday, but others encouraged him to take up a trade.

Instead, Hans moved to Copenhagen, where he tried singing, dancing and writing plays. Eventually, a group of sympathetic benefactors contributed money to send him away to school to learn some skills in his areas of interest. Hans, older than the other students, was ridiculed and made his way back to Copenhagen.

Prolific Writing Pays Off

Andersen traveled. And he wrote. He wrote plays. He wrote books. He wrote poems. Some met with marginal success, but nothing like the success he experienced when he started to write fairy tales. He had not written one before age 30. Once he started, he changed the world.

Andersen's fairy takes incorporated themes from his own childhood, and they were instantly well received. *The Ugly Duckling* reflected feelings about how awkward he felt as a young boy and how lonely he was at various points in his life. *The Little Match Girl* drew on experiences his mother had shared about times when she was required to beg in the streets as a young girl.

There is also a good degree of satire and political commentary woven through Andersen's tales. In *The Emperor's New Clothes*, for example, a vain ruler has two weavers dress him with an outfit that they say cannot be seen by those who are unfit for their positions or hopelessly stupid.

For those few unfamiliar with the story, everyone pretends to see clothes that are actually not there for fear of being exposed as unfit or ignorant. The emperor parades naked before his subjects before a little boy, immune to the pretense of the weavers' story, points out that "the Emperor has no clothes!"

The stories themes about pretense and going against popular opinion have made *The Emperor's New Clothes* and the saying, "the Emperor has no clothes," popular in many forms of art and literature since Andersen published the fairy tale in 1837. The same holds true for many of Andersen's 160-plus fairy tales.

Andersen was internationally acclaimed at the time of his death in 1875. His life and contributions have been commemorated in statue, stamp and numerous awards over the years. His was a rags-to-riches life, not unlike those of a fairy tale.

"'But he has nothing on at all,' said a little child at last. 'Good heavens! listen to the voice of an innocent child,' said the father, and one whispered to the other what the child had said.

'But he has nothing on at all,' cried at last the whole people."

Similar Sayings

"In composing, as a general rule, run your pen through every other word you have written; you have no idea what vigor it will give your style."

—SYDNEY SMITH

"An old tutor of a college said to one of his pupils: Read over your compositions, and wherever you meet with a passage which you think is particularly fine, strike it out."

—SAMUEL JOHNSON

"Whenever you feel an impulse to perpetrate a piece of exceptionally fine writing, obey it—whole-heartedly—and delete it before sending your manuscript to press. **Murder your darlings.***"*

—ARTHUR QUILLER-COUCH

"Omit needless words.

Vigorous writing is concise. A sentence should contain no unnecessary words, a paragraph no unnecessary sentences, for the same reason that a drawing should have no unnecessary lines and a machine no unnecessary parts. This requires not that the writer make all his sentences short, or that he avoid all detail and treat his subjects only in outline, but that every word tell."

—WILLIAM STRUNK, JR.

"Kill your darlings, kill your darlings, even when it breaks your ego-centric little scribbler's heart, kill your darlings."

—STEPHEN KING

Popular Saying Drawn from Many Sources

"All's fair in love and war." One of the most oft-quoted phrases has multiple origins but an agreed-upon meaning that's been debated for centuries.

❋   ❋   ❋   ❋

WAY BACK IN 1579, English poet John Lyly wrote a novel called *Euphues: The Anatomy of Wit* that contained the line, "the rules of fair play do not apply in love and war." Lyly is not always credited with authoring the "all's fair in love and war" credo, though his meaning could not be closer.

Cervantes, in the 1604 classic *Don Quixote*, wrote: "Love and war are all one … It is lawful to use sleights and stratagems to … attain the wished end." And the first known appearance of the quote in its "all's fair in love and war" grandeur comes from *Frank Fairleigh: Scenes from the Life of a Private Pupil*, an 1850 novel by Englishman Francis Edward Smedley about a schoolboy. It reads:

"You opened the letter!" exclaimed I.

"In course I did; how was I to read it if I hadn't? All's fair in love and war, you know …"

Now, more than four centuries after Lyly and more than 150 years after Smedley, all remains fair in love, war and famous quotes. The idea, of course, is that times of love and war change the rules of what's allowable and acceptable. True love and war victories are worth the price.

Or so it has been said.

Queen Victoria's Putdown: Fact or Fiction?

"There is a tale of the unfortunate equerry who ventured during dinner at Windsor to tell a story with a spice of scandal or impropriety in it. 'We are not amused,' said the Queen when he had finished."

✳   ✳   ✳   ✳

THE ABOVE ACCOUNT comes from Caroline Holland's 1919 *Notebooks of a Spinster Lady*. Its publication came 19 years after the Queen's death, so the long-reigning monarch was not around to verify its validity. Holland does not profess to have attended the dinner where the cheeky story was allegedly told.

Another version of the tale, said to have been told by Victoria's secretary Arthur Helps, contends that Victoria looked grimly at the entire group while those around the table chatted and laughed before settling them down with a cold, "We are not amused."

Research for the recent British television series *Victoria* brought about two more possibilities. One had Victoria cutting off Tom Hughes in mid-story as the young visitor tried to impress the Queen. Another had the remark directed toward Sir Arthur Bigge, who enjoyed telling inappropriate jokes and was thought to be having an affair with Victoria's daughter, Louise.

In any case, history can only speculate as to how, when, and even if the line was uttered. The thought of it, though, brings a smile to those who enjoy royal history.

Victoria Reigned for 63 Years

Queen Victoria, the daughter of Prince Edward, inherited the throne at age 18 in 1837 and ruled the United Kingdom of Great Britain and Ireland until her death in 1901. She was also known as the "Grandmother of Europe," as all nine of her children carried on royal or noble families across the continent.

Making her alleged dinner remark either ironic, telling, or both was the fact Victoria's reign— the Victorian Era—was known for its conservative, straight-laced morality. Those 63 years certainly saw tremendous growth in the areas of industry and science, along with the advancement of Great Britain in a number of political areas.

However, the matriarchal Victoria—standing no more than 5 feet tall—cast an imposing shadow over the country when it came to morality and behavior. She ran a smooth ship, and the tale of her casting off an inappropriate story or joke at the dinner table is one her subjects would have enjoyed telling and re-telling until it became part of history.

Unfortunately, the most likely scenario is that Victoria never delivered the line at all. Her granddaughter, Princess Alice, Countess of Athlone, gave an interview in 1976 in which she said Victoria claimed the famous story never happened.

"You know, I'm so disappointed," Alice said when asked about the tale. "I asked her, and she never said it."

Perhaps it was Queen Elizabeth I who shut down a risqué round of dinner table chatter. Perhaps Victoria delivered a more subdued scolding that benefitted from embellishment in its retelling. Perhaps it was a tall tale from the start, taken as fact with one author's writing and living on as others chronicled the life of the longest-reigning monarch. Or, just perhaps, the line was delivered as stated, with dramatic timing to boot.

In any of those cases, it has carried on as one of the most lasting royal quotes, making its way into movies, television shows, literature, and the stage for a century.

Warner Filled Churches with Song

"Jesus loves me—this I know,
For the Bible tells me so;
Little ones to him belong,—
They are weak, but he is strong."

✳   ✳   ✳   ✳

ONE OF THE most popular Christian hymns of all time comes from one of the most prolific and beloved hymn writers to ever belt out worship music. Anna Bartlett Warner, born on Long Island in 1827, lived to be 87 and filled most of those years with music.

Warner's father was a well-off lawyer in New York City, but he fell on hard times and moved his family to Constitution Island during Anna's youth. Anna and her sister, Susan, began writing short stories as a way to bring a little extra money in for the family. Anna also got a job teaching bible study at the U.S. Military Academy at nearby West Point.

While her sister became the more popular novelist of the two, Anna poured her heart and soul into religious poetry and had a gift for music. Songs of praise rolled off Anna's tongue and her pen. Accompanied by organ music, hymn after hymn found their way into churches around the northeast, and eventually across the country.

Written by Anna, "Jesus Loves Me" first appeared as a poem in one of Susan's novels, *Say and Seal*, in 1860. In the story, the words were spoken to bring comfort to a dying child. Two years after the book was published, William Batchelder Bradbury added music—along with the chorus "Yes, Jesus loves me"— and the song took flight, becoming one of the most popular children's hymns ever written.

Warner, Not Twain, Calls for Different Kind of Climate Change

"Everybody talks about the weather, but nobody does anything about it." Often attributed to Mark Twain, it was actually a close friend of his who offered it up. And as a New Englander, Charles Dudley Warner knew a thing or two about weather complaints.

✻ ✻ ✻ ✻

CHARLES DUDLEY WARNER was born in Massachusetts in 1829, lived in New York as a teenager, surveyed land in Missouri, studied law at Penn, and practiced in Chicago. After all that, however, he landed back in New England as a newspaper editor in Hartford, Connecticut.

Dudley and Mark Twain became close friends and, in 1873, they co-authored *The Gilded Age: A Tale of Today*. The book satirized corruption in post-Civil War America and is responsible for the name generally given to that period in U.S. history.

It was almost certainly Dudley who contributed the "weather" quote, though Twain started getting credit for it after using it in a lecture. Two published references from the 1880s attribute the quote to Dudley, whose references to the unpredictable New England weather were apparently common.

The saying showed up again in a *Hartford Courant* editorial in 1897 in this form: "A well-known American writer said once that, while everybody talked about the weather, nobody seemed to do anything about it."

Warner, toward the end of his career at the *Courant*, was almost certainly responsible for that editorial, meaning he referred to himself in the third person and accurately characterized himself as well known. And, of course, laid rightful claim to his own popular saying!

"The toad, without which no garden would be complete."

—CHARLES DUDLEY WARNER

'Forgotten Man' Never Far from Presidential Minds

The "Forgotten Man" has been portrayed in many ways since he was "born" as a lecture topic in 1883, including two completely opposite descriptions by U.S. presidents and politicians. One thing that he has not been, interestingly enough, is forgotten.

✳   ✳   ✳   ✳

THE "FORGOTTEN MAN" was first described by William Graham Sumner in an 1883 lecture. Sumner taught social sciences at Yale University and was one of the most prominent thinkers at the school. In today's terms, he would be called a conservative. He believed in a free-market economy, opposed imperialism, and was protective of the middle class.

His lecture, published posthumously as an essay in 1918, focused on those topics, with the Forgotten Man playing a leading role in the talk. He was the man left to pay the bill, Sumner argued, via taxes, for the social welfare and reformist programs put forth by liberals.

Sumner even offered a mathematical formula for the Forgotten Man's plight. He was C in the algebraic equation, where A and B get together and decide something needs to be done to alleviate the struggles of X. C is the Forgotten Man, who foots the bill for the assistance for X without a say in the matter.

Almost 50 years after the lecture, President Franklin Delano Roosevelt gave a 1932 radio address during the Great Depression to turn the tables on the Forgotten Man. FDR essentially made the Forgotten Man the X in Sumner's algebra.

"These unhappy times," Roosevelt said, "call for the building of plans that rest upon the forgotten, the unorganized but the indispensable units of economic power, for plans like those of 1917 that build from the bottom up and not from the top down, that put their faith once more in the Forgotten Man at the bottom of the economic pyramid."

Another Turn in Definition

While Roosevelt's Forgotten Man gained traction during the economic turbulence of the 1930s, showing up in songs, plays and films, the nation seemed to forget (pun intended) that Sumner's original Forgotten Man was not the downtrodden at all. He was the powerless middle-class man whose money was being redirected in support of Roosevelt's Forgotten Man.

However, the original Forgotten Man made something of a revival with Donald Trump's election to the White House in 2016. "Every single American will have the opportunity to realize his or her fullest potential," Trump declared in his victory speech. "The forgotten men and women of our country will be forgotten no longer."

Also nodding to the original Forgotten Man was a painting by conservative artist John McNaughton called "The Forgotten Man." It depicts a working-class American sitting on a bench with his head down, despondent, with money strewn about in front of him. In the background are several U.S. presidents, the Democratic ones presumably having forgotten about the man. President Barack Obama stands just a few paces from the bench, his arms folded and with one foot on the U.S. Constitution.

It might not have been exactly what Sumner envisioned when he addressed the crowd in Brooklyn more than 130 years ago, but it's closer than the FDR version of the Forgotten Man.

Spreading Light and Reflecting It

"There are two ways of spreading light: to be the candle or the mirror that reflects it."

Edith Wharton's ironic fiction about New York's high society that depicted the complex struggle of the individual within class constraints earned her a Pulitzer Prize in 1921 for her novel The Age of Innocence.

✳ ✳ ✳ ✳

EDITH WHARTON (NÉE Newbold) was born in New York City on January 24, 1862 to a family of old-money business elites. She was raised among the aristocracy of the City, and became familiar with its strict etiquette, snobbery and social taboos. She was educated at home by tutors. Her father had a large library, and Wharton read extensively. She began writing at a young age, and her poetry was noticed by Henry Wadsworth Longfellow, who recommended her parents allow her to publish it in *The New Atlantic*. Wharton completed her first novella, *Fast and Loose*, when she was sixteen. It was the first of many novels that perceptively mocked the manners of high society.

Literary Career

Edith married Edward Wharton, a wealthy Bostonian, in 1885. The couple lived on his inherited income, and traveled regularly to Europe. She continued publishing short stories in *Scribner's Magazine*, and two more novels, *The Valley of Decision* in 1902 and *The House of Mirth* in 1905.

The quote above also dates to that time period; in 1902, Wharton's long poem "Vesalius in Zante (1564)," which contains those lines, was published in *North American Review*. The Vesalius of the title was an anatomist and physician; he died on the Greek island on Zante in 1564.

The couple moved to France in 1907, where Wharton wrote *Ethan Frome*, one of her most celebrated novels, published in 1911. It is her only novel set in the countryside, and is loosely based on real events. As her reputation increased, she and Edward, who were never close, grew apart; his mental health deteriorated and they would eventually divorce in 1913. She continued to visit the United States, but would live in France for the rest of her life.

During World War I, Wharton was instrumental in establishing organizations to support refugees from the war. She also visited the war front on several occasions to distribute medical supplies, and wrote a number of essays that urged Americans to support the Allied war effort. The essays were published in *Fighting France from Dunkerque to Belfort* in 1915. She continued to do charitable work for war survivors and homeless in France in the years following the war.

Winner of the Pulitzer Prize for Fiction

Wharton wrote *The Age of Innocence* as a four-part serial in *Pictoral Magazine* in 1920. She became the first woman to be awarded the Pulitzer Prize for Fiction for the book. *Innocence* is set during the Gilded Age among the New York aristocracy, and subtly contrasts the extreme attention to outward manners and etiquette with the hidden social machinations among that class. It also contrasted the "old" world (before WWI) with the "new." The novel was published to universal acclaim in the United States and Europe. She received an honorary doctorate from Yale University in 1923.

In 1934 Wharton published her autobiography, *A Backward Glance*. She spent her later years living at *Le Pavillon Colombe* in northern France, where she continued to visit with many of the noted literary figures of the day. An extraordinarily prolific writer, she penned a total of sixteen novels, sixteen short story collections, eleven non-fiction books, six novellas and three books of poetry. Her novels have been adapted more than a dozen times into films and theatre productions. Wharton died in France, on August 11, 1937, and was buried at Versailles.

Quotes from Wharton

"It was part of her discernment to be aware that life is the only real counselor, that wisdom unfiltered through personal experience does not become a part of the moral tissues."

—*Sanctuary*

"The only way not to think about money is to have a great deal of it."

—*The House of Mirth*

"Life is always a tightrope or a feather bed. Give me the tightrope."

—*Journal*

"The worst of doing one's duty was that it apparently unfitted one for doing anything else."

—*The Age of Innocence*

"In the rotation of crops there was a recognized season for wild oats; but they were not sown more than once."

—*The Age of Innocence*

"In spite of illness, in spite even of the archenemy sorrow, one can remain alive long past the usual date of disintegration if one is unafraid of change, insatiable in intellectual curiosity, interested in big things, and happy in small ways."

—*A Backward Glance*

George Santayana

"Those who cannot remember the past are condemned to repeat it."

George Santayana was a Spanish-American cultural critic and philosopher who coined many popular aphorisms and originated the definition of beauty as "pleasure objectified."

✳ ✳ ✳ ✳

JORGE AGUSTÍN NICOLÁS Ruiz de Santayana y Borrás was born in Madrid on December 16, 1863. When he was nine, his family moved to Boston, where he attended the Boston Latin School. Santayana graduated from Harvard in 1886, and spent two years studying philosophy at the University of Berlin. In 1889, he received a PhD in philosophy and began teaching philosophy at Harvard. Santayana's students included luminaries such as T.S. Eliot, Robert Frost, Gertrude Stein, and W.E.B. Du Bois. He published *The Sense of Beauty*, a study of aesthetics, in 1896. This was the first major work on aesthetics writing in the United States. Santayana was later reported to have said he only wrote the book because he was under pressure to publish to be granted tenure.

He wrote his five-volume *The Life of Reason* in 1905–06. It is considered the first major work on the philosophy of Pragmatism and is the source of the quote above. He was made a full professor at Harvard in 1907, but following the death of his mother in 1912, he resigned his position and remained in Europe for the rest of his life, settling permanently in Rome in 1924. He wrote *The Realms of Being* from 1927–1942. The four-volume work deals with truth, materialism, and human consciousness. An atheist, he described himself as an "aesthetic Catholic," and had an affinity for the culture of the Roman church.

Santayana died on September 26, 1952.

Quotes from Santayana

"Beauty as we feel it is something indescribable: what it is or what it means can never be said."

—THE SENSE OF BEAUTY

"Happiness is the only sanction of life; where happiness fails, existence remains a mad and lamentable experiment."

—THE LIFE OF REASON

"That life is worth living is the most necessary of assumptions and, were it not assumed, the most impossible of conclusions".

—THE LIFE OF REASON

"Fanaticism consists in redoubling your efforts when you have forgotten your aim."

—THE LIFE OF REASON

"Progress, far from consisting in change, depends on retentiveness. When change is absolute there remains no being to improve and no direction is set for possible improvement: and when experience is not retained, as among savages, infancy is perpetual. Those who cannot remember the past are condemned to repeat it."

—THE LIFE OF REASON

"It is not society's fault that most men seem to miss their vocation. Most men have no vocation."

—THE LIFE OF REASON

"History is nothing but assisted and recorded memory. It might almost be said to be no science at all, if memory and faith in memory were not what science necessarily rest on. In order to sift evidence we must rely on some witness, and we must trust experience before we proceed to expand it. The line between what is known scientifically and what has to be assumed in order to support knowledge is impossible to draw."

—THE LIFE OF REASON

"There is no cure for birth and death save to enjoy the interval."

—SOLILOQUIES IN ENGLAND AND LATER SOLILOQUIES

Keeping One's Head

Widely considered one of the greatest British writers of the Victorian era, Nobel laureate Rudyard Kipling wrote beloved novels, poems, and short stories, including The Jungle Book, Kim, *and the poems "If-" and "Gunga Din."*

✳ ✳ ✳ ✳

RUDYARD KIPLING WAS born in Mumbai, India, on December 30, 1865. At the age of six, he was sent to Southsea, England, for his education. This time was difficult for Kipling; he did not fit in at school and his foster parents were cruel. He found solace in reading, and would later credit these years to his love of literature. Kipling returned to India in 1882, and began writing articles and short stories for the *Civil and Military Gazette* in Lahore. These would be collected in *Plain Tales from the Hills*, published in 1888.

The following year Kipling traveled through Singapore and Japan to the United States. He toured the U.S. extensively, writing articles for an American newspaper that were later collected in his second published volume. He met and married Carrie Balestier in 1891, and they settled in Brattleboro, Vermont. During their years in Vermont, he wrote *The Jungle Book* and *A Story of West and East*. In 1896, they returned to England. Kipling wrote *Kim* in 1901 and began working on *Just So Stories*.

"If-"

Kipling wrote "If-" in 1895, and it was published in *Rewards and Fairies* in 1910. The poem was inspired by the British colonial politician Leander Starr Jameson, who led a failed attack on the Transvaal government in South Africa that would help spark the Boer War. "If-" was written as paternal advice to Kipling's son John.

Kipling died on January 18, 1936.

The Text of "If-"

If you can keep your head when all about you
Are losing theirs and blaming it on you,
If you can trust yourself when all men doubt you,
But make allowance for their doubting too;
If you can wait and not be tired by waiting,
Or being lied about, don't deal in lies,
Or being hated, don't give way to hating,
And yet don't look too good, nor talk too wise:

If you can dream—and not make dreams your master;
If you can think—and not make thoughts your aim;
If you can meet with Triumph and Disaster
And treat those two impostors just the same;
If you can bear to hear the truth you've spoken
Twisted by knaves to make a trap for fools,
Or watch the things you gave your life to, broken,
And stoop and build 'em up with worn-out tools:

If you can make one heap of all your winnings
And risk it on one turn of pitch-and-toss,
And lose, and start again at your beginnings
And never breathe a word about your loss;
If you can force your heart and nerve and sinew
To serve your turn long after they are gone,
And so hold on when there is nothing in you
Except the Will which says to them: 'Hold on!'

If you can talk with crowds and keep your virtue,
Or walk with Kings—nor lose the common touch,
If neither foes nor loving friends can hurt you,
If all men count with you, but none too much;
If you can fill the unforgiving minute
With sixty seconds' worth of distance run,
Yours is the Earth and everything that's in it,
And—which is more—you'll be a Man, my son!

How Did the Cold War Begin?

An exploration of the factors that started the Cold War is outside the scope of this book. But the phrase comes to us from Bernard Baruch, an American businessman, philanthropist, and statesman who advised three United States Presidents and played a major role in crafting United Nations policy on the control of atomic energy.

* * * *

BERNARD BARUCH WAS born in Camden, South Carolina, on August 19, 1870. When he was eleven years old his family moved to New York City. Baruch studied at City College of New York. After graduating, he began working as a broker at a securities firm on Wall Street. He bought a seat on the New York Stock Exchange and made a fortune speculating on sugar prices. By 1910 he was one of Wall Street's most highly regarded brokers.

World War I

As it became increasingly apparent that the United States would be drawn into World War I, Baruch left his broker-age firm to advise Woodrow Wilson on the management of a wartime economy. He was appointed chairman of the War Industries Board in 1918, where he promoted the adoption of mass production of supplies for the war effort and successfully mitigated disputes between labor and management to prevent strikes from halting the manufacture of munitions. Following the war, Baruch was a member of the Supreme Economic Council at the Paris Peace Conference. He lobbied against the Allies' demands of economic reparations from Germany, and supported the creation of the League of Nations.

World War II

During the Great Depression, Baruch was a member of FDR's "Brain Trust" that advised him on creating the policies that shaped the New Deal and established the National Recovery

Administration. During World War II, Roosevelt considered appointing Baruch to the War Production Board but ultimately declined to do so. Although he did not hold an administrative post during the war, he continued to advise Roosevelt on matters of wartime economic policy.

His recommendations led to an increased role for civilian businessmen in determining the most efficient means of producing wartime supplies. He was widely credited with establishing policies that greatly increased the production of munitions and supplies and enabled the United States to invade Europe approximately two years sooner than it otherwise could have.

Naming the Cold War

Following the war, Harry Truman appointed him to represent the United States at the United Nations Atomic Energy Commission (UNAEC). In 1946, he presented a proposal to the Commission, called the Baruch Plan. The proposed plan would have seen the United States destroy its existing atomic weapons on the condition that an international system of controls was adopted. The controls would limit the use of atomic energy to only peaceful ends. Although the Commission passed the proposal, the Soviet Union abstained from the resolution on the proposal that was presented to the Security Council.

Because the United Nations could not convince the Soviet Union to agree to an atomic control treaty, the United States continued to develop its own nuclear arsenal. Relations between the United States and the Soviet Union deteriorated, as the Soviets rejected the Marshall Plan to rebuild Europe and the United States actively supported anti-communist partisans in the Greek Civil War. On October 24, 1947, while speaking before the Senate Special Committee Investigating the National Defense Program, Baruch first said "we are in a cold war that is getting warmer."

Baruch died on June 20, 1965, in New York City.

The Opiate of the People

Karl Marx, a nineteenth-century German philosopher, developed ideas regarding the nature of capitalism that would hugely impact events of the 20th century. Along with Friedrich Engels, he wrote the seminal treatise on class struggle, The Communist Manifesto, *and his work heavily influenced the Bolshevik Revolution and other Communist movements in the 20th century. He also left us some phrases that we use today without realizing their origin.*

* * * *

KARL MARX WAS born in Prussia on May 5, 1818. He studied for two semesters at the University of Bonn, before enrolling at the University of Berlin, where he studied philosophy and the law. There he was introduced to the philosophy of Hegel, whose theories on dialectics would largely influence the development of Marx's own philosophy of dialectical materialism. Marx became radicalized during his time at university, and when he received his doctorate in 1841, he was unable to secure a teaching position because of his politics.

He edited a liberal newspaper in Cologne until it was shut down by the government in 1843. He began working on a discussion of Hegel's philosophy of right, in which he described religion as the "opiate of the people." (The phrase is sometimes translated from the German as "the opium of the masses.") He saw religion as serving a structural function for society, in that it reduced the immediate suffering of people and made life more bearable—much like an opiate to a sick person—but also reduced their willingness to revolt against the oppressive reality of capitalism.

Marx married Jenny von Westphalen in 1843 and they moved to Paris, where he began collaborating with Friedrich Engels. In 1846, Marx moved to Brussels and began working with the Communist League, and in 1848 he and Engels published *The*

Communist Manifesto. He was expelled from Belgium, and found himself stateless, as neither France nor Prussia would accept him. He settled in London, where he began working on Das Kapital, his opus on the divisive and oppressive nature of capitalism, which was published in 1867.

Marx died on March 14, 1888, and is buried in London.

"Hegel remarks somewhere that all great world-historic facts and personages appear, so to speak, twice. He forgot to add: the first time as tragedy, the second time as farce."

—MARX'S *THE EIGHTEENTH BRUMAIRE OF LOUIS BONAPARTE*

Master of His Fate, Captain of His Soul

Henley was a British poet and literary critic who edited several literary journals that published many great British writers' early work in the late 19th century. He was the inspiration for the character Long John Silver in his friend Robert Louis Stevenson's book Treasure Island.

✳ ✳ ✳ ✳

WILLIAM ERNEST HENLEY was born on August 23, 1849, in Gloucester, England. At a young age, he was tutored by the poet T.E. Brown when he was a student at The Crypt School in Gloucester. When he was twelve, he contracted tuberculosis. The disease would later result in the amputation of his left leg below the knee in 1869. His other leg was saved by Joseph Lister, who treated him in Edinburgh; Lister's pioneering work in the use of antiseptic surgery would revolutionize medicine.

Henley was forced to stay in an infirmary for nearly two years in 1873–75, and while he was there he began writing poetry about hospital life. His poems were published in *The Cornhill Magazine* and later collected in 1888 in *A Book of Verses*.

"Invictus"

In 1875, he wrote "Invictus," one of his most famous poems; it was included in *A Book of Verses*. The work is representative of the value Victorian society placed on stoicism in the face of adversity, and it established Henley's reputation as a poet of note. The poem became well-known, and has been referenced throughout the twentieth century by notable figures. Winston Churchill paraphrased the poem in a speech to the House of Commons during World War II, and Nelson Mandela recited the poem to fellow anti-apartheid prisoners imprisoned on Robben Island. The poem has also been referenced numerous times in novels and films.

Literary Influence

When Henley recovered from his long stay in the hospital, he began editing several literary journals, starting with *The London* in 1877–78, and later the *Scots Observer* and *London Observer*. As editor, he had considerable control over which pieces would be published in these journals, and he was able to exert significant influence over the literary scene in Britain at the time. He published the early work of writers who would go on to great fame, including Thomas Hardy, H.G. Wells, Rudyard Kipling, William Butler Yeats, and George Bernard Shaw. The writers associated with him were sometimes referred to a "Henley's Regatta." He also edited *The Magazine of Art* from 1882–1886, and used his position to help the careers of James Whistler and Auguste Rodin.

Henley married Hannah Johnson Boyle in 1878. They had one daughter, Margaret Henley, who was the inspiration for Wendy Darling in the book *Peter Pan*, by the Henley's family friend J.M. Barrie. Margaret called Barrie her "fwendy-wendy," which inspired the name. A sickly child, Margaret died when she was only five, before the book was published.

Henley continued to publish volumes of poetry, including *London Voluntaries* in 1893, *Hawthorn and Lavender* in 1899, and *For England's Sake* in 1900. He died of tuberculosis on July 11, 1903, in Woking, England.

The Text of "Invictus"

Out of the night that covers me,
Black as the pit from pole to pole,
I thank whatever gods may be
For my unconquerable soul.
In the fell clutch of circumstance
I have not winced nor cried aloud.
Under the bludgeonings of chance
My head is bloody, but unbowed.
Beyond this place of wrath and tears
Looms but the Horror of the shade,
And yet the menace of the years
Finds and shall find me unafraid.
It matters not how strait the gate,
How charged with punishments the scroll,
I am the master of my fate,
I am the captain of my soul.

Drawing Circles

Edwin Markham, and educator and poet, was the Poet Laureate of Oregon from 1923 to 1931.

✳ ✳ ✳ ✳

CHARLES EDWIN MARKHAM was born in Oregon City on April 23, 1852, and was raised on a ranch in Northern California. He studied at California College and at Christian College in Santa Rosa, California. In 1872, he began teaching in Los Berros, and later in El Dorado county, near Sacramento. Markham was married three times. His first marriage fell apart due to his own infidelity. He remarried in 1887, but his second wife died in 1893. His third and final marriage, to Anna Catherine Murphy, was in 1898. She became his literary collaborator and editor, and they had a son together.

"The Man with the Hoe" and Other Works

Markham began publishing poetry in the 1880s, and sought the advice of other writers of the time, including Ambrose Bierce, who praised Markham's idealism. Markham's interest in the tribulations of poor and working-class people would be evident in "The Man with the Hoe," a fierce commentary on the hardships they faced:

"Bowed by the weight of centuries he leans
Upon his hoe and gazes on the ground,
The emptiness of ages in his face,
And on his back the burden of the world."

Inspired by an 1862 woodcut of the same title by the French artist François Millet, the poem was published in 1899 in the *San Francisco Examiner*. It not only described the oppression faced by day laborers, but also challenged society to address class disparities. It was consistent with the broader social reformist ideals of the time, and it quickly spread throughout the country as it was reprinted in dozens of publications.

The poem sparked a great deal of public discussion about the treatment of laborers in American society. It was included in Markham's first book of poetry, *The Man with the Hoe and Other Poems*, published the same year. The work includes poems that deal with Markham's mysticism, including "A Prayer," which examined his place in nature. Due to the success of the book, Markham was invited to write a poem that commemorated Abraham Lincoln for a birthday celebration in New York City at the turn of the century. "Lincoln, Man of the People," was well received, and he would publicly deliver it again at the dedication of the Lincoln Memorial in Washington, D.C. He included the poem in his second volume, *Lincoln and Other Poems*, published in 1901.

Markham's productivity slowed in the following years, but he remained an active literary figure and continued to teach. In 1908 he was elected to the National Institute of Arts and Letters, and in 1910, he founded the Poetry Society of America, which he spent much of his time administering. He did not publish another book of poetry until 1915: *The Shoes of Happiness and Other Poems* included the epigram "Outwitted," among others.

"He drew a circle that shut me out–
Heretic, a rebel, a thing to flout.
But Love and I had the wit to win:
We drew a circle that took him in!"

In 1920, he published *The Gates of Paradise,* and he published his final collection of poetry, *New Poems: Eighty Songs at Eighty,* in 1932. These were less well received than his earlier works, in part because he refused to adapt to the development of the modernist poetry movement, led by Ezra Pound, William Carlos Williams, and T.S. Eliot. Still he remained a significant literary figure, and he was honored by President Herbert Hoover at Carnegie Hall for his contributions to American literature on his eightieth birthday.

Markham died on March 7, 1940, at his home in New York.

The Horror, the Horror!

Joseph Conrad's novels Lord Jim, Heart of Darkness, *and* The Secret Agent, *explored the darker aspects of human nature and were loosely based on his own travels in South America, Asia, and Africa.*

✳   ✳   ✳   ✳

JOSEPH CONRAD (JOZEF Konrad Korzeniowski) was born in Berdychiv, Ukraine, on December 3, 1857. His parents were members of the Polish aristocracy, and supported the Polish independence movement against Russian rule. When he was four years old, Conrad's parents were arrested for their patriotic activities and sent to Vologda in northwest Russia. They died a few years later, and Conrad returned to Poland, where he was raised by an uncle. As a child, Conrad was tutored at home by his father, and upon his return to Poland he attended school in Krakow.

When he was sixteen years old, he travelled to Marseilles, France, where found work on merchant ships. He traveled to South America and served as a ship's apprentice and ship's steward, and may have taken part in international gunrunning. In his twenties, following a failed suicide attempt due to debts, he joined the British Merchant Navy, where he served for sixteen years. During his time as a merchant marine, Conrad sailed around the world, traveling to India, Singapore, Australia, and Africa. He was promoted multiple times and granted British citizenship.

Literary Career

Conrad began working on his first novel, *Almayer's Folly*, while he was in the Merchant Navy. The book is an adventure tale set in the jungles of Borneo. When he left the seafaring life in 1894, it was for several reasons, but his desire to begin a literary career was chief among them. He published *Almayer's* in 1895, and it received mixed reactions from critics due to the author's clear awkwardness with the English language. In 1896, he published *An Outpost of Progress*, a short story set in Belgium-controlled Congo, and *An Outcast of the Islands*, a novel set in Indonesia. Like his later novels, *Outpost* and *Outcast*, were both critical of colonialism.

Conrad married Jessie Emmeline George in 1896, and the couple had two children.

In 1900, Conrad published *Lord Jim* to critical acclaim. The book tells the story of a young sailor who, with his fellow crewmen, abandoned his ship while it was in distress, leaving the passengers to drown. The passengers are rescued, however, and Jim must grapple with the consequences of his cowardice. He travels to the South Pacific and eventually becomes the leader of a small country there.

In 1902, Conrad published what is perhaps his most famous novel, *Heart of Darkness*. Like Outpost, it is set in the Belgian Congo. The protagonist, an Englishman named Marlow, travels up the Congo River where he encounters a brutal and mysterious ivory trader named Kurtz, who has made himself the ruler of the native people in his area. *Heart of Darkness* examines the cruelty of humankind, and compares the "darkness" of both London and the Congo, arguing that civilized people have much in common with those they describe as "savage." The book is highly critical of colonial practices, which Conrad was familiar with from his years as a seafarer, and contains the lines, "The horror! The horror!" that have been referenced by multiple works through the decades that have followed, often in parody.

Conrad published several more novels during his lifetime, including *Nostromo* in 1904 and *The Secret Agent* in 1907, as well as collections of short stories. He died in Canterbury, England, an August 3, 1924.

No Free Lunch

The adage "there's no such thing as a free lunch" dates back until at least the 1930s in the United States. The idea originated in the practice of taverns offering a free lunch to drinking patrons.

✳ ✳ ✳ ✳

THE ADAGE REFERS to the belief that it is impossible to get something for nothing. Even if something appears free, the recipient, by choosing that, foregoes another alternative that they can no longer enjoy. This is called the *opportunity cost* in microeconomic theory. Milton Friedman popularized the phrase to describe opportunity cost in his 1975 book of the same name, and it remains central to capitalist economic theory. Friedman was one of the leaders of the Chicago school of economics, an affiliation of economic theorists associated with the University of Chicago. Friedman and his colleagues challenged classical Keynesian economic theory, developed by the British economist John Maynard Keynes during the Great Depression.

Friedman strongly opposed the principles of Keynesian government intervention during times of economic crisis. Friedman argued that there is a "natural" rate of unemployment, and that government intervention will lead to inflation. His 1975 book lays out many of his arguments in support of this theory. In 1976, he was awarded the Nobel Prize in Economics for his work. Friedman remained one of the most influential American economists until his death on November 16, 2006 in San Francisco.

The idea of a "free lunch" may have originated from the practice of American saloons offering a midday lunch buffet to customers who purchased a drink during the nineteenth century. Rudyard Kipling described the practice in his 1899 book *American Notes*. The economic position that contends there is no "free lunch" would observe that in this example, the patrons were paying for their drinks, which would likely be priced higher so the saloon could recoup the cost of the sandwiches.

The phrase first appeared in print in 1938, in a syndicated column in Scripps-Howard newspapers. The column was titled "Economics in Eight Words." The column was meant to satirize the economics of the New Deal, and described a fable of a kingdom that had fallen into poverty. The king called upon a council of economists to describe economic theory to him. After numerous attempts to explain the subject in shorter and shorter texts, the oldest economist turns to the king and utters the phrase.

The phrase later appeared in print Robert Heinlein's novel *The Moon Is a Harsh Mistress* in 1966. Heinlein was one of the first mainstream science fiction writers in the United States, and along with Isaac Asimov and Arthur C. Clarke, he is among the "Big Three" of American Science Fiction. *The Moon Is a Harsh Mistress* is one of the first science fiction novels to discuss libertarian ideas, and the third section of the book, *TNSTAAFL!* is an acronym of the phrase. *Mistress* was critically acclaimed, and along with *Starship Troopers* is considered among Heinlein's best works.

"No free lunch" remains a popular shorthand reference to the underlying principles of neoclassical economic theory.

Man Bites Dog

"When a dog bites a man, that is not news, because it happens so often. But if a man bites a dog, that is news."

This quote is widely attributed to John Bogart, the editor of the New York Sun, *but it may have been coined by the British newspaper magnate Alfred Harmsworth or by Jesse Lynch Williams in 1899.*

✳ ✳ ✳ ✳

John Bogart

JOHN BOGART WAS born in New York in 1848, and when he was sixteen he left home to join the Union Army in the Civil War. Following the war, he worked for a few years in a dry goods store before being hired as a reporter for the *New York Sun* in 1871. He was promoted to city editor after only five years at the paper. Bogart served as the city editor for seventeen years until he fell ill in 1890, forcing him to resign, but he continued to contribute articles to the newspaper for many years. Bogart was regularly quoted by fellow journalists, and he is most famously associated with the "man bites dog" quote. He died on November 17, 1921, and the quote was mentioned in his obituary in the *New York Times*.

Alfred Harmsworth

The quote is also attributed to Alfred Harmsworth, who was born in County Dublin, Ireland, on July 15, 1865. Harmsworth was educated in England from 1876–1878. In his twenties, he started his first newspaper, and acquired several periodicals, which he eventually built into the largest publishing company in the world at the time, Amalgamated Press. He bought *The Evening News* in 1894 and founded the *Edinburgh Daily Record*. In 1896, Harmsworth founded the *Daily Mail* in London; the paper remains in circulation to this day. In 1903 he founded *The Daily Mirror*, another London paper still in circulation, and purchased three more newspapers in 1905 and 1908.

His newspaper empire garnered him significant political influence. His newspapers were able to force the collapse of the government of the Liberal Prime Minister Herbert Asquith and helped to support the appointment of David Lloyd George as Prime Minister in 1916. In the run-up to World War I, his newspapers were ferociously anti-German, and the level of anti-German propaganda they reported was so immense that the Germans shelled his house during the war in an attempt to kill him. Harmsworth died in London on August 14, 1922.

Jesse Lynch Williams

Jesse Lynch Williams was a Pulitzer Prize-winning author and dramatist. He was born on August 17, 1871 in Sterling, Illinois. He started writing while he was attending Princeton College, and his first book, *Princeton Stories*, was published while he was still in college. Williams published *The Stolen Story and Other Newspaper Stories* in 1899, where the "man bites dog" phrase is found. An older reporter in the book named Billy Woods speaks the line as he is discussing the newspaper business with young protégés. This may have been the first time the quote appeared in print. Williams wrote five novels and three plays, including one based on *The Stolen Story*. This play may have led to the initial popularization of the phrase. Williams died on September 14, 1929.

Cold Cut Wisdom

"No matter how thin you slice it, it's still baloney."

New York Governor Al Smith has long been associated with the phrase, although its origins are unclear.

✳ ✳ ✳ ✳

ALFRED EMANUEL "AL" Smith was born on December 30, 1873 on the Lower East Side of Manhattan, New York. He had to drop out of school at the age of thirteen when his father died, and went to work at the Fulton Fish Market for the next seven years. Although he never attended school after that, he said he studied the customers at the market, and developed his oratorical skills while hawking fish.

Political Career

Smith began working as an investigator for Tammany Hall, the powerful New York Democratic organization, in 1895. In 1904, he won his first election to the New York State Assembly, where he worked to improve conditions for factory workers. He co-chaired the commission that investigated the Triangle Shirtwaist Factory fire in 1911, and the commission's findings led to the adoption of a series of labor and safety laws.

In 1915, Smith was elected to the Sheriff of New York County, a position that allowed him to consolidate his political power. The Sheriff controlled hundreds of patronage positions and effectively gave Smith control of an army of Democratic political workers.

In 1917 he leveraged his political connections to win election as President of the Board of Aldermen, and the following year he was elected Governor of New York. Although he lost his reelection campaign in 1920, he was reelected in the three subsequent elections. Smith ran on an anti-Prohibition platform, and embraced the Progressive Movement in the 1920s. While he was opposed by many teetotaling conservatives, many New

Yorkers who did not drink also supported him because of the gangland lawlessness that proliferated during Prohibition.

Smith was the Democratic candidate for U.S. president in 1928, and was the first Catholic nominee for the position. He attracted Catholic voters as well as women voters, who had just secured the vote after decades of suffragist agitation. But he was opposed by conservative white anti-Catholic Democrats in the Southern states, and many Protestants opposed him as well, fearing that he would be beholden to the Vatican. He was defeated by Herbert Hoover in a landslide. Hoover won six Southern states, and was the first Republican to win that many since the Civil War. In 1932, Smith again stood for the nomination of the Democratic party, but lost to his longtime rival Franklin D Roosevelt.

Smith was publicly critical of Roosevelt's New Deal, and supported Republican candidates in the 1936 and 1940 elections. He went so far as to deliver speeches on behalf of Wendell Winkie, the 1940 Republican candidate, during the campaign. He largely retired from public life following the 1940 election. Smith died on October 4, 1944, only a few months after his beloved wife Catherine died.

"It's Still Baloney"

Smith is widely associated with the phrase, but he may not have originated it. The phrase was widely popular among flappers during the 1920s, and appeared as early as 1926 in the Baltimore *Sun* in an article about contemporary slang. The article claimed that the phrase was so well-known that many flappers merely said "no matter how thin you slice it," with the second half of the phrase being implied. Al Smith often referred to the New Deal as "baloney dollars" following Roosevelt's devaluing of the dollar.

Chapter 11

The Quotables

As a Wise Man Once Said …

*If you hear someone say, "Mark Twain once said…," chances are
that what follows was never said by Twain.*

✳ ✳ ✳ ✳

MARK TWAIN IS a *quote magnet,* a person to whom quotations are often falsely ascribed. And the process of ascrib-
ing quotations to such people is sometimes called *Churchillian
drift,* a term coined by quotation maven Nigel Rees in reference to Winston Churchill, another powerful quote magnet.
Others who attract credit for a lot of quotes include Benjamin
Franklin, Yogi Berra, Abraham Lincoln, Oscar Wilde, Satchel
Paige, and George Bernard Shaw.

Examples of quotations falsely attributed to quote
magnets include:

✳ "The coldest winter I ever spent was a summer in San
Francisco." Falsely attributed to Mark Twain. No one knows
who first changed Twain's similar, but less eloquent, comment about Paris into this pithy form.

✳ "Donny Osmond has Van Gogh's ear for music." Falsely
attributed to Orson Welles, but actually said by Billy Wilder
in 1964 about actor Cliff Osmond (no relation): "Cliff has
the musical ear of Van Gogh."

* "If you're not a liberal when you're 25, you have no heart. If you're not a conservative by the time you're 35, you have no brain." Falsely attributed to Winston Churchill; probably a paraphrase of a quote by historian and statesman François Guizot.

Why are such people quote magnets? Well, often a quote can be "improved" by attributing it to a famous person. A pithy bit of wisdom sounds better if it comes from Abraham Lincoln rather than your Uncle Henry. Even a quote from a famed director like Billy Wilder can be improved by attributing it to an even more famous director (and changing the subject to a more famous Osmond).

The problem has worsened in the age of the Internet, where myths and false attributions multiply like viruses until it's almost impossible to find the truth.

Perhaps the subject of quote magnets is best summed up by George Bernard Shaw: "I tell you I have been misquoted everywhere, and the inaccuracies are chasing me around the world."

16 Quotes from George Bernard Shaw

Since we brought up George Bernard Shaw, here are 16 things he did write in his various works and plays...

* * * *

"Patriotism is, fundamentally, a conviction that a particular country is the best in the world because you were born in it..."

—*THE WORLD*

"People are always blaming circumstances for what they are. I don't believe in circumstances. The people who get on in this world are the people who get up and look for the circumstances they want, and, if they can't find them, make them."

—*MRS. WARREN'S PROFESSION*

"We have no more right to consume happiness without producing it than to consume wealth without producing it."

—CANDIDA

"We don't bother much about dress and manners in England, because as a nation we don't dress well and we've no manners."

—YOU CAN NEVER TELL

"There is only one religion, though there are a hundred versions of it."

—PLAYS PLEASANT AND UNPLEASANT

"The salvation of the world depends on the men who will not take evil good-humouredly, and whose laughter destroys the fool instead of encouraging him."

—QUINTESSENCE OF IBSENISM

"The fickleness of the women I love is only equaled by the infernal constancy of the women who love me."

—THE PHILANDERER

"Pardon him, Theodotus: he is a barbarian, and thinks that the customs of his tribe and island are the laws of nature."

—CAESAR AND CLEOPATRA

"When a stupid man is doing something he is ashamed of, he always declares that it is his duty."

—CAESAR AND CLEOPATRA

"The worst sin towards our fellow creatures is not to hate them, but to be indifferent to them: that's the essence of inhumanity."

—THE DEVIL'S DISCIPLE

"The only man I know who behaves sensibly is my tailor; he takes my measurements anew each time he sees me. The rest go on with their old measurements and expect me to fit them."

—MAN AND SUPERMAN

"A man's own self is the last person to believe in him, and is harder to cheat than the rest of the world."

—LOVE AMONG THE ARTISTS

"Geniuses are horrid, intolerant, easily offended, sleeplessly self-conscious men, who expect their wives to be angels with no further business in life than to pet and worship their husbands. Even at the best they are not comfortable men to live with; and a perfect husband is one who is perfectly comfortable to live with."

—*Love Among the Artists*

"He who confuses political liberty with freedom and political equality with similarity has never thought for five minutes about either."

—*Maxims for Revolutionists*

"The reasonable man adapts himself to the world: the unreasonable one persists in trying to adapt the world to himself. Therefore all progress depends on the unreasonable man."

—*Maxims for Revolutionists*

"Independence? That's middle-class blasphemy. We are all dependent on one another, every soul of us on earth."

—*Pygmalion*

Pop Quiz: Shakespeare or the Bible?

Each phrase below comes from either a Shakespeare play or sonnet or the Bible. Do you know which is which?

✳ ✳ ✳ ✳

1. A living dog is better than a dead lion.

a) Shakespeare

b) Bible

2. A house divided against itself cannot stand.

a) Shakespeare

b) Bible

3. Neither a borrower nor a lender be.

a) Shakespeare

b) Bible

4. Brevity is the soul of wit.

a) Shakespeare

b) Bible

5. Cry havoc and let slip the dogs of war.

a) Shakespeare

b) Bible

6. The game is afoot.

a) Shakespeare

b) Bible

7. Set my teeth on edge.

a) Shakespeare

b) Bible

8. Milk of human kindness

a) Shakespeare

b) Bible

9. Don't cast your pearls before swine.

a) Shakespeare

b) Bible

Answers: 1. Bible (Ecclesiastes 9:4); 2. Bible (Matthew 12:25); 3. Shakespeare (Hamlet); 4. Shakespeare (Hamlet); 5. Shakespeare (Julius Caesar); 6. Shakespeare (Henry IV); 7. Shakespeare (Henry IV); 8. Shakespeare (Macbeth) 9. Bible (Matthew 7:6).

The Bard vs. Bacon: Who Wrote Shakespeare?

"What's in a name? That which we call a rose, by any other name, would smell as sweet."

But would that which we call prose, by any other name, read as neat?

✳   ✳   ✳   ✳

THE QUOTE ABOVE was penned by William Shakespeare—or was it? Many scholars have raised doubts as to whether he really wrote some of the finest words in Western literature. Did other writers actually do the deed? Both sides believe they have the evidence to prove their point.

Meet Bill

William Shakespeare was born in Stratford-upon-Avon, England, in April 1564—the exact date is unknown. This and many other details of his life are vague, which has fueled the rampant speculation about authorship. It is generally accepted that he was the first in his family to read and write, although the extent of his education has been widely questioned. His father was involved in local politics, so it is likely that Shakespeare attended school until his early teens to study Latin and literature. At age 18, Shakespeare married Anne Hathaway, who was eight years older than he was and three months pregnant with their first child, Susanna. Twins Hamnet and Judith were born two years later.

The Bard's life story seems to disappear into the mist for more than seven years at this point, resurfacing in 1592, when he became involved in London theater. As a playwright and actor, he founded a performing troupe that was soon part of the court of King James I. Shakespeare retired in 1613, returning to his hometown with some wealth. He died in 1616 and was laid to rest in the Holy Trinity Church of Stratford-upon-Avon.

The Play's the Thing

While Shakespeare's plays were performed during his lifetime, they were not collected and published in book form until seven years after his death; *The First Folio* contained 36 of his theatrical works. Editors John Heminge and Henry Condell categorized the plays as tragedies, comedies, and histories. Many of Shakespeare's works, such as Hamlet and King Lear, were based on writings of former playwrights or even of Shakespeare's contemporaries—a common practice of the time. He also penned more than 150 sonnets, which often focused on love or beauty.

The diversity of this amazing body of work is what leads many to wonder whether Shakespeare had the education or ability to write it all. Certainly, they insist, others with better backgrounds and academic credentials were more likely to have actually written such great and timeless works of literature. Furthermore, they say, many of the plays displayed the acumen of a well-traveled writer—something Shakespeare was most likely not—someone who had a great knowledge of foreign languages, geography, and local customs. Who could have written such worldly plays?

Bringing Home the Bacon

Francis Bacon was born into a royal London family in 1561. Fragile as a young child, Bacon was schooled at home. He spent three years at Trinity College at Cambridge and traveled to Paris at age 15. Bacon became a lawyer and a member of the British Parliament in 1584. He soon joined the court of Queen Elizabeth and was knighted by King James I in 1603. Bacon eventually ascended to the positions of solicitor general and attorney general of the British government. He died of bronchitis in 1626.

Bacon is best remembered for his part in developing the scientific method, a process of systematic investigation. This standard prescribes defining a question, performing diligent research about the subject, forming a hypothesis, experimenting and collecting data, analyzing the results, and developing a conclusion. The progression has become commonplace in all types of scientific work, from grade school projects to research labs, and is still used today. But the multitalented Bacon was also a writer and essayist who once observed that "knowledge is power." His works include *Novum Organum, Astrologia Sana,* and *Meditationes Sacrae.* But could the man who penned these works be diverse and capable enough to also write *Much Ado About Nothing, Romeo and Juliet,* and words such as "If music be the food of love, play on"?

Something Is Rotten in the State of... Authorship

Speculation about the origin of Shakespeare's work began in the mid-1800s, as writers and scholars sought to demystify the works of the Bard. By the early 1900s, even the great American humorist Mark Twain had weighed in and questioned the authenticity of Shakespeare's plays and sonnets, albeit in his own way. In *Is Shakespeare Dead?*, Twain parodied those intellectuals who tried to discredit the man from Stratford-upon-Avon. The satiric piece questioned how biographers could write such detailed stories about their subject when so little solid information existed in the first place. But Twain also raised the question of whether Shakespeare could even write.

Similarities between the writings of Shakespeare and Bacon are abundant, and perhaps a bit too coincidental. For example, Shakespeare's Hamlet offers, "To thine own self be true, ... Thou canst not then be false to any man." In *Essay of Wisdom*, Bacon wrote, "Be so true to thyself as thou be not false to others." Plagiarism? Who can really say? In *Julius Caesar*, Shakespeare wrote, "Cowards die many times before their deaths." In Bacon's *Essay of Friendship*, he offered, "Men have their time, and die many times." Coincidence? Sure, maybe. The Bard wrote, "Tomorrow, and tomorrow, and tomorrow/ Creeps in this petty pace from day to day" in *Macbeth*. Bacon observed in *Religious Meditations*, "The Spanish have a proverb,

'To-morrow, to-morrow; and when to-morrow comes, tomorrow.'" Is it possible that Shakespeare knew of the same Spanish proverb? Certainly. While other similarities and questions proliferate, enough disbelief and lack of concrete evidence remain to thrill the world's doubting Thomases.

Parting Is Such Sweet Sorrow

Amid the swirl of controversy, most academics are convinced that Shakespeare himself wrote the plays and sonnets that made him famous. Of course, that conviction has done little to discourage those who have their doubts.

"Shall I set down the rest of the Conjectures which constitute the giant Biography of William Shakespeare? It would strain the Unabridged Dictionary to hold them. He is a Brontosaur: nine bones and six hundred barrels of plaster of paris.

In the Assuming trade three separate and independent cults are transacting business. Two of these cults are known as the Shakespearites and the Baconians, and I am the other one—the Brontosaurian.

The Shakespearite knows that Shakespeare wrote Shakespeare's Works; the Baconian knows that Francis Bacon wrote them; the Brontosaurian doesn't really know which of them did it, but is quite composedly and contentedly sure that Shakespeare didn't, and strongly suspects that Bacon did. We all have to do a good deal of assuming, but I am fairly certain that in every case I can call to mind the Baconian assumers have come out ahead of the Shakespearites. Both parties handle the same materials, but the Baconians seem to me to get much more reasonable and rational and persuasive results out of them than is the case with the Shakespearites."

—MARK TWAIN, *IS SHAKESPEARE DEAD?*

"If Shakespeare had owned a dog—but we need not go into that: we know he would have mentioned it in his will. If a good dog, Susanna would have got it; if an inferior one his wife would have got a dower interest in it. I wish he had had a dog, just so we could see how painstakingly he would have divided that dog among the family, in his careful business way."

—MARK TWAIN, *IS SHAKESPEARE DEAD?*

Shakespearean Quotes

"Now is the winter of our discontent."

—RICHARD III

"A horse! A horse! My kingdom for a horse!"

—RICHARD III

"What's in a name? That which we call a rose, / By any other name would smell as sweet."

—ROMEO AND JULIET

"The course of true love never did run smooth."

—A MIDSUMMER NIGHT'S DREAM

"Lord, what fools these mortals be!"

—A MIDSUMMER NIGHT'S DREAM

"I am a Jew. Hath not a Jew eyes? Hath not a Jew hands, organs, dimensions, senses, affections, passions; fed with the same food, hurt with the same weapons, subject to the same diseases, heal'd by the same means, warm'd and cool'd by the same winter and summer, as a Christian is? If you prick us, do we not bleed? If you tickle us, do we not laugh? If you poison us, do we not die? And if you wrong us, shall we not revenge?"

—THE MERCHANT OF VENICE

"Uneasy lies the head that wears a crown."

—HENRY IV, PART II

"Cowards die many times before their deaths; The valiant never taste of death but once."

—JULIUS CAESAR

"All the world's a stage, And all the men and women merely players: They have their exits and their entrances; And one man in his time plays many parts."

—AS YOU LIKE IT

"There is nothing either good or bad, but thinking makes it so."

—HAMLET

To be, or not to be—that is the question:
Whether 'tis nobler in the mind to suffer
The slings and arrows of outrageous fortune
Or to take arms against a sea of troubles,
And by opposing end them. To die—to sleep-
No more; and by a sleep to say we end
The heartache, and the thousand natural shocks
That flesh is heir to. 'Tis a consummation
Devoutly to be wish'd. To die—to sleep.
To sleep—perchance to dream: ay, there's the rub!
For in that sleep of death what dreams may come
When we have shuffled off this mortal coil,
Must give us pause. There's the respect
That makes calamity of so long life.
For who would bear the whips and scorns of time,
Th' oppressor's wrong, the proud man's contumely,
The pangs of despis'd love, the law's delay,
The insolence of office, and the spurns
That patient merit of th' unworthy takes,
When he himself might his quietus make
With a bare bodkin? Who would these fardels bear,
To grunt and sweat under a weary life,
But that the dread of something after death-
The undiscover'd country, from whose bourn
No traveller returns- puzzles the will,
And makes us rather bear those ills we have
Than fly to others that we know not of?
Thus conscience does make cowards of us all,
And thus the native hue of resolution
Is sicklied o'er with the pale cast of thought,
And enterprises of great pith and moment
With this regard their currents turn awry
And lose the name of action.

—*HAMLET*

"Something is rotten in the state of Denmark. "

—*HAMLET*

"The lady doth protest too much, methinks."

—*HAMLET*

"There are more things in heaven and earth, Horatio,
Than are dreamt of in your philosophy."

—*HAMLET*

"Some are born great, some achieve greatness, and some have
greatness thrust upon 'em."

—*TWELFTH NIGHT*

"Out, out, brief candle!
Life's but a walking shadow, a poor player
That struts and frets his hour upon the stage,
And then is heard no more. It is a tale
Told by an idiot, full of sound and fury,
Signifying nothing."

—*MACBETH*

Everybody Loves Bacon

*Since we brought up Francis Bacon—he may not have been
Shakespeare, but he was quotable in his own right, so let's take a
look at some words we know were his*

✳   ✳   ✳   ✳

"Knowledge itself is power."

—*SACRED MEDITATIONS*

"Nay, number (itself) in armies, importeth not much, where the
people is of weak courage; for (as Virgil saith) it never troubles the
wolf how many the sheep be."

—*ESSAYS OR COUNSELS CIVIL AND MORAL*

"Let great authors have their due, as time, which is the author of
authors, be not deprived of his due, which is, further and further to
discover truth."

—*THE ADVANCEMENT OF LEARNING*

"If a man will begin with certainties, he shall end in doubts; but if he
will be content to begin with doubts he shall end in certainties."

—*THE ADVANCEMENT OF LEARNING*

"They are ill discoverers that think there is no land, when they can see nothing but sea."

—*The Advancement of Learning*

"We cannot command nature except by obeying her."

—*Novum Organum*

"There are and can be only two ways of searching into and discovering truth. The one flies from the senses and particulars to the most general axioms, and from these principles, the truth of which it takes for settled and immovable, proceeds to judgment and to the discovery of middle axioms. And this way is now in fashion. The other derives axioms from the senses and particulars, rising by a gradual and unbroken ascent, so that it arrives at the most general axioms last of all. This is the true way, but as yet untried. "

—*Novum Organum*

"It is not the lie that passeth through the mind, but the lie that sinketh in and settleth in it, that doth the hurt."

—*Essays*, "Of Truth"

"Revenge is a kind of wild justice; which the more man's nature runs to, the more ought law to weed it out."

—*Essays*, "Of Revenge"

"Prosperity doth best discover vice, but adversity doth best discover virtue."

—*Essays*, "Of Adversity"

"In charity there is no excess."

—*Essays*, "Of Goodness and Goodness in Nature"

"If a man be gracious and courteous to strangers, it shows he is a citizen of the world, and that his heart is no island cut off from other lands, but a continent that joins to them."

—*Essays*, "Of Goodness and Goodness in Nature"

"I bequeath my soul to God... My body to be buried obscurely. For my name and memory, I leave it to men's charitable speeches, and to foreign nations, and the next age."

—His Will

A One-Man Wit and Wisdom Machine

Mark Twain's unique view of the world, uncanny way with words, and ability to connect with readers helped him become America's greatest literary treasure. Many of his sayings join his many brilliant works as true fabric of the nation's lexicon.

✳ ✳ ✳ ✳

THE SON OF a judge, Samuel Langhorne Clemens was born in the tiny town of Florida, Missouri, in 1835. The family moved east to Hannibal four years later, and its spot along the Mississippi River would shape Samuel's life and career in immeasurable ways.

Poor health kept the young Clemens indoors for much of his childhood. After his father died of pneumonia, however, a 13-year-old Samuel left school to become an apprentice to a printer. Two years later, he joined his brother Orion's newspaper as a printer and editorial assistant. Words already fascinated him, and he was about to embark on a journey that no one could have predicted.

That journey, of course, involved the mighty Mississippi. Clemens took a printer's job in St. Louis at age 17 and also picked up work as a river pilot's apprentice. Soon he earned his own river pilot's license and experienced the world like he never had before. His pen name, Mark Twain, was derived from a boating expression meaning "safe to navigate." That pen name became the most famous in the history of American writers.

The 'Great American Novel'

The Civil War crippled the river trade beginning in 1861, so Twain went to work as a newspaper reporter. He was witty and wise, cranking out copy that made him a favorite read among the local audiences. When his short story "The Celebrated Jumping Frog of Calaveras County" reached the pages of the

New York Saturday Press in 1865, Twain gained an almost immediate level of national and even international fame.

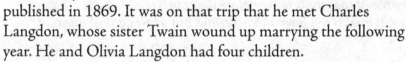

It was no fluke. Twain had a gift. He could be funny, poignant, or serious, sometimes all at once, and he did so while relating some of the most captivating stories ever told. They were stories about rather ordinary people, in tales frequently set along the Mississippi River.

His first book, *The Innocents Abroad*, was actually a collection of travel letters published in 1869. It was on that trip that he met Charles Langdon, whose sister Twain wound up marrying the following year. He and Olivia Langdon had four children.

Twain then changed the American literature landscape for good with *The Adventures of Tom Sawyer* in 1876 and *The Adventures of Huckleberry Finn* in 1885, stories about boys growing up on the Mississippi. The latter has been called the "Great American Novel." Characters like Tom, Huck, Jim, Becky Thatcher and Injun Joe became part of the American childhood experience, and remain so almost 150 years later.

In addition to the classics among his 28 books and numerous short stories, essays and letters, Twain is renowned for even smaller-sized nuggets of wisdom and wit in the form of quotes and sayings that have stood the test of time. His quips range from comical to political to societal, but they almost always carry a resonating piece of truth about life.

Though Twain died in 1910 and has no direct living descendants, his contributions to literature and Americana keep him relevant to this day. His childhood home in Hannibal is a museum, and many of the places he lived and wrote throughout the country have monuments or tributes in his honor.

Quotes from Mark Twain

"I haven't a particle of confidence in a man who has no redeeming petty vices whatsoever."

—*The Celebrated Jumping Frog of Calaveras County, and Other Sketches*

"Soap and education are not as sudden as a massacre, but they are more deadly in the long run."

—*Mark Twain's Sketches, New and Old*

"Barring that natural expression of villainy which we all have, the man looked honest enough."

—*Mark Twain's Sketches, New and Old*

"Is not this insanity plea becoming rather common? Is it not so common that the reader confidently expects to see it offered in every criminal case that comes before the courts? [. . .] Really, what we want now, is not laws against crime, but a law against insanity."

—*Mark Twain's Sketches, New and Old*

"Benjamin Franklin did a great many notable things for his country, and made her young name to be honored in many lands as the mother of such a son. It is not the idea of this memoir to ignore that or cover it up. No; the simple idea of it is to snub those pretentious maxims of his, which he worked up with a great show of originality out of truisms that had become wearisome platitudes as early as the dispersion from Babel."

—*Mark Twain's Sketches, New and Old*

"A baby is an inestimable blessing and bother."

—*Letter*

"All you need in this life is ignorance and confidence, and then Success is sure."

—*Mark Twain's Notebook*

"Weather is a literary specialty, and no untrained hand can turn out a good article on it."

—*The American Claimant*

"A round man cannot be expected to fit in a square hole right away. He must have time to modify his shape."

—*More Tramps Abroad*

"James Ross Clemens, a cousin of mine, was seriously ill two or three weeks ago in London, but is well now. The report of my illness grew out of his illness; the report of my death was an exaggeration."

—LETTER TO A REPORTER

"Get your facts first, and then you can distort them as much as you please."

—INTERVIEWED BY RUDYARD KIPLING

"He had only one vanity; he thought he could give advice better than any other person."

—"THE MAN THAT CORRUPTED HADLEYBURG"

"Work consists of whatever a body is OBLIGED to do, and . . . Play consists of whatever a body is not obliged to do."

—TOM SAWYER

"Persons attempting to find a motive in this narrative will be prosecuted; persons attempting to find a moral in it will be banished; persons attempting to find a plot in it will be shot."

—ADVENTURES OF HUCKLEBERRY FINN

"My kind of loyalty was loyalty to one's country, not to its institutions or its officeholders. The country is the real thing, the substantial thing, the eternal thing; it is the thing to watch over, and care for, and be loyal to; institutions are extraneous, they are its mere clothing, and clothing can wear out, become ragged, cease to be comfortable, cease to protect the body from winter, disease, and death."

—A CONNECTICUT YANKEE IN KING ARTHUR'S COURT

"Many a small thing has been made large by the right kind of advertising."

—A CONNECTICUT YANKEE IN KING ARTHUR'S COURT

"The radical invents the views. When he has worn them out the conservative adopts them."

—MARK TWAIN'S NOTEBOOK

"Familiarity breeds contempt — and children."

—MARK TWAIN'S NOTEBOOK

"In religion and politics, people's beliefs and convictions are in almost every case gotten at second-hand, and without examination, from authorities who have not themselves examined the questions at issue, but have taken them at second-hand from other non-examiners, whose opinions about them were not worth a brass farthing."

—*The Autobiography of Mark Twain*

Quotes Not by Twain

These quotes are often attributed to Twain, but those claims have not been verified by Twain scholars and should be viewed with skepticism.

"He who fights with monsters should look to it that he himself does not become a monster. And when you gaze long into an abyss the abyss also gazes into you."

—Real Source: Friedrich Nietzsche

"Be careful about reading health books. You may die of a misprint."

"The minority is always in the right. The majority is always in the wrong."

"Golf is a good walk spoiled."

"Censorship is telling a man he can't have a steak just because a baby can't chew it."

"Don't believe the world owes you a living. The world owes you nothing. It was here first."

"Politicians are like diapers: they should be changed often, and for the same reason."

"There are three kinds of lies: lies, damned lies, and statistics."

—Twain, in his autobiography, quotes this line himself but attributes it himself to Benjamin Disraeli, writing:

"Figures often beguile me, particularly when I have the arranging of them myself; in which case the remark attributed to Disraeli would often apply with justice and force:

'There are three kinds of lies: lies, damned lies, and statistics.'"

—*The Autobiography of Mark Twain*

Statesmen and Quote Sources

Benjamin Disraeli (1804–1881) was a Conservative politician who served as Prime Minister of England, alternating terms with influential Liberal William Gladstone (1809–1898). Both men left behind an influential legacy—and quotations!

✳ ✳ ✳ ✳

"I am a Conservative to preserve all that is good in our constitution, a Radical to remove all that is bad. I seek to preserve property and to respect order, and I equally decry the appeal to the passions of the many or the prejudices of the few."

—CAMPAIGN SPEECH BY DISRAELI

"Ignorance never settles a question."

—DISRAELI SPEECH IN THE HOUSE OF COMMONS

"What we anticipate seldom occurs; what we least expected generally happens."

—DISRAELI'S NOVEL, *HENRIETTA TEMPLE*

"Two nations; between whom there is no intercourse and no sympathy; who are as ignorant of each other's habits, thoughts, and feelings, as if they were dwellers in different zones, or inhabitants of different planets; who are formed by a different breeding, are fed by a different food, are ordered by different manners, and are not governed by the same laws: the rich and the poor."

—DISRAELI'S NOVEL, *SYBIL*

"All the people who pretend to take your own concerns out of your own hands and to do everything for you, I won't say they are imposters; I won't even say they are quacks; but I do say they are mistaken people."

—GLADSTONE SPEECH

"As the British Constitution is the most subtile organism which has proceeded from the womb and the long gestation of progressive history, so the American Constitution is, so far as I can see, the most wonderful work ever struck off by the brain and purpose of man."

—GLADSTONE, *KIN BEYOND SEA*

Voltaire's Defense

Voltaire, the infamous 18th-century French Enlightenment writer, is supposed to have said, "I disapprove of what you say, but I will defend to the death your right to say it." Noble as this concept may be, it was actually one of Voltaire's many biographers who penned the words.

✳ ✳ ✳ ✳

VOLTAIRE, ALSO KNOWN as François-Marie Arouet, was an outspoken and unwavering advocate of free speech. It is difficult to believe that the most powerful words ever written in support of this freedom cannot be attributed to the master himself, but the fact remains that the famous quote comes from Evelyn Beatrice Hall's 1907 book *The Friends of Voltaire*, which was published 129 years after Voltaire's death.

Hall wrote under the pseudonym Stephen G. Tallentyre at a time when it was difficult for women to publish nonfiction. At one point in the book, Hall discusses Voltaire's support of a fellow writer, Helvetius, who had been censored by the French government. The direct quote from Hall's book is: "The men who had hated [Helvetius' book] flocked round him now. Voltaire forgave him all injuries, intentional or unintentional... 'I disapprove of what you say, but I will defend to the death your right to say it,' was his attitude now."

Thus, through her indulgent dramatization of Voltaire's life, Hall inadvertently succeeded in summarizing his views on censorship in terms that were more eloquent than anything uttered by Voltaire himself (Hall later explained that the line was meant as a paraphrasing of his views).

Voltaire did, however, write a similar line in a 1770 letter, which translates as, "Monsieur l'abbe, I detest what you write, but I would give my life to make it possible for you to continue to write."

Some Things Voltaire Did Say

"Virtue is debased by self-justification."

"We should be considerate to the living; to the dead we owe only the truth."

"One always speaks badly when one has nothing to say."

"Thus, almost everything is imitation. The idea of The Persian Letters was taken from The Turkish Spy. Boiardo imitated Pulci, Ariosto imitated Boiardo. The most original minds borrowed from one another. Miguel de Cervantes makes his Don Quixote a fool; but pray is Orlando any other? It would puzzle one to decide whether knight errantry has been made more ridiculous by the grotesque painting of Cervantes, than by the luxuriant imagination of Ariosto. Metastasio has taken the greatest part of his operas from our French tragedies. Several English writers have copied us without saying one word of the matter. It is with books as with the fire in our hearths; we go to a neighbor to get the embers and light it when we return home, pass it on to others, and it belongs to everyone."

"Where there is friendship, there is our natural soil."

"The secret of being a bore is to tell everything."

"To hold a pen is to be at war."

"We all look for happiness, but without knowing where to find it: like drunkards who look for their house, knowing dimly that they have one."

"If God has made us in his image, we have returned him the favor."

"It is dangerous to be right in matters where established men are wrong."

"The husband who decides to surprise his wife is often very much surprised himself."

"Superstition is to religion what astrology is to astronomy, the mad daughter of a wise mother. These daughters have too long dominated the earth."

"Doubt is not a pleasant condition, but certainty is an absurd one."

"I always made one prayer to God, a very short one. Here it is: 'O Lord, make our enemies quite ridiculous!' God granted it."

"History is nothing more than a tableau of crimes and misfortunes."

"I am very fond of truth, but not at all of martyrdom."

"If this is the best of possible worlds, what then are the others?"

"Fools have a habit of believing that everything written by a famous author is admirable. For my part I read only to please myself and like only what suits my taste."

"A witty saying proves nothing."

Wilde Continues to Inspire

Had Oscar Wilde written only the novel The Picture of Dorian Gray, *he would be remembered as one of Ireland's all-time greats. The full breadth of his contributions to literature and life—even its terrible turns—makes him one of the most important writers in modern history.*

✻ ✻ ✻ ✻

WITH A NAME like Oscar Fingal O'Flahertie Wills Wilde, it's no wonder he stands as one of the most famous Irishmen to ever walk the earth. And what a walk it was. In addition to providing the world some of its great plays, poems, and memorable nuggets of wisdom, Wilde lived tragedy that defines him as one of literature's most sympathetic figures.

Wilde was born in Dublin in 1854, at the site where Trinity College's Oscar Wilde Centre now sits. His mother, of Italian descent, was a lifelong Irish nationalist who wrote poetry under the pen name "Speranza," meaning "Hope" in Italian. Wilde's father was a successful ear and eye surgeon who was knighted when Oscar was 10.

It was evident early that Wilde had greatness within him. He won a scholarship at Trinity, one of the most prestigious classical schools in the world, and finished atop his class in his first year. He earned the university's highest honor in Greek, which he had been studying for nearly a decade, and then landed a scholarship to attend Oxford.

Wilde became involved in two controversial movements while at Oxford: aesthetics and the decadent movement, which favored creativity over logic and societal standards. He wore his hair long, dressed lavishly, and decorated his rooms with blue china and peacock feathers, among other accoutrements.

Wilde was harassed by fellow students at times, once even attacked by a group of them. He also earned a rustication— a temporary suspension—for nonchalantly arriving late one semester upon his return from Greece with a professor.

Launching a Career

Wilde was taking Oxford by storm when his father died in 1876, leaving the family in a financial bind. Oscar's poem, "Ravenna," had won the prestigious Newdigate prize and earned him high honors at the school. He published his first collection, *Poems*, in 1881, and in December that year he set sail for New York to deliver a series of lectures on aesthetics. The lecture circuit lasted the better part of a year and gave Wilde an audience with the likes of Henry Longfellow and Walt Whitman.

Wilde's plays, poems, and prose were gaining a considerable following. After marrying Constance Lloyd in 1884, he established himself as a successful playwright with the likes of *A Woman of No Importance, An Ideal Husband* and *The Importance of Being Earnest*. His one and only novel, *The Picture of Dorian Gray*, created a firestorm of controversy when it appeared for the first time in an American magazine in 1890. Its homoerotic themes, which would later come to be used against him at trial, were considered immoral and reprehensible by some.

It was published as a novel in 1891. That summer, Wilde began a relationship with Oxford undergraduate Lord Alfred Douglas. Four years later, Wilde attempted to sue his lover's father for libel over the accusation of homosexuality. Wilde then decided to withdraw the suit, but he was arrested himself, convicted of gross indecency and sentenced to two years of hard labor.

"The Ballad of Reading Gaol," published between Wilde's release and the death of his wife in 1898, recounted the terror of his time as a prisoner. Wilde wandered Europe in his final years, contracted meningitis, and died in 1900. Numerous biographies have been written about his brilliant, eccentric life.

Quotes from Oscar Wilde

"Be warned in time, James, and remain, as I do, incomprehensible: to be great is to be misunderstood."

—LETTER TO JAMES MACNEILL WHISTLER

"A thing is not necessarily true because a man dies for it."

—"THE PORTRAIT OF MR. W.H."

"Consistency is the last refuge of the unimaginative."

—"THE RELATION OF DRESS TO ART'"

"A poet can survive everything but a misprint."

—"THE CHILDREN OF THE POETS"

"And, after all, what is a fashion? From the artistic point of view, it is usually a form of ugliness so intolerable that we have to alter it every six months."

—"THE PHILOSOPHY OF DRESS"

"All charming people, I fancy, are spoiled. It is the secret of their attraction."

—"THE PORTRAIT OF MR. W.H."

"All art is immoral."

—*INTENTIONS*

"People who count their chickens before they are hatched act very wisely because chickens run about so absurdly that it's impossible to count them accurately."

—LETTER

"The one duty we owe to history is to rewrite it."

—*THE CRITIC AS ARTIST*

"If Nature had been comfortable, mankind would never have invented architecture."

—*The Decay of Lying*

"Anybody can make history. Only a great man can write it."

—*The Critic as Artist*

"Man is least himself when he talks in his own person. Give him a mask, and he will tell you the truth."

—*The Critic as Artist*

"A dreamer is one who can only find his way by moonlight, and his punishment is that he sees the dawn before the rest of the world."

—*The Critic as Artist*

"The one duty we owe to history is to rewrite it."

—*The Critic as Artist*

"There is no sin except stupidity."

—*The Critic as Artist*

"Ah! Don't say you agree with me. When people agree with me I always feel I must be wrong."

—*The Critic as Artist*

"A little sincerity is a dangerous thing, and a great deal of it is absolutely fatal. "

—*The Critic as Artist*

"Sometimes the poor are praised for being thrifty. But to recommend thrift to the poor is both grotesque and insulting. It is like advising a man who is starving to eat less."

—*The Soul of Man Under Socialism*

"We are all in the gutter, but some of us are looking at the stars."

—*Lady Windemere's Fan*

"To speak frankly, I am not in favour of long engagements. They give people the opportunity of finding out each other's character before marriage, which I think is never advisable."

—*The Importance of Being Earnest*

The Vicious Circle

Sharp tongues and smooth martinis were standard fare in the Rose Room of Manhattan's Algonquin Hotel circa 1920, where some of the city's most prominent young literati—writers, critics, humorists, and artists—gathered daily to drink, dine, and dish. But visitors had to beware when this lunch bunch grabbed a bite.

✳ ✳ ✳ ✳

Joker's Wild

THE WHOLE THING started as a joke played on Alexander Woollcott, the *New York Times'* sharp-witted theater critic. In June 1919, publicist Murdock Pemberton organized a luncheon at the Algonquin Hotel under the guise of welcoming the caustic critic back from his overseas service as a war correspondent. In reality, Pemberton planned the event as a roast to poke fun at Woollcott and his tendency to drone on with lengthy war stories. Invitations were sent to Woollcott's friends, including well-known writers and critics such as *Vanity Fair's* Dorothy Parker and Robert Benchley. Ultimately, Woollcott had such a good time that he suggested the group meet at the hotel for lunch every day.

A Rose by Any Other Name

In addition to Woollcott, Parker, Pemberton, and Benchley, the group included a regular roster of up-and-comers on the Manhattan art scene. Novelist Edna Ferber; comedian Harpo Marx; playwrights Marc Connelly, George Kaufman, and Robert E. Sherwood; journalist Heywood Broun and his wife Ruth Hale; and *Times* columnist Franklin Pierce Adams were among the core group. Other friends and acquaintances made appearances as well, such as actress Tallulah Bankhead and playwright Noël Coward.

For more than a decade, the group lunched at the hotel six days a week (every day except Sunday). Initially they met in the Pergola Room, today known as the Oak Room. The hotel manager, Frank Case, served them complimentary celery, olives, and popovers and gave them their own designated waiter to ensure repeat business. Eventually, as more guests joined the party, Case designated a large round table just for them in the Rose Room at the back of the restaurant.

At first the group called itself The Board and its lunchtime liaisons "Board Meetings." When the group got a new waiter named Luigi, this quickly became the Luigi Board—a play on the popular Ouija board craze of the day.

Pun-Upsmanship

Witticism was the pet pastime of the Algonquin group, who were famous for their one-liners. In one story, Benchley entered the Rose Room on a rainy day and announced, "I've got to get out of these wet clothes and into a dry martini."

In another favorite game, group members challenged one another to use obscure words in a sentence—the goal, of course, to one-up each other with clever puns, the more terrible the better. According to lore, it was during this game that Parker notably uttered, "You can lead a horticulture but you can't make her think" and "Hiawatha nice girl until I met you."

Sometimes the barbs were launched at each other. The group skewered Connelly's play *Honduras* as "the big Hondurance contest" and openly trashed Ferber's novel *Mother Knows Best*. Once, the effete playwright Noël Coward commented on the masculine cut of Ferber's suit, allegedly saying she "almost looked like a man."

"So do you," retorted Ferber.

Members of the group often collaborated; one of the most famous projects being the *New Yorker*. Editor and friend of the Round Table Harold Ross launched the magazine in 1925 with funds provided by the hotel, hiring Parker as the magazine's book reviewer and Benchley as the drama critic.

For some visitors to the group, the constant verbal sparring proved too much, and they never came back. One guest claimed it was impossible to even ask for the salt without someone trying to make a "smartie" about it. The ruthless remarks inspired the group to call itself the Vicious Circle—although Ferber personally preferred Poison Squad. After a caricature of them appeared in the *Brooklyn Eagle* in 1920, the group publicly became cemented as the Algonquin Round Table.

The Bite Back

Naturally with so much success comes backlash, and artists outside the circle criticized the group deeply. Writer H. L. Mencken disparaged his contemporaries as "literati of the third, fourth, and fifth rate." Others complained group members were only interested in "self-promotion" and "back scratching." Still others accused the group of being too competitive and "forcing" its off-the-cuff humor, with some members even writing down one-liners in advance to casually toss out at the table.

Connelly once said that trying to remember the end of the Algonquin Round Table was like "remembering falling asleep"—it just sort of happened. But by the time the Great Depression of the 1930s hit, the Algonquin's boozy lunch bunch had all but disbanded. Some, such as Parker and Benchley, moved on to Hollywood to write for films.

Today, tourists can get a glimpse of the Algonquin Round Table's New York in a historic walking tour led by the president of the Dorothy Parker Society. Afterward, lunch is served at the hotel's restaurant, now named the Round Table after its legendary patrons.

They Said It

"Epitaph for a dead waiter: God finally caught his eye."

—GEORGE KAUFMAN

"I don't want you to think I'm not incoherent."

—HAROLD ROSS

"Being an old maid is like death by drowning, a really delightful sensation after you cease to struggle."

—EDNA FERBER

"Drawing on my fine command of the English language, I said nothing."

—ROBERT BENCHLEY

"I might repeat to myself, slowly and soothingly, a list of quotations beautiful from minds profound; if I can remember any of the damn things."

—DOROTHY PARKER

"Wit has truth in it; wise-cracking is simply calisthenics with words."

—DOROTHY PARKER

"Wit ought to be a glorious treat like caviar; never spread it about like marmalade."

—NOËL COWARD

Molly Ivins Can't Say That, Can She?

Say the word Texas to almost any journalist in the nation, and Molly Ivins's name is likely to come back in response, generally spoken with reverence. Well-known and loved around the country, she wrote columns that are still quoted. Molly Ivins stories abound and have not been slowed by her 2007 death at age 62 from breast cancer. But in Texas, where she was raised, this one-of-a-kind pundit is a legend.

✳ ✳ ✳ ✳

WRITER MOLLY IVINS could—and did—say practically anything, especially if it involved skewering the powerful, the poseurs, and the just plain politically dumb. And what she said over the course of nearly 40 years as an unabashedly liberal newspaper columnist and reporter was nearly always witty and often deliciously on target.

Ivins in Action

Take the title of this piece, which was also the title of her first book. When Ivins, writing for the *Dallas Times Herald*, said of Texas Republican congressman Jim Collins, "If his I.Q. slips any lower, we'll have to water him twice a day," she created an uproar. Advertisers cancelled. Readers (and the congressman) protested. And the newspaper rented billboards in her support, declaring, "Molly Ivins can't say that, can she?"

Or this, from the *Charleston Gazette* in 1994 about gun control. "I am not anti-gun, I'm pro-knife. Consider the merits of the knife. In the first place, you have to catch up with someone in order to stab him. A general substitution of knives for guns would promote physical fitness. We'd turn into a whole nation of great runners. Plus, knives don't ricochet. And people are seldom killed while cleaning their knives."

Ivins referred to the second President Bush as "Shrub" for years, and she once famously derided a speech by conservative Pat Buchanan: "It probably sounded better in the original German."

Starting Out

Ivins was born in California but moved as a young child to Houston with her family, who were staunch Republicans. After graduating from Smith College in 1966, she attended Columbia Graduate School of Journal-ism. Her first news-paper job was in the complaint department of the *Houston Chronicle*, followed by a stint at the *Minneapolis Tribune*, where she was the first woman to cover the police beat. In 1970, Ivins came home to Texas to become coeditor of the feisty independent *Texas Observer*, where she began her long career covering the antics of the Texas legislature—a goldmine of columns for the rest of her life. But she wasn't content to remain there.

A Legend Grows

It was no surprise when one of the country's great journalists joined the staff of one of its greatest papers. But Ivins wrote of *The New York Times*, where she worked from 1976 to 1982, that it was "a great newspaper: it is also No Fun." She was the *Times*'s Rocky Mountain bureau chief and covered major news stories for the paper, among them the Son of Sam and the death of Elvis Presley (she later joked that she was the only reporter on the scene whose stories referred to the late singer as "Mr. Presley"). But her idea of hell, she said, was "being edited by the *Times* copy desk for all eternity."

Back home in Texas in 1982, Ivins wrote for the *Dallas Times Herald*, despite the fact that she said Dallas "would have rooted for Goliath to beat David." After that paper folded, she moved on to the *Fort Worth Star-Telegram* before becoming a nationally syndicated independent columnist in 2001.

Ivins authored seven books, made innumerable television appearances, and was a tireless fund-raiser for causes she championed, particularly the *Texas Observer* and groups that supported the First Amendment, such as the American Civil Liberties Union.

A liberal voice heard around the world, she once said of her home, "I dearly love the state of Texas, but I consider that a harmless perversion on my part, and discuss it only with consenting adults."

The "First American"

Inventor, writer, postmaster, statesman, diplomat, and Founding Father, Benjamin Franklin helped write the Declaration of Independence, made important discoveries in the sciences, and left an enduring legacy. He is often called "The First American" for his contributions to the nation.

✳ ✳ ✳ ✳

BENJAMIN FRANKLIN WAS born in Boston on January 17, 1706. He attended the Boston Latin School until he was ten, when he began working for his father, a candlemaker. When he was twelve, his older brother Josiah apprenticed him at his printing shop. He left Boston in 1723 and settled in Philadelphia, where he found work in another printing shop. He traveled to London in 1724, returning to Philadelphia in 1726; the same year he developed his "Thirteen Virtues," which he attempted to practice for the rest of his life. He opened his own printing shop in Philadelphia in 1728. In 1730, he became common-law husband to Deborah Read, with whom he had had an on-again, off-again relationship for several years. Franklin founded a study and debate group called the *Junto*, and when its members ran out of books to read, Franklin helped found the first public library in America in 1731.

Publications and Experiments

Franklin began publishing *Poor Richard's Almanack* in 1732, and it quickly became very popular. The almanac provided weather forecasts, poetry, and essays, and it was where many of Franklin's popular aphorisms first appeared. Franklin would publish the almanac for a quarter century. He spent the next two decades growing his businesses, and by 1748 he was one of the wealthiest men in Philadelphia. He left his partner in charge of his printing business and began spending more time in scientific pursuits, and founded the American Philosophical Society. That same year, he bought his first slaves. Franklin's views on slavery would eventually change, and he freed them in the 1760s.

In 1751 Franklin published *Experiments and Observations on Electricity*, which compiled several years' worth of his investigations. The following year he proved that lightning was electricity with his famous key and kite experiment, and invented the lightning rod. Among his other inventions were bifocals, the rocking chair, the flexible catheter, and a public firefighting brigade.

American Revolution

In 1765 the British Parliament passed the Stamp Act, which imposed a tax on all printed material used in the colonies.

Franklin, serving as Pennsylvania's agent in London, delivered a passionate speech denouncing the Act in Parliament that contributed to its repeal the following year. In 1768, he wrote the pamphlet *Causes of the American Discontents Before 1768,* and in 1775 he returned to Philadelphia to assist in the cause of independence. He was elected to the Second Continental Congress that year, and in 1776 he helped write the Declaration of Independence. He was then sent to France to negotiate for the French King's financial and military support. He remained there for nine years, and became the informal American ambassador to Louis XVI's court. In 1783 he was instrumental in negotiating the Treaty of Paris, which ended the war and granted the colonies their independence.

Franklin returned to Philadelphia in 1785, and represented Pennsylvania at the Constitutional Convention of 1787. He played an integral role in developing the Great Compromise, which resulted in proportional representation for the States in the House of Representatives, and equal representation in the Senate. The compromise was vital for ensuring the ratification of the Constitution.

Benjamin Franklin died in Philadelphia on April 17, 1790.

Quotes from Franklin

"If all printers were determined not to print anything till they were sure it would offend nobody, there would be very little printed."

—"Apologies from Printers"

"Ambition has its disappointments to sour us, but never the good fortune to satisfy us."

—"On True Happiness"

"Sell not virtue to purchase wealth, nor Liberty to purchase power."

—Poor Richard's Almanack

"[A] great Empire, like a great Cake, is most easily diminished at the Edges."

—"Rules By Which A Great Empire May Be Reduced To A Small One"

"God grant, that not only the Love of Liberty, but a thorough Knowledge of the Rights of Man, may pervade all the Nations of the Earth, so that a Philosopher may set his Foot anywhere on its Surface, and say, 'This is my Country.'"

—LETTER

"Love your Enemies, for they tell you your Faults."

—POOR RICHARD'S ALMANACK

"Most People dislike Vanity in others whatever Share they have of it themselves."

—BENJAMIN FRANKLIN'S AUTOBIOGRAPHY

"In reality there is perhaps no one of our natural Passions so hard to subdue as Pride. Disguise it, struggle with it, beat it down, stifle it, mortify it as much as one pleases, it is still alive, and will every now and then peep out and show itself. You will see it perhaps often in this History. For even if I could conceive that I had completely over-come it, I should probably be proud of my Humility."

—BENJAMIN FRANKLIN'S AUTOBIOGRAPHY

"In 1736 I lost one of my Sons, a fine Boy of 4 Years old, by the Smallpox taken in the common way. I long regretted bitterly and still regret that I had not given it to him by Inoculation. This I mention for the Sake of Parents who omit that Operation on the Supposition that they should never forgive themselves if a Child died under it; my Example showing that the Regret may be the same either way, and that therefore the safer should be chosen."

—BENJAMIN FRANKLIN'S AUTOBIOGRAPHY

"Idleness and Pride Tax with a heavier Hand than Kings and Parliaments; If we can get rid of the former we may easily bear the Latter."

—LETTER

"Our Geese are but Geese tho' we may think 'em Swans; and Truth will be Truth tho' it sometimes prove mortifying and distasteful."

—"A DISSERTATION ON LIBERY AND NECESSITY, PLEASURE AND PAIN"

"In 200 years will people remember us as traitors or heros? That is the question we must ask."

—LETTER TO THOMAS JEFFERSON

"For my own part I wish the Bald Eagle had not been chosen the Representative of our Country. He is a Bird of bad moral Character. He does not get his Living honestly. You may have seen him perched on some dead Tree near the River, where, too lazy to fish for himself, he watches the Labour of the Fishing Hawk; and when that diligent Bird has at length taken a Fish, and is bearing it to his Nest for the Support of his Mate and young Ones, the Bald Eagle pursues him and takes it from him.

With all this injustice, he is never in good case but like those among men who live by sharping & robbing he is generally poor and often very lousy. Besides he is a rank coward: The little King Bird not bigger than a Sparrow attacks him boldly and drives him out of the district. He is therefore by no means a proper emblem for the brave and honest Cincinnati of America who have driven all the King birds from our country...

"I am on this account not displeased that the Figure is not known as a Bald Eagle, but looks more like a Turkey. For the Truth the Turkey is in Comparison a much more respectable Bird, and withal a true original Native of America... He is besides, though a little vain & silly, a Bird of Courage, and would not hesitate to attack a Grenadier of the British Guards who should presume to invade his Farm Yard with a red Coat on."

—LETTER

"Freedom of speech is a principal pillar of a free government; when this support is taken away, the constitution of a free society is dissolved, and tyranny is erected on its ruins. Republics and limited monarchies derive their strength and vigor from a popular examination into the action of the magistrates."

—"ON FREEDOM OF SPEECH AND THE PRESS"

Clarence Darrow

Clarence Darrow's work on many of the most important trials in the late 19th and 20th centuries made him one of the most well-known attorneys in American history.

✳   ✳   ✳   ✳

CLARENCE DARROW WAS born in Kinsman, Ohio, on April 18, 1857. He attended law school for only one year before passing the Ohio bar in 1878.

Practicing Law in Public

In 1887, he traveled to Chicago to take part in his first of many high-profile cases. The year before, at a demonstration for labor rights in the Chicago Haymarket, an unidentified person had thrown a bomb that killed several policemen. The organizers of the demonstration, known as the Haymarket Anarchists, were tried for the murders. Darrow later defended Eugene Debs, the leader of the American Railway Union, during the Pullman strike. Debs was convicted of contempt of court, and the charge was upheld on appeal. His work on the case, along with his successful defense of labor leader Big Bill Haywood and advocacy for striking miners in the Pennsylvania coal strike of 1903, cemented Darrow's reputation as a brilliant pro-labor, progressive attorney. In 1924 he defended Richard Loeb and Nathan Leopold, accused of the murder of 14-year-old Robert Franks, and succeeded in getting them spared from execution in spite of their guilt.

The Scopes Trial

Darrow is perhaps best known for his defense of John T. Scopes in Dayton, Tennessee in 1925. In what would become known as "The Scopes Monkey Trial," the high school teacher was tried for breaking a state law that prohibited teaching Darwin's Theory of Natural Selection. Scopes was found guilty, but the conviction was overturned on a technicality on appeal. The trial was fictionalized in the film *Inherit the Wind.*

Darrow died in Chicago on March 13, 1938.

Quotes from Clarence Darrow

"The objector and the rebel who raises his voice against what he believes to be the injustice of the present and the wrongs of the past is the one who hunches the world along."

—ADDRESS TO THE COURT, *PEOPLE VS. LLOYD*

"You can only protect your liberties in this world by protecting the other man's freedom. You can only be free if I am free."

—ADDRESS TO THE COURT, *PEOPLE VS. LLOYD*

"The Constitution is a delusion and a snare if the weakest and humblest man in the land cannot be defended in his right to speak and his right to think as much as the strongest in the land."

—ADDRESS TO THE COURT, *PEOPLE VS. LLOYD*

"I do not consider it an insult, but rather a compliment to be called an agnostic. I do not pretend to know where many ignorant men are sure — that is all that agnosticism means."

—SCOPES TRIAL

"If today you can take a thing like evolution and make it a crime to teach it in the public school, tomorrow you can make it a crime to teach it in the private schools, and the next year you can make it a crime to teach it to the hustings or in the church. At the next session you may ban books and the newspapers. Soon you may set Catholic against Protestant and Protestant against Protestant, and try to foist your own religion upon the minds of men. If you can do one you can do the other. Ignorance and fanaticism is ever busy and needs feeding. Always it is feeding and gloating for more. Today it is the public school teachers, tomorrow the private."

—SCOPES TRIAL

"When I was a boy I was told that anybody could become President. I'm beginning to believe it."

—*CLARENCE DARROW FOR THE DEFENSE*

"I have never killed any one, but I have read some obituary notices with great satisfaction."

—*THE STORY OF MY LIFE*

Maimonides

A Jewish philosopher, physician, and thinker of the medieval world, Maimonides wrote an influential book of Jewish law, and contributed to theology and medicine as well.

✳ ✳ ✳ ✳

MOSES MAIMONIDES WAS born in Córdoba, Spain, on March 30, 1135. He was tutored at a young age by his father and studied with other learned rabbis. In 1148, Córdoba was captured by the Almohads, and the Jews in the city were given the choice of converting to Islam or leaving. Maimonides' family remained in Córdoba for eleven years, practicing Judaism in secret. He continued his education and learned about science and philosophy as well as Judaic studies. In 1159, his family left Córdoba to settle in Fez, Morroco. In 1165, Rabbi Judah ibn Shoshan, Maimonides' teacher, was arrested for practicing Judaism and executed. The Maimons moved again, first to Palestine, then Egypt.

A Physician and Writer

Maimonides began practicing medicine in Cairo, and his skills as a physician led to him being appointed as court physician to Saladin. He became a leading figure in the Jewish community and was soon recognized as a gifted thinker and prolific writer as well. Maimonides wrote an authoritative commentary on the *Mishna*, the oldest set of Jewish laws. The *Kitab al-Siraj* offered clarifications on the meaning of passages in the *Mishna*, and included several essays in the introduction that explored the philosophical questions in the *Mishna*. Maimonides' major work on religious philosophy, *The Guide for the Perplexed*, took him fifteen years to complete and was finished in 1191. It argues for a rational philosophy of Judaism that allowed for accommodations for science and philosophy.

Maimonides died in Egypt on December 13, 1204.

Quotes from Maimonides

"One should accept the truth from whatever source it proceeds."

—*The Eight Chapters Of Maimonides On Ethics*

"For it is said, "You shall strengthen the stranger and the dweller in your midst and live with him," that is to say, strengthen him until he needs no longer fall upon the mercy of the community or be in need."

—*Mishneh Torah*

"Do not imagine that these most difficult problems can be thoroughly understood by any one of us. This is not the case. At times the truth shines so brilliantly that we perceive it as clear as day. Our nature and habit then draw a veil over our perception, and we return to a darkness almost as dense as before. We are like those who, though beholding frequent flashes of lightning, still find themselves in the thickest darkness of the night. On some the lightning flashes in rapid succession, and they seem to be in continuous light, and their night is as clear as the day."

—*Guide for the Perplexed*

"We suffer from the evils which we, by our own free will, inflict on ourselves and ascribe them to God, who is far from being connected with them!"

—*Guide for the Perplexed*

"Men frequently think that the evils in the world are more numerous than the good things; many sayings and songs of the nations dwell on this idea. ...Not only common people make this mistake, but even many who think they are wise."

—*Guide for the Perplexed*

"Anticipate charity by preventing poverty; assist the reduced fellow-man, either by a considerable gift, or a sum of money, or by teaching him a trade, or by putting him in the way of business, so that he may not earn an honest livelihood, and not be forced to the dreadful alternative of holding his hand out for charity. This is the highest step and the summit of charity's golden ladder."

—*Charity's Eight Degrees*

An Essayist for the Ages

Michel de Montaigne, a philosopher and writer during the French Renaissance, developed the essay as a literary genre in the 16th century.

✳   ✳   ✳   ✳

Michel de Montaigne was born on February 28, 1533, near Bordeaux, France, to a family of minor nobility. He spent the first three years of his life living with a family of peasants; his father believed it would help make him more sympathetic to the conditions of ordinary people. He spoke only Latin until he was six years old. When he was sixteen, he was sent to boarding school, and eventually studied law at the University of Toulouse. He held a seat on the Bordeaux Parliament beginning in 1557, and was a member of the court of Charles IX from 1561–1563.

While at Parliament he befriended Étienne de La Boétie, one of the founders of French political philosophy. The two often discussed philosophy, politics, and other subjects. Boétie's death in 1563 may have inspired Montaigne to write his essays as a means of communicating with is friend.

The Essays

In 1571, a few years after his father died, Montaigne retired from public life and moved to a tower ("Montaigne's Tower") near the family estate. He locked himself in the tower's extensive library and began writing personal and philosophical reflections on his life, religion, friendship, freedom, and love. He referred to these reflection as *essais*, French for "attempts." He published his first volume of *Essais* in 1580. He served as mayor of Bordeaux from 1581–1585, during which time he published his second volume of *Essais*. He would publish a third and final volume in 1588.

Montaigne died at his family estate on September 13, 1592.

Quotes from Montaigne's *Essays*

"I want to be seen here in my simple, natural, ordinary fashion, without straining or artifice; for it is myself that I portray . . . I am myself the matter of my book."

"In my opinion, every rich man is a miser."

"Things are not bad in themselves, but our cowardice makes them so."

"Whatever can be done another day can be done today."

"I want death to find me planting my cabbages."

"The day of your birth leads you to death as well as to life."

"Wherever your life ends, it is all there. The advantage of living is not measured by length, but by use; some men have lived long, and lived little; attend to it while you are in it. It lies in your will, not in the number of years, for you to have lived enough."

"I do not speak the minds of others except to speak my own mind better."

"If you press me to say why I loved him, I can say no more than it was because he was he, and I was I."

"Nothing is so firmly believed as that which we least know."

"A man of understanding has lost nothing, if he has himself."

"My trade and my art is living."

"When I play with my cat, who knows if I am not a pastime to her more than she is to me?"

"Those who have compared our life to a dream were right . . . We are sleeping awake, and waking asleep."

"Great abuses in the world are begotten, or, to speak more boldly, all the abuses of the world are begotten, by our being taught to be afraid of professing our ignorance, and that we are bound to accept all things we are not able to refute."

"Saying is one thing and doing is another."

"There were never in the world two opinions alike, any more than two hairs or two grains. Their most universal quality is diversity."

"Few men have been admired by their own households."

"I will follow the good side right to the fire, but not into it if I can help it."

"It (marriage) happens as with cages: the birds without despair to get in, and those within despair of getting out."

"Malice sucks up the greatest part of its own venom, and poisons itself."

"There is no wish more natural than the wish to know."

"He who remembers the evils he has undergone, and those that have threatened him, and the slight causes that have changed him from one state to another, prepares himself in that way for future changes and for recognizing his condition. The life of Caesar has no more to show us than our own; an emperor's or an ordinary man's, it is still a life subject to all human accidents."

"Let us give Nature a chance; she knows her business better than we do."

"As far as physicians go, chance is more valuable than knowledge."

"Physicians have this advantage: the sun lights their success and the earth covers their failures."

"Great abuses in the world are begotten, or, to speak more boldly, all the abuses of the world are begotten, by our being taught to be afraid of professing our ignorance, and that we are bound to accept all things we are not able to refute: we speak of all things by precepts and decisions. The style at Rome was that even that which a witness deposed to having seen with his own eyes, and what a judge determined with his most certain knowledge, was couched in this form of speaking: 'it seems to me.' They make me hate things that are likely, when they would impose them upon me as infallible."

"There is no man so good that if he placed all his actions and thoughts under the scrutiny of the laws, he would not deserve hanging ten times in his life."

"I have seen no more evident monstrosity and miracle in the world than myself."

"No matter that we may mount on stilts, we still must walk on our own legs. And on the highest throne in the world, we still sit only on our own bottom."

Blaise Pascal

Blaise Pascal was a French mathematician and theological philosopher who discovered many of the foundations of modern probability theory.

✳ ✳ ✳ ✳

BLAISE PASCAL WAS born in Clermont-Ferrand, France, on June 19, 1623. His father, a mathematician, educated him at home, recognizing that he was a prodigy at a young age. He initially did not teach Pascal mathematics out of a concern the boy would be so fascinated by geometry that he would neglect his other studies. But at the age of twelve, Pascal began studying geometry on his own. He began accompanying his father to meetings of mathematicians in Paris, and when he was sixteen, he delivered several of his early theorems to the group. The following year he published *Essay on Conic Sections*, and in 1642 he invented a mechanical calculator called the Pascaline, which used a series of wheels to perform calculations.

Pascal began experimenting in the physical sciences in the 1640s, and developed a proof that atmospheric pressure could be measured in terms of weight. He began working on a perpetual motion machine, and while he was unsuccessful, he accidentally invented the roulette wheel. Around the same time, he began corresponding with the mathematician Pierre de Fermat. The two independently came up with a rudimentary theory of probability.

Pascal's Wager

Pascal's family were Jesuits, having converted in 1646, and he became a religious apologist. His most famous argument for the existence of God, "Pascal's Wager," states that humans bet on God's existence with their own lives. Pascal argued that given what he saw as the infinite rewards for believing in God if God does exist, versus the relatively minor loss from believing if God does not, it is logical to believe in God.

Quotes from Pascal

"I made this [letter] very long only because I have not had the leisure to make it shorter."

—PROVINCIAL LETTERS

"People almost invariably arrive at their beliefs not on the basis of proof but on the basis of what they find attractive."

—THE ART OF PERSUASION

"It is necessary to have regard to the person whom we wish to persuade, of whom we must know the mind and the heart, what principles he acknowledges, what things he loves; and then observe in the thing in question what affinity it has with the acknowledged principles, or with the objects so delightful by the pleasure which they give him."

—THE ART OF PERSUASION

"The art of persuasion consists as much in that of pleasing as in that of convincing, so much more are men governed by caprice than by reason!"

—THE ART OF PERSUASION

"Do not imagine that it is less an accident by which you find yourself master of the wealth which you possess, than that by which this man found himself king."

—DISCOURSES ON THE CONDITION OF THE GREAT

"People are generally better persuaded by the reasons which they have themselves discovered than by those which have come into the mind of others."

—PENSÉES

"I lay it down as a fact that if all men knew what each said of the other, there would not be four friends in the world."

—PENSÉES

"Nature gives us ... passions and desires suitable to our present state. We are only troubled by the fears which we, and not nature, give ourselves ... "

—PENSÉES

"Man is to himself the most wonderful object in nature; for he cannot conceive what the body is, still less what the mind is, and least of all how a body should be united to a mind. This is the consummation of his difficulties, and yet it is his very being."

—Pensées

"Time heals griefs and quarrels, for we change and are no longer the same persons."

—Pensées

"Imagination cannot make fools wise, but it makes them happy, as against reason, which only makes its friends wretched: one covers them with glory, the other with shame."

—Pensées

Our nature consists in motion; complete rest is death."

—Pensées

"Time heals griefs and quarrels, for we change and are no longer the same persons."

—Pensées

"I have discovered that all human evil comes from this, man's being unable to sit still in a room."

—Pensées

"The heart has its reasons, which Reason does not know."

—Pensées

"Man is but a reed, the most feeble thing in nature; but he is a thinking reed. The entire universe need not arm itself to crush him. A vapour, a drop of water suffices to kill him. But, if the universe were to crush him, man would still be more noble than that which killed him, because he knows that he dies and the advantage which the universe has over him; the universe knows nothing of this."

—Pensées

"What a Chimera is man! What a novelty, a monster, a chaos, a contradiction, a prodigy! Judge of all things, an imbecile worm of the earth; depository of truth, and sewer of error and doubt; the glory and refuse of the universe."

—Pensées

Proverbs for the Ages

An English dramatist and poet, Heywood is best known for his collection of concise, poignant proverbs that endures to this day.

❋   ❋   ❋   ❋

JOHN HEYWOOD WAS born circa 1497 in Coventry; his family moved to London when he was a teenager. He attended Oxford, and while he was not as thoroughly educated as many of his contemporaries who attained literary fame, he was naturally gifted and quite intelligent. Heywood joined Henry VIII's Royal Court as a singer in 1520, and in 1523 he married Elizabeth Rastell. The Rastells were involved in the theatre, and Heywood soon was writing plays that were produced for the Royal Court. He would write and produce plays for four monarchs: Henry, Edward VI, Mary I, and Elizabeth I.

Not Just a Playwright

Heywood was outspoken during a time of political upheaval. Henry was asserting his authority as the head of the new Church of England, breaking with the Catholic Church, and Heywood made no secret of his Catholic sympathies. His wife's uncle, Thomas More, was executed for refusing to recognize Henry's supremacy in the Church, and Heywood narrowly escaped execution in 1543 for a plot against the Archbishop of Canterbury, Thomas Cranmer. While he remained a Court playwright through Elizabeth's ascendancy, he fled England in 1564 when anti-Catholic laws were passed.

The Proverb

He remains best known for his compilation of proverbs, published in 1546 in *The Proverbs of John Heywood*. Many (even most) may have been drawn from existing sources, what Heywood called "our common plaine pithie Proverbs olde." These became incredibly popular and remain some of the most famous aphorisms in English to this day. Heywood died around 1580, still in exile on the Continent.

Quotes from *Proverbs*

"Some things that provoke young men to wed in haste, Show after wedding, that haste makes waste."

"The more haste the less speed."

"Look ere ye leap."

"When the sun shines make hay, which is to say,
Take time when time comes, lest time steal away."

"The tide tarrieth no man."

"And while I at length debate and beat the bush,
There shall step in other men, and catch the birds,

And by long time lost in many vain words."

"When the iron is hot, strike."

"A hard beginning makes a good ending."

"When all candles are out, all cats are grey,
All things are then of one color, as who say."

"The nearer to the church, the farther from God."

"Two heads are better than one."

"Well aunt, said Ales, all is well that ends well.
Yes Ales, of a good beginning comes a good end."

"Ill weed grows fast."

"Be they winners or loosers,
… beggars should be not choosers."

"Throw no gift again at the giver's head,

For better is half a loaf than no bread."

"Who is worse shod, than the shoemakers wife,
With shops full of shoes all her life?"

"Children and fools cannot lie."

"Prove your friend ere you have need, but in deed.

A friend is never known till a man have need."

François, Duc de la Rochefoucauld

François was a French nobleman and writer who mastered the maxime, of which he wrote more than five hundred. These epigrams explore difficult or paradoxical truths, and François wrote them with unparalleled eloquence.

✳ ✳ ✳ ✳

FRANÇOIS WAS BORN in Paris on September 15, 1613 to a noble family at a time when Louis XIV was alternately attacking the French nobility and courting their support. François married Andrée de Vivone in 1628 and joined the army when he was sixteen to fight in the Franco-Spanish War. His family, like many nobles of the day, fell in and out of favor with the monarchy.

François participated in a plot against Cardinal Richelieu, Louis XIV's head minister, which resulted in him being imprisoned in the Bastille for eight days and exiled for two years. He participated in the second *Fronde*, an uprising of the nobility against the Crown, in 1648. The Royal forces and rebels were at war until 1653; François was wounded in the head at the battle of Faubourg Saint-Antoine in 1652 and retired to his family's estate.

The Maxims

In the late 1650s, Madeleine de Souvré, a noted writer, formed a *salon*, or gathering of like-minded literary figures, and invited François to join. It was at this salon that Francois began writing the *Maximes* for which he would become famous. The *Maximes* firmly established his reputation as a man of letters among the French elites. He also corresponded extensively, particularly with the Comtesse de La Fayette, who wrote one of the first novels in history. His *Letters*, along with his *Memoirs*, provide a glimpse of the life of French nobility in the 17th century.

He died in Paris on March 17, 1680.

Quotes from *Reflections;*
or Sentences and Moral Maxims

"Our virtues are most frequently but vices in disguise."

"What we term virtues are often but a mass of various actions and diverse interests, which fortune or our own industry manage to arrange; and it is not always from valour or from chastity that men are brave, and women chaste."

"Self-love is the greatest of all flatterers."

"Passion often renders the most clever man a fool, and even sometimes renders the most foolish man clever."

"We all have strength enough to endure the misfortunes of others."

"Philosophy triumphs easily over past and future evils; but present evils triumph over it."

"Neither the sun nor death can be looked at steadily."

"If we had no faults, we should not take so much pleasure in noting those of others."

"We promise according to our hopes; we fulfill according to our fears."

"Those who apply themselves too much to little things often become incapable of great ones."

"To succeed in the world we do everything we can to appear successful already."

"There is no disguise which can hide love for long where it exists, or simulate it where it does not."

"If we judge love by the majority of its results, it resembles hatred more than friendship."

"There is only one kind of love, but there are a thousand different versions."

"The love of justice is simply in the majority of men the fear of suffering injustice."

"Everyone complains about his memory, and no one complains about his judgment."

"Nothing is given so profusely as advice."

"Old men delight in giving good advice as a consolation for the fact that they can no longer provide bad examples."

'It is easier to be wise for others than for oneself."

"Some condemnations praise; some praise damns."

"The desire to appear clever often prevents one from being so."

"We often forgive those who bore us, but we cannot forgive those whom we bore."

"The stamp of great minds is to suggest much in few words, so, contrariwise, little minds have the gift of talking a great deal and saying nothing."

"We confess to little faults only to persuade ourselves we have no great ones."

Jean de la Fontaine

One of the most popular poets in France in the 17th century, Jean de la Fontaine is best remembered for his collection of Fables, *which he published from 1668 to 1694.*

✳   ✳   ✳   ✳

JEAN DE LA Fontaine was born on July 8, 1621, to an upper middle-class family. He was formally educated and attended the Oratory briefly before studying law. In 1652, he inherited his father's position as the maître des eaux et forêts, a manager of forests and waterways. Fontaine held the position until 1671, but by 1656 he was spending much of his time in Paris. He became interested in literary pursuits while he was in Paris, and as his position as maître was not very demanding, he had plenty of time to devote to his writing. Fontaine's first published work was an adaptation of *Eunuchus* by the Roman playwright Terrence, which he published in 1648.

In 1673, Fontaine joined the salon of Mademoiselle de la Sabliere, a noted intellectual of the day. He would spend twenty years there, publishing his *Fables* in twelve volumes over more than twenty years. His fables took place in pastoral settings, and were celebrated for their charm and wit. Fontaine touched on a diverse array of subjects, from social commentary to politics to simple moralistic fables. Like Aesop, after whose tradition he modeled his fables, Fontaine often used animal protagonists to represent human archetypes. The *Fables* garnered considerable fame for Fontaine, and in 1683 he was elected to the French Academy. Fontaine died in Paris on April 13, 1695.

Quotes from *Fables*

"The ant is no lender; that is the least of her faults."

"Be advised that all flatterers live at the expense of those who listen to them."

"'Tis thus we heed no instincts but our own;
Believe no evil till the evil's done."

"The argument of the strongest is always the best."

"By the work one knows the workman."

"The fastidious are unfortunate; nothing satisfies them."

"Patience and time do more than strength or passion."

"It is a double pleasure to deceive the deceiver."

"It is impossible to please all the world and one's father."

"There's nothing useless to a man of sense."

"Never sell the bear's skin before one has killed the beast."

"To win a race, the swiftness of a dart availeth not without a timely start."

"Help thyself and Heaven will help thee."

"Beware, as long as you live, of judging people by appearances."

"Man is so made that when anything fires his soul, impossibilities vanish."

"Nothing is as dangerous as an ignorant friend; a wise enemy is to be preferred."

"Our destiny is frequently met in the very paths we take to avoid it."

The Diary of Samuel Pepys

Pepys was a naval administrator who gained no literary fame during his life, but when his Diary *was published more than a century after his death, it was immediately recognized as a great work of literary consequence.*

✳ ✳ ✳ ✳

SAMUEL PEPYS WAS born on February 23, 1633, in London, to parents of a humble background. He attended St. Paul's School and then Trinity College at Cambridge. He received a Master's degree from Cambridge in 1660 and worked for several years in English government, first at Whitehall and later for the office of the Exchequer, George Downing, after whom Downing street is named. During the Anglo-Dutch War of 1665, Pepys began working in the administration of the Royal Navy, and in 1673 he was elevated to the position of chief administrator of the Navy.

Pepys began keeping the *Diary* on January 1, 1660, and continued until his failing eyesight made it impossible to do so. The final entry is on May 31, 1669. In those nine years, he wrote more than 1.25 million words in six volumes. More than a simple diary, Pepys crafted what is widely considered a groundbreaking work of art. The diary extensively discusses Pepys' life in the London of the English Restoration, and captures every scene is striking detail. Pepys appears to have been a man who was supremely fascinated by the mundanity as well as the grandeur of the world, and his interest in nearly everything he encountered is evident in the *Diary*. The work also describes pivotal events including the Fire of London, the Plague in London, and the Dutch War.

It was not published while he was alive, but the six volumes were included in his extensive library, which he gifted to Cambridge in his will. The diary was written in shorthand, and was transcribed in 1825 by John Smith.

From the Diary

"I went out to Charing Cross, to see Major-general Harrison hanged, drawn and quartered; which was done there, he looking as cheerful as any man could do in that condition."

"A good honest and painfull sermon."

"Then to the King's Theatre, where we saw Midsummer's Night's Dream, which I had never seen before, nor shall ever again, for it is the most insipid ridiculous play that ever I saw in my life."

"Methought it lessened my esteem of a king, that he should not be able to command the rain."

"Strange to see how a good dinner and feasting reconciles everybody."

"To church in the morning, and there saw a wedding in the church, which I have not seen many a day; and the young people so merry one with another, and strange to see what delight we married people have to see these poor fools decoyed into our condition, every man and woman gazing and smiling at them."

"The truth is, I do indulge myself a little the more in pleasure, knowing that this is the proper age of my life to do it; and out of my observation that most men that do thrive in the world, do forget to take pleasure during the time that they are getting their estate, but reserve that till they have got one, and then it is too late for them to enjoy it with any pleasure."

"This morning came home my fine Camlett cloak, with gold buttons, and a silk suit, which cost me much money, and I pray God to make me able to pay for it."

"He seems to be very well acquainted with the King's mind, and with all the several factions at Court, and spoke all with so much frankness, that I do take him to be my Lord's good friend, and one able to do him great service, being a cunning fellow, and one (by his own confession to me) that can put on two several faces, and look his enemies in the face with as much love as his friends. But, good God! what an age is this, and what a world is this! that a man cannot live without playing the knave and dissimulation."

Alexander Pope

An eighteenth-century poet who wrote biting satire, Alexander Pope's quotes remain popular in the English-speaking world.

✳   ✳   ✳   ✳

A LEXANDER POPE WAS born in London on May 21, 1688 to Catholic parents. Their religion prevented him from being able to attend public school or university, and so Pope mostly educated himself. He learned French, Latin, and Greek on his own, and read the *Odyssey* when he was only six years old. He wrote his first poem, "Ode to Solitude," when he was twelve. That year he also contracted a tuberculosis infection that would deform his spine and stunt his growth.

Master of the Heroic Couplet

Pope wrote *Pastorals* when he was sixteen, and they were published in 1710. The *Pastorals* catapulted him to literary fame. The following year he wrote "Essay on Criticism," a poem in which he first used the heroic couplet that would become his signature style. The "Essay" is the source of many of Pope's most famous quotations. It brought him to the attention of Jonathan Swift and John Gay, who with him formed the Scriblerus Club. The Club included writers who satirized ignorance in the fictional character Martinus Scriblerus, on whom Pope would later base the *Dunciad*.

In 1712, Pope wrote his most famous work, *The Rape of the Lock*. It is an epic poem that tells the story of two wealthy Catholic families who quarrel over a stolen lock of hair. In 1713, he began working on a six-volume translation of the *Iliad*, producing one volume a year. He sold the volumes by subscription, which allowed him to live comfortably on his writing alone. He went on to translate the *Odyssey* and wrote "Essay on Man" in 1734.

Pope died at his estate at Twickenham on May 30, 1744.

Quotes from Pope

*"For modes of faith let graceless zealots fight;
His can't be wrong whose life is in the right."*

—"An Essay on Man"

*"A little Learning is a dang'rous Thing;
Drink deep, or taste not the Pierian Spring:
There shallow Draughts intoxicate the Brain,
And drinking largely sobers us again."*

—"An Essay on Criticism"

*"True ease in writing comes from art, not chance,
As those move easiest who have learn'd to dance."*

—"An Essay on Criticism"

"To err is human, to forgive divine."

—"An Essay on Criticism"

*"'Tis with our judgments as our watches, none
Go just alike, yet each believes his own."*

—"An Essay on Criticism"

*"Let such teach others who themselves excel,
And censure freely who have written well."*

—"An Essay on Criticism"

*"Words are like leaves; and where they most abound,
Much fruit of sense beneath is rarely found."*

—"An Essay on Criticism"

"For fools rush in where angels fear to tread."

—"An Essay on Criticism"

*"Like following life through creatures you dissect,
You lose it in the moment you detect. "*

—Moral Essays

*"The fate of all extremes is such,
Men may read, as well as books, too much.
To observations which ourselves we make,
We grow more partial for th' observer's sake."*

—Moral Essays

Addison and Steele

"Addison and Steele" sounds a bit like the name of a cop show or a comedy duo. It's a little closer to the latter than the former. Richard Steele and Joseph Addison met at a young age at the Charter House School in England, and in the early 18th century they founded the Tatler and the Spectator, two of the first literary periodicals which gave rise to the Enlightenment-era public square of discussion.

✳   ✳   ✳   ✳

THE TATLER WAS conceived in 1709 by Richard Steele, an Irish writer born in Dublin in 1672. It was the first literary periodical to use an editorial pen-name; Steele wrote under the pseudonym "Issac Bickerstaff, Esq." The *Tatler* presented essays in the form of reporting on discussions in four coffeehouses in London, although it mixed actual coffeehouse gossip with Steele's own fictional accounts. Joseph Addison, an English poet, and Jonathan Swift later joined Steele in writing as Bickerstaff. The *Tatler* folded in 1711, and the same year Steele and Addison founded the Spectator. Its style was similar to the *Tatler's*, with members of a fictional "Spectator Club" writing on the authors' ideas about society.

The *Spectator* aimed to present articles that would stimulate discussion among its readers on issues of the day. In this regard, it was instrumental in the development of the public sphere, an Enlightenment concept that promoted public discourse about societal and political topics.

The *Spectator's* popularity soon spread to the American colonies, and influenced many of America's Founding Fathers, including James Madison. It was published for only a little more than a year, and the essays were collected in eight volumes. These continued to be read widely through the eighteenth and nineteenth century.

Addison in the *Spectator*

"If I can any way contribute to the diversion or improvement of the country in which I live, I shall leave it, when I am summoned out of it, with the secret satisfaction of thinking that I have not lived in vain."

"Thus I live in the world rather as a spectator of mankind than as one of the species."

"I shall endeavor to enliven morality with wit, and to temper wit with morality."

"True happiness is of a retired nature, and an enemy to pomp and noise; it arises, in the first place, from the enjoyment of one's self, and in the next, from the friendship and conversation of a few select companions."

"Of all the diversions of life, there is none so proper to fill up its empty spaces as the reading of useful and entertaining authors."

"The most violent appetites in all creatures are lust and hunger: the first is a perpetual call upon them to propogate their kind; the latter to preserve themselves."

"Books are the legacies that a great genius leaves to mankind, which are delivered down from generation to generation, as presents to the posterity of those who are yet unborn."

"I have somewhere met with the epitaph of a charitable man, which has very much pleased me. I cannot recollect the words, but the sense of it is to this purpose; 'What I spent I lost; what I possessed is left to others; what I gave away remains with me.'"

"A man must be excessively stupid, as well as uncharitable, who believes that there is no virtue but on his own side, and that there are not men as honest as himself who may differ from him."

"Some virtues are only seen in affliction and some in prosperity."

Addison in the *Tatler*

"Men may change their climate, but they cannot change their nature. A man that goes out a fool cannot ride or sail himself into common sense."

"Reading is to the mind, what exercise is to the body. As by the one, health is preserved, strengthened, and invigorated: by the other, virtue (which is the health of the mind) is kept alive, cherished, and confirmed."

"Cunning is only the mimic of discretion, and may pass upon weak men in the same manner as vivacity is often mistaken for wit, and gravity for wisdom."

Steele in the *Spectator*

"When you fall into a man's conversation, the first thing you should consider is, whether he has a greater inclination to hear you, or that you should hear him."

"When you fall into a man's conversation, the first thing you should consider is, whether he has a greater inclination to hear you, or that you should hear him."

"Among all the diseases of the mind there is not one more epidemical or more pernicious than the love of flattery."

"A favor well bestowed is almost as great an honor to him who confers it as to him who receives it."

"No man was ever so completely skilled in the conduct of life, as not to receive new information from age and experience..."

A Writer of Jests and Truths

Sterne's bawdy novel The Life and Opinions of Tristram Shandy, Gentleman *is considered one of the greatest comic works in English literature. The book influenced many later writers, including James Joyce, Karl Marx, and Virginia Woolf.*

✳ ✳ ✳ ✳

LAURENCE STERNE WAS born in Ireland on November 24, 1713, and attended Cambridge beginning in 1733. He received a Master of Arts degree in 1740 and became a vicar in Yorkshire the following year. His writing was limited to sermons for nearly twenty years until, in 1759, he wrote *A Political Romance* in support of his dean who was embroiled in a public quarrel. The book, a humorous satire of church figures, was controversial enough that Sterne left his position and turned to writing full-time.

He began writing his most famous novel, *The Life and Opinions of Tristram Shandy, Gentleman*, the same year. A lengthy work, it would be published over the next seven years in nine volumes.

Tristram Shandy is a humorous work that ostensibly tells the titular protagonist's life story, but is often interrupted by digressions and tangents. Sterne was well-read, and parts of the book parody other seventeenth and eighteenth century writers including Alexander Pope and Jonathan Swift. The book was quite popular, and was read by great minds of the nineteenth century, including Arthur Schopenhauer and Karl Marx.

Contemporary British abolitionists, including Ignatius Sancho, lobbied Sterne to write anti-slavery material because of the popularity of *Shandy*. Sterne's reply to a letter from Sancho, in which he lambasted the institution of slavery, became famous in abolitionist circles.

Sterne traveled to Europe in 1762, and published the novel *A Sentimental Journey through France and Italy* in 1768. He died shortly after it was published, on March 18.

Quotes from Sterne

"Only the brave know how to forgive . . . A coward never forgave; it is not in his nature."

—*Sermons*

"I wish either my father or my mother, or indeed both of them, as they were in duty both equally bound to it, had minded what they were about when they begot me."

—*Tristram Shandy*

"So long as a man rides his hobbyhorse peaceably and quietly along the King's highway, and neither compels you or me to get up behind him — pray, Sir, what have either you or I to do with it?"

—*Tristram Shandy*

"Digressions, incontestably, are the sunshine; — & they are the life, the soul of reading; — take them out of this book for instance, — you might as well take the book along with them."

—*Tristram Shandy*

"For every ten jokes, thou hast got a hundred enemies."

—Tristram Shandy

"'Tis known by the name of perseverance in a good cause — and of obstinacy in a bad one."

—Tristram Shandy

"Writing, when properly managed, (as you may be sure I think mine is) is but a different name for conversation."

—Tristram Shandy

"A man should know something of his own country too, before he goes abroad."

—Tristram Shandy

Malapropisms and Other Punchlines

Mrs. Malaprop, a character in Richard Brensley Sheridan's play The Rivals, *frequently misspoke, which gave rise to the term "malapropism."*

❋   ❋   ❋   ❋

RICHARD BRENSLEY SHERIDAN, an Irish satirist and play-wright, was born in Dublin on October 30, 1751. He was raised in a literary family: his mother Frances was a novelist and his father Thomas was an actor. Sheridan's family moved to London in 1758, and he was educated at the Harrow School and by a private tutor.

In 1772 he was involved in two duels with Thomas Mathews, who had written an article that attacked the character of his future wife, Elizabeth Linley. He won the first, but publicized it, which led Mathews to challenge him to a second in which Sheridan nearly lost his life. The couple married that year, but soon ran out of money, and in 1775 Sheridan wrote his first play, *The Rivals*, to make ends meet.

The Rivals was a disaster on its opening night, but Sheridan rewrote the play and produced it again two weeks later to significant critical acclaim. It was George Washington's favorite play, and was very popular in London as well. The play is a comedy of manners in which the character Mrs. Malaprop, a prim widow, is the guardian of Lydia, who has several suitors. Mrs. Malaprop's name references the word *malapropos*, or inappropriate, and she regularly misuses words that sound like what she means to say but in fact mean something completely different.

Sheridan owned managed the Drury Lane theatre from 1776 until it burned down in 1809, and wrote several other successful plays. He died in 1815 and was buried in the Poets' Corner at Westminster Abbey.

Quotes from Sheridan's Plays

"An apothecary should never be out of spirits."

—St. Patrick's Day

"Such protection as vultures give to lambs."

—Pizarro

"An oyster may be crossed in love."

—Clio's Protest

"'Tis safest in matrimony to begin with a little aversion."

—The Rivals

"A progeny of learning."

—The Rivals

"I know you are laughing in your sleeve."

—The Rivals

"He is the very pineapple of politeness!"

—The Rivals

"Illiterate him, I say, quite from your memory. "

—The Rivals

"Our ancestors are very good kind of folks; but they are the last people I should choose to have a visiting acquaintance with."

—*The Rivals*

"The quarrel is a very pretty quarrel as it stands; we should only spoil it by trying to explain it."

—*The Rivals*

"Be just before you're generous."

—*The School for Scandal*

"There is not a passion so strongly rooted in the human heart as envy."

—*The Critic*

"Certainly nothing is unnatural that is not physically impossible."

Joseph Joubert

Although he never published during his lifetime, Joubert's essays, collected in his private notebooks and published posthumously, explored morals, philosophy, and the human condition.

✳ ✳ ✳ ✳

JOSEPH JOUBERT WAS born in Montignac, France, on May 6, 1754. He attended college in Toulouse, and taught there in his early twenties. In 1778 he moved to Paris, where he met several literary figures who would become his lifelong friends, including Francois-René de Chateaubriand, a writer and diplomat who founded the Romanticist movement in French literature and published several novels, including the influential 1802 book *René*. Joubert married in 1793 and moved to Villeneuve-sur-Yvonne, but continued to correspond with Chateaubriand until his death on May 4, 1824 in Paris. Although he never published while he was alive, Joubert filled dozens of notebooks and scraps of paper with thoughts on literature, philosophy, politics and morality, which he stored in a trunk in his home.

Pensées

Following his death, Joubert's widow gave the notebooks to Chateaubriand, who edited and published them as *Recueil des Pensées de M. Joubert (Collected Thoughts of Mr. Joubert)* in 1838. The essays spanned more than forty years, and are wide-ranging and occasionally rambling, but show Joubert to have been a vibrant thinker.

Unlike many French writers of his day, who preferred to write tidy maxims, Joubert's notes are more oblique. Joubert discussed the thought not only of his own tumultuous historical period, but also explored the philosophy and history of previous centuries, and his *Pensées* influenced many thinkers of the 19th century.

Thoughts from Monsieur Joubert

"I had to grow old to learn what I wanted to know, and I should need to be young to say well what I know."

"We comprehend the earth only when we have known heaven. Without the spiritual world the material world is a disheartening enigma."

"Some find activity only in repose, and others repose only in movement."

"When you go in search of honey you must expect to be stung by bees."

"We use up in the passions the stuff that was given us for happiness."

"The direction of the mind is more important than its progress."

"Ask the young. They know everything."

"It is better to debate a question without settling it than to settle a question without debating it."

"It is easy to understand God as long as you don't try to explain him."

"Genius begins beautiful works, but only labor finishes them."

"To teach is to learn twice over."

"Don't cut what you can untie."

"All luxury corrupts either the morals or the taste."

"Do not choose for your wife any woman you would not choose for a friend if she were a man."

"Fear feeds the imagination."

"A part of kindness consists in loving people more than they deserve."

"There is nothing serious in civil life except good and evil, vice and virtue. Everything else in it should be a game."

"Those who never back down love themselves more than they love the truth."

"All gardeners live in beautiful places because they make them so."

"And perhaps there is no advice to give a writer more important than this: — Never write anything that does not give you great pleasure."

"To draw up in advance an exact and detailed plan is to deprive our minds of the pleasures of the encounter and the novelty that comes from executing the work."

"It is very difficult to be wise (through the mind); it is not difficult to be wise occasionally and by chance, but it is difficult to be wise assiduously and by choice."

"Few minds are spacious; few even have an empty place in them or can offer some vacant point. Almost all have narrow capacities and are filled by some knowledge that blocks them up. What a torture to talk to filled heads, that allow nothing from the outside to enter them! A good mind, in order to enjoy itself and allow itself to enjoy others, always keeps itself larger than its own thoughts. And in order to do this, this thoughts must be given a pliant form, must be easily folded and unfolded, so they are capable, finally, or maintaining a natural flexibility. All those short-sighted minds see clearly within their little ideas and see nothing in those of others; they are like those bad eyes that see from close range what is obscure and cannot perceive what is clear from afar."

"When we speak, we write what we are saying in the air."

"The important business of man is life, and the important business of life is death."

Mary Wollstonecraft

Mary Wollstonecraft was an 18th-century English educator and writer whose book A Vindication of the Rights of Woman was one of the first feminist philosophical works.

✳ ✳ ✳ ✳

MARY WOLLSTONECRAFT WAS born in London on April 27, 1759. Her father was abusive, and following her mother's death in 1780, she left home and established a school for women with her sister and her best friend. In 1787 she wrote *Thoughts on the Education of Daughters* based on her experiences at the school. After working as a governess in Ireland for a few years, she returned to London and began working with Joseph Johnson, who published socially progressive texts. She began contributing to Johnson's radical political journal the *Analytical Review* in 1788.

A Vindication

In 1792 Wollstonecraft published *A Vindication of the Rights of Woman*, which argued that women were not inferior to men, but merely appeared so because they were systematically denied educational opportunities. She argued that educational reform would liberate women from their confined existence and argued that they should be given the same access to education as men. These ideas were revolutionary for their time, and sparked a great deal of controversy. The work was generally well received by critics and was published in America and translated into French. Wollstonecraft also wrote the feminist novel *Maria: or the Wrongs of Woman* which her husband William Godwin published after her death. The novel criticized the institution of marriage as patriarchal and oppressive, and celebrated female sexuality.

Wollstonecraft died on September 10, 1797 after giving birth to her daughter Mary, who as Mary Shelley would write the novel *Frankenstein*.

Words from Wollstonecraft

"Independence I have long considered as the grand blessing of life, the basis of every virtue; and independence I will ever secure by contracting my wants, though I were to live on a barren heath."

—A Vindication of the Rights of Women

"Taught from their infancy that beauty is woman's sceptre, the mind shapes itself to the body, and roaming round its gilt cage, only seeks to adorn its prison."

—A Vindication of the Rights of Women

"It is justice, not charity, that is wanting in the world."

—A Vindication of the Rights of Women

"It is a melancholy truth; yet such is the blessed effect of civilization! the most respectable women are the most oppressed; and, unless they have understandings far superiour to the common run of understandings, taking in both sexes, they must, from being treated like contemptible beings, become contemptible."

—A Vindication of the Rights of Women

"It is vain to expect virtue from women till they are in some degree independent of men; nay, it is vain to expect that strength of natural affection which would make them good wives and mothers. Whilst they are absolutely dependent on their husbands they will be cunning, mean, and selfish."

—A Vindication of the Rights of Women

"No man chooses evil because it is evil; he only mistakes it for happiness, the good he seeks."

—A Vindication of the Rights of Men

"Virtue can only flourish amongst equals."

—A Vindication of the Rights of Men

"Every political good carried to the extreme must be productive of evil."

—The French Revolution

"We reason deeply, when we forcibly feel."

—Letters Written in Sweden

A Biography for the Ages

Samuel Johnson overcame incredible difficulties to become one of the most celebrated English literary figures of the 18th century, writing poignant biographies, witty essays, and compiling a dictionary.

✳ ✳ ✳ ✳

SAMUEL JOHNSON WAS born on September 18, 1709, in Staffordshire, England, the son of a bookseller. He contracted a form of tuberculosis that attacked his lymph system when he was a baby, and it resulted in impaired vision and hearing, as well as health problems, physical tics, and depression that plagued him for the remainder of his life. He underwent an unsuccessful operation when he was three that left scars on his face and body. Johnson also may have suffered from Tourette's syndrome. Johnson learned Latin at a young age, and read extensively. In 1728 he enrolled at Oxford, but lacking money, he was forced to drop out after only a year. He sought work as a teacher, but could not find any long-term positions. Lacking a job, he turned to writing to make ends meet. He married Elizabeth Porter in 1735, and with her savings he founded his own school, but the venture was a failure.

Literary Career

In 1737, Johnson moved to London with his friend and former pupil David Garrick; Porter joined him later that year. He found work as a writer, contributing to *The Gentleman's Magazine* and other publications. He published the poem "London," a political satire, and it enjoyed critical success, although he was often out of work and remained penniless. In 1746, he was hired by a group of publishers to write his first major work, *A Dictionary of the English Language*. It took him nine years to complete, and was published in 1755. Although he did not make much money from the Dictionary, it became the most widely used dictionary of English for the next

150 years, until the *Oxford English Dictionary* was published in the 20th century.

While he was working on the *Dictionary*, Johnson continued to write essays, publishing them in the twice-weekly paper *The Rambler* between 1750 and 1752. A collection of 208 articles from *The Rambler* increased his notoriety and placed him on par with similar periodicals such as the *Spectator*. His finances remained in dire straits, however, and in 1756 he was arrested for an outstanding debt. The publisher paid it for him, and they soon became friends. The same year Johnson began writing *The Literary Magazine* and published a collection of the works of Shakespeare. The collection took him two years to finish, and he finally did when his publisher paid to get him out of debtor's prison in 1758. In 1759, he published *The History of Rasselas, Prince of Abissinia*, in order to pay for his mother's funeral. The book was hugely popular, and has been referenced in numerous other novels, including *Jane Eyre* and *The House of Seven Gables*.

In recognition for his *Dictionary*,. King George granted Johnson a modest pension in 1762, which eased his financial troubles. In the 1770s, he began working on a series of biographical sketches of English poets that was collected as *The Lives of the Poets*.

Johnson died on December 13, 1784, in London, and was buried in Westminster Abbey. In 1791, his friend James Boswell published his biography, which is widely regarded as the greatest biography in the English language.

Quotes from *The Rambler*

"Men more frequently require to be reminded than informed."

"He that would pass the latter part of life with honour and decency, must, when he is young, consider that he shall one day be old; and remember, when he is old, that he has once been young."

"In order that all men may be taught to speak truth, it is necessary that all likewise should learn to hear it."

"A transition from an author's book to his conversation, is too often like an entrance into a large city, after a distant prospect. Remotely, we see nothing but spires of temples and turrets of palaces, and imagine it the residence of splendour, grandeur and magnificence; but when we have passed the gates, we find it perplexed with narrow passages, disgraced with despicable cottages, embarrassed with obstructions, and clouded with smoke."

"Curiosity is one of the permanent and certain characteristics of a vigorous intellect."

"No man is much pleased with a companion, who does not increase, in some respect, his fondness for himself."

"That he delights in the misery of others no man will confess, and yet what other motive can make a father cruel."

"Every man is rich or poor according to the proportion between his desires and his enjoyments."

From His Dictionary

"Every quotation contributes something to the stability or enlargement of the language."

"ESSAY — A loose sally of the mind; an irregular indigested piece; not a regular and orderly composition."

"GRUBSTREET — The name of a street near Moorsfield, London, much inhabited by writers of small histories, dictionaries, and temporary poems."

"LEXICOGRAPHER — A writer of dictionaries, a harmless drudge."

"PATRON, n. One who countenances, supports or protects. Commonly a wretch who supports with insolence, and is repaid in flattery."

From *The Idler*

"It is commonly observed, that when two Englishmen meet, their first talk is of the weather; they are in haste to tell each other, what each must already know, that it is hot or cold, bright or cloudy, windy or calm."

"Among the calamities of war may be justly numbered the diminution of the love of truth, by the falsehoods which interest dictates and credulity encourages."

"*The act of writing itself distracts the thoughts, and what is read twice is commonly better remembered than what is transcribed.*"

"*We are inclined to believe those whom we do not know, because they have never deceived us.*"

From *Lives of the English Poets*

"*Language is the dress of thought.*"

"*Whoever wishes to attain an English style, familiar but not coarse, and elegant but not ostentatious, must give his days and nights to the volumes of Addison.*"

"*'Paradise Lost' is one of the books which the reader admires and lays down, and forgets to take up again. None ever wished it longer than it is.*"

Boswell's *Life of Samuel Johnson*

"*A generous and elevated mind is distinguished by nothing more certainly than an eminent degree of curiosity.*"

"*This man, I thought, had been a Lord among wits; but, I find, he is only a wit among Lords!*"

"*If a man does not make new acquaintance as he advances through life, he will soon find himself left alone. A man, Sir, should keep his friendship in a constant repair.*"

"*A man of genius has been seldom ruined but by himself.*"

"*A man ought to read just as inclination leads him; for what he reads as a task will do him little good.*"

"*But if he does really think that there is no distinction between virtue and vice, why, Sir, when he leaves our houses let us count our spoons.*"

"*So far is it from being true that men are naturally equal, that no two people can be half an hour together, but one shall acquire an evident superiority over the other.*"

"*It matters not how a man dies, but how he lives. The act of dying is not of importance, it lasts so short a time.*"

"*That fellow seems to me to possess but one idea, and that is a wrong one.*"

"*Patriotism is the last refuge of a scoundrel.*"

"Johnson observed, that 'he did not care to speak ill of any man behind his back, but he believed the gentleman was an attorney.'"

"Knowledge is of two kinds. We know a subject ourselves, or we know where we can find information upon it."

"This is one of the disadvantages of wine, it makes a man mistake words for thoughts."

"Depend upon it, Sir, when a man knows he is to be hanged in a fortnight, it concentrates his mind wonderfully."

"When a man is tired of London, he is tired of life; for there is in London all that life can afford."

"I would rather be attacked than unnoticed. For the worst thing you can do to an author is to be silent as to his works."

A Novelist for the Best and Worst of Times

Considered one of the greatest novels of Victorian England, Charles Dickens was hugely popular during his lifetime. His novels Oliver Twist *and* Great Expectations, *and his novella* A Christmas Carol, *remain some of the best-loved and widely adapted literature of the 19th century.*

✳　✳　✳　✳

CHARLES DICKENS WAS born in Portsmouth in southern England on February 7, 1812 to a poor family. When he was ten, the family moved to London. Dickens' father was sent to debtors' prison in 1824, and Charles had to leave school and find work in a factory. The experience would inform much of his later writing. He was briefly able to return to school when his father received a small inheritance, but had to leave again when he was fifteen support the family. He began working as a freelance court reporter. By his early twenties, Dickens was contributing to major newspapers under the pseudonym "Boz," and his articles were collected in the book *Sketches by Boz* in 1836.

Writing Career

Dickens began publishing *The Posthumous Papers of the Pickwick Club* the same year *Sketches* was published. The short articles, collected as *The Pickwick Papers*, accompanied illustrations by Robert Seymour and catapulted him to fame. In his late twenties, Dickens began publishing *Bentley's Miscellany*, in which he would serially publish his first novel, *Oliver Twist*. The novel, about the adventures of an orphaned street urchin, became wildly popular in England and the United States, and each monthly installment was eagerly anticipated by Dickens' readers. Over the next few years, he published *The Life and Adventures of Nicholas Nickleby* and *The Old Curiosity Shop*, which were less popular than *Oliver Twist* but still enjoyed success.

In 1843, Dickens published *A Christmas Carol*, the story of curmudgeonly Ebenezer Scrooge whose Christmas Eve haunting inspired him to find a more charitable attitude toward his fellow man. Dickens was inspired to write the novella following a visit to the Ragged School, which served London's homeless children. The first edition sold out in less than a week, and thirteen editions were printed within a year. *A Christmas Carol* has inspired countless adaptations. The first stage play based on the book was produced in February 1844; by the end of the month eight rival adaptations were being produced in London alone.

America and Later Years

Dickens and his wife Catharine toured the United States and Canada. He delivered a series of widely attended lectures that were so popular they attracted ticket scalpers. He spoke out against slavery and for the adoption of international copyright laws. He enjoyed the celebrity at first, but soon grew tired of being the center of attention, and he resented the invasion of his privacy.

He wrote *American Notes for General Circulation* based on the trip, and in it he criticized the gregarious nature and crude habits of Americans. This led to criticism from U.S. readers, and on a second tour in 1867–68 he pledged to write a more generous description of Americans in future reprints.

In 1850 Dickens wrote *David Copperfield*. It was the first novel that discussed the daily life of a protagonist, and established the Dickensian style of literature. He followed it with *Bleak House* and *Hard Times* in 1853 and 1854. In 1859 he published *A Tale of Two Cities*, and in 1861 he completed his greatest novel, *Great Expectations*.

Dickens died on June 9, 1870, and was buried in Poets' Corner at Westminster Abbey.

Quotes from Dickens

"The dignity of his office is never impaired by the absence of efforts on his part to maintain it."

—*Sketches by Boz*

"The civility which money will purchase, is rarely extended to those who have none."

—*Sketches by Boz*

"It is strange with how little notice, good, bad, or indifferent, a man may live and die in London."

—*Sketches by Boz*

"It was a maxim with Mr. Brass that the habit of paying compliments kept a man's tongue oiled without any expense; and that, as that useful member ought never to grow rusty or creak in turning on its hinges in the case of a practitioner of the law, in whom it should be always glib and easy, he lost few opportunities of improving himself by the utterance of handsome speeches and eulogistic expression."

—*The Old Curiosity Shop*

"In love of home, the love of country has its rise."

—*The Old Curiosity Shop*

"If there were no bad people, there would be no good lawyers."

—*The Old Curiosity Shop*

"Now, what I want is, Facts. Teach these boys and girls nothing but Facts. Facts alone are wanted in life. Plant nothing else, and root out everything else. You can only form the minds of reasoning animals upon Facts: nothing else will ever be of any service to them. This is the principle on which I bring up my own children, and this is the principle on which I bring up these children. Stick to Facts, sir!"

—*Hard Times*

"In the little world in which children have their existence whosoever brings them up, there is nothing so finely perceived and so finely felt, as injustice. It may be only small injustice that the child can be exposed to; but the child is small, and its world is small, and its rocking-horse stands as many hands high, according to scale, as a big-boned Irish hunter."

—*Great Expectations*

"Life is made of ever so many partings welded together..."

—*Great Expectations*

"'Please, sir, I want some more.'"

—*Oliver Twist*

"'If the law supposes that,' said Mr. Bumble, squeezing his hat emphatically in both hands, 'the law is a ass — a idiot.'"

—*Oliver Twist*

"Old Marley was as dead as a door-nail. Mind! I don't mean to say that I know, of my own knowledge, what there is particularly dead about a door-nail. I might have been inclined, myself, to regard a coffin-nail as the deadest piece of ironmongery in the trade. But the wisdom of our ancestors is in the simile; and my unhallowed hands shall not disturb it, or the Country's done for."

—*A Christmas Carol*

"'Bah!" said Scrooge, "Humbug!"

—*A Christmas Carol*

"'I wear the chain I forged in life,' replied the Ghost. 'I made it link by link, and yard by yard; I girded it on of my own free will, and of my own free will I wore it.'"

—*A Christmas Carol*

"'Business!' cried the Ghost, wringing its hands again. 'Mankind was my business. The common welfare was my business; charity, mercy, forbearance, and benevolence were all my business. The dealings of my trade were but a drop of water in the comprehensive ocean of my business!'"

—*A Christmas Carol*

"And so, as Tiny Tim observed, God bless Us, Every One!"

—*A Christmas Carol*

"[A] loving heart was better and stronger than wisdom..."

—*The Adventures of David Copperfield*

"The pain of parting is nothing to the joy of meeting again."

—*Nicholas Nickleby*

"For nature gives to every time and season some beauties of its own; and from morning to night, as from the cradle to the grave, is but a succession of changes so gentle and easy, that we can scarcely mark their progress."

—*Nicholas Nickleby*

"It is a pleasant thing to reflect upon, and furnishes a complete answer to those who contend for the gradual degeneration of the human species, that every baby born into the world is a finer one than the last."

—*Nicholas Nickleby*

"It was the best of times, it was the worst of times, it was the age of wisdom, it was the age of foolishness, it was the epoch of belief, it was the epoch of incredulity, it was the season of Light, it was the season of Darkness, it was the spring of hope, it was the winter of despair, we had everything before us, we had nothing before us, we were all going direct to Heaven, we were all going direct the other way – in short, the period was so far like the present period, that some of its noisiest authorities insisted on its being received, for good or for evil, in the superlative degree of comparison only."

—*A Tale of Two Cities*

"It is a far, far better thing that I do, than I have ever done; it is a far, far better rest that I go to than I have ever known."

—*A Tale of Two Cities*

An Unforgettable Poet

Although she lived a reclusive life on her family's farm and rarely published during her lifetime, Emily Dickinson privately wrote nearly 1,800 poems, discovered by her sister after her death, that made her one of the most famous and important figures of American literature.

❊ ❊ ❊ ❊

EMILY ELIZABETH DICKINSON was born in Amherst, Massachusetts on December 10, 1830. Her grandfather founded Amherst College, which Dickinson attended for seven years before transferring to Mount Holyoke Seminary in 1847. She started writing as a teenager, after reading a book of Ralph Waldo Emerson's poetry. After leaving Mount Holyoke, she returned to Amherst, where she and her sister Lavinia cared for her mother until she died in 1882. Dickinson's best friend, Susan Gilbert, married her brother, and settled in Amherst near the family farm. Neither Emily nor Lavinia ever married.

Seclusion and Poetry

The reasons for Dickinson's reclusiveness are unknown; she may have suffered from depression or agoraphobia, or simply had to remain close to home in order to look after her ailing mother. She also received treatments for a painful condition of her eyes, and may have been unable to venture into sunlight as a result. From about 1865, Dickinson almost never left the family homestead, and later in life she rarely even left her own bedroom. She gained a reputation as an eccentric during her lifetime, and was reluctant to greet guests to the Homestead.

She did correspond widely with a number of friends. One of her epistolary companions, Judge Otis Phillips Lord, apparently became a romantic interest of Dickinson's before his death in 1884. It was also during this time that she began writing the bulk of her poetry. Dickinson would write small bundles of poetry that she apparently never shared with anyone during her lifetime, for reasons that are also unclear. Her chief companion during this time was a dog she named Carlo, who remained with her for sixteen years.

Dickinson died on May 15, 1886, of kidney disease and was buried in Amherst. Her sister Lavinia discovered her poems following her death, and in 1890 the first collection of Dickinson's poetry was published, although the poems were edited to conform to literary standards of the time. The alteration caused much of her original meaning to be lost. The first complete collection of her poems in their original form, *The Poems of Emily Dickinson*, was published in 1955. Her simple, poignant verse had a tremendous influence on 20th century American poetry. Dickinson was immediately recognized as one of the greatest poets in American literature.

Dickinson's poetry was far ahead of its time. She regularly used slant-rhyme, in which words nearly but do not precisely rhyme, and was unconventional in punctuation and capitalization. Her poems are often concerned with themes of death and immortality. Her writing is generally considered to fall into three distinct periods. Before 1861, her poetry was rather conventional for its time, with sentimental themes. From 1861–1865, she wrote the bulk of her poetry, with her production peaking in 1862 when she wrote more than 350 poems. From 1866 onwards her productivity declined.

The combination of Dickinson's soaring literary voice and her reclusive life have made her a figure of great interest. The homestead where she was born, lived in seclusion, wrote hundreds of poems, and was buried is now a museum.

Quotes by Dickinson

"If I read a book and it makes my whole body so cold no fire can ever warm me, I know that is poetry. If I feel physically as if the top of my head were taken off, I know that is poetry. These are the only ways I know it. Is there any other way?"

—LETTER

Success is counted sweetest
By those who ne'er succeed.

—"SUCCESS IS COUNTED SWEETEST"

"Hope" is the thing with feathers —
That perches in the soul —

—"'HOPE' IS THE THING WITH FEATHERS"

"Faith" is a fine invention
When Gentlemen can see —
But Microscopes are prudent
In an Emergency.

—"'FAITH' IS A FINE INVENTION"

I'm Nobody! Who are you?
Are you — Nobody — Too?

—"I'M NOBODY! WHO ARE YOU?"

The Soul selects her own Society —
Then — shuts the Door —
To her divine Majority —
Present no more —

—"THE SOUL SELECTS HER OWN SOCIETY"

Because I could not stop for Death —
He kindly stopped for me —
The Carriage held but just Ourselves —
And Immortality.

—"BECAUSE I COULD NOT STOP FOR DEATH"

Tell all the Truth but tell it slant —
Success in Circuit lies

—"TELL ALL THE TRUTH BUT TELL IT SLANT"

A little Madness in the Spring
Is wholesome even for the King.

—"A LITTLE MADNESS IN THE SPRING"

Parting is all we know of heaven,
And all we need of hell.

—"MY LIFE CLOSED TWICE BEFORE ITS CLOSE"

Definition of a Satirist

American journalist, satirist, and author, Ambrose Bierce is famous for his short story "An Occurrence at Owl Creek Bridge" and The Devil's Dictionary.

✻ ✻ ✻ ✻

A MBROSE GWINNETT BIERCE was born on June 24, 1824 in Ohio and grew up in Warsaw, Indiana. After attending high school for only about a year, he began working as a printer's apprentice. When the Civil War broke out in 1861, Bierce joined the 9th Indiana Volunteers and saw action in several major battles, including Shiloh, Chickamauga, and Kennesaw Mountain, where he was severely wounded. He remained in the Army until January 1865 and was promoted to Major.

Life and Career

Following the War, Bierce moved to San Francisco, where he began writing for the *News Letter* and a number of other periodicals in 1867. He began editing the *News Letter* the following year, and his reputation soon spread all over the West Coast. He published his first short story, *The Haunted Valley*, in 1871, and on Christmas Day of that year he married Mary Ellen Day. In 1872 the couple moved to London, where they lived for the next three years. While they were there, Bierce began contributing humorous and satirical pieces to magazines such as *Figaro* and Fun, and edited the *Lantern*. In 1873, he published a collection of the articles he wrote in London in *The Fiend's Delight*, and published *Nuggets and Dust Panned Out in California* in 1872 and *Cobwebs from an Empty Skull* in 1874.

Bierce and his wife returned to San Francisco in 1875, and in 1877 he began editing the *Argonaut*. After a brief stint as a local manager for a mining company in the Dakota Territory, he returned to San Francisco again, and in 1887 became a staff writer for the *San Francisco Examiner*, a newspaper published by William Randolph Hearst.

He would continue to write for Hearst newspapers until 1909. In 1888, Bierce discovered a cache of letters written to his wife by an admirer, and they separated, divorcing in 1904. Bierce left San Francisco in 1896, moving to Washington, D.C., where he continued to contribute to newspapers and magazines on the East Coast.

In October 1913, he travelled to Mexico, which at the time was in the turmoil of Pancho Villa's revolution. He joined Villa's army as an observer, and disappeared sometime after December 26. The date and circumstances of his death remain a mystery.

Literary Legacy

Bierce's principal work of fiction is *In the Midst of Life*, published in 1892. It includes the famous short stories "The Boarded Window," "A Horseman in the Sky," and "An Occurrence at Owl Creek Bridge." "Occurrence," which first appeared in the *San Francisco Examiner* and was also published in *Tales of Soldiers and Civilians*, is notable for its nonlinear timeline, twist ending, and use of stream of consciousness. The story has been adapted numerous times and influenced many later works that used a similar surprise twist ending.

The Devil's Dictionary, which Bierce wrote in a series of installments in magazines and newspapers over three decades beginning in 1867, is a collection of satirical definitions published in 1911. Bierce had begun including satirical definitions from time to time in his early essays, and published his first essay with multiple satirical definitions in *Webster Revisited* in 1869. He began working on the dictionary in earnest in 1875.

Although critical reception was initially mixed, it has since come to be considered one of the greatest satirical works in American literature.

Definitions from *The Devil's Dictionary*

"*Abnormal, adj.* Not conforming to standards in matters of thought and conduct. To be independent is to be abnormal, to be abnormal is to be detested."

"*Absurdity, n.* A statement or belief manifestly inconsistent with one's own opinion."

"*Alone, adj.* In bad company."

"*Birth, n.* The first and direst of all disasters."

"*Bore, n.* A person who talks when you wish him to listen."

"*Conservative, n.* A statesman enamored of existing evils, as opposed to a Liberal, who wants to replace them with others."

"*Dictionary, n.* A malevolent literary device for cramping the growth of a language and making it hard and inelastic. This dictionary, however, is a most useful work."

"*Education, n.* That which discloses to the wise and disguises from the foolish their lack of understanding."

"*Heaven, n.* A place where the wicked cease from troubling you with talk of their personal affairs, and the good listen with attention while you expound your own."

"*Laughter, n.* An interior convulsion, producing a distortion of the features and accompanied by inarticulate noises. It is infectious and, though intermittent, incurable."

"*Neighbor, n.* One whom we are commanded to love as ourselves, and who does all he knows how to make us disobedient."

"*Philosophy, n.* A route of many roads leading from nowhere to nothing."

"*Politeness , n.* The most acceptable hypocrisy."

"*Positive, adj.* Mistaken at the top of one's voice."

"*Quotation, n.* The act of repeating erroneously the words of another. The words erroneously repeated."

"*Success, n.* The one unpardonable sin against one's fellows."

"*Year, n.* A period of three hundred and sixty-five disappointments."

A Wit and a Clergyman

"As the French say, there are three sexes, — men, women, and clergymen." An Anglican clergyman left behind words of gentle wit that are still read.

✳ ✳ ✳ ✳

SYDNEY SMITH WAS born in England in 1771. He studied at Oxford and afterward took holy orders and became a curate. His first book was a collection of sermons. Afterward, he helped set up, edited, and wrote for *Edinburgh Review* before going to London.

In London, he was known as an entertaining and popular preacher and lecturer, speaking on the evils of slavery and other matters. He was stationed in different locations in England throughout his life, but was known for his wit and his engaging popularity with parishioners wherever he ended up.

He died in 1845.

Quotes from Smith

"Madam, I have been looking for a person who disliked gravy all my life; let us swear eternal friendship."

"Thank God for tea! What would the world do without tea?—how did it exist? I am glad I was not born before tea."

"Marriage resembles a pair of shears, so joined that they can not be separated; often moving in opposite directions, yet always punishing anyone who comes between them."

"He was a one-book man. Some men have only one book in them; others, a library."

"Have the courage to be ignorant of a great number of things, in order to avoid the calamity of being ignorant of everything."

"Among the smaller duties of life I hardly know any one more important than that of not praising where praise is not due."

"No man can ever end with being superior, who will not begin with being inferior."

"It is the greatest of all mistakes to do nothing because you can only do little."

"The object of preaching is, constantly to remind mankind of what mankind are constantly forgetting; not to supply the defects of human intelligence, but to fortify the feebleness of human resolutions."

A Master of Comedy

Moliere had his critics. Some disliked his style; others loathed his grammar. However, there was no mistaking the fact he revolutionized comedic literature and stage in the 17th Century and became known as the Father of French Comedy.

✳ ✳ ✳ ✳

MOLIERE WAS HIS stage name. The "Father of French Comedy" was born Jean-Baptiste Poquelin in Paris in 1622, and his career could have gone in several different directions. His father was an upholsterer and furniture merchant for the King. Jean-Baptiste was an accomplished student of Latin and Greek at a prestigious Jesuit school and went on to earn his law degree at the age of 20. He could have done well in his father's business, practiced law in Paris. or used his bright mind to embark on a lucrative career of his choice. So, naturally, he abandoned his class to launch a career in acting.

Poquelin joined actress Madeleine Bejart, who became his mistress, and founded the Illustre Theatre in 1643. It was around this time he adopted the name Moliere. It did not prevent his operation from struggling. After an unsuccessful season trying to drum up a following in Paris, his company went bankrupt and Moliere was imprisoned for a day over unpaid debts.

Over the next 12 years, he and Madeleine toured France as actors in several theatre companies. While Moliere was honing his acting skills, he was also displaying a true gift for mockery. He began writing plays with biting wit and extravagant scenes meant to ridicule that which Moliere found, well, ridiculous.

He was writing, acting, and administrating, and the success he enjoyed led him right back to Paris.

Making History at Home

Moliere's return to his hometown in 1658 marked a drastic change from his first Parisian theatre go-round. He performed for the King at the Louvre, and in 1659 the premiere of *The Affected Young Ladies* marked his first well-known satire of a French institution—in this case the French Academy. Moliere was on his way to becoming known for his comedy, and his reputation in the genre took on a life of its own.

Not everyone was a fan. Clergy took offense, thinking Moliere's plays were mocking the church. The best tragedy playwrights of the day were envious at the following Moliere's "buffoonery" was gathering. Certain members of the establishment were none too pleased with some of Moliere's farces. Moliere often responded by incorporating detractors as the unfortunate "punch lines" of future productions.

Moliere is credited with at least a dozen of the most lasting full-length satirical comedies ever written. Within his works, plays and pros, he also left a lasting legacy with some of the memorable quotes and lines that impart both wit and wisdom. Wrote famed English novelist Mary Wollstonecraft Shelley: "The more we learn of Moliere's career, and inquire into the peculiarities of his character, the more we are struck by the greatness of his genius. ... His dramas belong to all countries and ages."

In 1662, believing she was the sister of his former mistress, Moliere married Armande Bejart. She may have been Madeleine's illegitimate daughter by the Duke of Modena. Some of Moliere's critics put forth the notion that she was actually his own daughter. They had one daughter together.

Moliere developed lung issues a few years later, although he continued to write, act, direct and lead his troupe as his ailment grew worse. Shortly after a performance of *The Imaginary Invalid* in 1673, he died at 51.

Quotes from Moliere

"A witty woman is a devil at intrigue."

—L'École des Femmes

"Nearly all men die of their remedies, and not of their illnesses."

—Le Malade Imaginaire

"People do not mind being wicked; but they object to being made ridiculous."

—Tartuffe

"Those whose conduct gives room for talk
Are always the first to attack their neighbors."

—Tartuffe

"To esteem everything is to esteem nothing."

—Le Misanthrope

"The more we love our friends, the less we flatter them;
It is by excusing nothing that pure love shows itself."

—Le Misanthrope

"Doubts are more cruel than the worst of truths."

—Le Misanthrope

"Anyone may be an honorable man, and yet write verse badly."

—Le Misanthrope

"A learned fool is more foolish than an ignorant one."

—Les Femmes Savantes

"He's a wonderful talker, who has the art
Of telling you nothing in a great harangue."

—Le Misanthrope

"We die only once, and for such a long time!"

—Le Depit Amoreaux

Quotations about Quotations

What better way to close a book about quotations than with a set of quotations about quotations....well, we'll have one more entry after this one.

✳ ✳ ✳ ✳

"Classic quotation is the parole of literary men all over the world."

—SAMUEL JOHNSON

"Life itself is a quotation."

—JORGE LUIS BORGES

"A fine quotation is a diamond on the finger of a man of wit, and a pebble in the hand of a fool."

—JOSEPH ROUX

"A book that furnishes no quotations is...no book."

—THOMAS LOVE PEACOCK

"He wrapped himself in quotations—as a begger would enfold himself in the purple of emperors."

—RUDYARD KIPLING

"Next to the originator of a good sentence is the first quoter of it. Many will read the book before one thinks of quoting a passasge. As soon as he has done this, that line will be quoted east and west."

—RALPH WALDO EMERSON

"I hate quotations. Tell me what you know."

—RALPH WALDO EMERSON

"I always have a quotation for everything—it saves original thinking."

—DOROTHY SAYERS

"I have heard that nothing gives an Author so great Pleasure, as to find his Works respectfully quoted by other learned Authors. This Pleasure I have seldom enjoyed."

—BENJAMIN FRANKLIN

Carved in Stone:
11 Memorable Epitaphs

They might be six feet under, but a good epitaph means they'll never be forgotten. Here are some of our favorite gravestone inscriptions.

�֍ �֍ �֍ ✖

1. **Mel Blanc**: "That's all folks!" Arguably the world's most famous voice actor, Mel Blanc's characters included Bugs Bunny, Porky Pig, Yosemite Sam, and Sylvester the Cat. When Blanc died in 1989 at age 81, his epitaph was his best-known cartoon line.

2. **Spike Milligan**: "Dúirt mé leat go raibh mé breoite." The Gaelic epitaph for this Irish comedian translates as, "I told you I was ill." Milligan, who died of liver failure in 2002 at age 83, was famous for his irreverent humor showcased on TV and in films such as *Monty Python's Life of Brian*.

3. **Joan Hackett**: "Go away—I'm asleep." The actor, who was a regular on TV throughout the 1960s and '70s, appearing on shows such as *The Twilight Zone* and *Bonanza*, died in 1983 of ovarian cancer at age 49. Her epitaph was copied from the note she hung on her dressing room door when she didn't want to be disturbed.

4. **Rodney Dangerfield**: "There goes the neighborhood." This comedian and actor died in 2004 from complications following heart surgery at age 82. Dangerfield, master of self-deprecating one-liners, has an epitaph that's entirely fitting.

5. **Ludolph van Ceulen**: "3.14159265358979323846264338327950288..." The life's work of van Ceulen, who died in 1610 at age 70, was to calculate the value of the mathematical constant pi to 35 digits. He was so proud of this achievement that he asked that it be put on his tombstone.

6. **George Johnson**: "Here lies George Johnson, hanged by mistake 1882. He was right, we was wrong, but we strung him up and now he's gone." Johnson bought a stolen horse in good faith but the court didn't buy his story and sentenced him to hang. His final resting place is Boot Hill Cemetery, which is also "home" to many notorious characters of the Wild West, including Billy Clanton and the McLaury brothers, who died in the infamous gunfight at the O.K. Corral.

7. **John Yeast**: "Here lies Johnny Yeast. Pardon me for not rising." History hasn't recorded the date or cause of John Yeast's death, or even his profession. We can only hope that he was a baker.

8. **Lester Moore**: "Here lies Lester Moore. Four slugs from a 44, no Les, no more." The date of birth of this Wells Fargo agent is not recorded, but the cause of his death in 1880 couldn't be clearer.

9. **Jack Lemmon**: "Jack Lemmon in . . ." The star of *Some Like It Hot*, *The Odd Couple*, and *Grumpy Old Men* died of bladder cancer in 2001 at age 76. Lemmon's epitaph reads like a marquee right above his resting place.

10. **Hank Williams**: "I'll never get out of this world alive." The gravestone of the legendary country singer, who died of a heart attack in 1953 at age 29, is inscribed with several of his song titles, of which this is the most apt.

11. **Dee Dee Ramone**: "OK . . . I gotta go now." The bassist from the punk rock band The Ramones died of a drug overdose in 2002, at age 49. His epitaph is a reference to one of the group's hits, "Let's Go."

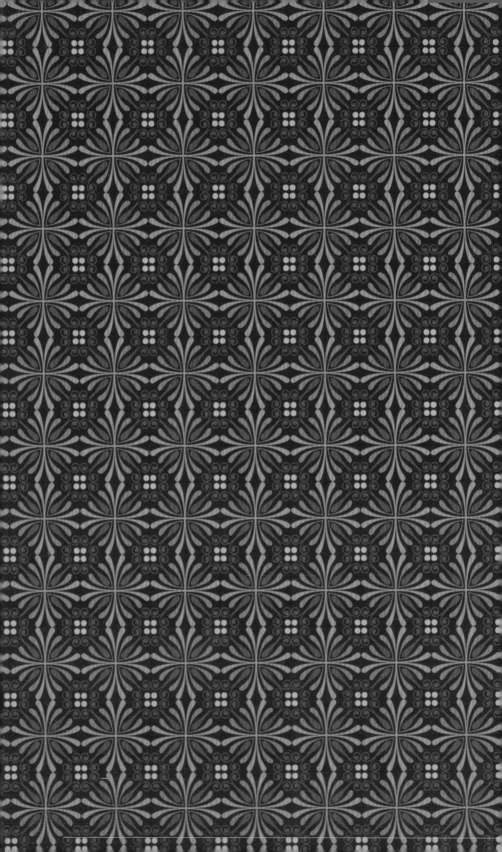